FORECASTING SYSTEMS FOR OPERATIONS MANAGEMENT

The BUSINESS ONE IRWIN/APICS Series in
Production Management

Supported by the American Production
and Inventory Control Society

OTHER BOOKS PUBLISHED IN THE BUSINESS ONE IRWIN
SERIES IN PRODUCTION MANAGEMENT

Attaining Manufacturing Excellence Robert W. Hall
Bills of Materials Hal Mather
Production Activity Control Steven A. Melnyk and Phillip L. Carter
Manufacturing Planning and Control Systems, Second Edition
Thomas E. Vollmann, William Lee Berry, D. Clay Whybark
Microcomputers in Production and Inventory Management
Thomas H. Fuller, Jr.
Shop Floor Control Steven A. Melnyk and Phillip L. Carter
The Spirit of Manufacturing Excellence Ernest Huge
Strategic Manufacturing, Dynamic New Directions for the 1990s
Patricia Moody
Total Quality: An Executive's Guide for the 1990s
The Ernst & Young Quality Improvement Consulting Group
*The New Performance Challenge: Measuring Operations for World-Class
Competition* J. Robb Dixon, Alfred J. Nanni, Thomas E. Vollmann
*Time-Based Competition: The Next Battle Ground in American
Manufacturing* Joseph Blackburn

The BUSINESS ONE IRWIN/APICS Series in
Production Management

APICS ADVISORY BOARD
L. James Burlingame
Eliyahu M. Goldratt
Robert W. Hall
Ed Heard
Ernest C. Huge
Henry H. Jordan
George W. Plossl
Richard Schonberger
Thomas E. Vollmann
D. Clay Whybark

FORECASTING SYSTEMS FOR OPERATIONS MANAGEMENT

**The BUSINESS ONE IRWIN
APICS Series in Production Management**

*Stephen DeLurgio
Carl Bhame*

Business One Irwin
Homewood, Illinois 60430

Senior editor: Jeffrey A. Krames
Project editor: Jess Ann Ramirez
Production manager: Diane Palmer
Compositor: Pam Frye Typesetting, Inc.
Typeface: 11/13 Century Schoolbook
Printer: Arcata Graphics, Kingsport

Library of Congress Cataloging-in-Publication Data

DeLurgio, Stephen A.
   Forecasting systems for operations management / Stephen A.
DeLurgio and Carl Bhame.
      p.   cm.
   Includes index.
   ISBN 1-55623-040-0
      1. Production management–Forecasting–Methodology. I. Bhame,
Carl. II. Title.
TS155.D464 1991
658.5'001'12–dc20   91–7386

Printed in the United States of America
1 2 3 4 5 6 7 8 9 0 K 8 7 6 5 4 3 2 1

To our wives
Ina and Linda
and our children
Steve and Patrick
Bill and Beth

PREFACE

The purpose of this book is to present the art and science of forecasting systems for operational management in a manner useful to manager and analyst alike. The methods and systems presented here are used by successful retailers, distributors, manufacturers, and many service organizations such as hospitals, utilities, government agencies, telecommunications companies, and financial institutions. We refer to these systems as operational forecasting systems. Specifically, this book will assist you in more effectively using, selecting, and designing operational forecasting systems. Of the hundreds of books on forecasting methods, none present both forecasting methods and systems in a manner that fulfills the purpose of this book.

This book is directed to all levels of management, because only through top-management leadership and middle-management involvement can forecasting systems be successfully implemented. As we show, the methods and systems of short-term forecasting are easier to understand and master than other, longer-term methods used in, for example, econometrics. In addition, there are many differences in the design of forecasting systems for short- to medium-term operational planning versus long-term strategic planning. Also, a good operational forecasting system is an essential part of a good strategic planning system.

Because the benefits from good forecasting systems are truly extraordinary, we share with you the principles, techniques, and designs of successful forecasting systems. This book helps you learn how to routinely and frequently forecast immediate (i.e., one-week to three-month) to medium-range (three-month to three-year) demands for many products or resources using predominantly automated systems.

FORECASTING SYSTEMS VERSUS FORECASTING METHODS

This book discusses both forecasting methods and forecasting systems; this distinction between methods and systems is important. A forecasting method is a mathematical or subjective technique that forecasts some future value or event. While many statistical forecasting software packages are implementations of forecasting methods, they are not forecasting systems. A forecasting system is a computer-based system that collects and processes demand data for thousands of items, makes forecasts using forecasting methods, has an interactive management-user interface, maintains a database of demands, detects out-of-control situations, and has report- and file-writing capabilities. We see that forecasting systems are considerably more complex than forecasting methods because the system has many essential support features, including the use of forecasting methods in a predominantly automated computer-based system. The requirements of a good operational forecasting system are much greater than those of a good statistical forecasting package. We study those requirements throughout this book.

THE PARTS OF THIS BOOK

This book is divided into six parts. Part 1 provides introductory information about forecasting methods and forecasting systems. It discusses the general principles and systems that are a foundation of the remaining chapters. Part 2 presents forecasting principles and concepts in six different operational environments—manufacturing, manufacturing-distribution, distribution, retailing, maintenance-utility, and remanufacturing. These six application areas are diverse enough to represent the forecasting needs of many other types of organizations, such as hospitals, government agencies, financial institutions, and telecommunications companies. Part 3 introduces the basics of forecasting methods in a straightforward, easily understood manner. Part 4 discusses 15 statistical methods of forecasting demand. While this is the most statistical part of the book, each of its chapters present some material suitable to all readers. Part 5 further develops forecasting system design. Chapter 17 combines the principles, concepts, and forecasting subsystems of the previous 16 chapters into an integrated system. In addition, Chapter 17 includes a forecasting system evaluation and selection checklist. This evaluation instrument is designed to help you select the best forecasting system for your application. Part 6 discusses important developments that will influence the future of forecasting systems. This part provides forecasts of forecasting systems.

In addition to this preview of the book, each of the six parts begins with an overview of its purpose and use. These provide a more in-depth statement of the content of each part. These overviews can be read now or as you read the remainder of this book.

HOW TO USE THIS BOOK

The six parts of this book can be used in at least two ways. If you are only interested in an overall understanding of forecasting systems without delving into the more technical, quantitative details, you can read the entire book with particular attention to all parts except Part 4. Part 4 should not be skipped but can be read for general information without spending much time on the technical or quantitative materials. In many cases, you might only skim the chapters of Part 4, paying particular attention to the forecasting principles. This suggestion is not meant to discourage you from studying the more technical and statistical material, even if you have no statistical background. We have tried to make the material here as meaningful and as accessible as possible so that all readers will benefit regardless of their statistical background. However, some chapters of Part 4 do present sophisticated forecasting methods that may require several readings to fully understand.

The second way in which the book can be used assumes that you desire a more technical understanding of forecasting systems. In this case, we suggest that you study all parts of the book in greater depth. Quantitative and system details should be studied in the examples of the book. To better reinforce newly acquired concepts, we strongly urge you to duplicate the techniques and tables presented and to experiment with your own spreadsheet programs.

FORECASTING SYSTEM PRINCIPLES

Interspersed throughout this book are italicized statements that typically precede or follow paragraphs. These statements are referred to as *forecasting system principles*. We, and others, have found them to be true in many forecasting situations. These important principles are in some cases very subtle or complex and in others, simple, self-evident truths that provide guidance in analyzing or designing a forecasting system. They often bridge the gap between the science and the art of forecasting and are, consequently, valuable guides. In addition to these principles, we have included general-interest cases and information in separate boxed areas in each chapter. These provide interesting and insightful examples of the practice of forecasting systems.

GLOSSARY

To assist you with terms needing clarification, we have included a glossary of the more technical terms of forecasting systems, production, and inventory management. Consequently, this glossary is an important part of learning about forecasting systems. Some of the terms and definitions were borrowed from the APICS dictionary; we appreciate the generous offer of the American Production and Inventory Control Society for allowing partial reproduction of its dictionary.

APICS CERTIFICATION PROGRAM

This book is also intended for use in preparation for the master planning module of the APICS certification program, and it has some value in preparing for the inventory-management examination. However, it is not sufficient in breadth to be the only reference for the master planning exam. The master planning module is one of six different modules in the APICS Certificate in Production and Inventory Management (CPIM) certification program. In addition, this book is useful in preparing for the Certificate in Integrated Resource Management offered by APICS. Those studying the master planning body of knowledge in preparation for APICS certification will benefit most from studying the entire book without attempting to master all the technical material of Part 4. However, we caution the reader to first consult the APICS educational materials for more specific guidance.

ACKNOWLEDGEMENTS

We are indebted to many who have supported our work and aided in developing this book. Our sincere thanks to the APICS headquarters personnel for their support in this effort, especially Michael Stack, Marcia Brown, and Charles Mertens. We particularly appreciate the encouragement, expertise, and insightful reviews of Henry (Hank) H. Jordan and Professor Richard Newman. Special thanks to Tom Detscher, Bob Holroyd, David Roth, and Julie Rhodes of American Software, Inc., and Professor N. K. Kwak of Saint Louis University for their contributions, comments, and recommendations on various topics. Particular thanks to Professors F. Dean Booth and S. Thomas Foster for contributing to Chapters 12 and 11, respectively. Several research assistants have endured formula and computation checking; of notable assistance were Srinivas Mandala, Jiguang Zhao, and Lin Zhang. Also, Carlene Martin of Westlake Hardware, Inc., and Wayne Reimer of Payless Cashways, Inc., provided useful managerial perspectives to this book.

Jeff Krames and Jess Ann Ramirez of Business One Irwin have been very helpful in preparing and editing the manuscript of this book. We wish to express special appreciation for the support and encouragement we have received from Dean William B. Eddy of the Henry W. Bloch School of Business, Vice Chancellor Eleanor Schwartz of the University of Missouri, Kansas City, and Jim Edenfield, President and CEO of American Software.

Finally, we owe a special thanks to our wives, Ina and Linda, and our families for their support, advice, patience, and understanding, particularly when we erred in forecasting the completion dates of many domestic chores.

Steve DeLurgio
Carl Bhame

CONTENTS

PART 1

INTRODUCTION TO FORECASTING SYSTEMS

The three chapters included in Part 1 have several important purposes and are prerequisites to all the other chapters in this book.

In Chapter 1, we discuss the strategic importance and benefits of forecasting systems for management. This chapter lays the foundation for understanding the important applications and commonality of forecasting systems, including their strategic and financial importance. Forecasting systems are common to almost all organizations—public, private, for-profit, and not-for-profit. Included in the appendix of that chapter is an important financial planning tool for justifying the acquisition of new computer-based systems.

Chapter 2 introduces forecasting, forecasting systems, and the hierarchical planning and control systems of good management. We can gain an important insight into management systems by studying the hierarchical structures presented in Chapter 2. (As will be shown in Chapter 3, good forecasting systems are hierarchical.) Chapter 2 also discusses what should be forecast and the six parts of a good forecasting system.

Chapter 3 introduces important concepts and principles related to achieving high levels of customer satisfaction in a variety of organizations. Achieving effective financial, marketing, and operational planning and control requires integrated forecasting systems. Important principles and the hierarchical forecasts needed to integrate planning are developed in this chapter. Three types of forecasts used in short-, medium-, and long-range planning are introduced. These three forecasts are important tools for integrating planning and forecasting in all organizations. Finally, the "pyramidal" hierarchical system of forecasting is developed.

CHAPTER 1

INTRODUCTION TO FORECASTING SYSTEMS

> Customer service begins with having the right product or service, in the right quantity, at the right time, in the right location. This is only achievable through excellence in operational forecasting systems.

The desire to forecast the future is one of the strongest cognitive motivations of modern society. The actualization of this dream has resulted in scientifically based forecasting models of human health, behavior, learning, economics, weather, horse racing, and corporate sales–to name only a few. Historically, early societies used forecasting methods that are now discredited; these included astrology, fortune telling, and predictions based on the entrails of animal sacrifices.

Despite the inherent desires of individuals to forecast, studies have shown that most companies—whether large or small—use highly subjective, nonquantitative forecasting methods. In contrast, we will show that the theory and practice of good operational forecasting can be learned and applied with relative ease.

There are many possible reasons why forecasting systems have not been fully implemented or utilized despite their success in many corporations. We believe that many of these reasons will disappear when those involved in forecasting have a good understanding of the basics of forecasting systems; it is for this purpose that we have written this book.

PURPOSE OF THIS BOOK

Top-management leadership and middle-management involvement are essential to forecasting system success.

The general purpose of this book is to present the art and science of forecasting systems for management in a manner that makes them useful to manager and analyst alike. The methods and systems presented here are used by successful retailers, wholesalers, large manufacturers, and many service organizations such as hospitals, utilities, government offices, financial institutions, and even school districts. We refer to these systems as *operational forecasting systems*. These forecasting systems provide important information to other planning systems, such as inventory management, production planning, labor scheduling, and capacity planning.

This book is directed to all levels of management; only through top-management leadership and middle-management involvement can forecasting systems be successfully implemented. As we will show, the methods and systems of short-term forecasting are considerably easier to understand and master than other, longer-term methods of forecasting, such as multiple regression and econometric methods.

Because the benefits from improved forecasting are truly extraordinary, we share with you the basics of successful forecasting systems. This book should help you learn how to routinely and frequently forecast immediate (i.e., one-week to three-month) to medium-range (three-month to three-year) demands for many products or resources using a predominantly automated system. In particular, we present successful forecasting system

Principles.

Design.

Implementation.

Benefits.

Costs.

The forecasting systems presented here are used in making immediate to medium-range operations, finance, and marketing decisions. We do not discuss long-range (i.e., 3- to 10-year) forecasting methods as presented in many other books. However, we do discuss the systems used to convert long-term group or aggregate forecasts into short-term forecasts of specific product or service demands.

Both the art and science of forecasting systems are essential for success.

We believe this book will contribute to the successful implementation or improvement of your company's forecasting process. Also, we hope your experiences will be as personally and professionally rewarding as those of others who have successfully

---

You Can't Sell from an Empty Cart.

This old marketing adage is one of the most important justifications for improved forecasting systems. Interestingly, this was recently summed up nicely by a quote from Joe Seigel of the National Retail Merchants Association.

"In half the cases where customers don't buy anything in a store, it's because the retailer doesn't have it in stock."

Most likely, this is also true for commercial and industrial buyers.

implemented operational forecasting systems. It is important to share with you not only the science but also the art of forecasting systems because presenting one without the other would considerably diminish the value of this presentation. As in most aspects of management, managers and analysts use both art and science in their professions.

Computer and Electronics Revolution

These are extraordinarily interesting and exciting times in the management of operations. The computer information and electronics revolution has now made it much more cost effective to collect and process data for use in integrated information systems. For example, electronic data interchange (EDI) and scanning devices of retailers, distributors, manufacturers, and hospitals enable businesses to collect and process data in extraordinary volumes in real time and on-line; never before has more useful data been available for operating decisions. However, data is useless if managers do not understand how to use it. This book presents many important uses of data in forecasting systems that are common to most organizations; these include applications in distribution and inventory management.

THE IMPORTANCE OF FORECASTING

For most companies, no other information system or investment has nearly as much immediate and long-range influence on profitability, customer service, and productivity as an operational forecasting system. A good forecasting system can dramatically improve operations. It is not uncommon for the payback from these systems to be less than a year. This is true because a good forecasting system is essential in eliminating waste such as inventory shortages or excesses, missed due dates, plant shutdowns, lost sales, lost customers, and expensive expediting. The advantages of operational forecasting systems are highlighted by the fact that the best manufacturers, distributors, retailers, and service organizations in the world are distinguished by the excellence of their forecasting/distribution systems.

Customers expect and receive better in-stock service levels today.

Giant™ Supermarkets

An Out-Of-Stock Item Can Send Five Customers to Another Store

Today's modern supermarket is one of the most extraordinary examples of modern management and prosperity. The first supermarket opened in 1930, and today there are 31,000 supermarkets that typically have about 22,000 stockkeeping units (SKUs) on their shelves. As an example of a larger supermarket, consider one of the 146 stores of the Giant Food Co.—their store #180 at Baileys Crossroads, Virginia. This supermarket does $53 million worth of business a year with 18 checkout lanes. "It uses 60,000 twist ties a week and recycles 6,000 pounds of scrap cardboard a day." Point-of-sale scanning devices make it possible for a checker to check out $5,000 a day with a gross dollar error rate of less than 0.04 percent (i.e., the checker is off $2 or less in $5,000).

This supermarket illustrates the importance of customer service and the systems used to achieve it. "One of Giant's guiding principles (which are ample enough to fill 27 three-ring binders . . .) is that an out-of-stock item can send five customers to another store." If a stockout occurs, the manager "will sometimes shop for it himself at a Safeway, Giant's archenemy in the Washington, D.C., area, and pass it on to the customer at cost."

With point-of-sale scanning equipment, the computer automatically tracks sales of items for inventory control and sales management. For example, the computer routinely calculates the past weekend's sales and then orders merchandise to be replenished on Sunday nights, thus assuring high levels of customer service. Also, the database from point-of-sale statistics is very important in making merchandising decisions. For example, if squeezable plastic bottles make ketchup in glass bottles unpopular in one store, the central merchandising department reduces the shelf space for ketchup in glass bottles in other stores in the chain also.

To ensure that goods are available and delivered in a timely fashion, the supermarkets are supplied by a large, highly automated distribution warehouse that handles 250 incoming truckload deliveries in the morning while distributing 7,200 cases an hour to supermarkets.

This integration of technologically advanced hardware and software provides managers with timely and accurate information for operational and strategic decision making. This information system is essential to the success of Giant™ food stores.

Source: Richard Conniff, "Any Business that Has to Do with Food, You Got to Keep Rolling," *Smithsonian*, November 1988, p. 40.

Many companies have found that it is no longer sufficient to have the right product, in the right quantity, in the right place only 80 or 90 percent of the time; customers now demand a level of service that is closer to 100 percent than it is to 95 percent. Thus, many customers who value their time more today than in the past expect retailers to be in stock 98 percent of the time. This in-stock condition is commonly called a 98 percent fill rate.

Large manufacturers, wholesalers, and retailers have been known to guard the designs of their forecasting and stock-replenishment systems with high levels of security because of the competitive advantages their systems provide. These systems provide timely and accurate information that can mean the difference between survival or demise, profitability or insolvency, world-class or lackluster performance.

Forecasting systems are of strategic importance.

An effective operational forecasting system is essential in achieving the strategic and operational goals of any organization. Forecasts drive the marketing, financial, and production information control systems. As discussed below, forecasts are central to almost all short-term decisions in organizations.

THE COMMONALITY OF OPERATIONAL FORECASTING

Operational forecasting is common to all organizations.

There is a commonality in the day-to-day control of organizations, whether it is the operation of a manufacturer or hospital. This commonality is the need to make effective decisions and resource allocations based on short-range forecasts. In all organizations, the demands for products, labor, materials, and other resources must be estimated using either formal or informal forecasting methods. We focus here on the essentials of planning, execution, and control of operations through the use of computer-based forecasting systems.

Figure 1–1 illustrates the commonality of forecasting in a va-

FIGURE 1–1
Commonality of Forecasting Systems in Resource Allocations

Type of Application	Data Acquisition	Information Processing	Forecasting Model	Operational Goals and Plans	Allocation Decisions
Supermarket chain	Cash register point of sale	Accumulation of store sales at distribution center	Forecasts of store demands by product	Keep probability of stockout to less than 2 percent	Shipments from distribution centers to stores
Hospital	Past and current patient admissions	Accumulation of demand by department and procedure type	Forecasts of the number of patients and the resources needed	Keep probability of stockout to approximately zero	Schedules of rooms, nurses, drugs, supplies, etc.
Manufacturer-distributor	Customer orders and EDI	Accumulation of demand for products by distribution center	Forecasts of demands by distribution center (DC)	Keep probability of DC stockout very low, less than 2–5 percent	Shipments from factory to DCs
School district	Student enrollment forms	Accumulation of demand for classes by school	Forecast number of continuing and migrating students	Assure that class sizes are reasonable; faculty, staff, and budget sufficient	Assign faculty, staff, budget, and students as necessary
Utility repair service	Past and current work orders	Accumulation of demand by procedure type	Forecast of number of customers and resource type	Keep probability of stockout to less than 1 percent	Schedules of stock items and work force needed

---

Customer Service Is Often the Competitive Edge

"Service, quality, and reliability are strategies aimed at loyalty and long-term revenue stream growth (and maintenance). The point of . . . a wonderful concomitant to a customer orientation is that the winners seem to focus especially on the revenue-generation side."

Source: Thomas J. Peters and Robert H. Waterman, Jr., *In Search of Excellence—Lessons from America's Best-Run Companies* (New York: Harper & Row, 1982), chap. 6, p. 157.

riety of organizations. As the figure shows, this common sequence is data collection, information processing, forecasting, applying operational goals, and resource-allocation decisions. Please review this figure before continuing.

Figures 1–2 and 1–3 illustrate two different systems where forecasts drive the allocation of resources. In Figure 1–2, a manufacturer-distributor-retailer uses actual and forecasted sales at each retail outlet to determine the orders for products supplied by four warehouses and two regional distribution centers (RDCs). These RDCs order products from two factory warehouses, which order products from the appropriate factory. The factories, in turn, order raw materials and parts from suppliers. As Figure 1–2 shows, the forecasts of sales at the retail level drive the total production-distribution system.

In contrast to Figure 1–2, Figure 1–3 illustrates the importance of forecasting in the allocation of elementary school faculty and staff. In this case, the forecasts and actual enrollments of each school are used by central administration in assigning faculty, staff, and budgets. The forecasts of class enrollments drive the allocation of resources in this operations management system.

While the central administration of the school district does not forecast as many items and as frequently as the manufacturer-distributor of Figure 1–2, the principles of forecasting system design and operation are very similar. In fact, the networks of Figures 1–2 and 1–3 are common to many types of organizations and their allocation decisions. These organizations use, or should use, forecasting systems for making immediate to medium-range resource allocations. Some of the typical problems and organiza-

FIGURE 1-2
Production-Distribution Network

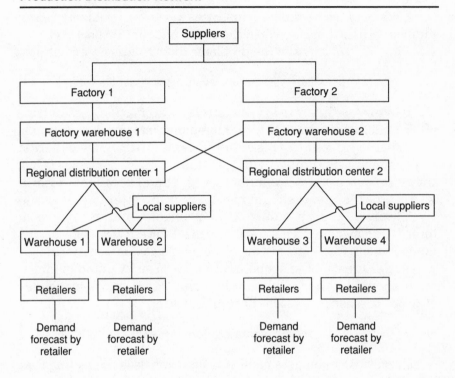

FIGURE 1-3
School District Faculty and Staff Distribution Network

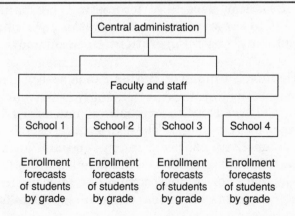

tions that we deal with in this book are illustrated by the case examples presented in the boxes on pages 13 and 14.

Each of these examples illustrates very real problems facing many organizations today. In the remainder of this book, we provide "how to" solutions to the problems facing these organizations.

Good forecasting systems are even more essential today.

The current interest in productivity, automation, just-in-time (JIT), quick response (QR), management information systems, manufacturing resource planning systems (MRPII), Distribution requirements planning (DRP), total quality control (TQC), computer-integrated manufacturing, and artificial intelligence/expert systems should not distract the attention of executives from an understanding of the principles and techniques of forecasting systems. These are essential for effective operations management. If the forecasting system is inadequate, performance will suffer greatly. Consequently, a high priority of top management should be the training of key employees in the principles of good forecasting system design and use.

All managers are forecasters.

Operations managers have at times expressed the feeling that forecasting is only indirectly related to their jobs and therefore of only minor concern to them, when, in fact, all managers need to study and understand forecasting. The growth and profitability of firms require that uncertainty and forecasts be better managed. While some managers may not need to know the technical, or statistical, aspects of forecasting, all managers and analysts need to know the basics of forecasting systems to better plan, execute, and control operations and resources.

Recent Trends Emphasize Better Forecasting

Several current trends make forecasting systems of great importance to the typical manager. These are concerns about cost containment, productivity improvement, just-in-time, quick response, the integration of computer-based management information systems, the introduction of microcomputers, telecommunications, spreadsheet programs, cost reductions in statistical/forecasting

---

Distribution Forecasting System Example

A distributor of nonfood products sold to retail grocery stores has had rapid growth in volume as a result of a successful marketing program and the acquisition of competitive routes. The plans for expansion of their eight distribution centers are being made and will include sophisticated material-handling, product-pricing, and labeling equipment. As the management committee reviews the firm's growth plans, the financial officer notes that inventory turnover has not increased in recent years and sometimes has declined. He asks of others on the committee, "What are you doing about reducing the slow-moving stock we keep seeing in greater quantities each quarter? Can't we reduce the level of stock on some of those items and improve both our profit margins and inventory turnover?" The merchandising manager replies, "We have reduced our stock on some items this past year, but we are also dealing with more variety of products. There are more products in stock, and forecasting is more difficult than before. We need a system that can handle the large variety and number of items stocked."

---

software, and last, but not least, the more sophisticated planning of competitors. Each of these concerns is briefly discussed below.

Cost Containment and Productivity Improvement
Historically, many organizations have not had to forecast as accurately as they do today; however, deregulation and competition (both domestic and international) have made improved forecasting necessary to more effectively and efficiently allocate managerial, informational, and operational resources. Airlines, the trucking industry, health-care providers, educational institutions, and manufacturing organizations all need more-effective forecasting systems to provide the information necessary to achieve profit and growth goals.

MIS Systems
The process of using an integrated production and information control system is very much dependent on the forecasts that drive the system. Computer-based management information systems,

Retail Hardware Store Example

A chain of 300 hardware stores struggles with inventory problems at regional distribution centers and retail store locations. Inventory buying is decentralized—individual store managers purchase some of their items directly from manufacturers and others directly from corporate regional distribution centers. Also, store managers are responsible for inventory control, profit, and loss, but not inventory investment. There is considerable difference in store performances as there is considerable difference in store managers.

Surveys of customers show that they feel that the price and quality of the stores' products are very competitive, the locations are convenient, and the store personnel are courteous. However, they complain about the larger percentage of items that are out of stock. Some customers feel they can only depend on getting 80 percent of the items they desire. Rarely are there only a few of any one item in stock—items seem to be either overstocked or out of stock. Store managers complain about long leadtimes from suppliers, out-of-stock conditions at the regional distribution center, and the inadequate inventory systems at the stores. Corporate financial managers complain about slow inventory turnover and declining profit margins.

Mail-Order Outdoor-Supply Example

A sporting goods mail-order company, Firm A, has experienced a declining market share because of the fierce competition of a new entrant in their industry, Firm B. Firm A is concerned about its operations. An experiment is performed whereby 100 randomly chosen items are ordered from each firm. On average, items from Firm A were received after 14 days, while those ordered from Firm B were received after 2 days; also, 10 percent of the items ordered from Firm A were out of stock, while only 1 percent of the items from Firm B were out of stock. These firms have very similar marketing, merchandising, and product mixes. Prior to the experiment, there was little agreement on the cause of the problem; now the management team understands the problem and must quickly agree on the solution. Their solution includes a better forecasting and inventory-management system.

integrated production information control systems, and marketing/financial information systems all require forecasts as inputs to planning, execution, and control. While the forecasting of aggregates (e.g., total sales) is discussed in many books, few deal with the focus of this book: product or service forecasting systems in which forecasting models are placed in an automated relationship with operational systems.

Microcomputers
The advent of the microcomputer has put almost unlimited analytical power in the hands of managers and analysts. Unfortunately, the idle microcomputers in many corporations attest to the inability of many users to apply analytical tools in meaningful systems. Users need to understand an application (e.g., forecasting) in the context of an appropriate system in order to implement successful systems.

Telecommunications
Recent telecommunications advances have dramatically reduced the cost and time of information processing and data transmissions. These advances have supported the introduction of EDI, JIT, and QR methods of retailing (see the EDI box on page 16). The telecommunications and teleprocessing activities of remote-terminal processing, distributed data processing, inquiry and response systems, remote data collection systems, remote batch processing, and data communications networks give the information specialist an almost unlimited number of approaches to worldwide data collection and information processing.

Productivity gains from technological improvements in telecommunications will continue to make more-rapid data collection, decision making, and resource allocations a necessary part of competitive operations management. This is highlighted in the EDI and UPC box.

Spreadsheet Programs
Programs such as Lotus 1-2-3™ and SuperCalc™ are being used primarily in financial forecasting (pro forma income and balance sheets) and operations planning. Both applications require an understanding of forecasting and simulation (what-if) analysis.

EDI and UPC

New electronic technology has dramatically changed operations management. These changes have affected all phases of operations—purchasing, production, and distribution. Electronic data interchange (EDI)—computer-application to computer-application communication—has reduced purchasing paperwork, decreased order-transmission leadtimes, and significantly reduced overall purchase leadtimes. For example, when EDI was used by a distributor, the cost of placing a purchase order dropped from $50 to approximately $15 an order. If a firm places 50,000 orders per year, then this reduces order costs by $1.75 million! Rapid data collection is further bolstered through the use of the universal product codes (UPC) and scanning devices.

The UPC are bar codes that are on almost all goods that we purchase in retail stores. These bar codes can reduce the time it takes to check out and collect point-of-sale (POS) information at the retail level. Also, use of the UPC results in significant productivity and accuracy gains in data collection in all phases of purchasing, production, distribution, and retailing.

Never before have so many people been *using and abusing* statistics and forecasts.

Dramatic Cost Reductions in Statistical Forecasting Software

Microcomputer-based statistical forecasting software now rivals that available on mainframe computers. For a few thousand dollars one can purchase forecasting software for a microcomputer that would have cost many thousands of dollars for a mainframe version. Compare, if you will, the cost of a mainframe spreadsheet program with a microcomputer spreadsheet program to appreciate the cost savings. Quite obviously, microcomputer software costs are a fraction of mainframe software costs because the system providers can spread the cost of the microcomputer software over a user base that numbers in the thousands instead of the hundreds for the mainframe version. The cost effectiveness of both mainframe- and microcomputer-based forecasting software has increased tremendously in recent years.

The More Sophisticated Planning of Competitors

Each of the trends above (cost containment, telecommunications, MIS integration, spreadsheets, and low-cost forecasting hardware and software) has made forecasting systems more essential for world-class competitiveness. Competitors are more effectively using systems that are driven by more-advanced forecasting systems.

These several trends place the highest priority on an understanding of forecasting and forecasting systems for operations managers.

FINANCIAL AND STRATEGIC IMPORTANCE OF FORECASTING

Nothing happens until somebody forecasts something.

The old marketing phrase "nothing happens until somebody sells something" is really more appropriately stated as "nothing happens until somebody forecasts something." Forecasts are essential to all plans and decisions because nothing happens until someone makes a forecast.

Better decisions come from better forecasts.

At first, profitability, productivity, and forecasting seem to be only slightly related concepts; however, there is a very strong relationship between them. The benefits from improved forecasting include:

Better marketing information.

Better financial information.

Better operations information.

Increased customer service.

Better allocation of scarce resources.

Increased manufacturing and operating efficiency.

Higher productivity.

Stability in planning.

Reduced finished-goods inventory.

Elimination of waste.

Computer Cost Justifications—The Early Days

The business computer has been in use since 1951, when the first commercial computer was installed in the U.S. Bureau of the Census. In the following three years, duplicates of this computer were being used by a few, very large companies at monthly rentals of about $25,000 (even more if we were to inflate to today's dollar). The Census Bureau finally retired its first computer to the Smithsonian Institution in 1964. In the early 1960s, the computer industry matured with a range of smaller and faster computers that rented for $700 to $300,000 per month. A 1964 book on computer applications provides this interesting perspective on the early days of computing.*

I. Desktop computers—Monthly rentals of $700 to $3,000. Examples: Monorobot X1, Autonetics Recomp III, IBM 1620. Punched Card Input-Output—Monthly rental of $1,500.

II. Small-scale computers—Monthly rentals of $2,000 to $7,000. Examples: Univac 80 and 90, RCA 301, CDC 160A, Burroughs 205, IBM 650. The IBM 650 had a magnetic drum with a capacity of 2,000, 10-digit words.

III. Medium-scale computers—Monthly rentals of $4,000 to $15,000. Examples: IBM 1401, GE 210, Honeywell H-400, NCR 315. The IBM 1401 had a 16,000-digit core storage capacity with 11.5 microsecond access.

IV. Large-scale computers—Monthly rentals of $15,000 to $300,000. Examples: IBM 704–7090, Univac 1105 and 1107, CDC 1604, Philco 2000. An IBM 7030 Stretch computer rented for $300,000 per month and could process tapes at 100,000 characters per second and execute instructions at 30,000 per second.

By today's standards, the above statistics are embarrassing; rental costs in 1964 were extraordinarily high while the performance measures were dismal compared to today's PCs. It is surprising that companies could justify the cost of computer applications; the improved competitive position or labor productivity gains were truly enormous for the large corporations. Today, the potential productivity gains from computer-based systems are not any less extraordinary. Current performance/cost ratios are thousands to millions of times greater than they were in 1964. It is considerably easier to justify the cost of new computer-based systems today than it was in 1964. The returns are truly extraordinary!

*Thomas H. Naylor and Eugene T. Byrne, *Linear Programming Methods and Cases* (Belmont, Calif.: Wadsworth Publishing, 1964), pp. 116–18.

More flexibility to respond to customer preferences.

Increased profitability.

Most important, increased return on investment.

Justifying New Systems–The Du Pont Model

An appendix to this chapter introduces the Du Pont financial model as a means of measuring the benefits and costs of implementing a new forecasting system. This model can be an important part of any cost-justification process, particularly when skeptics or the financial position of the firm make forecasting system purchases or development difficult. If you are developing or purchasing a forecasting system, we strongly recommend that you review this appendix.

Benefits from Improved Forecasting Systems– Some Actual Cases

The following actual cases were chosen as typical examples of successful applications of forecasting systems.

Automotive Manufacturer-Distributor
A manufacturer-distributor of automotive service parts with approximately 70,000 stockkeeping units reports a 30 percent reduction in inventory and a 50 percent reduction in required personnel to manage inventories while maintaining high levels of customer service.

Service Parts Distributor
A distributor having sales of $30 million of service parts and 10 distribution centers with approximately 6,000 parts in each reported a 20 percent increase in inventory turnover, an increase in customer service, and the ability to better control investment in inventory during business cycles. These benefits occur without offsetting negative changes in other performance variables.

Electrical Components Manufacturer-Distributor
A manufacturer-distributor of electrical components and construction supplies installed a forecasting and distribution system. Two

years after installation, there was a 70 percent decline in forecast errors, there were freight savings due to the ability to plan shipments for stock replenishments to branch warehouses, and inventory turnover improved from 4.5 to 6.5 times per year. The investment in inventory decreased by 30 percent, and leadtimes were better managed. Also, the improved planning of distribution inventories resulted in reductions in manufacturing and raw materials inventory investment. Finally, the percentage of orders shipped directly from stock increased from 85 to 95 percent.

Distributor and Food Processor

A distributor and processor of food commodities improved customer service by 8 points from 88 to 96 percent while reducing inventory by 30 percent. At the same time, it tripled the number of items in its catalog and increased sales by 36 percent.

Truck and Automotive Parts Distributor

A truck and automotive replacement parts distributor installed a forecasting/replenishment system. The forecasting error rate decreased by 50 percent (i.e., from 40 percent to 20 percent), and the return on investment from the software package was 350 percent after three years of use. The firm had five regional distribution centers that supplied 650,000 stockkeeping units. There were 13,000 parts at each regional distribution center representing a mix of 40,000 different parts. These 40,000 parts were members of 500 different part families.

Fashion Apparel Retailer

A fashion apparel retailer has approximately 250 stores supplied by four distribution centers. This retailer has approximately 5,000 different products in each store; thus, it manages 1,250,000 stockkeeping units. It installed an inventory system using electronic point-of-sale collection devices and after two years noted that the system had paid for itself at least three times. Management attributed the following benefits to use of the system: Buyers made better decisions, leadtimes decreased by 50 percent, inventory was

---

Modern Forecasting Systems and Inventory Management

Inventory management continues to be one of the least understood functions in modern organizations. Even in some of the larger companies, it has changed little over the last 40 years. A modern inventory-management system should:

1. Automatically manage each item carried in each warehouse or stock location.
2. Set the percentages of each item that will be in stock when demanded by customers.
3. Reorder quantities based on JIT techniques—such as the frequency of shipments, manufacturing cycles, and quick response—rather than on use of the economic order quantity.
4. Forecast each SKU using a combination of management and quantitative forecasting models.
5. Adjust the forecasts based on the effects of promotions and price changes.
6. Set buffer stocks using forecast errors so that the specified service level is achieved.
7. Update forecasts every planning cycle of once per month or week.
8. Provide for good inventory control by compiling excess and shortage lists of items needing managerial attention.
9. Effectively allocate scarce inventory over multiple stocking locations.
10. Be computer based.

These characteristics are essential if we are to achieve improved in-stock conditions and low investment in inventory.

---

reduced 30 percent, sales increased, and customer service increased. The company has been extremely pleased with system performance. The benefits it receives include more timely information, more-accurate forecasts, better distribution of the many different sizes and styles by region of the country, standardization of store operations, and the reduction of the time that management spends in tedious clerical data collection.

SUMMARY

This introductory chapter has discussed the importance of forecasting systems, customer service, the commonality of forecasting systems, typical examples of forecasting applications, recent trends in forecasting, and, finally, the financial and strategic importance of forecasting. As we showed, the typical benefits from new forecasting systems are numerous. The discussion of the Du Pont financial analysis model in the appendix to this chapter effectively demonstrates the benefits and justifies the costs of implementing new forecasting systems. The remaining chapters of this book provide technical and managerial principles of improved forecasting systems. While the benefits to be gained from improved forecasting methods are many, the demands on managers and employees are very high. Many of these demands are discussed in the remainder of this book.

APPENDIX: JUSTIFYING NEW FORECASTING SYSTEMS — THE DU PONT MODEL

The return on investment in forecasting systems is extraordinary.

Often, new computer-based systems have to be justified based on improvements in earnings and return on investment. Financial analysts and managers judge the performance of an organization on the basis of two important goals: high growth and stability of earnings. Obviously, a new forecasting system should help in achieving these goals. One of the most useful financial tools for judging the financial performance of a corporation and the impact of a new forecasting system is the Du Pont model of financial analysis introduced in Figure 1–4. This model is valuable in predicting the financial effects of changes in the accounts of the balance sheet and income statement.

While the Du Pont model is commonly used in business, it may be unfamiliar to some managers from the service sector. However, it is very useful for modeling the financial impact in a vari-

FIGURE 1-4
Returns with and without a New Forecasting System

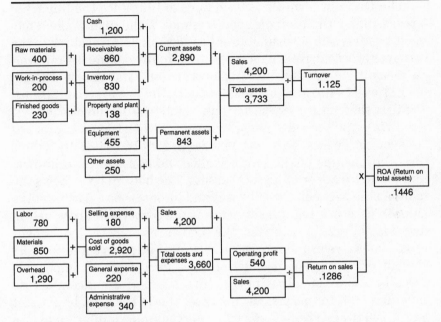

(a) Without new forecasting system

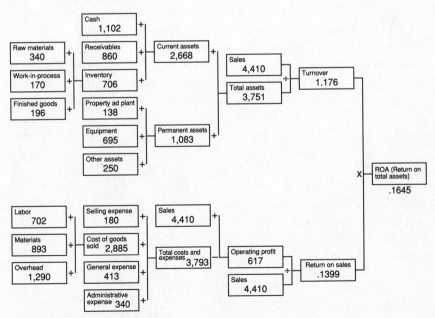

(b) With new forecasting system

ety of applications, including for-profit corporations, hospitals, and public agencies.

The Du Pont formula is used here to illustrate the impact of forecasting on the financial performance of the firm. Take a moment to study the several accounts and their relationships to the turnover of assets, return on sales, and, finally, an important overall measure of profitability—the return on total assets (ROA).

Figures 1–4(*a*) and (*b*) illustrate two Du Pont representations: The first shows company performance with the old forecasting system, while the second shows performance with the new forecasting system. The top half of the model in Figure 1–4(*a*) illustrates the relationships of the balance sheet accounts of an organization to the turnover of its total assets. The bottom half shows the relationship between the expenses and incomes of an income statement in determining the return that the corporation receives on its sales dollars. In this case, the firm turns its total assets over 1.125 times a year and receives a return on its sales equal to 12.86 percent per year. The product of these two yields an important overall measure of operating and financial performance, the rate of return on total assets; in this case, the ROA is 14.46 percent (i.e., 1.125 times 12.86). Let's run a very simple simulation to predict the results of investing in a new forecasting system.

Figure 1–4(*b*) is based on the assumption that the firm acquires a better forecasting system for $400,000. As a result, customer service increases because of a better mix of finished goods, which leads to a 5 percent increase in sales without any resultant increases in costs or investment; more-stable production schedules yield a 10 percent decrease in labor cost because of decreases in overtime and idle time; finally, investment in raw materials, work in process, and finished goods inventory each decline by 15 percent as a result of lower forecast errors. It costs the company 20 cents to hold each dollar of inventory for the year; thus, there are inventory-carry cost decreases with the new system. The net effects of these improvements are shown in Figure 1–4(*b*) assuming that the new forecasting system cost of $400,000 is amortized over three years at a 15 percent interest rate and is depreciated using an accelerated charge of 40 percent in the first year. (These are very conservative assumptions and resulting improvements; a slight modification of these figures can result in significantly greater improvements in financial performance.)

The first-year improvements in system performance are a 12 percent increase in return on sales (from 12.86 to 13.99), a 14 percent increase in return on assets (from 14.46 to 16.43), and a modest increase in turnover of all assets (from 1.125 to 1.176). These are significant improvements. Certainly, financial improvements like these will significantly increase the company's earnings per share of common stock.

Few projects have the potential ROI of better forecasting systems.

All of the figures used in these simple simulations were chosen to be conservative; it is not uncommon to see a 5 percent increase in sales, a 30 percent decrease in inventory, and similar improvements in other ratios as a consequence of improved forecasting. As shown by the Du Pont model, the financial benefits of improved operational forecasting are almost always very significant. If you do not already know how to use the Du Pont model and you need to justify new computer systems, then you should study it further.

CHAPTER 2

FORECASTING SYSTEMS IN OPERATIONS MANAGEMENT

System Control and Maintenance
Database Records
SUMMARY
REFERENCE

Plan your operations realistically, pay attention to detail, and
do not omit contingencies for unknowns.

In this chapter, we introduce important principles of forecasting
systems in operations management. We first discuss decision making as it relates to forecasting systems and then answer some very
basic questions concerning what a forecast is, why forecasts are
necessary, what should be forecast, and where one should forecast. In addition, we provide insights on how to integrate forecasts at different levels in the organization. The answers to these
questions provide important principles; and, as illustrated by the
box on the next page, these principles cannot be ignored without
serious consequences to the firm.

HIERARCHICAL
MANAGEMENT SYSTEMS

THE MANAGEMENT DECISION HIERARCHY

To better understand the many types and purposes of forecasts,
Figure 2–1 illustrates the management decision hierarchy of organizations. This hierarchy is represented by the triangular sequence of decisions that progress from highest-level decisions of
strategic business planning, managerial planning, and operational
control, to the lowest-level decisions, transaction processing. This
figure is a modification of a model that was popularized by Professor Robert Anthony of the Harvard Business School. It is important because it is generic to all organizations whether public or
private, product or service oriented. This hierarchical and sequential decision-making system is one that assists in understanding
the many functions and responsibilities in organizations; we use
it here to highlight the importance of forecasting.

The left-hand side of the figure presents the hierarchy of decisions of all organizations, while the far-right column denotes

Being Out of Stock Can Be Fatal!

The following is a full-page advertisement that recently appeared in several large metropolitan newspapers. This ad was part of a campaign to offset publicity concerning the out-of-stock conditions of a hardware store chain. We have changed the advertisement, name, and industry as a matter of courtesy to the original firm. This advertisement has meaning for all firms that do not have adequate controls and systems for assuring high levels of customer service.

We're Sorry!

We've disappointed our customers and that's almost unforgivable!

In the last 10 years, we've grown from a small chain of hardware stores to one of the largest retailers in the country. We've worked hard and fast, and we've also disappointed some of our customers more than once.

We've learned how to buy products in quantity at very low prices. We've created interesting and exciting stores. And we've learned how to attract customers with the right product and right price. Unfortunately, at times we've also run out of stock. Also, we've learned the hard way that it's faster and easier to ship a newspaper ad than a truckload of power saws or a trainload of ladders. We've disappointed a lot of customers and that's almost unforgivable.

As unpleasant as it is to want to buy something that's unavailable, it's equally painful for us to spend money on advertising only to disappoint and anger our customers. Solving this problem is our number-one corporate priority. To this end, we've built a new distribution center and we're bringing on-line a new state-of-the-art computerized inventory-management system. This system will help ensure that sufficient merchandise is in stock to support our advertising.

Even with these advanced systems and our commitment, we know that an occasional out-of-stock situation will occur. And no matter what the reason, whether it's a manufacturer's shipping delay or our own mistake, we want you to be satisfied. So, from this moment on, if we don't have an advertised product in stock, we'll give you a raincheck and a 5 percent discount, or we'll have a more expensive substitute available at the same price. In addition, if we can't fill your

---

Being Out of Stock Can Be Fatal!   (continued)

raincheck within 10 days, we'll discount your purchase an extra 10 percent when the product arrives. If we ever fail to live up to your expectations, we want to know. Ask for the store manager or call us on our customer satisfaction line. Simply dial (800)555-XXXX. We want you as our customer, and we're sorry.

Sincerely,

I. M. Responsible
Chairman and CEO
High Quality, Low Prices, Inc.

---

the important decisions in a manufacturing organization. As shown in the second column of Figure 2–1, forecasts drive all decisions. Of particular interest here is that all immediate to medium-horizon resource allocations are driven by the forecasting system. Take a moment to study the objectives and decisions of each hierarchy and place these in the context of your own business. You should be able to place the major decisions of your firm in this diagram.

All immediate to medium-horizon resource allocations are driven by the forecasting system.

Consider this figure in greater detail. The first column, Objectives of Management, identifies the responsibilities of the different levels of management. Quite obviously, these objectives cover the very strategic, top-management level to detailed day-to-day operations. The key idea conveyed by this figure is that managers are responsible for achieving these hierarchical objectives. Managers must coordinate these objectives to fulfill the overall goals of the organization.

The next column, Forecast Horizon Length, specifies the number of periods into the future that are planned at each level; for example, in business planning, the firm plans for 3 to 20 years

FIGURE 2–1
Hierarchy of Goals, Decisions, and Functions

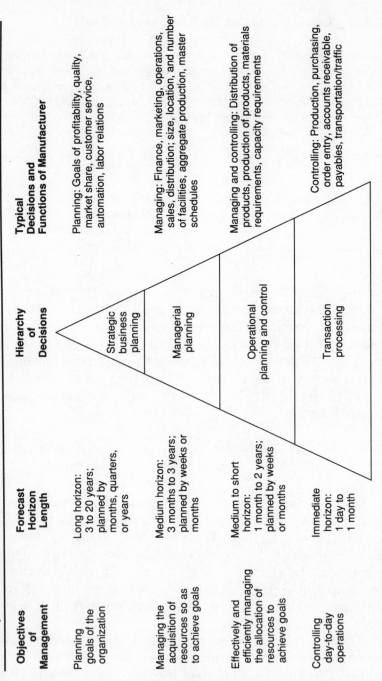

Objectives of Management	Forecast Horizon Length	Hierarchy of Decisions	Typical Decisions and Functions of Manufacturer
Planning goals of the organization	Long horizon: 3 to 20 years; planned by months, quarters, or years	Strategic business planning	Planning: Goals of profitability, quality, market share, customer service, automation, labor relations
Managing the acquisition of resources so as to achieve goals	Medium horizon: 3 months to 3 years; planned by weeks or months	Managerial planning	Managing: Finance, marketing, operations, sales, distribution; size, location, and number of facilities, aggregate production, master schedules
Effectively and efficiently managing the allocation of resources to achieve goals	Medium to short horizon: 1 month to 2 years; planned by weeks or months	Operational planning and control	Managing and controlling: Distribution of products, production of products, materials requirements, capacity requirements
Controlling day-to-day operations	Immediate horizon: 1 day to 1 month	Transaction processing	Controlling: Production, purchasing, order entry, accounts receivable, payables, transportation/traffic

into the future using either years or quarters. As one progresses down the hierarchy, the involvement of top management decreases and that of lower management increases. Also, as shown in the figure, the horizon length (i.e., how far one plans in the future) decreases as the level of detail increases.

The forecast horizon lengths shown in the figure are prescriptive of the way firms should plan and are descriptive of how the better-managed firms plan. The decision or function column (i.e., the far-right column) identifies the major activity of each level of a typical manufacturing firm. (If you are unfamiliar with manufacturing and the terms used here, you can skip this column or you can refer to the glossary at the end of this book.) Of particular interest here is that medium- to short-term forecasts are major inputs to the operational planning and control activities of production planning, distribution requirements planning (DRP), master production scheduling (MPS), and inventory management.

This top-down representation of the organization is very important in providing an organizational structure that will achieve common, yet hierarchical, goals. Almost all known systems are hierarchical, whether they are social, biological, physical, or ecological systems. Hierarchical systems have top-down dominance—decisions at a higher level place constraints on decisions at lower levels. Also, the decisions at one level are interdependent with decisions at all levels. As we will see, forecasting systems also have this hierarchical structure.

Hierarchical systems are effective because of their ability to handle exceedingly large numbers of complex relationships. Also, they require less information transmission and allow departments or subsystems to work somewhat independently toward subgoals that support higher-level goals.

As we progress down the decision hierarchy, the level of information and system detail increases. Hence, a pyramid is used to represent the system. Also, while moving down the pyramid, we move from ill-structured, nonprogrammable decisions of top management to programmable decisions at the lowest levels of the organization. The term *nonprogrammed* means that top-management decisions are not routine or repetitive. For example, prior to the early 1970s, the U.S. automobile industry had never faced serious international competition; few simple or routine rules existed to deal with this situation when it occurred. Consequently, considerable creativity was involved in responding to this situation. In fact, the strategies taken by Ford, GM, and Chrysler differed considerably.

In contrast to ill-structured decisions, the management of inventory at the lower levels of the hierarchy is normally a more-structured, repetitive decision process that is so programmable as to be compatible with high levels of automation. For example, in inventory management, once the computer-based management systems are in place, many of the decisions of inventory management can be automated. Only when exceptions are detected does management need to become part of the programmed decision process. We shall develop the programmed-decision and exception-reporting characteristics of these systems later.

In summary, as we progress down the hierarchy,

Decisions become less strategic.

Top-management involvement decreases.

Leadtimes of decisions decrease.

Forecast horizon lengths decrease from years to weeks.

Decisions become more programmable.

Levels of detail increase greatly.

Levels of automation increase.

Computers are used to support more repetitive decision making.

As we will show, a good forecasting system will be hierarchical in nature with most of the characteristics listed above.

A forecasting system should support hierarchical decision making.

A forecasting system should make routine decisions without human intervention.

A forecasting system should highlight exceptions for managerial intervention.

MANUFACTURING PLANNING AND CONTROL SYSTEMS

Figure 2–2 illustrates the management system of a manufacturer-distributor in considerable detail. The system illustrated in the figure is commonly called a manufacturing planning and control system (MPCS), a production and information control system (PICS), or a manufacturing resource planning system (MRPII). This comprehensive diagram is useful in understanding how forecasting is used in MPCSs to achieve hierarchical goals. You will notice in this diagram the same characteristics as the hierarchical diagram of Figure 2–1. Again, note that forecasts drive the planning and subsequent allocation of product, material, and capacity resources. Long-horizon forecasts drive business and sales planning, while medium- to short-horizon forecasts drive production planning, distribution requirements planning, and master production scheduling. All other plans and decisions are based on (i.e., dependent on) the plans at these higher levels.

After some study of Figure 2–2, you should be able to generalize it to your firm and better relate to the hierarchical nature of MPCSs and forecasting systems. For an explanation of terms, please refer to the glossary. We will return to the topic of systems later; for now we will discuss some very important basics of forecasting.

FORECASTING BASICS

WHY FORECAST?

Forecasts are necessary because of implementation leadtimes.

Forecasting is most often part of a larger process of planning and managing. A forecast is necessary to provide accurate estimates of the future for this larger process. We have seen that in the hierarchy of decisions, some decisions take considerably longer to implement than others. If a decision requires a long time to implement, then long-horizon forecasts are necessary to provide long-

FIGURE 2–2
Production Information Control System for Manufacturer-Distributor

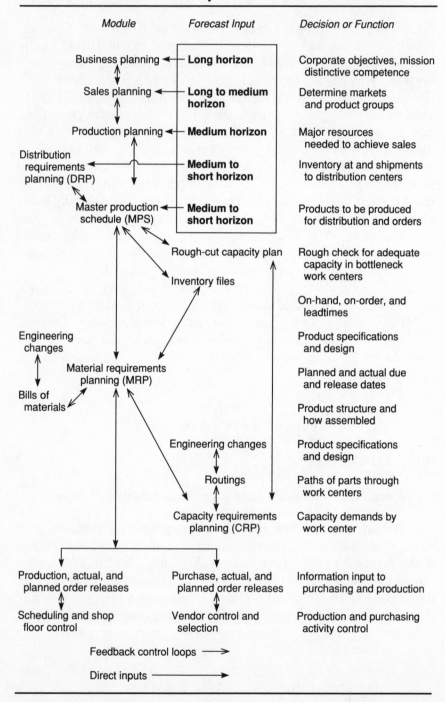

Module	Forecast Input	Decision or Function
Business planning	**Long horizon**	Corporate objectives, mission distinctive competence
Sales planning	**Long to medium horizon**	Determine markets and product groups
Production planning	**Medium horizon**	Major resources needed to achieve sales
Distribution requirements planning (DRP)	**Medium to short horizon**	Inventory at and shipments to distribution centers
Master production schedule (MPS)	**Medium to short horizon**	Products to be produced for distribution and orders
	Rough-cut capacity plan	Rough check for adequate capacity in bottleneck work centers
	Inventory files	On-hand, on-order, and leadtimes
Engineering changes		Product specifications and design
Material requirements planning (MRP)		Planned and actual due and release dates
Bills of materials		Product structure and how assembled
	Engineering changes	Product specifications and design
	Routings	Paths of parts through work centers
	Capacity requirements planning (CRP)	Capacity demands by work center
Production, actual, and planned order releases	Purchase, actual, and planned order releases	Information input to purchasing and production
Scheduling and shop floor control	Vendor control and selection	Production and purchasing activity control

Feedback control loops ⟶

Direct inputs ⟶

Horizon Length	Time Buckets*	Level of Detail	Computer Manufacturer Example
3–20 years	Years or quarters	Aggregate ($)	Strategic financial, quality, automation, and service goals
3–20 years	Quarters or months	Groups (families) or product lines	Market goals for mainframe, mini, and microcomputers
3–10 years	Quarters or months	Production lines and plants	Number, location, types of plants; production, labor, and $ at plants
1–2 years	Weeks or months	Disaggregate by products	Actual (planned) shipments of each type of computer at DCs
1–2 years	Weeks or months	Disaggregate by products	The build or assembly schedule of specific computers at plants
1–2 years	Weeks or months	Aggregate labor- and machine-hours	Planning and verifying sufficient assembly and fabrication capacity in constrained work centers
Database		Actual products, assemblies, and parts	Quantity on hand and on order of each computer type and components
Database		Defines all products, assemblies, and parts	Specifications of parts and assemblies used in computers
1–2 years	Weeks	All parts and assemblies	Requirements of all materials used in subassemblies and products
Database		Defines all products, assemblies, and parts	Product structure of different computers and components
Database		Defines all products, assemblies, and parts	
Database		All parts and assemblies	Routing of computer parts and assemblies through the shop
< 1 year	Weeks	All work centers in shop	Capacity requirements in all work centers by time period
Database		All purchases and produced parts	Planned and actual production and purchase orders
< 1 year	Weeks	All purchases and shop orders	Detailed scheduling of actual production and purchases

*Bucketless systems are now in use in which any activity is stored by date.

range information for planning purposes (e.g., business planning in Figure 2–1). In contrast, if a decision takes a short time to implement, then it only requires a short-horizon forecast as an input (e.g., operational planning and control in Figure 2–1). Operating decisions may have long or short leadtimes. For example, the decision to build a new plant may require five years to actually implement, while the decision to purchase additional parts or supplies may take only a day or two. Thus, forecasts are necessary to support decisions that will not be fully implemented until some future date.

Forecasts are necessary to reduce uncertainties about the future.

One of the major benefits from reducing implementation leadtimes is the resulting reduction in the horizon length of the forecast. For example, when the JIT philosophy is properly implemented, supplier and production leadtimes can be reduced significantly. Consider an example where order leadtime is reduced from 16 weeks to 2 weeks. In this situation, the forecast horizon decreases accordingly. As shown in Chapter 16, when the leadtime or forecast horizon decreases, the accuracy of the forecast increases. Thus, with reduced leadtimes, we have greater flexibility to change plans in the future (weeks 3 and later) and more-accurate forecasts with which to make decisions in the present (weeks 1 and 2). That is, the forecast of demand for the next 2 weeks will be more accurate than the forecast for the next 16 weeks. This relationship between leadtime and forecast accuracy yields the following principles.

Reducing forecast horizon lengths improves forecast accuracy.

Long leadtimes force future uncertainty on the present.

Long leadtimes require commitments of resources in the present despite the considerable uncertainty of the future.

Let us expand on this last principle. When a decision has to be made in the present, but there is considerable uncertainty because of the long leadtimes involved in implementing this decision (e.g., the decision to build a new electric power plant that will not be operational for 10 years), then the implementation leadtime forces management to assume much greater risk. Financial, marketing, and operating risks increase the further into the future we have to commit resources. The benefits of reducing leadtimes and uncertainty are illustrated in the box entitled "Why Made in America Is Back in Style."

WHAT IS A FORECAST?

A forecast should be a point, range, and probability estimate.

Because we all formally or informally make forecasts, we have an intuitive idea of what a forecast is—a forecast is an estimate or description of a future value or condition. While this is a good

---

Why Made in America Is Back in Style

"The ability to keep pace with fickle fashions is offsetting low wages as a lure for garment makers." Retailers in the fashion garment industry have learned that they have to respond very "quickly to the famous question: What do women want?" In order to better answer this question, apparel producers are moving production operations back to the United States in order to reduce the leadtimes in production and distribution. By reducing leadtimes, the producers can more quickly respond to demand at the retail level, a difficult task when minimum leadtimes for products from Asia are four months.

Until very recently, much apparel was produced offshore; however, some firms have been returning to the United States. Increased revenue generation has been cited as the justification for incurring 25 percent higher production costs in the United States. For example, by moving a production facility to the United States, the manufacturer can achieve shorter leadtimes and faster turnover and, consequently, increase profit margins by having fewer markdowns. The domestically produced garment generates 25 percent more retail profit margin than the imported garment. The manufacturer-distributor doesn't "have to project demand a year in advance, finance it with letters of credit, or worry about the vagaries of a typhoon knocking a ship out." Thus, the manufacturer can make better decisions because of reduced uncertainty of forecasts.

Source: *Business Week,* November 7, 1988, pp. 116–20.

general definition, formal planning and control require that a good forecast have three important dimensions. *A good forecast is a probabilistic estimate of a future value or condition that yields a mean, range, and probability estimate of the range.* The term *probabilistic* emphasizes that a forecast should not be a single number, but a range of numbers with a probability estimate. For example, a good forecast statement is "expected sales next month for a product is 400 with a 70 percent probability that sales will be 300 to 500 units" (i.e., a 35 percent chance of sales from 300 to 400 and a 35 percent chance from 400 to 500). The method used to arrive at this statement is shown in Chapter 7.

Forecasts are necessary to reduce the risk in decision making.

The probability estimates of forecasts are very important in contingency planning. Because forecasts always have errors, management should have plans for when errors occur, particularly when errors are large. For example, if sales are 300 units instead of 400, then management should have a plan that minimizes the negative effects of low sales. Likewise, when sales are 500 instead of 400, then management should have an alternative contingency plan. Forecasting is designed to reduce the uncertainty or risk in decision making; however, it cannot completely eliminate all uncertainty and risk. This is highlighted by the following principle.

Forecast accuracy is important, but valid contingency plans when the inevitable errors occur are more important.

All managers forecast. While most managers are not aware that they are making probability statements when they forecast, they are nonetheless implicitly doing so. For example, when someone forecasts that demand will be 900 units next month, they are making an implicit statement that there is a 50 percent chance that demand will be greater than 900 and a 50 percent chance demand will be less than 900. The probability dimension of forecasting should always be remembered, as highlighted by the following principle.

Forecasts are frequently wrong, and when right, they might be right for the wrong reasons.

Basic Assumption of Forecasting

Many different methods can be used to forecast the future. However, the basic underlying assumption of the most widely used forecasting methods is the same: Past patterns or relationships will continue in the future. Some managers think that their firms do not forecast; they simply assume that last month's sales will equal this month's sales; however, this is a simple method of forecasting. In fact, this highlights one of the most important assumptions of forecasting.

Almost all forecasts are based on the assumption that the past will repeat.

We will more fully develop this important principle in Chapters 7 to 14, where we show that simple projections of the past will often provide very effective forecasts.

WHAT SHOULD BE FORECAST?

Dependent versus Independent Demands

Forecast independent demands and then calculate the many dependent demands.

There is an important, yet simple, relationship concerning demands for products, services, and resources. *A demand is independent when it has to be forecast.* In contrast, dependent demands can be calculated directly from known physical or technical relationships. For example, a firm manufactures microcomputers, and the demand for their final assembly (called a system unit) must be forecast; therefore, it has independent demand. However, the demands for system circuit boards, disk drives, and computer housings do not have to be forecast, but instead can be calculated from the forecast of system units. Each forecasted system unit must have a circuit board, at least one disk drive, and a housing. Fortunately, most demands for resources in an organization are dependent and do not have to be forecasted, but instead can be calculated based on other forecasts.

Consider another example. If a company manufactures children's wagons, bicycles, and tricycles, then the demands for these products have to be forecast. However, the demand for the wheels, axles, and other parts of the wagons, bicycles, and tricycles do not have to be forecast, but instead can be calculated on the basis of the bill of materials for the product. The demand for wagon wheels is completely dependent on the assembly schedule for wagons. Since there are four wheels per wagon, the assembly of 100 wagons requires 400 wheels.

While this distinction between independent and dependent demands seems obvious, it was nonetheless ignored by many manufacturers until the early 1960s. Prior to that time, many firms forecasted the demand for wagons, wheels, axles, and so on without regard to this simple principle. Even more inappropriately, the demand for all these dependent items were forecasted independently. For example, the forecast for wagons might have been 100, while the forecast for wheels was 300. An order for 100 wagons could not be assembled with only 300 wheels in stock.

The independent-dependent distinction may at times be subtle. For example, a distributor-retailer might not recognize that the demand at regional distribution centers is completely dependent on the demands at the retail store. The distributor-retailer should forecast demand at the retail store and then calculate demand at the distribution center as the sum of the retail store demands. Dependent demands are difficult to forecast accurately; thus, a firm may be forecasting the wrong thing and doing it very badly. This yields the following principle.

Don't forecast dependent demands; forecast accuracy cannot be achieved with dependent demands.

Table 2–1 presents some other very simple relationships between independent and dependent demand items.

Forecasting Hierarchy – The Process of Aggregation/Disaggregation

The general planning process involves several different forecast dimensions. That is, there is not one forecast made in an organization, but a hierarchy of forecasts. Consider Table 2–2, which presents the hierarchy of forecasts for a computer manufacturer.

TABLE 2–1
Independent versus Dependent Demands

Organization	Independent Demands Forecasted	Dependent Demands Calculated
Manufacturer	Product demand at the factory	Parts in the product Labor schedules Machine schedules
Manufacturer-distributor	Product demand at distribution centers	Products at the factory and factory warehouse Labor and machine schedules
Wholesaler	Product demands at distribution centers	Demands at central warehouses or suppliers
Retailers	Product demand at each store	Demands for sales and service personnel
Distributor-retailer	Product demand at each store	Demands at distribution centers and warehouses
Hospitals	Number of patients by DRG or MDC	Number of nurses Material and drug demands Number of beds
Utilities	Kilowatt hours of power	Number of generating plants on-line, power purchased from other utilities
	New-home hookups Equipment breakdowns	Home watt meters Size of service crew
School district	Number of students by grade	Number of faculty, classes, laboratories
Universities	Number of students seeking a course	Number of faculty, classrooms, laboratories
Municipalities	Traffic counts on roads	Number and location of roads, lanes, bridges, and lights
	Applicants for licenses and permits	Number of employees

These forecasts are made of aggregate and disaggregate demands for the products of the firm. For example, the forecast hierarchy progresses from estimates of industry demand, to company demand, to product-line (i.e., group) demands, to companywide demands for specific products, and, finally, to specific product demands at particular locations.

TABLE 2-2
Multiple Forecasts of Demands for Computers – The Demand Hierarchy

Type of Demand	Example of Demand Forecasts
Industry demand	General demand for products of an industry, e.g., the industry demand for microcomputers, minis, and mainframes
Company demand	The company's market share
Product-line demand	Three product-line (micro, mini, and mainframe) demands need to be estimated at this level
Companywide product demands	National demand for 32-bit microcomputers; national demand for 64-bit minis; national demand for 64-bit mainframes
Demand for each product at each location	Demand for microcomputers at St. Louis distribution center, Los Angeles distribution center, New York distribution center

Consistent Forecasts – The One-Number Principle

When a firm makes may different forecasts of the same items, there is the possibility that the different forecasts are not equal. This is very likely unless a concerted effort is made to keep the forecasts consistent. The principle that higher-level and lower-level forecasts must be consistent is important. That is, the sum of the stockkeeping unit (SKU) demands should equal the companywide demands for that end-item group (a SKU is a specific item, for example, a 486 microcomputer, at a specific location such as retail store #47); the sum of end-item demands should equal product-line demands; and so forth up and down the product hierarchy. This principle of forecasting is sometimes called the *one-number* principle. This principle is important because, if different forecasts exist in different functional areas of the firm (e.g., marketing, finance, and operations), then the decisions of these functional areas will be inconsistent. For example, operations might plan the production of 1,000 units, finance might budget the acquisition of 900 units, while marketing might forecast 600 units. Efficient forecasting and effective decisions are made by assuring that a consistent forecast is used by all decision makers.

Table 2–3 illustrates an example of the one-number principle where the sum of forecasted regional distribution demands

TABLE 2-3
Consistent Forecasts at Different Levels of the Hierarchy

	Forecasted Demand	
Item	Units	Percent
Regional Distribution Demands		
Region I 486-microcomputer demand	1,307	21.3%
Region II 486-microcomputer demand	1,489	24.3
Region III 486-microcomputer demand	1,364	22.2
Region IV 486-microcomputer demand	1,977	32.2
Total regional demands	6,137	100.0%
National Demand		
486 microcomputers	6,137	
Revenue Forecasts		
6,137 486s @ $3,500	$21,479,500	

equals corporationwide demands and marketing revenue forecasts.
All of the six different forecasts listed in the table were generated independently and were initially not equal to each other.
However, it is important to reconcile the differences in the forecasts and to adjust each to be consistent with the other. As discussed in Chapter 3, there are several different ways to achieve
consistent forecasts.

The one-number principle—all forecasts of
the same product or activity should be equal.

Achieving Consistent Forecasts

There are several ways of generating consistent forecasts up and
down the hierarchy. These can be generated either from the top
down or from the bottom up. The top-down approach is used when
companywide demand is estimated for all products (e.g., 6,137 computers per year) and then historical ratios (e.g., 21.3% Region I,
24.3% Region II, 22.2% Region III, and 32.2% Region IV) are used
to generate specific demands for each region. In contrast, there

is a bottom-up approach to forecasting where the individual demands for each region are generated and accumulated upward to arrive at a company demand. There is a third way of forcing consistency; this approach and the two mentioned above are discussed fully in Chapter 3.

Discrete-Item Errors versus Cumulative-Group Errors

Cumulative-group errors are normally less than discrete-item errors.

The cumulative-group errors of forecasts are normally less than the errors of the individual items. For example, as shown in Table 2–4, the forecast errors for each item of a four-item group were typically −11 to 16.7 percent; however, the cumulative-group error for the total four-item group was only 2.5 percent (100/4,000). Therefore, individual forecast errors were sometimes high and sometimes low, and consequently the cumulative-group error is considerably less.

Short–Time-Period Errors versus Cumulative–Time-Period Errors

Cumulative–time-period errors are normally less than short–time-period errors.

Table 2–5 illustrates the errors over a four-week period. As shown, the forecast errors for the four-week periods varied from −11 to 16.7 percent; however, the cumulative-time error for the total four-week period was only 2.5 percent. Individual weekly forecast errors were sometimes high and sometimes low, yet the cumulative-time error for the four-week period was quite low, much less than the typical weekly error. Tables 2–4 and 2–5 intentionally use the same numbers in different settings because the principle of cumulative errors is applicable to both time and cumulative groups.

The cumulative-error principle is normally true but not always true for every item. The principle does not hold when the forecasts and errors are predominantly high or low, a condition

TABLE 2–4
Cumulative Errors Are Lower than Item Errors

					Cumulative		
Item	Actual	Forecast	Error	Percent Error	Actual	Error	Percent Error
1	1,000	900	100	10%	1,000	100	10 %
2	900	1,000	−100	−11.1	1,900	0	0
3	900	1,000	−100	−11.1	2,800	−100	−3.6
4	1,200	1,000	200	16.7	4,000	100	2.5
Total	4,000	3,900	100	n.a.	4,000	100	2.5%

n.a. = not available.
Error is actual minus forecast. Percent error is error divided by actual.

TABLE 2–5
Cumulative–Time-Period Errors Are Lower than Short–Time-Period Errors

					Cumulative		
Week	Actual	Forecast	Error	Percent Error	Actual	Error	Percent Error
1	1,000	900	100	10%	1,000	100	10 %
2	900	1,000	−100	−11.1	1,900	0	0
3	900	1,000	−100	−11.1	2,800	−100	−3.6
4	1,200	1,000	200	16.7	4,000	100	2.5
Total	4,000	3,900	100	n.a.	4,000	100	2.5%

n.a. = not available.
Error is actual minus forecast. Percent error is error divided by actual.

called bias or dependence. When this occurs, the cumulative error may not be lower than every item's error. Table 2–6 illustrates a situation in which there is considerable bias in the forecasts of the items; all forecasts are low. As we will show later, biased forecast errors should be avoided, detected, and eliminated. Chapter 14 discusses the statistical tools that can be used to detect and eliminate forecast bias.

Biased forecasts yield biased errors and biased cumulative errors.

TABLE 2-6
With Bias, Cumulative Errors Equal Typical Item Error

					Cumulative		
Week	Actual	Forecast	Error	Percent Error	Actual	Error	Percent Error
1	1,000	900	100	10%	1,000	100	10 %
2	1,000	900	100	10	2,000	200	10
3	900	800	100	11.1	2,900	300	10.3
4	1,200	1,000	200	16.7	4,100	500	12.2
Total	4,100	3,600	500	n.a.	4,100	500	12.2%

n.a. = not available.
Error is actual minus forecast. Percent error is error divided by actual.

Group Forecasts

Group forecasts are normally more accurate than individual forecasts.

Group demands are normally less random than individual demands.

Because group demands are normally less random than item demands, there is normally less error in group forecasts.[1] The group-error principle states that, in general, the error in a group forecast is normally less than the error in a specific product forecast. Consider a group that consists of four items (1, 2, 3, and 4) shown in Table 2-7. These items are each forecast individually as shown in the forecast line. In contrast, the actual demands of the four items are added together to yield the group demand of 1,703 in column 6. Using past group history, the group forecast was determined to be 1,842 (using a model of past group data). As shown in column 6, the error in the group demand forecast is less on a percentage basis than the typical percent error in the demand forecast of the individual items. This illustrates the group forecasting accuracy principle.

As shown by Item 3 of Table 2-7, the group error is not always lower than all individual-item errors. This is true because,

TABLE 2-7
Group Forecast Accuracy versus Individual Forecast Accuracy

	Item				Cumulative	Group
	1	2	3	4		
Actual	460	676	283	284	1,703	1,703
Forecast	351	853	294	328	1,826	1,842
Error	109	−177	−11	−44	−123	−139
Percent error	.24	−.26	−.04	−.15	−.07	−.08

Cumulative equals the sum of items 1, 2, 3, and 4.

if the demand for an individual item is large and not very random, then its individual-item errors may be less than its group error.

*When an item has low randomness, then its
error may be less than its group error.*

Cumulative Errors versus Group Errors

Table 2–7 also illustrates the cumulative principle of Tables 2–5 and 2–4 in the Cumulative column. As shown in column 5, the cumulative error is much lower than the typical error. It is important to note that normally both the cumulative and group errors are lower than the individual errors; however, the manner in which these two errors were calculated is considerably different. Group error results from a single group forecast, and cumulative error is the sum of several individual forecast errors. This difference is a subtle but important distinction, as shown in Tables 2–5 and 2–7. Both the cumulative and group principles are important in forecasting system design.

Using Groups in Forecasting Systems

Most forecasting systems use the cumulative error and group forecasting principles in their design. This is effective because the planning and forecasting processes are hierarchical. For example, because a group forecast is normally considerably better than an individual-item or individual-week forecast, it is possible to plan higher-level group decisions more accurately. Forecasts of groups of products or time periods use less-random data than those of individual products or time periods. Thus, forecasting and planning systems should be designed to take advantage of the increased accuracy of group errors across items and time. For example, dollar group forecasts will be more accurate than individual-item dollar sales forecasts. We shall develop more fully this and several other forecasting system design features in Chapter 3.

Forecasting systems should support more-accurate group forecasts.

WHAT IS AN OPERATIONAL FORECASTING SYSTEM?

In this book we distinguish between the terms *forecasting method* and *forecasting system*. A forecasting method is a mathematical or subjective technique for generating a forecast. Many statistical forecasting software packages are implementations of forecasting methods. In contrast, Figure 2–3 illustrates the six modules of a comprehensive forecasting system. The requirements of a good operational forecasting system are considerably greater than those of a good statistical forecasting package. A forecasting system is a computer-based system that typically

- Processes thousands of records accurately and quickly.
- Captures and maintains 24 to 36 months or more of demand data.
- Automatically provides 12 monthly forecasts for thousands of items.
- Groups items with low demand to achieve good group forecasts.
- Is capable of modeling demand with trends and seasonality.
- Collects data from geographically diverse locations.

FIGURE 2–3
The Modules of a Forecasting System

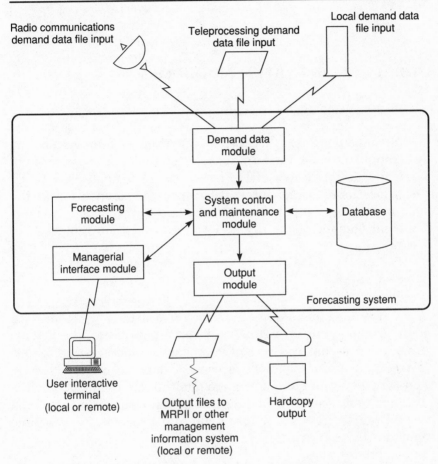

Radio communications demand data file input

Teleprocessing demand data file input

Local demand data file input

Demand data module

Forecasting module

System control and maintenance module

Database

Managerial interface module

Output module

Forecasting system

User interactive terminal (local or remote)

Output files to MRPII or other management information system (local or remote)

Hardcopy output

- Generates hierarchical reports for several levels of management.
- Provides ease of use to various types of users.
- Provides management with diagnostic, graphic, and interactive interfaces with the system.
- Is a means of integrating the market demand information needs of operations, marketing, and financial management.

The forecasting system modules of Figure 2–3 perform these and many other functions. We briefly review each of these modules below.

FORECASTING SYSTEM MODULES

Demand Data

The demand data module captures and processes demand before it is input to the demand database. It captures data via manual or electronic data entry, either locally or from geographically diverse locations. It also automatically checks to ensure that the data has not been input incorrectly or affected by unusual events. Unusual demand is highlighted and an exception reported.

Forecasting

The forecasting module selects a good forecasting model for each item, group, or entity managed by the firm. Thousands of items are in the database; consequently, thousands of forecasting models are selected and many more forecasts are made. Typically, forecasts are generated for 12 or more months into the future. In addition, the forecasting module generates group forecasts for a number of logical groupings, including product-line and low-demand items.

Managerial Interface and Interaction

The managerial interface and interaction module is the user interface to the forecasting system. It should provide a user-friendly graphical interface, screen displays, and navigational aids, thereby facilitating manager interaction with the forecasting system. In addition, it should provide good user help so that the system is easy to learn and use.

Output

The output module generates routine periodic batch reports and output files, including exception reports. These exception reports are important because they identify situations requiring human intervention in the forecasting process.

System Control and Maintenance

This module is the command center of the system that controls data and information flow between the modules. It is the operating and control system that directs user inputs, demand data, forecasts, and output to their correct destinations. This is why it is shown in the center of Figure 2–3. It also supports sophisticated user-system interactions, such as forecast simulations and other what-if analyses.

Database Records

The database records module holds actual demands, adjusted demands, seasonal information, and special event data for each item and group being forecast. This database can be quite large because it contains this information for the last 36 months or longer. Also, additional data–such as 12 or more monthly forecasts and the performance of past forecasts of all items and groups–are stored in this database. It is not uncommon, therefore, to have hundreds of thousands of item demands in the database. The database is updated periodically, typically every week or month.

Forecasting systems are considerably
more complex than forecasting methods.

Our above discussion of the modules in Figure 2–3 was necessarily brief at this time. We spend the next 18 chapters developing the functions of these modules. In addition to module functionality, we provide guidelines and principles of good forecasting systems. As you will see, all chapters of this book relate directly to one or more of these forecasting system modules.

Table 2–8 provides a more-comprehensive presentation of the modules of a good forecasting system and serves as a preview of the many topics we will study. For some of you, several of the

TABLE 2–8
The Modules of a Forecasting System

I. Demand data module.
　1. System input and output of local and remote demand data.
　2. Demand capturing.
　3. Logical filtering (demand versus supply or shipments).
　4. Special event filtering (promotions, price changes, and product introductions)
　5. Initial outlier detection, adjustment, and classification.
II. Forecasting module.
　1. System forecast model selection.
　2. Outlier detection, adjustment, and classification.
　3. Reasonableness test.
　4. Final forecast.
　5. Error measures.
　6. Tracking signal control.
III. Managerial interface and interaction module.
　1. Graphical user interface.
　2. Graphical presentations.
　3. Screen displays.
　4. Management forecasts.
　5. User help.
　6. Management feedback.
　7. User notepad.
　8. Expert advisory menu.
IV. Output module.
　1. File generation.
　2. Routine reports.
　3. Ad hoc reports.
　4. Exception reports.
V. System control and maintenance module.
　1. Navigation and system control of modules.
　2. Input/output control between modules.
　3. Simulation control.
　4. Database updating and maintenance.
　5. Detection of system malfunctions and bugs.
VI. Database.
　1. Actual and forecasted demand history.
　2. Adjusted demand history.
　3. Seasonal and promotional profiles.
　4. Performance measures.
　5. Item and group relationships and descriptions.

functions in Table 2–8 will be unclear until further study. Chapter 17 summarizes and integrates the characteristics of good forecasting systems. Our task now is to study the parts of a good forecasting system and how they relate to each other. Then we can integrate them into an effective system much greater than the sum of its parts.

SUMMARY

This chapter has presented important principles of forecasting system design. These principles include:

- Forecasting systems are hierarchical.
- Forecasts should be point, range, and probability estimates.
- Forecasts are necessary because of the leadtime in implementing decisions.
- The basic assumption of statistical forecasting is that the past repeats.
- Forecast independent demands, not dependent demands.
- The one-number principle denotes that all forecasts of the same item should be equal.
- Cumulative errors are lower than individual-item errors.
- Group forecasts are more accurate than individual forecasts.
- These principles should be incorporated in a good forecasting system.
- Forecasting systems are considerably more complex than forecasting methods.

The importance of several of these principles is more fully developed in the next chapter.

REFERENCE

1. A note for the statistician: *Less random* is a synonym for a lower coefficient of variation. The coefficient of variation is the ratio of the standard deviation to the mean.

CHAPTER 3

INTEGRATING
FORECASTING SYSTEMS

By dividing his problem into unsuitable parts, the inexperienced problem solver may increase his difficulty.

Leibnitz, *Philosophische Schriften*

The typical firm uses several formal or informal forecasting systems to predict demand. Frequently, these are redundant and uncoordinated systems that yield costly and ineffective decisions. The old saying that "the right hand does not know what the left hand is doing" is often true in such firms. In these situations, individual managers and departments try to perform as effectively as possible, but often decisions are made in a dis-integrated manner. Profits suffer and highly motivated managers are frustrated, feeling powerless to improve the situation. Effective management requires coordinated plans and efficient operations. Essential to achieving both of these goals is an integrated forecasting system. The principles of integrating forecasting systems for effective operations management are the focus of this chapter.

Having drawn on our own experiences in writing this chapter, many of you will recognize similarities to your own uses of forecasts. Chapter 2 developed the concepts of hierarchical systems; this chapter develops the concepts used to integrate the several forecasts needed to support this hierarchy.

As shown in Figure 2–3 in Chapter 2, three important parts of an effective forecasting system are an accurate common demand database, integrated hierarchical forecasts, and a demand data management system. The first two of these are discussed in greater detail in this chapter; Chapter 4, 5, 6, and 15 discuss demand data management.

It would seem that a good historical demand database is easily achieved; however, this is not so. Capturing demand history is the first topic of this chapter. Next, we define three types of hierarchical forecasts: Type 1, Type 2, and Type 3. Type 1 forecasts are those that support the short-horizon decisions of production and inventory control, and Type 2 forecasts are those that support the long-horizon, strategic business and sales plans. Finally, Type 3 forecasts integrate Type 1 and Type 2 forecasts to achieve more effective strategic short-term decisions. Our discussion of integrating forecasts is generic; thus, the topics of this chapter should be of value to all readers whether manufacturing or service oriented.

ACHIEVING CUSTOMER SATISFACTION AND SERVICE

In this section, we present several important forecasting principles and definitions relating to customer satisfaction. The end result of good forecasting is customer satisfaction and long-term

---

Where's Our Demand Database?

A hardware manufacturer experiences problems with late shipments to distributors. In addition, when customers make telephone inquiries about the availability of items, customer service personnel are unable to provide accurate information. Unfortunately, this problem has persisted for several years as the company's market share has declined from 20 percent in 1987 to 17 percent in 1990.

The company keeps a database of past monthly shipments as a measure of demand history; however, management believes that actual demand is much more seasonal than the recorded data. The company continues to measure demand using shipments. Also, there is an attitude that customers are not able to plan well, and this is why shipments are very erratic and less seasonal than anticipated.

Because of a retirement, a new CEO has been hired. While discussing problems of stockouts, inventory turnover, and market shares in a product line, the CEO raises his voice in frustration and asks, "Where is our demand database for this line? Where is demand? Show it to me!" Unfortunately, no one in the company recognized that customer service was poor because there was no adequate historical demand database. The shipments database was tainted, reflecting problems in supply and demand. This data will continue to lead this company toward missed sales, long customer leadtimes, poor in-stock conditions, and declining market share. The sales database should reflect customer's demands, not the company's shipment schedule. The CEO knows this and holds his executive committee accountable for their oversight.

---

profitability. The perception of customer service from the customer's viewpoint may be quite different than the company's. Recent surveys have identified that *responsiveness*, not just product quality or availability in the traditional sense, is essential to the image of good customer service. A direct answer to a customer's inquiry is important, regardless of whether the product is in stock or not. It is important to know when the product can be made available or shipped so that the customer can plan accordingly. Furthermore, for make-to-order products, the ability to ship immediately from stock is not necessary to achieve a positive image. It is more important to deliver when promised. Whether an

---

Customer Satisfaction and Service

L. L. Bean is a mail-order company that almost everyone has heard of. One of the attributes that makes it such a successful competitor is its 100 percent satisfaction policy. They'll accept returns any time for any reason during the life of the product. This was expressed by L. L. Bean in 1912.

> I do not consider a sale complete until goods are worn out and customer still satisfied.
> We will thank anyone to return goods that are not perfectly satisfactory.
> Should the person reading this notice know of anyone who is not satisfied with our goods, I will consider it a favor to be notified.
> Above all things we wish to avoid having a dissatisfied customer.

---

inventory of finished goods is available or not, much can be gained by communicating accurate estimates of available quantities and dates to inquiring customers.

> *Customer service has many dimensions, including accurate and timely communication of availability.*

Stockouts, Lost Sales, Backorders, and Backlogs

In retailing, distribution, and make-to-stock manufacturing, customer delivery promises can be made when the stock is already available. That is, inventory has been produced or ordered in anticipation of demand. Whether the inventory level is too high is a related question that can be answered in part by using statistical safety stock. Chapter 16 presents a statistical procedure to calculate safety stock. Also, many services such as fast food restaurants, banks, and government offices must have sufficient inventory to preclude stockouts; thus, their forecasting and safety stock problems are very similar to those of the distributor or make-to-stock manufacturer.

In any inventory system, there are times when stockouts occur. A stockout can result in a lost sale or a backorder depending on whether a customer will or will not wait. If a customer does not wait for future delivery, then a lost sale occurs. If a customer waits for an order, then a backorder occurs. A backorder is an order that when delivered was ordered "back" in the past; thus, it is filled later than when the customer desired. Backorders result in a backlog of unfinished late orders.

The unshipped customer orders in some companies are called *backlog* regardless of whether they are late (i.e., past due) or not. In other companies, only the late customer orders are considered a backlog. Because the term *backlog* is used two ways, the term *backorder* is used throughout this book to mean late orders.

Lost Sales
The topic of customer service often suggests the topic of lost sales. Ideally, forecasts can use past sales data as the demand database; however, inabilities to deliver items when requested, lost sales, and backorder shipments distort historical sales data so that it does not equal demand. Stated another way, the question is whether the sales data are really *demand* or *supply* data. Historical shipment and sales data is the lower of the supply or demand. For example, if the demand for a month is 1,000 units and the available inventory is 1,200, then sales reflect demand. In contrast, if demand is 1,000, and available inventory is 800, then sales would equal only 800, which is the supply of stock.

Historical shipment and sales data is the lower of supply or demand.

Order Processing Data Collection

In the make-to-order firm, customer orders are processed for future deliveries. When these orders are placed, the order quantities should be compared to the forecast and projected available stock for those dates. If the orders cannot be filled and will be late, the dates should be rescheduled to provide valid and truthful information to the customer. However, the original customer request date is the correct historical demand date, not the rescheduled date.

Backorders can distort shipments as a measure of demand.

Demand date equals requested ship date, not actual ship date.

Capture demand data, not shipment or sales data.

Let's expand on these principles. Historical data from the customer order processing system may be organized for forecasting purposes by actual ship date, requested ship date, or by order receipt date. While actual shipments or sales are nearly always the easiest of historical data to obtain, they reflect distortions due to inventory, capacity, or material shortages. Because inventory should be in stock when demanded, it is far better to collect data by *requested* ship date rather than by *actual ship date*. Similarly, the *requested quantity* is far superior to the *actual shipment quantity*. Only in the purely make-to-stock product line is it acceptable to record demand data as equal to the requested quantity by order receipt date. In this situation, few orders for future delivery are received, and the timing of customer order receipts is easily translated into the requested ship date. Only with clear and complete procedures to handle backorders and demand data will it be possible to make good delivery promises on the next customer order.

Requested quantity, not promised quantity, equals demand.

Estimating Demands during Stockouts

When a stockout occurs, there is no certain way to assess the demand that would have been booked. Some companies record requested quantities when processing orders for items that are out of stock. This can give an experienced manager some indication of lost sales, but it is also possible that the same demand is recorded more than once when stockouts last long enough for customers to inquire more than once. Also, it is likely that the quantity never gets recorded if the dialogue with the order entry person first indicates that the item is out of stock before a quantity is requested. Thus, when out-of-stock conditions occur frequently, demand data is difficult to collect and may be inaccurate unless we heed the principles stated below.

Capture customer request quantity before acknowledgment of stockouts.

Often a stockout of one item (e.g., 2 × 4 lumber) results in the lost sale of complementary items (e.g., nails, paneling, or screws). This occurs when the customer goes elsewhere to purchase all the goods needed to complete a project. This phenomenon is very common in the retail trades and some industrial and commercial industries. The out-of-stock item acts as a deterrent for the purchase of other items on the shopper's list. Thus, an out-of-stock item can result in very high lost sales.

The lost sales of complementary items are very difficult to estimate. Nonetheless, they represent further lost sales, lost profit, and the loss of an opportunity to serve the customer in several ways. In addition, these stockouts distort the historical demand for the out-of-stock item and its complements. Such distortions may be detectable for the out-of-stock item, but they are very difficult to detect for the complementary item.

A stockout of an item may cause lost sales of many complementary items.

A stockout of an item may distort the demand history of its complementary items.

Complementary lost sales from other item stockouts are very difficult to detect and measure.

Fortunately, when customer service (on-time shipments) is running at reasonably high levels according to industry standards of performance, the percentage of customers who remain loyal to the firm is high, even if they temporarily buy from a competitor. In this case, the short-term loss of sales for out-of-stock items can be estimated as an extension of the sales rate that existed before the stockout period, provided that the stockout is not lengthy. For example, if the daily demand rate before and after a five-day stockout is 35 units per day, then the lost demand is estimated at 175 (5 × 35).

Lost sales may equal units per day times days out of stock.

It is more difficult to estimate lost sales when customer service has been substandard for some time. The problem is that extended lost sales have affected more basic issues such as market share, customer perceptions, and customer loyalty. The sales that have been lost may have been lost forever because the firm has lost some customers.

Lengthy out-of-stock periods confound demand estimates.

Accurate Demand Databases

Some firms do not capture demand history that includes lost sales because they believe that it is unnecessary to retain actual sales, lost sales, and estimated demand for each forecasted item. They view this data as redundant or as a waste. Some data processing or management information systems departments highlight the cost of modifying programs and increasing disk storage, while not estimating the important net benefits from this data. However, *very few uses of data storage yield benefits greater than those of an accurate demand database.* We have been surprised by the large number of firms who do not know the demand for their products because they "can't afford" the database.

Effective forecasts require an accurate demand database.

An accurate demand database is a strategic resource.

Perpetual versus Periodic Records

Some firms persist in using periodic inventory systems despite the value of the data that is collected from a perpetual inventory record. A periodic review system counts and records inventory levels only periodically, such as once a month, instead of in real time. As an example of the benefits of perpetual inventory accounts, consider the effect of using a periodic review inventory system. With periodic review records, lost sales may occur and be unrecorded. This happens when lost sales are determined only from periodic monthly or quarterly counts of inventory, not from customer inquiries or orders. Consider the following scenario: An item is out of stock, and customer B places an order for 100 units but is denied; subsequently, customer A returns a previous order and the 100 units become available and could have been used for customer B; because inventory is counted only at the end of the month, inventory is recorded as 100. Consequently, the historical database does not show customer A's return, the lost sale, or the demand of customer B.

This sequence of events has tainted the historical demand database in two ways. The recorded demand in this example is 100 units lower than actual (we omitted customer B's demand),

and we have failed to record the stockout. Even with a perpetual inventory system, many firms do not adequately capture demand data because they do not attempt to do so. Demand, lost sales, and customer service cannot be managed without proper systems with which to capture data. When possible, lost sales should be captured at the time they occur, not retroactively from the inventory database.

Capture lost sales at customer inquiry time, not later.

As we have seen, how and when we capture demand data is very important in providing an accurate demand database. The internal data sources are many for the typical firm. Chapter 15 discusses data sources in several types of firms and transaction systems. For now, we discuss several types of forecasts that organizations make or should make.

INTEGRATING FORECASTS

Figure 3–1 introduces several generic forecasting systems and their relationships to forecast horizons, the number of forecasts, and the items to be forecast. As shown in the figure, with longer horizons, fewer items are forecast through the use of Type 2 forecasts. Also, these aggregate forecasts are *only* for medium to long-horizon strategic financial, marketing, and operations plans. In contrast, Type 1 forecasts are for short-horizon operations planning such as inventory management. In addition, most firms need short-horizon aggregate forecasts for strategic business units or profit centers. These are referred to as *Type 3 forecasts.* Type 3 forecasts may be produced in some firms using separate systems that should be, but often are not, integrated with the detailed Type 1 forecasting system. Regarding this dis-integrated process, one manager recently stated his problem this way:

> Our company suffers from a fragmented approach to the planning process. We fail to take into account marketing, sales, and customer projections. Our plans cannot be readily translated to product forecasts, so the planning process does not coordinate replenishment, purchasing, advertising, and financial commitments. As a result, customers are becoming dissatisfied because the available prod-

FIGURE 3-1
Three Types of Forecasting Systems

Forecasted unit	Forecast horizon			Number of forecasts to be prepared
	Short	Intermediate	Long	
Stockkeeping unit demand at DCs (units)	Type 1 forecasts	No forecasts		Large (3,000 and up)
Item national demand (units)				Medium (1,000–10,000)
Product-line demand (units or dollars)	Type 3 forecasts	Type 2 forecasts		Small (5–150)
Business entity ($)				Very small (1–20)

Type 1: Operating forecasts (e.g., forecasts for master scheduling)
Type 2: Planning forecasts (e.g., longer-horizon market, finance, and production plans)
Type 3: Short-term integration of Type 1 and Type 2 forecasts

ucts are in the wrong proportions—too much of some, not enough of others. In addition, management becomes concerned when forecasted demand differs from planned amounts and inventory turnover is too low.

Type 3 forecasting systems provide important information for coordinating short- and long-horizon decision making. Our purpose here is to define the principles and procedures whereby all three forecasts are integrated in a meaningful planning process.

Integrate and coordinate long-horizon aggregate
planning and short-horizon operating forecasts.

To better manage this situation, consider four aspects of Figure 3–1 that are discussed below.

1. The meaning and use of long-horizon, Type 2 forecasts,
2. The meaning and use of short-horizon, Type 1 forecasts,
3. The issue of integration/dis-integration of forecasts,
4. The migration of long-horizon forecasts to short-horizon, Type 3 forecasts.

TIME UNITS IN FORECASTS

Forecast the short horizon in weeks or months.

Forecast the long horizon in quarters or years.

Chapter 2 developed the idea of long-horizon, medium-horizon, and short-horizon forecasts. In the ongoing decisions of a business entity, a manager may plan the business volume and mix of a particular month (e.g., May 1991) several times as plans are revised and the future becomes the present. When the planning of a month is repeated, the forecasts are updated; this repetitive process is called *rolling the plan forward*. These longer-range, Type 2 forecasts, called *planning forecasts*, reach well into the future, typically 2 or more years.

One of the principles used to balance the benefits versus the costs of this planning (and replanning) process is to use larger time intervals, such as years or quarters (e.g., forecast annual or quarterly demand), for long-horizon, Type 2 forecasts and shorter time intervals, such as weeks or months (e.g., forecast weekly or monthly demand), for short-horizon, Type 1 forecasts. Long-horizon forecasts are used for planning purposes while short-horizon forecasts are used to make final commitments of time, materials, and labor to a production schedule of specific products. Short-horizon forecasts drive operating decision making; hence the term *operating forecasts*.

Planning forecasts use quarters or years.

Operating forecasts use weeks or months.

TYPE 2 AGGREGATE PLANNING FORECASTS

Forecast aggregates or groups for long-horizon planning.

A fundamental principle of forecasting is to use aggregate or group forecasts for long-horizon planning purposes. *Aggregate* and *group* are synonyms. Aggregate forecasts are those that apply to groups of similar products. For example, if a firm sold bicycles, then three possible aggregate forecast groups would be "adult multispeed," "teen multispeed," and "child multispeed." These logical groups have a common source of supply and demand; each group is produced on the same or similar equipment and requires many of the same or similar parts in assembly. Their demands originate from the same segments of the market.

As shown in Chapter 2, group forecasts are more accurate and less costly to maintain than specific product (disaggregate) forecasts. Typically, the decisions being made with long-horizon forecasts do not require specific product forecasts. For example, the automobile industry makes long-horizon forecasts for the sales of midsize, compact, and subcompact autos, and not for two-door, white, V-8, midsize automobiles or four-door, red, V-6, compact automobiles. There is no need for such detail in long-horizon forecasts. The percentage of two-door, white, V-8 automobiles or four-door, red, V-6 automobiles needs to be forecast, but automobiles with these options do not have to be planned or forecasted until immediately prior to assembly.

Table 3–1 illustrates a 12-month, Type 2 aggregate planning forecast for a company that produces briefcases. As shown in the table, the company has a product line with three different types of briefcases, vinyl, leather, and deluxe. The manufacturer's price for these briefcases is shown in the table. The forecast quantities are for all three briefcase types. After forecasting the aggregate, each month's aggregate forecast can be broken down (as shown later) to specific briefcase types using historical product ratios. The forecasted revenue in Table 3–1 is the product of the forecasted quantity and the price of the typical or average briefcase. The average briefcase price of $50 is a weighted average of the mix of briefcases sold in the last year. Thus, we see that Type 2 forecasts are aggregated groups expressed in average unit and dollar estimates.

TYPE 1 SHORT–HORIZON OPERATING FORECASTS

Short-horizon forecasts drive daily operations.

Short-horizon forecasts are used to manage the details of an operation. For example, the particular products that are purchased by a food distributor for resale will be bought in anticipation of

TABLE 3–1
Type 2 Aggregate Planning Forecast for Briefcases

Type	Price	As Percent of Past Demand
Vinyl	$40	65%
Leather	60	20
Deluxe	80	15

Average price = .65*$40 + .20*$60 + .15*$80 = $50

As of March 1990

Date	Quantity	Revenue ($50*Quantity)
April 90	350	$ 17,500
May 90	400	20,000
June 90	350	17,500
July 90	225	11,250
August 90	500	25,000
September 90	550	27,500
October 90	400	20,000
November 90	300	15,000
December 90	600	30,000
January 91	200	10,000
February 91	400	20,000
March 91	500	25,000
12-Month Total	4,775	$238,750

demand (customer orders), perhaps two weeks ahead of the customer orders. This is necessary because the food manufacturer requires that much time to deliver the products to the distributor's warehouse. This leadtime requires the distributor to forecast demand at least two weeks into the future. In contrast, the forecast horizon for other kinds of businesses can be very different depending on the replenishment leadtime. Some of the longest end-item leadtimes faced by business today are in the manufacture of automotive and aircraft service parts, especially those parts that are not used frequently in the current production of automobiles or aircraft. Some of the shortest leadtimes are for a grocery

TABLE 3–2
Type 1 Forecast as of January 1, 1991, for Briefcases

Date	Type	Quantity	Revenue
January 91	V	5	$ 200
	L	50	3,000
	D	20	1,600
Subtotal		75	$ 4,800
February 91	V	200	8,000
	L	125	7,500
	D	80	6,400
Subtotal		405	$ 21,900
March 91	V	280	$ 11,200
	L	140	8,400
	D	80	6,400
Subtotal		500	$ 26,000
April 91	. . .		
May 91			
June 91			.
Six-Month Total		2,000	$154,000

retailer, an automobile service station, and book or cassette retailers who can draw on distribution sources in the same city. The retail replenishment orders are often delivered one day after the order is placed, while special orders are sometimes delivered in four hours.

The first use of Type 1 forecasts is to make replenishment decisions by item and location.

Table 3–2 illustrates a Type 1 forecast for the briefcase manufacturer discussed previously. This Type 1 forecast projects demand for each briefcase for six months into the future. This six-month horizon is necessary to facilitate effective purchasing and production management. Note that this Type 1 forecast is much more detailed than the Type 2 forecast of Table 3–1. In Table

3-2, three different briefcases are forecast individually instead of the aggregate unit volume of Table 3-1.

Even though Type 1 forecasts are short term, they provide important information for marketing and financial planning.

The second use of Type 1 forecasts is to validate or modify the aggregate, Type 2 forecasts by product line, profit center, and business entity.

This second use involves a comparison and reconciliation of the long-horizon, Type 2 forecast with the short-horizon, Type 1 forecast. For example, the Type 2 forecasts of Table 3-1 can be compared to the Type 1 forecasts of Table 3-2. In this case, the long-range forecast as of March 1990 in Table 3-1 projected demands in January, February, and March of 1991 as 200, 400, and 500, respectively; the January 1991, short-range forecasts of Table 3-2 for these months are 75, 405, and 500, respectively. The outcome of such comparisons should highlight any unusual differences in volumes by item (i.e., a change in mix) and any resulting changes in sales, workloads, costs, and margins. Through the detection of significant deviations, management has greater control and time in which to take corrective action. In the case of Tables 3-1 and 3-2, the only significant difference in quantities occurs in January 1991 (75 versus 200). Management should investigate such differences to determine if they reflect shifts in consumer preferences or some other unusual event.

One of the difficulties in making comparisons between Type 2 long-horizon and Type 1 short-horizon forecasts is that they may be produced by separate systems using separate databases with only infrequent or ill-defined relationships between them. Such problems are highlighted below.

TYPE 3 INTEGRATED FORECASTS

The integration of Type 1 and Type 2 forecasts provides more effective plans and less waste.

Within a business entity, there may be two or more forecasting systems, perhaps a sales forecast, a production forecast, and a financial forecast, each prepared separately by different departments. In this situation, which is quite common, there may be some agreement on total forecasts between the departments at the start of the fiscal planning cycle, but less agreement as the fiscal year progresses. The reason for this is twofold. First, it is usually difficult and time consuming to forecast well enough to gain general acceptance across departmental lines. Second, the sharing of a common forecasting system for departments takes some degree of autonomy away from each department. But even more important, when there are two or more forecasting systems, each may be separately biased (intentionally perhaps) for the purposes of the using department.

The result of separate, uncoordinated forecasting systems is that buffers or cushions may be built into the separate business decisions of each department to protect against the uncertainty in the forecasts. For example, marketing may overforecast so as to place high expectations on sales and production, and production may try to guarantee that it can meet demand by having forecasts that are biased downward. However, the differences of these several perspectives may not be reconciled during the planning process, but are resolved only in the short horizon by default, if at all. These uncoordinated cushions are wasteful and can erode corporate profits and ROI. In such circumstances, we can expect a relatively low level of confidence in the forecasts made by other departments. Each department will continue to operate with their own system.

Separate forecasting systems erode confidence in the process of forecasting and in forecasts.

Below we illustrate a way that these several types of forecasts can be integrated.

Build forecasting confidence through integration and coordination using a common demand and forecast database.

The solution to the conflict between departmental forecast differences is to build coordination into the formal system. First, it is essential to use a common database. Second, the conversions in units of measure are part of the system so that pounds, cases, units, revenue dollars, and profits are in agreement. Finally, all forecasts should be the same so that all departments are planning by using the same expected demands. If we have this kind of unified forecasting system, then users can move from aggregate, long-horizon dollar forecasts to short-horizon units, cases, or pounds by item and location. As each month rolls into the short horizon, Type 2 forecasts in dollars by month and product line can be reconciled with the Type 1 forecasts of products in units by using Type 3 forecasts.

Integrated forecasting systems also facilitate interdepartmental communications through comparisons and projections as time passes. For example, if a long-horizon, Type 2 forecast made in March of 1990 was 50,000 units and $400,000 for March 1991, what does the short-horizon Type 1 forecast made as of the end of January 1991 indicate about the March volume and mix? Will the budget be achieved or exceeded? Will the mix achieve the contribution as budgeted? These types of questions are much more easily answered with integrated systems exemplified by the Type 3 forecasts.

Consider Tables 3–3 and 3–4 as examples of coordinating and integrating forecasting activities through the generation of Type 3 forecasts. Table 3–3 shows the results of Type 1 and 2 forecasting activities. At the top of the table are Type 2 forecasts of January 1991 through March 1991 that were made as of January 1991. These forecasts are important in achieving intermediate- to long-horizon plans and goals. These forecasts can be compared to the short-horizon, Type 1 forecasts as of January 1991. This disaggregate forecast provides important information about the product mix for this family. As shown, the two forecasts differ, and these differences should be resolved. The Type 2 forecasts were made using available aggregate demand data for the briefcase product line. In contrast, the Type 1 forecasts were made using the most-recent actual demands for specific briefcases.

There is considerable difference between the monthly and quarterly totals of the Type 1 and 2 forecasts of Table 3–3 (for example, quarterly totals of $52,700 and $60,500, respectively). The financial plans made using the longer-term forecasts may be greatly overestimating demand. In addition, if products are produced using the shorter-term, Type 1 forecast, and the Type 2 forecast is more accurate, then there will be considerable loss of sales and goodwill. The forecasting system should combine these

TABLE 3–3
Uncoordinated Briefcase Forecasts

Type 2 Forecast as of January 1, 1991

Date	Quantity	Revenue ($50*Quantity)
January 91	110	$ 5,500
February 91	500	25,000
March 91	600	30,000
Quarterly total	1,210	$60,500

Type 1 Forecast as of January 1, 1991

Date	Type	Quantity	Revenue
January 91	V	5	$ 200
	L	50	3,000
	D	20	1,600
Subtotal		75	$ 4,800
February 91	V	200	$ 8,000
	L	125	7,500
	D	80	6,400
Subtotal		405	$21,900
March 91	V	280	$11,200
	L	140	8,400
	D	80	6,400
Subtotal		500	$26,000
Quarterly total		980	$52,700

two so that the correct forecast is used for both planning and operating purposes.

Noting that each forecast was based on slightly different representations and assumptions about the same demand, one can infer that both forecasts contain useful information. This is often true. Interestingly, one way in which to handle this situation is to assume that each forecast is equally accurate (or inaccurate). This results in using a forecast that is the average of the two forecasts. This averaging process is illustrated in Table 3–4.

There are other ways that Type 1 and Type 2 forecasts can be combined. For example, in general, group forecasts such as Type

TABLE 3–4
Integrated Type 2 and Type 3 Forecasts

Initial Type 1 Forecast as of January 1, 1991 (from Table 3–3)

Date	Type	Quantity	Revenue
March 91	V	280	$11,200
	L	140	8,400
	D	80	6,400
Subtotal		500	$26,000

Type 2 Forecast as of January 1, 1991

Date	Quantity	Revenue ($50*Quantity)
March 91	600	$30,000

Type 3 Forecast as of January 1, 1991

Date	Quantity	Revenue (From Final Type 1)
March 91	(500 + 600)/2 = 550	$28,600

Final Type 1 Forecast as of January 1, 1991

Date	Type	Quantity	Revenue
March 91	V	550*(280/500) = 308@ $40	$12,320
	L	550*(140/500) = 154@ $60	9,240
	D	550*(80/500) = 88@ $80	7,040
		550	$28,600

2 forecasts are more accurate. Some forecasting systems use this fact when combining Type 1 and Type 2 forecasts by giving more weight to the Type 2. In fact, optimal weights can be determined, but this is normally too complex a procedure for routine forecasts. A popular method is to give zero weight to the Type 1 forecast and 100 percent weight to the Type 2 forecast.

Table 3–4 illustrates the corrected Type 1 and resulting Type 3 forecasts. The Type 3 forecast replaces the old Type 2 forecast for short-horizon planning. It is an average of the two forecasts and agrees with the new Type 1 forecasts.

In summary, note that the Type 2 forecast for the near term does not agree with the Type 3 forecast. Short-term uses of the Type 2 forecast have been replaced by the Type 3 forecasts. Let's expand on the method of combining forecasts.

Combining Forecasts: 1 + 2 = 3

As shown in Table 3–4, the Type 3 forecast equals the mean of the initial Type 1 and Type 2 forecasts. The final Type 1 forecast is the Type 3 forecast weighted by the original Type 1 product mix percentages.

Table 3–5 illustrates Type 1 and 3 forecasts related to our brief-case example. Take a moment to verify the calculations of this diagram. As you study these forecasts, remember the different purposes of the forecasts. Type 2 forecasts are much longer-term forecasts than 1 or 3. For example, we have used 6-month horizons for Type 1 and 3 forecasts and a 24-month horizon for the Type 2 forecast for this example. The Type 2 forecast is used in planning months 7 through 24.

PYRAMIDAL FORECASTING SYSTEMS

The forecasting sequence of Tables 3–2 through 3–5 illustrated the process of integrating and aggregating forecasts. There is another useful way in which to view this process, sometimes called the *pyramid principle*; Figures 3–2 and 3–3 illustrate the pyramid for our briefcase manufacturer. As shown there, the several forecasts in a company can be viewed from the top down or bottom up. The methods of integrating Type 1, 2, and 3 forecasts are part of this pyramidal system of forecasting.

As we show in Figure 3–2, the process of forecasting is hierarchical. At the peak of the pyramid is the original, January 1991 Type 2, group forecasts of 600 units at $50 per unit. In the middle of the pyramid, we see the dollar sales for each item; these dollar projections were calculated from the lowest level, Type 1 item forecasts. These two forecasts are uncoordinated at this time. This is apparent in the top section of the pyramid, which shows the Type 2 forecast at $30,000 versus the Type 1 forecast at

TABLE 3-5
Final Integrated Type 1 and Type 3 Forecasts

Type 3 Forecast as of January 1, 1991

Date	Quantity		Revenue (Based on Mix from Type 1)
January 91	(75 + 110)/2 =	93	$ 5,960
February 91	(405 + 500)/2 =	453	24,480
March 91	(500 + 600)/2 =	550	28,600
Quarterly total		1,096	$59,040

Final Type 1 Forecast as of January 1, 1991

Date	Type	Quantity		Revenue
January 91	V	93*(5/75) =	6@ $40	$ 240
	L	93*(50/75) =	62@ $60	3,720
	D	93*(20/75) =	25@ $80	2,000
Subtotal			93	$ 5,960
February 91	V	453*(200/405) =	224@ $40	$ 8,960
	L	453*(125/405) =	140@ $60	8,400
	D	453*(80/405) =	89@ $80	7,120
Subtotal			453	$24,480
March 91	V	550*(280/500) =	308@ $40	$12,320
	L	550*(140/500) =	154@ $60	9,240
	D	550*(80/500) =	88@ $80	7,040
Subtotal			550	$28,600
Quarterly total			1,096	$59,040

$26,000. These forecasts need to be integrated as shown in Table 3-5. This is illustrated using the pyramid of Figure 3-3.

The integration of forecasts requires two steps. The first step is referred to as the *roll-up step* and the second, the *force-down step*.

Figure 3-2 illustrates the roll-up of the Type 1 briefcase forecasts. This roll-up yields the aggregate unit and dollar forecasts of the second level (500 units and $26,000), which do not agree with the Type 2 group forecast (600 units and $30,000). The force-down step combines each of these so that they are consistent.

Figure 3-3 illustrates the force-down step. As shown in this figure, the Type 1 and 2 forecasts are averaged to yield the Type

FIGURE 3-2
Initial Roll-Up Forecasts—Forecasts of March 1991 as of January 1991

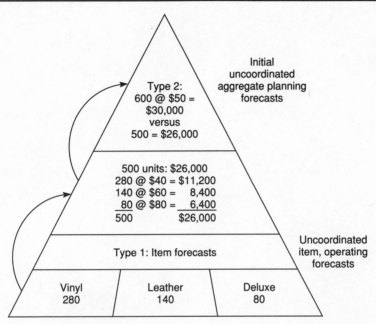

3 and final Type 1 forecasts. The mathematics of this example are shown in Table 3–5 and Figure 3–3. As noted previously, different weighting schemes are used in different systems. No matter what method is used, all forecasts are made consistent. Thus, each type of planning can proceed in harmony.

The pyramidal presentation is important because it is the basis of more-realistic and complex forecasting systems in manufacturing, distribution, retailing, and services. Because we have been discussing only manufacturers in this chapter, these figures do not illustrate pyramidal forecasts for distribution centers or warehouses. But, Figure 3–4 illustrates the results of integrating forecasts in a more complex manufacturing-distribution network. In this case, two product lines are produced by the manufacturer, overnight cases and briefcases. These two products are produced in vinyl, leather, and deluxe models. These six products are distributed through three regional distribution centers, RDC1, RDC2, and RDC3.

As we show in Figure 3–4, there are 18 stockkeeping units

FIGURE 3–3
Force-Down Forecasts—Forecasts of March 1991 as of January 1991

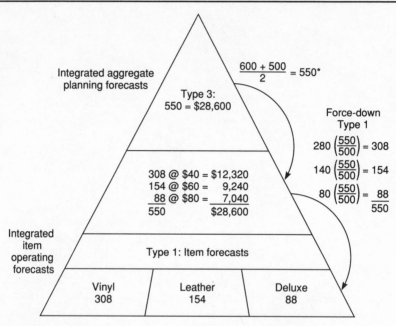

*This illustrates one of several ways to combine forecasts.

(SKUs) in the three distribution centers (6 products times 3 distribution centers). During the roll-up step, which is not shown here, the demand for each of these SKUs or items is forecast, each product line's demand is forecast at each distribution center, and national demand for each product line is forecast. Thus, 18 item forecasts, 6 product-line forecasts at the distribution centers, and 2 national product-line forecasts are made during the roll-up step. This roll-up step also provides an aggregate demand history at each level of the pyramid, from which forecasts are then made. Because these three levels of forecasts are not coordinated at this time, the sums of the SKU forecasts do not equal the product-line forecast. The next step, the force-down step, is used to provide a coordinated forecast. This step yields the forecasted quantities of Figure 3–4.

FIGURE 3-4
General Hierarchical Structure in Forecasting Systems—Forecasts of
March 1991 as of January 1991

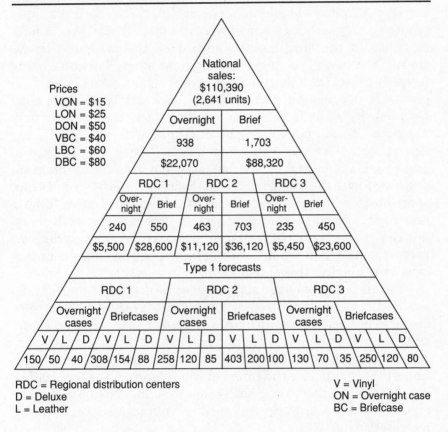

National
sales:
$110,390
(2,641 units)

Prices
VON = $15
LON = $25
DON = $50
VBC = $40
LBC = $60
DBC = $80

Overnight	Brief
938	1,703
$22,070	$88,320

RDC 1		RDC 2		RDC 3	
Over-night	Brief	Over-night	Brief	Over-night	Brief
240	550	463	703	235	450
$5,500	$28,600	$11,120	$36,120	$5,450	$23,600

Type 1 forecasts

RDC 1		RDC 2		RDC 3	
Overnight cases	Briefcases	Overnight cases	Briefcases	Overnight cases	Briefcases

V	L	D	V	L	D	V	L	D	V	L	D	V	L	D	V	L	D
150	50	40	308	154	88	258	120	85	403	200	100	130	70	35	250	120	80

RDC = Regional distribution centers   V = Vinyl
D = Deluxe   ON = Overnight case
L = Leather   BC = Briefcase

The benefits of coordinating forecasts and plans have already been stressed. However, we must emphasize that some process of combining or reconciling forecasts is essential to the effectiveness and survival of all firms that forecast in a multilevel product or distribution network. Group forecasts are inherently more accurate in total than item forecasts; however, item forecasts have important mix information that must be used in allocating items to locations. Plans should be coordinated and consistent, and this is only achieved if there is a common database of forecasts.

SUMMARY

Having a good demand database is essential to accurate forecasting and customer satisfaction. Generally, there are three types of forecasting activities and systems in most firms. Type 1 forecasts of item and stockkeeping units drive the day-to-day operations of the firm. Type 2 systems plan for longer horizons, using fewer forecasts than short-horizon operating forecasts. These forecasts are aggregated and are more accurate than short-term detailed operating forecasts. However, aggregate forecasts may not reflect actual or evolving product mixes. To better estimate actual demands in the short term, Type 3 forecasts are used to coordinate Type 1 and Type 2 forecasts. These forecasts integrate and coordinate the evolution of long-horizon, Type 2 forecasts into short-horizon, Type 1 forecasts. It is this integration of Type 1 and Type 2 forecasts that improves the operation of both short-horizon and long-horizon planning activities. The pyramidal representation and construction of forecasting systems is important in achieving this integration.

To this point, we have suggested some desirable characteristics and structures of forecasting systems as though they were operated by themselves, with little discussion to the data flow relationships with other systems and procedures. In fact, when viewing the diagrams that follow this chapter, it becomes increasingly important to consider the internal consistency of the forecasting system and its integration with other systems. The next chapter extends this hierarchy to specific planning processes in manufacturing.

PART 2

FORECASTING SYSTEM APPLICATIONS

Part 2 discusses several applications and principles of forecasting systems. These applications have many common features. These common features can be found in the forecasting systems of many organizations, both product and service oriented. Thus, no matter what your application, you will find important and useful principles of forecasting in these three chapters.

Chapter 4 introduces the use of forecasting in manufacturing. It discusses principles of forecasting related to the modules of an MRPII (manufacturing planning and control system). Make-to-stock and make-to-order manufacturing environments and their relationships to forecasting are developed. Those not involved in manufacturing per se will still benefit from this presentation.

Chapter 5 introduces manufacturer-distributor forecasting.

The forecasting needs of distributors are discussed first, followed by the manufacturer with a distribution network. Finally, the distribution requirements planning (DRP) tool is discussed relative to forecasting systems. Any firm on the manufacturer-distributor-customer supply chain will benefit from the principles presented in this chapter.

Chapter 6 develops forecasting in two types of businesses. The first half develops forecasting in retail operations. It presents principles for using forecasting to support merchandise planning by store, department, and item. Several principles of retail forecasting are highlighted. Many of the principles of Chapters 4 and 5 are also applicable to the retailer, but Chapter 6 focuses on those that are distinctly applicable to retail forecasting.

The second half of Chapter 6 develops forecasting in maintenance and remanufacturing operations. Several aspects of these operations make them unique, including the need to forecast both the supply and demand for service items. These types of operations are characterized by service and remanufacturing operations of public utilities, service-item manufacturing plants, airlines, truck lines, and so on.

CHAPTER 4

MANUFACTURER FORECASTING

No plan is perfect, yet plans are necessary if we are to avoid
  complete chaos.
        Edward T. Hall, *The Hidden Dimension*

This chapter introduces forecasting system principles and methods
that support the management of demand in manufacturing or-

ganizations. Good demand management is necessary to achieve the greatest benefits from improved forecasting systems. Because a forecasting system is only one part of a good demand management system, it is very wasteful to use sophisticated forecasting methods in an ineffective demand management system. In such cases, firms receive the costs of better forecasts and few of their benefits. Our purpose here is to preclude such mistakes by reviewing demand management systems and their relationship to forecasting systems.

DEMAND MANAGEMENT OVERVIEW

Figure 4–1 illustrates demand management subsystems and their relationships to forecasting in manufacturing firms. This diagram integrates demand forecasting of finished goods and service parts with other activities that are dependent on forecasts. (Service parts are items sold by some manufacturers for repair of their finished goods items, e.g., replacement motors for dishwashing machines.)

Demand management's objective is to manage the many sources of demand to assure that adequate supply will be available to fulfill these demands.

Sources of Demand

Customer orders, forecasts, marketing, stock plans, and engineering programs are all potential sources of demand for the products of a company. All of these sources of demand are represented in Figure 4–1 except engineering. Engineering is often viewed as external to the usual demand forecasting system. In the typical manufacturing firm, all sources of demand, whether usual or unusual, should be managed by a master scheduler. In addition to these activities, demand management in manufacturing often includes interplant transfers and distribution requirements. These are not illustrated in this example but are discussed in relation to forecasts and master scheduling in Chapter 5.

All sources of demand, usual and unusual, should be managed in master scheduling.

FIGURE 4–1
Forecasting Integration for Manufacturers

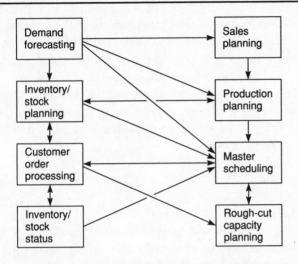

Forecast	Used by	Interval	Horizon
Type 2 and 3; longer-term by product line	Sales planning	Monthly or quarterly	Leadtime of marketing functions
Type 2 and 3; longer-term by product line, plant, and capacity group	Production planning	Monthly	Leadtime of major capacity changes
Type 1; short-term by item, plant, and need date	Master scheduling	Monthly or weekly	Cumulative leadtime for the product
Type 1; short-term by item, plant, and need date	Inventory/ stock planning	Monthly or weekly	Cumulative leadtime for the product
Type 1; short-term by item, plant, and need date	Rough-cut capacity planning	Monthly or weekly	Leadtime for load balancing in work centers

Consumers of Forecasts

All firms have consumers of forecast data, including those responsible for processing customer orders, planning inventory stock
replenishments, scheduling production, promoting sales, and planning production capacity. The information requirements of each

of these consumers should be met and coordinated through an integrated forecasting system. To understand how this is done, the activities of each module of Figure 4–1 are briefly introduced below. Following this, more detailed discussions will be made concerning those modules most directly related to demand management. Remember that the purpose of demand management is to ensure that there is an adequate supply of products to fulfill the many sources of product demands. The activities of Figure 4–1 are an important part of achieving this objective. Our purpose is not to fully develop these modules, but to relate them to effective forecasting systems.

Module Functions

Master Scheduling

Master scheduling is discussed first because it is the key function connecting the sources of demand with supply. The purpose of this activity is to schedule the production of finished goods (i.e., supply) so as to satisfy all sources of product demand, including customer orders, forecasted demands, and stock requirements. In manufacturing, the master schedule defines the quantities of products to be completed in each period of the planning horizon; it is frequently referred to as a *build schedule*. These production requirements are managed for several periods into the future. The existing stock on hand as recorded in the stock status system is the input to the master schedule to determine how many new items are needed to meet demand. The quantities scheduled in the master schedule are provided to the customer order processing system for use when promising future delivery dates on customer orders.

Customer Order Processing

Demand management requires that the quantities and delivery dates of customer orders be managed to achieve high-quality customer service. As we will see, these orders are very important inputs to the master schedule. During customer order processing, customer order quantities are accumulated for use in master scheduling and as a historical database of past demands. Also, as will be shown, customer orders are handled differently in make-to-stock and make-to-order environments.

Demand Forecasting

This module uses a historical demand database for forecasting. This demand history is accumulated from past customer orders recorded by customer order processing. These demands are then used to produce forecasts using a variety of methods, which are studied extensively in Chapters 7 through 14.

Rough-Cut Capacity Planning

This part of master scheduling examines the reasonableness of the work center capacities needed to achieve the master schedule. It answers the basic question, "Do we have enough capacity to fabricate and assemble the parts and products scheduled in the master schedule?" To answer this question, we only need to consider the few work centers that have been at or near capacity in the past. The capacity requirements of these important work centers are measured and used as key indicators of the feasibility of the master schedule. When the needed capacity exceeds the available capacity, then some corrective action is necessary.

The available capacity of work centers is typically constrained by the previously prepared production plans. By calculating the required capacity of constraining, bottleneck work centers, the feasibility of the master schedule can be determined before resources are allocated and schedules missed.

The term *bottleneck* refers to work centers that have caused material backlogs in the past and are therefore the work centers that may constrain output in the future. Typically, only a fraction of an organization's work centers are bottleneck centers, approximately 5 to 20 percent. To assure that the capacities of the centers are not being exceeded, it is relatively easy to do a quick check of the capacity required to meet demand. This will be illustrated later.

Production Planning

The production for several years in the future is planned in this module, typically using monthly periods. The objective of this planning process is to ensure that there is sufficient capacity in plant, labor, and equipment to achieve the longer-range goals of sales planning and the shorter-range goals of master scheduling. Consequently, this activity is supported by both Type 1 and Type 2 forecasts. To make this planning process less complex, appropriate groupings or aggregates of products and capacities are used in this planning process. Most frequently, an aggregate unit of analysis, such as a typical unit, dollar, labor hour, or machine hour, is used in this analysis. Normally, the specific aggregate unit that best represents the constraining capacity of the plant is chosen. Thus, forecasted demands for different products are converted into this aggregate unit. Planning proceeds using this unit to express the costs, revenues, and capacities of alternative means of achieving the production and sales plan.

Inventory/Stock Planning

In this function, finished goods inventory levels are set to achieve customer service goals and to provide inventory accumulations when production must occur well ahead of the date of need. This module includes methods of determining safety stocks through the use of statistical inventory control methods. These methods are more fully developed in Chapter 16.

Stock status is the database of finished goods inventory quantities in the stockroom or warehouse. The inventory on hand as recorded in the stock status file is used by master scheduling and production planning as a beginning inventory position. Also, customer order processing uses these on-hand quantities to commit goods for immediate shipment to customers.

Having previewed these functions, let us define several of them in greater detail.

MAKE–TO–STOCK DEMAND FORECASTING

There are four primary demand inputs to the master schedule in the make-to-stock firm. These are Type 1 and 2 forecasts, exceptional demands, and customer orders.

Type 1 Forecasts

Demands must be forecast by product, date, and quantity in a manufacturing firm. We have already discussed Type 1 and 2 forecasts in Chapter 3. As discussed there, these demands are often assumed to be the same as the historical shipments, but often this is not true because of stockouts or shipping delays.

The historical shipment data is rarely equal to historical demand.

The primary short- to medium-horizon, Type 1 forecasts for a manufacturing firm are forecasts by item and producing plant. As shown in Figure 4–1, this is an independent demand used to drive the activities in production planning and master scheduling. This demand forecast is for customer orders not yet received, so that the master schedule can provide finished goods in anticipation of those orders.

The routine, ongoing forecasts for products that have been produced for several months or years are usually the largest part of the forecasting effort. By automating much of the planning and execution of these forecasts, management will be free to attend to other, less easily programmed functions. For example, additional time can be given to the forecasts for new products and markets where demand is more difficult to estimate.

Automate routine forecasts—gain free time for the exceptions.

Exceptional and Managerial Inputs to Forecasts

Forecasts must include estimates for new markets, new products, new labels, and new business conditions. Forecasting models alone will not provide all the quantitative information for managing demand. Even though it is important to forecast the ongoing aspects of the company's business as well as possible, much of the information needed to forecast is not available from past data. Frequently, exceptional situations have significant impact on future demands. These events may not be predictable using historical demand because they did not occur in the past.

A good forecasting system should facilitate direct managerial input and adjustment of forecasts.

Changes in strategic plans may bring about changes in the plans for various markets, both domestic and international. Histor-

ical data may be available for domestic sales so that these forecasts are already prepared routinely. But what will be the demand
in a new international market, or for a new private label product? Will large contracts be part of the marketing direction for
the next fiscal year? These questions cannot be answered by forecasting models.

*Forecasting models alone do not provide
all data needed for managing demand.*

Management of demand occurs when forecasts are reviewed,
accepted, or changed to be consistent with the overall business
plans. This may involve evaluations of resource requirements,
costs, profit potentials, or alternate sales strategies. Managerial
adjustments to forecasts ought to be made frequently and routinely
in the planning process. Type 1, Type 2, and Type 3 forecasts must
reflect the same adjustments. Fortunately, adjustments are easily coordinated during the process of generating these three types
of forecasts.

Customer Orders

The final important input to the master schedule comes from the
customer order processing system. This is the input of actual unshipped customer orders, which are often called *open customer
orders*. In this way, the manufacturing system obtains information about demands already "in house" as well as demands not
yet received. The unshipped customer orders are often called the
backlog, but for some companies this term is reserved for orders
that are now past due (i.e., late).

MAKE–TO–ORDER FORECASTING

Depending on market and industry characteristics, a firm may
have customer orders for immediate and future shipment. When
the orders with future dates are dominant and their future dates
are at least as far ahead as the cumulative manufacturing leadtime, then the manufacturer is in a *make-to-order* situation. When

---

Remote Order Entry and Inquiry, Not a New Phenomenon

The idea of being on-line in real time at a customer's location is not a new phenomenon. In the late 1960s, several progressive corporations had salespeople who carried hardcopy terminals in briefcases. These thermal printing terminals had built-in modems for accessing the order entry systems of the home office of, for example, a manufacturer of industrial chemicals. The industrial salespeople would call on customers, make a sales presentation, and place orders while in the buyer's office. During periods of short supply for petroleum-based chemicals and plastics, the ability to get up-to-date price, quantity, and other available information was an important customer service. Some 1990s companies would do well to emulate these capabilities.

---

there are few if any orders with future requested ship dates, it is a *make-to-stock* situation. In reality, most manufacturers face a mix of orders for immediate and future delivery. Often overseas or special-pack private label orders are placed with delivery dates beyond the cumulative leadtime while domestic branded goods are ordered for immediate delivery from stock. Surveys have consistently found that the majority of firms are primarily make-to-stock operations with some make- or assemble-to-order options.

The make-to-order master schedule must be maintained at least as far ahead in time as the longest cumulative leadtime for the purchase and production of materials. When customer orders are placed at least this far ahead, there is little need for short-range item forecasts because the firm is operating in a make-to-order environment. However, it is still necessary to evaluate the mix of customer orders against work center capacities. Thus, necessary adjustments can be made in schedules or capacities by period. These longer-term capacity requirements may be determined by several methods, which are discussed later in this chapter, including the direct use of forecasts.

In the make-to-order firm, product demand may not be forecasted; however, demand for capacity should be.

MAKE–TO–STOCK MASTER SCHEDULING

The master schedule horizon length should be at least as long as the longest combined leadtime for procurement and manufacture.

When master scheduling in a make-to-stock situation, the demand inputs, stock plans, and stock status must all be considered together. While some master scheduling systems may calculate stock plans, Figure 4–1 assumes that stock planning is a separate function that feeds both production planning and master scheduling.

Stock planning in this situation is the system that manages finished goods stock quantities. Forecasts can be used to set stock targets with safety stock calculations, time supply, or other methods, or the plans may be set by direct management judgment if necessary. The forecasts by item and producing plant are used to help set the stock targets in most situations.

As shown in Figure 4–1, the master scheduling planning horizon is equal to or greater than the cumulative leadtime (CLT); the CLT includes the leadtime for purchased and manufactured parts. For example, if the longest total leadtime in the purchase, production, and distribution of a product is 15 weeks, then the master production schedule should be at least 15 weeks long.

To better understand the concept of cumulative leadtime, consider the bill of materials for the YO-YO of Figure 4–2. This YO-YO is assembled from one piece of string (STR), a wooden half (WH), and a wooden half subassembly (WHSA). The WHSA is assembled from a WH and a PEG. Finally, we see that there are three different purchased parts – wood blanks (WB) and peg blanks (PB), which are actually large dowel rods, and a roll of string (ROLL). These parts are purchased because they are not made from other components. The numbers shown in the parentheses are the quantities of each item that go into the next higher level item; for example, one WHSA is in every YO-YO. The number that follows the comma of each item is the leadtime that it takes to complete the purchase, fabrication, or assembly of that item. Thus, we see that the leadtime necessary to assemble a YO-YO is two weeks. Prior to assembling the YO-YO, it is necessary to have one WH, one WHSA, and one piece of string, STR, available. Each of these items has its own leadtime.

FIGURE 4–2
Bill of Materials for a Yo-Yo

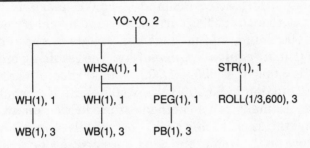

Upon inspection of the bill of materials, you should note that the longest cumulative leadtime is seven weeks. That is, the sequence that yields the longest leadtime is the purchase of WB (three weeks), the fabrication of WH (one week), the assembly of WHSA (one week), and the assembly of YO-YOs (two weeks). All of these processes must be completed in sequence, and this is the longest sequence of processes for this product. Thus, we see that the master production schedule should plan at least seven weeks into the future.

PRODUCTION PLANNING

While rough-cut capacity planning may be sufficient to manage capacity changes in some firms, most will require the higher-level, longer-term capacity information provided by a production plan. As illustrated in Figure 4–1, the inputs to this aggregate planning include Type 2 demand forecasts and stock plans.

Production planning is a longer-term check of the feasibility of sales plans. As such, it connects the longer-term sales planning process with the short-term master scheduling of specific parts.

A typical annual production planning procedure is to estimate required production by the formula:

Required aggregate production = End-of-year desired stock plan
+ Forecasted demand for the year
− Current stock on hand

These calculations can be made from aggregate forecast data

and expressed in terms of typical units, dollars, shift equivalents, hours, and pounds. For example, a production "season" of 12 months has a forecasted demand of 85,000 machine hours of equivalent production. The current on-hand inventory is equivalent to 1,000 hours, and management wants to end the season with 6,000 hours equivalent inventory. The resulting production quantity is 6,000 + 85,000 − 1,000 = 90,000 hours. The monthly rate of production is 90,000/12 = 7,500 hours per month.

There are many other methods of production planning that are beyond the scope of this book. Fortunately, there is a wealth of literature on this topic, and the interested reader should refer to Vollmann, Berry, and Whybark for further information.[1]

While we recognize the importance of production plans, often the most complex issues involve the conversion of the production plan to capacity requirements. Let's discuss methods of estimating long-term capacity requirements.

LONG–TERM CAPACITY REQUIREMENTS

Capacity planning beyond the horizon of the master schedule may be important in both make-to-order and make-to-stock companies. The leadtime for making major capacity changes may stretch well beyond the longest leadtime for materials. Consequently, the master schedule by item may not be prepared far enough into the future for capacity planning purposes.

Capacity leadtimes may be longer than material leadtimes.

There are several methods that can be used to forecast long-term capacity requirements; these include the following:

- Exploding production plans using historical mixes.
- Using long-term, Type 1 product forecasts.
- Capturing and forecasting capacity usage directly.

These alternative methods exist from necessity. For example, in some engineer-to-order environments, there are no product forecasts. In such cases, the demand for the capacity of the firm has to be estimated directly. In other situations, there are few products and the demand database is good enough that long-term, Type 1 item forecasts can be used directly for capacity planning. However, the usual method of capacity planning is to explode production plans using historical mixes to determine the capacity demands on key bottleneck work centers. Let's explore each of these methods below.

Exploding the Production Plan Using Historical Mixes

Long-term capacity plans can be calculated directly from long-term, Type 2 forecasts or from the production plan based on those forecasts. Both of these approaches make use of demand history aggregated by product line and management modifications to the product-line forecasts. These aggregate forecasts are converted to capacity and/or critical material requirements through a planning bill explosion. The planning bill for each product line is based on the historical mix of typical products and materials. In the explosion, the mix of the products, materials, and work centers for each product line will usually be assumed to be constant, even though it might vary somewhat from month to month.

Figure 4–3 illustrates a planning bill of capacity for a product line that has three products, A, B, and C, which pass through two work centers, W1 and W2. The numbers shown in parentheses for each of these products are the number of machine hours required in each of the work centers. Thus, each product C requires two hours of capacity in W1 and one hour of capacity in W2.

Assume that the Type 2 forecast or production plan for a month is 10,000 units. In the past, the historical mix of products has been

FIGURE 4–3
Planning Bill of Capacity

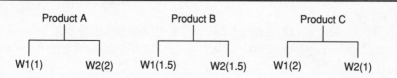

20 percent A, 30 percent B, and 50 percent C. Thus, the projected production mix is as follows:

Product A	2,000
Product B	3,000
Product C	5,000
Total units	10,000

Using the hours per unit from Figure 4–3, the total estimated load per month on the work centers is:

W1	W2
16,500	13,500

This approach works well when product mix changes are not significant. Also, it makes it easier to apply management judgment to the aggregate production plan and product-line forecasts, but it does not facilitate the analysis of trends within the mixes of specific product lines. However, product mixes do change significantly in some settings. For example, what if the product mix were to change as follows?

Product A	3,000
Product B	4,000
Product C	3,000
Total units	10,000

Then the revised capacity requirements in hours per month would be:

W1	W2
15,000	15,000

Thus, any mix changes may affect the feasibility of the production plan in regards to capacity. Significant product mix changes may invalidate this method.

Using Long-Term, Type 1 Forecasts

This second approach uses longer-term, Type 1 forecasts of each item's demand before converting demand to capacity requirements. This is applicable when make-to-stock items have sufficient history to forecast their volume individually so that these item forecasts can be used in production and capacity planning. Such forecasts allow for a changing mix of items in the future. This approach is essentially the same as rough-cut capacity planning, which begins with a master schedule by item, but this method extends further in the future than master scheduling.

The conversion of longer-term product forecasts to critical work center, resource, or material requirements can be handled by the manufacturing planning and control system directly using MRP or CRP. While specific item forecasts might be quite erroneous for longer horizons, management forecast overrides for the major product mixes may be used as an important control on the mix in future periods. Consequently, better product and capacity forecasts result because management's knowledge of market changes, engineering changes, and so on, is better reflected in the production planning forecasts.

The obvious disadvantage of this approach is its greater level of detail. The firm is no longer planning aggregates, but is instead performing disaggregate production and capacity planning. When the number of products is few, product mixes vary significantly, and the accuracy of specific product forecasts is high, then this method may be the most effective.

Capturing and Planning Capacity Directly

In this approach, capacity is forecasted and planned directly using a historical database of past capacity utilization. As mentioned previously, some firms have no forecastable products or their aggregate product forecasts are so unreliable as to be unusable. In these circumstances, demand history should be organized in the forecasting system by critical, constraining resources, that is, work center, material, or equipment. Then forecasts are made by critical resources directly from the demand history. This approach is advantageous where item history is sparse, which is especially typical of make-to-order businesses.

To provide these plans, the history of capacity or material demands must be organized in some appropriate way by type of work center, type of facility, critical component, feedstock, raw material, or some other variable. In the example of Figure 4–3, the aggregate unit is hours of capacity required in work centers. But the same concept can be extended to a critical material where the requirement is pounds per unit, or to any other essential and limited capacity or material. The database may be organized by specific unit of measure, machine, machine group, material, material type or class, and so on. Several alternate ways of accessing and summing the history should be available so that the planner may use the history to adapt the model to reflect current business constraints. With the database organized in this way, capacity and material resource history can be aggregated to the desired levels, and each capacity requirement (work center, plant, etc.) can be forecasted using this historical aggregated data.

PURCHASING USES OF FORECASTING

The purchasing department of a manufacturing firm is responsible for procurement of the materials required by the master schedule. However, the procurement process begins well ahead of the normal leadtime for placing purchase orders. Vendors must be selected, materials must be sent to vendors for bids, and contracts negotiated to assure price protection, quality, and good delivery responses.

These procurement activities cannot be based on historical material requirements alone. As products are changed, the material requirements must be anticipated, and, as the product mix changes, there may be an opportunity (and responsibility) to negotiate better prices and leadtimes for the purchase of old and new materials.

The forecasting system should support purchasing by estimating demand for critical or high-cost materials well ahead of normal leadtimes. The procurement process then can take advantage of these estimates to reduce costs and increase margins through better prices, shorter leadtimes, and speedier vendor service.

Purchasing needs long-term forecasts of critical and high-cost materials.

FINANCE AND MARKETING

Longer-term, Type 2 forecasts are necessary to support marketing and financial planning. Fiscal planning is dependent on forecasts for several months more than a fiscal year so that the assumptions and estimates in the fiscal plan can be verified and revised several times prior to the start of the fiscal year. Marketing plans for key products; old and new product-line volumes; advertising and promotional allowances; new product introductions; and estimates of selling expenses, discounts, returns, and other allowances will be needed. These estimates should be consistent with the production plan and should be based on the same forecasted volumes.

Marketing and production planning require the same Type 2 forecasts.

Financial executives will be concerned with profit projections after considering the revenues and costs of each department in the company. To the extent that profits are not satisfactory, there may be planned changes in volume or cost estimates so as to evaluate their impact on the profit plan. The requirements of these plans must not exceed the manufacturing capacities, material availability, labor requirements, or sales projections.

Fiscal plans prepared in this manner are usually supported by aggregate, Type 2 forecasts. The practicality of these forecasts is important, especially where top-down forecasts are used to drive fiscal planning. Out of this planning process, the budgeted sales volumes may be established for product lines and higher aggregations.

Budgets can be compared to actual performance as the fiscal year evolves. Mid-year or more frequent budget revisions are made in many companies where the forecasts, production plans, and profit plans can be readily brought together for review. More-efficient and effective financial planning tools use forecasts as their foundations. This is a rapidly evolving area in forecasting system design and support.

Effective financial planning requires Type 2 forecasts.

AN INTEGRATED PLANNING EXAMPLE

As an aid to reviewing the concepts of this chapter, consider a simplified planning example. Remember that we cannot fully develop all the details of production planning, master scheduling, and rough-cut capacity planning here. However, your basic understanding of these functions and their relationships to forecasting is essential to effective forecasting system design and use. To better understand the relationships between forecasting and planning functions in a manufacturing environment, consider Figure 4–4. This figure illustrates parts of several forecasting and planning documents for our luggage company. Type 1, 2, and 3 forecasts are shown using the information provided in Chapter 3. In addition, parts of the production planning, rough-cut capacity planning, customer order, and master schedule as of January 1, 1991, are shown.

As you will remember, this company produces three types of briefcases, vinyl, leather, and deluxe. In addition, they produce overnight cases, but these are not shown because they are unnecessary for the purpose of our discussion. As we show in Figure 4–4, the Type 1 and 3 forecasts are equal; however, the Type 2 forecast numbers are somewhat different, reflecting the forecasts of historical demand mixes.

The Type 1 and 3 forecasts are used for more-detailed short-term forecasts while the longer-term, Type 2 forecasts are used for longer-term plans. In this case, Type 1 forecasts are input to the master schedule for vinyl briefcases, while the Type 3 and 2 forecasts are used to develop the briefcase production plan. The Type 3 forecasts are used for the first 6 months, and the Type 2 forecasts for the last 18 months. Be sure to note which plans use which type of units. That is, note that the production plan uses typical briefcase units, customer orders are for the specific brief-case types, master scheduling is done for each type of case (only the vinyl case is shown), and, finally, the rough-cut capacity plan uses capacity hours in Work Center 13, Vinyl Fitting. Let us highlight the inputs and outputs of each planning step:

Type 1 forecasts are input to master scheduling.

Type 2 forecasts are input to long horizons of the production plan.

Type 3 forecasts are input to the short horizon of the production plan.

Customer orders come from the customer order processing system.

Customer orders are input to the master schedule.

The master schedule quantities are inputs to the rough-cut capacity plan.

The master schedule of Figure 4–4 uses common conventions in managing demand. The AVAIL row denotes the ending inventory of a period. For example, beginning January 1991, there were 50 units of vinyl briefcases in stock. These 50 units are available to fulfill the ordered demand for 13 (see ORDER row). Consequently, there were 37 units available as of the end of January 1991. The common convention is to calculate ending-period AVAIL as the difference between beginning inventory minus the larger of forecasted (FORE) or ORDER. In January 1991, the larger was ORDER with 13, while FORE is the larger in FEB through DEC 1991.

The AVAIL TO PRM (available to promise) row of the master schedule denotes the number of units that are available to promise to customers. The generally accepted procedure for available to promise is to use the difference between the master schedule quantity and the orders that are covered by that master schedule quantity. Consider March (MAR) as an example. The master schedule quantity for MAR is 308, while in March 1991 only 200 units have actually been ordered. Thus, 308 − 200 or 108 units of the 308 are still available to promise to customers. This logic is important in providing high levels of customer service. Our purpose is to have units available to promise when

FIGURE 4–4
Demand Management Hierarchy of Plans for Plant Supplying RDC1

BRIEFCASE MANUFACTURING

CURRENT DATE: JANUARY 1, 1991

TYPE 1 DEMAND FORECAST—SIX-MONTH HORIZON (FINAL FORECASTS)

PERIOD	1991					
	JAN	FEB	MAR	APR	MAY	JUN
TOTAL	93	453	550	405	410	370
VINYL	6	224	308	174	156	144
LEATHER	62	140	154	93	135	122
DELUXE	25	89	88	138	119	104

TYPE 2 FORECASTS FOR BRIEFCASES—24-MONTH HORIZON

PERIOD	1991					1992			
	JAN	FEB	MAR	NOV	DEC	JAN	FEB	MAR	DEC
TOTAL	110	500	600	400	600	200	400	600	700
VINYL	72	325	390		390	130	260	390	455
LEATHER	22	100	120		120	40	80	120	140
DELUXE	16	75	90		90	30	60	90	105
DOLLARS	5,480	25,000	30,000		30,000	10,000	20,000	30,000	35,000

TYPE 3 DEMAND FORECAST—SIX-MONTH HORIZON

PERIOD	1991					
	JAN	FEB	MAR	APR	MAY	JUN
TOTAL	93	453	550	405	410	370
VINYL	6	224	308	174	156	144
LEATHER	62	140	154	93	135	122
DELUXE	25	89	88	138	119	104
DOLLARS	5,960	24,480	28,600	23,500	23,860	21,400

BRIEFCASE PRODUCTION PLAN—24-MONTH HORIZON

PERIOD	1991					1992					
	JAN	FEB	MAR	…	DEC	JAN	FEB	MAR	…	NOV	DEC
FORE	93	453	550		600	200	400	600			700
ORDER	93										
INVENT 100	7	54	4	100	0	100	100	0		250	50
PROD	0	500	500		500	300	400	500			500

CUSTOMER ORDERS—12-MONTH HORIZON

PERIOD	1991									
	JAN	FEB	MAR	APR	MAY	JUN	JUL	AUG	…	DEC
TOTAL	98	301	300	260	180	102	93	50		
VINYL	13	131	200	100	100	60	70	30		
LEATHER	65	100	70	80	70	20	15	10		
DELUXE	20	70	30	80	10	22	8	10		

MASTER SCHEDULE FOR VINYL BRIEFCASES—12-MONTH HORIZON

PERIOD	1991											
	TYPE 1 INPUT						TYPE 2 INPUT					
	JAN	FEB	MAR	APR	MAY	JUN	JUL	AUG	SEP	OCT	NOV	DEC
FORE	6	224	308	174	156	144					260	390
ORDER	13	131	200	100	100	60					0	0
AVAIL 50	37	0	0	0	0	0						
AVAIL TO PRM	37	56	108	74	56	84					260	390
MPS	0	187	308	174	156	144					260	390

ROUGH-CUT CAPACITY PLANS—12-MONTH HORIZON

WORK CENTER 13—VINYL FITTING (.12 HOURS/VINYL CASE)

PERIOD	1991											
	JAN	FEB	MAR	APR	MAY	JUN	JUL	AUG	SEP	OCT	NOV	DEC
AVAIL	40	40	40	40	40	40					40	40
REQUIR		22.44	36.96	20.88	18.72	17.28					31.20	46.8
DIFF	40	17.56	3.04	19.12	21.28	22.72					8.80	-6.8

demanded. Because January 1991 is the first period in the plan, its AVAIL TO PRM equals the difference between beginning inventory (50 units) plus the MPS quantity (0 units) and the orders received for January (13). Thus, January's AVAIL TO PRM is 37 units. For further explanation of the AVAIL TO PRM, we recommend the review of this concept in other references.[2]

SUMMARY

In this chapter, we have discussed the important relationships between demand management and forecasting for manufacturers. The relationships and basic functions of forecasts in manufacturing activities were highlighted. Our purpose has been to clarify the importance of forecasts to those activities and to provide an understanding of the strategic and integrative nature of forecasting in manufacturing. In summary, good demand management requires several types of forecasts to achieve the profit and growth goals of the manufacturing organization. The next chapter develops these concepts for the manufacturer-distributor.

REFERENCES

1. Thomas E. Vollmann, William L. Berry, and D. Clay Whybark, *Manufacturing Planning and Control Systems,* 2nd ed. (Homewood, Ill.: Richard D. Irwin, 1988), chaps. 9 and 15.
2. Ibid., chaps. 8 and 14.

CHAPTER 5

MANUFACTURER–DISTRIBUTOR FORECASTING

Divide each difficult problem that you examine into as many
  parts as you can and as you need to solve them more easily.

Descartes, "Discours de la Methode," part II, *Oeuvres,* vol. VI, p. 18.

In Chapter 4 we discussed forecasting and planning in manufacturing. The manufacturer discussed in that chapter has no distribution responsibilities, only conversion responsibilities; that is, finished goods were sold and shipped only from the plant warehouse. This chapter extends forecasting to distributors and manufacturer-distributors. While many fundamentals of demand forecasting are the same among different kinds of operations, we point out some significant differences in the design of forecasting systems between a pure manufacturer and a manufacturer-distributor. Our purpose here is to develop several important principles of demand forecasting for distribution. Using these applications, you will be better positioned to determine your unique forecasting system requirements.

DISTRIBUTION FIRMS

Figure 5–1 illustrates an integrated forecasting system for a distributor. This figure is similar to that of a manufacturer except that the manufacturer's master scheduling and production planning functions are replaced by the distributor's purchasing systems. The distributor has no manufacturing operations but instead buys items for resale. Thus, it would seem that there is less complexity in such operations. However, the internal complexity of the manufacturer is replaced by the external complexity of the distribution network and the more complex vendor purchasing decisions that must be made.

Distributors are found in many industries including automotive service parts, electrical supplies, appliance parts, hardware, building materials, wholesale food, and office supplies, anywhere that industrial and consumer goods and commodities are involved. The distributor meets customers' needs for small quantities and mixes of products, often in shorter leadtimes than could be expected direct from the manufacturer. Were it not for the distributor, these orders would have to be placed with many different manufacturers at higher costs and higher quantities. The distributor also provides the market channel for smaller manufacturers who do not have their own distribution or direct sales operations.

In addition, distributors are organized in a more streamlined fashion. A "buyer" is typically responsible for the total materials

FIGURE 5–1
Forecasting Integration for Distributors

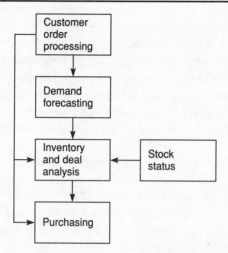

Forecast	Used by	Interval	Horizon
Type 1; demand by item and distributor location	Inventory management system	Monthly or weekly	Manufacturer's leadtime
Type 1; demand by item and distributor location	Deal analysis system	Monthly or weekly	Manufacturer's leadtime

management process. This includes forecast accuracy, the review and release of recommended purchase orders, the expedite/defer process, and actual order receipt.

EFFECTS OF SPECIAL PROMOTIONS AND DEALS

The effects of deals on demand forecasts should be analyzed.

Distributors depend on manufacturers for their stock, and many of those manufacturers compete for the same market share of the distributor's business. As an incentive to the distributor, and in many cases as an incentive to the retailer, many manufacturers offer special terms, discounts, free goods, and other kinds of financial "deals" to the distributor. The deals may be in the form of attractive incentives to the distributor, such as freight allowances to encourage a large order, special promotion offerings to retailers, off-invoice allowances, consumer rebates, or advertising allowances with proof of participation.

The deals offered to the distributor, which are typically passed on to customers, place a responsibility on the forecasting system and the distributor's buyers to anticipate each deal's effects on demand. Each deal will usually cause a change in the volume of the item being promoted, and it may also affect related products.

Deals and promotions will often affect more than one product.

A typical profile of a deal, when the deal is offered for a relatively short period of time, resembles Figure 5–2. Point A denotes the time when the deal that begins at Point B is announced. Point C denotes the end of the deal, and D is the point when demand returns to normal.

If the deal has a long duration and customers of the distributor choose to buy more than once, then there may be two peaks in the interval from B to C, or a less-pronounced, broader peak. A distributor will normally place a "first buy" purchase order to cover demand through the deal period. The first purchase order placed by the distributor after the deal begins is for the volume

FIGURE 5–2
Typical Deal Profile of Demand

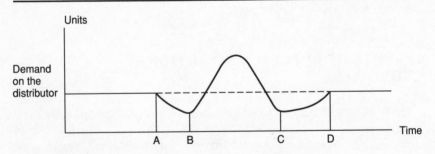

Point A: Deal is announced
Point B: Deal begins
Point C: End of deal
Point D: Demand returns to normal

of product that will be shipped during the deal period to customers of the distributor. When a second buy is allowed by the manufacturer, it will be made by the distributor just before the deal ends (at Point C). Distributor margins are enhanced significantly when they sell the product at its regular price after the completion of the deal.

When the deal is announced to the distributor's customers at point A, there is reluctance on the part of the customers to buy the deal item if they can wait for the deal to take effect. Thus, there is a slowdown from A to B. Similarly, the demand is lower from C to D because customers have increased their own retail stock levels, and demand will take some time to recover to the prediscount buying rate. The dotted line from A to D shows a likely level of business that would have occurred without the deal.

Deal Analysis

Without some understanding of the effect of a deal on the distributor's demand, the distributor would likely have too little stock during the deal period and too much after the deal was over. When it is understood that the profile of demand will be different from normal business, the deal periods of demand will be treated as what they are—a special event that needs to be isolated, specially recorded, and managed in the forecasting system.

Deals, promotions, and special events should be recorded in the demand history of the forecasting system.

Coordinating Promotional Timing and Inventory Is Critical

In 1983, the Osborne Computer Corporation announced that it would replace its fast-selling, small-screen Osborne 1 with a new and improved model in a few months. The Osborne 1 had been a great success in pioneering portable MS-DOS machines. However, because of the premature announcement, sales of the Osborne 1 immediately plummeted and the company soon went bankrupt. It failed because of the potential success of a new product that was announced before inventories of the existing product were depleted.

The graphical analysis in Figure 5-2 suggests one way to isolate deal effects, that is, to fit historical demand across the interval from point A to point D. The essential condition is to have enough demand periods that are not "promoted" so as to be able to reliably derive a regression line or other type of curve. The resulting curve provides a base line of "unpromoted" demand history. The difference between actual demand and the fitted line illustrates the profile and effect of the deal. By clarifying the two types of demand, regular and promotional, the firm can better model and forecast each source of demand in the future.

Deals will have different profiles depending on many factors such as the discount price, terms, free goods, and coupons. Distributors should develop a coding and classification scheme for the nature of the deals they have experienced. Similarly, the resulting demand should be kept in the history file along with descriptive remarks and characteristics about the deal. With this organized database of deal characteristics and quantified results, it becomes feasible to build causal models that "explain" a large percentage of the numerical impact of different types of deals. Then, using percentage profiles, deal analysis can supplement the forecasting of normal demand. Thus, most planned deals can be forecasted on the basis of their characteristics and the appropriate percentage volume effects can be applied to the base line of normal demand.

Demand forecasts should be modified by the type of deal or promotion.

Promotional Analysis

Deals that are essentially financial incentives to the distributor, and perhaps to the retailer, differ from promotions in which the product is packed in special sizes, special displays, labels that specify cents off the regular price, and so on. Promotional offers usually include some financial incentive to the distributor, but a second buy at the close of the promotional period may not be attractive to the distributor. This occurs when the goods, because of their marking, cannot be sold at regular prices. In some instances, it is appropriate for the distributor to carry promotional goods beyond the promotion period when they can be sold at regular prices, provided that the costs of carrying the inventory and any extra handling costs do not outweigh the financial incentives offered by the manufacturer.

The differences between deals and promotions do not change the basics of a demand profile. The illustration of Figure 5–2 applies to both deals and promotions; thus, these profiles are typically referred to as *promotional profiles*.

Divertors and the Grey Market

A distributor or retail chain may be able to procure inventory from alternate sources rather than the primary manufacturer. In particular industries, these alternate sources are often called *divertors* or *grey market* vendors. They represent a viable opportunity for distributors and retailers to procure inventory at reduced costs. Although this process is perfectly legal, it is generally handled in a somewhat discretionary manner due to its overall effect on the manufacturer, its salespeople, and, potentially, the distributors themselves.

The process typically begins when a manufacturer has a deal or plans to have a significant price increase. Divertors sometimes purchase inventory directly from the manufacturer, but, more typically, from a distributor or retail chain. The idea is for the divertor to procure the inventory at the reduced cost, then hold it until the deal is no longer available or the price increase has taken effect. As the distributor or retailer depletes their deal inventory, they have the opportunity to buy deal inventory from the divertor, who offers the product at less than the regular manufacturer's cost. The overall effect is an increase in inventory in the distribution pipeline.

> Hold back some goods for a thousand days and you will be
> sure to deal at a profit.
>
> Old Chinese proverb

The impact that diversion has on forecasting and inventory-management systems can be significant. The manufacturers may be producing promotional forecasts using the methods described previously. However, if the deal or price increase is quite lucrative, the grey market pipeline may cause promotional demand to far exceed the level that was predicted. It is for this reason that the diversion market becomes an important demand factor to consider when producing promotional forecasts at the manufacturing level.

> *Demands for products at the manufacturer can*
> *be distorted by changes in distribution practices.*

Distributors and retail chains have a different challenge. When the manufacturer is no longer offering the promotional prices, distributors and retail chains must determine if it is appropriate for them to purchase inventory from the manufacturer at regular cost or from the divertor at a reduced cost.

Several important business issues must be considered when making this decision. For example, consider the possibility that a distributor or retail chain is sharing their future requirements from distribution requirements planning (DRP) with the manufacturer in order to improve service levels and reduce costs for both parties. What is the impact on the accuracy of that information if the distributor or retail chain buys the requirements from the divertor? Conversely, should the opportunity to purchase the inventory at a lower cost be ignored?

Purchasing

Buying decisions will include the quantities needed to supplement normal demand during promotional or deal periods and the ongoing volume of regular business. Also, at the close of a promotion or deal period, the buyer may decide to carry extra low-cost stock bought at the better price. This decision depends on the economics of the situation, including the desirability of unique packages or price labels.

The decision to carry extra stock should include trade-offs between the cost of carrying inventory and the savings achieved by acquiring stock at the lower price; however, this analysis is complicated by factors such as the following:

- The shelf life of the item.
- The time value of the costs and savings, including return-on-investment analysis.
- The required minimum return on any investment in inventory.
- The expectation that another deal on the same item will be offered soon, when that will occur, and what the depth of that deal will be.
- The complication in any deal that offers several items in a "package" to achieve carload or truckload quantities or other minimums.
- The uncertainty of the demand forecasts for normal business beyond the deal.
- The uncertainty of the deal profile itself and the degree to which the market may have been saturated by the promotion.
- Considerations that impact carrying costs and required warehouse capacity.
- Number of buys allowed by the manufacturer.
- Item importance or obsolescence risk.
- Investment capital available.

Formal mathematical models are used to analyze these many considerations. Often, simple but effective formulas assume that demand is known during and after the deal. A good forecasting system should capture the data needed to use these formulas.

*The decision to buy extra stock during
a deal requires considerable analysis.*

When the analysis of deal items from a specific vendor-manufacturer has been completed, buyers can place purchase orders for the sum of normal stock replenishments and deal purchases. If a deal item is offered only in special packs, or with unique labels or markings, its deal purchase quantity will be clearly separated from regular-pack goods.

Total purchase requirements must include regular goods and promotional or deal items in quantities that cover known demand. These purchases should include orders placed in anticipation of upcoming retail promotions, customer orders for regular goods, as well as forecasted demand and shelf-stock requirements to protect against surges in demand on regular goods.

Stock Planning with Promotions

When customers expect immediate delivery on promoted items, then possible surges in the distributor's demand for that item should be covered in the distributor's inventory plans in the form

---

Order Optimization for Distributors

In addition to deals and promotions, distributors are frequently offered special discounts on the entire purchase order based on the relative size of that order. *Bracket pricing,* as it is called, is a method vendors use to encourage the distributor to increase the size of each purchase order.

There is obviously a cost associated with carrying the additional inventory. Therefore, the order should be "optimized," taking into consideration the associated costs (carrying costs and ordering cost) versus the additional savings generated by buying up to the next bracket. This process of order optimization is many times a manual inventory-management process performed by the buyer. However, distributors often manage hundreds of thousands of items, making automation of this function particularly attractive.

In this scenario, DRP can be used to calculate the pure time-phased requirements for each item/location. The order-optimization process summarizes those item/location requirements into vendor/location requirements. At this point, the requirements can be compared to vendor minimums, vendor prepaid freight minimums, and vendor bracket pricing opportunities in order to produce the most cost-effective order.

This concept allows distributors to take advantage of a more-proactive inventory-management tool in DRP, described later in this chapter, rather than the more-conventional, reactionary order-point method. Using DRP at the item/location level in conjunction with order optimization at the vendor level is an effective combination for distributors.

---

of safety stock. The regular and promotional demand forecasts are uncertain, but they should be used to determine the stock plans. The use of forecast errors and leadtimes to determine safety stock quantities is specifically discussed in Chapter 16.

MANUFACTURER WITH DISTRIBUTION NETWORK

The management of demand is more complex for the manufacturer-distributor because there are more sources of independent demand that must be managed. Next, we discuss these many different sources of demand and some principles of their management.

Figure 5–3 illustrates the demand management system for a manufacturer-distributor. This figure differs from that of the pure manufacturer in the following ways. Master scheduling and production planning have been combined and stock planning has been omitted for simplification, even though each has the same purpose as in Chapter 4. DRP has been added to help manage demand at the several warehouses or distribution centers.

To better understand the significance of the distribution network, consider Figure 5–4, which illustrates a simple, but common, two-echelon network of distribution centers that are replenished from two plants. The network shows the normal sourcing of replenishment shipments from the plants to the distribution centers (DCs) and the shipments to customers from both of the plants and from each DC.

Plant-Direct Shipments

When a manufacturer performs distribution functions, there are DC and plant-direct shipments to customers. Plant-direct shipments are often larger—full-truck or railcar shipments. These shipments take advantage of lower freight cost per unit, where possible, and avoid the storage and handling charges associated with goods that pass trough a DC on the way to a customer. Also included in Figure 5–4 as plant-direct are shipments to customers made from a warehouse at the plant site. The demand forecast

FIGURE 5–3
Manufacturer with Distribution Network

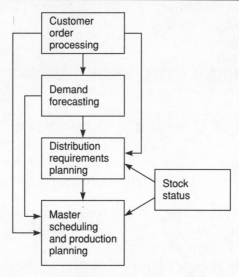

Forecast	Used by	Interval	Horizon
Type 1; demand by item and distribution center	Distribution requirements planning system	Weekly or daily	Leadtime required to obtain replenishments from the preferred source
Type 1; demand by item and plant for direct customer shipments	Master scheduling	Weekly or daily	Manufacturing leadtime

arrows at each plant are meant to include both direct, off-the-production-line loading of customer shipments and the plant-warehouse customer demand.

It is important to recognize that plant-warehouse shipments may be costlier than DC shipments when extra handling is required in the plant. These considerations are important in distribution network design. However, our purpose here centers on management of demand for finished goods and the forecasting system used to manage these at each location.

Both the master production scheduling (MPS) system and the distribution requirements planning (DRP) system use stock status data, as shown in Figure 5–3. Those inventories are used to

FIGURE 5-4
Two-Echelon Distribution Network

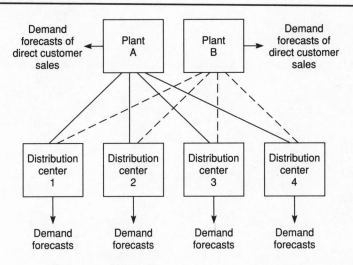

determine the *net* production requirements, after allowing for existing stock on hand. Consequently, it is important to coordinate the net distribution requirements with the net plant requirements. Inventory on hand at each plant warehouse and DC should be assigned to either the MPS system or the DRP system for management and calculation purposes. If the inventory at a plant warehouse is used in the calculations of the MPS, then that same location and its inventory should not be duplicated in the DRP system. To illustrate the typical choice of location assignments, consider Figure 5-4. Inventories of finished goods in the two plant warehouses (if any) should be assigned to the MPS system, and the four DCs and their inventories should be assigned to the DRP system.

An item/location should be managed by either DRP or MPS, but not both.

DISTRIBUTION REQUIREMENTS PLANNING

In general, the most-effective way to manage distribution demands is through distribution requirements planning. Figure 5-5 illustrates DRP for a manufacturer who produces a product at a sin-

FIGURE 5–5
Distribution Requirements Planning

REGIONAL DISTRIBUTION CENTER 1   LOS ANGELES
SKU NO. 11   PRODUCT 1   LT = 1 WEEK
ON HAND 60   ALLOCATED 10   SAFETY STOCK 50   ORDER QTY 400

WEEK	1	2	3	4	5	6	7	8	9
FORECAST ORDERS	96	128	159	175	187	187	202	280	337
ON HAND		304	176	17	242	55	268	66	186
RECEIPTS	400				400	(400)		400	400
RELEASES			400		(400)		400	400	

REGIONAL DISTRIBUTION CENTER 2   NEW YORK
SKU NO. 12   PRODUCT 1   LT = 2
ON HAND 100   ALLOCATED 5   SAFETY STOCK 50   ORDER QTY 600

WEEK	1	2	3	4	5	6	7	8	9
FORECAST ORDERS	173	208	172	172	279	199	198	278	239
ON HAND	45	472	264	92	520	241	42	444	166
RECEIPTS	600			600			(600)		600
RELEASES		600			(600)		600		

CUSTOMER DIRECT
SKU NO. 1C   PRODUCT 1   LT = 0

WEEK	1	2	3	4	5	6	7	8	9
FORECAST ORDERS		157	178	89	157	122	86	278	146
	74								
REQUIREMENTS	74	157	178	89	157	122	86	278	146
RELEASES	74	157	178	89	(157)	122	86	278	146

PRODUCT 1 DRP OUTPUT TO MASTER SCHEDULING MODULE

WEEK	1	2	3	4	5	6	7	8	9
REQUIREMENTS	74	757	578	89	(1,157)	122	1,086	678	146
ON HAND	90	16							
MPS		741	578	89	1,157	122	1,086	678	146

Note: On hand quantities are beginning inventory.
Beginning inventory of period 1 = On hand – Allocated – Safety stock.
Allocated = Promised units still in stock.
Safety stock = Units used only in emergency, not planned uses.

gle location. This product is sold directly to customers and through two regional distribution centers (RDCs), one in New York and one in Los Angeles.

The DRP records of Figure 5–5 show the plans at two RDCs, customer direct sales at the factory, and the resulting demand at the factory's master schedule. Consider week 5 for each of these locations. As shown, Los Angeles needs to receive 400 units of Product 1 at the beginning of week 6. In order to receive these, the factory must begin shipping these the beginning of week 5 (the leadtime (LT) from the factory to Los Angeles is one week). Thus, the transfer from the factory must be released in week 5 to arrive in Los Angeles in week 6. Similarly, New York needs to receive 600 units the beginning of week 7. Because the lead-time to New York is two weeks, the units must be released the beginning of week 5. The customer direct sales from the factory are shipped immediately, the customer service personnel having already offset the dates for customer order leadtime. Thus, we see that 157 customer direct units are to be shipped the beginning of week 5.

The sum of these three demands, 1,157 (that is, 400 + 600 + 157), is shown as the requirement in week 5 of the master schedule. The demand at the master schedule level is no longer forecast, but is instead a dependent demand calculated as the sum of the net requirements at the two distribution centers and customer direct sales. Thus, demand at the master schedule is called *requirements*.

DRP is such an important method because it manages the dependent demands in distribution networks. When a network has several distribution centers, DRP provides coordination of demand management information to the master scheduling system. The RDCs have forecasts of their gross requirements, since the demand on the warehouses is independent demand. Recognizing these dependencies in a distribution network is essential if we are to achieve high customer service without extraordinary investment in excess inventory.

DRP is essential in managing the dependent demands in a manufacturer-distributor network.

The DRP planning documents shown in Figure 5–5 may be used by distribution personnel in allocating available product and plant capacity. Without the use of this kind of centralized planning document, it is common to see distribution networks in which stock is misallocated across the network. Some locations have too much inventory while others are out of stock. With traditional order points, each location will try to pull as much inventory as possible for its needs. However, these order-point procedures do not give the scheduler any forward view of the real needs at the

RDCs or of the possible room for schedule adjustments. This is true because, as shown in our example, the RDCs request large quantities that, if supply were limited, could be broken into several smaller shipments, thus balancing demand over time and location. The central planner needs to be able to make such decisions. He or she will be able to make much better decisions with the information provided in a time-phased DRP.

DRP makes centralized allocation of scarce distribution inventories possible.

Without centralized allocation of inventories,
distribution inventories will be misallocated.

For those familiar with materials requirements planning, it is helpful to note that DRP provides several of the MRP techniques applied to distribution. Exception reporting, pegging, and firm planned orders are applicable in managing the replenishments in a network. Such detail is beyond our purposes; however, the interested reader can refer to Andre Martin's work.[1]

In summary, we see that through the use of DRP we can achieve a unified consideration of supply and demand across all locations. With DRP, we have made use of each location's forecast of independent demands.

Distribution Network Design

The choice of the number of plants and distribution centers in a distribution network may be quite simple in some cases where markets are geographically focused, such as an original equipment manufacturer (OEM) of automobile parts. In other industries, the network may become quite complex for competitive reasons. For example, where there are several channels of distribution (wholesale, customer direct, and retailers), there may be geographic overlap to serve different classes of trade. The demands of customers by each location and channel should be part of the input to network design and DC location studies. The need for forecasts to support this kind of analysis is obvious. The demand estimates for the network should be consistent with the forecasts used for other business planning purposes.

Managing independent demands in a network design is critical.

Out of this kind of analysis will come a set of distribution centers and plant-warehouse locations for managing customer shipments. This set can be determined using case analysis methods, simulation, or linear programming to suggest a least-cost or most-profitable set of stocking points. The distribution management and customer service personnel subsequently will be able to plan the assignment of different types of customer orders to each possible shipping point in the network. Some customer orders for truckload quantities may be shipped plant-direct, while smaller orders may be shipped from the preferred (perhaps the nearest) DC.

Demand management policies are part of network design.

The rules used for customer order assignment to shipping points should emulate the rules that were part of the network design analysis, otherwise the loads, stock levels, and so on, will be different than anticipated by the network analysis. Forecast accuracy may suffer if multiple forecast records are created when actual demands are not recorded in their preferred locations.

When customer orders are being processed correctly, the assigned customer demands will cause historical demand in the forecasting system to accumulate each period at the preferred shipping points. Accordingly, the forecast will change in response to those accumulated demands. As a company's business matures and evolves, however, the assignment of customer demands to preferred shipping points will also evolve. These changes to the demand forecasts may be gradual, because of the weight of historical demand, even though the preferred shipping points for some major customers have been permanently changed. We discuss this further in the section on demand history realignment below.

The distribution network design is used as the basis for ongoing operations as long as the economics of the business have not changed greatly. However, management may see ways to improve the distribution network design. Consequently, the network analysis might be repeated to see whether the demand assignment rules need to be changed among the existing locations, whether the network design should be changed, or both. This kind of planning may be done semiannually or annually, depending on the costs of the analysis, the benefits to be achieved, and the ease with which the recommended changes can be implemented in the forecasting and distribution systems.

DRP Uses of Forecasts and the Network Design

The DRP system used to manage distribution centers in Figure 5–4 uses forecasts of demands and calculates the inventory needs for each item at each location by date and quantity. It then uses the network design to pass those requirements to the assigned source locations (e.g., plants A and B), while recognizing the lead-times required to fulfill replenishment requests at each DC.

Electronic Clothing Network

Benetton is one of the most successful distributor-retailers in the global fashion industry. It sells products in 40 countries through 4,600 stores. Approximately 80 percent of its manufacturing is done by 450 vendors with 30 to 100 employees. Selling more than 50 million garments a year, it is the world's largest consumer of wool. Being a progressive company, it spends $12 million a year on computer systems and technology. To support its diverse market, it runs several IBM and Fujitsu mainframes and utilizes the General Electric Information Services (GEISCO) network for telecommunications.

Benetton stores are independently owned franchises in its global market of 75 geographic territories. Each territory is managed by an agent. The agents are tied to Benetton through an order handling system developed by GEISCO. This order system collects information from the agent's computers, updates product files, confirms orders, and sends the orders to the appropriate manufacturing location.

This efficient and effective manufacturing-distribution system has helped make Benetton one of the most responsive retailers in its industry.

Source: "A Clothing Network," *PC Week,* November 10, 1987.

When a DRP system is used to help manage the distribution network in this manner, the changes recommended by the network analysis should become part of the DRP system. The DRP system should reflect the preferred sourcing of each DC from a plant, a plant warehouse, or another DC. Furthermore, the demand forecasts of customer shipments should reflect the planned assignment of customer orders, if necessary by order type, to the preferred shipping locations. Figure 5–6 illustrates a rather complex network for a consumer goods firm. Customers may be assigned to a DC for mixed-load orders or directly to a plant for railcar or truckload orders. Thus it becomes critical to capture customer demands consistently so as to have a valid database of demand sources. If inconsistent demands are recorded, then forecast errors will increase significantly.

*Consistent and accurate sources of demand should
be managed and recorded in a DRP network.*

FIGURE 5–6
Consumer-Goods Distribution Network

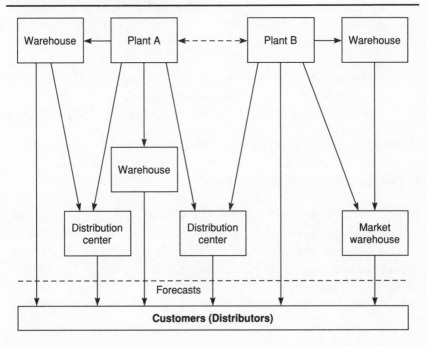

Substitution of Locations or Items

As a business evolves, some customer shipments may be made from locations other than the preferred locations. When a stock-out or quality problem occurs, items may be substituted if a satisfactory alternative is on hand at the preferred shipping location. When substitutions occur, on either the location or item code, it is important to record the demand history in such a way as to not distort the demand forecasts that will use that history. The responsibility for this data collection begins with the order processing system but must be carried out in the database used for demand forecasting.

Product or location substitutions should not distort true product demands.

The customer order processing system should maintain the customer-preferred shipping locations and may also designate alternate locations. When an order is accepted, the actual assigned location may differ from the preferred location, but, unless an override is made, the assigned location is set equal to the preferred location. Both the assigned and preferred locations are passed to the demand history file. Similarly, when item substitutions occur, the actual-item and the requested-item codes should be passed to the demand history file. The default, of course, is that both item codes are the same. With these procedures in place, the demand history is traceable to the order processing system data and has enough detail to support good forecasting by stockkeeping unit.

Demand history for forecasting should reflect preferred items and locations.

Demand History Realignment

When the DRP network is changed, or when customer demands are reassigned among the shipping locations, the DRP system should respond by replanning the stock levels and the replenishment requirements to meet the revised flow through the network. To achieve this, the forecasts used in DRP system calculations of stock requirements should be recalculated based on the revised customer assignments. For example, the demand associated with customer XYZ is shifted from the St. Louis DC to the Chicago DC. In this case, demand forecasts, stock plans, and replenishments will increase in Chicago and decrease in St. Louis, all other conditions being equal.

The DRP system should manage demand-location realignments to support accurate databases and forecasts.

Stock Planning

Demand forecasts, with their implicit customer assignments, are the basis for stock plans at each location. Each item must be planned in some way, either by a time supply rule, explicit use of forecasts, or anticipating immediate customer orders. Stock plans, especially those for safety stocks or minimum inventory levels, are an essential part of the DRP calculations.

DRP Net Requirements

Demand forecasts provided to the DRP system are for independent demands for items at specific locations (i.e., for SKUs). As customer orders are received, they are usually assigned to the preferred shipping locations based on customer, product, or type of order. As such, the customer orders are a realization of the forecasted demand on the SKU. Both open customer orders and forecasted demand are input to the DRP system. The net requirements of DRP equal customer orders and forecasted demands minus beginning on hand and receipts. The DRP receipts of Figure 5–5 are timed to cover these net requirements.

Master Scheduling

As shown in Figure 5–3, there are four inputs to the master scheduling system. While we have simplified the diagram in Figure 5–3, the other manufacturing planning systems are just as important to the manufacturer-distributor as they were in the pure manufacturer example of Figure 4–1, but they are omitted here.

The focus of the master scheduling at plant locations is to provide the replenishments needed by the distribution network, to prepare for forecasted plant-direct shipments to customers, and to cover any open customer orders already received.

The master schedule includes plant-direct and distribution requirements.

The master schedule provides production planners with product demands to be filled by the plant. Any open customer orders for immediate shipment may be satisfied by existing inventory at the plant or plant warehouse. Customer orders filled by the plant are usually a realization of the independent forecasted demand on the plant. Some of those customer orders may be for future shipping dates and may affect the total demand for those periods, depending on their volume relative to the forecast.

There are many other aspects of the forecasting and replenishment systems of manufacturer-distributors that are developed in other chapters of this book. These chapters are important in understanding and designing manufacturer-distributor forecasting systems.

SUMMARY

This chapter has developed important concepts and principles of forecasting systems for manufacturer-distributors. The importance of forecasts in supporting deal analysis, distribution network design, and distribution requirements planning (DRP) were discussed. The manufacturer-distributor faces many of the same problems of the pure manufacturing operation plus the problems of forecasting and demand management of the distribution network. The distributor must be aware of the importance of maintaining consistent product forecasts by distribution center location. How orders are processed, the origin of demand, and the preferred location of shipment must be accurately captured in demand databases so that accurate forecasts can be made of future demands. Without recognition of the principles of this chapter, a manufacturer-distributor faces relatively less accurate SKU forecasts and poorer customer service.

Having discussed manufacturers and manufacturer-distributors in Chapters 4 and 5, respectively, Chapter 6 extends our discussion of forecasting systems to retailers and service repair operations.

REFERENCE

1. Andre Martin, *Distribution Resource Planning*, 2nd ed. (Essex Junction, Vt.: Oliver Wight Limited Publications, 1990).

CHAPTER 6

RETAIL, MAINTENANCE, AND REMANUFACTURER FORECASTING

Success in the *next business upturn* comes from automating systems for forecasting, merchandising, and inventory control.

In the *next downturn,* those with good automated systems will have a significantly better chance of survival.

Retail Industry Experts

This chapter develops forecasting in retail, maintenance, and remanufacturing industries. It can be viewed as two separate chapters, one on retailing, the other on maintenance and remanufacturing operations. The requirements of these two different forecasting situations are unique in several ways. However, both of these topics are continuations of previous chapters; thus, an understanding of Chapters 1 through 5 is an important prerequisite to each topic of this chapter.

Retailers and service-item distributors must buy and sell many items at numerous places. The number of items at locations (i.e., stockkeeping units) can be several hundred thousands or millions in national retail chains. The planning decisions in retailing require that forecasts be organized by departments within individual stores, and frequently the demand patterns in different stores are unique, even for stores in the same city.

In contrast, maintenance operations and remanufacturers are distinguished from other industries in that important or expensive products are replaced or repaired (remanufactured) as scheduled or as needed. Typical examples of maintenance operations are those that service and replace items in public utilities, manufacturing plants, airlines, truck lines, and so on. These maintenance operations require labor and service items to achieve high levels of customer service. Those who repair these items are called remanufacturers. They receive broken, malfunctioning, or worn-out items for rebuilding and reassembly.

While many maintenance operations do not sell service items to customers, demand forecasting is needed to provide inventory for emergency or unscheduled repairs. Many service items have very low demands and are kept on hand as "insurance" spares. These may require special forecasting support. In addition, the sources of product supply and demand are somewhat different for maintenance operations. These differences require special forecasting and inventory management systems. These and other special aspects of service-item demand forecasting are discussed in this chapter. While the second half of this chapter focuses on maintenance/remanufacturing, the distributors of service items will benefit from the discussions of both sections of this chapter as well as from the discussion of the distribution forecasting systems in Chapter 5.

RETAIL OPERATIONS

You can't sell from an empty cart.

Nothing happens until somebody forecasts something.

Figure 6–1 illustrates demand forecasting in a major retail chain with many stores whose inventories are replenished from one or more regional distribution centers and vendors. The uniqueness of retail operations requires adaptations of the forecasting and planning functions presented earlier. The unique features of retail forecasting include:

- Store-level differences in market characteristics (i.e., demand patterns vary by store).
- Greater emphasis on event planning (promotions) and special seasonal merchandising.
- Style and trend-setting changes in design and fashion in some departments.
- High-volume transaction processing and many stock-keeping units across many stores.
- Frequent reliance on universal product code (UPC) marking and data collection.
- Availability of point-of-sale data.

We discuss several of these unique characteristics below.

Merchandise Planning

Demand forecasting must support merchandise planning in the retail trades. Merchandise planning includes management of product selections, inventory levels, gross margins, sales volume, display space, promotions, markdowns, stock turns, and open-to-buy (OTB) decisions. Forecasts can be used in some merchandise plan-

FIGURE 6–1
Illustration of Retail Forecasting Hierarchy

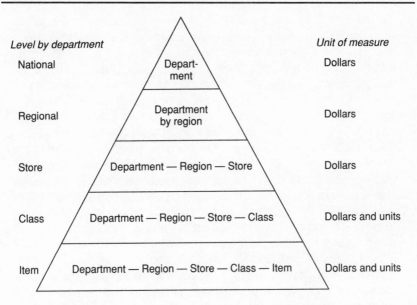

ning systems either "top-down" or "bottom-up." That is, department plans can be built upward from item forecasts (bottom-up) or they can be specified top-down by a general merchandise manager in total dollars. If top-down dollar or unit volumes are set as guidelines, the department manager develops merchandise plans so that the item plans sum to the required dollar or unit volumes. The discussions of forecast aggregation and disaggregation in Chapters 1, 2, and 3 are particularly relevant here. The important principles of those chapters assure that item plans are realistic and consistent with the department volume forecasts and plans.

Pyramidal forecasting principles are essential in merchandise planning.

> Plurality which is not reduced to unity is confusion; unity which does not depend on plurality is tyranny.
>
> Blaise Pascal

Fashion Goods and Electronic Processing

To increase customer service, decrease order leadtime, and stimulate quick response to changing customer demands, clothing manufacturers have developed electronic systems to connect customers with their order-processing systems. Some manufacturers sell their garments to approximately 15,000 retailers, many of whom use different computer systems and SKU pricing and identification systems. By coordinating garment-ordering and label-marking technology with manufacturers, some department store chains have reduced their leadtimes by 50 to 80 percent. Helping to reduce leadtimes are American National Standards Institute protocols for electronic data interchange (EDI) and national information services such as the General Electric Information Services (GEISCO) network. Manufacturers and their customers can rapidly communicate using electronics. To simplify automated order entry, manufacturers and customers use universal product codes and the National Retail Merchants Association universal vendor marking codes on their merchandise. For this reason, many retailers do not have to mark items separately. In addition, point-of-sale scanners and terminals keep track of clothing as it is sold.

The better merchandising decisions and shorter leadtimes allowed by these uses of technology and information result in significant profit increases and markdown reductions.

Forecasts by Department

The total demand volumes by department are usually analyzed historically in dollars and where possible in another convenient statistical measure such as the number of units, pairs, coordinated sets, pounds, and so on. Most often, forecasted volumes are in dollars directly unless a nondollar statistical unit is a more effective measure of demand. The advantages of using nondollar forecasts are twofold:

1. They highlight the required business volumes in units that are more closely related to demand, transaction volume, the number of customers, and the number of items required to achieve the department plans.

2. By using real-unit forecasts, the inflationary effects of price increases are isolated in the planning process. Dollar volumes are then calculated as the product of planned price levels and planned unit volumes. The realism of these dollar forecasts is therefore more easily determined when they are compared to nondollar forecasts.

When possible, use nondollar, real-unit
demand forecasts for planning purposes.

Concurrently, a forecast of dollar volumes based only on past dollar history can be provided by the forecasting system. This dollar forecast can be compared to the real-unit demand forecasts discussed above. The dollar forecasts and plans of product groups can be developed separately and then summed to provide the department totals.

The development and comparison of top-down and bottom-up
forecasts yield more-accurate and more-effective plans.

The proof of forecasting and planning realism is often in the details.

When we look at these several parallel approaches to business planning, we may be tempted to cast off all but one, perhaps choosing the easiest, which often is the top-down approach. But there is good reason to develop the detailed aspects of plans from the bottom up. This dual planning provides a "reality check" that is achieved by comparing aggregate dollars to unit details. Just as in a legal trial and its judgment, the proof of reality is often in the corroborating evidence provided by the details of the planned events.

Top-down and bottom-up planning provide an
internal consistency check on planning integrity.

Forecasts by Item

Forecasts of item demands are essential for long-leadtime items.

The practicality of item forecasting will vary between departments of a store. Item forecasts are appropriate for more-stable, larger-value items (e.g., white goods) but not appropriate for small-value items with short leadtimes. Where the department's success depends on a few major items, those items should be tracked, forecasted, and planned individually. These typically include the longer-leadtime items. The remaining items can be forecasted and planned as a group. Class or price-point groups of the remaining items may serve to organize the demand data in a useful way. For example, pens in a stationery department may be forecasted at each of several price points in total dollars: 49 cents, 89 cents, $1.79, $4.89, and so on. At these lower-price points where substitutions and various pack sizes are commonplace, the forecast should assure the purchase of enough units in a reasonable mix to achieve the planned sales volume. Some variations of pack sizes, and even brands, are usually acceptable to customers—thus, forecasting is simplified.

Some retail items are best forecast by groups.

Item forecasts are normally more effective and necessary for major retail items.

Whether to forecast items individually or as a group (or both) should depend on the value of the additional precision of item fore-

---

Tips for Retailing Goods

Businesses are taking advantage of low-cost technology and software to automate their inventory-management systems. The forecasting system of a retail inventory-management system is critical because it provides the information needed to keep the right product in the right place at the right time. This yields the right distribution of inventory within departments, between departments, and between stores. Having the total dollars of inventory allocated across all departments or stores is easy. It's much more difficult to have the unit volumes distributed to maximize departmental sales and customer service.

The old excuses for not having good inventory-management and forecasting systems are no longer valid. Computer-based systems are competitively priced and much more user-friendly today. Depending on your financial position, you can lease or buy inexpensive hardware and software.

As the old sales saying goes, "These systems don't cost you, they pay you."

casts. This additional precision is important when the merchandiser is making model stock and buying decisions. Will the merchandiser be able to allocate space, choose the items and their mix, and anticipate the changing mix of items without item forecasts? Will this be done well enough to achieve the sales, turnover, gross margin, and customer service objectives of the department? The immediate answer may depend on the skills and experience of the existing merchandiser in the short term. Forecasting system design, however, should be based on the realistic assessment of the skills of most ordinary merchandisers. Will these newer managers have adequate control with only group forecasts?

The choice of forecasting items separately or as a group is dependent on the benefits and costs of the increased control.

Aggregating low-cost, substitutable short-leadtime items can be more effective for forecasting than use of item forecasts.

Space Planning

When planning store layout and space, each department's allowed space must be organized to handle the planned number of items with designated types of displays and allotted areas. Forecasted volume by group and the planned number of items can be used to allocate the available display area. Higher-volume groups, and the higher-volume items within groups, should be allotted a greater percentage of the available space. This assures a reasonable stock turnover in the plan for both the higher- and lower-volume items while protecting against a stockout on the major items.

Typically, the plan of space use is drawn up as a "plan-o-gram," which graphically shows the table, shelf, and rack assignments for each group of merchandise. The term *plan-o-gram* is used with a variety of meanings, including simply the number of units of each item that should be in stock. However, we subscribe to the more technical use of the term, that is, graphical layout of stock.

Forecasts should be used in layout and allocation of retail space to items.

When individual-item forecasts are not available, such as in fashion goods, the historical average volume per item can be used to help plan the number of items required to meet the group or department volumes. The total department volume, number of items, and allotted space must be consistent. If the department has been achieving some sales volume per square foot and its overall space will not be increased, and if the merchandising objective is to increase dollar volume by 5 percent, then either more items must be displayed or greater sales dollars per item must be achieved. The value of good sales statistics by department cannot be overstated. Performance ratios on items, allotted space, and inventory investment are fundamental to good space planning.

Historical sales statistics by department and item are essential in achieving high departmental performance.

Sales Analysis

Historical data used for demand forecasting is also useful for some aspects of historical sales analysis. Sales analysis, however, is usually performed in much greater detail than the forecasting function. For example, sales analysis by employee can be very helpful, but ordinarily is not part of a demand forecasting system's projection of the future. However, sales performance per employee can be essential for departmental planning of staff requirements.

Sales analysis takes many forms, for example, markdown totals, volume sold on promotions, and volume by vendor. It is not our purpose here to develop the many forms of sales analysis, only to distinguish and highlight the greater detail needed in sales analysis from that needed in demand forecasting. Nonetheless, the department, group, and subgroup framework of good forecasting systems may be very useful in sales analysis. The insight provided by using the same organization of data for both purposes enables merchandise managers and buyers to better focus on the changing market opportunities.

Data used for sales analysis may be as detailed or more detailed than that used for demand forecasting.

Sales statistics by item also provide the basis for allocating the open-to-buy within a group of merchandise. As purchase commitments are being made by the buyer, the most popular items within a group should be given the larger proportion of the total dollars. Historical percentages by item may be used to calculate an initial purchase recommendation for the buyer. These historical percentages will be available from a well-designed forecasting system.

Most sales analysis is basically historical in its viewpoint.

The sensitivity of the buyer to trends within the group of merchandise becomes very important to department performance and profitability. Because historical averages often do not pick up the changing importance of items, it is much better to have item trend analyses (e.g., changing percentages of items within a group) or item forecasts for each item. This analysis makes management of changing mixes between items less difficult. Consequently, buying decisions can be based on the future mix, instead of the historical mix.

Get future item demand from the forecasting system, and
use historical percentages only if indicative of future demands.

Open-To-Buy

As stock plans are developed for a department, the inventory investments and associated stock turns will be estimated for the next season. The required purchases by date will also be set forth as part of the initial plan. The planned purchase commitments are called the *open-to-buy (OTB)*. Each period's forecasted sales and expected markdowns plus any increases in the planned inventory will suggest the planned amount to buy. Specific OTB figures are submitted for approval by the merchandise manager.

As the selling season progresses, actual sales are tracked, forecasts are changed, stock plans are revised, and the OTB is revised. The OTB then becomes a means to control the commitments of cash to inventories both in the preseason plans and their short-term revisions.

Open-to-buy decisions are driven by forecasts.

The buyer may choose items in several ways to complete purchase orders within the OTB limits of a merchandise group:

1. Historical averages of items within a group may be used. The same or similar items may be ordered to "fill-in" the merchandise group. Each item will be bought in proportion to its historical percentage, thereby creating a "buy" of the required total dollars.
2. Specific item plans for stock minimums may be based on forecasts by item, or judgment of the department manager or buyer.
3. Model stock plans by item may be used for new groups or departments.

Model Stock

When merchandise plans are set up for more-stable groups of products, the historical performance of the same group in similar stores may be used to create the individual store's item stock plans. This is called a model stock plan. This plan, which is normally based on some average-store product mixes, is used to guide the buyer while making purchase plans. Initial purchase quantities will fill in the stockkeeping units in proportion to the model stock with the OTB as the maximum total commitment. As the season develops, the more popular items will be replenished. Thus, the model stock essentially sets a minimum stock level for each item in the department of a given store.

Model stock revisions will be made as experience is gained; the resulting merchandise plans then reflect the demographics unique to the particular store. Forecasts by item can assist greatly when anticipating the changing mix of items within a group, rather than relying on historical averages alone.

Model stock is essentially a method to standardize minimum inventory planning across many stores.

Standardization of store inventories should be done cautiously; store differences are more common than store sameness.

Forecasting Many Stockkeeping Units

A single retailer may merchandise 15,000 or more items in any one store, and a chain store of national significance will manage hundreds or thousands of stores. A service-item distributor with several distribution centers may be dealing with 200,000 or more item locations. The resulting record volume, when viewed across all stores, suggests that the forecasting task be handled either at the store or regional levels to keep the processing volume and time from becoming excessive on any one computer.

Database sizes and run times may be important
concerns in retailing- and service-item forecasting.

An alternative approach is to forecast an item at the regional or chain level and to use percentages by store to allocate forecast totals to the stores for each item. This allocation process is appealing, but it requires some procedure to obtain and maintain the allocation percentages.

Even if a procedure is in use to maintain allocation percentages, they may be based on historical averages, such as the last six months' moving average of each store's sales. This is the most-often encountered method, but its weakness is that it assumes that there are no significant changes occurring in the mix between stores. The only cure for this weakness is to perform item forecasting, from which trends and any potential changes in the mix can be deduced. Simple moving averages have no capability to detect trends or changing seasonality.

Allocating stock to stores using regional or national percentages
often ignores important trends and changes in product mixes.

If it is correct to assume that the stores are going to sell the same relative percentages of items as sold in the recent past, then the number of item forecasts is reduced. For example, rather than producing forecasts for each of 50 stores in a region, forecasts of each item's regional total can be made. Then the regional total is allocated to individual stores using historical percentages. This yields a considerable reduction in file volume and run time.

When regional or national percentages are not used, millions of items must be forecasted and coordinated. The use of networks or distributed processing on several computers provides the computational power needed to achieve adequate capacity and responsiveness. This capacity is very important in managing and capturing the changing conditions in the individual stores. Where distributed or network connectivity is unnecessary, independent store computer systems can be used.

Distributed data processing, networks, or independent computers offer effective ways to forecast millions of stockkeeping units.

Having developed the use and uniqueness of forecasting in retailing, we now discuss another unique use of forecasting systems—forecasting demand for repairable items in maintenance and remanufacturing operations.

MAINTENANCE AND REMANUFACTURING OPERATIONS

The time to repair the roof is when the sun is shining.
John F. Kennedy, state of the union message, January 11, 1962

Some products or items are so critical to the safety or function of a system that, to preclude malfunctions, they are routinely replaced before failure. Many of these items are expensive and, consequently, are rebuilt or remanufactured for later sale. These items include aircraft engines, safety-control devices, and vehicle braking systems. Other items are so expensive that, after failing in service, they are replaced with rebuilt or remanufactured items. These products are used by public utilities, manufacturing plants, airlines, truck lines, automotive parts remanufacturers, and other industries. Consider the following example.

A commercial aircraft navigation device is discovered to be malfunctioning en route to Chicago. The pilot alerts the maintenance supervisor to be ready with a replacement. The defective unit is replaced and tagged for servicing, then sent to the appropriate maintenance base or remanufacturing plant. This particular unit may be one of many awaiting service at that base, but several units are already repaired. Consequently, there may be no need to hurry the repair of the unit that was just removed from service. There is no hurry because the demand had already been anticipated by the service-item forecasting inventory management system.

We call firms that replace items *maintenance operations (MOs)*. The firms that rebuild, repair, or remanufacture failed items are referred to as *remanufacturers*. The firms that distribute remanufactured or rebuilt items are referred to as *service-item distributors*. Finally, whether the items are new or used, we call them *service items*.[1]

The relationships between these three types of businesses and their functions are defined in Figure 6–2. We use the terms above and in Figure 6–2 throughout this chapter because they are the most common. We prefer to use the term *service items* for items that are replaced, rebuilt, or remanufactured even though the term *service parts* is used very frequently. We avoid the term *parts* because it is also used to refer to simple parts that are small and

FIGURE 6–2
Maintenance, Distribution, and Remanufacture Operations

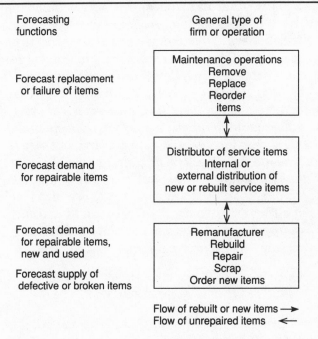

uncomplicated. In contrast, many of the items that are replaced in the field are large, complex assemblies. The use of the term *service parts* is a misnomer in this respect. Also, there are many other terms that are used for remanufacturers (e.g., rebuilders or repairers). We do not distinguish between these types of operations here. We hope that, by focusing on the functions defined in Figure 6–2, you will be able to relate your industry to our discussions.

Also, we depict maintenance operations (MOs) as external to the remanufacturer. This is the most general case. Very frequently, a MO is an internal department of the same company that remanufactures its own service items. Our discussion is relevant to both internal and external maintenance operations.

Finally, our discussion of the types of firms in Figure 6–2 is not meant to give comprehensive coverage of their missions or internal operations. Like other chapters, the discussion here is designed to highlight the forecasting principles that are relevant to them.

The left column of Figure 6–2 defines the forecasting functions of maintenance, distribution, and remanufacturing operations. Unlike many other industries, this network has material flow to *and* from customers (i.e., maintenance operations) and manufacturer-suppliers. This and several other aspects of these operations are unique. First, item availability in the maintenance and distribution firms is much more important than in other industries. If the item is not available (e.g., an aircraft engine), then a much larger piece of equipment (i.e., an aircraft) or system (i.e., airlines) may be unable to function. Second, the remanufacturer of service items should forecast not only demand, but also the supply of replacements for defective or failed items. Third, the demands for service items are normally much lower than the demands for products in other industries. These lower volumes make it more difficult to accurately forecast and maintain cost-effective inventory levels. We expand on these forecasting differences and problems in the remainder of this chapter.

A remanufacturer should forecast both the supply
of and demand for repairable service items.

Figure 6–3 provides more detail of the internal operations of a remanufacturer. It depicts the decision process of determining whether to buy, scrap, or rebuild items that are reusable. This type of inventory management process is common to aircraft "rotatable" and repairable items, telecommunications equipment, and many operations where the economics lead to a swap-now-repair-later policy.

As shown at the top of Figure 6–3, the remanufacturer supplies repairable service items to maintenance operations (upper left-hand corner) and to original equipment manufacturers (OEMs) (in the upper right-hand corner). The maintenance operations can be supplied with either new or repaired parts, while the OEM uses

FIGURE 6–3
Remanufacturer Material and Information System

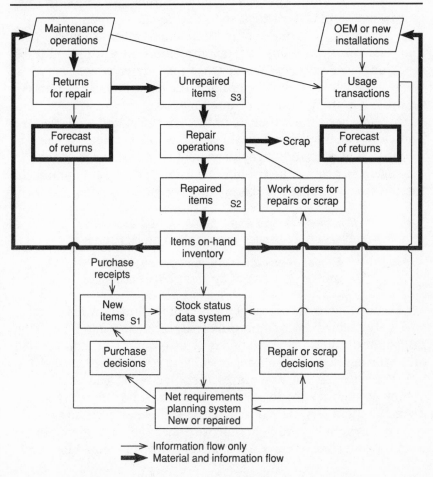

→ Information flow only
➡ Material and information flow

only new parts. The MOs return items in need of repair to the remanufacturer. In exchange, the MOs receive a lower price on the repaired item. The flow of material (i.e., items) is shown in Figure 6–3 using heavier lines and arrows (➖➤) than those depicting information flow only (⟶). Note that the upper left quarter of the figure shows the closed-loop material flow of items from the MOs to the remanufacturer back to the MOs. This material flow is distinguished by the heavier lines and arrows. Also, note that the material flow is only in the direction of the OEM and new installations block in the upper right-hand corner. Finally, note the net requirements planning system at the bottom-middle of the figure. We shall refer to these several blocks in the following sections.

Typically, where there is a pool of unrepaired units, the net requirements planner's task is to decide the following:

1. How many items should be in the new and repaired pool ready for immediate use? For example, not all units need to be repaired immediately if enough are already repaired. Alternatively, when new stock is demanded, the decision may be to issue an order for the purchase of new units.

2. Are there enough units in total in the closed-loop system? The closed-loop system has three states: in service, in the unrepaired pool, and in the repaired pool. The answer may lead to a decision to acquire additional units, if there aren't enough in the loop, or to dispose of excess units if there are too many.

> *In a closed-loop remanufacturing operation, the total pool of service items should be managed.*
>
> *Excess repairable service items should be sold or disposed of by some other means.*

Demand forecasts are important in predicting how many units will be returned for remanufacturing and how many will be needed or used. These demands may be estimated using several different methods. Some applications or regulations may stipulate that only new items can be installed, as in the production of new assemblies made to OEM standards, but in many situations the MOs have the option to install repaired items.

As shown in Figure 6–3, there are three sources of supply for items; new, repaired, and unrepaired stock shown as blocks S1,

S2, and S3, respectively. As mentioned, there are two forecasts needed to operate this system: the forecast of returns and usage; these are highlighted in bold blocks. The forecasts of usage include future demands for units to be put into service, either to replace in-service units for MOs or as new installations for OEMs. In the case of new installations, there will be firm orders, ideally placed beyond the normal order leadtime. But, in the case of replacement units, there is usually no order leadtime because replacement items are often needed immediately.

As shown in the figure, the net requirements planning function receives input from the two forecasts and current stock status. To balance supply and demand, the requirements planner (or master scheduler) issues purchase, repair, and scrap orders as needed to achieve effective operations.

In a closed-loop remanufacturing operation,
supply and demand should be equal.

Remanufacturing and Rebuilding Operations

Repairs normally require specialized skills, specialized equipment, or considerable work time; otherwise, the item could be repaired instead of being swapped out by service personnel. Effective scheduling and cost control require that repair decisions be set forth using work orders and schedules. In principle, these work orders are a master schedule for the remanufacturing process. To support this master schedule, a bill of materials shows an unrepaired unit as necessary to make the repaired unit.

Repair orders can be a remanufacturing master schedule.

The period-by-period relationships between the work order schedules, forecasts, buying operations, and stock transfers are very important and must be precise. Fortunately, they can be managed very well by an adaptation of a DRP or MPS system. The replenishment flow suggested in Figure 6–3 is typical of a remanufacturing operation in which the item code changes when the item is completed. This suggests the use of a bill of material (BOM) to show different stages of the item's progress through the shop. Instead, to reduce BOM complexity, the item part number may stay the same and a status flag on the data record for the unit may be used to recognize the change from unrepaired to repaired status. The three flagged statuses are new, unrepaired, and repaired.

Use Repaired Inventory where Possible

During planning and actual operations, the policy guidelines of when and where to use new or repaired stock must be applied consistently. Normally, the service personnel of the MOs should order and install repaired items if the stock is available. This is an important policy guideline–it minimizes the purchase of new items. The net requirements planning system of the remanufacturer should anticipate this policy by filling the demands for new or repaired items using repaired items. Otherwise, when the net requirements cannot be met through the repair operation, the system looks for new stock and, if necessary, recommends purchasing additional new stock. The conditional logic required in this planning process is denoted by the "or" condition in the net requirements planning system block at the bottom of Figure 6–3. This logic distinguishes this planning process from those in the typical MPS or DRP situations.

Where policy, economics, and availability permit, net requirements of repair-service operations should be met using repaired stock.

Stock Planning

As shown in Figure 6–3, the planner should manage the three types of items, new, repaired, and unrepaired. Demand forecasts should be used to help determine the desired minimum stocks. When there is sufficient stock of repaired items, new stock is not used for repaired stock demands. On the occasions where MOs' replacements must be made using new stock even though repaired items are acceptable to the customer, there is a withdrawal from new stock that might jeopardize the availability of new stock for new installations or for OEMs unless the planning system foresees this.

The policy of using available repaired units is usually the lower-cost policy.

Because net requirements for repaired stock are met with new stock only when repaired stock is not available, the purchasing decision should provide new stock to cover the anticipated shortages. If the purchasing leadtime is longer than the repair leadtime, then the master schedule of repairs must be planned through the longer purchasing leadtime. Also, it should be validated against the likely availability of unrepaired stock, and the resulting net requirements for new stock used to recommend purchase quantities.

The net requirements plan in remanufacturing should have a planning horizon equal to the longer of remanufacturing or purchasing leadtimes.

In the life cycle of items that are repairable, some will be scrapped and others repaired. As a stock of unrepaired items builds over time, the planner should decide how much inventory should be retained on specific items. The long-term need for an item can be used to decide this retention quantity. Various writers have formulated the cost trade-offs in this decision.[2] A convenient way to handle this decision is to set the maximum time supply on the unrepaired stock. As an example, set two years as the maximum time supply of stock that will be retained. This time supply is simply calculated as the number of units in stock divided by the demand rate, for example, 5 units in stock/(1 unit/month) = 5 months of stock.

In a closed-loop remanufacturing operation, the demand for repaired items is uncertain, so safety stocks are needed.

Repaired stock levels will normally be set to assure enough inventory to cover any forecasted demand through the repair leadtime, plus safety stock. The demand forecasts and their forecast errors are obtained directly from the forecasting system for use in calculating the desired repaired stock levels.

Forecasting Returns for Repair

Up to this point, the forecasts described in this chapter have been for and based on usage or customer-maintenance demands. It is possible, however, to use the historical data on removals of items to project the continuing returns of repairable service items from

MTBF or MTBR?

The time spent by an item in service on an aircraft depends on the design and stress on the item, variations of materials used to make the item, the replacement policy, and so on. The replacement policy should be determined by comparing the cost of failure in service to the cost of preventive maintenance.

As frequent air travelers, we appreciate the regulations that require rigid inspections and scheduled replacements of critical assemblies such as the engines on the aircraft. Where there is little or no redundancy and the cost of failure is very high, the scheduled removals are the only proper choice. The policy in this case is to schedule a removal after either a maximum number of engine hours or start-up cycles. The calendar time elapsed between removals is a function of the aircraft utilization. The intent of the policy is to prevent failures in service.

Other types of items such as radios are less critical because there are back-up units on the aircraft. They may be removed for service when they fail, or when they seem to be malfunctioning. Any hint of poor performance is usually enough reason to remove the unit, even before outright failure. Units that are allowed to fail in service will experience a distribution of service life, such as shown here:

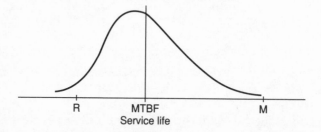

R   MTBF   M
Service life

The mean of this distribution is called the *mean time between failures* (MTBF). When policies don't force replacements before items fail, there will be some empirically observed maximum point M by which time all units will fail. But, when scheduled-replacement policies are set to preclude failure in the field, the intent is to set the service time between removals at some much lower value such as point R above. This gives a high degree of assurance that few if any units will fail in service.

It is common to use the measure mean time between removals (MTBR) (e.g., point R above) as a way to schedule preventive main-

MTBF or MTBR?   (continued)

tenance removals, replacements, and repairs. Because the MTBR is set to preclude failures in the field, its value is considerably lower than the MTBF. Fortunately, when the MTBR is a policy variable, its use stabilizes the demand forecasting process because replacements are scheduled instead of being dependent on actual failures. This scheduling of preventive maintenance also stabilizes the maintenance and remanufacturing operations, thus making them more cost effective.

some population of equipment. Using this data, time series forecasting models can be used to model the historical patterns of failures. These forecasts are sometimes supplemented with engineering estimates of rates of replacement. Such estimates are based on mean time between removals (MTBR), perhaps using population size and age and the estimated service hours of the population.[3]

Our purpose in forecasting returns for repairs is multifold. This forecast assists in estimating the supply of unrepaired items and the resulting demand placed on the repair operations to repair those items. Also, and very important, in many situations a usable relationship exists between the supply of returned repairable items and the demand for repaired items. In those situations, a forecast of repairable returns is also a forecast of the demand for repaired or new items. For example, when each returned item is accompanied by an order for a repaired item, then a forecast of returned items is also a forecast for repaired or new items. Thus, we see that a forecast of returns provides information useful for several purposes.

Neither time series analysis of returns nor more-complex engineering-based forecasting methods should be viewed as providing the final answer, because, when used together, each method provides different insights. When the size of the working population is reasonably well known, time series analysis can predict changes taking place in either the MTBR or the number of service hours being consumed in the population. Time series methods are also used to predict the changes in the working population through new sales and equipment retirements. Using both time series and engineering estimates together provides a better prediction of service-item demands.

Time series forecasting and engineering–failure-rate models should be used in a complementary way.

Forecasting with Removal Rates

Figure 6–4 illustrates the use of actual removal rates to estimate the MTBR using two different methods on two different items. Figure 6–4(*a*) illustrates the calculation of the MTBR using a known population of units and the number of units removed. The MTBR is calculated as the ratio of the population in a period divided by the number of removals in that period. For example, in Period 1, 2 units out of a population of 25 were removed. Consequently, the MTBR was 25 unit-periods divided by 2 units removed. This yields:

$$\text{MTBR} = (25 \text{ unit-periods})/(2 \text{ units removed})$$
$$= 12.5 \text{ periods/removal}$$

In contrast, Figure 6–4(*b*) illustrates the calculation of MTBR using an activity-based measure such as hours. As shown for Period 1, the MTBR is equal to the base number of hours in service divided by the number of removals:

$$\text{MTBR} = (1,500 \text{ hour-units})/(4 \text{ removed units}) = 375 \text{ hours/removal}$$

One purpose of using these two methods is to update the values for MTBR or MTBF that were used during initial provisioning of service items. Suppose, for example, that a large motor bearing is expected to operate 10,000 hours by the engineer who designed it. In practice, its real life may average 12,000 hours. Thus, the MTBF and MTBR can be measured more precisely based on historical data. We can and should take advantage of that fact to adjust our plans for stocking the bearing.

A second purpose of the methods illustrated in Figure 6–4 is to manage two aspects of the environment in which items operate.

1. The first aspect is the number of units that have been put into service. How many motors are in use today? How many will

FIGURE 6–4
Illustration of Mean Time between Removals (MTBR)

(a) Population-Based Demand Rates

Period	1	2	3	4	5	6	7	8
Population (units)	25	25	30	30	35	35	40	40
Removals	2	2	2	3	3	3	4	4
Ratio (removals/unit-period)	.080	.080	.067	.100	.086	.086	.100	.100
MTBR (unit-periods/removal)	12.5	12.5	15.0	10.0	11.7	11.7	10.0	10.0
Cumulative MTBR	12.5	12.5	13.3	12.2	12.1	12.0	11.6	11.3

(b) Activity-Based Demand Rates

Period	1	2	3	4	5	6	7	8
Population (units)	30	30	30	30	30	30	30	30
Base (UOM)*	1,500	2,000	1,800	2,200	2,500	2,000	2,400	2,300
Removals	4	5	4	5	5	4	6	5
Removals per 1,000-base UOM	2.67	2.50	2.22	2.27	2.00	2.00	2.50	2.18
MTBR (base measure)	375	400	450	440	500	500	400	460

*The base unit of measure (UOM) could be operating hours, cycles, takeoffs, and so on.

be in use next year? Is the population constant? This provides the basis for population-based demand rates. [See Figure 6–4(a).]

2. The second aspect is the stress on the equipment as measured by its use. Are all motors running all of the time? Are the operating hours recorded as a way to reflect the stress? This provides the basis for activity-based demand rates. [See Figure 6–4(b).]

In the simplest of situations, the population size is essentially constant and the operating stress is shared equally by all motors in the population. In these simplest cases, time series analysis (using the removals history alone) will model the rate of change in bearing removals as the population ages. If the population also has a distribution of ages (because the motors were put into service over a course of several years), then the MTBR will eventually approach a steady state as the bearings are replaced.

However, the population may be changing as shown in Figure 6–4(a), or the service hours may be changing as shown in Figure 6–4(b). The data obtained from history allows the system to develop better MTBR values, using just the population (a) or using the total "base" or measured service stress (b). The more comprehensive model, which is activity based [Figure 6–4(b)], lends itself to forecasting a total number of removals in the future in more than one way:

1. We can apply simple time series forecasting to the number of removals, as mentioned above. The methods for doing so are developed in Chapters 10 through 13.

OR

2. We can apply time series forecasting to the MTBR historical values to develop future MTBR values, and then apply those future MTBR values to the future anticipated activity base, which itself may be changing. Suppose also that the population size may be managed, for example, by decisions to retire older units. Then we need to change the future population size and reflect that change on the expected activity base.

OR

3. We may have little, if any, control of the population size in some business situations, for example, the fleet of 1987–91 automobiles that use a particular brake rotor. In this case, we may wish to forecast not only the future MTBR values but the population size also. This becomes a dual time series model. The future base of activity [row 3 of Figure 6–4(b)] must be forecast and the MTBR [row 6 of Figure 6–4(b)] must be forecast. The final forecast of the future rate of removals is the base of activity forecast divided by the forecasted MTBR value. Alternatively, this forecast can be the product of the future rate of removal times the number of the base activity. Consider the example of Figure 6–5.

Figure 6–5 presents an example of forecasts developed from MTBR data. This MTBR data is estimated using a removal rate expressed simply as the "number per 1,000 hours" of base activity; as shown in the figure, this is the reciprocal of the MTBR. The MTBR is shown for comparison only and is not used in the calculations. The forecasting procedure of Figure 6–5 uses two forecasts, the forecast of the failure rates or removal per 1,000 of base hour activity (row 4) and the forecast of the number of base hours of activity (row 2). The forecasted number of removals in periods 6, 7, 8, and 9 is calculated as the forecasted number of base hours multiplied by the forecasted number of failures per 1,000 base hours. While we have not shown how the forecasts of rows 2 and

FIGURE 6–5
Forecast Adjusted for Future Base Activity Hours

	History				
Period	1	2	3	4	5
Base (hours)	1,000	1,500	2,000	2,000	2,000
Number removed	3	2	4	5	3
Number/1,000	3.00	1.33	2.00	2.50	1.50
MTBR	333	750	500	400	677

	Future			
Period	6	7	8	9
Base (hours)	2,000	2,500	2,800	3,000
Number removed	4	5	6	6
Number/1,000	2	2	2	2
MTBR	500	500	500	500

4 were derived, the methods for doing so are more fully developed in Chapters 10 through 13.

Brown presents useful suggestions and methods for estimating declining populations of aging machinery.[4] These suggestions and methods may apply to the task of estimating the remaining active population size and the declining base hours of activity.

FORECASTING LOW–VOLUME DEMANDS

We have not discussed how the forecasts of Figure 6–5 are derived, but these are discussed in Chapters 10 through 13. As in most forecasting endeavors, the method of forecasting is determined after gaining some understanding of the underlying patterns in the data. The forecasts of service items often involve very low demand volumes having unique demand patterns. Low-volume demands are very common in many forecasting applications, including service-items distribution, manufacturing, service repair operations, and some retail items. To assure that we have adequate inventory in the low-volume applications requires a good understanding of low-volume demand patterns and models. These concepts are discussed in Chapters 10 and 16.

SUMMARY

Retail forecasting has been presented in this chapter not only for its differences with but also for its similarities to the systems discussed in previous chapters. It is different in terminology, emphasis on dollar forecasts, the frequent use of promotions, highly seasonal demands, and the very large number of item locations (i.e., stockkeeping units). Retail demand management is similar to other businesses in the need for hierarchical views of the data, forecasts, and the use of management judgment.

The methods outlined here for repair operations forecasting are special cases of low-volume demand items. Many service items are rarely needed in repair operations if the populations of equipment using these items are small. But, we must forecast these item demands even if such forecasts are not as accurate as those of high-volume demands. However, when the population is large or known, or if the total activity of the population is measured regularly, then the demand for low-volume service items can be forecasted more accurately.

We devote the next eight chapters to the process of actually selecting, fitting, and evaluating forecast models. We hope that you will find this process intriguing and gratifying.

REFERENCES

1. W. B. Lee and E. Steinberg, *Service Parts Management* (Falls Church, Va.: American Production Control Society, 1984).
2. R. G. Brown, *Advanced Service Parts Inventory Control* (Thetford, Vt.: Materials Management Systems, 1982), chap. 4.
3. J. H. Greene, *Production and Inventory Handbook,* 2nd ed. (New York: McGraw-Hill, 1987); and G. Salvendy, *Handbook of Industrial Engineering* (New York: John Wiley & Sons, 1982).
4. Brown, *Advanced Service Parts Inventory Control.*

PART 3

INTRODUCTION TO FORECASTING METHODS

Part 3 introduces some important concepts and principles of forecasting methods and systems. These chapters are prerequisite for both managers and analysts.

Chapter 7 introduces the fundamentals of statistics for forecasting. While some of you may be intimidated by this topic, we urge you to give this chapter a try. We have tried with much diligence to make this chapter on statistical analysis for forecasting easy to understand. Some basic comfort with simple arithmetic is all that is necessary to study this chapter. We have made this topic as intuitive and meaningful as possible. It has relevance for all. If, however, you do have problems with this chapter, do not give up on Part 3. The two remaining chapters involve no mathematics or statistics but instead introduce forecasting methods in nonquantitative and intuitive ways.

Chapter 8 introduces forecasting methods without involving mathematics. It presents common time series demand patterns in an intuitive manner. It presents modeling and forecasting purposes and methods so that everyone can understand them no matter what their mathematical backgrounds are. All time series methods are based on the assumption that past demand follows some pattern. By identifying these past demand patterns, we can more-effectively model future demand patterns. This chapter is unique in its intuitive approach to describing simple and complex demand patterns and the principles used to forecast them. In addition, the second half of the chapter introduces in the same intuitive way several different methods of forecasting. *Under no circumstances should you skip this chapter if you are unfamiliar with its topics.*

Chapter 9 compares many different methods of forecasting, including criteria used to select one approach over others. This chapter is meant to be an overview of forecasting techniques in general and for the remainder of this book in particular. It is presented early because of its general and accessible concepts and principles. The discipline of forecasting is rich with many techniques, and this overview surveys those techniques.

CHAPTER 7

STATISTICAL FUNDAMENTALS
FOR FORECASTING

DESCRIPTIVE STATISTICS
    Descriptive and Graphical Tools
    Probabilities
    Probability Distributions in Forecasting
    Disadvantages of Graphical Tools
SUMMARY STATISTICS
    Predicting Demand Using Mean, Median, and
      Mode
    Comparisons of Measures
    Properties of Central Values
    Mean Forecast Error
MEASURES OF FORECAST ERROR – STANDARD
  DEVIATION AND MAD
NORMAL DISTRIBUTION
    Characteristics of the Normal Distribution (ND)
    The Mean and Standard Deviation Describe the
      Whole ND
    Describing All Normal Distributions
    Confidence Intervals
    MAD – An Easily Calculated Measure of Scatter
    A Forecasting Example Using Sales of Product A
    Frequency Distribution Solution
    Using the ND to Set Inventory Levels
SUMMARY

After all, the higher statistics are only common sense reduced
to numerical appreciation.
Karl Pearson

If it can't be quantified, then it is not relevant. Almost anything can be quantified using statistics.

Understanding statistics is essential in forecasting.

This chapter develops the fundamentals and principles of statistical analysis for forecasting. It is designed to make these concepts
as accessible and relevant as possible to both manager and analyst. This is an important chapter because almost all employees
can benefit from an understanding of statistics as they apply to
decision making, forecasting, and statistical quality control. As
we will see, statistical measures of forecast errors and the normal distribution are central to forecasting systems. This chapter
develops the mean, standard deviation, mean absolute deviation,
and normal distribution as widely used measures of actuals, forecasts, and forecast errors.

The general reader seeking an overall understanding of forecasting systems may not need to fully understand all that is
presented in this and other forecasting methods chapters; however, the forecasting analyst is advised to study these concepts
in more depth. Our purpose here is to present the essential concepts of forecasting methods so that one can select forecasting systems or, with further study, design one's own.

DESCRIPTIVE STATISTICS

Statistical analysis models the past to predict the future.

One of the first steps in forecasting is to describe (model) the behavior of the past. All methods of forecasting include the assumption that the past behavior of demand or its relationship to other
values (e.g., demand versus personal income) will continue into the
future. The first step in modeling historical demand data for forecasting purposes is to plot the series versus time. Figure 7–1 illustrates the demand for boxes of computer paper. This series and
five others, which are introduced later, are used throughout the
text to illustrate different forecasting models and systems; the
actual values and plots of these series are given in Appendixes
A and B, respectively.

FIGURE 7-1
Demand for Product A (Boxes of Computer Paper): A Series with Random Sales

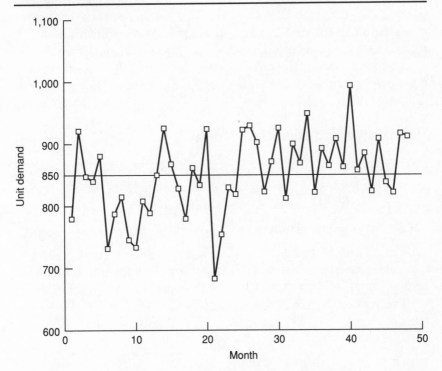

The plot of Figure 7-1 is very random, having no pattern; because of this, we can forecast the series relatively accurately by scaling an average from the graph. We simply draw a straight line through the approximate center of points as an estimate of the future. A study of the plot yields 850 as representative of the past and, consequently, as a forecast for month 49. While this forecast may be accurate for this data, most series have nonrandom patterns that must be modeled using more sophisticated methods than simply estimating a typical value; these methods are discussed here and in the next several chapters.

Plotting the data is a first step in forecasting.
Sample the past to predict the future.

In forecasting, the most recent history of a product's demand is used as a representative sample of all past and future demands.

We are forced to use the past in prediction because a random sample of the future is impossible; next month's demand is unknown until next month occurs. This is why almost all forecasts are based upon the assumption that the past behavior of the series will continue into the future. That is, forecasts use samples of past demands as estimates of all possible past and future demands. To a surprising extent, the past repeats itself, thus forecasts become good predictors. Below, we discuss ways to model the past to predict the future.

Descriptive and Graphical Tools

In a forecasting context, statistical analysis is used to extract information from the past so that a forecast can be made. Based on more-accurate forecasts, more-effective decisions are possible:

Raw data ⟶ Information ⟶ Forecast ⟶ Better decisions

Graphs and bar charts (e.g., Figure 7–1 and Table 7–1) are typical descriptive devices in forecasting. In addition, tools such as frequency and probability distributions are very useful.

Frequency distributions such as Table 7–1 are useful tools for summarizing the past. For example, it illustrates that demands

TABLE 7–1
Frequency/Probability Distribution of Demands for Product A

Demand Interval	Interval Midpoint	Frequency Distribution	Frequency Distribution	Percentage Frequency	Cumulative Percentage Frequency Below
≥ 1,025			0	0.00%	
975 to 1,024	1,000	*	1	2.08	100.00%
925 to 974	950	****	4	8.33	97.94
875 to 924	900	************	12	25.00	89.61
825 to 874	850	**************	14	29.20	64.61
775 to 824	800	************	12	25.00	35.41
725 to 774	750	****	4	8.33	10.41
675 to 724	700	*	1	2.08	2.08
≤ 674			0	0.00	0.00
Total			48	100.00%	

Note: There may be some round-off error in totals.
≥ denotes greater than or equal to, ≤ denotes less than or equal to.

have varied between 675 to 1,024, approximately 30 percent (29.20 percent) of past demands have been between 825 and 874, only 2.08 percent of demands were above 974, and 0 percent of the demands were above 1,024. Approximately 80 percent (25 + 29.2 + 25) of the time demands have been between 775 and 924.

When this frequency distribution is combined with the plot of Figure 7–1, one has a good graphical representation of the series. Such graphical devices are important because the ability of humans to detect patterns is extremely good. Consequently, it is very important that a forecasting system supports graphical representation of the data being forecasted. Also, as discussed below, graphics are very important in detecting unusual events including outliers, promotions, and seasonal influences.

A good forecasting system should provide good graphical support.

Probabilities

Because probabilities model uncertain future events, they are used extensively in forecasting. As shown below, there are two very simple ways to estimate probabilities.

Use past percentage frequencies as probability estimates.

A percentage frequency is equal to the number of times that a specific event has occurred (e.g., days it rained) divided by the total number of events that have occurred (e.g., total number of days). For example, if in the past there has been rain on 600 out of 1,000 days like tomorrow (i.e., days having the same climatic conditions as tomorrow), then the probability of rain tomorrow is 600/1,000, .6, or 60 percent. Mathematically, this is expressed as:

$$P(Rain) = 600/1,000 = .6 = 60\%$$

The .6 probability can be confusing because it will either rain or not rain tomorrow; however, the essential concept of a probability lies in the percentage statements of the future. Because in the past 6 out of every 10 days like tomorrow have had rain, it can be generalized that 6 out of every 10 days in the future with similar climatic conditions will experience rain. When we assume the past frequency distribution predicts the future, then it becomes the basis of probability statements and is called a *probability distribution.*

Use subjective judgment to estimate probabilities.

Another way that probabilities can be estimated is through subjective estimates. Decision makers or experts subjectively estimate the probability of an event based on their experience. For example, merchandising managers are often forced to subjectively estimate the probability of a new product being successful even though there is no past record of sales. Based on subjective judgment, the decision maker states his or her probability estimate of the future.

These subjective probability estimates are very important in forecasting because some events may not have ever occurred before. For example, in estimating the influence of a new sales promotion, a firm may have no alternative but to make a subjective estimate of the effects. A decision maker may state that he or she is 60 percent sure that sales will increase by 100 to 500 units and only 40 percent sure that sales will increase by more than 500 units. A good forecasting system should facilitate the inclusion of such subjective forecasts.

A good forecasting system should support the inclusion of subjective estimates of demand.

Probability Distributions in Forecasting

A frequency distribution of past demands (e.g., Figure 7–1) becomes a probability distribution of future demands when the following assumptions are accepted:

Assumption 1: Past demands are indicative of future demands. That is, the past demands will repeat themselves.

Assumption 2: Past demands are accurately represented by the sample of the past. For example, we assume that the 48 observations of Figure 7–1 accurately represent the past.

Consider the following examples using a percentage frequency distribution in making probability statements. Given that the sales of Product A in Table 7–1 are indicative of the sales of this product next month, then what is the probability that sales will be in the range of 825 to 874? In the past, 29.2 percent of the months have had sales in the range of 825 to 874; therefore, 29.2 percent of the time, future sales will be in this range. Alternatively, we can state that there is a 29.2 percent probability that sales will be in this range. Also, the probability that sales will be greater than 974 is 2.08 percent, while the probability that sales will be greater than 1,024 is nearly zero because past demands have never been above 1,024.

The use of probability statements is very important in forecasting because a forecast should consist of three statements: an average (e.g., 850), a range (e.g., 825 to 874), and a probability statement (e.g., 29.2 percent).

A forecast should include an average, a range, and a probability estimate.

Another way that probability distributions are represented is given in Figure 7–2. This figure is simply the frequency distribution of Table 7–1 turned on its side. Note the two left-hand columns represent the frequency and percentage frequency (probability) of sales shown on the horizontal axis. For example, a demand of 850 (really 825 to 874) has a probability of 29.2 percent, or alternatively, 29.2 percent of the time in the past, a demand of 850 has occurred.

Disadvantages of Graphical Tools

Graphical tools are important in many forecasting situations; however, they are expensive to use because they require human intervention. Use of graphs is not cost effective for routine analysis of all items in forecasting systems where thousands of items are forecasted frequently. Fortunately, human intervention is not needed in the vast majority of forecasts because sample statistics can be used to model and judge the validity of forecasts with-

FIGURE 7–2
Probability Distribution of Demands for Product A

Frequency	Percentage Frequency (Probability)	7	7.5	8	8.5	9	9.5	10
14	29.2 %				*			
13	27.1				*			
12	25.0			*	*	*		
11	22.9			*	*	*		
10	20.8			*	*	*		
9	18.7			*	*	*		
8	16.7			*	*	*		
7	14.6			*	*	*		
6	12.5			*	*	*		
5	10.4			*	*	*		
4	8.33		*	*	*	*	*	
3	6.3		*	*	*	*	*	
2	4.2		*	*	*	*	*	
1	2.08	*	*	*	*	*	*	*
48	100.00%	7	7.5	8	8.5	9	9.5	10

(Units in 100s)

out analysis by humans. Only when exceptional uncertainty exists in forecasts should a human analyst process the forecasting data. Consequently, it is important to detect exceptions and provide human analysts with the tools to solve these problems. Several statistics that are important in managing the routine and the exceptional forecasting situations are discussed below.

A forecasting system must detect unusual demands.

SUMMARY STATISTICS

Summary statistics are used to forecast future values.

Frequently, it is effective to summarize a large amount of data through the use of summary statistics. For example, managers monitor average monthly sales as useful summaries of performance. These statistics provide important information about the past and the future.

Is Forecasting a Game of Chance?

The oldest probabilistic game is that of casting four-sided bones or *lots* as they were called. It is estimated that as long ago as 40,000 years, cave dwellers were tossing cube-shaped bones in games of chance. Dice, as we know them, have been around for at least 3,400 years. In fact, the study of probability owes its start to the analysis of dice games. Galileo, Pascal, and Cardano, in about 1600, studied the probabilities of dice games after being requested to do so by disillusioned participants. It is accurate to view statistical forecasting as a game of chance in which our objective is to reduce the uncertainty associated with future events such as a product's demand. Just as in dice games, we can never know with certainty what the next demand will be; however, by looking at frequency distributions of past demands or "tosses," we can state probabilities of future values. For example, in tossing a six-sided die, we see a ⅙ probability of each side occurring. Thus, the probability of any single side (e.g., a one) occurring is ⅙ or 16.67 percent. Therefore, we should also be able to make such probability statements when forecasting.

Predicting Demand Using Mean, Median, and Mode

The mean is the center of deviations.

The *mean,* also called the *arithmetic average,* is a statistic that is learned in elementary school as a typical value. It measures that value about which 50 percent of the deviations are above and 50 percent of the deviations are below. That is, the sum of deviations about the mean equals zero. This concept is illustrated below.

Time $t =$	1	2	3	4	5	6	7
Values $X_t =$	11	4	5	12	9	2	6

where X_t is the sales of a product in each of the last seven months, which are numbered from 1 to 7. The mean sales for the last 7 months is the following:

$$\overline{X} = \frac{\Sigma X_t}{n} = \frac{11 + 4 + 5 + 12 + 9 + 2 + 6}{7} = \frac{49}{7} = 7 \quad (7\text{-}1)$$

where ΣX_t denotes the summation process from $t = 1$ to $t = 7$. (The equation number of this formula is given in parentheses.)

To illustrate the concept of the mean, deviations (d_t) are calculated below. A *deviation* (d_t) is defined as an observed value (X_t) minus the mean. For this data, the deviations are the following:

$$X_t - X = d_t$$
$$(11 - 7) = 4$$
$$(4 - 7) = -3$$
$$(5 - 7) = -2$$
$$(12 - 7) = 5$$
$$(9 - 7) = 2$$
$$(2 - 7) = -5$$
$$(6 - 7) = -1$$
$$\text{Sum of } d_t = 4 - 3 - 2 + 5 + 2 - 5 - 1 = 0$$

The median is the center of data—50 percent of the values are above, 50 percent of the values are below.

The *median* is an important summary statistic about which 50 percent of the values are above and 50 percent of the values are below. As shown below, it is the middle value.

2   4   5   6   9   11   12

It is easy to see that of the seven observations, three are above 6 and three are below 6; therefore the median is 6. Fifty percent of the time in the past, sales have been greater than 6, and 50 percent of the time, sales have been less than 6. When an even number of observations exist, the median equals the mean of the middle two values.

The mode is the most frequent value.

The *mode* is that number or group of numbers that occurs most often. In the data below, the mode is 6 because it appears most frequently.

1   2   5   6   6   7   10   11

For the data in Table 7–1, the most frequent range of numbers (i.e., the modal range) is 825 to 874, which occurs 14 months out of 48 months. In general, a mode is expressed as a modal range such as 825 to 874.

Comparisons of Measures

Each of the above measures of central values has slightly different advantages or uses in forecasting. However, note that for any distribution that is symmetrical (i.e., the right and the left sides are mirror images), the mean, median, and mode are all equal. The series of Figure 7–1 is symmetrical, as is the following data set, which has mean, median, and mode all equal to 6.

$$1 \quad 2 \quad 5 \quad 6 \quad 6 \quad 7 \quad 10 \quad 11$$

Finally, it is important to note that the most important distribution in forecasting, the normal distribution, is symmetrical. Consequently, its mean, median, and mode are equal.

Properties of Central Values

Because it is the center of deviations, the mean is influenced by extreme values. For example, a very large deviation will greatly change the value of the mean. This creates very serious problems in forecasting. It is unwise to use these extreme values when forecasting. Thus, the mean is not the most appropriate statistic to use without first eliminating or adjusting the extreme values, a process called *outlier adjustment*.

In contrast to the mean, the median is much less affected by extreme values and is therefore useful in describing the center of highly skewed data (*skewed* meaning a data set that has a few extremely high or low values, but not both). Finally, the mode, while not often used, does describe the most frequent number and is unaffected by extremes in the data.

Consider this time series data as a basis for forecasting period 9.

Period $t =$	1	2	3	4	5	6	7	8
Value $X_t =$	100	70	90	110	1,200	110	130	80

In ascending order, the series is as follows:

70   80   90   100   110   110   130   1,200

As shown by this data, sales have typically been in the range of 70 to 130; however, in Period 5, something extraordinary happened, a sale of 1,200 units. Which of the following statistics is the best typical value for forecasting Period 9?

$$\text{Mean} = \frac{100 + 70 + 90 + 110 + 1,200 + 110 + 130 + 80}{8}$$

$$= 236.25$$

$$\text{Median} = (100 + 110)/2 = 105$$

$$\text{Mode} = 110$$

The effect of the 1,200 is rather dramatic on the mean, while, in contrast, the median and mode are much less affected. Assuming that the 1,200 is a typical value representative of the past and the future, then the mean of 236.25 would be the best forecast. In contrast, the following discussion assumes that the occurrence in Period 5 is a very abnormal one that is unlikely to recur and the median would be the best choice for a typical value and the best forecast for Period 9. However, it is normally better to use the mean after adjusting the extreme values.

The 1,200 is referred to as an *outlier,* which is a nontypically large or small value that is not expected to recur in the future. As we have seen with this data, outliers can have dramatic impacts on the mean. The mean has little value in forecasting this data without first explaining and adjusting the 1,200 value. Formal methods of detecting and adjusting outliers will be discussed in Chapter 14. For now, recognize that outliers should almost always be investigated to determine the cause and relevancy of the observation. Is the 1,200 a seasonal phenomenon (e.g., Christmas sales), a data entry error, or the result of some unusual promotional activity? After determining the cause, then appropriate action can be taken.

One could eliminate the fifth value or adjust it to a meaningful value. It is more appropriate to adjust the outlier to an estimated value than to eliminate it. In this example, assume that the best estimate of the fifth value is 130; the new statistics for this data are calculated below.

$$\text{Mean} = \frac{100 + 70 + 90 + 110 + 130 + 110 + 130 + 80}{8}$$

$$= 102.5$$

$$\text{Median} = 105$$

$$\text{Mode} = 110$$

A good forecast of sales for this product is the new mean of 102.5. This is the suggested summary statistic for this series and the one that would be used by a good forecasting system.

As done in this example, it is recommended that an outlier be replaced with a typical value to retain the time series continuity of the past data in order to forecast the future. That is, eliminating the fifth value in the series would imply that demand was zero; as shown later, this will cause serious problems in forecasting.

Outlier adjustment is critical in statistical forecasting.

Adjust outliers to typical values.

A good forecasting system should detect and facilitate outlier adjustments.

Outlier Adjustments Are Essential

Conditions of Normality are achieved through conscious and intelligent identification and elimination of the abnormal.

Mean Forecast Error

The mean is used in forecasting systems as a measure of the typical error. A good forecasting model should have an average error of zero because it should overforecast and underforecast approximately the same number of times with the same magnitude. Thus, the mean error is used primarily as a measure of systematic error, called *bias*. Bias is consistent over- or underforecasting that will create large cumulative errors. Thus, it is very undesirable. Near the end of this chapter, we discuss ways to use the mean error and standard deviation to detect bias.

MEASURES OF FORECAST ERROR – STANDARD DEVIATION AND MAD

The measures of central values (i.e., mean, median, and mode) discussed previously give only one dimension of the distribution of data, the typical or center value. Other, equally important measures are the standard deviation and the mean absolute deviation (MAD). Four different distributions of demand are shown in Figure 7–3, each with considerably different scatter. As shown in this figure, a higher standard deviation denotes that there is more scatter and vice versa. The standard deviation measures the scatter of data about the mean and thus is used as a measure of the potential error in using the mean to predict future values. In general, the standard deviation is the preferred statistic to measure scatter; however, the MAD, which is more easily calculated, is a carryover from precomputer days and continues to persist as a measure of data scatter. Nonetheless, as is discussed later, the MAD is inferior to the standard deviation.

The *standard deviation* is the square root of the mean of the squared deviations, sometimes referred to as the *mean of the squared errors* (MSE) *or deviations* (MSD). When calculating the standard deviation, it is important to distinguish between two standard deviations – the sample standard deviation (S) and the population standard deviation (σ). We do not discuss the calculation of standard deviation of the population (σ) because this requires a 100 percent sample or census, which is costly to perform. Also, it is rare that the population formula is used in statistical analysis. Most σs are estimated using the mean and standard deviation of large samples. It is rarely necessary to perform a complete census because the mean and standard deviation of large samples (i.e., a sample size greater than 30) are accurate in estimating σ.

The formula for the best estimate of σ is the sample standard deviation (S) formula, given below.

$$S = \sqrt{\frac{\Sigma(X_t - \overline{X})^2}{n - 1}} \qquad (7\text{--}2)$$

where $\overline{X}$ is the sample mean that is used to estimate the population mean. The X_t values are the actual values from a sample of the population, and $n - 1$ denotes that the sample was performed

FIGURE 7–3
Four Distributions with the Same Mean but Different Scatter

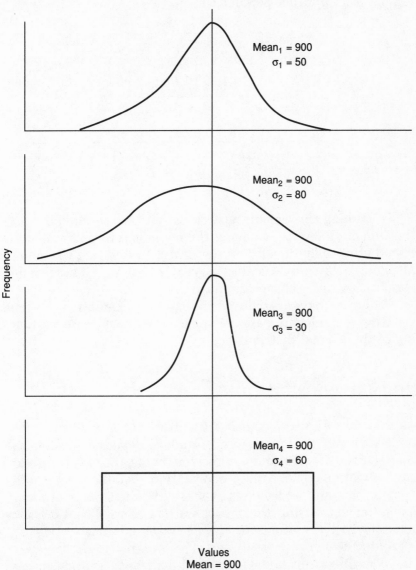

Values
Mean = 900
In order of most scatter to least scatter, distribution 2>4>1>3

using n observations included in the calculations (subtracting 1 makes S a better estimator of σ). A summation process of all n values from $t = 1$ to $t = n$ is denoted by Σ.

The sample standard deviation is calculated below using a simple data set. Assume that these seven observations represent a sample from a larger population.

$t =$	1	2	3	4	5	6	7
$X_t =$	11	4	5	12	9	2	6

$\overline{X} = 7$

$$S = \sqrt{\frac{(11-7)^2+(4-7)^2+(5-7)^2+(12-7)^2+(9-7)^2+(2-7)^2+(6-7)^2}{7-1}}$$

$S = 3.742$

In making this calculation, deviations are squared because the sum of all deviations about the mean is zero; this was illustrated previously in defining the mean. In contrast, the sum of all squared deviations is always greater than zero if at least one observation differs from the mean.

While we have introduced the standard deviation, its true meaning and relevance are not apparent without an understanding of the normal distribution.

NORMAL DISTRIBUTION

As shown in Figure 7–3, it is difficult to compare two distributions with different means and standard deviations unless the shapes of the distributions are known. That is, the mean and standard deviation do not convey information about the shape of the distribution, and, consequently, it is difficult to make probability statements using the mean and standard deviation. Fortunately, in many situations, means and standard deviations are presented as summary statistics of known distributions. One of the most important and widely used distributions and concepts in statistical analysis and forecasting is the normal distribution (ND). This distribution is important because of its usefulness in describing a wide variety of phenomena, including the error when using a good forecasting model. That is, the error in forecasting will be normally distributed when one uses a good forecasting model. To better understand these examples, the ND is discussed in more detail.

Characteristics of the Normal Distribution (ND)

1. The ND is a symmetrical, bell-shaped distribution with equal mean, median, and mode. Figure 7–4 illustrates a normal distribution. Symmetry is important because an estimate of one central value (e.g., mean) equals the other central values (e.g., median and mode).

2. ND phenomena are the result of a relatively large number of minor, independent, chance (random) influences working together. For example, if the diameters of a turned shaft are influenced by a large number of small or minor events (e.g., temperatures of the shaft, cutting tool, machine, or room; minor variations in the material of the shaft, cutting tool, or machine setting) that act independently of each other, then the variations of the shaft diameter will be a ND. "Independent" denotes that influences do not act together. Some influences will increase the

---

Forecasting Is the Origin of the Normal Distribution

The ND has its origins in the forecasting field. Carl Friedrich Gauss (1777–1856) developed the concept of the ND (also known as the *Gaussian distribution*) as a measure of error in predicting the orbits of planets. It was common then, as it is today, to repeat scientific measurements and then calculate the mean of the many measures as the typical value. Gauss went one step further and plotted the frequency of different values. When the error was random, denoting a good experimental measure, the frequency distribution normally looked bell-shaped as shown in Figure 7–4. This was an extraordinary discovery, and we owe much of our understanding of forecasting methods to him. Gauss is also known for another important development, the concept of least squares regression analysis. We discuss this concept in Chapter 11.

FIGURE 7–4
Normal Distribution Area

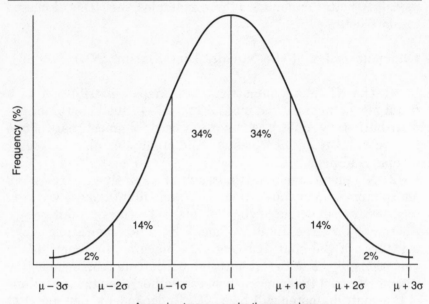

Approximate areas under the normal curve

Interval	Percent of Observations
$\mu \pm Z\sigma$	
$\mu \pm 1\sigma$	68.26%
$\mu \pm 1.96\sigma$	95.00
$\mu \pm 2\sigma$	95.55
$\mu \pm 2.33\sigma$	98.00
$\mu \pm 2.58\sigma$	99.00
$\mu \pm 3\sigma$	99.73

diameter, while others will decrease the diameter. This is true because the tool design engineers have eliminated all the large, major influences in the machine and tool design, and, therefore, only small, minor influences remain; consequently, the output of the shaft turning process is a ND. Likewise, if the forecasting system has been well designed, then all of the large, major patterns of the series have been modeled, and, therefore, differences between the actual value and the forecasted value, the error, will be a ND.

3. The errors in taking large samples from any population, no matter how it is distributed, are ND; *large* is defined as a sample size greater than 30.

Other examples of ND events include the errors in estimating the percentage of voters in favor of a political candidate, the percentage of individuals in favor of one product over another, and the differences between actual demand and forecasted demand (i.e., errors).

4. A ND is fully defined by its mean and standard deviation. For example, given a mean of 850 and a standard deviation of 40, one and only one ND is defined.

The Mean and Standard Deviation Describe the Whole ND

The table in Appendix C describes all possible NDs as a function of their mean and standard deviation. This table is referred to as a *Z table,* where *Z* represents the number of standard deviations that an observation is above or below the mean of its distribution. That is, the numbers in the table represent the area under the normal distribution between the mean and the mean plus (or minus) *Z* standard deviations; this is also illustrated in Table 7–2. The *Z* value is frequently called a *safety factor.* The information in the tables of Appendix C at the end of the book and in Table 7–2 are known facts that should be accepted as true; proof of these is beyond our purpose.

Describing All Normal Distributions

A specific example is used to describe the ND; however, all results of this discussion can be generalized to any ND. Thus, "If you have seen one ND, you have seen them all." A firm uses a model that forecast a mean error of 0 and a standard deviation of 40. By definition, *forecast error* is the difference between the actual demand and forecasted demand.

$$\text{Forecast error} = \text{Actual} - \text{Forecast} \qquad (7\text{--}3)$$

The forecasted demand for next month is 1,000 units and the mean error is expected to be zero because the model sometimes

TABLE 7–2
Some Standard Confidence Intervals for the Normal Distribution

Interval $\overline{X}$ – ZS to $\overline{X}$ + ZS	Percentage of Values in Interval from Z Table*	Example* $\overline{X}$ = 1,000 S = 40 Forecast – ZS to Forecast + ZS
$\overline{X}$ – 1.00S to $\overline{X}$ + 1.00S	68%	1,000 – 40 to 1,000 + 40
$\overline{X}$ – 1.96S to $\overline{X}$ + 1.96S	95	1,000 – 78.4 to 1,000 + 78.4
$\overline{X}$ – 2.33S to $\overline{X}$ + 2.33S	98	1,000 – 93.2 to 1,000 + 93.2
$\overline{X}$ – 2.58S to $\overline{X}$ + 2.58S	99	1,000 – 103.2 to 1,000 + 103.2
$\overline{X}$ – 3.00S to $\overline{X}$ + 3.00S	99.73	1,000 – 120.0 to 1,000 + 120.0
> $\overline{X}$ + 2.06S	2	> 1,082.4
> $\overline{X}$ + 2.33S	1	> 1,093.2
> $\overline{X}$ + 3.00S	(100 – 99.73)/2 = .135	> 1,120
< $\overline{X}$ – 3.00S	(100 – 99.73)/2 = .135	< 880

*Given a forecasting model with mean forecast of 1,000 with a standard deviation of the forecast errors equal to 40.

overforecasts and other times underforecasts. Based upon this information, we can describe the distribution of errors using common confidence intervals, which are taken from the table in Appendix C. These intervals are universally true for all NDs and are commonly used to describe and make probability statements about the forecasts.

The mean plus and minus 1 standard deviation contains 68 percent of the ND.

For any ND, the interval defined by the mean plus and minus one standard deviation contains approximately 68 percent of the population. In this case, 68 percent of the errors produced by the forecast model are in the interval 0.0 plus and minus 40; that is, the interval of −40 to +40 contains 68 percent of the past errors and, we hope, 68 percent of future errors. For example, approximately 7 (i.e., 6.8) of every 10 forecasts will have an error between −40 and +40 units, or, alternatively, 7 out of 10 actual demands will be within 40 units of the forecast. Approximately 7 out of 10 times the actual demand will be in the interval of 1,000 plus and minus 40 units. This interval is called a *confidence interval* because we have confidence that 68 percent of the time the forecast interval will contain the actual demand.

7 out of 10 times actual demand will be in the interval of the forecast plus and minus 1 standard deviation of the errors.

Actual demand = 1,000 + and − 40 = 960 to 1,040,
7 out of 10 times

The mean plus and minus 1.96 standard deviations contains 95 percent of the ND.

In this case, 95 percent of the forecasts will have an error in the interval of 0.0 plus and minus 1.96(40), that is, approximately −80 to +80. Approximately 9.5 out of 10 forecasts will have an error of −80 to +80 units. Another view is that approximately 9.5 out of 10 times the actual demand will be in the range of 1,000 plus and minus 80 units; that is, 920 to 1,080. [Note: 1.96(40) equals 78.4, but 1.96 is commonly rounded to 2; therefore, 80 is used instead of 78.4.]

Actual demand = 1,000 + and − 80 = 920 to 1,080,
95 out of 100 times

The mean plus and minus 2.58 standard deviations contains 99 percent of the ND.

In a similar manner, 99 out of 100 forecasts will have an error in the range of 0.0 plus and minus 2.58(40), that is, − 103.2 to +103.2 units. Approximately 99 percent of future demands for next month will be in the range of 1,000 plus and minus 103.2.

Actual demand = 1,000 + and − 103.2 = 896.8 to 1103.2, 99 out of 100 times

The mean plus and minus 3 standard deviations contains 99.73 percent of the ND.

Finally, 99.73 out of 100 forecasts will have an error of −120 to +120 units. Alternatively, 99.73 percent of future demands will be in the range of 1,000 plus and minus 120, that is, 880 to 1,120. Thus, in planning, one can be very confident that demand will be at least 880 and not greater than 1,120, except on very rare occasions. These and other common intervals are summarized in Table 7–2.

Confidence Intervals

The intervals of Table 7–2 are called *confidence intervals*. For example, given that the forecasting model is valid and the past repeats itself, then 68 percent of all forecasts will have a mean error in the range of −40 to +40 units. The −40 to +40 interval is called a 68 percent confidence interval. In a similar manner, one can state that there is a 68 percent chance that next month's actual demand will be within 40 units of the forecasted value. These confidence intervals yield important probability statements.

Confidence intervals are very useful in controlling statistical processes such as forecasts and industrial processes. If, in the example, the actual demand were greater than 1,000 plus 120 (greater than the mean + 3 standard deviations), then there is cause for concern. If the forecasting process were in control (i.e., adequate), then 99.73 percent of the time the demand will be within 3 standard deviations and only .27 percent of the time (or 27 out of 10,000 times) will the demand be outside 3 standard deviations, an extremely low number. Therefore, when an actual demand falls outside the 3-standard-deviation interval, the only logical conclusion is that the forecasting process is out of control (i.e., inadequate). To infer that the process is in control would not be logical because only 27 out of 10,000 times would it be in control. This use of the 3-standard-deviation interval is important in detecting outliers. This is illustrated in the example that follows the discussion of the MAD.

Uncertainty Reduction Is Important in All Endeavors

The ND is an important tool in reducing uncertainty about the future. Our general, if not mystical, interest in reducing that uncertainty by studying the past may be more deeply rooted in our psyches than we realize. As Sigmund Freud said, "The less a man knows about the past and present, the more insecure must be his judgment of the future."

MAD–An Easily Calculated Measure of Scatter

Before modern computers and handheld calculators were available, calculating the squares and square roots of the standard deviation was tedious and time consuming. An alternative measure of dispersion popular at that time was the mean absolute deviation. This measure of dispersion is easily calculated and has an approximate relationship to S.

$$MAD = \frac{\Sigma \mid X_t - \overline{X} \mid}{n} \tag{7-4}$$

$$MAD =$$

$$\frac{\mid 11-7 \mid + \mid 4-7 \mid + \mid 5-7 \mid + \mid 12-7 \mid + \mid 9-7 \mid + \mid 2-7 \mid + \mid 6-7 \mid}{7}$$

$$= 3.143$$

Where $\mid$ denotes the taking of absolute values (i.e., ignoring the sign of the deviations). The MAD of this data denotes that the average absolute deviation is 3.143. As in the case of the standard deviation, the MAD is not a particularly intuitive concept. It is more easily interpreted in the context of the ND. It can be shown that, for the ND, the MAD is approximately 80 percent of the standard deviation.

$$MAD = .80S \tag{7-5}$$
$$S = 1.25MAD \tag{7-6}$$

MAD intervals are used just like S intervals. In generating MAD intervals, we use K to designate the safety factor of MAD as we used Z values for the standard deviation. Table 7–3 shows confidence intervals of the ND in terms of MADs. Again, these values are givens and are not intuitively or easily derived.

A comparison of Table 7–2 with Table 7–3 illustrates that the same numerical confidence intervals can be determined with either MADs or standard deviations. This is further demonstrated with the equivalent confidence intervals given below.

Calculate a 99.73 percent confidence interval given a ND with an S of 40 and a MAD of 32. In terms of S, the following interval results:

TABLE 7–3
Standard Confidence Interval for the ND in Terms of MADs

Interval	Percentage of Values in Interval from D Table	Example*
$\overline{X} - K*MAD$ to $\overline{X} + K*MAD$		Forecast + K*MAD to Forecast − K*MAD
$\overline{X}$ − 1.25 MAD to $\overline{X}$ + 1.25 MAD	68%	1,000 − 40 to 1,000 + 40
$\overline{X}$ − 2.5 MAD to $\overline{X}$ + 2.5 MAD	95	1,000 − 80 to 1,000 + 80
$\overline{X}$ − 3.0 MAD to $\overline{X}$ + 3.0 MAD	98.4	1,000 − 96 to 1,000 + 96
$\overline{X}$ − 3.75 MAD to $\overline{X}$ + 3.75 MAD	99.73	1,000 − 120.0 to 1,000 + 120.0

*Given a forecasting model with a mean forecast of 1,000 with a MAD of the forecast errors equal to 32, which is equivalent to a standard deviation of 1.25 * 32 = 40.

$$\text{Mean} + \text{and} - 3.00S = \text{Mean} + \text{and} - 3.00(40)$$
$$= \text{Mean} + \text{and} - 120$$

The same interval in terms of MAD is:

$$\text{Mean} + \text{and} - 3.75\text{MAD} = \text{Mean} + \text{and} - 3.75(32) =$$
$$\text{Mean} + \text{and} - 120$$

In these examples, it appears that MAD and S are equivalent measures of dispersion, but this is only true for normally distributed populations. Because the statistical properties of the standard deviation are well known and utilized in many applications of forecasting, it is the preferred measure despite the popularity of the MAD.

Now that all of the summary statistics of this chapter have been defined, an example is used to reinforce their application.

A Forecasting Example Using Sales of Product A

Consider the following forecasting example using Series A of Figure 7–1, Table 7–1, and the table in Appendix A at the end of the book. A firm desires to forecast sales so that they are 98 percent confident that there is enough inventory available to preclude an out-of-stock condition next month. Given the facts below, what inventory level should be in stock?

Because the series varies randomly about a constant mean of 850 without any systematic pattern, an effective forecast is 850.

$$\text{Forecast} = 850$$
$$\text{Error} = \text{Actual} - \text{Forecast} = \text{Actual} - 850$$

This calculation yields the frequency distribution of Table 7–4. We will first use this distribution to solve the problem graphically, and then we will use the concept of the ND.

Frequency Distribution Solution

From Tables 7–1 and 7–4, it is clear that only 2.08 percent of the time has actual demand exceeded 850 by more than 125 units. That is, if inventory were set equal to 975, then only 2.08 percent of the time will we have insufficient stock. Thus, from the frequency distribution of Table 7–4, we can assure that approximately 98 percent of the demands will be met if we stock 850 plus 125 units. This graphical approach is an effective way to set inventory levels. However, there is a much more efficient way of setting stock under conditions of the normal distribution.

Using the ND to Set Inventory Levels

The mean error and standard deviation of the errors were calculated using the actual data of Series A of Appendix A at the end of the book. The standard deviation of the errors using the for-

TABLE 7–4
Frequency Distribution of Forecast Errors for Product A
(Forecasted demand = 850; Error = Actual − 850)

Error In Units	Mid-point	Frequency Distribution	Frequency Units	Percentage Frequency	Cumulative Percentage Frequency
125 to 174	150	*	1	2.08%	100.00%
75 to 124	100	* * * *	4	8.33	97.94
25 to 74	50	* * * * * * * * * * * *	12	25.00	89.61
− 25 to 24	0	* * * * * * * * * * * * * *	14	29.20	64.61
− 75 to − 24	− 50	* * * * * * * * * * * *	12	25.00	35.41
− 125 to − 74	− 100	* * * *	4	8.33	10.41
− 175 to − 124	− 150	*	1	2.08	2.08
Total			48	100.00%	

Note: There may be some round-off error in totals.

mula for the sample standard deviation of Equation 7–2 is 64.53. The errors are nearly normally distributed, where the term *nearly* is used because it is rare that forecast errors are exactly normally distributed. Based on these error statistics, a confidence interval can be calculated to achieve the desired product availability.

Table 7–2 illustrated important intervals of the normal distribution. As shown here, the mean plus 2.06 standard deviations has approximately 98 percent of the observations below that value and about 2 percent above. Thus, we can set inventory using the following relationships.

$$\text{Forecast} + 2.06S = 850 + 2.06(64.53) = 983$$

Then, only 2 times out of 100 will demand exceed this number. Thus, there should be sufficient stock about 98 percent of the time to meet customer demand. The forecast calculated using the normal distribution assumption is very nearly equal to the one that was calculated using the frequency distribution of Table 7–4. Herein lies the power of forecasting summary statistics under conditions of the normal distribution. Our ability to model the past and project the future using probabilities and intervals yields a very powerful set of statistical tools. These statistical tools will be refined further in the remainder of this book. When these tools are placed in an effective computer-based forecasting system, there can be dramatic impacts on the effectiveness of the firm; it is to this end that this book is directed.

SUMMARY

This chapter has presented statistical concepts that are essential to understand the statistical forecasting methods discussed in Chapters 8 through 14. These statistics will be used throughout the forecasting methods chapters of this book. This chapter has presented some very basic statistics as an introduction to essential statistical concepts in forecasting. It may be too detailed for some readers, and, as suggested, it can be skimmed or skipped. However, this chapter is an important beginning of a study of statistical forecasting since the concepts of mean, median, mode, outliers, and probability statements are inherent in all forecasting and forecasting systems. Chapters 10 through 14 extend the concepts of this chapter to forecasting models. The next two chapters introduce forecasting models using intuitive explanations and definitions.

CHAPTER 8

INTRODUCTION TO FORECASTING METHODS

COMMON TIME SERIES DEMAND PATTERNS
    Random Patterns
    Trend Patterns
    Seasonal Patterns
    Cyclical Patterns
    Autocorrelated Patterns
    Outliers
    Promotional and Planned Patterns
    Modeling Combinations of Patterns
INTRODUCTION TO FORECASTING METHODS
    Intrinsic (Time Series) Forecasting Methods
    Extrinsic (Causal) Forecasting Methods
    Qualitative Forecasting Methods
    Management Intuition and Involvement—
       The Art of Forecasting
SUMMARY

> The earth is degenerating these days. Bribery and corruption
> abound. Children no longer mind parents. Everyman wants
> to write a book, and it is evident that the end of the world
> is approaching fast.
>
> Assyrian Tablet 2800 B.C.

This chapter introduces forecasting models by illustrating several
different demand patterns and forecasting methods. The most common methods of forecasting make estimates of the future based

on past patterns, past relationships, or subjective predictions concerning the future. These three ways to estimate the future are used to classify forecasting methods as *intrinsic* (i.e., forecasts using past patterns), *extrinsic* (i.e., forecasts using past relationships), and *qualitative* (i.e., forecasts using subjective judgments). Intrinsic methods are the most widely used in operational forecasting systems; thus, we first discuss the common demand patterns that are modeled by intrinsic methods. These demand patterns include random, trend, seasonal, cyclical, autocorrelated, outlier, promotional, and combinations of these patterns. We then discuss the characteristics of each of the three different classes of forecasting methods. It should be stressed that by far the most widely used methods for short-term, operational forecasting systems are intrinsic methods, which will be discussed in several chapters of this book.

*Almost all operational forecasting systems use
intrinsic (time series) forecasting methods.*

COMMON TIME SERIES DEMAND PATTERNS

A *time series* is an uninterrupted set of data observations that have been recorded and ordered in time in equally spaced intervals (e.g., one per month). When a time series is plotted, common patterns are frequently found. There are many possible cause-and-effect relationships that might explain why a time series behaves in a certain way; these will be highlighted for each pattern. Some common patterns are shown below in Figures 8–1 through 8–7, which illustrate demands for hypothetical products. These time series have been chosen to clearly illustrate specific demand patterns.

Random Patterns

Random time series patterns are the result of many influences that act independently so as to yield nonsystematic and nonrepeating patterns about some average value. Random patterns have

FIGURE 8-1
Demand for Computer Paper, Series with Random Sales (Series A, Boxes of Computer Paper)

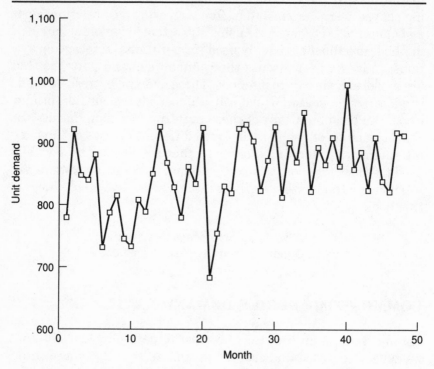

a constant mean and no systematic pattern in the data. Figure 8-1 illustrates random demand for a product. For random series, simple forecasting models are often the most accurate. In this case, one appropriate forecasting model would be to estimate future demand as equal to the overall mean of the series (i.e., 850). Alternatively, if demand was randomly increasing or decreasing very slowly over time, then an average of the most-recent observations could be used. For example, an average of the last 12 months of Series A yields a mean of 882 (see Appendix A at the end of the book for the actual data). There are other simple but effective methods that can be used to forecast this series; these are discussed in Chapter 10.

Random patterns are modeled best by using simple smoothing models.

Trend Patterns

A trend is a general increase or decrease in a time series that lasts for approximately seven or more periods (e.g., seven months). Trends are caused by long-term population changes, growth during product and technology introductions, changes in economic conditions, and so on. Figure 8–2 illustrates a series with a trend. In this case, the trend is a period-to-period increase that follows a straight line, a pattern called *linear trend.* Trends are not necessarily linear because there are a large number of nonlinear influences that might cause a series to have a nonlinear increase or decrease; the large number of relationships that can be used to model nonlinear and linear trends are discussed in Chapter 11.

Trend patterns are modeled best by using trend models.

FIGURE 8–2
Demand for a Product with Trend (Series C, Demand for Advanced Microcomputers)

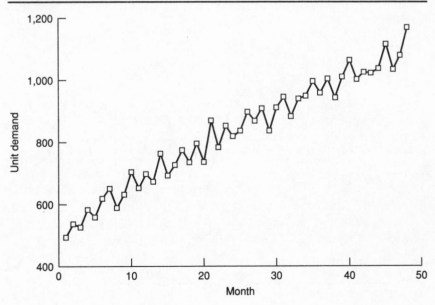

Seasonal Patterns

Figure 8–3 illustrates a demand with pronounced seasonality. *Seasonal demands* are caused by events that are periodic and recurrent (e.g., 12-month periods recurring each year). The most-common seasonal influences are those that occur because of climatic seasons, human habits, holidays, new-product announcements at conventions, and so on. Seasonality can occur by week of the year, day of the month (e.g., pay day), day of the week (e.g., absenteeism on Friday or the greater demand on weekends), and hour of the day (e.g., telephone usage by hour). A seasonal period may be for a year, month, day, and, for some activities, even an hour. In some cases, the seasonal cycle may last for four years (e.g., the demand for Olympic athletic equipment). When seasonal influences are present, then seasonal forecasting models should be used to forecast; these models are discussed in Chapters 11 through 13.

FIGURE 8–3
Demand for a Product with Strong Seasonality (Series D, Demand for a Brand of Diet Soft Drinks)

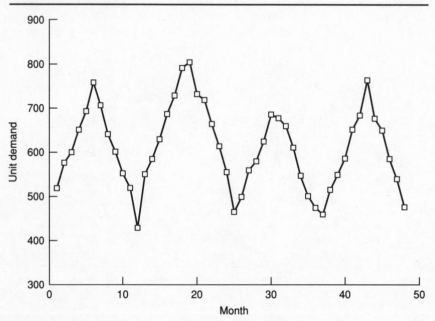

Seasonal patterns are best modeled by using seasonal models.

Seasonal patterns are recurrent and periodic.

Cyclical Patterns

Economic and business expansions (increasing demand) and contractions (recessions and depressions) are the most frequent causes of cyclical influences on the demand for a product or service. Cyclical influences most often last for two to five years and recur, but with no known period. In the search for explanations of cyclical movements, many theories have been proposed, including sun spots, positions of the planets, stars, long-wave movements in weather conditions, population life cycles, growth and decay of

---

A Good Forecast Requires a Good Backcast

There is an insightful relationship between forecasting and the oldest known sport, fishing. In fishing as in forecasting, one casts a "line" forward. This cast is called a *forward cast* or *forecast*. As in fly fishing, a good forecast requires a good backcast. As shown below, a backcast in fishing is the toss of a line backward overhead. This is analogous to the concept of modeling past demands in forecasting. In statistical forecasting, we model patterns of the past (i.e., the backcast) in order to throw those patterns forward when forecasting. Thus, as in fly fishing, the most important determinant of a good forecast is a good backcast.

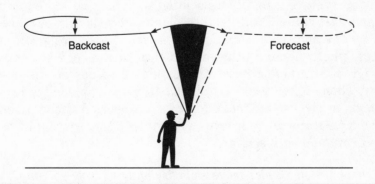

new products and technology (e.g, Beta VCRs), product life cycles, and the economy. Cyclical influences are difficult to forecast because, unlike seasonal demands, which are periodic and recurrent, cyclical demands are recurrent but not periodic. Because cyclical demands are the most difficult to forecast and their duration is for several years, few, if any, item-level forecasting systems attempt direct modeling and prediction of cyclical influences.

Cyclical influences are extremely difficult to forecast.

Autocorrelated Patterns

Another pattern that is often seen in the demand for a product is a concept called *autocorrelation.* Correlation measures the degree of dependence or association between two variables. The term *autocorrelation* means that the demand in one time period is very much related to (e.g., equal to) the demand in a previous period. In this example, there is an automatic (self-) correlation between adjacent observations in the series. For example, if there is high positive autocorrelation, then the demand in June is very nearly equal to the demand in May. This automatic association occurs because of the momentum of demand. Customer preferences, brand loyalty, sales force loyalty, and so on may change slowly; thus, changes in demand may move slowly. Also, when demand is the result of many customers, it may move slowly up and down due to the momentum of the number of customers. Autocorrelated demands are most frequently high-volume demands.

Figure 8–4 illustrates a series that is highly autocorrelated; each observation is highly associated with (i.e., nearly equal to) the previous value. Positive autocorrelated series are characterized by the smooth pattern of the series. Autocorrelation is a general phenomenon in that any of the patterns of Figures 8–1 through 8–3 could also have autocorrelated values. As discussed below, when high autocorrelation exists, very simple but accurate methods can be used to make forecasts one period ahead. Highly positively autocorrelated series without trends or seasonality are called *random-walk series.*

High autocorrelated series move smoothly and randomly up and down.

FIGURE 8–4
Demand for Common Stock with a Highly Autocorrelated, Random-Walk Pattern (Series B, Price of a Common Stock)

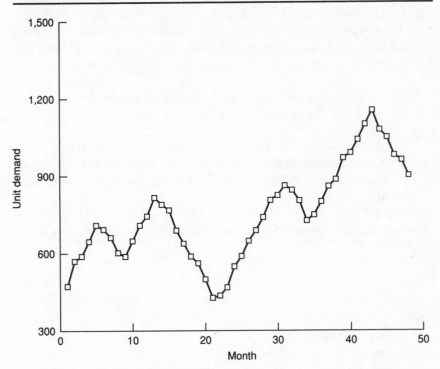

Although negatively autocorrelated series exist, they are rare. Such series consist of alternating high and low values such that a high value follows a low value, and vice versa. When they do occur, it is because of nonrandom processes (e.g., supply problems) that yield alternating highs and lows.

Accurate short-horizon forecasts are possible with high positive autocorrelations (i.e., random walks) and no seasonality or trend.

Some decision makers state that they do not forecast, but instead assume that sales in the following month will equal sales of the current month. However, the decision maker is really forecasting using a model that assumes sales to be highly autocorrelated. In fact, one very accurate short-horizon forecasting model with highly autocorrelated series is to equate the demand for next month to the demand of this month. Figure 8–5 illustrates this situation using Series B of Figure 8–4. As Figure 8–5 shows, the forecasted values track the actual values with a one-period lag; the actuals are just moved one period to the right to become forecasted values. As in all such plots, the vertical distance between the actual and predicted values is the forecast error.

> *Accurate one-period-ahead forecasts of random*
> *walks are possible using the most recent actual.*

While very accurate short-horizon (one period ahead) forecasts are possible using simple models with highly autocorrelated series, long-horizon forecasts (e.g., 10-period-ahead forecasts) will

FIGURE 8–5
Forecast Equals Previous Actual with High Autocorrelation (Series B)

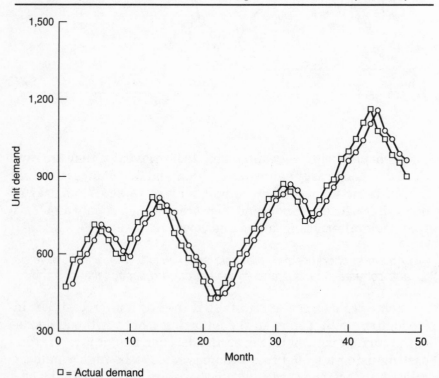

□ = Actual demand
○ = Forecast using previous actual

be very inaccurate. Consider using the previous actual as a forecast of the demand of the next and many subsequent periods in
Figure 8–4; this is shown as Figure 8–5. When using this or other
simple models, the long-horizon forecasts are a constant, equal
to some simple function of the most-recent actuals. In this case,
the forecasts for Periods 25 through 30 would all equal the actual demand in Period 24. The actual demand in Period 24 is 558
(see Appendix A at the end of the book); therefore, the forecasts
for Periods 25 through 30 would all equal 558; however, the actuals in Periods 25 through 30 are 597, 654, 696, 746, 814, and,
finally, 826. The actual of Period 24 is very accurate in forecasting period 25; however, it is a very poor forecast of Periods 26
through 30.

Multiperiod-ahead forecasts are inaccurate with random-walk series.

A series that behaves as Series B in Figure 8–5 is called a
random walk because it moves randomly and smoothly about without a constant mean. When the mean of the series is always changing, the series is called a *nonstationary series*. Unfortunately,
because Series B is a series that walks randomly about, there are
no good forecasting methods for long horizons. This is a problem
that plagues all forecasters facing random walks, particularly
those wanting to predict prices or product demands more than
one period ahead.

Outliers

The analysis of past data is made very complex by the fact that
past data includes values that are not typical of the past or future. These nontypical values are called *outliers*. Outliers are very
large or small observations that are not indicative of repeating
past or future patterns. Outliers include deviations that occur because of unusual events such as supply interruptions, strikes,
earthquakes, floods, wars, plant shut-downs, and oil spills. However, in some cases, the cause of the outlier may be an unknown
event. Figure 8–6 illustrates the data of Figure 8–1 before a low
outlier was removed in Period 31. As shown there, demand in
Period 31 was originally 450 units, which is an unusually low

FIGURE 8-6
Demand for Computer Paper, Series with Outlier (Series A, Boxes of Computer Paper)

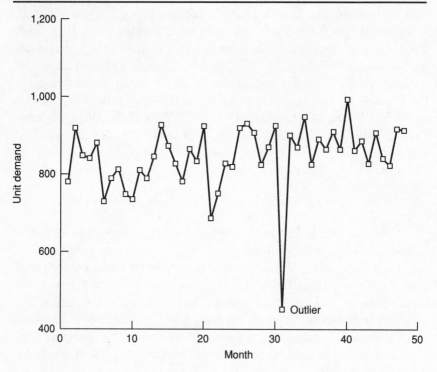

number. This value is so low as to be considered an outlier. Consequently, as shown, it was adjusted to a more typical value, 811.

We must stress the importance of adjusting outliers prior to and during the analysis of a times series. The old adage that "if you put garbage in a model, then you will get garbage out" is very accurate in describing the effects of outliers. Outliers are the worst type of forecasting garbage; consequently, it is very important to adjust these outliers. Later, in Chapter 14, we discuss "scientific" methods of adjusting outliers; however, these scientific methods often are not more accurate than "eyeballing" a new value as was done with the observation for Period 31 of Figure 8-6. When analyzing data in forecasting, a significant amount of computer programming or analyst time is devoted to detecting and removing outliers.

*Outliers confound pattern-identification
processes and should always be adjusted.*

*Automated outlier detection procedures are an
essential feature of a good forecasting system.*

Promotional and Planned Patterns

Most often, the patterns of past data reflect many planned events such as product or price promotions. When these occur, their effects should be modeled so that their future impact can be anticipated. As discussed in Chapter 5, promotional effects will affect demand before, during, and after the promotional time period. Some demands are dominated by promotional influences. Consequently, it is important to be able to track promotions and promotional effects. Promotional increases and decreases may be mistakenly identified as an unexplainable outlier unless promotional timing and effects are recorded in the system. Sometimes the promotional effect can simply be measured as the difference between the expected demand (e.g., 1,000) and the actual demand (e.g., 1,600). This difference (600, in this case) should be captured by the forecasting system. It will be useful in predicting future promotional demands, and its identification eliminates a past outlier.

A good forecasting system should track and model promotional effects.

Modeling Combinations of Patterns

In general, a time series can possess a combination of patterns such as those shown in Figures 8–7 and 8–8. Figure 8–7 shows Series E with a slight trend and considerable randomness about that trend. In contrast, Figure 8–8 illustrates Series F with both pronounced trend and seasonality. The method chosen to forecast Series F should model the trend and seasonality patterns to accurately predict the future. Fortunately, as discussed in Chapters 11 through 13, there are a number of methods that will accurately represent series with trend and seasonality.

*If a series has a combination of patterns,
a model of it should include these patterns.*

FIGURE 8–7
Demand for a Product with Slight Trend (Series E, 3.5-inch Brand X Floppy Diskettes)

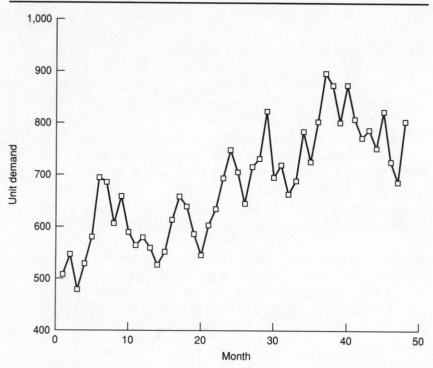

INTRODUCTION TO FORECASTING METHODS

Three classifications of forecasting methods—intrinsic, extrinsic, and qualitative—are discussed below.

Intrinsic (Time Series) Forecasting Methods

Intrinsic forecasting methods, which are also known as *time series methods,* use the past, internal patterns in data to forecast the future. Intrinsic methods include time series, smoothing, exponential smoothing, decomposition, Fourier series analysis, ARIMA (i.e., Box-Jenkins), linear trends, and nonlinear growth models, among others. The purpose of these methods is to model

FIGURE 8-8
Demand for a Product with Pronounced Trend and Seasonality (Series F, AM/FM Personal Radios)

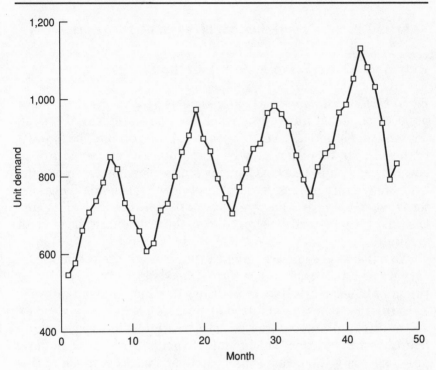

the patterns of past demands in order to project them into the future. Where costs and accuracy of short- to medium-horizon forecasts are important, intrinsic methods are almost always the most cost effective. As mentioned, these methods are almost always used in operational forecasting systems. The basic concept of intrinsic forecasting is that future values of the series will follow some mathematical function (f) of past values of the series. Mathematically, this is:

$$\text{Future value} = f(\text{Past values}) \qquad (8\text{–}1)$$

For example, consider a simple two-month average forecast model.

$$\begin{array}{l}\text{Forecast} \\ \text{of June} \\ \text{sales}\end{array} = \frac{\text{April sales} + \text{May sales}}{2} = \frac{600 + 500}{2} = 550 \qquad (8\text{–}2)$$

Chapters 10 to 13 are devoted to intrinsic forecasting methods; we will therefore not discuss them in detail here. Also, Chapter 11 discusses causal (extrinsic) forecasting methods.

Intrinsic methods model demands based on past demands alone.

Extrinsic (Causal) Forecasting Methods

Extrinsic forecasting methods, also known as *causal methods,* make projections of the future by modeling the relationship between demand and other "external" variables. For example, the forecast of the sales of furniture may be based upon a relationship with economic indicators such as housing starts, personal income, number of new marriages, and number of new households. These external variables are called *predictor* or *independent variables,* and the furniture demand is referred to as the predicted or dependent variable.

Extrinsic forecasts are important in making projections of aggregate demands such as the total sales dollars of a corporation, the sales of a product line, or the sales in a region of the country. These methods include simple- and multiple-regression, econometric, multiequation econometric, multivariate time series, and a few other more advanced techniques. In general, extrinsic methods are more costly to develop than intrinsic methods; much of this additional cost results from necessary external data collection and human analyst time. Currently, extrinsic methods are rarely used in operational forecasting systems; they are only used to forecast the demand for a few major product groups or families.

General mathematical statements of simple extrinsic models are:

Dependent variable = f(Independent predictor variables)

OR

Future values = f(Past values, past values of other variables)

$$(8\text{--}3)$$

Consider a simple three-variable model for furniture demand:

Forecast of
June demand = 50 + .2*LMS + 1*API + .5*NHS   (8–4)
= 50 + .2*600 + 1*250 + .5*200 = 520

where the independent predictor variables are as follows:

LMS = Last month's furniture sales (i.e., sales in May)
API = Average personal incomes
NHS = New housing starts

The term *extrinsic* makes reference to the use of external variables as predictor or explanatory variables. Also, the synonym for extrinsic methods, *causal methods*, indicates that the purpose of extrinsic methods is to model the causes of demand so as to better predict future demand. However, modeling cause-and-effect relationships in business and economics is very costly and difficult. Also, when judged by the accuracy of short- to medium-term forecasts, extrinsic models are not cost effective for operational forecasting, except when used to forecast a very few major product groups. Finally, extrinsic methods have the distinct disadvantage that the independent variables (i.e., LMS, API, and NHS) need to be forecasted in order to predict the future value of the dependent variable (demand). However, if one wants to explain the cause-and-effect relationships of demand (for example, in the context of strategic planning), then no better method than extrinsic methods exists.

Extrinsic methods require forecasts of a dependent variable and one or more independent variables.

Extrinsic methods are rarely used in operational forecasting systems.

The important differences between the purposes of extrinsic and intrinsic models should be emphasized further. Intrinsic models are designed to model the past with mathematical relationships that mimic, but do not explain, past patterns. In contrast, extrinsic methods are designed to model the cause-and-effect relationships of the past so as to forecast and explain demand. Explanation of demand (e.g., demand for furniture) as a function of other variables is the forté of extrinsic methods. By explaining the sales of a product as a function of external, independent variables, managers receive valuable information that can be used for short- to long-horizon decisions, including important strategic-management decisions.

Extrinsic methods can be effective in explaining causes and effects of demands.

Seven Laws of Economic Forecasting

The following laws are presented for their relevance to short- and long-term forecasting.

1. History repeats itself; history does not repeat itself.
2. From time to time, major shocks throw the economy off course, and these are often not only unforecasted, but unforecastable. (Economists fail to forecast large or unusual events such as wars, strikes, earthquakes, and technological breakthroughs.)
3. The consensus of economists' forecasts is more often right than wrong. (Over time, the average of several forecasts is more often better than any single forecast.)
4. Adherence to a single economic theory can be dangerous to your forecasting health. (The assumptions surrounding formal and informal theory may change without being anticipated in the forecast.)
5. Economic forces work relentlessly but on an uncertain timetable. (One might predict that demand will increase six months from now; however, demand increases one year later. This supports the old forecasting joke, "Give them a number or a date, but not both.")
6. Beware when something goes off the drawing board of historical experience. (When a ratio or trend departs dramatically from its historical bounds, we need to find out why and what risks it poses. Outlier detection is an essential part of this process.)
7. "The road is more important than the inn." (In general, the process of forecasting is more important than the final numbers. Improved decisions should result from a good process. The value in causal (i.e., extrinsic) forecasting methods is in the assumptions made, the reasoning employed, the uncertainties described, and the factors identified as affecting the outcome.)

Source: Adapted from Gilbert Hebner, "Seven Laws of Economic Forecasting," National Association of Business Economists.

Our presentation of extrinsic models in this book is not extensive because they are not used extensively in forecasting systems and because there are many excellent publications on extrinsic methods. Nonetheless, Chapter 11 does discuss extrinsic methods in enough detail for users of operational forecasting systems.

Qualitative Forecasting Methods

Qualitative forecasting methods are based on the judgment and opinions of others concerning future trends, tastes, and technological changes. Qualitative methods include Delphi, market research, panel-consensus, visionary, and historical-analogy methods of predicting the future. These methods are as expensive as, and in some cases more expensive than, extrinsic methods. A very simple example of qualitative forecasting is illustrated by a group of executives agreeing upon the forecast for the following month. Consider a consensus forecast of a three-executive panel.

$$\text{June forecast} = \frac{\overset{\text{Manager 1}}{\text{forecast}} + \overset{\text{Manager 2}}{\text{forecast}} + \overset{\text{Manager 3}}{\text{forecast}}}{3}$$

$$= \frac{400 + 600 + 600}{3} = 533 \tag{8-5}$$

Qualitative methods are useful in forecasting demands when there is little data to support quantitative methods. They are used to forecast new products, new market shares, the cost or development time for a new product, or the best competitive business strategy. They are sometimes called *technological forecasting methods* because of their frequent use in projecting long-run technological changes; however, technological forecasting is best viewed as a subset of qualitative methods. Qualitative methods are most frequently used to make long-run forecasts when there is little objective data concerning relevant past patterns or relationships (i.e., it can't be assumed that past relationships and patterns will repeat).

Qualitative methods are not used much in forecasting systems because of their higher cost, lower accuracy, and the ready availability of data for intrinsic forecasting. However, they are used rather informally in item-level forecasting systems to estimate the effects of new-product introductions, promotions, price changes, competition, and so on. For example, a product manager might subjectively estimate that demand will be 50 percent higher in May because of special promotional effects. Because these subjective methods are used in item-level forecasting in informal and intuitive ways, they are briefly defined below. The methods that we briefly discuss here include Delphi, market research, panel consensus, and historical analogy.

Qualitative methods are necessary when
there is little or no past objective data.

The *Delphi method* is a popular means of forecasting that is based on a structured questioning of a panel of experts who respond independently to questions. These experts iteratively fill out questionnaires concerning the future and thereby reveal facts that are important in influencing and forecasting the future. The results of the first questionnaires are used to generate the next set of questions. These questionnaires are generated sequentially so that the experts' opinions can be tabulated and shared with all participants. That is, the results of all independently completed

---

Long-Term Technological Forecasting Is Difficult

The following humorous forecasting blunders exemplify the difficulty of making accurate technological forecasts even when experts are making the projections.

"Everything that can be invented has been invented."
Charles H. Duell, Director of U.S. Patent Office, 1899

"Who the hell wants to hear actors talk?"
Harry Warner, Warner Bros. Pictures, 1927

"Sensible and responsible women do not want to vote."
Grover Cleveland, 1905

"There is no likelihood man can ever tap the power of the atom."
Robert Millikan, Nobel prize in physics, 1923

"Heavier-than-air flying machines are impossible."
Lord Kelvin, President of the Royal Society, 1895

"Home mortgage rates will never go below 10 percent in this century."
Many financial experts, 1980

questionnaires are shared with all experts. The independence of questionnaire responses eliminates much of the bias that might take place if the experts were to openly try to influence each other. In the end, we seek a defensible conclusion based on the evidence provided by the independent expert opinions.

Market research is characterized by a systematic, formal, and objective application of the scientific method to estimate market data. Formal hypotheses are proposed and tested using a wide variety of statistical analyses of data collected by mail, telephone, and personal surveys.

The *panel-consensus method* is based on the assumption that the consensus of several experts will yield a better forecast than a single expert's opinion. In contrast to the Delphi method, there is little secrecy because communications and interaction are encouraged. However, the openness might yield forecasts that are influenced (i.e., biased) by the social pressures of the group dynamics and therefore may not reflect an objective consensus.

The *historical-analogy method* is a popular means of making short- to long-term forecasts of products that have characteristics that are very similar to other products for which we have objective data. For example, the demand during the introduction and growth of a new product might be expected to follow the demand patterns of similar products. Similar patterns are expected in the new product's demands because of its similarities to the old products and customers. The use of historical analogy can be very important and effective in modeling the expected seasonal demand for a new product that is replacing an old one, or for a product that will have the same seasonal demand pattern as an established product.

A forecasting system should support the use of historical analogies for new or low-volume products.

Management Intuition and Involvement— The Art of Forecasting

The several qualitative methods discussed above involve the subjective judgments of one or more individuals. It is important to highlight the very common practice of managerial "guestimates" when data is unavailable or other methods are incapable of modeling operational demands. Such procedures can be invaluable when necessary. Not every manager is capable of successfully practicing the art of forecasting; however, many managers are very successful. These individuals have insights concerning appropriate assumptions and factors in a forecast. When sufficient data are not available, then subjective management judgment is probably better than placing false hopes on sophisticated forecasting models that do not have an adequate database.

The forecasting system should provide a method
for input of subjective information from managers.

While operational forecasts are often made by the computer in an automated environment, there are many times when management should have direct input to the forecasts. This management intervention may be prompted by an exception report highlighting a problem in the system. This problem may reflect a problem with outliers or the inability of the forecasting system to incorporate all relevant information about demand. The intervention might be initiated by management because he or she knows of an event that will occur in the future that will be different than past data patterns in the time series.

A forecasting system should prompt and support managerial intervention.

Even when a model's forecast is accepted, in the end, management is responsible for the forecast consequences. Important future events like promotions are not included in the simple assumptions of forecasting methods. Consequently, management involvement continues during all phases of the forecasting process. The system must be monitored, improved, and maintained. If the system is ineffective, then it will be the managers who are held accountable for system failures. Conditions change too quickly and too often to depend solely on an automated forecasting system. An operational forecasting system should routinely and accurately forecast 80 to 90 percent of the items. When the 10 to 20 percent exceptional errors occur, then the system should detect these and facilitate management involvement in the correction of these errors.

If a forecasting system is ineffective, so might
be the managers supported by the system.

SUMMARY

This chapter has introduced a number of fundamental concepts in forecasting. Common demand patterns were introduced. These demand patterns include random, trend, seasonal, cyclical, autocorrelated, outlier, promotional, and combinations of these patterns. Forecasting systems must be capable of modeling each of these patterns simultaneously. Chapters 10 through 14 will present the models and systems that are capable of this complex modeling task. Finally, this chapter introduced the concepts of intrinsic, extrinsic, and qualitative forecasting methods. These concepts are further developed in Chapter 9 where a detailed comparison will be made between several different methods.

CHAPTER 9

COMPARING AND SELECTING FORECASTING METHODS

HORIZON LENGTH (*a*)
ACCURACY AT EACH HORIZON (*b*)
COST OF APPLICATION (*c*)
DATA PERIOD USED (*d*)
FREQUENCY OF REVISION (*e*)
TYPE OF APPLICATION (*f*)
AUTOMATION POTENTIAL (*g*)
USE OF EXTERNAL AND SUBJECTIVE DATA (*h*)
    Data Availability
    Primary versus Secondary Sources of Data
DEMAND PATTERN CAPABILITY (*i*)
NUMBER OF OBSERVATIONS REQUIRED (*j*)
    New- and Low-Demand Product Forecasts
SUMMARY
REFERENCES

> Forecasters are far more artists than scientists, and the com-
> plexity of their methods should not obscure the simplicity
> of their underlying assumptions.
> Practical forecasters of the 20th century

This chapter presents the characteristics of many forecasting
methods discussed in Chapter 8. It is difficult to generalize about
the differences between forecasting methods because of the diver-
sity of their applications; however, some useful generalizations
are possible.[1] Table 9–1 presents the general characteristics of

several forecasting methods for management; these include short-range through long-range methods. While several of these methods are not suitable for use in Type 1, operational forecasting systems, they are important methods of long-term forecasting in operations management.

The selection of the best forecasting method depends on many factors, such as time horizon, data characteristics, needs of the organization, the potential benefits from better forecasts, and resources of the organization. The forecaster should evaluate the methods that make the best use of the data available. If an acceptable forecast using existing data is not available, then a more costly and complex method may be necessary.

In selecting the best method for preparing forecasts, there will be many trade-offs, some of which will be easy to make and others that will take considerable thought. For example, the forecaster may need to resolve the choice between a very simple and inexpensive method that provides a good forecast and a complex and expensive method that may provide a more accurate forecast.[2] The forecaster must then determine if the incremental gain in forecast accuracy is worth the increased cost of the latter method. For example, increased accuracy in operational forecasts is likely to lead to lower safety stocks. Thus, the forecaster must determine if the costs of a more accurate forecast will be offset by lower costs associated with lower safety stocks.

Many times, these types of estimates and decisions will be made subjectively based on the forecaster's knowledge and experience. Although much of forecasting is an art, the characteristics listed in Table 9–1, which are gleaned from published research and our experience, should be helpful in the selection of a forecasting method.

Ultimately, a corporation should choose the technique that provides the greatest return on investment. The appendix to Chapter 1 introduced the Du Pont model as a tool in this decision process. It models not only revenues and costs associated with forecasts but also the return that the firm receives from its investment in a forecasting method or system. If the method or system is an important investment, then the use of the Du Pont model is important. However, simpler models of the trade-offs can be used in the less complex setting.

TABLE 9–1

Comparison of Forecasting Methods for Management

Methods	(a) Horizon Length				(b) Accuracy at Each Horizon				(c) Cost				(d) Data Period Used					(e) Frequency of Revision			
	Immediate (< 1 month)	Short (1–3 months)	Medium (3 months–2 years)	Long (> 2 years)	Immediate	Short	Medium	Long	Very Low ($.10)	Low ($10)	Medium ($100)	High ($1,000)	Days	Weeks	Months	Quarters	Years	Weekly	Monthly	Quarterly	Yearly
Intrinsic:																					
Simple smoothing	•	•			H	M	L	V	•				•	•	•			•	•		
Complex smoothing	•	•	•		H	H	M	L	•	•			•	•	•	•		•	•		
Extrinsic:																					
Multiple regression	•	•	•		H	H	M	L		•				•	•	•	•		•	•	
Single-equation econometric	•	•	•		M	H	H	M			•				•	•	•		•	•	
Multiequation econometric	•	•			L	H	H	M			•				•	•	•			•	•
Qualitative:																					
Delphi		•	•		M	M	M	M		•						•	•			•	•
Market research		•	•		M	H	M	M		•					•	•	•			•	•
Panel consensus		•	•		V	L	L	V	•	•					•	•	•			•	•
Historical analogy		•	•	•	M	M	M	M	•	•					•	•	•			•	•

H = High accuracy.   M = Medium accuracy.   L = Low accuracy.
V = Very low accuracy.

(f) Type of Application					(g) Automation Potential				(h) Use of External and Subjective Data	(i) Demand Pattern Capability					(j) Number of Observations Required		
Item-Level Plan	*Production Plan*	*Aggregate Plan*	*New-Product Plan*	*Strategic Plan*	*Very Low*	*Low*	*Medium*	*High*		*None*	*Trend*	*Seasonal*	*Cyclical*	*Explanatory*	*Low (< 36)*	*Medium (24–48)*	*High (> 48)*
•	•						•		No	•					•		
•	•	•	•				•		No	•	•				•		
•	•	•	•		•				Yes	•	•		•			•	•
•	•	•	•		•				Yes	•	•	•	•			•	•
•	•	•	•		•				Yes	•	•	•	•			•	•
	•	•	•		•				Yes subjective	•		•	•		•		
	•	•	•		•				Yes	•	•	•	•			•	•
	•	•	•		•				Yes subjective	•		•	•		•		
•	•	•			•				Yes subjective	•	•	•				•	•

Because the benefits can vary widely by application, this chapter only discusses the relative costs and accuracies of different methods. However, these relative measures are important in the initial forecasting method selection process.

The forecasting model characteristics of interest to general management are listed in the columns of Table 9–1. This table presents three general types of forecasting methods: intrinsic, extrinsic, and qualitative. Each column presents a different characteristic of these methods and is discussed in detail below under a separate heading. The letters after the section headings correspond to the column letters in Table 9–1.

HORIZON LENGTH (a)

Different forecasting methods have evolved in order to forecast different horizon lengths. As shown in Table 9–1, the effective horizon length of different methods increases for those that are lower in the table. That is, the effective horizon lengths are longer as we move from intrinsic to qualitative methods. In Chapter 8, we explained that intrinsic methods simply utilize objective information internal to the series being forecasted, whereas extrinsic methods rely on objective information external to the series, and that qualitative methods use many sources of both subjective and objective information.

In general and for our purposes, forecasting methods are defined as either immediate, short-, medium-, or long-term methods.

Origin of the Term *Forecasting*

One of the first written uses of the word *forecasting* was in 1400. The term is a combination of the Middle English words *fore* and *casten.* A literal synonym for the term is to "throw forward" or to cast a set of dice forward as in a game of chance. Thus, a forecaster is one who will cast predictions forward in time. As shown in Table 9–1, there are many different ways to cast forward. Most methods simply cast past patterns or relationships forward into the future.

The horizons of these forecasts are, respectively, 1 day to 1 month, 1 to 3 months, 3 months to 2 years, and 2 to 10 years. Your definitions might overlap these because there are no universally accepted ranges for these terms. As discussed in Chapter 1:

*The forecasting horizon length is determined
by the leadtime of the decisions.*

ACCURACY AT EACH HORIZON (*b*)

There is considerable difference in the accuracy of different methods at different horizons. As mentioned above, longer-horizon accuracy increases for methods lower in the table. The term *accuracy* here refers to the relative accuracy of methods; however, no percentage error is given because accuracy, as measured by percentages, is dependent on the variability of the series and future influences. We can generalize by noting that short-horizon forecasts are typically more accurate than longer-horizon forecasts. Long-horizon accuracy can vary dramatically depending on the validity of the forecasting model and the uncertainty of that being forecast. For example, next month's demand can be forecasted much more accurately than the demand 36 or 48 months from now.

Short-range forecasts are more accurate than long-range forecasts.

The accuracy of the forecast is dependent on the accuracy and representativeness of past data. The forecaster must be aware of and adjust for any nonrecurring events such as sales promotions, manufacturing interruptions, or lost sales caused by out-of-stock conditions. If such nonrecurring events are not adjusted for properly in input data, then accuracy suffers greatly.

To a very large extent, forecast accuracy is dependent on the ability of the model and data to represent the past patterns that will recur in future values. Thus, input data and model structure should reflect the repeating patterns of the data in the future.

*Forecasts will be more accurate if input data and model
structure reflect the repeating patterns of future values.*

COST OF APPLICATION (*c*)

The operating costs of intrinsic methods are the lowest, while extrinsic and qualitative methods can be very costly, depending on the method and application.

When choosing one forecasting method over another, the net benefit of each method is the most relevant measure to use. However, it is very difficult to generalize about the net benefit of one method over another.

$$\text{Net benefit} = \text{Benefit from use} - \text{Cost of use}$$

The benefits of a particular forecasting method result from the improved decisions provided by the more accurate predictions or insightful information. Increased accuracy yields a lower standard deviation or mean absolute deviation of the forecast errors. This results in lower uncertainty in any plans derived from the forecast projections.

Somewhat surprisingly, there are times when methods are not chosen for their lower errors, but for the insights resulting from the structure of the model. For example, intrinsic methods are sometimes more accurate than extrinsic methods for immediate to short-horizon forecasts. However, an extrinsic forecasting model might be chosen because it provides causal explanations of the relationship between demand and other variables. That is, even though an extrinsic model may be more costly to construct than an intrinsic model, and might not be more accurate, it may nonetheless provide significantly higher benefits because of its ability to explain cause and effect relationships. Consequently, management is provided with an improved framework for their decisions.

Forecast accuracy is only one characteristic of a good forecasting model.

The insights provided by extrinsic models may be more important than forecast accuracy.

Additionally, the forecaster should consider developmental and operating costs separately. Developmental costs are associated with start-up costs of the forecasting method, which may include data gathering, data entry, program acquisition, program modification, and development of ongoing data-gathering processes. Operating costs are those costs associated with producing the next forecast using the same technique. These costs will vary by company and technique and should be evaluated separately when determining the best technique.

To keep costs as low as possible, the forecaster should evaluate all internal data sources prior to purchasing external data, since external data is generally expensive. A cost-benefit analysis is helpful to determine the need for external data.

Intrinsic methods are frequently more accurate than more-costly extrinsic methods.

The net benefits of using extrinsic methods for longer-term forecasts should offset their costs.

DATA PERIOD USED (*d*)

The data period (i.e., week, month, quarter, or year) analyzed should increase as the forecast horizon increases. The extrinsic and qualitative methods shown lower in Table 9–1 are more effective with longer horizons and are therefore used with larger data periods (e.g., quarters or years versus weeks or months).

The size or length of the individual forecast period is an important determinant of the forecasting method and system design. Should weekly, monthly, quarterly, or yearly demand data be forecasted? If a general rule could be stated, it would be to choose the largest data period that will give meaningful results. The trade-off in selecting a data period size involves the relationship between the number of periods per year versus the number of years being forecast. For example, if five-year projections of demand are necessary, it is unlikely that daily or weekly demand periods will be forecasted; instead, monthly, quarterly, or annual data should be used. In other words, the further into the future one needs to forecast, the larger the data period used in the model. If a forecast is to be made to describe demand for the next three years, it is best to use monthly or quarterly data. In contrast, to control inventory levels in a warehouse over the next month, most likely weekly or monthly data will be used. As we showed in Chapter 2, forecasts of groups of periods are more accurate than individual-period forecasts. Normally, the forecast of a single four-week period will be more accurate than the individual forecast of one of those weekly periods.

The further in the future one forecasts, the larger the data period used (e.g., weeks, months, quarters, or years).

By far the most widely used period of analysis in operational forecasting has been the month. Then, typically, these monthly forecasts are disaggregated to weekly projections using simple rules based on the number of weeks or days per month. Unfortunately, the number of working days per month varies from month to month (e.g., the number of working days in June versus July), and even year to year (e.g., the number of working days in May 1991 versus May 1992). This variation in the number of days per month frequently causes complexity in the design of the forecasting system. Several different approaches are used to compensate for these differences.

Simple Ratios

If decisions and allocations are made weekly, then it would seem that weekly forecasts are most appropriate. However, because monthly forecasts are more accurate than weekly forecasts, it can be more effective to forecast the demand for a month and then decompose that forecast into weekly forecasts using (1) simple ratios such as 4.33 weeks per month (52 weeks/12 months = 4.33), (2) historical ratios of a week's sales to a month's sales, or (3) the number of working days in each week of the month. These ratios are effective if monthly totals are not greatly influenced by large holiday influences that only affect one week of the month (e.g., the week of Labor Day and its effect on September).

Use of Average Daily Demand

Another solution to the problem requires forecasts of average daily demand per month and then converts this average to total monthly demand based on the number of days in the month. For example, assume that a forecast is based on a simple model that predicts that the May 1992 daily sales rate will be equal to that of May

1991. However, these two months do not have the same number of selling days. Assume that May 1991 has 22 selling days, while May 1992 has 23 selling days. To forecast sales for May 1992, first divide sales of May 1991 by 22, then multiply that answer by 23. Assume that the sales of May 1991 were 2,500.

Forecast May 1992 = (Daily sales May 1991)*(Days in May 1992)
Forecast May 1992 = (2,500/22)*23 = 2,613.6

The forecast based on daily average sales is considerably different than the total May 1991 sales of 2,500, and, in general, this method is superior to simply ignoring monthly differences. This is a very popular method, one that is used in forecasting systems, especially in retail businesses where the number of selling days is so important.

13-Period Years
Another solution to the problem of forecasting nonstandard months is to divide the year into 13 periods or months of four weeks each. While this approach greatly reduces the month-to-month variations in sales, it does not completely eliminate variations. However, when a firm operates seven days per week, including holidays, each of the 13 months contains the same number of working or operating days. This method has been very popular with utilities and some larger corporations that operate during holidays.

Quarterly, 4-4-5–Week Months
Another method divides the year into 12 "months" that have a repeating pattern of months with four, four, and five weeks starting with January. Thus, each month no longer follows the calendar, but instead follows a 13-week quarter in which the first two months have 4 weeks and the last month has 5 weeks. A disadvantage of this approach is that it introduces an artificial seasonality to the data. That is why average daily demand or 13-period years are more frequently used.

Use of Weekly Forecasts
Finally, there has been some movement from monthly forecasting periods to weekly forecasting periods. This helps eliminate

the differences in the number of days in each month. On average, weeks are much more homogeneous from year to year. However, to forecast one year into the future requires projecting 52 weeks. Herein lies the basic trade-off when choosing the forecast period: choosing shorter periods of analysis requires projections over larger numbers of periods. Consequently, when weeks are used for immediate to short-term forecasting, months may be used to forecast longer-term demands, for example, demands by month next year.

In general, choose the largest size of data period that will give meaningful results.

FREQUENCY OF REVISION (*e*)

Logically, the very expensive methods may be applied only once or twice a year because of their cost. The frequency of revision decreases for methods lower in Table 9–1 because they are more expensive to apply. Intrinsic methods can be applied weekly or even daily. In contrast, qualitative methods may be applied only annually due to the high cost of data gathering. Revisions of forecasts are not made more frequently than the period of the data; a forecast using monthly data is not normally revised weekly simply because too little new data are available to warrant the effort each week.

TYPE OF APPLICATION (*f*)

In Table 9–1, the applicability of methods for operational forecasting and inventory control decreases while the use of methods for higher-level management considerations increases as we move down the table. Higher-level decisions (e.g., planning new distribution centers) are normally decisions that take a long time to implement. Extrinsic and qualitative methods are more useful for longer horizons and are therefore more useful for higher-level decisions. The required forecast horizon is important in choosing an appropriate forecasting method.

The main focus of this book is operational forecasting. Thus, as shown in Table 9-1, the three most popular methods for operational forecasting are simple smoothing, complex smoothing, and multiple-regression techniques.

While we have been discussing planning applications in this section as if the forecasting needs of different applications were independent of each other, this is not true. As we discussed in Chapter 3, the forecasts of the same demands (e.g., product A in January 1992) used in different planning applications should be equal; this is a requirement of the one-number principle. This equality is important across different departments in the organization (e.g., marketing versus operations) as well as over different time periods. Thus, the monthly forecasts for three years (i.e., a Type 1 forecast) should be consistent with the quarterly forecasts for years 1 to 10 (i.e., a Type 2 forecast). These two forecasts should be coordinated through the use of Type 3 forecasts.

Short-leadtime decisions need short-horizon forecasting methods.
Long-leadtime decisions need long-horizon forecasting methods.

AUTOMATION POTENTIAL (*g*)

The degree to which forecasting methods are used to make automated decisions decreases for methods lower in the table. This is true because, as we move down the table, the applications of the forecasting methods of Table 9-1 evolve from the highly programmable decisions (e.g., inventory control) to the ill-structured decisions (e.g., strategic business planning). As the complexity of the decision increases, the less likely will be its automation.

Causal methods such as regression and econometric techniques are complex to apply. It is not normally cost effective to make inventory-control decisions using the causal modeling methods of multiple-regression and econometric techniques. Causal modeling requires too much analyst time and expense.

Extrinsic methods are rarely used in automated decision processes.

Extrinsic and qualitative modeling processes cannot be automated because of their need for significant analyst involvement.

USE OF EXTERNAL AND SUBJECTIVE DATA (*h*)

The use of external and subjective data increases for methods lower in the table.

Data Availability

One of the important factors in choosing a forecasting method is the availability of data. As shown in Table 9–1 and discussed below, the data needs of methods differ considerably. One of the distinct advantages of intrinsic forecasting methods is that the required data may be readily available from company records. However, this is not to say that there are no data-availability problems, a topic discussed in Chapter 15. In contrast, extrinsic data are frequently costly to obtain. Also, in order to make forecasts of demand, it is necessary to make a forecast of the predictor or independent variables of the model. The necessity to obtain reliable forecasts of independent variables can make data availability problematic and very costly.

Qualitative data requirements vary considerably by the method chosen. In general, the external-data requirements are high and costly. Frequently, data are collected from many sources, including published government documents, sample surveys, and other database searches.

Primary versus Secondary Sources of Data

There are two classifications of data sources, primary and secondary data. Secondary data refers to data that have already been collected and published for reasons other than for use in a specific forecast system. Secondary data include all data collected and published by corporations and governmental and commercial organizations for general use. In contrast, primary data are collected to support the forecasting or research task at hand. Through research, sample surveys, and on-line computerized data collection devices, data is collected to support a specific forecasting system. Intrinsic and extrinsic methods normally use secondary data in their databases. The data for a forecasting system using intrinsic methods will probably exist in a perpetual inventory or order processing system. However, it does cost to collect intrinsic data, particularly during system startup. One of the more costly aspects of qualitative methods is that they frequently require the collection of expensive external primary data.

DEMAND PATTERN CAPABILITY (*i*)

The ability to model different demand patterns is dependent on the method chosen. Different methods are designed to model different components of demand patterns. It is important to match a method's capability to the demand patterns of the series being forecasted. Operational forecasting systems are designed to detect different demand patterns and to subsequently choose the appropriate forecasting model. A forecasting method should not be used to predict demand unless that method is capable of modeling the patterns in the demand. If a demand pattern is not modeled, then significant forecast errors will occur.

If a method does not model relevant demand
patterns, then its forecasts will be less than relevant.

Another aspect of demand pattern capability is the ability to predict turning points. Turning points reflect changes in the current trend or cyclical variations. These changes in direction are very difficult to predict. Examples of turning points are the cyclical expansions and contractions of the gross national product (GNP) and their effects on industrywide demands. Long-term forecasting of GNP turning points is very subjective, and experts frequently disagree as to the timing of those turning points. Short-term forecasting such as item-demand turning points are even more difficult to predict. The forecaster responsible for identifying turning points must be aware of the difficulty of predicting turning points and the potential for significant error. The models in Table 9–1 that are identified as having a cyclical pattern capability have a better chance of predicting turning points than other methods. However, these methods are normally too expensive to be used for short-term item forecasts. Forecasting systems employ tracking signals to detect turning points; these are discussed in Chapter 14.

The turning points in demand are extremely difficult to predict.

NUMBER OF OBSERVATIONS REQUIRED (j)

The number of observations required to use the methods of Table 9–1 varies considerably. In general, at least 36 and, more effectively, at least 48 observations of data should be available to model seasonal data using intrinsic methods. In contrast, trends can be estimated with as few as seven observations. As shown in Table 9–1, the number of required observations for extrinsic methods is the highest of all methods.

In general, all methods are more accurate when more observations are available. However, this increased accuracy will diminish when the oldest observations become irrelevant in representing future demand patterns. When seasonality exists in the demand for an item, a method that can model seasonality should be used. Most seasonal forecasting methods require three to four seasonal cycles for accurate forecasts. Thus, it is recommended that the forecasting systems be capable of storing at least three years of weekly data (i.e., 156 observations) or a minimum of three years of monthly data (i.e., 36 observations). Almost all popular operational forecasting systems can accommodate this number.

A good forecasting system should accommodate
three to four years of seasonal data.

Data Collection Is the First Step

It is a mistake to theorize before one has data.
Sir Arthur Conan Doyle, *The Adventures of Sherlock Holmes,*
"Scandal in Bohemia," 1891

New- and Low-Demand Product Forecasts

During the startup of a forecasting system, there will be many items for which three to four years of data are unavailable. Also, many products have such low demands that patterns are hard to identify; nonetheless, patterns do exist. These problems need to be recognized and appropriate techniques used to ensure relatively accurate forecasts for trend and seasonal patterns. The methods that are used in these situations include family trend and seasonal profiles and historical analogies; these are discussed in more detail in Chapter 17.

A good forecasting system supports the use of family trend and seasonal profiles and historical analogies.

SUMMARY

The characteristics of the methods illustrated in Table 9–1 are very important in choosing one method over another; however, other factors enter into the choice. These include the availability of data, the expertise of the analyst, the availability of software and hardware, the benefits from increased forecast accuracy, and the costs of forecast errors. Fortunately, the choice of the forecasting method for operational forecasting systems is quite easy, and intrinsic methods are by far the most cost effective. This is true because they are relatively inexpensive to use, have very high accuracy in immediate to medium-range forecasts, and lend themselves to automated applications. In contrast, extrinsic and qualitative methods are unsuitable for the routine forecasting of hundreds or thousands of items because of their use of costly analyst time and effort.

Long-horizon forecasts are the basis of corporate long-horizon planning, including functional areas of finance, marketing, operations, and logistics. These forecasts provide information for budgetary planning and cost control. Marketing depends on short- to long-horizon demand forecasts to plan new products and allocate sales and distribution resources. Production uses long-term forecasts to make long-term decisions involving process selection, capacity planning, and facility layout. Short-horizon forecasts are needed by production to support decisions about production planning, scheduling, and inventory control. Also, logistical plans depend on long-horizon forecasts for warehouse and transportation planning.

Because forecasts always have errors, rather than search for the perfect forecast, it is far more important to continuously review forecasts to achieve relatively accurate and unbiased predictions. By building low-cost, but effective buffers for these inaccurate forecasts, overall system costs can be minimized despite the inaccuracy of the forecasts. This is not to say that we should not try to improve the forecasting model or system, but that we should try to find and use the most cost-effective forecasting method available for our application.

Buffers against uncertainty are a good method of planning for contingencies.

For long-horizon forecasts that lead to large financial commitments, greater care is justified in forecasting. Extrinsic methods such as multiple-regression analysis and econometrics are important explanatory and policy planning tools. The aggregate effects of economic factors, product trends, growth factors, and competition should be modeled. Then these effects can be used to adjust the product demand forecasts to reflect the influence of each.

Aggregate economic influences should be
used to adjust intrinsic operational forecasts.

Short- to medium-horizon forecasts, such as required for inventory control, staffing, and master scheduling, may use intrinsic methods, such as exponential smoothing models, that incorporate trend and seasonal adjustment procedures. In such applications, there are usually thousands of items to forecast. The forecasting routine should therefore be simple and run efficiently on a computer. The routines should also detect and respond rapidly to definite short-term changes in demand while ignoring at the same time the occasional outliers in demand. The remaining chapters of this book will develop the forecasting methods and systems that have these attributes and are most cost effective in operational forecasting for management.

REFERENCES

1. R. G. Murdick and D. M. Georgoff, "How to Choose the Best Technique – or Combination of Techniques – to Help Solve Your Particular Forecasting Dilemma," *Harvard Business Review,* January–February 1986, pp. 110–20.
2. J. Holton Wilson and Barry Keating, *Business Forecasting* (Homewood, Ill.: Richard D. Irwin, 1990).

PART 4

FORECASTING METHODS

Part 4 is the largest section in this book. Some sections may not be of interest if you desire only a managerial perspective of forecasting systems. Consequently, below we highlight those chapter sections that are most technical. Chapters 10, 11, 14 and parts of Chapters 12 and 13 should be read by all. If you are interested in the more-statistical details of forecasting, you will benefit from more-detailed study of the technical material in Chapters 12 and 13. Finally, several chapters have technical appendixes that can be skipped without loss of continuity.

Chapter 10 is intended for all of us regardless of our mathematical background. It presents a variety of simple smoothing methods that are effective when only simple random patterns exist in the data. Specifically, it presents the most widely discussed method of forecasting random demands, single exponential smoothing. Your familiarity with single exponential smoothing is a good foundation on which to build an understanding of its limitations and of the need for more-sophisticated methods. Also, this chapter presents the formal principles and processes of selecting forecast model parameters. Since these principles and processes are at the heart of any forecasting system, Chapter 10 is important for everyone. The final section discusses principles for forecasting low-volume and erratic demands.

Chapter 11 is a general-interest chapter that presents two of the most widely used methods of forecasting—multiple regression and classical time series decomposition. Both are presented in a manner making them accessible to all. Multiple regression is the most widely used extrinsic method for short- to long-term forecasting. It is also used in operational forecasting systems to estimate group forecasts. The discussion of seasonal indexes in the second half of Chapter 11 is important for all readers. Like Chapter 10, this chapter presents essential foundation material for the more-advanced forecasting methods discussed in Chapters 12 and 13.

Chapter 12 presents simple and sophisticated trend and seasonal models of forecasting. The methods of modeling trends and seasonality using differences is an interesting and easily understood, yet powerful, set of techniques. Holt-Winters' three-parameter model of random, trend, and seasonality is an important technique for operational forecasting systems. While this material is some of the most technical in the text, it should nonetheless be studied or reviewed by all, particularly those using or considering using Holt-Winters' method of forecasting. This method has been effective in a wide variety of forecasting environments.

Chapter 13 presents Fourier series analysis models and a new approach to forecasting systems, multimodel simulation methods. You may find Fourier series analysis to be the most technical topic in this book. We have attempted to present it as simply as possible. While it is based on trigonometric functions, those desiring a more-technical presentation of forecasting should not have great difficulty understanding or applying this technique as presented here.

In contrast to Fourier series analysis, multimodel simulation methods are intuitive methods that are more easily understood. This exciting new approach to forecasting integrates a long history of simple, intuitive forecasting methods. Those of you familiar with – or desiring more information about – systems like Focus Forecasting™ will find this topic interesting.

Chapter 14, the final chapter in Part 4, is one of the most important in this book. The techniques, principles, and systems discussed there are of great importance to all users of forecasting systems. The first section of the chapter is a nontechnical presentation of essential material about the accuracy of different forecasting methods. This insightful material will assist you in understanding principles and issues related to technique accuracy. The performances of 25 different forecasting methods are reviewed in this section.

The second section of Chapter 14 discusses forecasting system control devices, including ways to use tracking signals to detect outliers and out-of-control situations. The final section of this chapter presents an integrated system flow chart for a simple operational forecasting system. Understanding this system flow chart is essential for mastering and integrating the many concepts learned throughout the book. This flow chart provides a system-wide perspective of the parts of the system and how they relate.

CHAPTER 10

SIMPLE SMOOTHING METHODS

I know of no way of judging the future but by the past.
Patrick Henry, Virginia Convention, 1775

Because of their almost exclusive use in forecasting systems, four chapters of this book are devoted to intrinsic forecasting methods. This chapter develops elementary smoothing methods of moving averages, weighted moving averages, and single exponential smoothing. These are effective methods when short-run forecasts are projected for series that do not have trends and seasonality. Chapter 11 presents seasonal and trend methods using decomposition techniques; Chapter 12 presents more-advanced smoothing methods including Winters' method; and Chapter 13 presents Fourier series analysis. If you are unfamiliar with the concepts and principles presented in this chapter, then reading it should be a prerequisite to studying the other intrinsic methods of this book. Finally, the last section of this chapter discusses principles of forecasting low-volume and erratic demands. These demands are often forecasted using the methods presented in this chapter.

Simple smoothing methods are not important as general forecasting approaches, but instead they are the foundation on which we can build an understanding of more-sophisticated general approaches to forecasting. Simple methods only forecast simple series accurately. They do not accurately forecast series with trends or seasonality. However, single exponential smoothing has been found to be a particularly effective method when used with deseasonalized data.

*When seasonal patterns exist without trends, simple
smoothing methods work well with deseasonalized data.*

Intrinsic forecasting methods are those that use the past behavior of a series to predict the future value of that same series. The term *intrinsic* denotes that the information used to forecast the series is internal or within the series. The terms *time series analysis, univariate forecasting methods,* and *smoothing methods* are often used as synonyms for intrinsic methods. We have a preference for the term *univariate forecasting methods;* however, the term *intrinsic methods* is used because of its widespread and historical usage in operational forecasting.

MOVING AVERAGES

SIMPLE MOVING AVERAGES (SMA)

One of the simplest methods of forecasting demand is to assume that a future demand will equal the average of past demands. This is the essential assumption of the moving average. The moving average is useful in modeling a random series (i.e., one without trend or seasonality) because it averages or smooths the most recent actual values to remove the unwanted randomness.

The SMA is one of the easiest calculated forecasts. Table 10–1 illustrates the actual demand of a series and shows the forecasts and errors for two-, four-, and eight-period moving averages. As the table shows, the simple moving average used to forecast May Year 1 is easily calculated:

$$SMA(May) = (Jan + Feb + Mar + Apr)/4$$
$$= (120 + 124 + 122 + 123)/4 = 122.25$$

This simple formula is used to forecast each month in the four-period moving average column of Table 10–1.

In general, an n-period moving average will equal the average of n prior periods. The term *moving* denotes that each new forecast moves ahead one period by adding the newest actual and dropping the oldest actual. For example, the forecast for June Year 1 is:

$$SMA(Jun) = (Feb + Mar + Apr + May)/4$$
$$= (124 + 122 + 123 + 125)/4 = 123.50$$

At the bottom of Table 10–1, several statistics are shown for each of the three different SMAs. These error statistics (the mean error, the sum of the squared errors, and the standard deviation of the errors) are used to compare the accuracy of the different models. They are defined as follows:

$$\text{Mean error} = \frac{\Sigma(A_t - F_t)}{n} = \bar{e}_t = \frac{\text{Sum of errors}}{\text{Number of errors}} \quad (10\text{–}1)$$

$$\text{Sum of squared errors} = \Sigma e_t^2 = \Sigma(A_t - F_t)^2 \quad (10\text{–}2)$$

TABLE 10–1
2-, 4-, and 8-Period Simple Moving Averages

Month	Period (t)	Actual	Two-Period SMA	Two-Period SMA Error	Four-Period SMA	Four-Period SMA Error	Eight-Period SMA	Eight-Period SMA Error
YEAR 1								
JAN	1	120.00						
FEB	2	124.00						
MAR	3	122.00	122.00	.00				
APR	4	123.00	123.00	.00				
MAY	5	125.00	122.50	2.50	122.25	2.75		
JUN	6	128.00	124.00	4.00	123.50	4.50		
JUL	7	129.00	126.50	2.50	124.50	4.50		
AUG	8	127.00	128.50	−1.50	126.25	.75		
SEP	9	129.00	128.00	1.00	127.25	1.75	124.75	4.25
OCT	10	128.00	128.00	.00	128.25	−.25	125.88	2.13
NOV	11	130.00	128.50	1.50	128.25	1.75	126.38	3.63
DEC	12	132.00	129.00	3.00	128.50	3.50	127.38	4.63
YEAR 2								
JAN	13	131.00	131.00	.00	129.75	1.25	128.50	2.50
FEB	14	132.00	131.50	.50	130.25	1.75	129.25	2.75
MAR	15	133.00	131.50	1.50	131.25	1.75	129.75	3.25
APR	16	130.00	132.50	−2.50	132.00	−2.00	130.25	−.25
MAY	17	132.00	131.50	.50	131.50	.50	130.63	1.38
JUN	18	134.00	131.00	3.00	131.75	2.25	131.00	3.00
JUL	19	134.00	133.00	1.00	132.25	1.75	131.75	2.25
AUG	20	133.00	134.00	−1.00	132.50	.50	132.25	.75
SEP	21	131.00	133.50	−2.50	133.25	−2.25	132.38	−1.38
OCT	22	135.00	132.00	3.00	133.00	2.00	132.38	2.63
NOV	23	137.00	133.00	4.00	133.25	3.75	132.75	4.25
DEC	24	138.00	136.00	2.00	134.00	4.00	133.25	4.75
Mean		129.88	129.57	1.02	129.68	1.73	129.91	2.53
Sum of squared errors (for t = 9 to 24)				67.50		77.88		147.47
Standard deviation of errors (for t = 9 to 24)				2.12		2.28		3.14

$$\text{Standard deviation of errors} = \sqrt{\frac{\text{Sum of } e_t^2}{n-1}} \quad (10\text{–}3)$$

where

$$A_t = \text{Actual demand}$$
$$F_t = \text{Forecasted demand}$$
$$n = \text{Number of errors}$$

The mean error of Equation 10–1 is important in judging whether the forecasting model is consistently over- or underforecasting, a condition called *bias*. That is, a good forecasting model should not consistently overforecast or underforecast; consequently, the mean error will not vary greatly from zero.

An unbiased forecasting model has a sum of
errors that is not significantly different than zero.

The sum of the squared errors is used to calculate the standard deviation of the forecast errors as in Equation 10–3. This is a very important measure of the accuracy of a forecasting model and a statistic used to choose the best forecasting model. The importance of the standard deviation was presented in Chapter 7, and we expand on that concept below. The formula in Equation 10–3 is used throughout this book for calculating the standard deviation of the errors. In contrast to the formula of Chapter 7, the standard deviation of the errors is based on the assumption that the mean error is always equal to zero, whether it is or not. You should note this because if you use a statistical program or spreadsheet to calculate the standard deviations of the errors, your solutions will not agree with those shown here unless you use Equation 10–3. Equation 10–3 is the formula used to calculate the standard deviation of errors in all statistical programs that generate errors in fitting or forecasting models.

The best forecasting model is the one with the
smallest standard deviation of the forecast errors.

Using the statistics at the bottom of Table 10–1, it is evident that the two-period moving average is the best forecasting model of the three.

Choosing the Best Forecasting Model

The criteria used to choose one forecasting model over another are discussed here, in Chapter 7, and in Chapter 14. As discussed in Chapter 7, one of the most important general objectives in forecasting is to decrease the width of the confidence intervals used to make probability statements about future values. A probability statement for the next actual value is shown below using a confidence interval.

Actual demand =
Forecast demand +/− Z*Standard deviation of errors

The probability that the actual value will be in this interval is determined by the Z value of the normal distribution. If a Z of 1.96 is used, then 95 percent of the actual demands for one-period-ahead forecasts will be in this range. (This is discussed in Chapter 7.) For example, using a two-period moving average, the 95 percent confidence interval for the actual demand in period $t = 25$ (i.e., January of Year 3) can be calculated using the last two actuals in Table 10-1:

Actual Jan ($t = 25$) = (Nov + Dec)/2 +/− 1.96*Standard
deviation of errors
= (137 + 138)/2 +/− 1.96*2.12
= 137.5 − 4.16 to 137.5 + 4.16
= 133.34 to 141.66

Thus, because 95 percent of the past demands were within 1.96 standard deviations, there is a 95 percent chance that the above one-period-ahead forecast interval will contain the actual demand. (This assumes that the future is a repeat of the past pattern.)

Because of the importance of probability statements, the most frequently used criterion for selecting the best forecasting model is the minimization of the standard deviation of errors. This minimizes the width of the confidence interval and maximizes forecast accuracy. There are several other important considerations in choosing one model over another. These considerations were discussed in Chapter 9, and others will be discussed in Chapter 14.

As shown in Table 10-1, the two-period simple moving average is the most accurate of the three models. Its standard deviation of the errors (2.12) is slightly lower than that of the four-period simple moving average (2.28), and significantly lower than that of the eight-period simple moving average (3.14). For this data, the standard deviations of the errors are 50 percent higher for the eight-period moving average than the two-period moving average. Thus, we see that there are significant benefits to be derived from choosing the best moving average.

Optimal Number of Periods in the Average

In general, the optimal number of periods to have in a forecasting model is that number that minimizes the standard deviation of the forecast errors. As mentioned for the three models of Table 10–1, the optimal number of periods to include is two. Figure 10–1 confirms that the two-period moving average most closely follows that actual series. This figure illustrates that the number of periods in the moving average determines the length of the "mem-

FIGURE 10–1
Two-, Four-, and Eight-Period Moving Averages for Data of Table 10–1

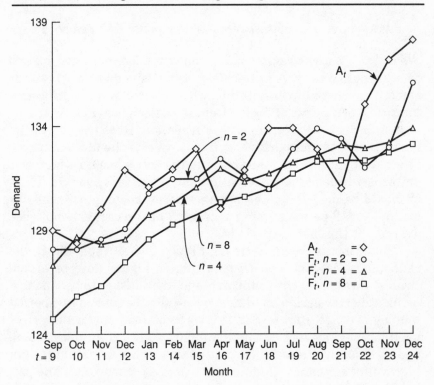

ory" of the average. A two-period moving average only has a memory of two periods, while an eight-period moving average includes the most recent eight observations in its calculations.

As shown in Figure 10–1, the longer the moving average period, the more the randomness is smoothed. A long-period moving average yields the lowest standard deviation when the series is very random and erratic (i.e., does not possess high levels of autocorrelation). However, if the series is random and moves smoothly up or down (i.e., is highly autocorrelated), then a shorter-period moving average will yield a lower standard deviation. The series in Figure 10–1 does move rather smoothly up over time; thus, a short-period moving average model works best for this series. Below we present an objective way to choose the best number of periods.

When to Use Simple Moving Averages

Moving average models work well with patternless demands.

We define a *patternless demand* as one that does not have a trend or seasonality in it. A patternless series is random with either smooth or erratic variations (i.e., with or without high autocorrelation). When demand for an item is patternless and erratic as shown in Series A, Figure B–1 of Appendix B (at the end of the book), then a longer-period moving average is the more-accurate forecasting model. This is so because the series has no systematic patterns; the demands are erratic about a constant average. Thus, it should be modeled using a longer-period moving average, for example, a 12-period moving average. The forecast is simply the average of the last 12 periods.

If, in contrast, as in Series B, Figure B–2 of Appendix B, the randomness is very smooth resulting in highly autocorrelated "walks" away from the grand average, then it should be modeled using a shorter-period moving average, for example, a two-period moving average. Figure B–2 is a very common pattern of prices for items sold in very competitive markets, such as stock, bond, and commodity markets. Also, it describes the demand for very high-volume products that are not trending or seasonal. The pattern is referred to as a *random walk* because the series randomly walks up and down without any predictable pattern. As discussed in Chapter 8, random walks are characterized by high degrees of autocorrelations.

Use long-period moving averages with erratic random series. Use short-period moving averages with smooth random (i.e., random-walk) series.

WEIGHTED MOVING AVERAGES (WMA)

It is normally true that *the immediate past is most relevant in fore-casting the immediate future.* For this reason, weighted moving averages are used to place more weight on the most recent obser-vations. The simple moving average gives equal weight to each observation, while a weighted moving average uses different weights on each observation. The only restriction on the weights is that their sum equals one. Using a four-month moving aver-age with weights of .4, .3, .2, and .1 and the data of Figure 10–1 yields the following forecast for May Year 1.

$$\text{WMA(May)} = .1*\text{Jan} + .2*\text{Feb} + .3*\text{Mar} + .4*\text{Apr}$$
$$= .1*120 + .2*124 + .3*122 + .4*123 = 122.6$$

An advantage of the weighted moving average is that the weights placed on past demands can be varied. However, the deter-mination of the optimal weights can be difficult and costly. Ta-ble 10–2 and Figure 10–2 illustrate a comparison of a four-period weighted moving average versus a four-period simple moving aver-age for the example of Figure 10–1. As shown in Table 10–2 and Figure 10–2, the weighted moving average is slightly more ac-curate than the simple moving average. The weighted moving average standard deviation of the errors is slightly less than that of the four-period simple moving average. Consequently, it is the superior method of the two.

Limitations of the SMA and the WMA

The most distinct disadvantage of all moving average or smooth-ing methods is that they do not model the seasonality or trend of a series. An operational forecasting model should have the capa-bility to model seasonal and trend movements of a series. Histor-ically, the main disadvantage of moving averages has been that all the data necessary to calculate the average must be stored.

TABLE 10–2
4-Period Simple Versus 4-Period Weighted Moving Average Forecasts

Month	Period (t)	Actual Demand	Four-Period			
			SMA	SMA Error	WMA	WMA Error
YEAR 1						
JAN	1	120				
FEB	2	124				
MAR	3	122				
APR	4	123				
MAY	5	125	122.25	2.75	122.6	2.4
JUN	6	128	123.5	4.5	123.7	4.3
JUL	7	129	124.5	4.5	125.5	3.5
AUG	8	127	126.25	.75	127.3	−.3
SEP	9	129	127.25	1.75	127.6	1.4
OCT	10	128	128.25	−.25	128.3	−.3
NOV	11	130	128.25	1.75	128.2	1.8
DEC	12	132	128.5	3.5	128.9	3.1
YEAR 2						
JAN	13	131	129.75	1.25	130.3	.7
FEB	14	132	130.25	1.75	130.8	1.2
MAR	15	133	131.25	1.75	131.5	1.5
APR	16	130	132	−2	132.2	−2.2
MAY	17	132	131.5	.5	131.4	.6
JUN	18	134	131.75	2.25	131.6	2.4
JUL	19	134	132.25	1.75	132.5	1.5
AUG	20	133	132.5	.5	133.2	−.2
SEP	21	131	133.25	−2.25	133.4	−2.4
OCT	22	135	133	2	132.5	2.5
NOV	23	137	133.25	3.75	133.3	3.7
DEC	24	138	134	4	134.8	3.2
Mean		129.88	129.68	1.73	129.98	1.42
Sum of squared errors (for t = 9 to 24)				77.88		68.27
Standard deviation of errors (for t = 9 to 24)				2.28		2.13

If a 12-period moving average is to be used, then a historical database of 12 observations must be used to calculate the mean of 12 observations. While this created a serious data storage problem several decades ago when computer memory and calculations were so expensive, it is no longer a matter of great concern. Today, it is recommended that a minimum of 36 to 48 observations be stored for monthly series, regardless of the forecasting method.

FIGURE 10-2
Four-Period Simple versus Four-Period Weighted Moving Average Forecasts

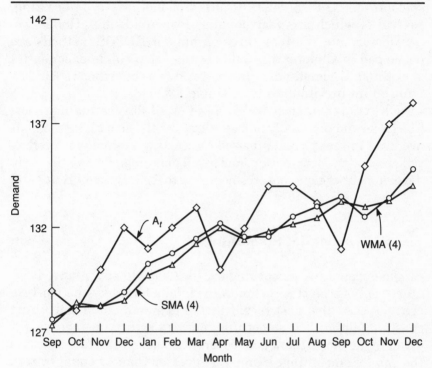

The most important reason for not using moving averages is that exponential smoothing is as accurate as moving averages while at the same time computationally more efficient. When using a moving average, it is more difficult to determine the optimal number of periods to include in the average. In contrast, it is somewhat easier to find the optimal number of periods using the exponential smoothing model. This optimization procedure is discussed below.

EXPONENTIAL SMOOTHING

SINGLE EXPONENTIAL SMOOTHING

As mentioned above, when computer storage capacity was expensive, exponentially weighted moving averages (best known as *exponential smoothing*) became popular. They are still very popular today, even though storage cost is not as significant a concern. (We will use the abbreviation EXPOS for the phrase *exponential smoothing*.) EXPOS refers to a set of methods of forecasting, several of which are very popular. Brown's double, Holt's two-parameter, and Winters' three-parameter EXPOS methods are developed in Chapter 12. Below we develop single exponential smoothing. Understanding the more advanced methods should be built on an understanding of single EXPOS.

EXPOS is the most widely used of all forecasting methods. The trend and seasonally adjusted exponential smoothing methods are used in many computerized forecasting systems for production, inventory, distribution, and retail planning. We owe the early development of exponential smoothing to R. G. Brown,[1] Holt,[2] and Winters.[3]

Single Exponential Smoothing

Single exponential smoothing (SES) is easy to apply since it requires only three pieces of data to make a forecast—the most recent forecast, the most recent actual demand, and a smoothing constant (alpha). The smoothing constant determines the weight given to the most recent past observations and therefore, controls the rate of smoothing. It must be greater than or equal to zero and less than or equal to one.

The equation for a SES forecast is the following:

$$F_t = \alpha * A_{t-1} + (1 - \alpha) * F_{t-1} \qquad (10\text{--}4)$$

where

F_t = Exponentially smoothed forecast for period t
A_{t-1} = Actual demand in the prior period
F_{t-1} = Exponentially smoothed forecast of the prior period
α = Smoothing constant, called alpha, restricted to be
  greater than or equal to 0 and less than or equal to 1.

Suppose a firm desires to forecast demand for a product using SES with an alpha of .3. Last month's actual demand was 1,000, while the forecast was 900. Therefore, the forecast for this month is:

$$F_t = \alpha * A_{t-1} + (1 - \alpha) * F_{t-1}$$
$$= .30 * 1,000 + (1 - .30) * 900 = 300 + 630 = 930 \text{ units}$$

This formula states that the current forecast is equal to a weighted average of the most recent actual and forecasted values. Alpha (α) provides the relative weight given to each term in Equation 10–4. With alpha equal to .3, the forecast is 30 percent of the most recent actual and 70 percent of the most recent forecasted value. As we will show, the alpha value can be chosen to achieve the desired level of averaging or smoothing. A high alpha smooths the previous actual very little by giving more weight to it, while it greatly smooths the previous forecast by giving little weight to it.

Continuing the numerical example above, suppose that the demand for period t actually was 980. What is the forecast for period $t+1$? Since

$$F_t = \alpha * A_{t-1} + (1 - \alpha) * F_{t-1}$$
$$= .30 * 1,000 + (1 - .30) * 900 = 300 + 630 = 930 \text{ units}$$

and

$$A_t = 980$$

then

$$F_{t+1} = \alpha * A_t + (1 - \alpha) * F_t$$
$$= .30 * 980 + (1 - .30) * 930 = 294 + 651 = 945 \text{ units}$$

Another equally simple way to calculate the SES equation is:

$$F_t = F_{t-1} + \alpha * (A_{t-1} - F_{t-1}) \qquad (10-5)$$

According to this formula, the current forecast is equal to the old forecast plus a fraction (alpha) of the error in the previous forecast. However, note that Equations 10–4 and 10–5 are the same equations written with terms combined in different ways. Equation 10–4 is the preferred way of viewing SES in our discussions here. However, the reader will find that both equations are used in practice and should understand both of them.

To start using SES requires the choice of a smoothing constant, an initial forecast, and an actual value. The choice of a smoothing constant has been categorized by many as being arbitrary; however, this is not true. What is true is that the best choice of a smoothing constant *might* not be critical in some situations and often values between .1 to .5 are acceptable. However, there are many times when the choice of alpha can be very critical. With low-cost computers and the high costs of forecast errors, it is no longer advisable to choose a convenient or typical alpha value, but, instead, the best alphas should be chosen. We provide explicit guidelines for choosing the best alpha later. For now, we use an alpha of .3.

Optimal values of alpha should be used in exponential smoothing.

After choosing a smoothing constant, the next step in application is to choose an initial forecast value. Very frequently, the first actual value is chosen as the forecast for the second period. Consider the situation below.

Period	Actual Values
1	900
2	1,000

To get SES started, we assume that the initial forecasted value is for Period 2 and equals the actual value for Period 1. It is now possible to forecast Period 3.

$$F_2 = A_1 = 900$$
$$F_3 = \alpha * A_2 + (1 - \alpha) * F_2$$
$$= .3 * 1,000 + (1 - .3) * 900 = 300 + 630 = 930 \text{ units}$$

While there are other methods of arriving at an initial forecast, this method is very popular and effective.

The Smoothing Constant

The function of the smoothing constant is to give relative weights to the most recent actual and forecasted values. Smoothing and averaging are synonyms in forecasting; consequently, exponential smoothing might also be called *exponential averaging*. While it is not evident from our examples, *an exponentially smoothed value is actually a weighted moving average of all past* actual *demand values.* The exponential weights of the past actuals are completely determined by the smoothing constant, alpha. The first four weights, when alpha is .3, are given below.

Actual Demand	Weight
Most recent	$\alpha = 0.300$
One period old	$\alpha(1 - \alpha) = 0.210$
Two periods old	$\alpha(1 - \alpha)(1 - \alpha) = 0.147$
Three periods old	$\alpha(1 - \alpha)(1 - \alpha)(1 - \alpha) = 0.1029$

(To better understand where these weights come from please refer to the appendix of this chapter. The appendix can be skipped by those not interested; however, you should be able to use it, regardless of your mathematical background.)

Table 10–3 illustrates the values of the weights given to past actuals for smoothing constants of .1, .3, .6, and .9. These were calculated in the appendix. As shown in the table, if an alpha value of .1 is chosen, then the demand in the last period (i.e., $t-1$) will be given a weight of 10 percent, while, if an alpha of .9 is chosen, last period's demand will be given a weight of .9. Using an alpha of .1 results in weights of .1, .09, .081, .0729, and .0656 for periods 1, 2, 3, 4, and 5, respectively. The second column of Table 10–3 defines the mathematical weighting term for each past value when using exponential smoothing. The determination of this term is illustrated in the appendix to this chapter.

As shown in Table 10–3, if greater weight is to be given to the most recent actual values, then a high smoothing constant is chosen. This is referred to as *low smoothing.* An alpha of 1.0 provides no smoothing because the forecast equals the most recent actual value. This is called zero smoothing.

$$F_t = \alpha*A_{t-1} + (1 - \alpha)*F_{t-1} = 1*A_{t-1} + (1 - 1)*F_{t-1} = A_{t-1} \quad (10-6)$$

An alpha of 1 yields a one-period simple moving average. In contrast, a low smoothing constant yields low response to the recent actual and a great amount of smoothing or averaging; consider the values in Table 10–3 and the example below, which uses a smoothing constant of .1.

TABLE 10-3
Exponential Weights of Actual Demand with Different Smoothing Constants

Period	Term	Weight When Alpha Equals			
		.1	.3	.6	.9
$t - 1$	α	.1	.3	.6	.9
$t - 2$	$\alpha*(1 - \alpha)$	.09	.21	.24	.09
$t - 3$	$\alpha*(1 - \alpha)^2$	.081	.147	.096	.009
$t - 4$	$\alpha*(1 - \alpha)^3$	.0729	.1029	.0384	.0009
$t - 5$	$\alpha*(1 - \alpha)^4$	.0656	.0720	.0154	.00009
$t - 6$	$\alpha*(1 - \alpha)^5$	.0590	.0504	.0061	.000009
$t - 7$	$\alpha*(1 - \alpha)^6$	.0531	.0353	.0025	.0000009
$t - 8$	$\alpha*(1 - \alpha)^7$	.0478	.0247	.0010	.00000009
$t - 9$	$\alpha*(1 - \alpha)^8$	.0430	.0173	.0004	.000000009
$t - 10$	$\alpha*(1 - \alpha)^9$	.0387	.0121	.0002	.0000000009

CHOOSING THE BEST ALPHA

Alpha Based on Autocorrelation

With high (low) autocorrelations use a high (low) alpha. With high (low) smoothness in demand use a high (low) alpha.

There are several ways to choose an optimal value for forecasting a particular data series. Using judgment and the two principles above, alpha can be selected subjectively. If a great amount of smoothing is desired, then a small alpha should be chosen. For example, a low alpha would be most appropriate for Series A in Figure B-1 of the book appendix. In contrast, a very high alpha should be chosen for Series B in Figure B-2. This choice was based upon the desire to greatly smooth the data of Figure B-1 and not smooth the data of Figure B-2.

Use a low alpha for a very random series.
Use a high alpha for a very smooth series.

Alpha Based on Desired Simple Moving Average

There is an approximate relationship between alpha and the number of periods included in a simple moving average. This relationship is expressed as follows:

Managers Are Using Exponential Smoothing and Don't Know It!

We have heard managers state that they do not forecast; they simply assume that this month's demand will equal last month's demand. However, this form of "not forecasting" is actually the use of exponential smoothing with a smoothing constant of 1. When alpha equals one, then the forecast equals the value of the most recent actual. This form of forecasting works well when the series is very smooth, without significant seasonality or trend. Even with a smooth series, these managers might be much better off by using an alpha that is chosen using one of the methods described below.

$$\alpha = 2/(n + 1) \text{ or } n = 2/\alpha - 1 \qquad (10\text{--}8)$$

This is only an approximate relationship; consider the use of the following alphas:

For alpha of .1: $n = 2/.1 - 1 = 19.00$
For alpha of .3: $n = 2/.3 - 1 = 5.67$
For alpha of .6: $n = 2/.6 - 1 = 2.33$
For alpha of .9: $n = 2/.9 - 1 = 1.22$

This method of choosing alpha can be useful when converting to or from simple moving averages. However, because there are better ways to set alpha, the use of Equation 10–8 is not recommended.

Alpha Based on Minimum Standard Deviation

The alpha that yields the most-accurate forecasts is the one that achieves the lowest standard deviation errors. In other words, when choosing alpha, the object is to reduce the standard deviation of the forecast errors to as low as possible. The standard deviation of the forecast errors was given previously in Equation 10–3.

The standard deviation is minimized when the sum of the squared forecast error is minimized. This is why in most forecasting systems alpha is chosen so as to minimize either the standard deviation or the sum of squared forecast errors. To achieve this, search methods are used to find the optimal alpha. That is, different alpha values are actually tried in forecasting and the alpha that achieves the lowest standard deviation of the forecast errors is the best. A crude search using three alpha values is illustrated in Table 10–4 using the data of Table 10–1. As we show in Table 10–4, the best alpha for this data is .9 with a standard deviation of 1.97, while an alpha of .1 is much less accurate with a standard deviation of the errors equal to 5.72. There is little difference between the alphas of .6 and .9. The best alpha may not be .9; to refine our estimate will require additional searching between .6 and 1.0.

Figure 10–3 graphically illustrates the function of alpha and

TABLE 10–4
Simple Exponential Smoothing Using Alpha of .1, .6, and .9

Month	Period (t)	Actual	Alpha = .1 Forecast	Alpha = .1 Error	Alpha = .6 Forecast	Alpha = .6 Error	Alpha = .9 Forecast	Alpha = .9 Error
YEAR 1								
JAN	1	120						
FEB	2	124	120.00		120.00		120.00	
MAR	3	122	120.40		122.40		123.60	
APR	4	123	120.56		122.16		122.16	
MAY	5	125	120.80	4.20	122.66	2.34	122.92	2.08
JUN	6	128	121.22	6.78	124.07	3.93	124.79	3.21
JUL	7	129	121.90	7.10	126.43	2.57	127.68	1.32
AUG	8	127	122.61	4.39	127.97	−.97	128.87	−1.87
SEP	9	129	123.05	5.95	127.39	1.61	127.19	1.81
OCT	10	128	123.65	4.35	128.36	−.36	128.82	−.82
NOV	11	130	124.08	5.92	128.14	1.86	128.08	1.92
DEC	12	132	124.67	7.33	129.26	2.74	129.81	2.19
YEAR 2								
JAN	13	131	125.41	5.59	130.90	.10	131.78	−.78
FEB	14	132	125.96	6.04	130.96	1.04	131.08	.92
MAR	15	133	126.57	6.43	131.58	1.42	131.91	1.09
APR	16	130	127.21	2.79	132.43	−2.43	132.89	−2.89
MAY	17	132	127.49	4.51	130.97	1.03	130.29	1.71
JUN	18	134	127.94	6.06	131.59	2.41	131.83	2.17
JUL	19	134	128.55	5.45	133.04	.96	133.78	.22
AUG	20	133	129.09	3.91	133.61	−.61	133.98	−.98
SEP	21	131	129.48	1.52	133.25	−2.25	133.10	−2.10
OCT	22	135	129.63	5.37	131.90	3.10	131.21	3.79
NOV	23	137	130.17	6.83	133.76	3.24	134.62	2.38
DEC	24	138	130.85	7.15	135.70	2.30	136.76	1.24
Mean		129.88	125.27	5.38	129.07	1.20	129.44	.83
Sum of squared errors (t = 9 to 24)				490.80		61.33		58.05
Standard deviation (t = 9 to 24)				5.72		2.02		1.97

FIGURE 10–3
Single Exponential Smoothing with Various Alpha Values

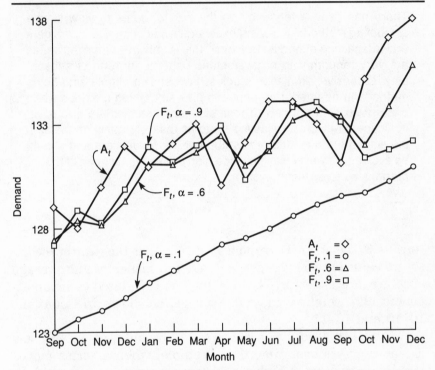

the inferiority of the forecasted values using alpha of .1. Obviously, the value of alpha can greatly affect the accuracy of the forecasts.

ADAPTIVE RESPONSE–RATE EXPONENTIAL SMOOTHING (ARRES)

There are several methods of automatically choosing the alpha value based on the errors of previous time periods; these are called *adaptive response-rate exponential smoothing methods* because the smoothing constant adapts to the data. Trigg and Leach[4] have suggested setting alpha by increasing alpha when errors are high and reducing alpha when errors are low. As shown below in Equa-

---

Simple Smoothing Methods Do Not Work Well with Patterns

There has been a tendency on the part of some to view simple smoothing methods, including exponential smoothing, as good, general forecasting methods. However, this is only true when the series are very random with no systematic patterns in trend or seasonality. Extensive simulation studies have shown simple smoothing methods to be inferior to more-complex smoothing methods when patterns exist in the data. These simulation studies are discussed in Chapter 14. Any forecasting systems that rely solely on the simple smoothing methods of this chapter are insufficient and should be avoided. However, simple smoothing is an important part of a comprehensive forecasting system.

---

tion 10–9, the adaptive response rate (TST$_t$) is the ratio of the absolute value of two averages, average forecast error and average absolute forecast error. These means are calculated using an exponentially weighted moving average, as shown in Equations 10–10 and 10–11.

We call this ratio a *tracking signal* because, as we will see, it tracks errors over time. For example, when a series moves rapidly up or down, a high alpha value is automatically used. In contrast, if the series moves slowly and has low forecast errors, then a low alpha value is used. Also, if the model is systematically under- or overforecasting, then the alpha value is increased. (Note: If you are not interested in the technical aspects of ARRES, then you can proceed to the section entitled Accuracy of ARRES without loss of continuity.)

$$TST_t = \left| \frac{SAD_t}{MAD_t} \right| \tag{10–9}$$

$$SAD_t = ß*(A_t - F_t) + (1 - ß)*SAD_{t-1} \tag{10–10}$$

$$MAD_t = ß*|A_t - F_t| + (1 - ß)*MAD_{t-1} \tag{10–11}$$

where

TST_t = Tracking signal in period t used for alpha in period $t + 1$

ß = Beta, a smoothing constant for SAD and MAD typically chosen to be .2

SAD_t = An exponentially weighted average
deviation (mean forecast error) in
period t

MAD_t = An exponentially weighted mean
absolute deviation (mean absolute
forecast error) in period t

| | Denotes absolute values

Thus, alpha is replaced by the value of Equation 10–9, and single exponential smoothing becomes

$$F_t = F_{t-1} + TST_{t-1}*(A_{t-1} - F_{t-1}) \qquad (10\text{--}12)$$

The value of TST can never be greater than 1 or less than 0; this is also the constraint on alpha. Because it adapts to the magnitude of the errors, TST is referred to as an adaptive alpha. Note that SAD_t and MAD_t are simply weighted moving averages of past forecast errors and absolute values of errors. If the model is forecasting accurately, then SAD_t will be nearly equal to zero and the ratio, TST_t, will therefore be low. However, if a model consistently under- or overforecasts, then SAD_t will approach the value of MAD_t.

Research has shown that if alpha is set equal to this tracking signal, then under some conditions the forecast will more closely track the actual. Table 10–5 and Figure 10–4 illustrate the use of adaptive response-rate exponential smoothing (ARRES) for the example of this chapter. As shown there, after the initialization phase of periods 1 to 3, the adaptive alpha has varied from .23 to as high as .76. The forecasts are quite accurate and follow the data well; however, one has to be cautious when using TST for alpha when the series is very random.

The use of ARRES requires initial values of SAD, MAD, and TST. There are several procedures for doing so. When there is little information about these values, an arbitrary value of alpha can be used to initiate the process for several periods until representative values of SAD, MAD, and TST can be used in the calculations. Thus, in Tables 10–5 and 10–6, we set alpha equal to .2 for the first two forecasting periods (periods 2 and 3). Thereafter, alpha is determined using TST. Also, as is true for single exponential smoothing, the first actual value (120) is used to forecast demand for period 2. Finally, so that the initialization process will rapidly converge on a steady-state value, SAD_1 and MAD_1

TABLE 10–5
Adaptive Response-Rate Exponential Smoothing (Random Series)

Month	Period (t)	Actual (A_t)	SAD_t	MAD_t	Adaptive Alpha (TST_t)	Forecast (F_t)	Error ($A_t - F_t$)
			Beta = .2				
YEAR 1							
JAN	1	120	.000	4.000	.200		
FEB	2	124	.800	4.000	.200	120.000	4.000
MAR	3	122	.880	3.440	.256	120.800	1.200
APR	4	123	1.082	3.131	.346	121.107	1.893
MAY	5	125	1.514	3.152	.480	121.762	3.238
JUN	6	128	2.148	3.458	.621	123.317	4.683
JUL	7	129	2.273	3.322	.684	126.225	2.775
AUG	8	127	1.594	2.882	.553	128.124	-1.124
SEP	9	129	1.574	2.605	.604	127.503	1.498
OCT	10	128	1.178	2.166	.544	128.408	-.4085
NOV	11	130	1.305	2.095	.623	128.186	1.814
DEC	12	132	1.581	2.213	.714	129.316	2.684
YEAR 2							
JAN	13	131	1.218	1.817	.670	131.233	-.233
FEB	14	132	1.159	1.638	.708	131.077	.923
MAR	15	133	1.181	1.565	.755	131.730	1.270
APR	16	130	.408	1.790	.228	132.689	-2.689
MAY	17	132	.310	1.447	.215	132.077	-.077
JUN	18	134	.637	1.545	.412	132.060	1.940
JUL	19	134	.737	1.465	.503	132.859	1.141
AUG	20	133	.503	1.258	.400	133.433	-.433
SEP	21	131	-.050	1.459	.034	133.260	-2.260
OCT	22	135	.324	1.530	.212	133.183	1.817
NOV	23	137	.945	1.911	.495	133.568	3.432
DEC	24	138	1.303	2.075	.628	135.266	2.734
Mean		129.88	1.070	2.259	.473	129.008	1.296
Standard deviation		4.64					2.316

are estimated. SAD_1 is estimated to be zero, because we expect the mean error to be zero. MAD_1 is estimated to be some typical value based either on the first several periods (e.g., periods 1 and 2) or, when past history is available, on the MAD of the past. We have chosen 4 as a typical MAD in period 1.

TST and Erratic Series

Adaptive response-rate exponential smoothing has a serious disadvantage, it does not work very well for data that is very random and erratic (i.e., with low autocorrelation). Table 10–6 and Figure 10–5 illustrate a series with more randomness than previ-

FIGURE 10–4
Adaptive Response-Rate Exponential Smoothing

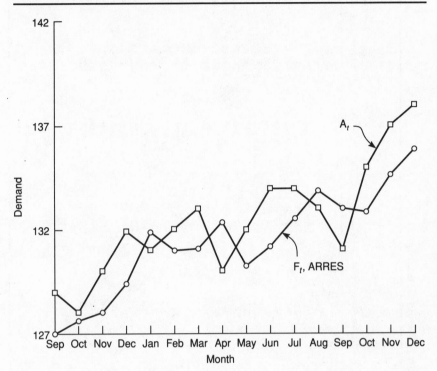

ous series. As shown there, ARRES does not forecast as well as simple exponential smoothing. This is evident by the very large forecast errors in several periods. The last two columns of Table 10–6 illustrate the use of SES with a fixed alpha of .2. As seen by the standard deviations of forecast errors, the model with a fixed alpha has performed much better than ARRES.

While the series of Figure 10–5 is very random, it is not as erratic as many series controlled by operational forecasting systems; it runs from a low of 98 to a high of 180. For the many series that are much more erratic than this one, the ARRES results in extraordinary errors. This is not to say that ARRES is not applicable in some situations; however, the forecaster that uses it must do so cautiously in order to avoid extremely inaccurate forecasts.

TABLE 10-6
Adaptive Response-Rate Exponential Smoothing (Random Series)

Beta = .2

Month	Period (t)	Actual (At)	SADt	MADt	Adaptive Alpha (TSTt)	Forecast (Ft)	Error (At − Ft)	Single Forecast	EXPOS* Error
YEAR 1									
JAN	1	120	.000	4.000	.200	120.000	4.000	120.00	4.00
FEB	2	124	.800	4.000	.200	120.800	47.200	120.80	47.20
MAR	3	168	10.080	12.640	.798	158.441	−35.441	130.24	−7.24
APR	4	123	.976	17.200	.057	156.430	−16.430	128.79	11.21
MAY	5	140	−2.505	17.046	.147	154.015	−53.015	131.03	−30.03
JUN	6	101	−12.607	24.240	.520	126.442	40.558	125.03	41.97
JUL	7	167	−1.974	27.504	.072	129.353	50.647	133.42	46.58
AUG	8	180	8.550	32.132	.266	142.830	−13.830	142.74	−13.74
SEP	9	129	4.074	28.472	.143	140.851	39.149	139.99	40.01
OCT	10	180	11.089	30.607	.362	155.035	−57.035	147.99	−49.99
NOV	11	98	−2.536	35.892	.071	151.006	−6.006	137.99	7.01
DEC	12	145	−3.230	29.915	.108	150.357	−19.357	139.40	−8.39
YEAR 2									
JAN	13	131	−6.455	27.804	.232	145.863	−.863	137.72	7.28
FEB	14	145	−5.337	22.416	.238	145.658	−35.658	139.17	−29.17
MAR	15	110	−11.401	25.064	.455	129.438	.562	133.34	−3.34
APR	16	130	−9.008	20.164	.447	129.689	50.311	132.67	47.33
MAY	17	180	2.856	26.193	.109	135.174	12.826	142.14	5.86
JUN	18	148	4.850	23.520	.206	137.819	−37.819	143.31	−43.31
JUL	19	100	−3.684	26.380	.140	132.537	9.463	134.67	7.35
AUG	20	142	−1.055	22.996	.046	132.971	25.029	136.12	21.88
SEP	21	158	4.162	23.403	.178	137.422	−2.422	140.49	−5.49
OCT	22	135	2.845	19.207	.148	137.064	31.937	139.40	29.60
NOV	23	169	8.663	21.753	.398	149.783	−14.783	145.32	−10.32
DEC	24	135	3.974	20.359	.195				
Mean		139.92	.13	22.62	.24	139.96	.83	135.73	5.05
Standard deviation		25.26				32.71			28.82

*Alpha is fixed at .2 for the single exponential smoothing model.

FIGURE 10-5
Adaptive Response-Rate EXPOS versus Simple EXPOS

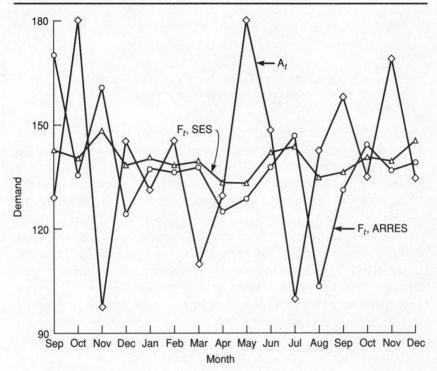

Accuracy of ARRES

An article by Gardner and Dannenbring[5] has questioned the accuracy of adaptive smoothing models. In a simulation study using 9,000 time series, the adaptive response weight models more frequently generated unstable forecasts, even when average demand was relatively stable. They recommended the use of trend-adjusted models to hedge against sudden changes in demand. Trend-adjusted models were shown to be more stable and more accurate than the adaptive models under a variety of conditions. These models are studied in Chapter 12. Gardner and Dannenbring's conclusions were confirmed by Makridakis et al.,[6] who compared the accuracy of a variety of forecasting models using 1,001 actual time series. The Makridakis study found that adaptive smoothing models were significantly less accurate than models using fixed parameters.

ARRES is not recommended as a forecasting method for routine forecasts.

FORECASTING LOW–VOLUME AND ERRATIC DEMANDS

In many forecasting situations, some items or services have very low or erratic demands. When this occurs, the selection of a good forecasting model can be difficult. Low and erratic demands are characterized as having very high standard deviations relative to the mean of the series. In statistics, the ratio of the standard deviation to the mean is called the *coefficient of variation*. Thus, when the coefficient of variation is high and no seasonal or trend patterns account for this high variation, it may be difficult to identify an accurate forecasting model. There are two solutions to this problem: (1) forecast the series as well as possible or (2) when a meaningful group can be identified, group the demands to improve the group forecast accuracy. However, no matter which solution is chosen, the standard deviation of the forecast errors is likely to be very high relative to mean demand.

Low-volume or erratic demands need to be handled differently than high-volume or patterned demands.

Patterns in Low-Volume Demands

It is common to find demands that are relatively low but nonetheless possess patterns and are, consequently, more easily forecasted than those without patterns. This results because of regularity in the demand process. For example, the low demand might be the result of having many customers who individually demand only a few units. In contrast, in many situations only a few customers may demand the product, but their demand is very erratic. In such situations, the resulting demand to the supplier will be very erratic (i.e., infrequent and lumpy).

Large numbers of customers often, but not always, enhance pattern identifiability and reduce errors in forecasting demands.

Low-Volume and Erratic Demands

If there are no repeating patterns in a demand, then simple smoothing methods are the best forecasting models. Single exponential smoothing with a low alpha value or simple moving averages with a large number of periods may be the best approach to forecasting such items. However, it is important to measure the errors and their standard deviations. The typically large standard deviations are very important in setting forecast error confidence intervals and contingency plans. Contingency plans include keeping the best level of buffer stocks to preclude stockouts and also excess inventory reports to preclude gross overstock conditions. The tracking signals and control devices discussed in Chapter 14 become critical tools of monitoring and controlling the forecast of low-volume or erratic demands. The level of low-volume or erratic demands may shift, and we need to detect such shifts as soon as possible.

*The uncertainty in low-volume or erratic demand should
be managed through error measures and contingency plans.*

Group Patterns in Low-Volume or
Erratic Demands

While an item may have a very erratic or low-volume demand, it may nonetheless be subject to some seasonal or trend patterns that are hidden by its high error variability. In such situations, it can be helpful to combine this item's demand with similar items that are all members of a common group. Accumulating group demands makes it easier to identify the seasonal patterns of demands and to preclude a stockout. As shown in the simple relationship below, the patterns in individual demands may not be pronounced enough to be identified, but when several demands are added together, the resulting group demand pattern may be quite discernible. Individual demands may, on average, be influenced 20 percent by patterns and 80 percent by random demands. Thus, the individual pattern demand may be difficult to identify. However, when this item is a member of a group, the demand patterns reinforce each other (i.e., are all high or all low in any given time period), while the random demands may cancel each other out. Thus, we may see that the group demand is influenced 60 percent by patterns, such as trends and seasonality, while the random demands account for only 40 percent of the group demand variation.

Individual demand = f(20 percent from pattern + 80 percent from random)

Group demand = f(60 percent from pattern + 40 percent from random)

The group demand pattern is then used to generate the individual demand patterns with the methods discussed in Chapter 3.

Grouping low-volume-demand items with similar demand patterns may improve the pattern-recognition process and reduce forecast errors.

Extremely Low-Volume Demands

In many situations, mean demand is extremely low, sometimes a fractional unit per month. In such situations, demand and the errors in forecasting demands should be modeled with different methods. These methods include the use of distributions other than the normal distribution. We discuss these extremely low-volume-demand situations in Chapter 16 using the Poisson distribution. The methods discussed in Chapter 16 are an important part of a good forecasting system that faces extremely low mean demands.

Extremely low demands require special forecasting procedures and buffer stock calculations.

SUMMARY

This chapter has introduced several methods of averaging or smoothing data for short-term forecasting. All smoothing methods except ARRES work adequately with patternless data for short-horizon forecasts of one or two periods. Because of its computational and storage efficiency, SES is the preferred method of those discussed here. However, all methods of this chapter suffer from an inability to model demands with seasonal and trend patterns. Because these patterns are not modeled, SES is inadequate for even short-horizon forecasts of trend and seasonal data. Fortunately, there are simple ways to incorporate growth and seasonality in exponentially weighted moving averages. These ways are discussed in the next three chapters.

REFERENCES

1. R. G. Brown, *Statistical Forecasting for Inventory Control* (New York: McGraw-Hill, 1959).
2. C. C. Holt, "Forecasting Seasonal and Trends by Exponentially Weighted Moving Averages," *Research Memorandum 52* (Office of Naval Research: 1957).
3. P. R. Winters, "Forecasting Sales by Exponentially Weighted Moving Averages," *Management Science* 6, 1960, pp. 324–42.
4. D. W. Trigg and D. H. Leach, "Exponential Smoothing with an Adaptive Response Rate," *Operational Research Quarterly* 18, 1967, pp. 53–59.
5. E. S. Gardner, Jr., and D. G. Dannenbring, "Forecasting with Exponential Smoothing: Some Guidelines for Model Selection," *Decision Sciences* 11, 1980, pp. 370–83.
6. S. Makridakis et al., "The Accuracy of Extrapolation (Time Series) Methods," *Journal of Forecasting* 1, no. 2, April–June 1982, pp. 111–53.

APPENDIX: DERIVATION OF EXPONENTIAL WEIGHTS FOR PAST ACTUALS

The basic exponential smoothing model is the following:

$$F_t = \alpha * A_{t-1} + (1 - \alpha) * F_{t-1} \qquad (10\text{--}13)$$

Thus, the following equations are also true:

$$F_{t-1} = \alpha * A_{t-2} + (1 - \alpha) * F_{t-2} \qquad (10\text{--}14)$$
$$F_{t-2} = \alpha * A_{t-3} + (1 - \alpha) * F_{t-3} \qquad (10\text{--}15)$$
$$F_{t-3} = \alpha * A_{t-4} + (1 - \alpha) * F_{t-4} \qquad (10\text{--}16)$$
$$F_{t-4} = \alpha * A_{t-5} + (1 - \alpha) * F_{t-5} \qquad (10\text{--}17)$$

Therefore, by substituting the right side of Equation 10–14 for F_{t-1} in Equation 10–13, we obtain Equation 10–18.

$$F_t = \alpha*A_{t-1} + (1 - \alpha)*[\alpha*A_{t-2} + (1 - \alpha)*F_{t-2}] \qquad (10\text{--}18)$$

Equation 10–18 denotes that the forecast in t is equal to a weighted moving average of the actuals in Periods $t - 1$ and $t - 2$ and the forecast of Period $t - 2$. This moving average is expanded by substituting the right side of Equation 10–15 for F_{t-2} in Equation 10–18; this yields Equation 10–19.

$$F_t = \alpha*A_{t-1} + (1 - \alpha)*[\alpha*A_{t-2} + (1 - \alpha)*(\alpha*A_{t-3} + (1 - \alpha)*F_{t-3})] \quad (10\text{--}19)$$

Simplified, this is:

$$F(t) = \alpha*A_{t-1} + (1 - \alpha)^1*\alpha*A_{t-2} + (1 - \alpha)^2*\alpha*A_{t-3} + (1 - \alpha)^3*F_{t-3}$$
$$(10\text{--}20)$$

Now the forecast in t is equal to a weighted moving average of the past three actuals and a forecast of Period $t-3$. This process of substitution can continue indefinitely, in a theoretical sense. Mathematically, continuing this substitution process yields the following equation:

$$F(t) = \alpha*A_{t-1} + (1 - \alpha)^1*\alpha*A_{t-2} + (1 - \alpha)^2*\alpha*A_{t-3} + (1 - \alpha)^3*\alpha*A_{t-4}$$
$$+ (1 -\alpha)^4*\alpha*A_{t-5} + (1 - \alpha)^5*\alpha*A_{t-6} + (1 - \alpha)^6*\alpha*A_{t-7}$$
$$+ \ldots + (1 - \alpha)^n*F_{t-n}$$

$$(10\text{--}21)$$

where

$$F_{t-n} = \text{Initial forecast in period } t - n$$

While Equation 10–21 seems complex, it simply states that the forecast in period t is equal to a weighted moving average of all past actual values and one initial forecast. Fortunately, this long equation is used only in textbooks to demonstrate that the simple exponential smoothing formula of Equation 10–13 yields an exponentially weighted moving average of all past actual demands. In other words, Equation 10–13, which is very simple, gives a numerical value that is equal to the solution of Equation 10–21. The sum of the weights do equal 1 when this equation is expanded to a very large number of lags.

CHAPTER 11

REGRESSION AND DECOMPOSITION METHODS

> Ain't got no future, cause I ain't got no past.
>
> 60s folk song

This chapter introduces two important forecasting methods, regression analysis and classical decomposition methods. These are important techniques for different reasons. Regression analysis is used in many forecasting systems and is one of the most popular methods for medium- to long-term forecasting (i.e., Type 2 forecasts). It is an important method for forecasting aggregate or group demands such as total company or product-line demands.

The classical decomposition method is important because it is the conceptual foundation on which more-sophisticated methods are based. These more-sophisticated methods include the Department of Commerce's Census Method II–X11 method of arriving at seasonal indexes[1] as well as the very important Winters' method and Fourier series analysis discussed in Chapters 12 and 13, respectively. The methods model time series as functions of trend and seasonal influences. The seasonal indexes that result from decomposing a series are essential for accurate forecasts in many situations.

Regression analysis is a general approach to modeling the causal relationships between one variable, such as product demand, and one or more other variables, such as price, industry sales, or other economic variables. Causal methods are sometimes referred to as extrinsic methods because they use external data. They differ from intrinsic methods in that extrinsic methods predict the future by modeling the past relationships between a dependent variable and one or more independent variables. The independent variables are considered "external," hence the term *extrinsic*.

Extrinsic methods use variables external to a time series.

Below, we discuss simple linear regression and then multiple linear regression. Finally, we introduce the decomposition method and seasonal indexes. The information and insights that these methods provide are important for short- to long-range planning activities.

REGRESSION ANALYSIS

SIMPLE LINEAR REGRESSION ANALYSIS

Dependent and Independent Variables

Causal methods such as regression analysis distinguish between the variable that is being predicted, called the *dependent variable,* and the variables used to predict that dependent variable, called *independent variables.* The dependent variable is commonly denoted by Y and the independent variables by X or some other more meaningful notations such as A for advertising or C for competition.

A dependent variable is one that is explained by the statistical model.

Consider the following situation as an example of a causal modeling application. The manager of the Big City Bookstore is reviewing sales of past years. She notes that sales have fluctuated over time. Her experiences tell her that there are several factors that can affect sales such as cyclical influences, advertising expenditures, the level of competition, the popularity of book reading (which tends to be cyclical), and population. To better understand these influences, she seeks a model that will relate book demand to important market and demographic variables.

There are a number of variables that the manager of the Big

City Bookstore may consider as predictors of total dollar book demand. These include:

Cyclical influences (*C*).

Advertising expenditures (*A*).

Competition from other bookstores (*O*).

Population (*P*).

These four independent variables should be very useful in explaining and predicting the dependent variable (*Y*). Note that in this case the dependent variable is the sales (in dollars) for all books sold, not the sales demand for a specific book or product. However, regression will work well on item forecasts as well. Conceptually, the manager believes that demand for books is dependent on the values of these other independent variables. Mathematically, this dependency is expressed by the following formula:

$$Y = f(C,A,O,P) \qquad (11\text{--}1)$$

This statement says that *Y* is a function of or dependent on *C, A, O,* and *P*. While it may seem obvious in this example, the following principle is nonetheless important.

The first step in constructing a linear regression model is correct identification of the dependent and independent variables.

Table 11–1 illustrates a number of independent-dependent variable examples. As you might imagine, it can be very difficult to model and understand all of the interactions of the many variables that influence demand. Thus, in most situations, it is very difficult to model true cause and effect relationships. Typically, the most a company can do is to model how several independent variables are useful in predicting a single dependent variable and hope that true cause and effect relationships are being modeled.

Some theory explaining the dependent variable should be the basis of selecting independent variables.

TABLE 11-1
Simple Dependent and Independent Variables

Dependent Variables as functions of *Independent Variables*

Product demand	Advertising, economic conditions, competition
Crop yield	Rainfall, temperature
Computer paper sales	Computer printer sales
Demand for consumer products	Population, price, competition
High-resolution TV	Price, economic conditions, popularity, competition

---

Causal regression relationships are much more difficult to identify than are useful predictive relationships.

Simple linear regression models have one dependent variable and only one independent variable.

Scatter Plots

Figure 11-1 shows graphs of matched pairs of independent and dependent variables; these are called *scatter plots*. In forecasting, graphical tools are extremely important because they reveal patterns about two- and three-dimensional relationships. In general, there are a variety of different relationships that can exist between two variables; several are shown in Figure 11-1.

In Figure 11-1, (*a*) illustrates a perfect positive linear relationship. The term *perfect* refers to the fact that all the points will lie perfectly on a single line. *Positive* refers to the direction of the line as being up or positive to the right. In contrast, Plot (*c*) refers to a perfect negative relationship between variables X and Y. Plots (*b*) and (*d*) are referred to as nonlinear relationships because the algebraic equations between the dependent and independent variables are nonlinear. In Plot (*b*) the squared values of the independent variable are related to Y:

$$Y = 30 + 2X^2 \tag{11-2}$$

FIGURE 11–1
Types of Relationships between Independent and Dependent Variables

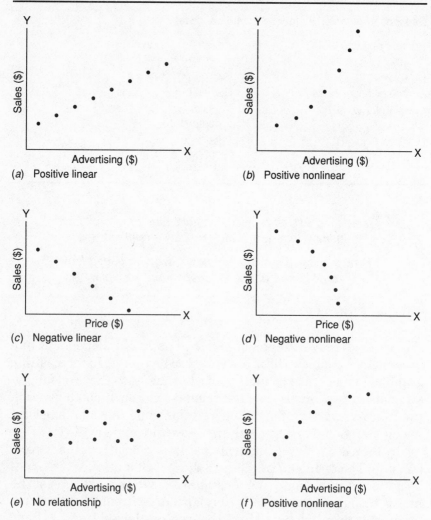

(a) Positive linear

(b) Positive nonlinear

(c) Negative linear

(d) Negative nonlinear

(e) No relationship

(f) Positive nonlinear

The interpretation of Plot (b) is that, as advertising expenditures increase, sales increase *at an increasing rate.* Plot (e) shows an instance where advertising has no influence on sales. Thus, sales and advertising are unrelated. Scatter Plot (f) shows a nonlinear relationship where each additional dollar of advertising increases sales but at a decreasing rate.

The dependent variable is on the vertical scale called Y and the independent variable is on the horizontal scale called X.

There are many possible linear and nonlinear relationships between a dependent variable and one or more independent variables.

Returning to the Big City Bookstore situation, suppose that the manager has gathered the data of Table 11–2 from the previous years. Based on this data, she decides to predict sales using only advertising expenditures [i.e., $Y = f(X)$, where X is advertising]. This model involves one dependent variable (demand) and one independent variable (advertising) as shown in Figure 11–2. We see in Figure 11–2 that high sales are associated with high advertising and low sales are associated with low advertising expenditures. This is a positive linear relationship. Having decided to model this relationship, she applies linear regression techniques.

PURPOSES OF REGRESSION ANALYSIS

Simple linear regression analysis has three general purposes:

1. To identify the relationship between the dependent variable Y and independent variable X.

TABLE 11–2
Big City Product Demands and Advertising Expenditures

Year	Demand (Y) ($000s)	Advertising Expenditures (X) ($000s)
1979	27	20
1980	23	20
1981	31	25
1982	45	28
1983	47	29
1984	42	28
1985	39	31
1986	45	34
1987	57	35
1988	59	36
1989	73	41
1990	84	45

FIGURE 11–2
Scatter Plot, Big City Bookstore

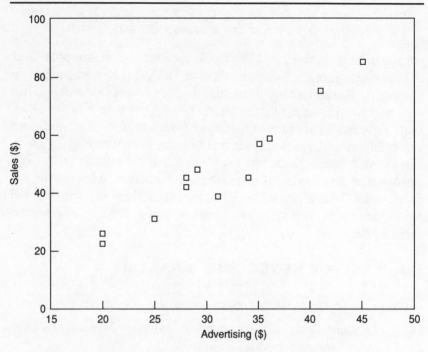

2. To measure the error in using that relationship to predict values of the dependent variable.
3. To measure the degree of association between the two variables.

We will illustrate each of these purposes in the context of the Big City Bookstore. The first purpose is illustrated below in our discussion of the method of least squares. The second purpose is illustrated through the use of a standard deviation called the standard error of estimate. The third objective is presented through discussion of the coefficients of correlation and determination.

METHOD OF LEAST SQUARES

The primary objective in simple linear regression is to model the relationship between the dependent and independent variables as accurately as possible. As will be shown, the most accurate relationship is one that has the minimum sum of squared errors, hence the term *method of least squares.*

To define the best relationship between sales and advertising in Figure 11-2 requires finding the line that best represents the data. One might assume that the most representative line would be the one that has the sum of the errors above the line equal to the sum of the errors below the line. However, it can be shown that any line that passes through the mean of X and mean of Y will have a sum of errors equal to zero. This is shown in Figure 11-3 where there are many lines with the sum of errors above and below being equal. Therefore, using this criterion is not sufficient. However, there is only one line passing through the means that yields *a minimum value when the errors are squared.* This is called the *least-squares regression line.*

A least-squares straight line is defined by the following formulas:

FIGURE 11-3
Possible Least-Squares Lines, Big City Bookstore

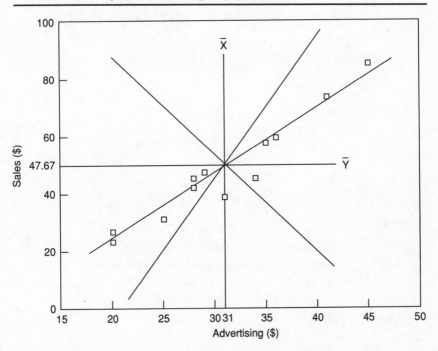

$$Y = a + bX + e \qquad (11\text{--}3)$$

$$\hat{Y} = a + bX \qquad (11\text{--}4)$$

$$e = Y - \hat{Y} \qquad (11\text{--}5)$$

where

Y = Actual value of sales
$\hat{Y}$ = Predicted or forecasted value of Y
a = Value of Y when X is equal to zero
b = Change in Y resulting from a one-unit change in X
e = Error that remains after fitting the model

The objective of minimizing the sum of squared errors is shown in Equation 11–6. By minimizing these squared errors, this method minimizes the squared deviations between the actual and predicted values of Y. The values of a and b that minimize errors are called *least squares estimators* and are calculated using Equations 11–7 and 11–8.

$$\text{MIN[Sum } (Y - \hat{Y})^2] = \text{MIN[Sum } (Y - a - bX)^2] \quad (11\text{--}6)$$

The least-squares regression line minimizes the squared deviations between actual and predicted values of Y.

In summary, the least-squares regression line is expressed as:

$$\hat{Y} = a + bX$$

where

$$a = \overline{Y} - b\overline{X} \qquad (11\text{--}7)$$

and

$$b = \frac{\Sigma XY - n\overline{X}\,\overline{Y}}{\Sigma(X^2) - n\overline{X}^2} \qquad (11\text{--}8)$$

where

$\overline{Y}$ = Mean of the dependent variable = 47.67
$\overline{X}$ = Mean of the independent variable = 31
a = Value of Y when X equals zero
b = Slope of the least-squares regression line

Referring back to the Big City Bookstore example:

$$\Sigma Y = 572$$
$$\Sigma X = 372$$
$$\Sigma XY = 19{,}205$$
$$\Sigma(X^2) = 12{,}178$$

which yields:

$$b = \frac{19{,}205 - 17{,}732}{12{,}178 - 11{,}532} = 2.280 \qquad (11\text{--}9)$$

$$a = 47.667 - 2.2802(31) = -23.02 \qquad (11\text{--}10)$$

$$\hat{Y} = -23.02 + 2.280X \qquad (11\text{--}11)$$

This final expression is the best-fit relationship for the sales and advertising data of Table 11–2. The b value of 2.280 denotes that every \$1 spent on advertising yields a \$2.28 increase in demand for books. The a in Equation 11–11 is mathematically the value of Y when X equals zero. However, practically and theoretically, this is a meaningless statement. The a values in most regression analyses are not interpretable. This is true because rarely are X values of zero included in the data. How can we know what Y equals when X equals zero if there have never been observed values of X equal to zero? The interpretation of a in this case is that sales will equal $-\$23{,}020$ when advertising is zero. Such a conclusion is illogical; there is no meaning to negative sales. In fact, the a in regression analysis is there just to position the line so that it fits the matched pairs of X and Y.

The "a" values in most regressions cannot be interpreted literally.

Table 11–3 and Figure 11–4 illustrate how closely the predicted and actual values of Y are. In Figure 11–4, the error in fitting the relationship is equal to the distance between the actual values and the regression line. Table 11–3 is the regression output of the Big City Bookstore program using a simple spreadsheet program. The column of errors shows the actual Y value minus the value that is predicted by the regression equation. The term *residual* is often used in regression analysis to denote the difference between the true value of Y and the predicted

TABLE 11–3
Actual, Fitted, and Error Terms for Big City Bookstore

Year	Actual Demand (000s)	Predicted (000s)	Error
1979	27	22.585	4.415
1980	23	22.585	0.415
1981	31	33.985	−2.986
1982	45	40.826	4.174
1983	47	43.106	3.894
1984	42	40.826	1.174
1985	39	47.667	−8.667
1986	45	54.507	−9.507
1987	57	56.787	0.213
1988	59	59.068	−0.068
1989	73	70.469	2.531
1990	84	79.589	4.411
Average	47.67		0.00
Standard deviation	18.12		5.039

value of Y for each value of X. In other words, *error* and *residual* are synonyms:

$$\text{Residual} = \text{Error} = (Y - \hat{Y}) \qquad (11\text{–}12)$$

Standard Error of Estimate

Having computed the relationship between sales and advertising, we are interested in knowing how closely the actual data fits the regression line. The best measure of fit is the standard deviation of the errors (residuals), also known as the *standard error of the estimate*. This standard deviation measures the scatter of actual values about the regression line. The standard error of the estimate is the same as the standard deviation of errors discussed in Chapter 10 except for a slight difference in the denominator. As such, it is a measure of dispersion of the actual values about the predicted values of Y. The formula for the standard error of the estimate is:

FIGURE 11–4
Least-Squares Line, Big City Bookstore

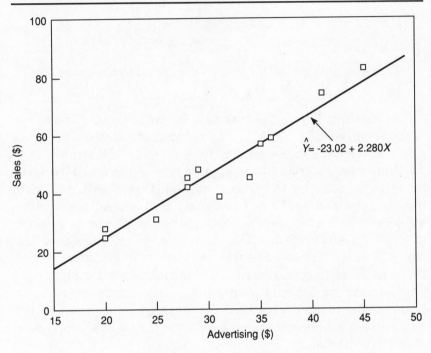

$$S_{YX} = \sqrt{\frac{\Sigma(Y - \hat{Y})^2}{n - k}} = \sqrt{\frac{\Sigma e^2}{12 - 2}} = 5.039 \quad (11\text{–}13)$$

where

Y, $\hat{Y}$, and e^2 were defined previously

n = Number of observations

k = Number of estimated parameters (a and b); in this case, 2

Note that the standard error of estimate is minimum when the sum of squared errors is minimum; hence the term *method of least-squared deviations*. A lower standard error of estimate means that the regression line is a better predictor of Y values when given X and hence a more accurate forecasting tool. Conversely, a higher standard error of estimate will tend to yield a less accurate predictor of future values of Y.

*The standard error of estimate is the standard
deviation of actual values about the predicted values.*

For the Big City Bookstore example:

$$S_{YX} = 5.039$$

This standard deviation can be compared to that of sales (Y).

$$S_Y = 18.12$$

By relating Y to X, the standard deviation has declined from 18.12 to only 5.039. Thus, X has reduced the scatter of Y from 18.12 to 5.039 as measured by these standard deviations.

To better understand the significance of the standard error of estimate, consider the process of predicting Y with and without the relationship. Prior to relating Y to X, confidence intervals about future values of Y are based on the standard deviation of Y, 18.12. After relating Y to X, confidence intervals about future values of Y are based on the standard error of estimate, which gives us smaller confidence intervals and greater accuracy.

Not knowing Y's relationship with X, let us generate a 95 percent confidence interval for Y. The confidence interval equals the mean value Y plus and minus two times the standard deviation of Y (see Chapter 7).

$$\overline{Y} +/- 2S_Y = 47.667 +/- 2(18.12) = 47.667 +/- 36.24$$

The actual Y value is expected to be in the range 11.43 to 83.91.

Now, knowing Y's relationship with X, let us generate a 95 percent confidence interval for Y given an X value of 25. This confidence interval is the predicted Y plus and minus two standard errors of estimate.

$$Y = \hat{Y} +/- 2S_{YX} = -23.02 + 2.28X +/- 2S_{YX}$$
$$Y = -23.02 + 2.280(25) +/- 2(5.04) = 33.98 +/- 10.08$$

Y, given $X = 25$, is expected to be 23.90 to 44.06.

The confidence interval with the forecasting model is considerably narrower than that without the model. In making confidence interval statements, it is not uncommon to use one standard error of estimate (5.04). This yields a 68 percent confidence interval. Thus, the sales projection is expected to be within $5,040 of the actual sales 68 percent of the time.

A good forecasting model should reduce the width of the confidence interval for future values of the dependent variable.

Coefficient of Determination

The standard error of estimate is an absolute measure of the fit of the forecasting model. A very useful measure of relative fit is the coefficient of determination, which compares the square of the standard error of estimate to the square of the standard deviation of Y. (The squares of standard deviations are called variances.) As shown below, this measure has a useful and intuitive meaning. The coefficient of determination equals the proportion of the variance in the dependent variable (Y) that is explained or eliminated by the independent variable X. The coefficient of determination is also known as R-square. It is computed as follows:

$$R^2 = \frac{\text{Explained variation}}{\text{Total variation}} = 1 - \frac{\text{Unexplained variation}}{\text{Total variation}}$$

$$= 1 - \frac{S_{YX}^2}{S_Y^2} = 1 - \frac{5.039^2}{18.122^2} = 1 - \frac{25.392}{328.334} = .923 \quad (11\text{--}14)$$

In this case, the variance of Y equals 328.33 while the variance of the errors is only a fraction of this, 25.392. Thus, by relating Y to X, we have explained or eliminated 92.3 percent of Y's original variance. The term *explained* means that there is much less scatter of Y values about the regression line than about the mean of Y. This was obvious when we considered confidence intervals above.

An R-square of 1 means that all of the variance of Y has been eliminated because the standard error of estimate is zero; all points are on the regression line. An R-square of zero indicates that the standard error of estimate equals the standard deviation of Y. When the R-square equals zero, the regression model does not predict better than the mean of Y; in other words, the regression model is useless as a predictor.

R-square is a general statistic that can be used to judge the relative accuracy of any forecasting model. For example, in using single exponential smoothing (as in Chapter 10) on a time series W, assume that the standard deviation of the errors is 10 and the standard deviation of W is 40. Then the R-square for this model is:

$$R^2 = 1 - 10^2/40^2 = 1 - 100/1600 = .9375 \text{ or } 93.75\%$$

Thus, single exponential smoothing has explained 93.75 percent of the original variance of W. The R-square statistic is very useful when judging the accuracy of forecasting models.

The R-square calculated in Equation 11–4 is called an *adjusted* R-square because the denominator of S_{YX} is adjusted for the degree of model complexity (i.e., number of parameters). As shown in Equation 11–13, $n - k$ is used. Thus, more-complex models have higher values for S_{YX} because of higher ks.

Unadjusted R-squares do not adjust S_{YX} for model complexity. Thus, S_Y and S_{YX} have the same denominator, $n - 1$. Adjusted R-square is the better statistic to use.

Frequently, another statistic, the correlation coefficient (r), which is the square root of the R-square, is used to measure the strength of the relationship between X and Y. (By convention, the correlation coefficient for a two-variable relationship is designated by a lower-case r.) The values of the correlation coefficient will always range between 1 and -1. It serves the same purpose as R-square because it can always be squared to yield the R-square. However, it provides information about the direction of the relationship. R-square is always positive; in contrast, the correlation coefficient, r, takes on the sign of the relationship. If the relationship between X and Y is positive, then the correlation coefficient is positive. If the relationship is negative, then r is negative as shown below.

If $r = -1$, then there is a perfect negative relationship.

If $r = 0$, then there is no relationship.

If $r = 1$, then there is a perfect positive relationship.

The coefficients of correlation and determination both measure the degree of association between dependent and independent variables.

The R-square and r of other relationships are not always as high as those calculated here. In such situations, the question then arises at to whether there is a significant relationship between variables with a low r. That is, if R-square or r does not equal a high value, does this denote no relationship between Y and X or is there a statistically significant relationship between Y and X? This question can be answered through a simple hypothesis test.

A hypothesis test can be used to determine whether a variable is statistically significantly different than another selected value. For example, we can perform a test to determine whether the correlation coefficient is statistically significantly different than zero. If r is significantly different from zero, then this denotes that there is a significant relationship between Y and X. In the case of the Big City Bookstore, the hypothesis test will help to determine if advertising and sales are significantly correlated.

Below, find a common procedure used in statistical hypothesis testing in simple linear regression. A test statistic will be calculated. If there are more than 30 observations used to fit the relationship, then a Z table is used to perform the test. If there are 30 or fewer observations, then a t table is used to perform the test. (We do not develop the theory surrounding these t- and Z-tests; nonetheless, you should be able to apply them validly based on the explanation.) As shown below, the formulas used in the test are the same whether a t or Z table is used.

$$t_r = \frac{|r|}{\sqrt{\dfrac{1 - r^2}{n - 2}}} \qquad Z_r = \frac{|r|}{\sqrt{\dfrac{1 - r^2}{n - 2}}}$$

where

$|\quad|$ denotes absolute values

Using the previously calculated r value, a t-test is performed on the significance of r. The statistical hypothesis that is being tested is given below:

$$H_0: r = 0 \qquad\qquad H_1: r \neq 0$$

The explanation is as follows: The null hypothesis (H_0) states that the two variables (advertising and sales) are not related. The alternative hypothesis (H_1) states that they are related and r is significantly different from zero. Obviously, the manager in this case hopes to reject the null hypothesis, accept the alternative, and conclude that advertising and sales are positively correlated.

If advertising and demand are unrelated, then the calculated t or Z value should not be very high, for example, less than 2. In contrast, if they are related, then the calculated t or Z value will be greater than 2. The question of how high t or Z should be before we can comfortably conclude that there is a relationship between demand and advertising is answered one of two ways.

A significant t or Z value is a value that is so high that it is very unlikely that it could have come from a relationship that has zero correlation. For example, we infer that there is a relationship between sales and advertising if the t value is inconsistent with t values expected from a no-correlation relationship. If the dependent and independent variables are unrelated, then the calculated t or Z values should be low. High t or Z values come from related dependent and independent variables. The bounds of high and low are defined in Table 11–4.

TABLE 11–4
Critical Values of t and z for .05 and .01 Probabilities

	t *Value*		Z *Value*	
n–k	.05	.01	.05	.01
1	12.73	63.66	n.a.	n.a.
2	4.30	9.92	n.a.	n.a.
3	3.18	5.84	n.a.	n.a.
5	2.57	4.03	n.a.	n.a.
8	2.31	3.56	n.a.	n.a.
10	2.23	3.17	n.a.	n.a.
15	2.13	2.95	n.a.	n.a.
20	2.09	2.85	n.a.	n.a.
30	2.04	2.75	n.a.	n.a.
40	2.02	2.70	1.96	2.58
50	2.01	2.68	1.96	2.58
100	1.98	2.63	1.96	2.58
500	1.96	2.58	1.96	2.58

n.a. = Not applicable.
  Probability of t or z being greater than these values is given by the column headings, either .05 or .01, respectively, when there is no relationship between variables.

Table 11–4 illustrates the t and Z values when Y and X are unrelated. As shown in the table, when 12 matched pairs of Xs and Ys are regressed and there is no relationship, then only 1 out of 100 times will the calculated t value be greater than 3.17. This t-value is found in the row where $n - k = 10$. That is, if there is no relationship between Y and X, then 99 times out of 100, the absolute t value will be less than 3.17. If an absolute t value exceeds 3.17, then the most logical inference is that Y and X are related.

The value of k in $n - k$ equals the number of parameters that are being estimated in the model. For example, k equals 2 for simple linear regression because a and b had to be estimated, and k equals 1 for single exponential smoothing because only alpha had to be estimated. Let us run this test for the Big City Bookstore. The t statistic for the Big City Bookstore is:

$$t = \frac{|\,r\,|}{\sqrt{\dfrac{1 - r^2}{n - 2}}} = \frac{|\,.961\,|}{\sqrt{\dfrac{1 - .923}{12 - 2}}} = 10.95$$

Since 10.95 is greater than the critical value of 3.17 from Table 11–4 for $n - k$ of 10, then we conclude that advertising and sales are significantly correlated. We conclude that the relationship is useful in predicting future values of Y. (As always, these predicted values will be true only if the relationship continues into the future. Statistically, there is no way to be sure what the future will bring.) Finally, let us emphasize that this t-test is only valid when using a single independent variable to predict the dependent variable. The test is not valid for relationships using multiple independent variables.

Statistical t tests on r and R-square can confirm the significance of the relationship between dependent and independent variables.

Cause and Effect

In the case of the Big City Bookstore, a scatter plot showed that the two variables had a positive linear relationship. This was confirmed by the standard error of the estimate, the r value, and the t-test. We may be tempted to state that there is a cause-and-effect relationship between advertising and sales; in other words, an increase in advertising expenditures will lead to an increase in sales. While this seems logical, it is a mistake to assume that this is a true cause-and-effect relationship without spending considerable time analyzing the relationship further. Other factors that influence sales may have been in operation during the time sales and advertising were measured. We expect a causal relationship between sales and advertising, but statistical significance is not sufficient to prove this. However, statistical significance is necessary to detect causality.

Correlation is association between Y
and X, not causality between Y and X.

In reality, there may be a third factor that influences both the dependent and the independent variables. Consider the following hypothetical situation. In the Big City Bookstore example, sales and advertising expenditures might seem highly correlated, but each is independent of each other. The relationship may seem significant, but, in fact, is not, because sales have been increasing due to the increase in the population surrounding the store. Because sales have been increasing, the manager has been increasing advertising, not knowing that advertising has no effect. These conditions make it appear that sales and advertising have a true cause-and-effect relationship and that we have measured that relationship. Thus, we should always be careful to remember the principle stated below.

A high r or R-square value does not mean
there is a cause-and-effect relationship.

In terms of cause and effect, past studies have shown a high correlation between skirt length and stock market performance, church attendance and beer consumption, and the price of scotch and clergy salaries. These nonsensical examples illustrate the need for care in concluding that a cause-and-effect relationship exists between two variables simply because they are highly correlated. Only if we have measured and controlled for other influencing factors on the dependent variable can we be confident that there is a cause-and-effect relationship. We explore this situation in the next section after reviewing the steps of regression analysis.

Review of Regression Analysis Steps

In summary, these are the steps to follow in performing a simple linear regression:

1. Determine the dependent and independent variables. Theory should dictate what independent variables should be included.
2. Develop a scatter plot of X and Y. Determine if the relationship appears to be linear or nonlinear. Transform the variables if nonlinearities are present (see section below concerning nonlinearities).
3. Compute the regression equation.
4. Compute the standard error of the estimate. This provides a measure of the "fit" of the data to its regression line.
5. Compute the coefficient of determination. This is a measure of the amount of variation in Y that is caused by X.
6. Perform a hypothesis test using the t-statistic to determine if the X and Y variables are significantly correlated.
7. Interpret the significance of the relationship, practically and theoretically.

MULTIPLE LINEAR REGRESSION

Multiple linear regression involves one dependent variable and more than one independent variable.

When using regression analysis, it is almost always better to build models that relate the dependent variable to more than one independent variable. As you will recall, in the Big City Bookstore example, the manager originally identified several variables that could affect sales—cyclical influences, advertising expenditures, competition, and population.

Assume that the manager is concerned about advertising and competition effects on sales. The effect that competition has had on demand at her store might be a function of the total square feet of competitor stores in her area. The number of square feet of competitive bookstores in her area is shown in Table 11–5.

Multiple regression is important because it can measure the simultaneous effects of several independent variables on a depen-

TABLE 11–5
Big City Product Demands and Advertising Expenditures

Year	Demand (Y) ($000s)	Advertising (X) ($000s)	Competitor Display (Z) (000s of square feet)
1979	27	20	10
1980	23	20	15
1981	31	25	15
1982	45	28	15
1983	47	29	20
1984	42	28	25
1985	39	31	35
1986	45	34	35
1987	57	35	20
1988	59	36	30
1989	73	41	20
1990	84	45	20

dent variable. As we mentioned, if we measure demand only as a function of advertising over the last 12 years, then we may be misled. As shown in Table 11–5, competitor square footage has varied during this time period. Normally, the demand at a store is affected by the number and size of competing stores. To better understand the problem of not accounting or controlling for competition when studying advertising influence, consider the following three relationships.

$$\hat{Y} = -23.02 + 2.280X \qquad (11\text{--}15)$$
$$(t_b = 11.5) \qquad\qquad t_r = 10.95 \quad R^2 = .923$$

$$\hat{Y} = 37.34 \quad + .477Z \qquad (11\text{--}16)$$
$$(t_b = .687) \qquad\qquad t_r = .686 \quad R^2 = .045$$

$$\hat{Y} = -18.80 + 2.525X \quad - .545Z \qquad (11\text{--}17)$$
$$(t_b = 19.50) \quad (t_b = -4.31) \quad t_r = \text{N.A.} \quad R^2 = .973$$

where

$$Y = \text{Demand in \$1,000s}$$
$$X = \text{Advertising in \$1,000s}$$
$$Z = \text{Competition in 1,000s of square feet}$$
$$t_b = b/S_b \text{ as explained below}$$

Equation 11–15 has already been discussed and is consistent with the theory that increased advertising will increase sales. In contrast, Equation 11–16 is confounding. Based on theory, one would expect that increased competition would yield lower sales. However, the value of the b-coefficient for Z is positive (.477). It denotes that every 1,000 square feet of competitor space will yield a \$477 increase in demand for books. This is inconsistent with theory, which states that increased competition in a market will normally drive demand down at any one store. Herein lies the problem with our understanding of the effects of competition. The problem with Equation 11–16 is that we have a flawed model. It does not measure the changes in demand that result from simultaneous changes in competition and advertising. Equation 11–16 does not control for the influence of advertising on demand. Fortunately, multiple regression exists to measure the simultaneous influence of several variables.

Multiple regression measures the simultaneous influence of several independent variables on the dependent variable.

Equation 11–17 is the result of multiple regression. As the equation shows, the influence of advertising is positive, while the influence of increased competition is negative. As measured by the R-square, the latter relationship is the most significant and accurate.

Statistical Tests on Regression Coefficients

Equations 11–15 to 11–17 show another statistic under each b-coefficient. This statistic is a t_b value that measures the number of standard deviations the regression coefficient is away from the "no-relationship" coefficient of zero. That is, if a regression coefficient (i.e., b value) is near zero, then that variable is not related to the dependent variable. These t values are calculated by dividing the regression coefficient (b) by a standard deviation (S_b), which we do not develop here. If there is a relationship between two variables, then their regression coefficient (b) should be statistically significantly different than zero. The simple t- or Z-test is easily performed as b divided by S_b. The results of that test are the t_b values given in parentheses below each coefficient. Remembering that t values that are greater than 2 standard deviations are significant, we see that in Equation 11–15 the t value of 11.5 denotes that the coefficient of advertising, X, is 11.5 standard deviations away from zero. Thus, there is a very significant relationship between advertising (X) and sales (Y). This is also confirmed by the t_r value.

In contrast, the t_b value of the regression coefficient for Equation 11–16 is very low, .687. This denotes that the regression coefficient for competition is not significantly different than zero. There appears to be no relationship between competition and sales. This is also confirmed by the t_r value. As we mentioned above, this is not the right conclusion theoretically.

Equation 11–16 has not shown there to be a relationship between competition and sales because the influence of advertising is not measured in Equation 11–16. We have not controlled for advertising when measuring the influence of competition. The R-square for Equation 11–16 is extremely low, and we have found that there is no relationship between competition and sales as measured by Equation 11–16.

Controlling for the influences of other variables is essential to achieve correct results in regression analysis.

Finally, and most important, Equation 11–17 illustrates a more valid approach to measuring advertising and competition effects on sales. As the equation shows, the R-square of this relationship is highest, the t values of the regression coefficients are all very significantly different than zero (i.e., greater than 2), and the signs of the coefficients are all in the right directions. Advertising has a positive effect on sales, and competition has a negative impact. Finally, we see that the effect of advertising is greater after we have controlled for competition in the relationship. Each dollar of advertising is associated with a $2.53 increase in sales. Only by simultaneously controlling for (i.e., including) each independent variable in the relationship were we able to measure the true relationships between demand, competition, and advertising.

The t_r test developed for the two-variable equations (11–15 and 11–16) is not valid for multiple-regression relationships, such as Equation 11–17. Individual t_b and another test (called an F-test) are used to test the significance of multiple-regression relationships. A full development of these is beyond our purpose.

General Multiple-Regression Equation

The general form of the multiple-regression model is:

$$Y = a + b_1X_1 + b_2X_2 \ldots b_nX_n + e \qquad (11\text{--}18)$$

where the notation is similar to the notation already defined above. The number of independent variables included in a regression relationship should rarely exceed six or seven, because there are seldom six or seven significant independent variables.

Dummy Variables for Modeling Events

Multiple regression is a versatile technique for measuring the relationships between variables. One of its capabilities in operational forecasting is modeling the effects of qualitative attributes or events on the dependent variable. It does this through the use of dummy variables (also called *dichotomous variables*). Important uses of dummy variables include the modeling of promotions, outliers, and other special events. In addition, dummy variables can model seasonal effects.

Dummy variables have only two values, zero and one. These variables denote the occurrence of special events, such as outliers, promotions, price increases, or new product introductions. These dummy variables are treated like any other variables in regression analysis. Consider the following simple example.

A firm has experienced the following 12 months of demand for a product. This product is not seasonal; but in period 7, a special promotion was run on the product. Management would like to measure the effect of the promotion.

Time (t)	1	2	3	4	5	6	7	8	9	10	11	12
Demand (D)	13	16	18	22	24	28	42	34	39	41	44	46
Special promotion (P)	0	0	0	0	0	0	1	0	0	0	0	0

This data was used in a multiple-regression relationship of the following form.

$$\hat{D}_t = a + b_1 t + b_2 P_t$$

The following relationship was found:

$$\hat{D}_t = 9.36 + 3.13t + 10.75P_t$$
$$(t_b = 48.48) \quad (t_b = 13.34)$$
$$R^2 = .996 \quad \text{Standard deviation of errors } (S_{yx}) = .77$$

This relationship has a simple interpretation. The trend for this product has been increasing by 3.13 units per month, as measured by b_1 for t. In addition, in Period 7, demand increased an additional 10.75 units, as measured by b_2 for P_t. This is the result of the promotional influence, P_7. Note that P_t is equal to zero for all periods except 7; therefore, the promotional effect was zero for all periods except 7. This example can be generalized to modeling any events that can be represented through zeros and ones.

This is such a simple example, you no doubt could have estimated the effect of the promotion with little difficulty. However, we need an objective way to measure these in an automated environment that processes data that is not nearly as simple as our example. Multiple regression is invaluable in such applications.

There is another important operational forecasting use of dummy variables. It is possible to use dummy variables to measure the seasonal effects on demand. Because this involves concepts that are developed later in this chapter, we defer the discussion of seasonal dummy variables to the appendix to this chapter.

*The use of dummy variables provides
important measures of special event effects.*

Nonlinear Relationships in Linear Regression

Even though regression analysis is known as linear regression, it can model many different types of nonlinear relationships. While we cannot develop these methods extensively, the use of logarithms and other transformations of dependent variables can be used to model a wide variety of nonlinear functions. To apply linear regression to nonlinear relationships, the independent or dependent variables must first be transformed to yield a linear relationship. Consider Equations 11–19 through 11–22.

$$Y = a + b\log X \qquad (11\text{--}19)$$

$$Y = a + bX + cX^2 \qquad (11\text{--}20)$$

$$Y = a + bX + cX^2 + dX^3 \qquad (11\text{-}21)$$

$$\log Y = a + b \log X \qquad (11\text{-}22)$$

Equation 11-19 is transformed to a linear relationship by taking logarithms of X and regressing those versus Y. Equation 11-20 is fitted by creating a new variable with the values of X^2; the same is true in Equation 11-21. Finally, Equation 11-22 can be fitted by taking logs of both Y and X. Then, linear regression can proceed as shown above.

Advantages

The advantages of regression analysis include the ability to relate a single dependent variable to one or more independent variables. Its ability to find apparent causal relationships that not only predict but explain demand makes it a very powerful technique. It is the only causal or extrinsic method that is commonly used in forecasting systems. Also, its many error statistics help to assure that valid relationships result from its use. Being widely and easily applied by computers, regression methods are the most accurate method for forecasting medium- to long-range demands. They are used in many forecasting systems for event filtering and are an important technique used in Fourier series analysis in Chapter 13. Finally, regression software is very inexpensive.

Regression methods are versatile.

Disadvantages

The biggest disadvantage of regression methods in forecasting is that, in order to forecast Y, future values of the independent variable must be known. Thus, multiple forecasts are needed to apply regression analysis. To the extent that the independent variables influence the dependent variables in later time periods (e.g., $Y_t = f(X_{t-2})$), this problem is lessened. Because of the cost and complexity of developing extrinsic models, they are generally used in long-range forecasts. Even after considerable time and effort have been expended to fit regression models, we do not have assurance that we have found the best causal model. Finally, there is considerably greater art and science in applying regression methods. Consequently, before applying multiple regression, it is suggested that you study it further in one or more references.[2]

Other Extrinsic Forecasting Methods

There are a variety of extrinsic methods other than multiple linear regression that are used in forecasting. These include econometric, multiequation econometric, and multivariate autoregressive–moving-average methods. While these methods are important in short- to long-term forecasting, they are considerably more difficult to understand and apply than the methods of this text. They cost more and require a larger research department than many firms have today. These methods are not used for routine forecasting of many thousands of items. Improvements in forecasting system intelligence may someday make these methods important in operational forecasting systems.

DECOMPOSITION AND SEASONAL INDEXES

CLASSICAL TIME SERIES DECOMPOSITION METHOD

A forecasting method that is commonly used in short- to long-term aggregate or group forecasting is the classical time series decomposition method.[3] In decomposition, we describe a time series through a multicomponent model. The model is:

$$Y_t = f(T,C,S,e)$$

where

Y_t = Actual value of the time series at time t
f = Mathematical function of
T = Trend
C = Cyclical influences
S = Seasonal influences
e = Error

T, C, S, and e were defined in Chapter 8.

Past Relationships May or May Not Remain Constant

Causal or extrinsic models are based on the assumption that the past relationships between dependent and independent variables remain constant. Of course, some believe the only thing that remains constant in the long run is change. There are times when changes affect our company, industry, country, or world. One notable event that made many extrinsic forecasts invalid throughout the world was the 1973 oil embargo. Middle Eastern suppliers restricted the flow of oil to the United States.

Gasoline, plastic, and many other products that are petroleum based, including pharmaceutical drugs, had very rapid price increases because the price of oil increased dramatically over a short period of time. Thus, the short-term forecasts of the price and demand for products throughout the world were very inaccurate.

However, there also were long-term effects from this crisis. The embargo and resulting price increases caused a near global effort to conserve oil and energy. The electric power industry was impacted significantly from the long-term effects of the oil embargo. Prior to the embargo, energy demand was increasing at the rate of about 3 percent a year. After the embargo and the nationwide efforts to reduce energy demands, the rate of growth in the electric power industry went to approximately zero. Although the rate of growth has increased recently, it has not rebounded back to its previous pre-embargo rate.

While we as a society will benefit from this conservation effort, not everyone is better off. The leadtimes in the electric power industry are very long. Nuclear power plants take more than 10 years to plan and construct. Many electric companies did not or could not change their plans for new nuclear power plants. The result was an oversupply of electricity capacity and the last-minute cancellation of nuclear power plants. The problems in overcapacity persist even today. Demands for electricity remain below their historical growth trends, and conservation and environmental concerns will continue to keep these demands low. Neither of these events were predicted by the electric power industry prior to 1973.

Trend-cyclical variations are commonly modeled together and referred to as *trend-cyclical components*. We will only model the trend and seasonal components in the examples of this chapter. This is so because cyclical variations are still being studied and researched, but there is as yet no simple modeling technique to predict future cyclical values.

Typically, seasonal variations are thought of as being only quarterly or monthly, but there are seasonal variations that occur every 4 years (e.g., Olympics), every 12 months, every 4 quarters, every 52 weeks, every 13 weeks, every 7 days, every 24 hours, and so on. The key to identifying seasonal influences is whether the influence is recurrent and periodic.

Error is the residual component of a time series that is not explained by *T, C,* and *S.* Large errors can be caused by irregular influences. Irregular influences in a time series are unpredictable and can be caused by random events such as weather, earthquakes, wars, floods, hurricanes, governmental action (domestic or foreign), and labor unrest. The error component of a time series is a "catchall" for all the unexplained variation in a time series. It is also referred to as *residual error.*

There are two general types of decomposition models, an additive and a multiplicative.

$$\textit{Additive: } Y = T + C + S + e$$
$$\textit{Multiplicative: } Y = T \times C \times S \times e$$

Since the multiplicative model is used most frequently, we will develop it here. Below we will provide guidelines for choosing between multiplicative and additive models. In the multiplicative model, Y is the product of the four components, $T, C, S,$ and $e.$ The $C, S,$ and e are indexes that are proportions centered on 1. For example, if a period has a seasonal factor of 1.10, this denotes that demand is 10 percent higher than the typical value. Similarly, a cyclical component of .92 illustrates a below-average cyclical effect for the period $t.$ Only the trend (T) is measured in the same units as the item being forecast. For example, the forecast of a product group for the month of April might be:

$$\hat{Y}_{\text{April}} = T \times C \times S = 240,000 \times 1.36 \times .98 = 319,872$$

where the cyclical effect is above normal and the seasonal effect below normal.

When forecasting, e is unknown and therefore assumed to be equal to 1.0. Figure 11–5 illustrates the four components of a multiplicative time series. The procedure for identifying these is illustrated below.

FIGURE 11-5
Anatomy of a Time Series

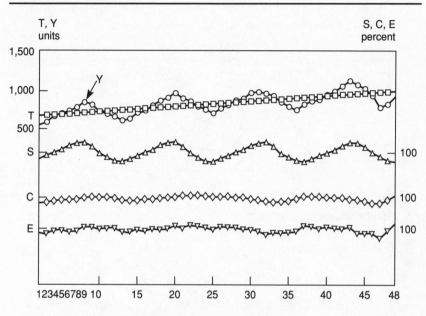

Multiplicative versus Additive Models

Additive models are used when it is evident from plots of the data that seasonal and cyclical influences are unrelated to the general level of demand. That is, an additive seasonal model denotes that demand for soft drinks in July is always 100 units higher than the trend in July. A multiplicative model is used when the seasonal influence is a percentage of the trend in July (for example, 10 percent higher than the trend). Figure 11-6 illustrates each of these situations.

The determination of whether seasonal influences are additive or multiplicative is usually evident from a graph of the data. As shown in Figure 11-6(a), if the differences of the peaks and troughs get greater as the trend increases, then a multiplicative model is used. In contrast, as shown in Figure 11-6(b), if the differences between the peaks and troughs stay the same—that is, are independent of the level of the series—then an additive model is the correct choice. There are statistical tests that can be used in an automated environment to determine which model is correct.

FIGURE 11–6
Additive and Multiplicative Seasonal Influences

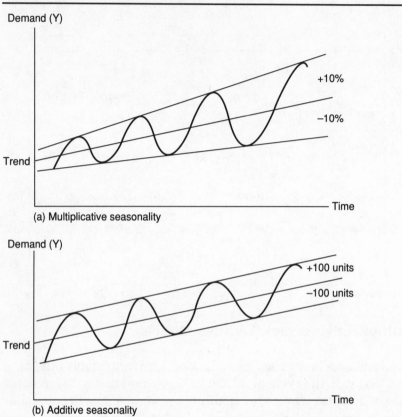

(a) Multiplicative seasonality

(b) Additive seasonality

However, as already mentioned, most series are multiplicative; therefore, most operational forecasting systems assume that all series will be modeled using multiplicative models.

Seasonal Variation–The Ratio to Moving Average Method

Seasonal indexes provide a very important insight regarding demand. When pronounced seasonality exists in a time series, we normally have a powerful tool for short-term forecasting. It is very important to model seasonality because detection and anticipation of peak seasonal demands can mean the difference between a profitable and an unprofitable year.

Anticipating peak-season demand is essential to accurate planning.

In addition, seasonal indexes are important because the best way to identify trend components of a time series is to first deseasonalize the time series. The calculation of seasonal indexes is accomplished through the use of centered moving averages using a method called the *ratio to moving average method.* It is necessary to measure seasonality first because it is very difficult to measure the trend of a highly seasonal series. By calculating seasonal indexes first, we can then estimate the trend.

To decompose a series is easy because the multiplicative time series model yields several simple identities that are used to estimate individual components. For example, given

$$Y_t = TCSe$$

then

$$Se = \frac{Y_t}{TC} = \frac{T\!\!\!/C\!\!\!/Se}{T\!\!\!/C\!\!\!/}$$

This denotes that the actual value of period t divided by the trend and cyclical components equals the seasonal and error components. As shown below, the combined trend and cyclical components are estimated using moving averages.

Let us return to the Big City Bookstore example. Suppose the manager desires to identify the trend and seasonality of her business. In order to do this, she plots the past four years' quarterly sales data (in Figure 11–7) and computes a centered moving average and seasonal factors.

In order to compute an annual centered moving average for quarterly data, first compute four-period moving averages. Four-period moving averages are used because the four-quarter total is a full year and, therefore, the average is neither seasonally high nor seasonally low. In other words, because the sum of four quarters is neither seasonally high nor seasonally low, the average will not be seasonally high or low. For example, the four-period moving averages for Periods 2 and 3 are:

$$\text{Moving average} \atop \text{for Periods 1–4} = \frac{72 + 110 + 117 + 172}{4} = 117.750$$

$$\text{Moving average} \atop \text{for Periods 2–5} = \frac{110 + 117 + 172 + 76}{4} = 118.750$$

FIGURE 11–7
Big City Bookstore

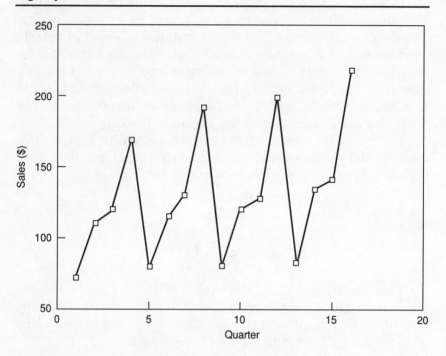

As shown in Table 11–6, the four-period moving average for Periods 1 to 4 will be centered between Periods 1 and 4, which is the beginning of Period 3 and the end of Period 2. Also, the moving average for Periods 2 to 5 will be centered at the beginning of Period 4 and the end of Period 3. In order to get the average centered on Period 3 (i.e., $t = 3.5$), the mean of these two moving averages is calculated as shown below.

$$\text{Centered moving average for Period 3} = \frac{117.75 + 118.75}{2} = 118.250$$

Because it contains no seasonality, the centered moving average for Period 3 equals the combined trend and cyclical components for that period. Using the identity $Se = Y/(TC)$, we then find the combined seasonal and error component for Period 3, which is:

$$\frac{T\!\!\!/C\!\!\!/Se}{T\!\!\!/C\!\!\!/} = Se = \frac{Y_3}{TC_3} = \frac{117}{118.250} = .989$$

TABLE 11-6
Seasonal Indexes Percent of Centered Moving Averages

Period (t)	Year	Quarter	Sales	Four-Period Average Simple	Four-Period Average Centered	Percent MA
1	1	1	72			
2		2	110	117.750		
3		3	117	118.750	118.250	.989
4		4	172	119.250	119.000	1.445
5	2	1	76	122.500	120.875	.629
6		2	112	128.000	125.250	.894
7		3	130	128.500	128.250	1.014
8		4	194	130.250	129.375	1.500
9	3	1	78	129.750	130.000	.600
10		2	119	131.500	130.625	.911
11		3	128	132.250	131.875	.971
12		4	201	136.000	134.125	1.499
13	4	1	81	139.250	137.625	.589
14		2	134	143.000	141.125	.950
15		3	141			
16		4	216			

Quarters	Average		Unadjusted Seasonal Indexes		Final Seasonal Indexes
1	(.629 + .600 + .589)/3	=	.606		.606
2	(.894 + .911 + .950)/3	=	.918	Times	.919
3	(.989 + 1.014 + .971)/3	=	.992	4.000	.993
4	(1.445 + 1.500 + 1.499)/3	=	1.481	3.997	1.482
			3.997		4.000

where

$$Y_3 = \text{Actual value for Period 3}$$
$$TC_3 = \text{Centered moving average for Period 3}$$

After the combined seasonal and error (Se) components are computed for all of the available periods, they are averaged to reduce the error and to isolate the seasonal component as shown at the bottom of Table 11-6. The final computation performed at the bottom of the table is to adjust the seasonal factors so that they equal 4.0, which is the number of periods per year. This is required because the average seasonal factor must equal 1 (i.e., the sum of all seasonal factors should total the number of periods per year). Otherwise, the final forecast would not be correct. In order to accomplish this, we divided 4.0 by 3.997 and multiplied this factor by each of the seasonal indexes.

Interpreting Seasonal Indexes

The seasonal indexes for the Big City Bookstore are indicative of a repeating pattern. As shown at the bottom of Table 11–6, the first, second, and third quarters of the year are seasonally low, while the fourth quarter is seasonally high. The interpretation of the index for Quarter 1 is that its sales are only 60.6 percent of the average quarterly sales of the year centered on Quarter 1. In other words, the sales for Quarter 1 are typically only 60.6 percent of the trend-cyclical values of that quarter. In contrast, the average sales for Quarter 4 are 48.2 percent higher than the trend-cyclical value of that quarter.

Seasonal indexes give good insight into the factors influencing demand.

In the brief time that it takes to calculate seasonal indexes, management can gain important knowledge about the demand for their products. As we will see later, seasonal indexes are an important part of any good forecasting system. Also, seasonal indexes are used by Winters' and Fourier series methods discussed in Chapters 12 and 13, respectively.

Deseasonalizing Demand to Identify Trend

Having identified the seasonal component of demand, the trend of the series can be estimated. Decomposing trend is illustrated in the equation below.

$$\frac{Y}{S} = \frac{TCSe}{S} = TCe \qquad (11\text{–}23)$$

where

$$S = \text{Seasonal index for period } t$$

Using the identity of Equation 11–23, Table 11–7 shows deseasonalized sales for the four-year period. These values are

TABLE 11-7
Deseasonalized Sales

(1) Period (t)	(2) Year	(3) Quarter	(4) Y_t	(5) S_t	(6) Deseasonalized Sales (TCe)	(7) Trend (T_t)
1	1	1	72	.606	118.81	115.63
2		2	110	.919	119.70	117.49
3		3	117	.993	117.83	119.35
4		4	172	1.482	116.06	121.20
5	2	1	76	.606	125.41	123.06
6		2	112	.919	121.87	124.91
7		3	130	.993	130.92	126.77
8		4	194	1.482	130.90	128.63
9	3	1	78	.606	128.71	130.48
10		2	119	.919	129.49	132.34
11		3	128	.993	128.90	134.19
12		4	201	1.482	135.63	136.05
13	4	1	81	.606	133.66	137.91
14		2	134	.919	145.81	139.76
15		3	141	.993	141.99	141.62
16		4	216	1.482	145.75	143.48

$T_t = 113.776 + 1.85t$, where $t = 1$, Quarter 1 of Year 1.

shown in column 6. These deseasonalized values are important in identifying movements in the trend over time. That is, just as we track deseasonalized inflation and unemployment rates in the economy, we should track deseasonalized demands in our organizations.

*Management should track deseasonalized
demands to detect trend changes early.*

Using Simple Linear Regression to Forecast Trend

Having calculated deseasonalized sales, simple linear regression can now be used to estimate the trend in sales. Figure 11-8 shows deseasonalized sales calculated above versus time on the X axis. In addition, we see a trend line that was estimated using the method of least-squared deviations. The resulting relationship is:

FIGURE 11–8
Deseasonalized Values and Trend, Big City Bookstore

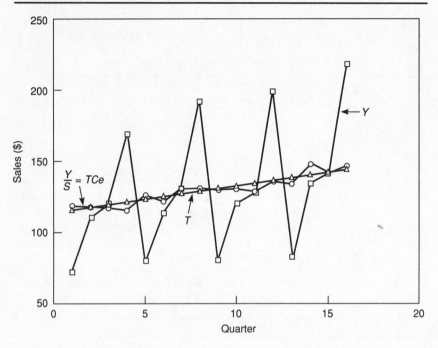

$$\text{Trend} = T_t = 113.78 + 1.85t$$

where $t = 1$, Quarter 1 of Year 1. The resulting T_t values are shown in column 7 of Table 11–7.

Having decomposed sales into trend and seasonal components, let us see how well the model fits the data. Table 11–8 shows the calculation of fitted values using T and S. Columns 5 and 6 show the seasonal indexes and trend values, respectively. The products of these two are shown in column 7 and are called the fitted values of sales. Finally, column 8 shows the resulting error from this fitting process. These errors are quite low, and, as shown at the bottom of the table, the coefficient of determination, R-square, is quite high. Of the original variance of Y (45.341^2), 99 percent has been removed by decomposing it into seasonal and trend components. The standard deviation of the errors shown in Table 11–8 is only 3.57, and its square (i.e., variance) is 12.75. This is an ex-

TABLE 11-8
Fitted Decomposition Time Series Model

(1) Period (t)	(2) Year	(3) Quarter	(4) Sales	(5) Seasonal (S)	(6) Trend (T)	(7) Fitted Values TS	(8) Error
1	1	1	72	.606	115.632	70.073	1.927
2		2	110	.919	117.489	107.972	2.028
3		3	117	.993	119.345	118.509	-1.509
4		4	172	1.481	121.201	179.620	-7.620
5	2	1	76	.606	123.057	74.573	1.427
6		2	112	.919	124.913	114.795	-2.796
7		3	130	.993	126.769	125.882	4.118
8		4	194	1.481	128.626	190.623	3.377
9	3	1	78	.606	130.482	79.072	-1.072
10		2	119	.919	132.338	121.619	-2.619
11		3	128	.993	134.194	133.255	-5.255
12		4	201	1.481	136.050	201.627	-.627
13	4	1	81	.606	137.907	83.571	-2.571
14		2	134	.919	139.763	128.442	5.558
15		3	141	.993	141.619	140.628	.372
16		4	216	1.481	143.475	212.630	3.370
Mean			130.06				-.020
Standard deviation			45.341				3.570

$$R^2 = 1 - \frac{3.570^2}{45.341^2} = .99 = 99\%$$

traordinarily good fit, a fact that we discuss later in the section on disadvantages below.

To this point, we have only fitted past history using decomposition. Table 11–9 illustrates forecasting two years into the future using the seasonal indexes of Table 11–6 and the trend equation. The patterns of the forecasted values very closely match the pattern of the past data.

Steps in Classical Decomposition

The steps to forecast using the classical decomposition method are:

1. Perform a moving average in accordance with the appropriate number of periods.
2. Center the moving average.
3. Compute the actual as a percentage of the centered moving average to obtain the seasonal factor for each period.

TABLE 11–9
Forecast of a Decomposed Time Series

(1) Period (t)	(2) Year	(3) Quarter	(4) Seasonal (S)	(5) Trend (T)	(6) TS
17	5	1	.606	145.328	88.069
18		2	.919	147.184	135.262
19		3	.993	149.040	147.997
20		4	1.482	150.896	223.628
21	6	1	.606	152.752	92.568
22		2	.919	154.608	142.085
23		3	.993	156.464	155.369
24		4	1.482	158.320	234.630

Adjust the total of the seasonal factors to equal the number of periods per year.

4. Deseasonalize the time series as in Table 11–7.
5. Compute the trend-cyclical regression equation using deseasonalized data.
6. Multiply the forecasted trend values by their appropriate seasonal factors for a more accurate forecast.

While completing each of these steps, always check and adjust for outliers. Methods for doing so are discussed in Chapter 14.

Table 11–10 illustrates the use of the decomposition method on Series F from Appendix B at the end of this book. We leave it to the reader to verify each of the above steps in this table. Finally, as discussed in the box on the next page:

Medium- to long-term forecasts should include cyclical influence adjustments.

Advantages

Classical decomposition of a time series is easily understood and applied. It provides management with an important perspective on the underlying cause-and-effect relationships in a time series. By decomposing a time series into its components, management can analyze and identify the causes of these variations. Also, this

---

Two-Year-Ahead Forecasts Should Include Cyclical Influences

Sometimes it is surprising how well time series methods like decomposition, Winters', and Fourier series forecast the next several months and, frequently, the next year or two. A good track record during one time period does not ensure a good track record in future time periods. *Any company that forecasts ahead for two or more years without a business cycle correction is defying the laws of economics and documented history.* Cyclical influences are rarely directly included in forecasts generated by operational forecasting systems because they are so difficult to forecast. It is, however, still very important to have aggregate and group forecasts that reflect cyclical influences. It is even more important to have contingency plans that are effective when significant changes in business cycles occur. The value of future cyclical indexes can be estimated using sophisticated forecasting and econometric methods. These indexes can then be used to adjust the forecasts resulting from any of the techniques developed in this book.

---

method is easily implemented by simple spreadsheet programs, and the interpretation and use of seasonal indexes are intuitive yet insightful. The most sophisticated decomposition method is the Department of Commerce's Census II-X11 method. This method is so computationally intense that routinely using it is not feasible in operational forecasting. However, it is the best technique for decomposing an important time series, and its popularity is increasing as it becomes available from many microcomputer software vendors. Finally, we highlighted that the use of deseasonalized values is an important early detection tool of management.

Disadvantages

Because of the manner in which seasonal indexes and trends are calculated, it is more likely to overfit a model using the decomposition method than when using other methods. This is true because the form of the model is decided before any analysis is done

TABLE 11-10

Classical Decomposition Method Using Centered 12-Month Moving Averages, Seasonal Indexes, and Simple Linear Regression for Trend – Series F

Month	Period	Demand	12-Month Total	12-Month Total	Centered 12-Month	12-Month Average	Percent 12-Month Average
JAN	1	546					
FEB	2	578					
MAR	3	660					
APR	4	707					
MAY	5	738					
JUN	6	781					
JUL	7	848	8,358	8,441	8,399.5	699.9583	1.2115
AUG	8	818	8,441	8,574	8,507.5	708.9583	1.1538
SEP	9	729	8,574	8,643	8,608.5	717.375	1.0162
OCT	10	691	8,643	8,734	8,688.5	724.0417	.9543
NOV	11	658	8,734	8,857	8,795.5	732.9583	.8977
DEC	12	604	8,857	8,979	8,918	743.1667	.8127
JAN	13	629	8,979	9,099	9,039	753.25	.8350
FEB	14	711	9,099	9,175	9,137	761.4167	.9337
MAR	15	729	9,175	9,306	9,240.5	770.0417	.9467
APR	16	798	9,306	9,407	9,356.5	779.7083	1.0234
MAY	17	861	9,407	9,488	9,447.5	787.2917	1.0936
JUN	18	903	9,488	9,583	9,535.5	794.625	1.1363
JUL	19	968	9,583	9,727	9,655	804.5833	1.2031
AUG	20	894	9,727	9,834	9,780.5	815.0417	1.0968
SEP	21	860	9,834	9,976	9,905	825.4167	1.0418
OCT	22	792	9,976	10,060	10,018	834.8333	.9486
NOV	23	739	10,060	10,158	10,109	842.4167	.8772
DEC	24	699	10,158	10,234	10,196	849.6667	.8226
JAN	25	773	10,234	10,221	10,227.5	852.2917	.9069
FEB	26	818	10,221	10,252	10,236.5	853.0417	.9589
MAR	27	871	10,252	10,235	10,243.5	853.625	1.0203
APR	28	882	10,235	10,233	10,234	852.8333	1.0342
MAY	29	959	10,233	10,240	10,236.5	853.0417	1.1242
JUN	30	979	10,240	10,363	10,301.5	858.4583	1.1404
JUL	31	955	10,363	10,447	10,405	867.0833	1.1013

Month	No.	Year 1	Year 3		Max	Min	Final Seasonal Index
AUG	32	925	10,447	10,505	10,476	873	1.0595
SEP	33	843	10,505	10,593	10,549	879.0833	.9589
OCT	34	790	10,593	10,692	10,642.5	886.875	.8907
NOV	35	746	10,692	10,784	10,738	894.8333	.8336
DEC	36	822	10,784	10,929	10,856.5	904.7083	.9085
JAN	37	857	10,929	11,047	10,988	915.6667	.9359
FEB	38	876	11,047	11,142	11,094.5	924.5417	.9474
MAR	39	959	11,142	11,232	11,187	932.25	1.0286
APR	40	981	11,232	11,229	11,230.5	935.875	1.0482
MAY	41	1,051	11,229	11,313	11,271	939.25	1.1189
JUN	42	1,124	11,313	11,413	11,363	946.9167	1.1870
JUL	43	1,073					
AUG	44	1,020					
SEP	45	933					
OCT	46	787					
NOV	47	830					
DEC	48	922					
Averages	24.5	827.44					

Seasonal Indexes

Season	Percent 12-Month MA			Unadjusted Index Mean	Max	Min	Final Seasonal Index
	Year 1	Year 2	Year 3				
S(1)	.83505	.9069665	.9359301	.8926482	.9359301	.8350481	.8874672
S(2)	.93379	.9589215	.9474965	.9467346	.9589215	.9337857	.9412396
S(3)	.94670	1.020354	1.028694	.9985835	1.028694	.9467020	.9927876
S(4)	1.0235	1.034200	1.048217	1.035292	1.048217	1.023460	1.029283
S(5)	1.0936	1.124212	1.118978	1.112271	1.124212	1.093623	1.105815
S(6)	1.1364	1.140416	1.187010	1.154604	1.187010	1.136385	1.147903
S(7)	1.2115	1.203107	1.101394	1.172000	1.211501	1.101394	1.165198
S(8)	1.1538	1.096876	1.059565	1.103416	1.153805	1.059565	1.097011
S(9)	1.0162	1.041898	.9589535	1.005685	1.041898	.9589535	.9998483
S(10)	.95436	.9486924	.8907681	.9312752	.9543650	.8907681	.9258699
S(11)	.89773	.8772381	.8336748	.8695482	.8977318	.8336748	.8645013
S(12)	.81274	.8226756	.9085801	.8479980	.9085801	.8127383	.8430761
Sum				12.07006			12.0

TABLE 11-10 (continued)

Period (t)	Actual (Y_t)	Seasonal Index (S)	Deseasonalized (Y_t/S)	(X·X)	(X·Y)	Trend	Forecast (S × T)	Error (e)	Percent Error (e/Y_t)	Squared Errors (e^2)	Z-Value of e*
1	546	.88746	615.2340	1	615.234	663.8587	589.15	-43.15	-.0790	1,862.10	-1.120
2	578	.94123	614.0838	4	1,228.168	670.8607	631.44	-53.44	-.0924	2,855.90	-1.387
3	660	.99278	664.7948	9	1,994.384	677.8626	672.97	-12.97	-.0196	168.31	-.337
4	707	1.0292	686.8858	16	2,747.543	684.8646	704.91	2.08	.00294	4.33	.054
5	738	1.1058	667.3809	25	3,336.905	691.8666	765.07	-27.08	.0366	733.14	-.703
6	781	1.1479	680.3714	36	4,082.228	698.8685	802.23	-21.23	-.0271	450.83	-.551
7	848	1.1651	727.7733	49	5,094.413	705.8705	822.47	25.52	.03009	651.32	.663
8	818	1.0970	745.6624	64	5,965.299	712.8725	782.02	35.97	.04397	1,293.90	.934
9	729	.99984	729.1106	81	6,561.995	719.8744	719.76	9.23	.01266	85.28	.240
10	691	.92586	746.3252	100	7,463.252	726.8764	672.99	18.00	.02605	324.25	.468
11	658	.86450	761.1325	121	8,372.457	733.8783	634.43	23.56	.03580	555.13	.612
12	604	.84307	716.4241	144	8,597.089	740.8803	624.61	-20.62	-.0341	425.12	-.535
13	629	.88746	708.7586	169	9,213.862	747.8823	663.72	-34.72	-.0552	1,205.50	-.901
14	711	.94123	755.3868	196	10,575.42	754.4842	710.52	.47	.00066	.22	.012
15	729	.99278	734.2961	225	11,014.44	761.8862	756.39	-27.39	-.0375	750.27	-.711
16	798	1.0292	775.2969	256	12,404.75	768.8882	791.40	6.59	.00826	43.51	.171
17	861	1.1058	778.6111	289	13,236.39	775.8901	857.99	3.00	.00349	9.05	.078
18	903	1.1479	786.6522	324	14,159.74	782.8921	898.68	4.31	.00477	18.63	.112
19	968	1.1651	830.7601	361	15,784.44	789.8941	920.38	47.61	.04919	2,267.30	1.236
20	894	1.0970	814.9416	400	16,298.83	796.8960	874.20	19.79	.02214	391.88	.514
21	860	.99984	860.1305	441	18,062.74	803.8980	803.77	56.22	.06537	3,161.10	1.460
22	792	.92586	855.4118	484	18,819.06	810.9000	750.78	41.21	.05203	1,698.40	1.070
23	739	.86450	854.8281	529	19,661.05	817.9019	707.07	31.92	.04319	1,019.00	.829
24	699	.84307	829.1067	576	19,898.56	824.9039	695.45	3.54	.00506	12.55	.092
25	773	.88746	871.0181	625	21,775.45	831.9059	738.28	34.71	.04490	1,204.80	.901
26	818	.94123	869.0067	676	22,595.73	838.9078	789.61	28.38	.03470	805.80	.737
27	871	.99278	877.3277	729	23,687.85	845.9098	839.80	31.19	.03581	972.89	.810
28	882	1.0292	856.9071	784	23,993.40	852.9117	877.88	4.11	.00466	16.91	.107
29	959	1.1058	867.2335	841	25,149.77	859.9137	950.90	8.09	.00844	65.52	.210
30	979	1.1479	852.8599	900	25,585.80	866.9157	995.13	-16.13	-.0164	260.32	-.419

Trend Calculation | Forecast and Error

31	955	1.1651	819.6032	961	25,407.70	873.9176	1,018.2	−63.29	−.0662	4,005.20	−1.643
32	925	1.0970	843.2002	1,024	26,982.41	880.9196	966.37	−41.38	−.0447	1,712.10	−1.074
33	843	.99984	843.1279	1,089	27,823.22	887.9216	887.78	−44.79	−.0531	2,005.80	−1.162
34	790	.92586	853.2516	1,156	29,010.56	894.9235	828.58	−38.58	−.0488	1,488.60	−1.001
35	746	.86450	862.9253	1,225	30,202.39	901.9255	779.71	−33.72	−.0451	1,136.70	−.876
36	822	.84307	975.0010	1,296	35,100.03	908.9275	766.29	55.70	.06776	3,103.00	1.446
37	857	.88746	965.6695	1,369	35,729.77	915.9294	812.85	44.14	.05150	1,948.50	1.146
38	876	.94123	930.6876	1,444	35,366.13	922.9314	868.69	7.30	.00833	53.30	.190
39	959	.99278	965.9670	1,521	37,672.71	929.9334	923.22	35.77	.03730	1,279.70	.929
40	981	1.0292	953.0905	1,600	38,123.62	936.9353	964.37	16.62	.01695	276.50	.432
41	1,051	1.1058	950.4300	1,681	38,967.63	943.9373	1,043.8	7.17	.00683	51.55	.186
42	1,124	1.1479	979.1772	1,764	41,125.44	950.9393	1,091.5	32.41	.02883	1,050.60	.842
43	1,073	1.1651	920.8735	1,849	39,597.56	957.9412	1,116.1	−43.19	−.0402	1,865.40	−1.121
44	1,020	1.0970	929.7991	1,936	40,911.16	964.9432	1,058.5	−38.55	−.0377	1,486.30	−1.001
45	933	.99984	933.1415	2,025	41,991.37	971.9452	971.79	−38.80	−.0415	1,505.20	−1.007
46	787	.92586	850.0114	2,116	39,100.53	978.9471	906.37	−119.4	−.1516	14,251.00	−3.099
47	830	.86450	960.0911	2,209	45,124.28	985.9491	852.35	−22.35	−.0269	499.71	−.580
48	922	.84307	1,093.614	2,304	52,493.48	992.9510	837.13	84.86	.09204	7,202.30	2.203
1,176	SUM		39,763.43	38,024	1,038,706.					68,236.04	

Trend coefficients   b = 7.0020   a = 656.86

Sum of squared errors   68,236.04
Standard deviation of errors   38.515
Standard deviation of series   130.97
R-square   .915

*Z value of error is error divided by the standard deviation of the errors.

on the time series. There may be a tendency for decomposition methods to model large random variations as either true seasonal or trend influences. Also, a large random error in one period will influence the estimate of the seasonal and trend values. Therefore, when calculating seasonal indexes, it is important to eliminate any extraordinarily high or low indexes as well as the actual values that cause those unusually high or low indexes. Also, if there are more than three seasons of indexes, then a modified mean or a median of seasonal indexes should be used.

Another serious problem when deseasonalizing data and calculating trends is that the division by seasonal indexes might create extremely large values. This creates large errors when actually forecasting as well as in fitting models. Consequently, it is important to check for outliers in each step of the method. We have seen a commercial system in which this is not done. The statistical tests for outliers discussed in Chapter 14 should be applied to each of the deseasonalized trend values.

Because of these problems, the R-squares of the fitted decomposition model may be quite high relative to the actual R-square values realized when forecasting. Also, the multiperiod-ahead forecast of a decomposition model may be greatly influenced by future changes in the trend or cyclical influences. Consequently, we very cautiously forecast one to two seasonal cycles into the future using decomposition methods. We are even more cautious in forecasting several years into the future. Although this method has serious disadvantages, it is useful in conjunction with other models of trend and cyclical variations. The more sophisticated the decomposition program, the better.

Very cautiously forecast using decomposition methods.

SUMMARY

This chapter has introduced two important methods of forecasting in business, regression analysis and classical decomposition time-series analysis. We have not presented this material in a statistically rigorous way. Instead, we have focused on the essential knowledge that a manager or analyst needs to be a user of good operational forecasting systems. Those interested in implementing causal methods of regression analysis should refer to other references. This chapter prepares you to use regression methods as important parts of the forecasting systems discussed in Chapters 12 and 13. We have studied simple linear regression, statistical significance tests, correlation measures, and multiple regression. However, we have presented only the essential information needed by you to use or further study these topics.

The concept of classical decomposition time series methods was presented in the second half of this chapter. This is an important method because it can be used to forecast short- and medium-term demand. The appendix of this chapter presents regression methods for decomposing a time series using additive and multiplicative models. This illustrates the power and versatility of multiple-regression applications in operational forecasting systems.

This chapter lays the groundwork for seasonal indexes in Winters' method and Fourier series analysis. The theoretical relationships between these methods are very strong. Each decomposes demand into trend, seasonality, and randomness. While the methods of estimating these components differ, the underlying model remains the same. We will highlight this in the next two chapters.

REFERENCES

1. J. Shiskin, A. H. Young, and J. C. Musgrave, "The X-11 Variant of the Census II Method Seasonal Adjustment Program," *Technical Paper No. 15* (Washington, D.C.: U.S. Bureau of the Census).
2. S. Makridakis, S. C. Wheelwright, and V. E. McGee, *Forecasting: Methods and Applications,* 2nd ed. (New York: John Wiley & Sons, 1983); J. Holton Wilson and Barry Keating, *Business Forecasting* (Homewood, Ill.: Richard D. Irwin, 1990); and R. S. Pindyck and Daniel L. Rubinfeld, *Econometric Models and Economic Forecasts,* 2nd ed. (New York: McGraw-Hill, 1981).
3. Makridakis et al., *Forecasting: Methods and Applications;* and Wilson and Keating, *Business Forecasting.*

APPENDIX: CLASSICAL TIME SERIES DECOMPOSITION USING REGRESSION ANALYSIS

As mentioned previously, multiple-regression techniques are versatile in modeling a variety of relationships. This section illustrates their use in decomposing a time series using dummy (dichotomous) variables on the quarterly data of Table 11–6. This data is presented in Table 11–11. As previously mentioned, this firm desires to measure the trend and seasonal influences on the quarterly demand for its product. To do so, it must create seasonal dummy variables. These dummy variables will be used to model the seasonal increases or decreases in demand in each quarter.

As Table 11–11 shows, four new variables have been created to perform the decomposition of this quarterly demand. Column 3 introduces a time variable, Trend, which is used to measure the long-run change in demand over time. Three columns (4, 5, and 6) have been created to represent the four quarterly influences on demands. These three variables are $Q2$, $Q3$, and $Q4$. Only three variables are necessary to measure

TABLE 11–11
Decomposition Using Multiple Regression

(1) Time	(2) Demand	(3) Trend	(4) Q2	(5) Q3	(6) Q4
1	72	1	0	0	0
2	110	2	1	0	0
3	117	3	0	1	0
4	172	4	0	0	1
5	76	5	0	0	0
6	112	6	1	0	0
7	130	7	0	1	0
8	194	8	0	0	1
9	78	9	0	0	0
10	119	10	1	0	0
11	128	11	0	1	0
12	201	12	0	0	1
13	81	13	0	0	0
14	134	14	1	0	0
15	141	15	0	1	0
16	216	16	0	0	1

the effect of four quarters because, as we will see, when all three of these variables are zero, demand is the result of first-quarter influences.

As shown in Periods 1, 5, 9, and 13, each first quarter has columns 4, 5, and 6 equal to zero. More important, for mathematical reasons, multiple regression will not work if four dummy variables are used to represent four dependent events. That is, to represent p mutually exclusive, collectively exhaustive events (e.g., 4 quarters), we must use only p minus 1 dummy variable (i.e., $4 - 1 = 3$ dummies). To use p dummy variables for p events will result in an indeterminate regression result—the solution method will not be able to identify the best regression coefficients.

The seasonal influences on demand in Table 11–11 can be modeled using either an additive model, Equation 11–24, or a multiplicative model, Equation 11–25. We briefly present both models.

$$\hat{D}_t = a + b_1 T_t + b_2 Q2_t + b_3 Q3_t + b_4 Q4_t \qquad (11\text{--}24)$$

$$\widehat{Ln(D_t)} = a' + b'_1 T_t + b'_2 Q2_t + b'_3 Q3_t + b'_4 Q4_t \qquad (11\text{--}25)$$

where

$$D_t = \text{Demand in period } t$$
$$T_t = \text{Time value in period } t$$
$$Q2_t, Q3_t, Q4_t = \text{Dummy variables for each quarter}$$
$$a, b_i, a', b'_i = \text{Relevant regression coefficients, where } i \text{ equals 1 to 4}$$
$$Ln(D_t) = \text{Logarithm of demand to the base of the natural number } e$$

Additive Seasonal Regression Models

Using the data of Table 11–11, the following additive multiple-regression relationship resulted:

$$\hat{D}_t = 62.88 + 1.98 T_t + 40.12 Q2_t + 48.29 Q3_t + 113.06 Q4_t \qquad (11\text{--}26)$$
$$\quad\quad\quad\;\; (5.62) \quad\;\; (8.96) \quad\;\;\; (10.71) \quad\quad (24.71)$$

$R^2 = .981$ Standard deviation of errors $= 6.296$

The interpretation of this model is that demand increases 1.98 units each quarter, as measured by T_t. The additive seasonal influences of each quarter are interpreted relative to quarter 1. That is, each quarterly value is related to quarter 1. For example, the demand in quarter 2 is, on average, 40.12 units higher than the demand in quarter 1. Similarly, quarters 3 and 4 are 48.29 and 113.06 units higher than quarter 1, respectively. Remember that at most only one of $Q2$, $Q3$, or $Q4$ is nonzero at time t, and the parenthetical values below bs are t_bs.

From a statistical standpoint, this is a very good model of demand. Its R-square is high, the standard deviation is low, and all of the regression coefficients are statistically different than zero. The classical decomposition method of Table 11–7 had a standard deviation of 3.570; that of this method is 6.296. Also, Figure 11–7 confirms that this data is better modeled using a multiplicative model because the magnitudes of the seasonal peaks and troughs are a constant percentage of the level of the series. Thus, we choose the multiplicative model of Table 11–7 over the additive model of Equation 11–26.

However, as shown below, multiplicative regression models can be used to represent percentage-growth influences using logarithmic transformations.

Multiplicative Seasonal Regression Models

The modeling of percentage-growth relationships is most easily done using logarithms. To model the demand of Table 11–11 as a multiplicative model, first take natural logarithms of demand (i.e., logs to the base e), then use multiple regression to relate the logarithmic demand to the independent variables in Equation 11–25.

Equation 11–27 illustrates the results of this multiple-regression model. As shown, all regression coefficients are statistically significantly different than zero.

$$\widehat{Ln(D_t)} = 4.239 + .01434T_t + .420Q2_t + .489Q3_t + .891Q4_t \quad (11\text{–}27)$$
$$\phantom{\widehat{Ln(D_t)} = 4.239 + } (8.49) \qquad (19.59) \qquad (22.61) \qquad (40.56)$$

$$R^2 = .992 \qquad \text{Standard deviation of errors} = .030224$$

Unfortunately, the interpretation and comparison of these results are complicated by the use of logarithms. To better interpret this model, we need to transform the log model using antilogs.

Equation 11–28 is the result of taking the antilogs of the right and left sides of Equation 11–27. This was accomplished by taking the natural number e to the power of each side of the equation. Because the addition of logs is the equivalent of multiplication of antilogs, we see that Equation 11–28 is a multiplicative model.

$$\hat{D}_t = (e^{4.239})(e^{.01434T_t})(e^{.420Q2_t})(e^{.489Q3_t})(e^{.891Q4_t}) \quad (11\text{–}28)$$

Interpretation of this relationship is best accomplished by calculating a few examples. Let us consider the last four quarters of data in Table 11–11. (Remember as we fit demands using Equation 11–28 that any number taken to the zero power equals 1. Thus, when $Q2$ equals zero, e to the power of zero equals one.)

First quarter, $t = 13$, $T_t = 13$, $Q2_{13} = Q3_{13} = Q4_{13} = 0$.

$$\hat{D}_{13} = 69.338\ (e^{.01434(13)})\ (e^{.420(0)})(e^{.489(0)})(e^{.891(0)})$$
$$= 69.338\ (1.2049) = 83.55$$

From Table 11–11: $D_{13} = 81$; $\text{Error}_{13} = 81 - 83.55 = -2.55$.
Second quarter, $t = 14$, $T_t = 14$, $Q2_{14} = 1$, $Q3_{14} = Q4_{14} = 0$.

$$\hat{D}_{14} = 69.338\ (e^{.01434(14)})\ (e^{.420(1)})(e^{.489(0)})(e^{.891(0)})$$
$$= 128.99$$

From Table 11–11: $D_{14} = 134$; $\text{Error}_{14} = 134 - 128.99 = 5.01$.
Third quarter, $t = 15$, $T_t = 15$, $Q2_{15} = 0$, $Q3_{15} = 1$, $Q4_{15} = 0$.

$$\hat{D}_{15} = 69.338\ (e^{.01434(15)})(e^{.489}) = 140.20$$

From Table 11–11: $D_{15} = 141$; $\text{Error}_{15} = 141 - 140.2 = .8$.

Fourth quarter, $t = 16$, $T_t = 16$, $Q2_{16} = Q3_{16} = 0$, $Q4_{16} = 1$.

$$\hat{D}_{16} = 69.338\ (e^{.01434(16)})(e^{.891(1)}) = 212.60$$

From Table 11–11: $D_{16} = 216$; $\text{Error}_{16} = 216 - 212.60 = 3.40$.
These fitted values are quite accurate.

As shown below, the coefficients b'_1, b'_2, b'_3, and b'_4 are meaningful. Trend percentage growth:

$$e^{b'_1} - 1 = e^{b'_1} - 1 = e^{.01434} - 1 = .0144$$

denotes that there is a 1.44 percent increase in demand each quarter.
Quarterly demands versus quarter 1 demands:

$$e^{b'_2} = 1.522$$

denotes that quarter 2 demand is 1.522 times quarter 1 demand.

$$e^{b'_3} = 1.631$$

denotes that quarter 3 demand is 1.631 times quarter 1 demand.

$$e^{b'_4} = 2.438$$

denotes that quarter 4 demand is 2.438 times quarter 1 demand.

As shown below, these quarterly demand ratios nearly equal those of the ratios of the seasonal indexes of Table 11–6.

$$\frac{\text{Seasonal index quarter 2}}{\text{Seasonal index quarter 1}} = \frac{.918}{.606} = 1.515$$

$$\frac{\text{Seasonal index quarter 3}}{\text{Seasonal index quarter 1}} = \frac{.992}{.606} = 1.637$$

$$\frac{\text{Seasonal index quarter 4}}{\text{Seasonal index quarter 1}} = \frac{1.482}{.606} = 2.446$$

Thus, we see that the regression multiplicative model of Equation 11–27 is nearly identical to the classical decomposition time series model of Table 11–8. This near equivalency is not limited to classical decomposition and regression multiplicative models, but is common in the several models which we discuss in Chapters 12 and 13.

CHAPTER 12

TREND-SEASONAL AND WINTERS' SMOOTHING

REFERENCES
APPENDIX: TEST OF SIGNIFICANT TREND
WHEN USING DIFFERENCES

When we mean to build, we first survey the plot, then draw
the model.

William Shakespeare

The ability to forecast trend and seasonal patterns in demand is essential. Some have mistakenly been led to believe that the simple exponential smoothing methods of Chapter 10 are sufficient for many short-term forecasting situations. Most often, this is not true. It has been our experience that at least 50 percent of product demands possess either a trend or seasonal pattern, or both.

There are many methods of estimating trends and seasonality. Our purpose here is to illustrate several methods so that you can be a better user and evaluator of forecasts and forecasting systems. There are a variety of statistical methods for estimating trends and seasonality; some are rather simple and some complex. Somewhat surprisingly, the simple methods are very effective. In this chapter, we discuss the following methods of estimating trends: first differences, double moving averages, Brown's double exponential smoothing, Holt's two-parameter model, and Winters' three-parameter model. In addition, we discuss two methods of estimating seasonality, the use of seasonal differences and Winters' method. Winters' method is the most versatile method of this chapter because it models the level, trend, and seasonality of demand. As we will show, Winters' method is a decomposition method very similar to those studied in Chapter 11. The use of differences to model trends and seasonality is discussed first.

ESTIMATING TRENDS WITH DIFFERENCES

As discussed in Chapter 8, a *trend* is an increase or decrease in a series that persists for an extended time. For nonseasonal data, many use a rule of thumb that a trend exists when seven or more observations show a consistent increase or decrease. However, we must be cautious in using such rules. Trends can be difficult to detect when a series has significant randomness and seasonality. To better understand this, consider Figure 12-1, which shows two series with trends and one without.

The process of using differences to estimate trends is a simple one. However, the results are as meaningful as those of much more-complex models. Remembering that a trend is a consistent increase or decrease over time, we see that using differences identifies trends. Definitionally, first differences are:

$$Y_t - Y_{t-1} = \text{Change from Period } t-1 \text{ to } t$$

Consider the three series of Table 12-1 plotted in Figure 12-1. As shown in columns 3, 6, and 9 of Table 12-1, the process of using first differences yields actual period-to-period increases or decreases over time.

If a series exhibits a trend, then on average the first differences should equal the increasing or decreasing trend by being greater than or less than zero, respectively. That is, if first differences yield changes that are primarily above zero as measured by the mean, then the series has been increasing (Series G of Table 12-1). In contrast, if differences yield a series with values primarily below zero, then the series has a decreasing trend (Series H). Finally, if the mean of first differences yields a series that is random about zero, then we infer that there is no trend (Series I).

As shown at the bottom of Table 12-1, the mean of the first differences of Series G is 2.94. This denotes that Series G is increasing on average 2.94 units per period. The mean of first differences of Series H is −2.92, while the mean of first differences of Series I is −.25. Based on these numbers and an inspection of Figure 12-1, we infer there is no trend in Series I, while G and H do have trends. We use these statistics to illustrate the computation of future values of Series G. Columns 4, 7, and 10 of Table 12-1 illustrate fitted values (i.e., $t=1$ to $t=31$) and forecasted values (i.e., $t=32$) for each series. The computation of fitted and forecasted values for Series H and I forecasts is left to the reader.

Forecasting with Differences

The forecasting equation for first differences is very simple.

$$\hat{Y}_t = Y_{t-1} + \text{Mean of the differences} \qquad (12\text{-}1)$$

Let's designate the mean of the differences as b.

FIGURE 12–1
Series G, H, and I

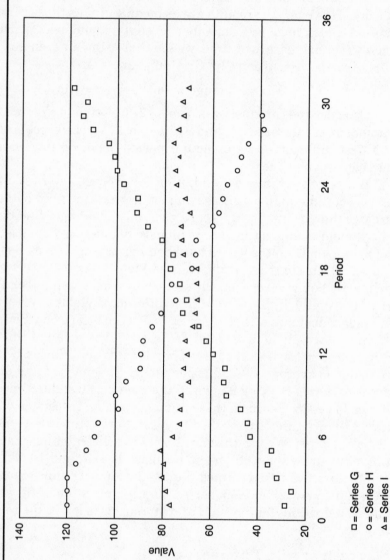

□ = Series G
o = Series H
△ = Series I

$$\hat{Y}_t = Y_{t-1} + b \tag{12-2}$$

$$\hat{Y}_{t+m} = Y_t + m*b \tag{12-3}$$

where m is the number of periods forecast into the future.

Let's forecast Series G using these equations. Assume that it is now the end of Period 25 and we want to forecast periods 26 through 28. The results of forecasting are shown below.

$$\hat{Y}_{26} = Y_{25} + b = 99.96 + 2.94 = 102.90$$
$$\text{Actual } Y_{26} = 100.91$$
$$\text{Error} = 100.91 - 102.90 = -1.99$$
$$\hat{Y}_{27} = Y_{25} + 2*2.94 = 99.96 + 2*2.94 = 105.84$$
$$\text{Actual } Y_{27} = 103.30$$
$$\text{Error} = 103.30 - 105.84 = -2.54$$
$$\hat{Y}_{28} = Y_{25} + 3*2.94 = 99.96 + 3*2.94 = 108.78$$
$$\text{Actual } Y_{28} = 109.99$$
$$\text{Error} = 109.99 - 108.78 = 1.31$$

As shown, this is a very simple method for forecasting future values.

While applying Equation 12–3, we assumed that the mean of the first differences reflects a trend. The mean could have been the result of random influences. To have more confidence in our trend estimates, we must answer the statistical question of whether a mean of first differences is or is not different than zero. The value of zero is important because if the mean is nearly equal to zero, then this is consistent with the assertion that there is no trend in the data. Table 12–2 illustrates frequency distributions of the three series of Figure 12–1. As shown, Series G rarely has period-to-period changes less than zero, Series H rarely has period-to-period changes greater than zero, while the number of positive and negative period-to-period changes of Series I is exactly equal, hence the mean of near zero.

One of the advantages of using differences to estimate trends is that simple statistical tests can prove that a trend is significant. We can perform this test on the mean of the first differences of each series shown in Table 12–1. It can be proven that Series G and Series H have trends while Series I does not. The statistical analysis and hypothesis test necessary to prove or disprove that trends exist is shown in the appendix of this chapter. It is

TABLE 12–1
Three Series: Two with Trends and One Without

(1) Period (t)	(2) Series G Value	(3) First Difference	(4) Fitted Value	(5) Series H Value	(6) First Difference	(7) Fitted Value	(8) Series I Value	(9) First Difference	(10) Fitted Value
1	29.64			119.72			77.42		
2	27.14	-2.50	32.58	120.18	.46	116.80	78.79	1.37	77.42
3	32.70	5.56	30.08	120.72	.54	117.26	80.07	1.28	78.79
4	36.53	3.83	35.64	116.56	-4.16	117.80	79.53	-.54	80.07
5	34.96	-1.57	39.47	112.13	-4.43	113.64	81.17	1.64	79.53
6	44.00	9.04	37.90	108.78	-3.35	109.21	75.78	-5.39	81.17
7	45.17	1.17	46.94	107.49	-1.29	105.86	72.80	-2.98	75.78
8	48.02	2.85	48.11	98.99	-8.50	104.57	72.78	-.02	72.80
9	53.73	5.71	50.96	100.40	1.41	96.07	72.37	-.41	72.78
10	55.02	1.29	56.67	95.86	-4.54	97.48	69.24	-3.13	72.37
11	54.58	-.44	57.96	90.11	-5.75	92.94	71.48	2.24	69.24
12	59.49	4.91	57.52	89.90	-.21	87.19	69.77	-1.71	71.48
13	62.34	2.85	62.43	89.06	-.84	86.98	70.60	.83	69.77
14	65.41	3.07	65.28	85.12	-3.94	86.14	67.34	-3.26	70.60
15	72.23	6.82	68.35	81.34	-3.78	82.20	66.61	-.73	67.34

16	70.66	-1.57	75.17	75.50	-5.84	78.42	65.80	-.81	66.61
17	73.59	2.93	73.60	77.02	1.52	72.58	66.11	.31	65.80
18	77.50	3.91	76.53	68.63	-8.39	74.10	66.83	.72	66.11
19	76.78	-.72	80.44	67.10	-1.53	65.71	71.80	4.97	66.83
20	81.07	4.29	79.72	67.04	-.06	64.18	72.55	.75	71.80
21	87.15	6.08	84.01	60.30	-6.74	64.12	72.81	.26	72.55
22	91.78	4.63	90.09	57.52	-2.78	57.38	69.26	-3.55	72.81
23	91.29	-.49	94.72	55.95	-1.57	54.60	71.11	1.85	69.26
24	97.13	5.84	94.23	54.02	-1.93	53.03	74.57	3.46	71.11
25	99.96	2.83	100.07	49.75	-4.27	51.10	75.13	.56	74.57
26	100.91	.95	102.90	48.16	-1.59	46.83	73.81	-1.32	75.13
27	103.30	2.39	103.85	45.37	-2.79	45.24	75.82	2.01	73.81
28	109.99	6.69	106.24	38.84	-6.53	42.45	74.03	-1.79	75.82
29	113.93	3.94	112.93	39.69	.85	35.92	71.51	-2.52	74.03
30	112.28	-1.65	116.87	34.99	-4.70	36.77	72.12	.61	71.51
31	117.86	5.58	115.22	32.21	-2.78	32.07	69.83	-2.29	72.12
32			120.80			29.29			69.83
Mean	71.81	2.94		77.69	-2.92		72.54	-.25	
Standard deviation	26.29	2.92		26.80	2.73		4.01	2.22	

TABLE 12–2
Frequency Distributions of Differenced Series G, H, and I

Difference Range	Series G	Series H	Series I
− 10 to − 8		2	
− 8 to − 6		2	
− 6 to − 4		7	
− 4 to − 2	1	6	6
− 2 to 0	5	8	8
0 to 2	4	5	11
2 to 4	9		3
4 to 6	7		1
6 to 8	3		
8 to 10	1		
Total	30	30	30

not necessary for you to study the appendix unless you want to know more about the statistical aspects of this method. Frequently, your intuitive judgment or other empirical information may be all that is necessary to confirm that a trend exists. However, we must be cautious whenever basing forecasts on intuition or other subjective information.

Advantages and Disadvantages of Forecasting with Differences

Using differences to model trends has advantages and disadvantages. The advantages are (1) the trend is easily calculated; (2) the trend is easily interpreted; and (3) the significance of the trend can easily be tested using the simple hypothesis tests shown in the appendix.

The disadvantages of using differences arise from this method's weakness in dealing with outliers. Differences do not smooth out the effects of extreme outliers as much as smoothed averages, such as double moving averages and double exponential smoothing. In addition, when applying Equation 12–3, the value Y_{t-1} is critical in forecasting future values. Thus Y_{t-1} should not be an unusual or outlier value. If it is, all future forecasts will be adversely affected. Instead, a typical or smoothed value should be used as the point from which forecasts are made.

Because it does not smooth unusual values or outliers as much as smoothing methods, differences are not frequently used to estimate trends in automated forecasting systems. Instead, methods such as double moving averages or double exponential smoothing are used. We discuss these more fully below. Despite its disadvantages, differencing is a very powerful method for estimating trends when used intelligently.

Nonlinear Trends and Second Differences

The process of differences can be used to forecast nonlinear trends using either multiple differences or logarithms. Both of these methods are illustrated in Table 12–3. The actual data in Table 12–3 has a slight nonlinearity as shown in Figure 12–2.

Logarithms are useful when the trend is a percentage growth function and double differences are useful when modeling quadratic functions. The formula for using second differences is:

$$Y_t - Y_{t-1} = \text{First differences} \qquad (12\text{–}4)$$
$$(Y_t - Y_{t-1}) - (Y_{t-1} - Y_{t-2}) = \text{First differences of first differences}$$
$$\text{(called } second\ differences)$$

Thus, second differences yield the following:

$$Y_t - 2Y_{t-1} + Y_{t-2} \qquad (12\text{–}5)$$

First differences and second differences are shown in columns 3 and 4 of Table 12–3.

In forecasting form, the process of second differences is:

$$\hat{Y}_t = 2Y_{t-1} - Y_{t-2} + b = Y_{t-1} + (Y_{t-1} - Y_{t-2}) + b \quad (12\text{–}6)$$

where b is the mean of the second differenced series and represents a trend estimate. This mean is shown at the bottom of column 4. Upon inspection, you should see that Equation 12–6 has an intuitive explanation: Y_t equals Y_{t-1} plus the increase or decrease of $(Y_{t-1} - Y_{t-2})$ plus an additional constant of b, assuming that it is statistically significantly different than zero. Using the quadratic trend data from Table 12–3, the forecast for Period 32 is:

$$\hat{Y}_t = 110.42 + 2.87 + .10 = 113.39$$

Logarithms

Logarithms are used to model percentage trends or percentage seasonality (seasonal uses are discussed later). To use logs in mod-

TABLE 12–3
Second Differences and Logarithms for Nonlinear Trends

(1) Period (t)	(2) Actual Y(t)	(3) First Difference	(4) Second Difference	(5) Fitted Values	(6) Two- Difference Error	(7) Log (Y)	(8) Difference Log (Y)	(9) Fitted Values	(10) Error
1	31.16					3.439			
2	31.03	-.13				3.435	-.004	32.50	-1.47
3	34.57	3.54	3.67	31.00	3.57	3.543	.108	32.37	2.20
4	38.73	4.16	.62	38.21	.52	3.657	.114	36.06	2.67
5	40.15	1.42	-2.74	42.99	-2.84	3.693	.036	40.40	-.25
6	45.09	4.94	3.52	41.67	3.42	3.809	.116	41.88	3.21
7	48.01	2.92	-2.02	50.13	-2.12	3.871	.063	47.03	.98
8	48.67	.66	-2.26	51.03	-2.36	3.885	.014	50.08	-1.41
9	54.11	5.44	4.78	49.43	4.68	3.991	.106	50.77	3.34
10	55.21	1.10	-4.34	59.65	-4.44	4.011	.020	56.44	-1.23
11	60.50	5.29	4.19	56.41	4.09	4.103	.091	57.59	2.91
12	62.82	2.32	-2.97	65.89	-3.07	4.140	.038	63.11	-.29
13	65.83	3.01	.69	65.24	.59	4.187	.047	65.53	.30
14	65.32	-.51	-3.52	68.94	-3.62	4.179	-.008	68.67	-3.35
15	71.25	5.93	6.44	64.91	6.34	4.266	.087	68.13	3.12

16	72.27	1.02	-4.91	77.28	-5.01	4.280	.014	74.32	-2.05
17	73.37	1.10	.08	73.39	-.02	4.296	.015	75.38	-2.01
18	79.71	6.34	5.24	74.57	5.14	4.378	.083	76.53	3.18
19	80.18	.47	-5.87	86.15	-5.97	4.384	.006	83.14	-2.96
20	84.30	4.12	3.65	80.75	3.55	4.434	.050	83.63	.67
21	84.02	-.28	-4.40	88.52	-4.50	4.431	-.003	87.93	-3.91
22	87.55	3.53	3.81	83.84	3.71	4.472	.041	87.64	-.09
23	90.74	3.19	-.34	91.18	-.44	4.508	.036	91.32	-.58
24	92.76	2.02	-1.17	94.03	-1.27	4.530	.022	94.65	-1.89
25	95.40	2.64	.62	94.88	.52	4.558	.028	96.76	-1.36
26	98.18	2.78	.14	98.14	.04	4.587	.029	99.51	-1.33
27	101.41	3.23	.45	101.06	.35	4.619	.032	102.41	-1.00
28	102.55	1.14	-2.09	104.74	-2.19	4.630	.011	105.78	-3.23
29	105.30	2.75	1.61	103.79	1.51	4.657	.026	106.97	-1.67
30	107.55	2.25	-.50	108.15	-.60	4.678	.021	109.84	-2.29
31	110.42	2.87	.62	109.90	.52	4.704	.026	112.18	-1.76
Mean	71.55	2.64	.10	74.34	.00	4.205	.042	73.28	-.38
Standard deviation	24.45	1.84	3.31	23.00	3.31	.383	.037	24.77	2.18

FIGURE 12–2
Slight Nonlinear Trend

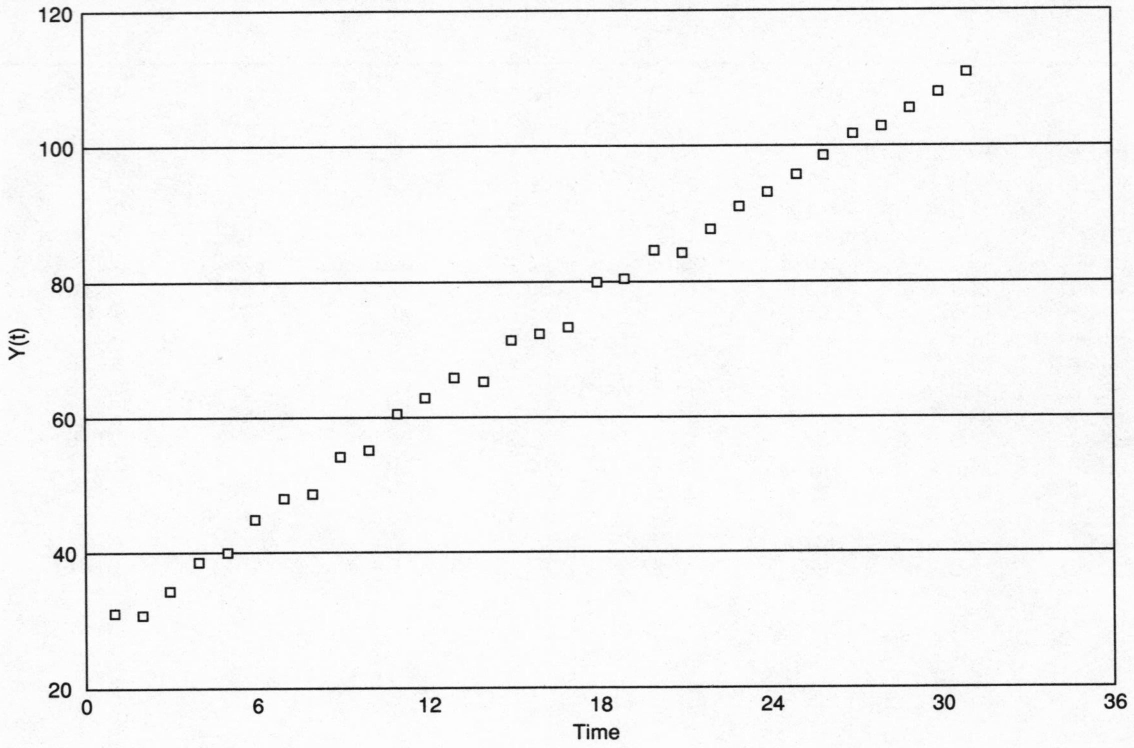

eling nonlinear trends, first take logarithms of the series (column 7 of Table 12–3), then take first differences of the logarithms (column 8), and finally perform a statistical significance test on the mean of the first differences. When the mean of first differences is significant, the following model results.

$$\widehat{Ln(Y_t)} = Ln(Y_{t-1}) + b \qquad (12\text{–}7)$$

where Ln is the process of taking the natural logarithm of Y to the base e, and b is the resulting mean of the first differences. (Note: all logarithms in this book are taken in the base e.) After forecasting the Ln of Y, the actual value of Y is calculated by taking the antilog of the Ln of Y. This is as simple as taking the natural number e to the power of the forecasted value of $Ln\,(Y_t)$. This is written mathematically as:

$$\hat{Y}_t = \widehat{e^{Ln(Y)}} \qquad (12\text{–}8)$$

Finally, there is a simple yet powerful interpretation of the b value for logarithmic relationships. The antilog of $b - 1$ is equal to the percentage change of the series.

Using the example of Table 12–3 yields the following forecasting form and interpretation of b.

$$\widehat{Ln(Y_{32})} = Ln(Y_{31}) + b = 4.704 + .042 = 4.746$$
$$\hat{Y}_{32} = e^{4.746} = 115.12$$

The antilog of b yields the following interpretation.

$$e^b - 1 = 1.0429 - 1 = .0429$$

The series of Table 12–3 has a period-to-period trend of approximately 4.29 percent.

Seasonal Differences to Estimate Trends

The method of estimating and testing for trends in data can be generalized to data that is highly seasonal. In such cases, we do not estimate trends using first differences, but instead use seasonal differences. Table 12–4 illustrates the use of 12th differences to model the trend and seasonality of a series. This is a very powerful method that is incorporated in the smoothing methods of more-sophisticated forecasting software. Note that the process of taking seasonal differences follows the theory and intuitive expla-

TABLE 12–4
Seasonal Differences for Modeling Seasonal Data

Period (t)	Actual Value	12th Difference	Fitted Value	Error Actual – Fitted
1	15.29			
2	22.10			
3	28.25			
4	41.75			
5	52.19			
6	60.46			
7	68.87			
8	59.73			
9	56.73			
10	48.12			
11	58.33			
12	73.69			
13	31.12	15.83	50.76	– 19.64
14	38.71	16.61	57.57	– 18.86
15	57.28	29.03	63.72	– 6.44
16	76.65	34.90	77.22	– .57
17	95.56	43.37	87.66	7.90
18	103.76	43.30	95.93	7.83
19	121.21	52.34	104.34	16.87
20	103.22	43.49	95.20	8.02
21	87.12	30.39	92.20	– 5.08
22	78.44	30.32	83.59	– 5.15
23	93.33	35.00	93.80	– .47
24	120.43	46.74	109.16	11.27
25	45.18	14.06	66.59	– 21.41
26	62.92	24.21	74.18	– 11.26
27	88.50	31.22	92.75	– 4.25
28	110.08	33.43	112.12	– 2.04
29	136.14	40.58	131.03	5.11
30	153.23	49.47	139.23	14.00
31	171.46	50.25	156.68	14.78
32	148.21	44.99	138.69	9.52
33	124.46	37.34	122.59	1.87
34	109.42	30.98	113.91	– 4.49
35	126.11	32.78	128.80	– 2.69
36	161.07	40.64	155.90	5.17
37			Forecast = 80.65	
Mean =	101.82	35.47		.00
Standard deviation =	37.45	10.47		10.47

nations of those used for first differences. Because of this, we do not develop seasonal differences further. However, please note that the process of taking seasonal differences includes performing a statistical test on the mean of the differences. If this mean difference is statistically significantly different than zero, then trend exists in the series. Thus, we have a very simple model that includes trend and seasonal patterns.

$$\text{Forecast} = \text{Seasonal estimate} + \text{Trend}$$
$$\hat{Y}_t = Y_{t-12} + b$$

where

$$b = \text{Mean of 12th differences } (Y_t - Y_{t-12})$$

For quarterly data, the following model may be appropriate.

$$\hat{Y}_t = Y_{t-4} + b$$

where

$$b = \text{Mean of 4th differences } (Y_t - Y_{t-4})$$

The process of using differences to estimate trends and seasonality is an intuitive, yet effective, statistical method. Through application of logarithms and second differences, it is possible to represent nonlinear trends and percentage growth in seasonality. Those desiring more information about differencing as a modeling method are encouraged to review Wilson and Makridakis.[1]

DOUBLE MOVING AVERAGES

As noted in Chapter 10, simple moving averages do not work well with data series involving trends. They lag behind series values, and, when used to forecast future values, this lag becomes even more pronounced. This section describes a modification to the simple moving average procedure that includes an adjustment for the lag as well as for the trend.

Table 12–5 illustrates a simple trending series with 12 observations showing a trend of three units from period to period. All random error has been removed so that the trend can be more easily identified. A three-period moving average [MA(3)] is used to forecast the series; thus, the first three periods are used to forecast the fourth period. As shown in column 6, the forecasts produced by this three-period simple moving average reflect a systematic error of six units. Half of this error, three units, is the inherent lag in the moving average because the moving average for the first three periods cannot be computed until the end of Period 3. That is, the average is centered on Period 2. Thus, the

TABLE 12–5
Forecasting a Trended Series Using a Three-Period Simple Moving Average

(1) Period (t)	(2) Observed Value	(3) Computed MA(3)	(4) Lag (2) − (3)	(5) Forecast MA(3)	(6) Error (2) − (5)
1	120	—	—	—	—
2	123	—	—	—	—
3	126	123	3	—	—
4	129	126	3	123	6
5	132	129	3	126	6
6	135	132	3	129	6
7	138	135	3	132	6
8	141	138	3	135	6
9	144	141	3	138	6
10	147	144	3	141	6
11	150	147	3	144	6
12	153	150	3	147	6

moving average lags the series by the trend of one period; it is centered on Period 2 instead of Period 3. Using the moving average computed at Period 3 as a forecast for Period 4 creates an additional period of lag and increases the systematic error to the trend over two periods. For a MA(3), this trend is the difference between two adjacent moving averages. Below we develop a general formula for estimating trends.

To eliminate the systematic error just described, a method of *double moving averages,* sometimes called *linear moving averages,* has been developed. This method essentially involves calculating a second moving average from the original moving averages. This is annotated as MA(M×N), an M-period moving average of N-period moving average. For example, a three-period moving average of three-period moving average is written as MA(3×3).

Table 12–6 illustrates double moving averages using the data of Table 12–5. The difference between the simple moving average and the double moving average for any period is added to the simple moving average together with the trend estimate to get the forecast for the following period. For example:

$$F_{10} = (MA(3) \text{ at Period } 9) + (MA(3) - MA(3×3) \text{ at Period } 9)$$
$$+ \text{ Trend}$$
$$= 141 + 3 + 3 = 147$$

TABLE 12–6
Forecasting a Trended Series Using a Double Moving Average [MA(3 × 3)]

(1) Period (t)	(2) Observed Value	(3) MA3	(4) Difference (2) – (3)	(5) MA(3 × 3)	(6) Difference (3) – (5)	(7) Forecast (3) + (6) + Trend	(8) Error (2) – (7)
1	120	—	—	—	—	—	—
2	123	—	—	—	—	—	—
3	126	123	3	—	—	—	—
4	129	126	3	—	—	—	—
5	132	129	3	126	3	—	—
6	135	132	3	129	3	135	0
7	138	135	3	132	3	138	0
8	141	138	3	135	3	141	0
9	144	141	3	138	3	144	0
10	147	144	3	141	3	147	0
11	150	147	3	144	3	150	0
12	153	150	3	147	3	153	0

where the trend is estimated from the following formula:

$$\text{Trend} = \frac{2}{N-1}\,(MA(3) - MA(3 \times 3))$$

and where N is the length of the simple moving average.

This trend formula is necessary because the lag between the simple and double moving averages is dependent on the number of periods in the averages. That is, the lag between these two averages may be greater than one period, and so their difference may represent a multiperiod trend. The adjustment, $2/(N-1)$, assures that the trend is adjusted to be only a one-period trend, not a multiperiod trend.

This example illustrates that with trending items, the systematic error produced by a simple moving average can be removed from the forecast. The level of systematic error and the ability to adjust the forecast for it are a function of the amount of random error (variation around a linear trend line) present in the data series.

In summary, the double moving average is computed as follows:

1. Compute a simple moving average and a double moving average at time t (hereafter annotated as S'_t and S''_t).
2. Add to the simple moving average the difference between the simple and double moving averages.

3. Add the linear trend from Period t to Period $t+1$ (or to Period $t+m$ for forecasting m periods ahead).

This procedure is best generalized through the following set of equations:

$$S'_t = \frac{Y_t + Y_{t-1} + \ldots + Y_{t-N+1}}{N} \qquad (12\text{-}9)$$

$$S''_t = \frac{S'_t + S'_{t-1} + \ldots + S'_{t-M+1}}{M} \qquad (12\text{-}10)$$

$$a_t = S'_t + (S'_t - S''_t) = 2S'_t - S''_t \qquad (12\text{-}11)$$

$$b_t = \frac{2}{N-1} (S'_t - S''_t) \qquad (12\text{-}12)$$

$$F_{t+m} = a_t + b_t m \qquad (12\text{-}13)$$

where

a_t = Smoothed level
b_t = Smoothed trend
m = Number of periods forecasted into the future (i.e., forecast horizon)

Table 12–7 is a more complete example of the application of double moving averages to a data set of 30 values of weekly demand. With $N=3$, the table shows the results of the intermediate steps as well as the final forecast value. Figure 12–3 shows these same results in graph form. One can see in Figure 12–3 that the double moving forecast follows the actual data fairly closely; the single moving forecast, however, is low most of the time. The double moving average forecasts are above and below the actual values denoting that both positive and negative errors occur (i.e., it is unbiased). This indicates that the systematic error of the simple moving average has been eliminated.

Advantages

When trend and randomness are the only significant demand pattern, then this is a useful method. Because it smoothes larger random variations more than the method of first differences, it is less influenced by outliers.

TABLE 12-7
Double Moving Averages: Fitted and Forecasted

Period (t)	(1) Weekly Demand	(2) Three-Period Moving Average of (1)	(3) Three-Period Moving Average of (2)	(4) Value of a	(5) Value of b	(6) Fitted Value of a + b(m) (m = 1)	Error
1	63						
2	64						
3	66	64.33					
4	64	64.67					
5	68	66.00	65.00	67.00	1.00		
6	70	67.33	66.00	68.67	1.33	68.00	2.00
7	67	68.33	67.22	69.44	1.11	70.00	-3.00
8	69	68.67	68.11	69.22	.56	70.56	-1.56
9	74	70.00	69.00	71.00	1.00	69.78	4.22
10	72	71.67	70.11	73.22	1.56	72.00	.00
11	73	73.00	71.56	74.44	1.44	74.78	-1.78
12	78	74.33	73.00	75.67	1.33	75.89	2.11
13	77	76.00	74.44	77.56	1.56	77.00	.00
14	80	78.33	76.22	80.44	2.11	79.11	.89
15	83	80.00	78.11	81.89	1.89	82.56	.44
16	81	81.33	79.89	82.78	1.44	83.78	-2.78
17	86	83.33	81.56	85.11	1.78	84.22	1.78
18	88	85.00	83.22	86.78	1.78	86.89	1.11
19	85	86.33	84.89	87.78	1.44	88.56	-3.56
20	87	86.67	86.00	87.33	.67	89.22	-2.22
21	92	88.00	87.00	89.00	1.00	88.00	4.00
22	95	91.33	88.67	94.00	2.67	90.00	5.00
23	93	93.33	90.89	95.78	2.44	96.67	-3.67
24	97	95.00	93.22	96.78	1.78	98.22	-1.22
25	99	96.33	94.89	97.78	1.44	98.56	.44
26	96	97.33	96.22	98.44	1.11	99.22	-3.22
27	102	99.00	97.56	100.44	1.44	99.56	2.44
28	101	99.67	98.67	100.67	1.00	101.89	-.89
29	103	102.00	100.22	103.78	1.78	101.67	1.33
30	105	103.00	101.56	104.44	1.44	105.56	-.56
Mean	82.60					86.07	.05
Standard deviation	13.16					11.58	2.47

Disadvantages

In general, this method is too simplistic to be used by itself; it does not model the seasonality of the series. Also, as we see below, there are computationally simpler methods that are as effective as this method. Moving averages require more computations than other methods such as exponential smoothing. Finally, when using this method, one faces the problem of determining the optimal number of periods to use in the simple and double moving averages.

BROWN'S DOUBLE EXPONENTIAL SMOOTHING

A method very similar to double moving averages is double exponential smoothing. This method has the capability to account for trend and retains the advantage of requiring less data than moving averages, an attribute of all exponential smoothing methods.

Brown's double exponential smoothing model is very much like the double moving average model discussed in the previous section.[2] It uses a single parameter, alpha, for both smoothing operations. As in double moving averages, this method computes the difference between single and double smoothed values as a measure of trend. It then adds this value to the single smoothed value together with an adjustment for current trend. Brown's model is implemented with the following set of equations: (As before, S'_t denotes a single smoothed value and S''_t denotes the double smoothed value).

$$S'_t = \alpha Y_t + (1-\alpha) S'_{t-1} \qquad (12\text{--}14)$$

$$S''_t = \alpha S'_t + (1-\alpha) S''_{t-1} \qquad (12\text{--}15)$$

$$a_t = S'_t + (S'_t - S''_t) = 2S'_t - S''_t \qquad (12\text{--}16)$$

$$b_t = \frac{\alpha}{1-\alpha} (S'_t - S''_t) \qquad (12\text{--}17)$$

$$F_{t+m} = a_t + b_t m \qquad (12\text{--}18)$$

where

$$m = \text{Forecast horizon}$$

The application of this model is illustrated in Table 12–8, the results of which are shown in graph form in Figure 12–4.

Starting Values of S'_t and S''_t

The equations below illustrate our choice of starting values for Brown's linear exponential smoothing.

$$S'_1 = S''_1 = Y_1$$
$$a_1 = Y_1$$
$$b_1 = \frac{(Y_2 - Y_1) + (Y_4 - Y_3)}{2}$$

FIGURE 12–3
Single and Double Moving Averages

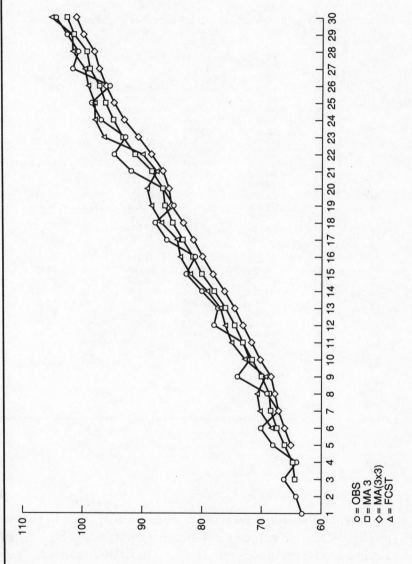

o = OBS
□ = MA 3
◇ = MA(3x3)
△ = FCST

TABLE 12-8
Brown's Double Exponential Smoothing Model (Alpha = .15)

Period (t)	Weekly Demand	Single Exponential Smoothing	Double Exponential Smoothing	Value of a	Value of b	Fitted Value of a + b(m) (m = 1)	Error
1	63	63.000	63.000	63.000	1.500		
2	64	63.150	63.023	63.278	.023	64.500	-.500
3	58	62.378	62.926	61.829	-.097	63,300	-5.300
4	60	62.021	62.790	61.252	-.136	61.733	-1.733
5	75	63.968	62.967	64.969	.177	61.116	13.884
6	70	64.873	63.253	66.493	.286	65.145	4.855
7	64	64.742	63.476	66.007	.223	66.778	-2.778
8	67	65.080	63.717	66.444	.241	66.231	.769
9	80	67.318	64.257	70.380	.540	66.685	13.315
10	74	68.321	64.866	71.775	.610	70.920	3.080
11	66	67.973	65.332	70.613	.466	72.384	-6.384
12	68	67.977	65.729	70.224	.397	71.079	-3.079
13	80	69.780	66.337	73.224	.608	70.621	9.379
14	81	71.463	67.106	75.821	.769	73.831	7.169
15	74	71.844	67.816	75.871	.711	76.590	-2.590
16	75	72.317	68.491	76.143	.675	76.582	-1.582
17	87	74.520	69.396	79.643	.904	76.818	10.182
18	84	75.942	70.378	81.506	.982	80.548	3.452
19	76	75.950	71.213	80.687	.836	82.488	-6.488
20	74	75.658	71.880	79.435	.667	81.523	-7.523
21	93	78.259	72.837	83.681	.957	80.102	12.898
22	91	80.170	73.937	86.404	1.100	84.638	6.362
23	85	80.895	74.981	86.809	1.044	87.504	-2.504
24	84	81.361	75.938	86.783	.957	87.852	-3.852
25	97	83.706	77.103	90.310	1.165	87.740	9.260
26	95	85.400	78.348	92.453	1.245	91.475	3.525
27	89	85.940	79.486	92.394	1.139	93.698	-4.698
28	86	85.949	80.456	91.443	.969	93.533	-7,533
29	103	88.507	81.664	95.350	1.208	92.412	10.588
30	101	90.381	82.971	97.791	1.308	96.558	4.442
Mean	78.803						1.952
Standard deviation	12.143						7.0524

Because we have 30 periods of historical data in this example, the starting values have little influence on the forecast for Period 31. In instances where there is little historical data and the smoothing constant is small (close to zero), the choice of the initialization procedure will have significant influence on the resulting forecasts for several future time periods.

FIGURE 12-4
Single (SES) and Double (DES) Exponential Smoothing

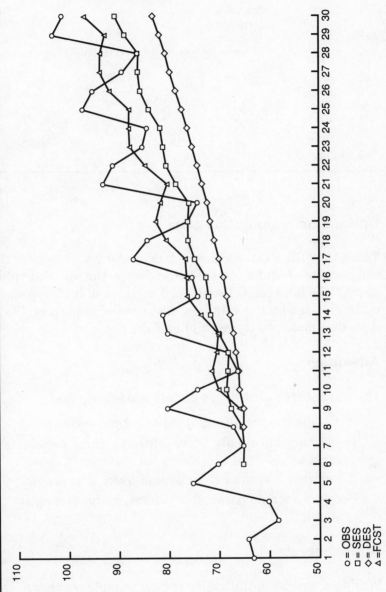

o = OBS
□ = SES
◇ = DES
△ = FCST

TABLE 12–9
A Search for a Good Alpha Value: Brown's Double Exponential Smoothing

Alpha	Standard Deviation of Errors	Alpha	Standard Deviation of Errors
.05	10.02	.16	7.06
.02	14.76	.18	7.10
.10	7.43	.20	7.18
.12	7.16	.25	7.44
.14	7.06	.30	7.74
.15*	7.05	.70	10.47

*The best value of those calculated.

Optimal Smoothing Constant

Table 12–9 illustrates a simple trial and error search for the optimal value of alpha. As the table shows, the optimal value appears to lie between 0.1 and 0.2. The value of 0.15 appears to be optimal based on the standard deviation of the errors. We leave it to the reader to try an alpha of .17.

Advantages

The advantages of Brown's double smoothing are:

It models the trend and level of a time series.

It is computationally more efficient than double moving averages.

It requires less data than double moving averages.

Because a single parameter is used, parameter optimization is simple.

Disadvantages

While parameter optimization is made simple because of the use of one parameter, there is some loss of flexibility because the best smoothing constant for the level and trend components may not be equal. Brown's double smoothing model is not a full model in that it does not model the level, trend, and *seasonality* of a series. Many time series have these three components. Thus, it is not recommended that Brown's method be used unless the data is first deseasonalized, a procedure that was discussed in Chapter 11.

The next method we discuss is easier to understand than Brown's and has the flexibility of using two smoothing constants, one for trend and one for the level of the series.

HOLT'S TWO-PARAMETER TREND MODEL

Holt's two-parameter double exponential smoothing model, as the name implies, differs from Brown's model in that it allows the use of a second smoothing constant to separately smooth the trend.[3] Holt's model further adjusts each smoothed value for the trend of the previous period before calculating the new smoothed value. Holt's two-parameter trend model is implemented using the following set of equations:

$$S_t = \alpha Y_t + (1-\alpha)(S_{t-1} + b_{t-1}) \qquad (12\text{-}19)$$

where

α = Normal smoothing constant
S_t = Smoothed level in Period t

$$b_t = \gamma(S_t - S_{t-1}) + (1-\gamma) b_{t-1} \qquad (12\text{-}20)$$

where

γ = Trend smoothing constant
b_t = Smoothed trend in Period t

$$F_{t+m} = S_t + b_t m \qquad (12\text{-}21)$$

Notice that in Equation 12–19, the smoothed level (S_{t-1}) from Period $t-1$ is adjusted by the trend (b_{t-1}) from that period. This eliminates some of the natural lag of the process. The first smoothing constant, α, is then used to smooth the new demand and trend-adjusted previous smoothed level. The second smoothing constant, γ, is used to smooth out or average the trend in Equation 12–20. This removes some of the random error that would otherwise be reflected in the unsmoothed trend $(S_t - S_{t-1})$.

TABLE 12–10
Holt's Two-Parameter Trend Model

(1) Period (t)	(2) Weekly Demand	(3) Smoothed Level	(4) Smoothed Trend	(5) Forecast (m = 1)	(6) Error
1	63	63.000	−.500		
2	64	62.800	−.320	62.500	1.500
3	66	63.184	.102	62.480	3.520
4	64	63.429	.188	63.286	.714
5	68	64.494	.714	63.617	4.383
6	70	66.166	1.289	65.208	4.792
7	67	67.364	1.234	67.455	−.455
8	69	68.679	1.283	68.599	.401
9	74	70.769	1.767	69.961	4.039
10	72	72.429	1.703	72.536	−.536
11	73	73.906	1.567	74.132	−1.132
12	78	75.978	1.870	75.473	2.527
13	77	77.679	1.769	77.848	−.848
14	80	79.558	1.835	79.447	.553
15	83	81.714	2.028	81.393	1.607
16	81	83.193	1.699	83.742	−2.742
17	86	85.114	1.832	84.892	1.108
18	88	87.156	1.958	86.945	1.055
19	85	88.292	1.464	89.115	−4.115
20	87	89.205	1.134	89.756	−2.756
21	92	90.671	1.333	90.339	1.661
22	95	92.603	1.693	92.004	2.996
23	93	94.037	1.537	94.296	−1.296
24	97	95.859	1.708	95.574	1.426
25	99	97.854	1.880	97.567	1.433
26	96	98.987	1.432	99.734	−3.734
27	102	100.735	1.622	100.419	1.581
28	101	102.086	1.459	102.357	−1.357
29	103	103.436	1.394	103.545	−.545
30	105	104.863	1.414	104.829	.171
31				106.277	
Mean	82.6				.550
Standard deviation	13.39				2.361

Alpha = .20
Gamma = .60
Starting trend = −.50 = $(Y_2 − Y_1 + Y_4 − Y_3)/2$
Starting base = 63 = Y_1

Holt's model is illustrated in Table 12–10 and Figure 12–5, using the data from the previous examples. We can see in Table 12–10 that adjusting the previous smoothed level for trend as in

FIGURE 12–5
Holt's Two-Parameter Exponential Smoothing

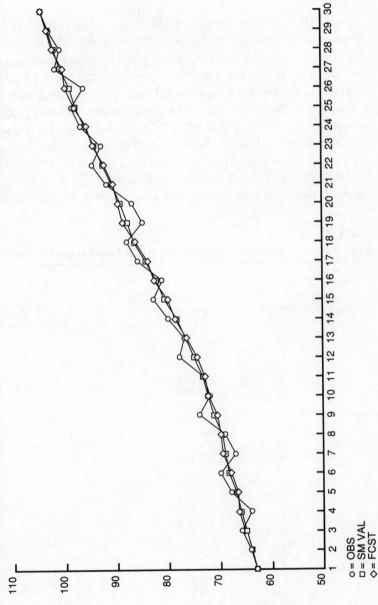

o = OBS
□ = SM VAL
◇ = FCST

Equation 12–21 brings the new smoothed level (i.e., forecast) closer to the actual value. This is shown in columns 3, 4, and 5 of Table 12–10.

As with any exponential smoothing model, there are two basic questions to be answered for Holt's model. These are: What smoothing constant(s) should be used and how should the exponential smoothing process be initialized? In our example, several values of α and γ were tried until the apparent best values of $\alpha = .2$ and $\gamma = .6$ were found. The results with various parameter values are shown in Table 12–11. In initializing the process, we need an initial value for both S_1 and b_1. For S_1, we can simply use Y_1, the observed value for Period 1. The initial trend estimate is a little more difficult. Some possible values are: the difference between the first two observed values, some average of the ob-

TABLE 12–11
Good Values of Alpha and Gamma for Holt's Two-Parameter Model

Alpha	Gamma	Standard Deviation of Errors
.3	.3	2.465
.3	.2	2.701
.3	.1	3.373
.25	.45	2.374
.25	.40	2.424
.25	.35	2.491
.25	.3	2.586
.2*	.6	2.361
.2	.55	2.395
.2	.5	2.442
.2	.45	2.505
.2	.4	2.590
.2	.35	2.704
.2	.3	2.859
.2	.25	3.068
.2	.2	3.360
.2	.1	4.565
.1	.3	4.798
.1	.2	5.889
.1	.1	8.544

*Best combination of alpha and gamma of those tried.

served slope for the first several periods, or an estimate of the series slope from a plot of the data. Any of these possible methods will work well if the data is consistent from period to period. However, if the data is not well behaved, that is, shows a significant drop at some point when the general trend is upward, inclusion of such irregularities in the initial slope estimate can require the use of a lengthy time period to overcome their impact. In such instances, it would be better to estimate the longer-range-trend slope from the data plot. In this case, we used the common starting conditions shown below.

$$S_1 = Y_1$$

$$b_1 = \frac{(Y_2 - Y_1) + (Y_4 - Y_3)}{2}$$

Advantages

Holt's method has the same advantages as Brown's double smoothing. In addition, Holt's is more flexible in that the level and trend can be smoothed with different weights.

Disadvantages

Holt's requires that two parameters be optimized. Thus, the search for the best combination of parameters is more complex than for a single parameter. Holt's suffers the same limitation as other methods presented above in that it does not model the seasonality of a series. This is a serious limitation, which is eliminated by the method described below.

WINTERS' THREE–PARAMETER EXPONENTIAL SMOOTHING

Both Brown's one-parameter model and Holt's two-parameter model perform well when a series has significant trend and no seasonality. However, they do not perform well with seasonal data. Winters' smoothing model extends Holt's two-parameter model to the seasonal case by including a third smoothing operation (and

The Dilemma of Random Walks and Trends

The old adage that "What goes up must come down" is often true in short- to medium-term forecasting. Also, we can add the complement of this adage, "What goes down may come up." This is true because for some time series, the short- to medium-term behavior is a random walk. A random walk is characterized by its slow meanderings up and down over time. If graphs of six months to a year are studied, random walks appear to have very strong upward or downward trends. That is, if we confine our analysis to only one short period of time, we may be misled into believing the time series has a sustainable trend. Herein lies a dilemma facing the forecaster and the forecasting system.

In general, it is assumed that the most recent past is the best predictor of the immediate future. Depending on our definition of immediate future and the consequences of random walks, this may or may not be true. The dilemma is that detecting random walks requires more than a year of data. However, we view the last year of data as the most relevant. In general, this dilemma puts us in a difficult position. If we include enough data (i.e., several years) to predict the random walk for some time series, we may miss the recent trend for other nonrandom-walk series. Or, if we do not include large amounts of data and predict trends for trending and random-walk series both, then we are correct for the trending series and grossly incorrect for the random-walk series.

How can a statistical model distinguish between a short-run period of a random walk and a trend? It can't.

The solution to this dilemma in most forecasting systems has been to use three years of data to identify forecasting models. If a trend is strong enough or long enough to sustain a three-year influence, then it will be identified as a trending model. This strategy may result in some trends being missed and some random walks being misidentified as trends, but it nonetheless appears to be a reasonable trade-off. The problem has not been eliminated, but we hope it has been reduced to a cost-effective solution.

When random walks exist, we might have accurate one- or two-period-ahead forecasts. But as horizons get longer than, for example, three-period-ahead forecasts, there will be extremely large errors.

a third parameter) to adjust for seasonality.[4] This method is sometimes called the *Holt-Winters'* method. This is a very important approach to operational forecasting.

The underlying structure of Winters' model assumes that:

$$Y_{t+1} = (S_t + b_t) I_{t-L+1} + e_t \qquad (12\text{--}22)$$

where

S_t = Nonseasonal level of the series in Period t
b_t = Trend in Period t
I_{t-L+1} = Seasonal index for Period $t+1$
e_t = Error in Period t

That is, Y_{t+1}, the actual value of a series, equals a smoothed level value S_t plus an estimate of trend b_t times a seasonal index I_{t-L+1}. These three components of demand are each exponentially smoothed values available at the end of Period t. Thus, we see that this model is very similar to the decomposition method described in Chapter 11. The equations used to estimate these smoothed values are given below.

$$S_t = \alpha \frac{Y_t}{I_{t-L}} + (1 - \alpha)(S_{t-1} + b_{t-1}) \qquad (12\text{--}23)$$

$$b_t = \gamma (S_t - S_{t-1}) + (1 - \gamma)b_{t-1} \qquad (12\text{--}24)$$

$$I_t = \beta \frac{Y_t}{S_t} + (1 - \beta) I_{t-L} \qquad (12\text{--}25)$$

$$\hat{Y}_{t+m} = (S_t + b_t m) I_{t-L+m} \qquad (12\text{--}26)$$

where

Y_t = Value of actual demand in Period t
α = Smoothing constant used for S_t
S_t = Smoothed value in Period t after adjusting for seasonality
γ = Smoothing constant used to calculate the trend (b_t)
b_t = Smoothed value of trend
I_{t-L} = Smoothed seasonal index
L = Length of the seasonal cycle (e.g., 12 or 4 for monthly or quarterly data, respectively)
β = Smoothing constant used to calculate the seasonal index in Period t

I_t = Smoothed seasonal index

m = Horizon length of the forecasts of Y_{t+m}

Let's study each of these equations. Equation 12–23 calculates the overall level of the series as in other exponential smoothing models. It differs from single exponential smoothing models in two ways. First, the most recent actual value (Y_t) is deseasonalized by dividing it by I_{t-L}, and, second, the most recent trend b_t is added to the previous smoothed value prior to smoothing. Thus, S_t in Equation 12–23 is the trend-adjusted, deseasonalized level at the end of Period t. S_t is used in Equation 12–26 to generate forecasts. As the equation shows, a trend estimate is added to S_t; the resulting term is then multiplied by an appropriate seasonal index to yield a final forecast.

As in Holt's and Brown's methods, Equation 12–24 provides an estimate of the trend by smoothing the difference between the smoothed values S_t and S_{t-1}. This is an estimate of the period-to-period change (trend) in the overall level of Y_t.

Equation 12–25 illustrates the calculation of the smoothed seasonal index, I_t. The denominator of the first term of this equation uses the most recent smoothed value of S_t. This value reflects only the trend and level patterns of Y_t, not the seasonal influence. By dividing Y_t by S_t, we have an estimate of an unsmoothed seasonal index for this period as shown below.

$$Y_t/S_t = (\$_t)I_t/\$_t = I_t \qquad (12\text{--}27)$$

Then Equation 12–25, which is repeated below, smooths this estimate by averaging it with the index of the same period last year.

$$I_t = \beta \frac{Y_t}{S_t} + (1 - \beta) I_{t-L}$$

This seasonal factor is calculated in preparation for the next cycle of forecasting and used to forecast demand one or more full seasonal cycles ahead.

The forecast (Equation 12–26) is made by adding trend from Equation 12–24 to the deseasonalized value (from Equation 12–23) and then multiplying this result by the appropriate seasonal index. These forecasts can be readily extended beyond L periods in the future by reusing the L seasonal factor.

Table 12-12 is an example of the application of Winters' method to a data set that reflects both trend and seasonality. A plot of actual values and forecasts is shown in Figure 12-6.

The bottom of Table 12-12 summarizes the errors realized during the parameter-fitting process (Periods 13 through 36) and the forecasting process (Periods 37 through 48). As shown, these errors are comparable: the standard deviations of the errors were nearly equal. Interestingly, the error statistics for forecasting (i.e., Periods 37 to 48) are actually 1- through 12-period-ahead forecast errors. Each of the forecasts of Periods 37 through 48 were made at the end of Period 36. Thus, these represent full-year-ahead forecasts.

As Table 12-12 shows, the mean error during this 12-month period was −29.997; thus, the total cumulative error for the period is about −360 units (i.e., −30*12) during a period when cumulative demand was actually 11,413. This yields a cumulative percent error of 360/11,413, or about 3 percent. While we cannot generalize from this result, we can nonetheless recognize that for this series of repeating patterns, Winters' method forecasted for 12 months quite accurately.

The exact procedure illustrated in Table 12-12 would not be used in actual practice because it used unadjusted seasonal indexes in the calculations. That is, the sum of the seasonal indexes for each year were not forced to equal 12, as was done in Chapter 11. The indexes were not adjusted because to do so would have made the computations more complex than necessary for our purposes. In actual practice, the final seasonal adjustment procedure used in Chapter 11 can be applied to the seasonal indexes of Table 12-12.

Initialization of Parameters

Table 12-12 reflects a combination of techniques in addition to the straightforward application of Equations 12-23 through 12-26. Some method must be used to derive initial b_t, S_t, and I_ts. In this case, the differences in the value of the series over three 12-month periods (Period 13 − Period 1, Period 14 − Period 2, and Period 15 − Period 3) are summed and then divided by 36 to get an average monthly trend value of 7.9167. The average

TABLE 12–12
Winters' Three-Parameter Exponential Smoothing (Additive Trend, Multiplicative Seasonal, and Smoothed Model: $\alpha = .2$, $\beta = .65$, $\gamma = .5$**)**

| Period | Y_t | Smoothed Trend | | $S_t + b_t$ | Seasonal | $\hat{Y}_t$ |
		S_t	b_t		I_t	
1	546			652.96	.836	
2	578			660.87	.875	
3	660			668.79	.987	
4	707	Initial $S_t + b_t =$		676.71	1.045	
5	738	for initial I_t		684.62	1.078	
6	781			692.54	1.128	
7	848			700.45	1.211	
8	818			708.37	1.155	
9	729			716.29	1.018	
10	691			724.21	.954	
11	658			732.12	.899	
12	604	604.000	7.917	611.917	.816	
13	629	639.977	21.947	661.924	.932	511.681
14	711	692.128	37.049	729.177	.974	578.917
15	729	731.084	38.002	769.086	.994	719.591
16	798	768.031	37.475	805.505	1.041	803.513
17	861	804.150	36.797	840.947	1.073	868.304
18	903	832.902	32.775	865.677	1.099	948.361
19	968	852.458	26.165	878.623	1.162	1,048.020
20	894	857.736	15.722	873.458	1.082	1,014.594
21	860	867.768	12.877	880.644	1.000	888.954
22	792	870.528	7.818	878.347	.925	840.263
23	739	867.127	2.209	869.336	.869	789.417
24	699	866.757	.919	867.676	.810	709.526
25	773	860.106	−2.866	857.240	.910	808.257
26	818	853.788	−4.592	849.196	.964	834.809

value of the first 12 periods (696.5) becomes a base upon which S_t and b_t are projected. This average value is centered on the Period 6.5 [i.e., (12+1)/2]. Thus, to get the $S_t + b_t$ value for any particular month, we must use the appropriate multiplier on the trend value of 7.9167. Therefore, $S_t + b_t$ for Period 1 is 696.5 − 5.5(7.9167) = 652.96. $S_t + b_t$ for Period 2 is 696.5 − 4.5(7.9167) = 660.87 and so on. Each successive $S_t + b_t$ value is approximately 7.9167 greater than its preceding value. The actual values for Periods 1 to 12 are then divided by their respective $S_t + b_t$ values to obtain the initial seasonal factors shown in Periods 1 to 12. S_t for Period 12 is the observed value for that period while b_t for Period 12 is the average trend as estimated earlier. Fitted values

TABLE 12–12 (continued)

Period	Y_t	Smoothed Trend S_t	b_t	$S_t + b_t$	Seasonal I_t	$\hat{Y}_t$
27	871	854.689	−1.846	852.843	1.010	843.716
28	882	851.722	−2.406	849.316	1.037	887.836
29	959	858.164	2.018	860.182	1.102	911.519
30	979	866.241	5.047	871.288	1.119	945.692
31	955	861.427	.117	861.544	1.127	1,012.284
32	925	860.271	−.520	859.752	1.077	931.886
33	843	856.335	−2.228	854.108	.990	860.088
34	790	854.039	−2.262	851.776	.925	790.320
35	746	853.208	−1.547	851.661	.872	739.784
36	822	884.328	14.787	899.115	.888	689.722
37	857					818.378
38	876					880.632
39	959					938.112
40	981					978.826
41	1,051					1,056.015
42	1,124					1,089.236
43	1,073					1,113.534
44	1,020					1,080.310
45	933					1,007.252
46	787					954.908
47	830					913.293
48	922					942.467

Fitted Values Periods 13–36   Forecasted Values Periods 37–48
  Mean error = −1.29390   Mean error = −29.9970
         MAD = 43.40864   MAD = 46.0716
Standard error = 61.51383   Standard error = 64.2464

for the next 24 time periods (i.e., Periods 13 to 36) were used to determine the values of alpha, beta, and gamma that minimize the sum of the squared errors. The selected values of the parameters are then used to forecast the series for a full 12 periods ahead (Periods 37 to 48), with Period 36 as the origin of all 12 forecasts. In general, as the future rolls into the past, these forecasts are revised as each new observed value becomes known.

In practice, Winters' method is used as follows.

1. At the end of Period t, the actual demand, Y_t, is recorded.
2. Apply this value in Equation 12–23 to calculate the smoothed value at time t. Note that all values in Equation 12–23 are known at this time.

FIGURE 12-6
Winters' Three-Parameter Exponential Smoothing

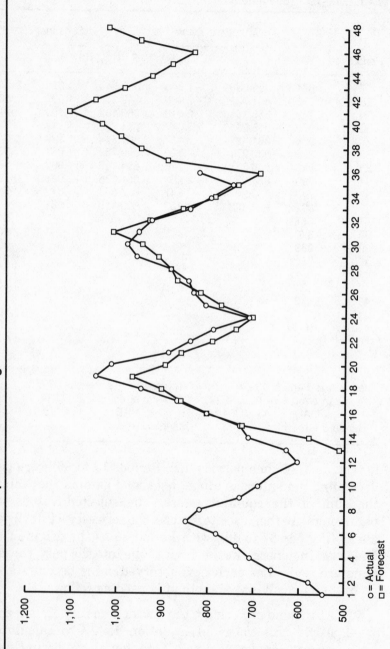

o = Actual
□ = Forecast

Your Winter Blues May Be SAD

The underlying causes of seasonal demands for products can be complex. Demands for products such as pharmaceuticals are greatly influenced by changes in temperature, humidity, and precipitation. While some of us thrive on these changes in the seasons, some do not. One of the stranger seasonal influences is SAD (seasonal affective disorder). The American Psychiatric Association believes that approximately 10 million U.S. citizens (about 4 percent) are severely affected by this disorder. An additional 25 million people (about 14 percent) are mildly affected or hampered by the disorder. SAD affects people primarily during winter months and is apparently caused by the hormonal and neurological changes that occur with decreases in the number of hours of daylight. The severely affected individuals may gain or lose weight, be lethargic, or have difficulty concentrating on their jobs. It is believed that having fewer daylight hours in the winter affects different parts of the brain, hormones, and biological rhythms. Fortunately, the disorder can be treated with therapies that typically involve exposure to special fluorescent lights.

3. Next calculate the newest value of the seasonal index, I_t. Then adjust this and previous indexes for the past year so that they sum to the number of periods per year. These values will be used in the next forecast cycle.
4. Calculate the new trend, b_t.
5. Forecast future sales using Equation 12–26.

Each of these steps is illustrated in Table 12–12. Table 12–12 shows the results using Winters' method with alpha equal to .2, beta equal to .65, and gamma equal to .5. Using a crude search method, these were found to be good values of the three smoothing constants.

Additive and Multiplicative Factors

Equation 12–26 assumes that trend is additive and that the seasonal influence is multiplicative. When a model results in the multiplication of two factors to yield a forecast, this is referred to as a *multiplicative forecasting model*. In Equation 12–26, the seasonal index is multiplied times the current smoothed and trend values. In contrast, the trend in Equation 12–26 is additive. Holt-Winters' method can be used to model four different combinations of trend and seasonal influences. Winters' method is most commonly used to model additive trend and multiplicative seasonality as in Equations 12–26 and 12–29.

Additive trends are more popular than multiplicative trends because long-horizon forecasts that extrapolate a multiplicative trend have a tendency to significantly over- or underforecast demand. Because of this over- or underforecasting, multiplicative models are either avoided or dampening of the trend is used. Dampening is discussed next in this chapter.

Equations 12–28 through 12–31 illustrate four different forecasting equations for the situations of Figure 12–7.

$$F_{t+m} = S_t + b_t m + I_{t-L+m} \qquad (12\text{–}28)$$

$$F_{t+m} = (S_t + b_t m)\, I_{t-L+m} \qquad (12\text{–}29)$$

$$F_{t+m} = S_t b_t^{\ m} + I_{t-L+m} \qquad (12\text{–}30)$$

$$F_{t+m} = S_t b_t^{\ m} I_{t-L+m} \qquad (12\text{–}31)$$

Data Requirements

Because Winters' method models seasonality, its data requirements are greater than other methods discussed in this chapter. To adequately measure seasonality, at least three seasons of monthly data (36 months), four or five seasons of quarterly data (16 to 20 quarters), and three seasons of weekly data (156 weeks) are the minimums recommended.

FIGURE 12–7
Four Combinations of Trend-Seasonal Models

		Seasonality	
		Additive	Multiplicative
Trend	Additive	Equation 12–28	Equation 12–29
	Multiplicative	Equation 12–30	Equation 12–31

Advantages

Winters' powerful method models trend, seasonality, and randomness using an efficient exponential smoothing process. Its seasonal indexes are easily interpreted; also, when these indexes are group indexes, they can be applied to new or low-volume products in the group. Because this is an exponential smoothing model, parameters can be updated using computationally efficient algorithms. The model formulation of Equation 12–29 is easily interpreted and understood by management. The relationship between Winters' method and simple decomposition methods makes it more intuitive than other methods such as Fourier series analysis. Because of these advantages, Winters' model is used in several commercially available forecasting systems.

Disadvantages

Winters' model may be too complex for series that do not have identifiable trends and seasonality. The simultaneous determination of the optimal values of three smoothing parameters can be computationally intense. Thus, the initial fitting of parameters using Winters' model may take more time than regression, classical decomposition, or Fourier series analysis. However, after fitting a model, these parameters can be updated very efficiently.

TREND DAMPENING

Forecasters have noted the times that forecasts have been dramatically in error. One problem noted has been the tendency of trend models to grossly overforecast the positive or negative trends of the past when long-term forecasts are made. Some believe that this occurs because it is difficult to distinguish between the trend and cyclical variations in a time series; consequently, most modeling methods do not adequately decompose a series into separate trend and cyclical influences. Thus, trend and cyclical influences are modeled together in a single trend component (the trend may be higher or lower than it should be because of the cyclical up- or downturn). *Dampening* is the process of reducing the trend value in proportion to the length of the forecast horizon. Thus, it offsets the over- and underforecasting caused by trend extrapolation.

The underlying assumption in justifying dampened trends is that the trend reflects the effects of the business cycle. These effects are not expected to extend indefinitely into the future. There is not much research on the use of trend dampening. However, the empirical evidence of many users suggests that dampening is more effective than not. Dampening is done by multiplying the trend estimate by a fractional constant to the power of m, the number of periods forecast into the future. The modified forecast equations are shown below.

$$F_{t+m} = (S_t + p^m b_t m) + I_{t-L+m} \qquad (12\text{-}32)$$

$$F_{t+m} = (S_t + p^m b_t m) I_{t-L+m} \qquad (12\text{-}33)$$

$$F_{t+m} = (S_t p^m b_t^m) + I_{t-L+m} \qquad (12\text{-}34)$$

$$F_{t+m} = S_t p^m b_t^m I_{t-L+m} \qquad (12\text{-}35)$$

where

$$p = \text{Fractional dampening constant}$$

Table 12–13 illustrates selected values of p^m for different values of p and m.

We have seen little research on choosing the best dampening constant, p. It is suggested that very high values of p be used to avoid unrealistically low projections for long-term values unless there is strong evidence to support rapid declines in the trend. Much subjective insight is needed in selecting p. The systematic

TABLE 12–13
p^m **for Selected Values of** p **and** m

				m		
p	1	2	3	6	12	24
.7	.7	.49	.343	.118	.014	.0002
.8	.8	.64	.512	.262	.069	.0047
.9	.9	.81	.729	.531	.282	.0800
.95	.95	.903	.857	.735	.540	.292
1.0	1.0	1.0	1.0	1.0	1.0	1.0

bias caused by p values can be very misleading when p is used across all items in an automated forecasting environment. We should be able to identify those groups of items that will have sustainable trends and those that will not. In all cases of dampening, we do not allow it to reverse the trend. Additive trends are not allowed to reverse their signs, nor are multiplicative trends allowed to go below 1.00 or above 1.00 for increasing and decreasing trends, respectively. Thus, zero is an additive trend dampening bound, and 1.00 is a multiplicative trend dampening bound.

SUMMARY

This chapter has illustrated a number of forecasting methods. The method of using first, second, and seasonal differences to model trend and seasonal patterns is simple and effective. However, because differences do not average or smooth the past, one must be cautious in using these methods since unusual values or outliers can adversely affect resulting forecasts. The trend-adjusted methods of linear moving averages, double exponential smoothing, and Holt's two-parameter exponential smoothing are effective methods of modeling trends. However, many series have seasonal demand patterns. Thus, these methods are inappropriate when used with data that is seasonal. The most widely used method discussed here is Winters' method.[5] This method is a powerful one that models randomness, trend, and seasonality, and it is used in several commercially available forecasting systems.

REFERENCES

1. J. Holton Wilson and Barry Keating, *Business Forecasting* (Homewood, Ill.: Richard D. Irwin, 1990); and Spyros Makridakis, Steven C. Wheelwright, and Victor E. McGee, *Forecasting: Methods and Applications,* 2nd ed. (New York: John Wiley & Sons, 1983).
2. R. G. Brown, *Smoothing, Forecasting and Prediction* (Englewood Cliffs, N. J.: Prentice-Hall, 1963).
3. C. C. Holt, "Forecasting Seasonal and Trends by Exponentially Weighted Moving Averages," *Research Memorandum 52* (Washington, D.C.: Office of Naval Research, 1957).

4. P. R. Winters, "Forecasting Sales by Exponentially Weighted Moving Averages," *Management Science* 6, 1960, pp. 324–42.

5. Everette S. Gardner, "Exponential Smoothing: The State of the Art," *Journal of Forecasting* 4, no. 1 (1985), pp. 1–28.

APPENDIX: TEST OF SIGNIFICANT TREND WHEN USING DIFFERENCES

This appendix develops a simple test to determine whether the mean of differences is statistically significantly different than zero. While this test illustrates the test on first differences, it can be generalized to any type of differences. We present the test using classical hypothesis-testing procedures.

$$\text{Null hypothesis: On average, } Y_t - Y_{t-1} = 0$$

In other words, there is no trend.

If this hypothesis is proven wrong, then we accept the alternative hypothesis that:

Alternative hypothesis: On average, $Y_t - Y_{t-1}$ is either <0 or >0

In other words, there is a negative or a positive trend.

We make these inferences by comparing the mean of the differences to two times the standard deviation of the differences divided by the square root of the number of differences. Letting d equal the level of differences ($d=1$ for first differences, $d=2$ for second differences, and $d=12$ for monthly seasonal differences), the number of differences taken, $n-d$, will always be less than the sample size because we lose one or more observations when differencing.

If | Mean difference | $\leq 2(S/\sqrt{n-d})$, then accept the null hypothesis.

If | Mean difference | $> 2(S/\sqrt{n-d})$, then accept the alternative hypothesis and infer that there is a significant trend (a positive trend if the mean difference is positive or a negative trend if the mean difference is negative).

where | | denotes the absolute value of the mean differences and S denotes the standard deviation of the differences. The quantity $S/\sqrt{n-d}$ is called the *standard error of the mean differences,* hereafter called the *standard error of the mean.*

This test is based on the fact that, if there is no trend and the differences of the series are normally or nearly normally distributed, then 95.5 percent of the period-to-period changes will lie within two standard errors of the mean value of zero (remember that zero indicates no trend). As we discussed in Chapter 7, only 4.5 times out of 100 will values be more than two standard deviations away from their mean. In this test, the mean is selected to be the hypothesized mean of zero. It is very unlikely to get a value more than two standard errors away when the true mean difference is zero. Consequently, we infer that the hypothesized value of zero is not the correct value and that the null hypothesis is false. We logically infer that the mean is significantly different than zero because there is a systematic trend. This is summarized through the following decision rules.

If $|$ Mean difference $| \leq 2(S/\sqrt{n-d})$, then there is no trend.

If (Mean difference) $> 2(S/\sqrt{n-d})$, then there is a positive trend.

If (Mean difference) $< -2(S/\sqrt{n-d})$, then there is a negative trend.

Let's perform this test for the data of Table 12–1. For Series G, $S/\sqrt{n-d}$ equals $2.92/\sqrt{31-1}$ equals .533.

Mean difference of Series G $= 2.94 > 2$ Standard errors $= 2(.533) = 1.07$

Consequently, there is a positive trend.

For Series H, $S/\sqrt{n-d} = 2.73/\sqrt{31-1} = .498$

Mean difference of Series H $= -2.92 < -2$ Standard errors $=$
$$-2(.498) = -.997$$

Consequently, there is a negative trend.

For Series I, $S/\sqrt{n-d} = 2.22/\sqrt{31-1} = .405$

Mean difference of Series I $= |-.25| \leq 2$ Standard errors $=$
$$2(.405) = .81$$

Consequently, there is no trend. These conclusions are consistent with our intuitive interpretations of Figure 12–1 and Table 12–1.

The statistical test for trend is a powerful test. At least one mainframe item-level forecasting system uses this test to confirm that a trend exists in the data. When this test is automated, we have a powerful tool that can help us identify trends.

CHAPTER 13

FOURIER SERIES AND MULTIMODEL SIMULATION METHODS

Everything should be as simple as it can be, but not simpler.

Albert Einstein

The power of computers has made it cost effective to routinely use sophisticated methods of forecasting such as Winters' method and the approaches presented here. This chapter describes two methods of forecasting. The first method is known by several names, including Fourier series analysis, spectral analysis, and harmonic smoothing. We have chosen to use the most common name—Fourier series analysis (hereafter referred to as FSA).

The second method, the multimodel simulation method (MSM), is developed in the last half of this chapter. While some characteristics of this method are several decades old, the integration of old and new forecasting approaches with powerful computer systems makes this an exciting new method.

The two forecasting methods of this chapter are presented independently; thus, you can choose which to study first.

FOURIER SERIES ANALYSIS

Some have found FSA hard to understand because it uses trigonometric functions. Consequently, we have written this chapter to make FSA much more easily understood by actual and potential users. Because FSA has advantages in operational forecasting, it is used in several commercially available software packages; as all methods, it does have some disadvantages.

The mathematics of FSA methods were developed by Joseph Fourier, a French mathematician and physicist, in about 1880. He showed that any periodic observations can be represented by a series of trigonometric functions of sine and cosine terms. Fourier series techniques are used extensively in science and engineering to model the behavior of mechanical and electrical systems. The repeating patterns of alternating current, vibrating springs, and the oscillations of structures are similar to patterns of seasonal and cyclical demands for products.

One of the most important advantages of FSA is its simple way of modeling series with seasonality. It estimates a complex seasonal model in a computationally efficient way; then it facilitates simplification of the model if necessary. For example, FSA can be used to model a seasonal variation that includes one, two, three, and four seasonal peaks per year. Based on statistics that are generated during the modeling process, the unimportant seasonal patterns of the model are dropped without any necessity to reestimate the remaining model. That is, if a seasonal term in the model is not necessary, it is dropped, and the remaining terms are used to forecast. Most other methods require a refitting of the model when one or more terms are dropped.

MULTIPEAK SEASONALITY

We may tend to think that seasonal influences result in only one peak and trough per year; however, many seasonal series have multiple peaks per year. Consumer items can have several peaks during the year, for example, in the summer and at Christmas. The classical decomposition method and Winters' approach allow multiple peaks per year also, and there are no serious disadvantages to those methods as compared to FSA. However, FSA is somewhat more methodical in identifying significant and insignificant peaks and eliminating those that are not significant. The ability to model a series as if it were a complex one and to eliminate the nonsignificant peaks is a distinctive advantage of FSA. As we will see, this provides an efficient and effective final forecasting model.

Finally, let us emphasize that you do not have to know advanced mathematics to use and understand FSA. However, a basic understanding of simple trigonometric function behavior is important for any consumer of FSA.

UNDERSTANDING TRIGONOMETRIC FUNCTIONS

Understanding sine and cosine function behavior will greatly increase your understanding of FSA. Figure 13–1 and Table 13–1 illustrate a simple sine function.

FIGURE 13–1
Y = sin(X)

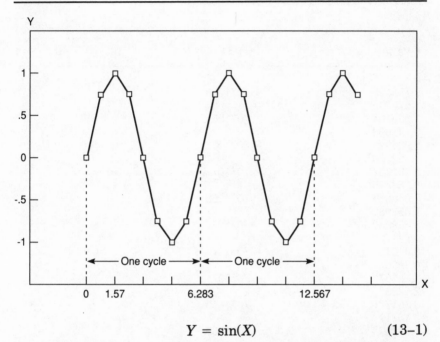

$$Y = \sin(X) \qquad (13\text{–}1)$$

A sine wave is a repeating pattern that goes through one cycle every 6.283185 (i.e., every 2π) units of time. Thus, we can view a sine function as a mathematical function that converts a number (X) into another number $\sin(X)$.

As shown in Table 13–1, the value of $\sin(X)$ varies smoothly from 0 to +1 to 0 to −1 to 0 as X varies from 0 to 1.5708 to 3.14 to 4.71 to 6.283185. This pattern repeats again at 6.283185, that is, the $\sin(6.283185 + X)$ varies smoothly from 0 to +1 to 0 to −1 to 0 as X varies from 0 to 1.5708 to 3.14 to 4.71 to 6.283185. This is confirmed by noting that the repeating patterns of Figure 13–1 are identical for X values of 0 to 6.2832 versus 6.2832 to 12.5664. It is this ability of trigonometric functions to vary smoothly from 0 to +1 to 0 to −1 to 0 that makes them useful in modeling the repeating patterns of seasonal sales. To better understand the anatomy of a sine wave, consider Figure 13–2 and Table 13–2 discussed below.

TABLE 13–1
Y = sin(X)

X Values	sin(X)	sin(X) Graph −1	0	+1
0	0		•	
.785398	.7071068			•
1.570796	1			•
2.356194	.7071068			•
3.141593	0		•	
3.926991	−.707107	•		
4.712389	−1	•		
5.497787	−.707107	•		
6.283185	0		•	
7.068583	.7071068			•
7.853982	1			•
8.639380	.7071068			•
9.424778	0		•	
10.21018	−.707107	•		
10.99557	−1	•		
11.78097	−.707107	•		
12.56637	0		•	
13.35177	.7071068			•
14.13717	1			•
14.92257	.7071068			•

Sine-Wave Phase Shifts

Different time series have peaks and troughs in different months of the year; these differences are called *phases*. Figure 13–2 and Table 13–2 show two sine waves with different phases.

$$Y = \sin(X) \tag{13–1}$$

$$Z = \sin(X + 1.5708) \tag{13–2}$$

Series Y is the sine function previously plotted in Figure 13–1, while Z is the same sine wave shifted to the left by 1.5708 units. This 1.5708 shift is called a *phase shift*. Different constants (i.e., phases) can be added to or subtracted from the X value of sine or cosine functions to change the location of the series peaks and troughs. Note that the shift in Y to Z is a shift of 1.5708 units. That is, the shape of Z starting at $X = 0$ is the same shape of

FIGURE 13-2
$Y = \sin(X)$ and $Z = \sin(X + 1.5708)$

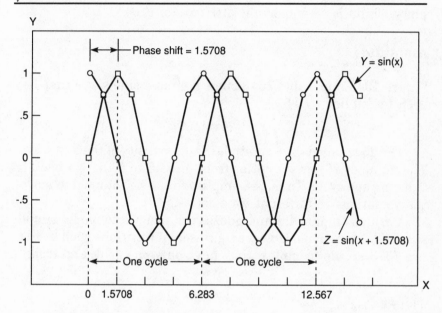

TABLE 13-2
$Y = \sin(X)$ and $Z = \sin(X + 1.570796)$

X Values	y sin(X)	sin(X) Graph			z sin(X + 1.5708)	sin(X + 1.5708) Graph		
		-1	0	+1		-1	0	+1
0	0		•		1			•
.785398	.7071068			•	.7071068			•
1.570796	1			•	0		•	
2.356194	.7071068			•	-.707107	•		
3.141593	0		•		-1	•		
3.926991	-.707107	•			-.707107	•		
4.712389	-1	•			0		•	
5.497787	-.707107	•			.7071068			•
6.283185	0		•		1			•
7.068583	.7071068			•	.7071068			•
7.853982	1			•	0		•	
8.639380	.7071068			•	-.707107	•		
9.424778	0		•		-1	•		
10.21018	-.707107	•			-.707107	•		
10.99557	-1	•			0		•	
11.78097	-.707107	•			.7071068			•
12.56637	0		•		1			•
13.35177	.7071068			•	.7071068			•
14.13717	1			•	0		•	
14.92257	.7071068			•	-.707107	•		

Y starting at $X = 1.5708$; Z's pattern is the same as Y's pattern shifted 1.5708 units to the left. The ability to identify different phase shifts is an important attribute of FSA.

Amplitude

Figure 13–3 and Table 13–3 show a simple sine wave that has been multiplied by 25.

$$Y = 25*\sin(X) \tag{13–3}$$

The 25 is called the amplitude (A) or intensity of the sine wave. The value of $25*\sin(X)$ varies from 0 to 25 to 0 to -25 back to 0 during one cycle. Thus, the amplitude can be changed to model the variations in different time series.

Various amplitudes and phases can be used to model simple sinusoidal functions. However, sinusoidal functions such as Figure 13–3 are not complex; they have only one peak and trough

FIGURE 13–3
$Y = 25*\sin(X)$, Amplitude = 25

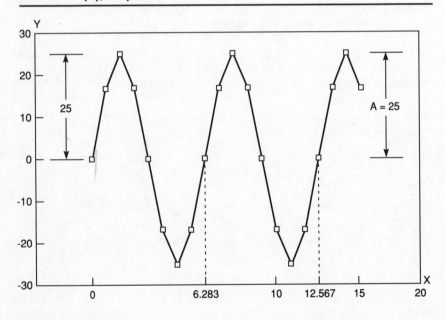

TABLE 13-3
Selected Sine Wave Values for Figures 13-1 and 13-3

X Value	Figure 13-1 sin(X)	Figure 13-3 25*sin(X)	25*sin(X) Graph −25	0	+25
0	0	0		•	
.7853982	.7071	17.68			•
1.570796	1	25			•
2.356194	.7071	17.68			•
3.141593	0	0		•	
3.926991	−.7071	−17.68	•		
4.712389	−1	−25	•		
5.497787	−.7071	−17.68	•		
6.283185	0	0		•	
7.068583	.7071	17.68			•
7.853982	1	25			•
8.639380	.7071	17.68			•
9.424778	0	0		•	
10.21018	−.7071	−17.68	•		
10.99557	−1	−25	•		
11.78097	−.7071	−17.68	•		
12.56637	0	0		•	
13.35177	.7071	17.68			•
14.13717	1	25			•
14.92257	.7071	17.68			•

per year. These two parameters are not sufficient to model more-complex seasonal behavior. Few seasonal cycles are as regular as this, where the peak season is a mirror image of the off-season (i.e., +25 to −25). Fortunately, more-complex seasonality can be modeled by adding additional trigonometric functions. We will discuss these more-complex functions below.

Combining Amplitude, Phase, Frequency, and Wavelength

Trigonometric functions such as sine waves have four characteristics that make them useful in modeling seasonal demand patterns: frequency, phase, amplitude, and wavelength. We see these concepts in the following general form of the terms in FSA.

$$Y_t = \text{Amplitude} * \sin[(\text{Frequency}*\text{Time}/n)6.283185 + \text{Phase}]$$

$$Y_t = A * \sin\left(\frac{ft}{n} \, 6.283185 + P\right) \qquad (13\text{--}4)$$

where

t = Time ($t = 1, 2, 3, \ldots, n$)

Y_t = Value of the time series at time t

A = Amplitude or intensity of the series

f = Frequency (number of peaks or troughs) in n observations

n = Number of periods in the time series

6.283185 = Constant that yields one complete sine cycle = 2π

P = Phase shift that determines the horizontal position of the repeating pattern

(Frequency/n)6.283185 is often known as ω or omega.

In previous equations, the sine of a single parameter, X, was calculated. Equation 13–4 presents a more general representation of six different parameters that are useful in defining a FSA model; these are A, f, t, n, 6.283185, and P. While this representation may at first appear very complex, upon further inspection and use, these parameters should be understandable and provide insight. Consider each below.

A, the *amplitude* of the wave, determines the magnitude of the seasonal effect on the series. It is the height of peaks and depths of troughs about the mean value of the series.

f, the *frequency*, is the number of peaks or troughs in the whole series. For example, with monthly data, a frequency of 4 is expected if there is one peak and trough per year and four years of data in the series. Two peaks per year would yield a frequency of eight in 48 months, that is two peaks every 12 months. It is common to use frequency per year and per whole series, so we need to relate the frequency to its relevant time frame, n.

P, the *phase*, refers to the horizontal position of the sine wave at its start. The phase determines where peaks or troughs occur relative to time.

L, the *wavelength*, is expressed in time units and is inversely related to the frequency. It represents the number of periods from one peak or trough to the next; for monthly data, the wavelength is typically 12 periods between peak and trough. L is the number of observations (n) in the series divided by the frequency (f).

$$L = \frac{n}{f} = \frac{48}{4} = 12 \tag{13-5}$$

$$L*f = n \tag{13-6}$$

Figures 13–4 and 13–5 illustrate several different functions with different wavelengths, phases and amplitudes. The equations

FIGURE 13–4
Two Seasonal Patterns with Different Phases and Amplitudes

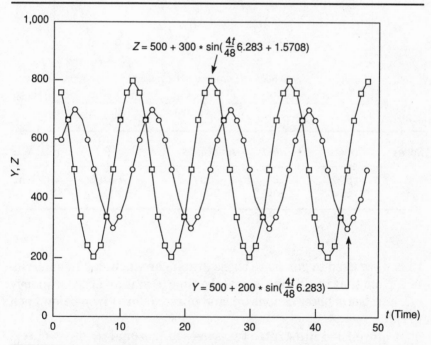

Series	Constant	Amplitude	f	P	n	L
Z	500	300	4	1.5708	48	12
Y	500	200	4	0	48	12

FIGURE 13–5
Two Trend-Seasonal Patterns

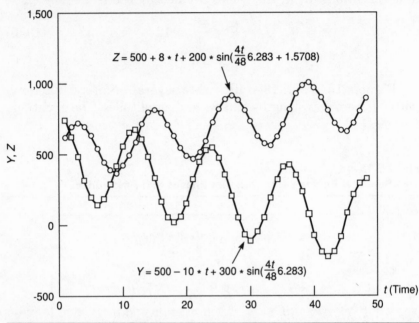

$$Z = 500 + 8 * t + 200 * \sin(\frac{4t}{48}6.283 + 1.5708)$$

$$Y = 500 - 10 * t + 300 * \sin(\frac{4t}{48}6.283)$$

Series	Constant	Trend	Amplitude	f	P	n	L
Z	500	8	200	4	1.5708	48	12
Y	500	−10	300	4	0	48	12

that were used to generate these graphs are included in each figure. Note that the X axis is now the time (t) axis and the frequency (f), number of observations (n), and phase (P) are given below each graph.

Figure 13–4 illustrates two series of seasonal monthly observations with two different amplitudes and phases. Figure 13–5 illustrates two series with trend and seasonal influences. The trends are linear, equaling 8 and −10 units per month for Z and Y, respectively. How these parameters were estimated is discussed below.

MODELING PARAMETERS

To fit a sine function such as Equation 13–7 to a time series requires estimation of several parameters. Consider Equation 13–7.

$$Y = A*\sin\left(\frac{ft}{n} \, 6.283185 + P\right) = A*\sin(\omega t + P) \qquad (13\text{–}7)$$

where

$$\omega = \frac{f}{n} \, 6.283185 = \frac{f}{n} \, 2\pi$$

All of the parameters in Equation 13–7 are known before a model is estimated except for A and P, the amplitude and the phase shift, respectively. The frequency (f), time (t), and n are known prior to model fitting. However, as Equation 13–7 is currently defined, it is difficult to simultaneously estimate A and P. Fortunately, there is a theorem of trigonometry that makes it possible to estimate A and P. This theorem is illustrated in Equation 13–8.

$$A*\sin(\omega t + P) = a_1\cos(\omega t) + a_2\sin(\omega t) \qquad (13\text{–}8)$$

As Equation 13–8 shows, a single sine function is equal to the sum of a sine and cosine function. (Note: A cosine function behaves just as a sine function with a phase shift of 3.1416 units.)

While the FSA model of Equation 13–8 contains two terms in *sin* and *cos* as opposed to one in Equation 13–7, it is much easier to estimate its parameters using multiple-regression procedures (which we will illustrate in a moment).

After estimating a_1 and a_2, the value of the amplitude (A) can be estimated from Equation 13–9.

$$A = \sqrt{a_1{}^2 + a_2{}^2} \qquad (13\text{–}9)$$

Also, if we are interested in determining the phase shift (P), then the following relationships can be used.

$$\sin(P) = a_1/A \qquad (13\text{–}10)$$

$$\cos(P) = a_2/A \qquad (13\text{–}11)$$

Finally, there is a simple but powerful test to determine if an amplitude (A) should be included in a FSA model. This test denotes that statistically significant A's are at least one half of the standard deviation of the errors. If an A is less than this, then its frequency is not a statistically significant contributor to explaining the seasonal component of the series. Also, it can be shown that the highest frequency in a FSA model should be the number of observations per season divided by 2. When this is an even number, then the last term involving sin is always zero and can be omitted.[1]

COMBINING FUNCTIONS IN FOURIER SERIES ANALYSIS

When modeling an actual time series, the amplitudes of the seasonal peaks and troughs are rarely equal. To model these various amplitudes and phases requires combining several trigonometric terms in a single model. Equation 13–12 illustrates the general FSA model used in forecasting time series.

$$\hat{Y}_t = a_1 + a_2 t + a_3 \cos(\omega t) + a_4 \sin(\omega t) + a_5 \cos(2\omega t)$$
$$+ a_6 \sin(2\omega t) + a_7 \cos(3\omega t) + a_8 \sin(3\omega t) + \ldots \qquad (13\text{--}12)$$

where

$\hat{Y}_t$ = Fitted or forecasted value at time t

a_1 = Constant term used to set the level of the series

a_2 = Trend estimate of the series

$a_3, a_4, a_5 \ldots$ = Parameters defining the amplitudes and phases of seasonal demands

ω = $(f/n)*6.283185$ and is known as omega and defines the frequency of the seasonal influence

As shown in Equation 13–12, it is easy to add a constant (a_1) and a trend (a_2) term to the relationship to model three patterns of demand—the average, trend, and seasonal. These patterns are the same as those modeled by Winters' exponential smoothing and the classical decomposition methods discussed previously. For most series, the results from using these different methods will be very similar, if not identical.

In order to estimate parameters in this model, it is necessary to use least-squares regression analysis. To better understand how this method fits past demand patterns, consider the model for Series F shown in Equation 13–13, Figure 13–6, and Table 13–4.

FIGURE 13–6
Composition of Four-Term FSA for Series F

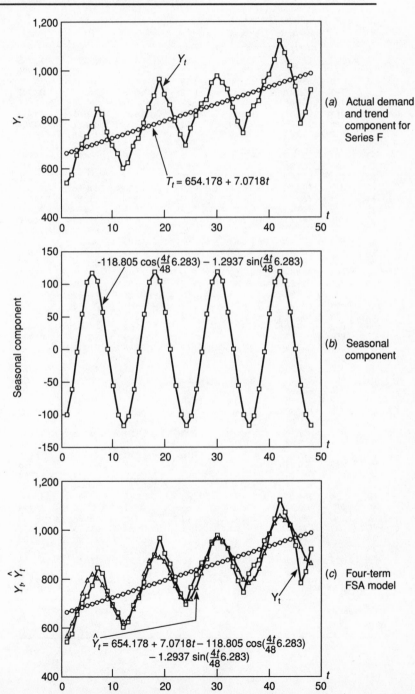

(a) Actual demand and trend component for Series F

$$T_t = 654.178 + 7.0718t$$

$$-118.805 \cos\left(\frac{4t}{48}6.283\right) - 1.2937 \sin\left(\frac{4t}{48}6.283\right)$$

(b) Seasonal component

(c) Four-term FSA model

$$\hat{Y}_t = 654.178 + 7.0718t - 118.805 \cos\left(\frac{4t}{48}6.283\right)$$
$$- 1.2937 \sin\left(\frac{4t}{48}6.283\right)$$

TABLE 13–4
Four-Parameter FSA Model for Series F

t	Y_t	$a_1 + a_2 * t$	$a_3 cos(\omega t)$	$a_4 sin(\omega t)$	Amplitude	$\hat{Y}_t$	Error	Squared Errors
1	546	661.25	−102.89	−.65	−103.53	557.71	−11.715	137.24
2	578	668.32	−59.40	−1.12	−60.52	607.80	−29.799	887.96
3	660	675.39	.00	−1.29	−1.29	674.10	−14.100	198.80
4	707	682.47	59.40	−1.12	58.28	740.75	−33.747	1,138.88
5	738	689.54	102.89	−.65	102.24	791.78	−53.778	2,892.11
6	781	696.61	118.81	.00	118.81	815.41	−34.414	1,184.31
7	848	703.68	102.89	.65	103.53	807.22	40.784	1,663.37
8	818	710.75	59.40	1.12	60.52	771.28	46.724	2,183.20
9	729	717.82	.00	1.29	1.29	719.12	9.882	97.66
10	691	724.90	−59.40	1.12	−58.28	666.61	24.386	594.68
11	658	731.97	−102.89	.65	−102.24	629.73	28.273	799.39
12	604	739.04	−118.81	.00	−118.81	620.23	−16.235	263.56
13	629	746.11	−102.89	−.65	−103.53	642.58	−13.576	184.32
14	711	753.18	−59.40	−1.12	−60.52	692.66	18.339	336.34
15	729	760.26	.00	−1.29	−1.29	758.96	−29.961	897.68
16	798	767.33	59.40	−1.12	58.28	825.61	−27.609	762.25
17	861	774.40	102.89	−.65	102.24	876.64	−15.640	244.61
18	903	781.47	118.81	.00	118.81	900.28	2.724	7.42
19	968	788.54	102.89	.65	103.53	892.08	75.922	5,764.27
20	894	795.61	59.40	1.12	60.52	856.14	37.863	1,433.62
21	860	802.69	.00	1.29	1.29	803.98	56.020	3,138.30
22	792	809.76	−59.40	1.12	−58.28	751.48	40.524	1,642.24
23	739	816.83	−102.89	.65	−102.24	714.59	24.411	595.94
24	699	823.90	−118.81	.00	−118.81	705.10	−6.096	37.16
25	773	830.97	−102.89	−.65	−103.53	727.44	45.562	2,075.90
26	818	838.04	−59.40	−1.12	−60.52	777.52	40.478	1,638.47
27	871	845.12	.00	−1.29	−1.29	843.82	27.177	738.59
28	882	852.19	59.40	−1.12	58.28	910.47	−28.471	810.57
29	959	859.26	102.89	−.65	102.24	961.50	−2.501	6.26
30	979	866.33	118.81	.00	118.81	985.14	−6.137	37.66
31	955	873.40	102.89	.65	103.53	976.94	−21.939	481.31
32	925	880.48	59.40	1.12	60.52	941.00	−15.998	255.95
33	843	887.55	.00	1.29	1.29	888.84	−45.841	2,101.41
34	790	894.62	−59.40	1.12	−58.28	836.34	−46.337	2,147.12
35	746	901.69	−102.89	.65	−102.24	799.45	−53.450	2,856.87
36	822	908.76	−118.81	.00	−118.81	789.96	32.042	1,026.70
37	857	915.83	−102.89	−.65	−103.53	812.30	44.700	1,998.13
38	876	922.91	−59.40	−1.12	−60.52	862.38	13.616	185.41
39	959	929.98	.00	−1.29	−1.29	928.68	30.315	919.03
40	981	937.05	59.40	−1.12	58.28	995.33	−14.332	205.41
41	1,051	944.12	102.89	−.65	102.24	1,046.36	4.636	21.50
42	1,124	951.19	118.81	.00	118.81	1,070.00	54.001	2,916.15
43	1,073	958.27	102.89	.65	103.53	1,061.80	11.199	125.43
44	1,020	965.34	59.40	1.12	60.52	1,025.86	−5.860	34.34
45	933	972.41	.00	1.29	1.29	973.70	−40.703	1,656.71
46	787	979.48	−59.40	1.12	−58.28	921.20	−134.20	18,009.28
47	830	986.55	−102.89	.65	−102.24	884.31	−54.311	2,949.72
48	922	993.02	−118.81	.00	−118.81	874.82	47.180	2,226.01

Mean   827   .0004   1,719.27
Standard deviation   39.70

$a_1 = 654.178$ $a_2 = 7.07$ $a_3 = -118.805$ $a_4 = -1.2937$
$f = 4$ $n = 48.00$ $\omega = .52$

Table 13–4 illustrates the input data for this series, which is described by the following equation:

$$\hat{Y}_t = 654.18 + 7.07*t - 118.81*\cos(.52t) - 1.294*\sin(.52t) \qquad (13\text{--}13)$$

where

$a_1 = 654.18 = $ Constant

$a_2 = 7.07 = $ Trend

$\left.\begin{array}{l} a_3 = -118.81 \\ a_4 = -1.294 \end{array}\right\}$ Determine the amplitude and phase.

$n = 48$

$f = 4$

$\omega = (f/n)*6.283185 = (4/48)*6.283185 = .52$

We describe the modeling process used to identify this relationship later. For now, our purpose is to understand the components of this model.

Figure 13–6(a) through (c) illustrates the patterns of Equation 13–13. Figure 13–6(a) illustrates the constant and trend components of the relationship. As shown, the trend relationship fits the general movement of the series, but does not follow its seasonal pattern. As shown in Figure 13–6(b), the trigonometric terms of Equation 13–13 model the seasonal movement of the series. The parameters of this component, a_3 and a_4, were determined using least-squares regressions, which are described below. Finally, we see in Figure 13–6(c) the sum of the trend and seasonal models, that is, the fitted values, $\hat{Y}_t$, plotted with the actual series values, Y_t.

The statistical method used to estimate the parameters of this relationship is described below and in Brown.[2]

MODEL FITTING AND PARAMETER ESTIMATES

As we discuss the steps of FSA, Tables 13–5 and 13–6 will be used to illustrate each step. The column numbers of these tables will be referred to as the steps are explained. The general steps of this method include estimating trends using seasonal differencing, es-

TABLE 13–5
Input Data for Six-Term FSA Model

					Fourier Terms			
(1)	(2)	(3)	(4)	(5)	(6)	(7)	(8)	(9)
	Actual	Differences	Trend	Detrended				
t	Y_t	$Y_t - Y_{t-12}$	T_t	$Y_t - T_t$	$cos(\omega t)$	$sin(\omega t)$	$cos(2\omega t)$	$sin(2\omega t)$
1	546		661.250	−115.250	.8660	.5000	.5000	.8660
2	578		668.322	−90.3220	.5000	.8660	−.5000	.8660
3	660		675.394	−15.3938	0	1.000	−1.000	0
4	707		682.466	24.5344	−.5000	.8660	−.5000	−.8660
5	738		689.537	48.4626	−.8660	.5000	.5000	−.8660
6	781		696.609	84.3908	−1.000	0	1.000	0
7	848		703.681	144.319	−.8660	−.5000	.5000	.8660
8	818		710.753	107.247	−.5000	−.8660	−.5000	.8660
9	729		717.825	11.1754	0	−1.000	−1.000	0
10	691		724.896	−33.8964	.5000	−.8660	−.5000	−.8660
11	658		731.968	−73.9682	.8660	−.5000	.5000	−.8660
12	604		739.040	−135.040	1.000	0	1.000	0
13	629	83.00	746.112	−117.112	.8660	.5000	.5000	.8660
14	711	133.00	753.184	−42.1836	.5000	.8660	−.5000	.8660
15	729	69.00	760.255	−31.2554	0	1.000	−1.000	0
16	798	91.00	767.327	30.6728	−.5000	.8660	−.5000	−.8660
17	861	123.00	774.399	86.6010	−.8660	.5000	.5000	−.8660
18	903	122.00	781.471	121.529	−1.000	0	1.000	0
19	968	120.00	788.543	179.457	−.8660	−.5000	.5000	.8660
20	894	76.00	795.614	98.3856	−.5000	−.8660	−.5000	.8660
21	860	131.00	802.686	57.3138	0	−1.000	−1.000	0
22	792	101.00	809.758	−17.7580	.5000	−.8660	−.5000	−.8660
23	739	81.00	816.830	−77.8298	.8660	−.5000	.5000	−.8660
24	699	95.00	823.902	−124.902	1.000	0	1.000	0
25	773	144.00	830.973	−57.9734	.8660	.5000	.5000	.8660
26	818	107.00	838.045	−20.0452	.5000	.8660	−.5000	.8660
27	871	142.00	845.117	25.8830	0	1.000	−1.000	0
28	882	84.00	852.189	29.8112	−.5000	.8660	−.5000	−.8660
29	959	98.00	859.261	99.7394	−.8660	.5000	.5000	−.8660
30	979	76.00	866.332	112.668	−1.000	0	1.000	0
31	955	−13.00	873.404	81.5958	−.8660	−.5000	.5000	.8660
32	925	31.00	880.476	44.5240	−.5000	−.8660	−.5000	.8660
33	843	−17.00	887.548	−44.5478	0	−1.000	−1.000	0
34	790	−2.00	894.620	−104.620	.5000	−.8660	−.5000	−.8660
35	746	7.00	901.691	−155.691	.8660	−.5000	.5000	−.8660
36	822	123.00	908.763	−86.7632	1.000	0	1.000	0
37	857	84.00	915.835	−58.8350	.8660	.5000	.5000	.8660
38	876	58.00	922.907	−46.9068	.5000	.8660	−.5000	.8660
39	959	88.00	929.979	29.0214	0	1.000	−1.000	0
40	981	99.00	937.050	43.9496	−.5000	.8660	−.5000	−.8660
41	1,051	92.00	944.122	106.878	−.8660	.5000	.5000	−.8660
42	1.124	145.00	951.194	172.806	−1.000	0	1.000	0
43	1,073	118.00	958.266	114.734	−.8660	−.5000	.5000	.8660
44	1,020	95.00	965.338	54.6624	−.5000	−.8660	−.5000	.8660
45	933	90.00	972.409	−39.4094	0	−1.000	−1.000	0
46	787	−3.00	979.481	−192.481	.5000	−.8660	−.5000	−.8660
47	830	84.00	986.553	−156.553	.8660	−.5000	.5000	−.8660
48	922	100.00	993.625	−71.6248	1.000	0	1.000	0

Mean 827.4 84.86 827.4
12-month trend = 84.86 Monthly trend = 7.07176

TABLE 13-6
Regression Output and Amplitude Calculation for a Full Model

(1)	(2)	(3)	(4)	(5)	(6)	(7)
				Standard	A	
			Frequency (f)	Deviation of	Standard	
Variable	Parameter	A	per Year	Errors	Deviation	Significant
a_3	118.80					
a_4	1.29	118.81	1	39.67	3.00	Yes
a_5	6.74					
a_6	22.32	23.31	2	39.67	.59	Yes
a_7	3.01					
a_8	3.64	4.72	3	39.67	12	No
a_9	4.12	'				
a_{10}	1.15	4.27	4	39.67	.11	No
a_{11}	2.08					
a_{12}	.62	2.17	5	39.67	.05	No
a_{13}	1.72	1.72	6	39.67	.04	No

An amplitude is significant if A/(Standard Deviation) is greater than .50.
All standard deviations are equal because only one model was fitted.

timating Fourier seasonal parameters, eliminating those parameters that are insignificant, and, finally, forecasting future values. Our approach uses a method that is slightly different than Brown's. Brown's method is discussed in an appendix of this chapter. Both methods yield nearly identical results.

Applying Fourier Series Analysis

1. *Take seasonal differences to estimate the annual trend* (see Chapter 12 for an explanation of this method). For the monthly data of Table 13–5, the mean of the 12th differences shown in column 3 is 84.86.

$$\text{Mean}(Y_t - Y_{t-12}) = 84.86$$

Thus, demand has increased an average of 84.86 every 12 months.

2. *Calculate the monthly trend* by dividing the mean of the annual seasonal differences by the length of the seasonal cycle, 12.

$$\frac{\text{Mean}(Y_t - Y_{t-12})}{12} = \frac{84.86111}{12} = 7.0718$$

Thus, the monthly trend is 7.0718 units.

3. *Center the trend on the mean of* Y_t *and the mean of time* (t). This is done by finding the value of a_1 which forces the trend line through the intersection of the mean of the actual series Y_t and t. Best-fit trend lines normally go through this intersection. The mean of t is:

$$\frac{\text{Ending value } t + \text{Beginning value } t}{2} = \frac{48 + 1}{2} = 24.5$$

The mean of Y_t is:

$$\text{Mean}(Y_t) = 827.4375$$

The best-fit trend line will have the form:

$$T_t = a_1 + 7.0718t$$

We determine a_1 from the relationship below.

$$T_{24.5} = 827.4375 = a_1 + 7.0718\bar{t} = a_1 + 7.0718*24.5$$

Therefore,

$$a_1 = 827.4375 - 7.0718*24.5 = 654.178$$

and the trend line is:

$$T_t = 654.178 + 7.0718t$$

4. *Calculate the trend values from* t = 1 *to* t = 48. See column 4 of Table 13–5.

5. *Calculate the deviations from the trend* by subtracting the projected trends from each actual observation to yield a new series that is centered on zero. The resulting series is called a *detrended series* and is shown in column 5 of Table 13–5. (Alternatively, when seasonality is believed to be a percent of trend, the actual observations can be divided by the trend series, or natural logarithms can be used as described in Chapter 12.)

6. *Input the detrended series and trigonometric values to a multiple-regression program;* i.e., detrended actual values, $\cos(\omega t)$, $\sin(\omega t)$, $\cos(2\omega t)$, and $\sin(2\omega t)$ are shown in columns 5, 6, 7, 8, and 9 of Table 13–5, respectively. The values of the sine and cosine are easily calculated using computer software such as spreadsheets or programming languages. Almost all statistical forecasting packages provide this capability. Table 13–5 only shows 4 trigonometric terms, but 11 trigonometric terms were input in the actual computer analysis discussed below. These 11 terms are:

$a_3\cos(\omega t) + a_4\sin(\omega t) + a_5\cos(2\omega t) + a_6\sin(2\omega t) + a_7\cos(3\omega t) + a_8\sin(3\omega t) + a_9\cos(4\omega t) + a_{10}\sin(4\omega t) + a_{11}\cos(5\omega t) + a_{12}\sin(5\omega t) + a_{13}\cos(6\omega t)$

where

$$\omega = (4/48)*6.283185 = .52$$

7. *Fit FSA model parameters* to the detrended series using a multiple-regression program that determines the values of a_3, $a_4, a_5, \ldots, a_{13}$ and that minimizes the sum of the squared errors. This is done using any general multiple-regression procedure, including those supplied with spreadsheet systems.

Column 2 of Table 13–6 illustrates a single model with 11 fitted regression coefficients that were estimated using a general statistical package.

8. *Calculate the amplitudes of each frequency.* These values are calculated in column 3 of Table 13–6. The values of a_i are transformed to amplitudes A_i in order to test their significance.

$$A_1 = \sqrt{a_3^2 + a_4^2} = \sqrt{118.8^2 + 1.29^2} = 118.81$$

9. *Discard all insignificant frequencies above the highest significant frequency.* When analyzing the amplitude of each frequency, we are trying to determine if a frequency should be included in the model. The statistic in column 6 of Table 13–6 is used to determine whether an amplitude of a frequency is sufficient to justify inclusion of that frequency.

Consider each of the columns of Table 13–6 in more detail. These are the variable, parameter estimate, resulting amplitude, frequency per year, standard deviation of the errors, the ratio of the amplitude to the standard deviation, and whether that amplitude is significantly different than zero or not. As the table shows, some of the amplitudes are not very high relative to the standard deviation of the errors. The amplitudes at frequencies 3, 4, 5, and 6 per year (i.e., 12, 16, 20, and 24 cycles per four years, respectively) are only 4.72, 4.27, 2.17, and 1.72, respectively. If the amplitude of a frequency is greater than one half of the standard deviation of the errors, then it is a statistically significant part of the seasonal pattern. If the amplitude is smaller than one half of the standard deviation of the residuals, then it should be eliminated. The amplitudes of frequencies 3, 4, 5, and 6 cycles per year are insignificant and are dropped as shown previously in Table 13–5. It is standard practice to use all frequencies up to and including the highest frequency that has a statistically significant amplitude.

Table 13–7 illustrates the standard deviations of the errors for seven different FSA models. The most complex model was fitted with 13 terms. Then these terms were eliminated frequency by frequency. As shown, the standard deviation of the errors does not change much except when going from a two-term model to a four-term model, then from a four-term to a six-term model. As shown, the six-term model has the lowest standard deviation of errors. This also confirms our decision to include only six terms in the model.

10. *Forecast the withheld or out-of-sample values by projecting the trend-seasonal components.* Having selected a six-term FSA model (a_1 through a_6) to forecast demand, it is a relatively simple matter to project the trend and seasonal function of that relationship into the future. Table 13–8 and Figure 13–7 illustrate the fitted values of the six-term model along with the resulting errors.

As shown in Table 13–8, the fitted values are calculated in column 9 by adding the trend of column 3 to the seasonal estimate in column 8. The seasonal estimate is the sum of four trigonometric functions in columns 4, 5, 6, and 7. Note the repeating pattern of seasonality in column 8. This is an additive seasonality for each month of the year. The magnitudes of the seasonal-

TABLE 13–7
Standard Error of FSA Models of Series F

Terms in Model	Standard Deviation of Errors	f	Amplitude of Last Term	Significant Frequency	Pattern Modeled
Two	94.29	0	n.a.*	Yes	Trend only
Four	39.70	1	118.81	Yes	Trend and seasonal
Six	36.76	2	23.31	Yes	Trend and seasonal
Eight	37.46	3	4.72	No	Trend and seasonal
Ten	38.24	4	4.27	No	Trend and seasonal
Twelve	39.17	5	2.17	No	Trend and seasonal
Thirteen	39.67	6	1.72	No	Trend and seasonal

*n.a. = Not applicable. A two-term FSA model has only a constant and trend in the equation.

ity of column 8 are easily interpreted as the quantity by which a month is higher or lower than the trend. (Note: Multiplicative models can be modeled using ratios or logs as illustrated in the appendix to Chapter 11.)

The error in column 10 is the difference between the actual in column 2 and the fitted in column 9. Because minimizing the sum of squared errors is the criterion used to select the best model, these squared errors are shown in column 11.

Table 13–9 illustrates the process of forecasting. This process is identical to that of calculating the fitted values of Table 13–8. Because we are forecasting, the actual values are unknown as shown in column 2. The sum of the trend, column 3, and the seasonal, column 8, yields the fitted values of column 9. As shown in Figure 13–7, these fitted values seem very reasonable in projecting past behavior forward into the future. However, it is always important to perform a reasonableness check of any forecast. This check has to be built into any forecasting system.

11. *Update model parameters.* To this point, we have illustrated the generation of a forecasting model. We have not discussed how this model would be used in a forecasting system. In general, it is not efficient to refit model parameters each week or month. It is suggested that some form of smoothing or averaging be used to generate new model coefficients. As Brown points out, an efficient smoothing process might require only 5 percent of the computer resources needed to estimate and diagnose the original model. Thus, it is inefficient to reestimate models every month.[3] We suggest reviewing Brown for those implementing a FSA model in an operational forecasting system.

Overfitting and the Number of Parameters to Include

As parameters are added to a model, it becomes more complex, more difficult to estimate, more accurate in fitting past demands, and *possibly* less accurate in forecasting future demand. That is, additional terms that increase historical fit might not forecast the future well—this is called *overfitting*. Added terms might mistakenly model events such as outliers that occurred in the past, but are not going to occur in the future. Thus, the significance

TABLE 13-8
Fitted Values of Six-Term FSA for Series F

(1) t	(2) Y_t	(3) $a_1 + a_2 \cdot t$ Trend	(4) $a_3\cos(\omega t)$	(5) $a_4\sin(\omega t)$	(6) $a_5\cos(2\omega t)$	(7) $a_6\sin(2\omega t)$	(8) Seasonal Amplitude	(9) Trend and Seasonal $\hat{Y}_t$	(10) Error	(11) Squared Errors
1	546	661.25	-102.89	-.65	3.37	19.33	-80.84	580.41	-34.412	1,184.16
2	578	668.32	-59.40	-1.12	-3.37	19.33	-44.57	623.75	-45.755	2,093.50
3	660	675.39	.00	-1.29	-6.74	.00	-8.03	667.36	-7.359	54.15
4	707	682.47	59.40	-1.12	-3.37	-19.33	35.59	718.05	-11.051	122.11
5	738	689.54	102.89	-.65	3.37	-19.33	86.29	775.82	-37.822	1,430.52
6	781	696.61	118.81	.00	6.74	.00	125.55	822.15	-41.155	1,693.69
7	848	703.68	102.89	.65	3.37	19.33	126.23	829.91	18.087	327.16
8	818	710.75	59.40	1.12	-3.37	19.33	76.48	787.23	30.768	946.71
9	729	717.82	.00	1.29	-6.74	.00	-5.45	712.38	16.622	276.32
10	691	724.90	-59.40	1.12	-3.37	-19.33	-80.98	643.92	47.082	2,216.80
11	658	731.97	-102.89	.65	3.37	-19.33	-118.20	613.77	44.229	1,956.26
12	604	739.04	-118.81	.00	6.74	.00	-112.06	626.98	-22.975	527.86
13	629	746.11	-102.89	-.65	3.37	19.33	-80.84	665.27	-36.273	1,315.75
14	711	753.18	-59.40	-1.12	-3.37	19.33	-44.57	708.62	2.383	5.68
15	729	760.26	.00	-1.29	-6.74	.00	-8.03	752.22	-23.221	539.20
16	798	767.33	59.40	-1.12	-3.37	-19.33	35.59	802.91	-4.912	24.13
17	861	774.40	102.89	-.65	3.37	-19.33	86.29	860.68	.316	.10
18	903	781.47	118.81	.00	6.74	.00	125.55	907.02	-4.016	16.13
19	968	788.54	102.89	.65	3.37	19.33	126.23	914.77	53.226	2,833.01
20	894	795.61	59.40	1.12	-3.37	19.33	76.48	872.09	21.907	479.92
21	860	802.69	.00	1.29	-6.74	.00	-5.45	797.24	62.761	3,938.97
22	792	809.76	-59.40	1.12	-3.37	-19.33	-80.98	728.78	63.221	3,996.94

23	739	816.83	-102.89	.65	3.37	-19.33	-118.20	698.63	40.368	1,629.58
24	699	823.90	-118.81	.00	6.74	.00	-112.06	711.84	-12.837	164.79
25	773	830.97	-102.89	-.65	3.37	19.33	-80.84	750.13	22.865	522.82
26	818	838.04	-59.40	-1.12	-3.37	19.33	-44.57	793.48	24.522	601.33
27	871	845.12	.00	-1.29	-6.74	.00	-8.03	837.08	33.917	1,150.42
28	882	852.19	59.40	-1.12	-3.37	-19.33	35.59	887.77	-5.773	33.34
29	959	859.26	102.89	-.65	3.37	-19.33	86.29	945.55	13.454	181.03
30	979	866.33	118.81	.00	6.74	.00	125.55	991.88	-12.878	165.84
31	955	873.40	102.89	.65	3.37	19.33	126.23	999.64	-44.636	1,992.34
32	925	880.48	59.40	1.12	-3.37	19.33	76.48	956.95	-31.955	1,021.09
33	843	887.55	.00	1.29	-6.74	.00	-5.45	882.10	-39.100	1,528.84
34	790	894.62	-59.40	1.12	-3.37	-19.33	-80.98	813.64	-23.640	558.86
35	746	901.69	-102.89	.65	3.37	-19.33	-118.20	783.49	-37.494	1,405.77
36	822	908.76	-118.81	.00	6.74	.00	-112.06	796.70	25.301	640.17
37	857	915.83	-102.89	-.65	3.37	19.33	-80.84	835.00	22.003	484.16
38	876	922.91	-59.40	-1.12	-3.37	19.33	-44.57	878.34	-2.339	5.47
39	959	929.98	.00	-1.29	-6.74	.00	-8.03	921.94	37.056	1,373.16
40	981	937.05	59.40	-1.12	-3.37	-19.33	35.59	972.64	8.364	69.97
41	1,051	944.12	102.89	-.65	3.37	-19.33	86.29	1,030.41	20.593	424.07
42	1,124	951.19	118.81	.00	6.74	.00	125.55	1,076.74	47.260	2,233.57
43	1,073	958.27	102.89	.65	3.37	19.33	126.23	1,084.50	-11.497	132.19
44	1,020	965.34	59.40	1.12	-3.37	19.33	76.48	1,041.82	-21.816	475.95
45	933	972.41	.00	1.29	-6.74	.00	-5.45	966.96	-33.962	1,153.42
46	787	979.48	-59.40	1.12	-3.37	-19.33	-80.98	898.50	-111.50	12,432.67
47	830	986.55	-102.89	.65	3.37	-19.33	-118.20	868.36	-38.355	1,471.12
48	922	993.62	-118.81	.00	6.74	.00	-112.06	881.56	40.439	1,635.39

$a_1 = 654.2$ $a_2 = 7.07$ $a_3 = -118.81$ $a_4 = -1.2937$ $a_5 = 6.74$ $a_6 = 22.3163$

$f = 4$ $n = 48.00$ $\omega = .52$

FIGURE 13–7
Six-Term FSA Model for Series F

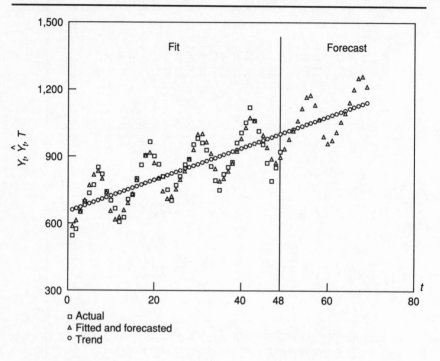

□ Actual
△ Fitted and forecasted
○ Trend

test on the choice of frequencies that should be included in the model is an important tool in model selection. However, it is not an infallible one. Overfitting is a general problem that may occur no matter which forecasting approach is used.

Disadvantages

The primary disadvantage of this method is that it may be difficult to relate the model parameters to commonly used or intuitive explanations of seasonal profiles. We have found the use of graphs very useful in describing the seasonal behavior of FSA. Also, these seasonal profiles can be used to express the amplitudes of each period as either an additive or percentage of the trend for that period. See column 8 of Table 13–8 for the additive interpretation.

TABLE 13–9
Forecasted Values Using Six-Term FSA for Series F

(1) t	(2) Y_t	(3) $a_1 + a_2 \cdot t$ Trend	(4) $a_3 cos(\omega t)$	(5) $a_4 sin(\omega t)$	(6) $a_5 cos(2\omega t)$	(7) $a_6 sin(2\omega t)$	(8) Seasonal Amplitude	(9) Sum of Trend and Seasonal $\hat{Y}_t$
49	1,000.70	−102.89	−.65	3.37	19.33	−80.84	919.86
50	1,007.77	−59.40	−1.12	−3.37	19.33	−44.57	963.20
51	1,014.84	.00	−1.29	−6.74	.00	−8.03	1,006.81
52	1,021.91	59.40	−1.12	−3.37	−19.33	35.59	1,057.50
53	1,028.98	102.89	−.65	3.37	−19.33	86.29	1,115.27
54	1,036.06	118.81	.00	6.74	.00	125.55	1,161.60
55	1,043.13	102.89	.65	3.37	19.33	126.23	1,169.36
56	1,050.20	59.40	1.12	−3.37	19.33	76.48	1,126.68
57	1,057.27	.00	1.29	−6.74	.00	−5.45	1,051.82
58	1,064.34	−59.40	1.12	−3.37	−19.33	−80.98	983.36
59	1,071.41	−102.89	.65	3.37	−19.33	−118.20	953.22
60	1,078.49	−118.81	.00	6.74	.00	−112.06	966.42
61	1,085.56	−102.89	−.65	3.37	19.33	−80.84	1,004.72
62	1,092.63	−59.40	−1.12	−3.37	19.33	−44.57	1,048.06
63	1,099.70	.00	−1.29	−6.74	.00	−8.03	1,091.67
64	1,106.77	59.40	−1.12	−3.37	−19.33	35.59	1,142.36
65	1,113.85	102.89	−.65	3.37	−19.33	86.29	1,200.13
66	1,120.92	118.81	.00	6.74	.00	125.55	1,246.46
67	1,127.99	102.89	.65	3.37	19.33	126.23	1,254.22
68	1,135.06	59.40	1.12	−3.37	19.33	76.48	1,211.54
69	1,142.13	.00	1.29	−6.74	.00	−5.45	1,136.69
70	1,149.20	−59.40	1.12	−3.37	−19.33	−80.98	1,068.23
71	1,156.28	−102.89	.65	3.37	−19.33	−118.20	1,038.08
72	1,163.35	−118.81	.00	6.74	.00	−112.06	1,051.28

$a_1 = 654.2$ $a_2 = 7.07$ $a_3 = -118.81$ $a_4 = -1.2937$ $a_5 = 6.74$ $a_6 = 22.3163$
$f = 4$ $n = 48.00$ $\omega = .52$

There are those who claim that FSA will overfit models and therefore not perform well in forecasting. As mentioned, overfitting is the identification and use of models that are more complex than they should be (e.g., have too many terms in them). Therefore, we must delete insignificant terms. Nonetheless, there is still the possibility of overfitting—even when parameters appear significant, it may be random error that appears significant. Overfitted models fit past data well, but they do not forecast future values well.

Finally, another disadvantage of FSA is that analysts and managers do not relate to the trigonometric functions of this approach. We hope this chapter will help rectify that situation. However, FSA will still remain foreign to some users.

Advantages

An advantage of spectral analysis over other trend-seasonal methods is that it divides the variance of the time series into frequencies whose components are statistically independent so that we can remove or manipulate each component without affecting the others.[4]

For example, we used FSA to model a 13-term trend-seasonal model for Series F. Based on statistics that were generated during the modeling process, the seasonal terms for a_7 through a_{13} of the model are dropped without any necessity to reestimate the remaining model. In general, if all amplitudes are insignificant, then all will be dropped and the model will no longer include seasonal patterns. Finally, if the trend parameter (a_2) is found to be insignificant, it too can be dropped to yield a simple level model. Most other methods require a refitting of the model when one or more terms are dropped from the model. This makes FSA a versatile approach to modeling time series in operational forecasting systems.[5]

MULTIMODEL SIMULATION METHODS

From its beginning, the forecasting literature has discussed criteria for choosing the best from alternative forecasting models. The most commonly used criterion for choosing the best model is the minimization of the standard deviation or the sum of the squared-error terms. Some forecasting systems use several different models to forecast recent actuals of the same time series. After forecasting these, then the best of the several models is chosen using the minimum-sum-of-squared-errors criterion. Then, this best model is used to predict future values of the time series. Because we are unaware of any generic name for such methods, we call them *multimodel simulation methods (MSM)*. Research by Makridakis[6] in 1990 and previous research by Smith[7] are examples of MSM. Some MSM ideas are in a system sold under the trademark of Focus Forecasting™. We discuss MSM using a very general example.

The following example of MSM employs an algorithm that is not unlike those used in the electric power industry several decades ago. That method was used to forecast electricity demand using Winters' three-parameter model. A typical procedure is as follows:

1. Divide the time series history into two groups of data. Group one is used to fit models. Group-two data are used to measure the forecast accuracy of those models. For example, with 48 months of data, group-one data include the first 36 months, and group-two data, the last 12 months.
2. Fit multiple models to the group-one data. For example, fit 10 different models to the 36 months of data.
3. Use the fitted models from Step 2 to forecast the withheld (or sometimes called *out-of-sample*) group-two data. For example, use each of the 10 different models to forecast the remaining 12 months of data.
4. Collect the sum of squared errors of each model from Step 3.
5. Based on the criterion of the minimum sum of squared errors, choose the best single model or group of models to forecast the next 12 months. Alternatively, the choice of the best method might vary by horizon length. For example, one model could be chosen to forecast 1 to 6 months into the future, and another model, 7 to 12 months into the future.
6. Update any parameters for the best models and forecast the next 12 months using those models (i.e., months 49 to 60).
7. Repeat this process every month or quarter.

This procedure is illustrated below using four simple models to forecast the demand for a simple quarterly time series. A short quarterly time series is used for clarity and computational ease. The four simple models are:

$$\text{Model 1: } Y_t = Y_{t-1} + b \qquad (13\text{--}14)$$

where
$$b = \text{Mean}(Y_t - Y_{t-1})$$

$$\text{Model 2: } Y_t = Y_{t-4} + B \qquad (13\text{--}15)$$

where $$B = \text{Mean}(Y_t - Y_{t-4})$$

$$\text{Model 3: } (Y_t = Y_{t-1}/Y_{t-5}) * Y_{t-4} \tag{13-16}$$

$$\text{Model 4: } Y_t = (Y_{t-1} + Y_{t-2} + Y_{t-3} + Y_{t-4})/4 \tag{13-17}$$

We have chosen these four models, not because they are the best, but because these represent those that might be used in a MSM forecasting system. These models have the capability to model the following demand patterns.

Model 1 is a random-walk if $b = 0$ or a quarterly trend model if $b \neq 0$.

Model 2 is a seasonal random-walk if $B = 0$ or an annual trend model if $B \neq 0$.

Model 3 is a seasonal model with multiplicative trend (Y_{t-1}/Y_{t-5}).

Model 4 is a simple four-period moving average model.

Table 13–10 illustrates this method using data from the Big City Bookstore quarterly data of Chapter 11. In this example, we fit models to the first two years of data, forecast the third year, and, based on the minimum sum of squared errors, choose the two best models to forecast Year 4.

Fitting All Models

Table 13–10 illustrates the process of forecasting Year 3 data with each of the four models. The first step is to estimate the trend parameters of Models 1 and 2 using Year 1 and 2 data. As the table shows, the average quarterly trend estimate for Model 1 is 5.5 units, and the annual trend estimate for Model 2 is 10.25 units. Given these estimates, the second section of Table 13–10 illustrates the process of forecasting Year 3 (i.e., $t = 9$ to 12).

Year 3 forecasts using Models 1, 3, and 4 require some explanation because the data needed to forecast more than one quarter in the future are unknown and must be estimated. When a model requires a value that is unknown at the time of forecasting, then the most recent forecast of that value should be used. Thus, in Models 1, 3, and 4, forecasted values are used for unknown ac-

TABLE 13–10
Multimodel Simulation Method—Big City Bookstore Quarterly Sales

Fitting b and B to Models 1 and 2

t	Year/Quarter	Actual Demand	Y_{t-1}	Trend	Y_{t-4}	Trend
1	1/1	72				
2	1/2	110				
3	1/3	117				
4	1/4	172				
5	2/1	76	172.00	−96.00	72.00	4.00
6	2/2	112	76.00	36.00	110.00	2.00
7	2/3	130	112.00	18.00	117.00	13.00
8	2/4	194	130.00	64.00	172.00	22.00
Average trend				b = 5.50		B = 10.25

Forecasting Year 3 Demands Using All Four Models

			Model 1		Model 2		Model 3		Model 4	
t	Year/Quarter	Actual Demand	Forecast	Error	Forecast	Error	Forecast	Error	Forecast	Error
9	3/1	78	199.50	−121.50	86.25	−8.25	85.72	−7.72	128.00	−50.00
10	3/2	119	205.00	−86.00	122.25	−3.25	126.32	−7.32	141.00	−22.00
11	3/3	128	210.50	−82.50	140.25	−12.25	146.62	−18.63	148.25	−20.25
12	3/4	201	216.00	−15.00	204.25	−3.25	218.82	−17.82	152.81	48.19
Average error				−76.125		−6.75		−12.86		−11.02
Sum of squared errors (SSE)				29,190		239		777.45		5,716

Using minimum SSE, the two best models are Models 2 and 3.

tual values. This is called *conditional forecasting*. Consider the conditional forecasts for Period 10 using Model 1. As shown below, Y_{10} is determined by Y_9, but Y_9 is unknown at the end of Period 8 (or if you prefer the beginning of Period 9). To forecast Period 10, the forecasted value of Period 9 is substituted for the unknown actual of Period 9. This substitution is used in Models 1, 3, and 4 for forecasts for periods 10 through 12.

Model 1: $\hat{Y}_t = Y_{t-1} + 5.5$

$\hat{Y}_9 = Y_8 + 5.5 = 194 + 5.5 = 199.5$

$\hat{Y}_{10} = \hat{Y}_9 + 5.5 = 199.5 + 5.5 = 205$

$\hat{Y}_{11} = \hat{Y}_{10} + 5.5 = 205 + 5.5 = 210.5$

$\hat{Y}_{12} = \hat{Y}_{11} + 5.5 = 210.5 + 5.5 = 216.0$

Model 2: $\hat{Y}_t = Y_{t-4} + 10.25$
$\hat{Y}_9 = Y_5 + 10.25 = 76 + 10.25 = 86.25$

$\cdots$

$\hat{Y}_{12} = Y_8 + 10.25 = 194 + 10.25 = 204.25$

Model 3: $\hat{Y}_t = (Y_{t-1}/Y_{t-5})*Y_{t-4}$

$\hat{Y}_9 = (Y_8/Y_4)*Y_5 = (194/172)*76 = 85.72$

$\cdots$

$\hat{Y}_{12} = (\hat{Y}_{11}/Y_7)*Y_8 = (146.62/130)*194 = 218.82$

Model 4: $\hat{Y}_t = (Y_{t-1} + Y_{t-2} + Y_{t-3} + Y_{t-4})/4$

$\hat{Y}_9 = (Y_8 + Y_7 + Y_6 + Y_5)/4 = (76 + 112 + 130 + 194)/4 = 128$

$\cdots$

$\hat{Y}_{12} = (\hat{Y}_{11} + \hat{Y}_{10} + \hat{Y}_9 + Y_8)/4 = (148.25 + 141 + 128 + 194)/4 = 152.81$

As shown at the bottom of Table 13–10, Models 2 and 3 have the two lowest sums of squared errors, 239 and 777, respectively. Since our criterion of best model is minimum sum of squared errors for all four forecasted quarters, Models 2 and 3 will be used to forecast Year 4 (i.e., $t = 13$ to 16).

Forecasting with the Two Best Models

Table 13–11 illustrates the process of forecasting Year 4 using Models 2 and 3. As the table shows, Model 2's trend parameter is reestimated using Year 3 data alone. The new trend parameter, B, equals 3.5. Because Model 3 has no parameters, it can forecast Year 4 solely on Year 2 and 3 data. The bottom section of the table illustrates the resulting forecasts. These forecasts are averaged to yield the combined forecast in the last column of the table. While we have shown the actual demands for Year 4 as if they were known during this process, in actual applications,

TABLE 13–11
MSM Forecasting Using Two Best Models

t	Year/ Quarter	Demand
5	2/1	76
6	2/2	112
7	2/3	130
8	2/4	194

Fitting the B Parameter for Model 2 Using the Most Recent Year — Year 3

t	Year/ Quarter	Actual Demand	Model 2 Y_{t-4}	Model 2 Trend $Y_t - Y_{t-4}$
9	3/1	78	76	2.00
10	3/2	119	112	7.00
11	3/3	128	130	−2.00
12	3/4	201	194	7.00

$$B = \text{Mean}(Y_t - Y_{t-4}) = 3.50$$

Forecasting Demand for the Following Year Using Two Best Models

t	Year/ Quarter	Actual Demand	Model 2 Forecast	Model 3 Forecast	Combined Forecast
13	4/1	81	81.50	80.81	81.16
14	4/2	134	122.50	123.29	122.90
15	4/3	141	131.50	132.62	132.06
16	4/4	216	204.50	208.25	206.38

they would be unknown. As shown, the forecasts are quite accurate.

General Comments about MSM

Several comments should be made about this example. First, there are many possible models that could have been used during the model-selection process of Table 13–10. One commercially available package uses 20 different methods as possible best models. An advantage of this method is that the user can customize the forecasting methods for his or her application. Yet, this is also a disadvantage when the user is uncomfortable in selecting models. While there is considerable art involved in deciding on the models to include, this process can be easier than choosing a single best model for a system. Also, research continues on the MSM so that better selections can be made.

The most important criterion for deciding which models to include in a system is to make sure that all possible combinations of demand patterns are included. Therefore, all demand patterns are candidates for being chosen.

We have chosen to illustrate MSM using a selection procedure that selects the two best models. Some systems only use one best model. This is inferior to selecting several best models. As discussed in Chapter 14, several research studies have shown that taking the mean of several good models is much better than using only one model to forecast.

Combining the forecasts of several good
models is better than using only one model.

Table 13–10 illustrates the selection of models based on the minimum sum of squared errors for forecasts of the last year (i.e., four forecasts). Other implementations of MSM choose the best model based only on the last period's forecast accuracy. Our experiences and other research have shown that the sum of squared errors should be collected for a longer period, for example, a minimum of one year of squared errors. Unless a year's worth of data is used, there is the possibility that an effective seasonal model may be overlooked. We suggest this because when models are chosen based on one-period-ahead forecast accuracy, some simple models like Models 1 and 4 appear to perform better than they actually do. They appear to be better because they use much more-recent data in their calculations. Compare the age of data used in Model 1 versus Model 2.

$$\text{Model 1:} \quad \hat{Y}_t = Y_{t-1} + b$$

$$\text{Model 2:} \quad \hat{Y}_t = Y_{t-4} + B$$

Most decisions that are based on operational forecasts are made for more than one period into the future. Should not a forecasting model be judged on its accuracy in forecasting the same number of periods into the future? The obvious answer is yes. Models should be selected using criteria related to the decisions that will be based on the model's forecasts. For example, let us assume that we forecast to make decisions that influence the next three months. Should not our forecast model predict the next three months accurately? Yes, the designer of the forecasting system should, therefore, select forecast accuracy of one to three months ahead as the criterion of best fit. Some models are inherently multiperiod-ahead forecasts. Consider Model 2 above. This model is actually providing forecasts four quarters ahead, not one period ahead. It is much richer than the simple four-period moving average of Model 4.

Models should be chosen based on multiperiod-ahead forecast accuracy, not one-period-ahead accuracy.

Finally, this example illustrated selection of models based on their average performance over one horizon length. It has been suggested that it is effective to choose different models for different horizon lengths. For example, one model can be chosen to forecast one to three months ahead, other models four to six months ahead, and so on. While this increases computation time, it has been suggested that the payoff in terms of greater accuracy for longer-horizon decisions may be worth the effort. Also, in many cases, we believe that it is possible to identify a best model for all horizons. That is, for many short to medium-term forecasts, the best model(s) is(are) not dependent on the chosen horizon length. Research continues on this topic, so we suggest using a "show me" attitude at this time.

Disadvantages of MSM

There are several disadvantages of the MSM procedure. First, it is possible and common that different models are chosen as best each time the models are refitted. This is particularly true when one-period-ahead forecast accuracy is used as a selection criterion. If refitting is done each period, the system will use more time to calculate forecasts that may be less accurate than those that would have resulted without refitting (i.e., with the old models). When multiperiod-ahead forecasts are the basis of model selection, then this "fickle" tendency is reduced.

Another disadvantage of the method is that the system developers must decide which models to include in the system. This may require considerable time, effort, and expertise.

Finally, there might be excessive computational time if too many or too complex models are included as potential candidates. To offset long computational times, the models included in commercial MSM packages are typically very simple models, including many models that are parameterless like Models 3 and 4.

Advantages of MSM

The selection of any one method in the multimodel situation is not as critical as the selection of a single model in the conventional forecasting system situation. Theoretically and empirically appealing models can be chosen. Forecast model performance and applicability can be monitored in the system. Thus, the system can evolve to a best system; however, this evolution requires additional cost and effort.

Simple models like those used in Focus Forecasting™ are not necessarily less effective than other, more-complex procedures. This is discussed further in Chapter 14. Thus, MSM provides a simple, flexible, and powerful method for modeling demands in operational forecasting systems.

MSM Research

While MSM have been used for some time, their applications have only recently been reported in the forecasting literature. In 1990, Makridakis proposed an approach to time series analysis that encompasses the following characteristics.[8] First, models are selected based on how well they predict out-of-sample or withheld data, as was illustrated in predicting Year 3 demand in Table 13–10. Second, multiple models compete to be chosen best; this is shown above when forecasting with four models and then choosing the best of the models. Finally, different models may be chosen for each horizon length separately; thus, different models may be used to predict each of m different horizon lengths. As discussed in the next chapter, the Makridakis approach outperformed 24 other methods in an actual forecasting competition.

In summary, we see that there is not one approach to multimodel simulation methods, but many. MSM possess several of the following characteristics.

1. Several models are used to forecast past demands.
2. Model selection is based on actual out-of-sample forecast accuracy using criteria like the minimum sum of squared errors.
3. The out-of-sample forecast accuracy measure is based on m-period-ahead forecasts, not simply one-period-ahead forecasts.
4. Different models can be selected for different horizons.
5. The forecasts of different models are averaged to yield a combined forecast.

The MSM reported by Makridakis has all five of these characteristics, while other MSM systems may not. There has not been much discussion of MSM systems in the forecasting literature to date. Yet, new research is showing that MSM may yield improved forecasting systems. This research is discussed further in the next chapter.

SUMMARY

FSA remains a popular method of forecasting item-level demands. We have seen that the method is different—it uses trigonometric functions and is therefore somewhat more difficult to understand than other trend-seasonal methods. In fact, Winters' method, classical decomposition, and FSA are all very similar in their structure. That is, they each model a time series as a function of trend, seasonality, and randomness. As any method, FSA has its advantages and disadvantages. Several mainframe vendors of operational forecasting systems rely on this method.

Because FSA was not used in the much-reported forecasting competition of Makridakis et al.,[9] it is a little more difficult to make generalizations about its accuracy. Because it is as flexible as Winters' method in modeling patterns, we infer that it is comparable to that method. Other research has suggested that the advantages of FSA discussed above make it a more effective method of forecasting. We feel that this may be a moot issue and believe that there is no best method of forecasting; however, there are best systems of forecasting. The forecasting methods used in good systems are, in general, less important than their intelligent use.

Finally, this chapter has discussed very recent research on multimodel simulation methods. Parts of this general approach to forecasting have been applied for decades in many different systems. The integration of these many different parts by Makridakis may have provided exciting new approaches to forecasting. We review the forecasting effectiveness of MSM and 24 other forecasting methods in the next chapter.

REFERENCES

1. R. G. Brown, *Advanced Service Parts Inventory Control,* 2nd ed. (Thetford, Vt.: Materials Management Systems, 1982).
2. Ibid.
3. Ibid.
4. Hung Chan and Jack Hayya, "Spectral Analysis in Business Forecasting," *Decision Sciences* 7, no. 1 (January 1976), pp. 137–51.

5. James E. Reinmuth and Michael D. Geunts, "Using Spectral Analysis for Forecast Model Selection," *Decision Sciences* 8, no. 1 (January 1977), pp. 134–50.
6. Spyros Makridakis, "Sliding Simulation: A New Approach to Time Series Forecasting," *Management Science* 36, no. 4 (April 1990), pp. 505–11.
7. Bernard Smith, *Focus Forecasting—Computer Techniques for Inventory Control* (Boston: CBI Publishing, 1984).
8. Makridakis, "Sliding Simulation."
9. S. Makridakis, A. Andersen, R. Carbone, R. Fildes, M. Hibon, R. Lewandowski, J. Newton, E. Parzen, and R. Winkler, "The Accuracy of Extrapolation (Time Series) Methods: Results of a Forecasting Competition," *Journal of Forecasting* 2, April–June 1982, pp. 111–53.
10. Brown, *Advanced Service Parts Inventory Control.*

APPENDIX: BROWN'S FSA FITTING PROCESS

The following is a simple overview of the steps in the model fitting process developed by Brown[10]:

1. Deseasonalize the data using centered moving averages as described in Chapter 11.
2. Fit a trend line, using least squares, to the data of Step 1.
3. Subtract this trend from each actual value to yield the seasonal component of demand.
4. Fit a Fourier series model to the detrended series using least squares regression of Step 3 data.
5. Add the seasonal and trend projections for each period to get the full model-fitted values.
6. Eliminate those seasonal terms that are not significant.
7. Forecast future values not in the original sample.
8. Use smoothing methods to update parameter values.

We suggest Brown's approach for forecasting hundreds or thousands of items because of its efficiencies. The serious user of FSA should consult Brown for more information about his methods.

CHAPTER 14

FORECAST ACCURACY AND SYSTEM CONTROL

FORECASTING SYSTEM OPERATION AND CONTROL
SUMMARY
REFERENCES

To err is human and to blame it on a computer is even more so.

To a surprising extent, the effectiveness of forecasting systems is dependent on how well they handle unusual demands. Relatively well behaved patterns in demand are effectively and efficiently handled by forecasting methods that model trend, seasonal, and random components of demand. However, unusual demands present serious problems unless they are adjusted prior to forecasting.

Forecasting system performance is determined in
great part by its ability to handle the unusual.

The first section of this chapter presents a discussion of research concerning the accuracy and effectiveness of different time series forecasting methods. This is presented in a very nontechnical manner. As we will see, the forecasting performances of many methods are comparable. Also, there is not one best forecasting method.

There is not one best forecasting method—
many methods seem to perform equally well.

Next, this chapter develops three forecasting tools that detect and control unusual demands and forecast errors. These tools are outlier detection/adjustment methods, tracking signals, and forecast-reasonableness tests. Each of these is an essential part of an effective system. A forecasting system must detect outliers; otherwise, the old adage "garbage in, garbage out (GIGO)" will soon describe system operations and the views of users. Large outliers must be removed from the data; otherwise, these unusually large deviations will adversely affect the forecasting process.

Unmanaged outliers and unusual demands are garbage into a system and probably will result in some garbage out—GIGO.

Even if large outliers are eliminated, the forecasting process can go out of control. In order to detect out-of-control situations as soon as possible, early warning devices called *tracking signals* are used. This chapter develops several tracking signals that are essential to effective forecasting systems. These monitor forecast accuracy and highlight when human intervention is necessary.

Tracking signals provide early warning of out-of-control forecasts.

There are times when unreasonably high or low forecasts occur, even though everything appears correct prior to forecasting. These occur because of the interactions of several unusual demands. These unusual forecasts should be detected and eliminated before any harm is done. Unless forecast reasonableness is checked prior to the decision process, unreasonably high and costly errors may occur.

*Verifying forecast reasonableness is necessary
to ensure good forecasts and good decisions.*

Finally, this chapter presents an operational forecasting system flow chart. This flow chart illustrates the major processes and decisions of a good operational forecasting system, including the control devices of this chapter. It assists you in understanding and integrating the functions and principles that are discussed throughout this book. Studying this system diagram is an essential part of your understanding of the design and operation of operational forecasting systems.

FORECAST ACCURACY

ACCURACY OF TIME SERIES METHODS

Many forecast accuracy studies have been completed over the years. Overall, the results of these studies suggest that more-complex and more-expensive methods do not necessarily provide significantly more accurate forecasts than simple time series methods. (The methods of Chapters 11, 12, and 13 are not considered complex in this context.)

Complex forecasting methods are not significantly more accurate than simpler methods that include correct demand patterns.

M-Competition

Two of the most comprehensive studies of forecasting method accuracy were completed by Makridakis and Hibon in 1979[1] and Makridakis, et al., in 1982.[2] The first study investigated the accuracy of 21 different methods in forecasting 111 different series. A second study conducted by Makridakis, et al., involved seven experts who used 24 forecasting methods. They analyzed 1,001 different actual time series. This competition is now commonly called the *M-competition*. The 1,001 series varied by type (e.g., industry data, national data) and the time period analyzed (e.g., month, quarter, and year). The results of this study are presented in Table 14–1.

Because of the cost and time of applying some methods, not all 24 were used with all 1,001 series. To reduce application time, 111 series were randomly selected from the 1,001 series. The procedures of the Box-Jenkins, Lewandowski, and Parzen methodologies were added to the 21 methods. These three procedures require more time and effort to apply than other methods. Thus, Table 14–1 reports results of 21 methods, while Table 14–3 reports the findings from 111 time series with 24 models; we discuss Table 14–3 later.

In the M-competition, the lengths of the forecast horizons ranged from 1 to 18 periods into the future. Thus, 21 methods were used to forecast 1,001 series for 18 horizons, a total of 378,378 forecasts (1,001*18*21). The accuracy of these 1- to 18-period-ahead forecasts was measured using five different statistical measures. We report model performance using one of these measures–the forecast accuracy rank shown in Table 14–1. The table shows the average rank of methods using 1 to 21 for lowest to highest average errors. For example, a rank of 10 for one-period-ahead forecasts indicates that, on average, nine other methods had errors

TABLE 14–1
Average Ranking of 21 Models Using 1,001 Series

Methods	Model Fitting	Forecasting Horizons								Average of All Forecasts
		1	2	3	6	9	12	15	18	
Naive 1	15.8	11.9	12.4	12.3	12.0	11.6	10.0	11.1	11.2	11.62
Moving Average	13.3	11.8	12.3	11.9	11.5	10.8	10.9	10.4	10.6	11.28
Single EXP	12.9	11.9	12.2	11.9	11.6	10.4	10.6	10.5	10.6	11.18
ARR EXP	18.3	12.8	14.0	12.4	12.4	10.7	11.5	11.1	10.9	11.82
Holt EXP	10.5	10.9	10.9	11.0	11.0	11.7	11.3	12.0	11.8	11.41
Brown EXP	12.4	10.8	10.9	10.9	11.4	12.0	11.9	12.3	12.6	11.68
Quad. EXP	13.8	11.8	12.0	12.5	13.1	13.8	14.5	15.1	15.7	13.68
Regression	15.6	14.2	13.4	12.8	11.4	11.9	11.8	11.3	11.1	12.08
Naive 2	11.1	10.4	10.5	10.6	10.6	10.5	10.0	10.2	9.9	10.36
D Moving Average	8.1	11.4	11.9	12.3	11.6	11.2	10.9	10.8	10.8	11.34
D Sing EXP	7.6	10.3	10.4	10.6	10.5	9.6	9.8	9.7	9.4	10.00
D ARR EXP	13.6	11.4	12.4	11.6	11.5	10.4	10.5	10.3	10.0	10.87
D Holt EXP	4.8	9.4	8.9	9.3	9.9	10.7	10.7	10.7	10.7	10.09
D Brown EXP	6.6	9.4	9.0	9.5	10.0	10.6	10.9	11.0	11.3	10.29
D Quad. EXP	8.3	10.2	10.2	11.0	11.9	12.9	13.7	14.1	14.6	12.44
D Regress	12.3	13.3	12.0	12.1	10.9	11.4	11.2	10.7	10.0	11.21
Winters'	7.2	9.4	9.0	9.3	9.8	10.8	10.4	10.7	10.3	9.96
Autom. AEP	9.1	9.8	9.8	10.2	10.0	10.7	10.4	10.2	10.3	10.32
Bayesian F	15.6	11.0	10.0	10.1	10.4	10.3	10.6	10.5	10.7	10.38
Combining A	6.7	9.0	8.8	8.9	9.4	9.4	9.4	9.3	9.1	9.17
Combining B	7.5	9.8	10.0	10.0	10.1	9.7	9.8	9.6	9.6	9.80
Average	11.0	11.0	11.0	11.0	11.0	11.0	11.0	11.0	11.0	11.00

Source: Spyros Makridakis et al., "The Accuracy of Extrapolation (Time Series) Methods: Results of a Forecasting Competition," *Journal of Forecasting* 1 (1982), pp. 111–53.

that were lower. Each method receives a rank at each horizon length for each of 1,001 series. Then, the mean of the 1,001 rankings is recorded.

To increase the relevance of Table 14–1, Table 14–2 relates the methods used in the M-competition to those that are presented in this book. Table 14–2 shows that 17 out of the 24 methods are presented in this text. The remaining seven methods are not developed in this book because they are currently either too sophisticated, too costly, or too ineffective for use in automated item-level forecasting systems.

To better understand Table 14–1, consider the example of single exponential smoothing (Single EXP) and single exponential smoothing using deseasonalized data (D Sing EXP). The average ranking of 1,001 forecasts using Single EXP for one-period-ahead forecasts is 11.9 and for six-period-ahead forecasts, 11.6. When each of the 1,001 series is deseasonalized using the ratio-to-moving average method described in Chapter 11, Table 11–6, then the rankings of D Sing EXP are 10.3 and 10.5, respectively, for one- and six-period-ahead forecasts.

Table 14–3 provides summary results of Table 14–1. We report the rank of each method using the 18-month average of all forecast horizons. This is shown in column 2 of Table 14–3 and is the same as the last column of Table 14–1. That average ranking is then ranked from best to worst in column 3 of Table 14–3. Finally, for comparison purposes, we have reported the all-horizon, average rankings of the 111 series using all 24 methods in columns 1, 4, and 5 of Table 14–3. Let's study the results and conclusions of Tables 14–1 and 14–3.

Conclusions from M-Competition

The conclusions of the M-competition were consistent with those of other studies. There was not one method that was best for all series or all forecast horizons. Some methods are better than others at short-horizon lengths, others at long-horizon lengths. There was a general conclusion that simple methods do better than the more sophisticated methods, particularly over short-horizon lengths. While there is not one method that is best for all series and forecast horizons, we believe that there are better methods.

TABLE 14–2

Relationship between M-Competition 24 Models and this Book

Name Used in Table 14–1*	Description of Method	Chapter(s) where Method(s) Discussed
Naive 1	$Y_t = Y_{t-1}$	8 and 10
Moving Average	n-period moving average where n is chosen to minimize sum(e²)	10
Single EXP	Single (simple) exponential smoothing with optimal alpha	10
ARR EXP	Adaptive response-rate exponential smoothing	10
Holt EXP	Holt's two-parameter exponential smoothing with optimal parameters	12
Brown EXP	Brown's single-parameter trend smoothing with optimal parameters	12
Quad. EXP	Brown's single-parameter quadratic, triple smoothing with optimal parameters	Not developed here
Regression	Simple linear regression with time as independent variable	11
Naive 2†	Deseasonalized data used in Naive 1 model	10 and 11
D Moving Average†	Moving average using deseasonalized values	10 and 11
D Single EXP†	Single EXP using deseasonalized values	10 and 11
D ARR EXP†	ARR EXP using deseasonalized values	10 and 11
D Holt EXP†	Holt EXP using deseasonalized values	12 and 11
D Brown EXP†	Brown EXP using deseasonalized values	12 and 11
D Quad. EXP†	Quad. EXP using deseasonalized values	Not developed here
D Regress†	Regression using deseasonalized values	11
Winters'	Winters' three-parameter exponential smoothing with optimal parameters	12
Autom. AEP	An automatic adaptive estimation procedure developed by Carbone-Longini	Not developed here
Bayesian F	An adaptive Bayesian procedure developed by Harrison and Stevens	Not developed here
Combining A	A simple average of D Sing EXP, D ARR EXP, D Holt EXP, D Brown EXP, Winters', and Autom. AEP	10, 11 and 12
Combining B	A weighted average of methods used in Combining A, weights determined by percentage error of each	10,11, and 12
Box-Jenkins‡	ARIMA model building methods	Not developed here
Lewandowski‡	Lewandowski's FORSYS system	Not developed here
Parzen‡	Parzen's ARARMA methodology	Not developed here

*The methods are presented in the order used in Table 14–1.

†The method of ratio to centered moving averages developed in Chapter 11 was used to determine seasonal indexes. Then the series were deseasonalized, forecasted using specified methods, and reseasonalized by multiplying the deseasonalized forecasts times the relevant seasonal indexes.

‡These three methods are not included in Table 14–1, but are in Table 14–3.

TABLE 14-3
Rankings of Methods Based on Forecast Errors

(1) Method	(2) All-Horizon Average Rank 1,001 Series	(3) Rank-Rank 1,001 Series	(4) All-Horizon Average Rank (111 Series)	(5) Rank-Rank 111 Series
Combining A	9.17	1	10.40	1
Lewandowski	n.a.	n.a.	10.87	2
Combining B	9.80	2	11.30	6
Winters'	9.96	3	11.26	5
D Sing EXP	10.00	4	11.57	9
Parzen	n.a.	n.a.	11.22	4
D Holt EXP	10.09	5	11.15	3
D Brown EXP	10.29	6	11.47	7
Box-Jenkins	n.a.	n.a.	11.53	8
Autom. AEP	10.32	7	11.77	10
Naive 2	10.36	8	12.32	12
Bayesian F	10.38	9	11.90	11
D ARR EXP	10.87	10	12.72	13
Single EXP	11.18	11	13.20	16
D Regress	11.21	12	12.94	14
Moving Average	11.28	13	13.09	15
D Moving Average	11.34	14	13.86	21
Holt EXP	11.41	15	13.25	18
Naive 1	11.62	16	13.83	20
Brown EXP	11.68	17	13.30	19
ARR EXP	11.82	18	13.95	22
Regression	12.08	19	14.61	23
D. Quad. EXP	12.44	20	12.23	17
Quad. EXP	13.68	21	15.27	24

n.a. = Not applicable.

Source: Spyros Makridakis et al., "The Accuracy of Extrapolation (Time Series) Methods: Results of a Forecasting Competition," *Journal of Forecasting* 1 (1982), pp. 111–53.

*No one forecasting method is best for all series and forecast horizons.
While best forecasting methods do not exist, better methods do.*

One of the more surprising results of this study is the effectiveness of combining forecasting methods. As shown in Tables 14–1 and 14–3, Combining A and Combining B methods achieve much better performance than using only one method. Combining A method consists of deseasonalized exponential smoothing, deseasonalized ARR exponential smoothing, deseasonalized Holt, deseasonalized Brown, Winters, and autom. AEP. These are all easily implemented forecasting methods, and, except for the last method, all have been presented in this book. This suggests that it may be better to combine a few methods than to rely on the chance that a forecasting system can isolate a best method.

Combining the forecasts of several different
methods improves forecast accuracy.

One common method of combining forecasts is to average the forecasts of several methods. Combining B method of forecasting was a weighted average of the methods used in Combining A, where the weights are inversely proportionate to the errors of the methods. As shown in Tables 14–1 and 14–3, the additional complexity of calculating weights did not yield more accurate forecasts.

Simple average combinations of several good forecasting
methods work better than weighted average combinations.

Another important conclusion of the study is that the sophisticated methods not currently used in forecasting systems do not appear to be significantly better than simple methods. This is apparent when comparing the performance of the top eight methods of columns 4 and 5 of Table 14–3. Their performance rankings vary from only 10.40 to 11.53. There is no significant difference between the most sophisticated methods of Lewandowski (10.87), Parzen (11.22), and Box-Jenkins (11.53) and the simpler methods of Combining A (10.40), Winters (11.26), and D Holt EXP (11.15).

More-sophisticated and more-costly methods are not necessarily better.

While not presented here, Markridakis et al. presented the results of forecasting 60 seasonal series out of the 1,001 series. These results illustrated that, for the seasonal data of these 60 series, there is very little difference between the performance of the seasonally adjusted methods. "A hypothesis may be advanced at this point stating that statistically sophisticated methods do not do better than simple methods (such as deseasonalized exponential smoothing) when there is considerable randomness in the data. . . . Finally, it seems that seasonal patterns can be predicted equally well by both simple and statistically sophisticated methods."[3]

Multimodel Simulation Method Accuracy

There have been few forecast accuracy studies involving the multimodel simulation methods discussed in Chapter 13. A few have used the commercial forecasting system, Focus Forecasting™.[4] Some of those results were contradictory. In 1990, Makridakis completed additional research using MSM on the 111 series of the M-competition.[5] The research results of this study were not reported using ranks as in Tables 14–1 and 14–3. However, based on several other statistics, Makridakis concluded that the MSM "approach outperforms the best methods of the M-competition by a large margin when tested empirically with the 111 series subsamples of the M-competition data." Several characteristics of MSM were found to be very effective in forecasting systems. The following tentative principles resulted from this study.

Choosing models based on out-of-sample (withheld) multiple-period-ahead forecasts is better than using historical fit.

Choosing different models for different horizon lengths appears better than using a single model for all horizon lengths.

Combining the forecasts of several different methods is a very effective way to increase forecast accuracy.

Limitations of the M-Competition

For our purposes, the greatest limitations of the M-competition are the small number of series and that Fourier series analysis (FSA) was not included in the study. We do not know how different methods perform when forecasting demands for tens of thousands of items. Also, because FSA is a very popular method in item-level forecasting systems, its performance relative to other methods is very important. A previous study by Makridakis and Hibon[6] used FSA along with 20 other methods. FSA did not perform well in that study. However, it remains a very popular method. We have difficulty accepting the conclusions of Makridakis and Hibon concerning the ineffectiveness of FSA methods. Additional published research is needed to provide more conclusive comparisons.

Finally, we think it is important to highlight that the accuracies of methods are greatly influenced by how they are actually used in the forecasting systems. If the method models the correct demand patterns and is used intelligently, then it should perform reasonably well in the forecasting system. In general, we cannot choose a forecasting system based only on the method(s) used; but, more importantly, our choice should be based on how well the method(s) is(are) used in the system.

Forecasting method performance is dependent on how that method is used in a system.

As users and designers of forecasting systems, our research for a best method should include multiple criteria. Certainly other considerations such as cost, versatility for modeling many types of patterns, ease of use, and understandability are important considerations. Those methods that would appear to possess these attributes include Combining A, Combining B, D Holt EXP, D Brown EXP, Winters, MSM, and, while not reported here, Fourier series analysis.

FORECASTING SYSTEM CONTROL

OUTLIERS

Detecting when a forecasting model is no longer representative of demand is an important ability of a good forecasting system. A model can go out of control because of large, one-time abnormal occurrences (i.e., outliers) or because of several minor events that cause the model to consistently over- or underforecast (i.e., bias). Both of these influences cause a large difference between the actual and expected demands. These differences may result from problems in either the forecast or actual demand. The remainder of this chapter discusses ways to detect and control outliers and biased forecasts. We first discuss outliers, then biased forecasts.

Outliers are extremely large or small relative to the actual or expected demand patterns.

Outliers and bias can be caused by abnormal demands and forecasts.

Because they are large deviations from the dominant patterns in demand, outliers distort and confound the pattern-recognition process of forecasting. While outliers do cause problems, they also provide important information that is worth retaining.

Outliers confound the pattern-identification process of forecasting.

There is often a causal explanation for the difference between the outlier and the dominant pattern.

While it may seem that outliers are easily detected, this is not necessarily true. When a series has considerable randomness in trend or seasonality, visual inspection of the data might not reveal the outlier. Also, outliers are difficult to detect because they can affect or arise in each step of forecasting. Figure 14–1 illustrates the major parts of a simple forecasting system. As shown, outliers affect all parts of the system, particularly the demand data, forecasting, managerial interface, and database modules.

Causes of Outliers and Out-of-Control Forecasts

Outliers are caused by data entry errors, unusual events, unknown influences, planned events, incorrect forecasting models, and changes in demand patterns. These are discussed below.

1. *Data entry errors.* Data entry outliers can occur during any data input to the system. Many of these are due to human error, including keyboard errors, inconsistent measuring units (e.g., dozens versus units), rounding errors, and recording the wrong item.

Data entry errors and their causes must be eliminated before an accurate database of demand will be achieved.

2. *Unusual or irregular events.* Sometimes demands change dramatically because of unusual events. For example, natural disasters, strikes, competitors' out-of-stock situations, and competitors' promotional campaigns will likely cause demands to vary from expected values.

Adjust outliers caused by unusual events, but retain outlier information if it is likely to repeat in the future.

FIGURE 14–1
The Parts of a Forecasting System

___

I. Demand data module
 System input and output of local and remote demand data
 Demand capturing
 Logical filtering (demand versus supply or shipments)
 Special event filtering (promotions, price changes, product introductions)
 Initial outlier detection, adjustment, classification

II. Forecasting module
 System forecast model selection
 Outlier detection, adjustment, classification
 Reasonableness test
 Final forecast
 Error measures
 Tracking signal control

III. Managerial interface and interaction module
 Graphical user interface
 Graphical presentations
 Screen displays
 Management forecasts
 User help
 Management feedback
 User notepad
 Expert advisory menu

IV. Output module
 File generation
 Routine batch reports
 Ad hoc reports
 Exception reports

V. System control and maintenance module
 Navigation and system control of modules
 Input/output control between modules
 Simulation control
 Database updating and maintenance
 Detection of system malfunctions and bugs

VI. Database record module
 Actual and adjusted demand
 Demand forecasts and performance measures
 Promotional and seasonal profiles
 Item and group relationship structure
 Item descriptions

___

 3. *Unknown events.* There are outliers that are caused by unknown influences. Because they have unknown causes, the usual correction is to simply adjust demand back to normal values.

When failing to explain outliers, adjust them anyway.

4. *Planned events.* Unless we manage demands that result from changes in prices, promotions, and so on, these demands may be viewed as outliers.

Promotional and price effects should be managed in the forecasting system; otherwise, their effects will appear as outliers.

Effects from planned events should be modeled separately from dominant demand patterns.

5. *Incorrect forecasting models.* An outlier or out-of-control condition can occur when the wrong forecasting model is being used. It might be wrong because past demand was not representative of the future or because the model selection process failed. For example, this could result in using single exponential smoothing on a series with significant trend and seasonality. The simpler model might appear to be performing well between seasonal peaks or troughs, but it over- or under-forecasts during those peaks and troughs. We need tools to detect such out-of-control situations.

An incorrect model may forecast badly only during some periods, yet these might be the most important periods of peak demands.

6. *Changes in demand patterns.* It is important to detect changes in demand patterns as soon as possible. Almost all products go through life cycles that result in considerable differences in trends and seasonality. A series that has had a positive trend might suddenly have a negative one. Or, a random series might

---

Coincidences and Outliers

"It is no great wonder if, in the long process of time, while fortune takes her course hither and thither, numerous coincidences should spontaneously occur."

Plutarch

It is no great wonder that outliers should occur spontaneously. The causes of these outliers are sometimes unknown and unknowable.

suddenly change from having a mean demand of 1,000 to 2,000 per month. The sooner these can be detected, the sooner the proper decisions will be made.

A good forecasting system should
detect changes in a product's life cycle.

Outlier Detection

Formal statistical tests and informal judgment can be used to detect outliers. Both of these approaches use simple statistical tools such as time plots, frequency distributions, and simple *t*-tests to detect outliers. Below, we discuss these as practical methods of outlier detection. Our ultimate purpose is to understand how automated and judgmental outlier detection and adjustment procedures work. Both are important.

To better understand the practical problems of detecting outliers, consider the seasonal data of Table 14–4. If we were to examine this data using simple frequency distributions like those illustrated in Chapter 7, we might not find any outliers because the order of data is lost in the distribution. All the data would appear to be typical values; none are very unusual when viewed as a single group. However, by dividing the data into quarterly groups as in Table 14–4, our ability to detect outliers improves.

To detect seasonal outliers requires
detecting deviations from seasonal patterns.

TABLE 14–4
Detecting Outliers with Seasonal Presentations

	1986	*1987*	*1988*	*1989*	*1990*	*1991*
Quarter 1	31	32	34	36	39	42
Quarter 2	40	41	45	53	58	60
Quarter 3	58	65	67	37	74	78
Quarter 4	42	44	49	51	52	53

By scanning the data of Table 14–4 by quarters (i.e., by row), we can see that the value of 37 in Quarter 3 of 1989 is very unusual. This is even more evident in Table 14–5, which shows each observation with its seasonal difference in parentheses. For example, the parenthetical value for Quarter 1, 1988 is Quarter 1, 1988 minus Quarter 1, 1987 (i.e., 34 − 32). The outlier of Quarter 3, 1989 is evident now because of its extremely low value (−30). Interestingly, this single outlier creates two inconsistent seasonal values. Note that the seasonal differences of Quarter 3 in 1989 and 1990 are distorted by the single outlier. It is not hard to imagine how a forecasting system might have problems in identifying the correct demand patterns when several outliers cause multiple problems like those in Table 14–5.

Outliers distort more than one observation
when there are seasonal or trend patterns.

Plotting Values to Detect Outliers

One very effective way to detect outliers is to plot values of the data over time. Such plots can include those of the original data, appropriate transformations, differences, or seasonal graphs (e.g., plot Quarters 1, 2, 3, and 4 data on separate graphs). Figure 14–2 illustrates a plot of the data of Table 14–4. The outlier in Period 15 is easily detected with this graph. In addition, we might plot

TABLE 14–5
Detecting Outliers with Seasonal Differences (in parentheses)

	1986	1987	1988	1989	1990	1991
Quarter 1	31	32 (1)	34 (2)	36 (2)	39 (3)	42 (3)
Quarter 2	40	41 (1)	45 (4)	53 (8)	58 (5)	60 (2)
Quarter 3	58	65 (7)	67 (2)	37 (−30)	74 (37)	78 (4)
Quarter 4	42	44 (2)	49 (5)	51 (2)	52 (1)	53 (1)

FIGURE 14–2
Quarterly Demand of Table 14–4 Data

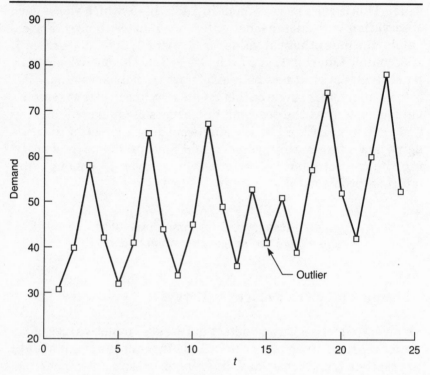

seasonally differenced data for each season on separate graphs. These simple extensions are left to the reader.

*Plots of various transformations of demands
are essential in outlier detection.*

Statistical Tests for Outliers

In Chapter 7, we developed the concept of the standard deviation and the mean as they relate to the normal distribution. One powerful way to detect outliers is to measure each observation as a standardized deviation from its mean. Assuming that demand is approximately normally distributed without pronounced seasonality or trend, then actual observations should not deviate greatly from the mean. We can perform a simple Z-or t'-test to detect the outlier. (We use t' to distinguish the statistical concept of a t value from the use of t for time period.) The t' value is:

$$t_Y = \frac{Y_t - \overline{Y}_t}{S_Y} \qquad (14\text{–}1)$$

where

$t_Y = t'$ value of each observation, Y_t
$\overline{Y}_t = $ Mean of Y_t
$S_Y = $ Standard deviation of the observations

This calculated t_Y value is compared to some value of K from the normal distribution (ND). We infer that an observation is an outlier when the calculated t' value exceeds the chosen K value. For the ND, approximately 95 percent of the values will be within two standard deviations (i.e., $K = 2$). Approximately 99.73 percent will be within three standard deviations, (i.e., $K = 3$). It is common to use K values of 3 to detect outliers.

*Outliers in patternless or random series
can be detected with simple t'-tests.*

Table 14–6 illustrates the calculation of two t' values for the data of Table 14–5: one for the original data, the other for seasonal differences. The actual demand is shown in column 2; the t' values of each of these is in column 3. Assume we use a K value of 3 to identify an outlier. As shown in column 3, no t' value is greater than 3; thus, it appears that there are no outliers in the data. Using a simple t'-test on the original data is not sufficient to detect a seasonal outlier.

*Simple t'-tests on raw data are insufficient
to detect seasonal and trend outliers.*

When data are highly seasonal or trending, then the check for outliers is more complex. In such cases, we can fit appropriate seasonal or trend models to the data and thereby search for unusual differences between the actual and forecast. An effective way of defining seasonal outliers is to use seasonal differences. Also, a way to detect outliers in trends is to use first differences. We discussed differencing in Chapter 12.

TABLE 14–6
Detection of Outliers Using Regular and Seasonal t' Values

(1)	(2)	(3)	(4)	(5)	(6)	(7)	(8)
						Outlier	
			Seasonal	Seasonal	Adjusted	Effect	Type of
Time (t)	Demand	t' Value	Differences	t' Values	Demand	(2) – (6)	Outlier*
1	31	–1.40			31		
2	40	–.71			40		
3	58	.67			58		
4	42	–.55			42		
5	32	–1.32	1	–.19	32		
6	41	–.63	1	–.19	41		
7	65	1.21	7	.35	65		
8	44	–.40	2	–.10	44		
9	34	–1.17	2	–.10	34		
10	45	–.32	4	.08	45		
11	67	1.36	2	–.10	67		
12	49	–.02	5	.17	49		
13	36	–1.01	2	–.10	36		
14	53	.29	8	.44	53		
15	37	–.94	–30	–3.00	71	–34	(a)
16	51	.14	2	–.10	51		
17	39	–.78	3	–.01	39		
18	58	.67	5	.17	58		
19	74	1.90	37	3.07	74		
20	52	.21	1	–.19	52		
21	42	–.55	3	–.01	42		
22	60	.83	2	–.10	60		
23	78	2.21	4	.08	78		
24	53	.29	1	–.19	53		
Mean	49.21	.00	3.10	.00	50.63		
Standard							
Deviation	13.04	1.00	11.04	1.00	13.49		

*Explanation of outlier types:
  (a) Promotion.
  (b) Price increase.
  (c) Other influence.
  (d) Unknown cause.

*Appropriate differencing is an important
method of detecting seasonal and trend outliers.*

In Table 14–6, the t' values of seasonal differences in column 5 denote two potential outliers. These t' values were calculated using Equation 14–1 on the fourth-order differences of column 4 (i.e., $Y_t - Y_{t-4}$). The first value is the actual outlier at Period 15, while the highest t-value is in Period 19; however, this second outlier is a result of the first outlier at Period 15. The Period 15 outlier should be adjusted so as to preserve the integrity of the seasonal pattern. As this example illustrates, simple approaches to outlier detection may be insufficient to properly identify and adjust outliers.

Caution is necessary when automating outlier adjustments.

Comparing Actual to Forecast

The above methods of detecting outliers are particularly important in judgmental methods or during the initialization of a new forecasting system or new items. After system initialization, a more effective way to detect outliers is to compare actual demand with the forecast of a good model. If the difference between actual and forecast is large, then there may be a problem with either the forecast or demand. This is discussed more in the next section on outlier adjustment.

The most common way of detecting outliers
is to compare actual and forecasted values.

Adjusting Outliers

When outliers are detected, the next step is to replace them with good observations. When the outlier is due to measurement or human error, replacing the observation with the correct value solves the problem. When an outlier must be replaced with a hypothetical value, then we need some guidance in how to replace it.

In time series forecasting, never delete an outlier; always adjust it.

The correct adjustment of outliers is often apparent after some thought. Typically, understanding the underlying pattern of demand provides the information necessary to adjust the value. Consider the following simple methods.

1. If a reliable forecast exists for a series, then an outlier can be replaced with the forecast.

Frequently, replacing the actual value with the forecasted value is the best method for adjusting outliers.

2. If the series has no seasonality or trend, then we can replace outliers with several possible values. If the series is completely random, then the outlier can be replaced with the mean of the series. In contrast, if the series has a random walk or trend, then it can be replaced with the mean of the two adjacent values as in Equation 14–2, which uses the data of Table 14–6.

$$(Y_{t-1} + Y_{t+1})/2 = (Y_{14} + Y_{16})/2 = (53 + 51)/2 = 52 \qquad (14\text{–}2)$$

However, this is not the correct adjustment for this data because of its strong seasonality.

3. If the series is seasonal, then replace the outlier with the mean of the two seasonally adjacent values. In Table 14–6, this is:

$$\begin{aligned}(Y_{t-4} + Y_{t+4})/2 &= (Y_{11} + Y_{19})/2 \\ &= (67 + 74)/2 = 70.5 = 71\end{aligned} \qquad (14\text{–}3)$$

This is the best procedure for the data of Table 14–6.

The mean of two adjacent seasonal values can be an effective outlier replacement.

4. If the analyst wants to preserve the unusually high or low value of the outlier, then he or she could use the above rules, but add or subtract some additional quantity. The adjusted number would not be an outlier, but it would still preserve some of its extreme value. This can be valuable when it is believed that future demands will also be extreme, but not as high or low as the outlier.

Retaining Actual, Adjusted, and Outlier Demands

It is important to retain both actual demand (i.e., unadjusted demand), adjusted demand, and the outlier effect. These are shown in columns 2, 6, and 7 of Table 14–6. The difference between the adjusted demand and the actual demand can provide important information about the outlier effect. For outliers that might reoccur in the future, it is important to retain the outlier effect with the notation of the cause of the outlier. This notation can be simply done, as shown in column 8 of Table 14–6.

*Retention of actual and adjusted demand
provides valuable outlier information.*

FORECAST MONITORING AND TRACKING SIGNALS

Individual Outlier Errors

One of the simplest ways to detect outlier errors is to compare them to zero. It is expected that errors are approximately normally distributed with a mean of zero and a constant standard deviation. To detect an out-of-control situation, a simple t'-test is performed. The t' value is calculated as:

$$t_I = \frac{e_t - 0}{Se} \tag{14–4}$$

where

t_I = t' value of an individual error, e_t
Se = Standard deviation of forecast errors

For clarity, we show the value of zero in Equation 14–4 to denote that individual errors should not deviate much from zero. In detecting outliers, this calculated t_I value is compared to some chosen K value as discussed previously. In practice, it is not uncommon to choose K values of 2 or more.

This t_I statistic detects very large one-time errors. There are many possible explanations for out-of-control errors and appropriate corrective actions. Detecting these out-of-control situations is something a forecasting system must do. This process is called demand filtering, and it is used by almost all forecasting systems when new demands are recorded.

While demand filtering is an essential part of a good forecasting system, it does not measure and control cumulative errors over time. Measuring cumulative errors is important because their effects can be much more detrimental than a single large error. Also, very important, the bias of cumulative errors can be indicative of fundamental changes in the demand pattern, changes that we want to detect as soon as possible.

Biased errors can be indicative of
fundamental changes in demand patterns.

Tracking Signals–Detecting Biased Cumulative Errors

The major concern in monitoring forecasts is to ensure that the forecast model is still valid and demand is behaving as expected. We infer that this is true when forecasts have small errors individually and cumulatively over time. Large cumulative errors can be detected by use of a tracking signal (TS). This statistical measure detects cumulative errors that are significantly different than zero. If a forecast is in control, then its mean error, cumulative errors, and tracking signal should not vary much from zero. However, when a forecast goes out of control, bias occurs if the errors are primarily positive or primarily negative, but not both.

The way to detect out-of-control forecasts is to set K values, called *trip points,* to identify when an error or groups of errors are collectively outliers. When the TS exceeds some constant K,

---

The Whole Distribution Is Important, So Be Cautious When Dealing with Averages.

The average error of a good forecasting model should not be significantly different than zero. However, a model with a mean error of zero is not necessarily a good forecasting model. Remember the example of the woman who states that on average she is comfortable because she has her head in the refrigerator and her feet in the oven. A good forecast model has errors with an average of approximately zero and, more important, a low standard deviation or mean absolute deviation.

we infer that the forecasts are biased and the mean of the errors deviates significantly from the expected value of zero. We thus infer that the sum of errors is not random, but is caused by some large or consistent over- or underforecasting influences. There are a number of theoretically and empirically derived rules of thumb for setting these TS trip points (i.e., setting K). However, the most common way is to choose K directly from actual system performance. This is so because controlling forecasts involves complex probabilistic trade-offs.

Unbiased (in-control) forecast errors have
mean and cumulative errors of zero.

A way to monitor forecasts is to use the sum of errors over time, sometimes called a *cumulative summation* (CUSUM). The summation of past errors is simply:

$$\text{CUSUM}_t = \Sigma \; e_t = \text{CUSUM}_{t-1} + e_t \qquad (14\text{--}5)$$

If the forecasting situation is running smoothly, then the CUSUM should fluctuate about zero. The CUSUM can be controlled using a simple t-test when errors are normally and independently distributed. Under these conditions, the standard deviation of the CUSUM is equal to the standard deviation of the errors times the square root of the number of errors. That is,

$$\text{Standard deviation (CUSUM)} = Sc = Se \; \sqrt{n} \qquad (14\text{--}6)$$

where

Sc = Standard deviation of the CUSUM
Se = Standard deviation of errors in period t
n = Number of errors in the calculation of CUSUM_t

This results in the following t-test, which we call *tracking signal cumulative sum* (TSC).

$$\text{TSC}_t = \frac{\text{CUSUM}_t - 0}{Sc_t} \qquad (14\text{--}7)$$

The calculated TSC value can be compared to a chosen K value using the t-distribution or normal distribution as was done using t_I in Equation 14–4.

While the TSC is a useful test statistic, it is not commonly used because Sc_t gives equal weight to all past errors. Because the immediate past is a better indication of the immediate future, more-recent errors should be given more weight than old errors. For example, consider the use of TSC based on 36 observations when the forecasting system shifts out of control in Period 36. This shift will be diluted by the other 35 observations; thus, it may be some time before the out-of-control situation is detected. For this reason, it is suggested that a smaller number of observations be used in the equations above; but how many?

The MAD and standard deviation should be weighted to more-recent errors because these errors are more relevant to the immediate future.

The question of how many periods to include in the Sc is very much like the question of how many periods to include in an exponential smoothing model. If too many are included in TSC, then it may not be responsive enough to errors; if too few are included, then the system may be too responsive. Not surprisingly, we find a popular method of detecting out-of-control situations is to use averages that are exponentially smoothed values.

Tracking Signal–CUSUM₍/MAD₍

Considerable research has been devoted to the best tracking signal and ways in which to use them. Brown[7] defined a tracking signal that is a simple extension of TSC. We call this a tracking-signal-cumulative using MAD (TSM). This is defined as:

$$TSM_t = \frac{CUSUM_t - 0}{MAD_t} \qquad (14\text{--}8)$$

where

$$MAD_t = \alpha|e_t| + (1 - \alpha)MAD_{t-1} \qquad (14\text{--}9)$$

and where CUSUM is the cumulative sum of forecast errors that have occurred since the forecasting model was selected or reestimated. The value of CUSUM is set to zero whenever the tracking signal is tripped or a major change is made in the forecasting environment. When tripped, the forecasting situation is investigated, corrected, and the CUSUM$_t$ reset to zero; however, the MAD$_t$ is not reset to zero.

The theoretical standard deviations of TSC and TSM are not well defined when errors are not normally and independently distributed. Most often when smoothing models are used, errors are significantly dependent. Because of this, it is not easy to theoretically set the K value of TSM, TSC, or TST (which is discussed below). Consequently, in most applications, the K value is determined empirically, based on actual system performance. This determination is based on the feasibility of attending to all of the exceptions. If too many models are tripped, making managerial or automated interventions an impossible task, the K value should be increased. Common values of K are from 4 to 7. When the calculated TSM exceeds this value, then the forecasting situation is identified as one that is out of control.

Most time series models have dependent (autocorrelated) errors that complicate selection of TS trip points.

TS trip points are often empirically derived.

Note that in Equation 14-8, the TSM is presented using MAD$_t$ as opposed to the standard deviation. However, the denominator of Equation 14-8 could include an exponentially smoothed standard deviation instead of MAD. Brown makes a very strong case for the use of the standard deviation instead of MAD.[8] Brown advocates the use of the square root of the mean squared error, RMSE$_t$ (a variable that is actually equal to a smoothed Se).

$$\text{MSE}_t = \alpha e_t^2 + (1 - \alpha)\text{MSE}_{t-1} \qquad (14\text{--}10)$$

$$\text{RMSE}_t = \sqrt{\text{MSE}_t} \qquad (14\text{--}11)$$

While this appears to be a best measure of error variation, there is some debate regarding the use of RMSE$_t$. Some have suggested that an advantageous characteristic of the MAD$_t$ over the use of the RMSE$_t$ is that it responds less to forecast errors that are almost, but not quite, outliers. This results from the fact that MAD$_t$ involves no squared errors. Thus, MAD$_t$ does not increase as rapidly as RMSE$_t$. In contrast, some argue the opposite problem exists, that the MAD$_t$ is not responsive enough and should

---

Not Mad about MAD

R. G. Brown developed the concept of MAD in the late 1950s to measure the variation of forecast errors. MAD was designed to reduce the computational intensity on primitive data processing systems that were not capable of taking square roots. With modern computers, there are no problems in using the standard deviation instead of MAD. Brown stresses that it is mad to continue using MAD instead of the standard deviation.[9]

---

be replaced by $RMSE_t$. Also, MAD_t is much more easily calculated than $RMSE_t$. As we will soon see, this debate is not important because we will not recommend the use of TSM. Also, we agree with the persuasive arguments of Brown in favor of using $RMSE_t$ in all statistical calculations.

The standard deviation ($RMSE_t$) is a better error measure than MAD_t.

Trigg Tracking Signal

Trigg[10] has provided another tracking signal based on the smoothed average of the forecast error (SAD_t) and the MAD_t. The SAD_t is calculated as:

$$SAD_t = \alpha e_t + (1 - \alpha)SAD_{t-1} \qquad (14\text{--}12)$$

SAD_t is nothing more than a weighted moving average of past errors. The resulting Trigg tracking signal is as follows:

$$TST_t = \frac{SAD_t}{MAD_t} \qquad (14\text{--}13)$$

This tracking signal varies from -1 to $+1$. For unbiased errors, TST should fluctuate about zero. But when bias occurs, the TST will approach either $+1$ or -1 depending on the direction of bias. If error terms are approximately normally and independently distributed, then the approximate standard deviation of SAD_t ($SSAD_t$) is:

$$SSAD_t = Se \sqrt{\frac{\alpha}{2 - \alpha}} = 1.25MAD_t \sqrt{\frac{\alpha}{2 - \alpha}} \qquad (14\text{--}14)$$

This standard deviation is used to set trip points for the TST as shown below. When using MAD_t and an α of .1, a 95 percent trip point for TST is:

$$2*1.25 \sqrt{\frac{\alpha}{2 - \alpha}} = 2*1.25 \sqrt{\frac{.1}{2 - .1}} = .574 \qquad (14\text{--}15)$$

Thus, when the TST_t exceeds .57, this indicates that an out-of-control forecasting situation exists. However, as discussed previously, most errors are not independently distributed. Thus, empirically derived K values for TST should be used in an actual system. Brown suggests an initial setting of trip points based on an empirically derived formula for the standard deviation of TST (STST):

$$STST_t = .55 \sqrt{\alpha}$$

With $\alpha = .10$,

$$STST = .55 \sqrt{.1} = .174 \qquad (14\text{--}16)$$

Applying the ususual two standard deviations for K, when TST exceeds .35 (i.e., 2 times .174), the system is deemed to be out of control. While this trip point is not universally applicable, it has been found to be a good initial value. However, the final trip points will be determined empirically from actual system performance.

An Example Application of TSM and TST

Table 14–7 simulates the use of the tracking signals of Brown and Trigg over a 24-month period. Brown's TSM is shown in column 5, while Trigg's TST is shown in column 7. To apply these tracking signals requires starting values for MAD_t, $CUSUM_t$, and SAD_t. It is correct to set initial values, $CUSUM_0$ and SAD_0, to zero as shown in Period 0; these are expected to vary about zero. However, it is not logical for MAD to be zero. An initial value of MAD_0 must be estimated. This initial value can be estimated from the initial forecast model fitting process or from some past mean absolute errors. In this case, MAD_0 was chosen using the past 10 errors (these are not shown). The trip points (i.e., K values) for the two tracking signals are 4 and .35, respectively, the trip point of TST being derived from Equation 14–16. The values of SAD_t and MAD_t are calculated using an alpha of .10.

TABLE 14-7
Use of Brown's TSM and Trigg's TST Tracking Signals

	(1) Period (t)	(2) Error,	(3) MAD,	(4) CUSUM,	(5) TSM,	(6) SAD,	(7) TST,
	0		59.22	.00	.00	.00	.00
	1	-83.30	61.63	-83.30	-1.35	-8.33	-.14
	2	78.60	63.33	-4.70	-.07	.36	.01
	3	-9.50	57.94	-14.20	-.25	-.62	-.01
	4	-42.60	56.41	-56.80	-1.01	-4.82	-.09
	5	-82.10	58.98	-138.90	-2.36	-12.55	-.21
	6	-96.00	62.68	-234.90	-3.75	-20.89	-.33
Tripped	7	-50.00	61.41	-284.90	-4.64	-23.80	-.39

Correct the System and Set CUSUM and SAD to Zero

	(1)	(2)	(3)	(4)	(5)	(6)	(7)
	7	-50.00	61.41	.00	.00	.00	.00
	8	52.30	60.50	52.30	.86	5.23	.09
	9	-21.50	56.60	30.80	.54	2.56	.05
	10	-73.10	58.25	-42.30	-.73	-5.01	-.09
	11	35.70	56.00	-6.60	-.12	-.94	-.02
	12	-57.30	56.13	-63.90	-1.14	-6.57	-.12
	13	-5.50	51.06	-69.40	-1.36	-6.47	-.13
	14	-94.30	55.39	-163.70	-2.96	-15.25	-.28
	15	68.60	56.71	-95.10	-1.68	-6.86	-.12
	16	-87.80	59.82	-182.90	-3.06	-14.96	-.25
Tripped	17	-88.00	62.64	-270.90	-4.33	-22.26	-.36

Correct the System and Set CUSUM and Sad to Zero

	(1)	(2)	(3)	(4)	(5)	(6)	(7)
	17	-88.00	62.64	.00	.00	.00	.00
	18	49.20	61.29	49.20	.80	4.92	.08
	19	-80.20	63.18	-31.00	-.49	-3.59	-.06
	20	94.30	66.29	63.30	.95	6.20	.09
	21	-72.80	66.95	-9.50	-.14	-1.70	-.03
	22	15.90	61.84	6.40	.10	.06	.00
	23	-89.60	64.62	-83.20	-1.29	-8.91	-.14
	24	72.70	65.42	-10.50	-.16	-.75	-.01

$\alpha = .10$ Trip point TSM = 4   Trip point TST = .35

As shown in Period 7 of Table 14-7, both tracking signals tripped because of the bias of Periods 3 through 7 (all five periods had negative errors). At the end of Period 7, the situation was investigated, and the system was corrected and reset. As shown by the second Period 7 of the table, $CUSUM_7$ and SAD_7 were both reset to zero. The system continued to forecast without problems until Period 17. At that point, both TSM_{17} and TST_{17} tripped because of another run of negative errors. Again, the system was reset and the forecasting process continued without problems through Period 24.

Choosing a Simple Tracking Signal

Gardner provides an excellent review of tracking signals.[11] He has found that TST is more widely used than TSM. An advantage of TST is that it is less sensitive to certain types of false trips. It can easily be shown that if a very large error is followed by several small errors, the TSM will be tripped by the several smaller errors. This occurs because the larger error has increased $CUSUM_t$ while the smoothed MAD_t becomes smaller as a result of the several very small errors. Thus, we see that the numerator of Equation 14–8 increases while the denominator decreases. It is very dysfunctional to have a tracking signal trip because the latest forecast errors are nearly zero. To trip when forecast errors are low is unacceptable. However, the TST is not adversely affected by this behavior. As the MAD_t decreases because of smaller errors, so does the SAD_t. It is for this reason that TST_t is used more frequently than TSM_t.

The TST_t is more reliable than the TSM_t tracking signal.

Backward CUSUM *V*-Mask Tracking Signal

A problem with the above tracking signals is that smoothing SAD_t and MAD_t results in some time delay in the detection process. A system goes out of control in time t, but is not detected until time $t + L$, where L is the length of delay. More-advanced tracking signals using cumulative summation techniques based on the use of *V*- or parabolic masks are designed to detect bias within a specific number of periods.[12] These are derived from the sequential sampling techniques of Wald and are very effective methods.[13] This TS is a popular method that is successfully implemented in many forecasting systems. We strongly recommend that developers consider incorporating it into their designs.

Backward CUSUM techniques are the best tracking signal.

Graphical Support and Expert System Control

Automated controls are an essential part of an operational control system, but it is always important to have support for human review and modification. The highest degree of control in forecasting systems normally comes from periodical human intervention when the tracking signal trips or other exceptions occur. This is accomplished by having master schedulers or product managers review plots of actual demands versus forecasted demands as well as plots of errors. The pattern-recognition capabilities of the human mind are very good; thus, graphical presentations are an important part of a good forecasting system.

Human pattern-recognition abilities provide powerful tracking signals.

If the cost consequences of errors are low, then it may not be effective to allocate analyst time to all exceptions; this is why trip

---

Regression toward the Mean and Outliers

The term *regression* was coined during the study of natural phenomena such as child heights in relation to parent heights. It was found that child heights regress toward the mean heights of all individuals. For example, if a child's parents are tall, then it is likely that the child will also be tall, but not quite as tall as his or her parents. Likewise, if a child's parents are short, then it is likely that the child will also be short, but not quite as short as his or her parents. This is not a universal principle, as we all can attest, yet it is a common phenomenon that describes more situations than not. So, too, in forecasting we often see unusual behavior in a time series, unusually high or low demands that yield unusually high or low forecast errors. In a majority of cases, these unusual behaviors will regress (i.e., return) to normal values. Thus many series may have outliers during one month or period followed by normal values in the next periods.

However, when several periods of outliers occur, then the property of regression toward the mean is not operating. There is some systematic bias in the forecasting process. In this situation, we must detect and eliminate the cause of the bias.

points are set empirically. However, an out-of-stock condition is always a serious matter to the customer, and overstock conditions yielding poor liquidity are always a concern of the owners. Therefore, there should be controls to ensure that we have balanced inventory. The methods used to ensure in-stock conditions are discussed in Chapter 16.

With the advent of more-powerful forecasting hardware and software, we have the opportunity to develop better automated methods of detecting and adjusting out-of-control situations. While it is not easy to duplicate the pattern-recognition capabilities of humans, expert systems are being developed to assist in this regard. These combine the best objective control techniques with the subjective assessment of management. Artificial intelligence and expert systems (AI/ES) are already used in some systems to help identify, diagnose, and adjust out-of-control situations. Chapter 18 discusses AI/ES applications in operational forecasting.

REASONABLENESS TESTS

Even though the forecasting process has been monitored through the use of outlier adjustments and tracking signals, there are times when the predicted values of otherwise good models yield unreasonable forecasts. These unreasonable forecasts can result from the interaction of several near outliers that greatly affect the next forecasted value. The statistical tests discussed in this chapter are important tools in precluding gross errors. These tools can be applied directly to demand or to percentage change measures of future demands as discussed below.

Even when the system performs properly,
unreasonable forecasts may result.

Unreasonable forecasts need to be detected and
corrected during their generation, not afterward.

Reasonableness tests typically involve simple rules of thumb that result in exception reports. These exception reports prompt human intervention into the forecasting process. For example, it would be unusual for an item to grow at a 100 percent annual rate. While this does occur, it may be decided that any item with a projection this high should be highlighted to management. The basic question of a reasonableness test is, "Does this projected demand seem reasonable when compared to past demands and future expectations?" Thus, one simple rule could be to highlight or identify as an exception any item with a deseasonalized monthly growth rate in excess of some number considered much too large, such as 25 percent.

The definition of reasonable can be item or product-line specific. thus, there are many ways we can answer this question. Almost all answers involve simple rules of thumb.

FORECASTING SYSTEM OPERATION AND CONTROL

Figure 14–3 illustrates a macro-system flow chart for a generic operational forecasting system. This flow chart illustrates only the major steps and parts of a forecasting system. The first 14 chapters of this book have developed many principles and functions of forecasting systems. Figure 14–3 integrates these details by illustrating the sequence of processes and decisions used in executing and controlling a forecasting system. As shown, this process includes all the major functions of operational forecasting systems discussed in Chapters 1 through 14.

Each of the blocks in Figure 14–3 is numbered for purposes of our discussion. Blocks 1 through 4 represent the process of validating and filtering demand for use in the forecasting system. After validation, the system classifies the item as either a new item (Yes in block 5) or a previously forecasted item (No in block 5) and either a forecastable or unforecastable item (in blocks 6 or 8). If a new item has sufficient data to be forecast, then a forecasting model is fitted in block 7. If an item has insufficient data with which to forecast (No in blocks 6 and 8), then it is referenced to a hierarchical group forecast (block 23). During the hierarchical group forecasting process, this item's demand can be forecasted as a percentage of the group forecast. While not shown here, at times an item may not be forecasted by the system.

If an item has been forecasted previously (Yes in block 8), then a tracking signal is calculated. If the tracking signal is out of control, then appropriate actions are taken (see blocks 10, 11, 12, 13, 14, and 16). These actions include refitting a model, as shown in block 16. If the tracking signal is in control, then a check is made to see whether it is time to refit a model. Such refitting is done only rarely (for example, once a year when a new model has not been fitted during the past year).

After forecasts have been generated in either blocks 7, 16, or 17, they are checked for reasonableness in block 18. If found unreasonable, then an adjustment and/or warning to the user is made in block 19. When the system forecast is found to be reasonable, it may be adjusted for special or planned events (such as promotions, as shown in block 20). After adjustment for these special events, the system model is combined with subjective forecasts of management (input from block 22 to block 21). If the item forecasted is a member of a larger group or is used in hierarchical roll-up or force-down forecasting, this process is represented by block 23. Finally, as shown in block 24, the forecast database is updated, and this forecasting cycle is completed for all items in the demand database. As noted in block 25, this process will be repeated in the next forecast period (i.e., either next month or next week).

The interactions of management during this process are represented by the management interface module of block 26. These processes are designated by the C:. As shown by the C:s, management interventions take place in five of the block processes (blocks 4, 10, 14, 19, and 22). The direction of information flows involving management (i.e., the C:s) are bidirectional, denoting the interactions of management with the system. Four of these exceptions (blocks 4, 10, 14, and 19) are generated by the control devices presented in this chapter. As this diagram shows, these are essential to the effective functioning of an operational forecasting system.

Familiarity with operation of the forecasting system in Figure 14–3 will assist you in understanding the relationships of the many forecasting principles presented throughout this book. Also, understanding the system will prepare you for your study of the remaining six chapters. These chapters extend many of the principles presented in Chapters 1 to 14. Chapters 17, 18, and 20, however, relate most directly to the design of forecasting systems as depicted here.

FIGURE 14–3
Operation of a Simple Forecasting System

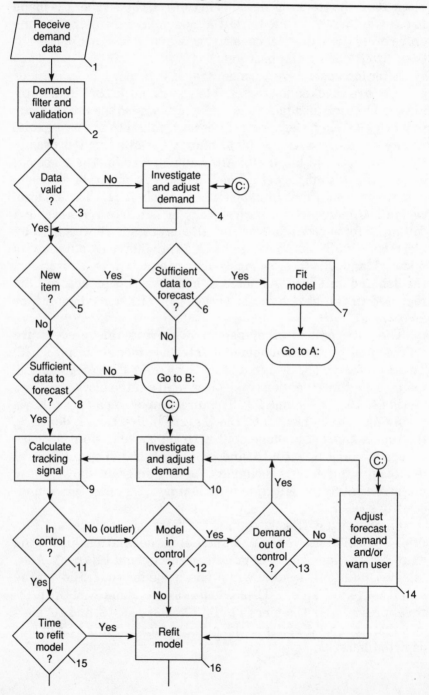

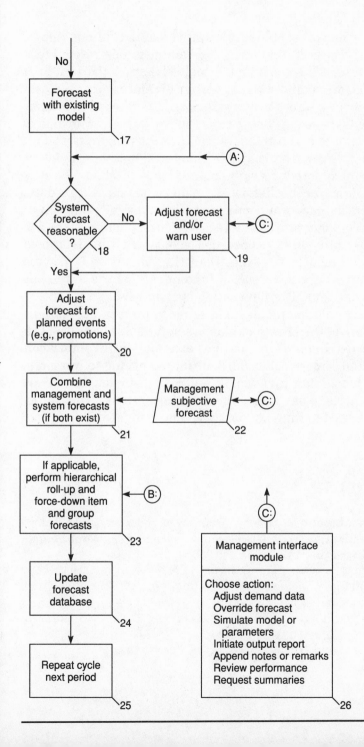

SUMMARY

This chapter has presented important research findings related to the effectiveness of time series forecasting in operational forecasting systems. This research has yielded many important principles of good forecasting systems. Many new and exciting research studies regarding forecasting systems and methods have taken place in the last decade. These research thrusts will continue as more attention is given to operational forecasting systems.

The second major topic of this chapter is methods of detecting out-of-control forecasts using manual and automated system controls. As is shown, outlier detection and adjustment procedures are an essential part of a good forecasting system. While large, one-time errors can decrease forecast accuracy and system performance, we are equally concerned about bias, that is, consistent over- or under-forecasting. Detecting bias is so important because it is usually the result of fundamental shifts in the pattern of the demand. The forecasting system needs to be able to detect these fundamental shifts in order to provide accurate information. Also, the effects of bias are significant because of its cumulative detrimental impact. For example, in inventory control, over- and understock conditions may continue to worsen as a result of bias. High investment and low customer service are too costly a price to pay for poor forecasting systems. The control devices presented in this chapter are essential for achieving a good forecasting system.

REFERENCES

1. S. Makridakis and M. Hibon, "Accuracy of Forecasting: An Empirical Investigation (With Discussion)," *Journal of the Royal Statistical Society* A, no. 142 (1979, Part 2), pp. 97–145.
2. S. Makridakis et al., "The Accuracy of Major Extrapolation (Time Series) Methods," *Journal of Forecasting* 1, no. 2 (1982), pp. 111–53.
3. Ibid.
4. Bernard Smith, *Focus Forecasting—Computer Techniques for Inventory Control* (Boston: CBI Publishing, 1984).
5. Makridakis and Hibon, "Accuracy of Forecasting."

6. Ibid.
7. R. G. Brown, *Smoothing, Forecasting and Prediction* (Englewood Cliffs, N. J.: Prentice-Hall, 1963).
8. R. G. Brown, *Advanced Service Parts Inventory Control,* 2nd ed. (Thetford Center, Vt.: Materials Management Systems, 1982).
9. Ibid.
10. D. W. Trigg, "Monitoring a Forecasting System," *Operational Research Quarterly* 15, 1964, pp. 271–74.
11. E. S. Gardner, "CUSUM versus Smoothed-Error Forecast Monitoring Schemes: Some Simulation Comparisons," *Journal of the Operational Research Society* 36, 1985, and "Automatic Monitoring of Forecast Errors," *Journal of Forecasting* 2, no. 1 (1983), pp. 1–22.
12. R. G. Brown, "Detection of Turning Points in a Time Series," *Decision Sciences* 2, 1971, pp. 383–403.
13. P. J. Harrison and O. L. Davies, "The Use of Cumulative Sum (CUSUM) Techniques for the Control of Routine Forecasts of Product Demand," *Operations Research* 12, 1963, pp. 325–33.

FORECASTING SYSTEM DESIGN AND APPLICATION

Part 5 discusses the design of good forecasting systems. All of the topics of these chapters are suitable for readers whether they are managers or analysts.

Chapter 15 continues the discussion of Chapters 2 through 6 by expanding on the topics of what and where to forecast. Specific internal sources and needs for demand data are discussed for several types of businesses. The transaction systems that provide internal data are discussed as sources of demand data. These transaction systems include order processing, accounting, work order, and material-requisitioning systems.

Chapter 16 discusses customer service and inventory as they relate to forecasting systems. As we show, customer service has many dimensions. Several popular measures of customer service

---

are defined in the chapter. The second half of the chapter illustrates the statistical inventory control methods that are so important in achieving customer service goals. The integration of forecasting and inventory management is an important and common application in a wide variety of organizations. The last section of this chapter discusses inventory management of low-demand items.

Chapter 17 integrates the principles and concepts of the previous 16 chapters and refines the six modules of forecasting systems. In addition, this chapter includes an important forecasting system evaluation and selection checklist. This evaluation instrument provides a useful method of deciding which capabilities your forecasting system should have. Using this checklist will help you define the best system for your application. Also, it will help you rank competing systems in a forecasting system procurement process.

CHAPTER 15

WHAT AND WHERE
TO FORECAST

What is laid down, ordered, factual is never enough to em-
brace the whole truth; life always spills over the rim of every cup.

               Boris Pasternak, 1890–1960

The questions of what to forecast and where to forecast are very
basic; however, many firms have not adequately answered these
two questions. Proper plans cannot be made unless appropriate
demand data is available to support these plans. At times, we have

seen top managers view item-level forecasting as an operational issue with little strategic impact on the firm's profitability, survival, or success. Nothing could be further from the truth.

This chapter extends the discussions of Chapters 3, 4, 5, and 6 by discussing what demand forecasts should be made, and, in greater detail, where these forecasts should be made.

When comparing or contrasting industry forecasting needs, there are more similarities than differences. Also, there are similarities in the application of forecasting systems in both businesses and government agencies where much can be gained in terms of better resource planning and allocation. For example, the U.S. Postal Service has a distribution system that anticipates its needs for equipment and service parts across the country. This distribution system saves money, labor, freight, and so on, by having the correct material in distribution centers, thus achieving higher customer service at lower costs. This program began with a new system for forecasting demands by item and distribution center. Each distribution center is responsible for specific maintenance and repair service for which they must have the related service parts, personnel, and facilities to perform the operations.

BUSINESS DIFFERENCES AND SIMILARITIES

Different management objectives in demand forecasting result in several different types of users of forecasts. Users may come from sales, marketing, operations, finance, distribution, purchasing, or other departments. While we would hope that the business plans that are developed and carried out by each department are based on consistent companywide forecasts, such is often not the case. More often, the different departmental users will suggest that the appropriate forecasts should be their own, regardless of the implications for the rest of the firm. This creates a situation where each department applies their own forecast, and, therefore, there are inconsistencies in plans between departments. For example, if the finance department is projecting cash flow based on some historical mix of product volumes and contribution margin, then a problem arises if marketing plans on changing that product mix. These aspects of change may not be reflected in the projected margins unless the system provides for this level of coordination and integration.

For marketing purposes, forecasts may not need to be by product but perhaps only by product line. For instance, if new products are introduced, some initial estimates may be needed for planning purposes, and as products are discontinued, the product mix may change. Forecasts by major account or by industry group are often needed to assess the planned market share inherent in the forecasts. Thus, we see the following principle:

Many marketing purposes may require only product-line forecasts.

Sales plans are usually broken down by sales regions or territories and compared to marketing estimates. Some reconciliation will be made at least for fiscal planning purposes between marketing and sales (sales usually estimating demand from the bottom up and marketing using top-down forecasts). Quite often, sales estimates are built up from major-account estimates prepared by each sales representative. The feasibility of this approach needs to be decided by each company's situation. Some of the key questions are:

How many major customer accounts need to be analyzed to cover most of the sales volume?

How many products represent most of the sales volume to the major customer accounts?

Does the demand history of these major products and customer accounts lend itself to a routine process of forecasting?

In major-appliance, capital equipment, computers, industrial chemicals, and other industries, the number of products is usually small enough to forecast item demands by each customer account. However, when some customer accounts are not worth itemizing, these can be grouped and treated as one large account.

Forecasting demand by major accounts may be effective.

The process of bottom-up forecasting should be designed to facilitate routine updating. The data system must support the process so that the forecasts are current and reflect the latest situations known to the sales representative. Only then can we expect these bottom-up forecasts to be widely accepted as a basis for operational decisions.

Sales planning forecasts should reinforce accountability by sales region and territories.

Operations management, on the other hand, is interested in plant loads, engineering work, unusual technology or materials, and longer-range needs for plant and equipment. Forecasts for new products again take on a great significance. Forecasts of shipments to customers by product and producing plant are necessary unless distribution centers buffer the plants from all customer requirements. Even with distribution centers, most plants have some customer-direct shipping responsibilities, for example, to ship full truckloads of customer orders.

Operations require forecasts by product and plant or distribution center.

Finance departments need demand forecasts in dollars so that revenue and contribution margin projections can be provided by accounting period. While it may seem to be a very high expectation, much can be done to build financial projections upon product demand forecasts by locations. For example, the product forecasts in units can be multiplied by the average selling price of each product to obtain the revenue forecast. If discounts and allowances vary greatly from time to time, it may be worthwhile to track the historical average selling price. Since the forecasted contribution margin requires that we have a projected cost that can be subtracted from the revenue, we may need to adjust any standard cost for each product by cost variances. In many cases, however, the use of standard costs will be acceptable as a basis for the calculation of contribution margins by product. Once these revenues and contribution margins are calculated by product, they can be summed to their appropriate product-line totals.

Finance may require forecasts by product line in dollars.

Distribution planning and execution responsibilities can be carried out best by starting with forecasts by item and shipping location. These forecasts will result in greater accuracy in the development of stock plans, service-level plans, replenishment plans, transportation plans, warehouse sizing, and other distribution plans.

Distribution requires forecasts by item and location.

The coordination and updating of the several different forecasts must be provided routinely by the system in order for the business to be most profitable. In addition, the forecasting procedure should accommodate subjective managerial modifications to these integrated forecasts. Several different types of businesses are described below to illustrate these points.

*Coordination of the different departmental
forecasts is necessary for profitability.*

TYPES OF BUSINESSES

Figure 15-1 presents a simplified view of the relationships between several types of firms in a supply chain. We use the company classifications of this figure to discuss the forecasting needs of these firms.

Manufacturers of Capital Goods

Manufacturers of capital goods make trucks, construction equipment, stamping and printing machines, tools and dies, textile and apparel plant machinery, robotics, computers, and so on. By definition, these goods have long useful lives so that they are capitalized (i.e., depreciated over time), rather than charged as current expenses at the time of acquisition. Also, the typically larger unit costs of these goods may mean that fewer units of any one product are made and sold. In most instances, these capital goods are assembled to customer order.

In this industry, a forecast is made by operations management to provide enough capacity for a diverse mix of products that might be purchased by customers. Large variations in customer order

FIGURE 15–1
Manufacturer-Distributor Material Flow Network

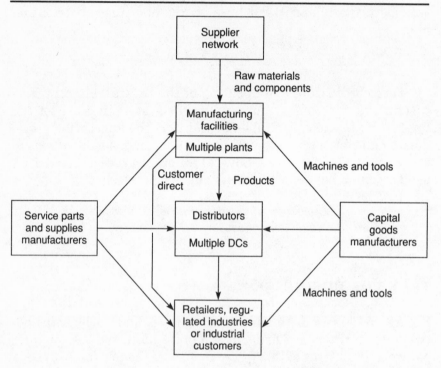

size, mix, and value are not uncommon; thus, specific product mixes may be unforecastable. Many larger firms are seeing this especially in their overseas markets. While most capital goods are ordered and then manufactured (i.e., made to order), there must be enough planning to purchase materials and achieve a reasonable customer order leadtime. Thus, purchasing management requires material volume estimates for the purpose of negotiating contracts for various types of components.

The required operational forecasts that may suffice are by product line and plant. Distribution of finished goods is not a concern in this make-to-order situation. Purchasing estimates of major component volumes (such as engines or computer chips) can be derived from planning bills of materials for the typical mix of products sold in each product line. Marketing and sales must partici-

---

**Electronic Data Interchange (EDI) Yields Improved
Forecasting and Paperless Inventory Cycle**

EDI is a computer-application to computer-application exchange of
information used to move organizations to paperless inventory cycles. The process does not use paper for reordering, shipping, and
receiving merchandise, but instead processes everything electronically. As an example, an apparel manufacturer/retailer already has
an EDI system coded with the universal product code bar codes.
Several things happen when the cashier scans the label on a
garment:

1. The customer gets a receipt with item name, description, regular price, and sale price.
2. The system records the product's size, color, and SKU number.
3. In real time, the product's inventory level at the store is
   decreased (or increased for returns), and, if the item on-hand
   level drops below the reorder point, it is reordered from the
   distribution center.
4. Because of the short leadtimes in reordering, the merchandise
   is restocked quickly. (As a result of bar coding and EDI, the
   leadtimes from distribution centers to stores have been
   decreased, for example, from 30 days to 10 days.)
5. Customer service increases as measured by percent fill and
   checkout times.
6. Average inventory levels decline.
7. Demands are captured in real time, enabling patterns and shifts
   in demand to be analyzed quickly, with resulting improvements
   in forecast accuracy and percent fill customer service.

---

pate in the forecasting process in order to communicate any
expected or planned changes in the product mix. These changes
may affect both the typical mix expressed in the planning bills
as well as the product-line volumes. (See Table 15–1 for an example of a planning bill.) Also, production capacity requirements
can be estimated from the product-line forecasts by using a generic
capacity bill, which identifies the major work centers and the load
produced by the average mix on those centers. The generic data

TABLE 15–1
Example of a Planning Bill of Materials

	Product Line: Large Dump Trucks	
Engines:	Size A	0.20
	Size B	0.45
	Size C	0.35
Chassis:	Size A	0.30
	Size B	0.20
	Size C	0.50
Suspension:	50 tons	0.40
	80 tons	0.35
	100 tons	0.25

accomplishes essentially the same results that Joseph Orlicky first described through the use of load profiles.[1] Table 15–2 illustrates a generic capacity bill for an "average truck."

> *In make-to-order operations, forecasts by product lines may provide sufficient detail for planning.*

Manufacturers of Service Parts

Manufacturers of service parts often sell simultaneously to the original equipment manufacturers (OEMs) and the replacement markets. In the replacement markets, those who buy the original equipment will look to the manufacturer to provide particularly unique service parts, especially where the frequency of the part's failure is low and the alternate channels of distribution have not found it economical to handle the part.

When the replacement market is large, as with automotive service parts, the competition for sales will require that the larger-volume parts be available quickly to the next echelon in the distribution (or supply) chain. Automotive parts may be stocked by national parts houses, franchised repair shops, major independent shops, automobile service stations, and so on.

As the service part manufacturers plan for this business volume, they must be clear as to the plans for stock availability. Will

TABLE 15–2
Example of a Generic Capacity Bill and Routing

Product Line: Large Dump Trucks	
Hours per Truck	
Bed forming	3
Bed welding	20
Chassis assembly	30
Engine installation	14
Stationary testing	2
Field testing	1

the OEM orders be filled on a make-to-order basis? Will there be any channel to the replacement market that requires them to stock parts? Will those stocks be at locations other than their own plants? If the answers to these questions are all yes, then the manufacturer should be using a replacement-market demand forecast by part number at each of the stocking locations and at each plant that ships direct to the replacement market. In addition, the manufacturer will require OEM market forecasts for capacity and materials planning purposes.

Service parts manufacturers require separate
forecasts of OEM and replacement market demands.

The replacement market forecasts are then used to prepare stock plans and related business plans by distribution center and by plant. Note that the OEM demand forecasts are separate from the replacement market forecasts even though some relationship between these two forecasts may exist over time. Thus, each type of demand should be properly included in plans for materials, capacity, and finished goods.

Distribution has come to play a large role in this type of business. This makes the business more complex and detailed in terms of forecasting as compared to the manufacturer of capital goods. Purchasing decisions of the service parts manufacturer, however, may be based on the forecasts by part number and may not require maintenance of planning bills. Thus, in contrast to the capital goods manufacturer, planning bill estimates of component volumes are not required for service parts that have separate demand forecasts.

*Service parts that compete for market share should
be forecasted by part number and distribution center.*

Because many service parts demands (perhaps the great majority) are very low in volume, this makes forecasting very difficult. This is one of the distinguishing marks of the service parts business that was discussed in Chapter 6. Furthermore, when demand is very low for a distributor, consumer, or manufacturer — for anyone in the supply chain — forecasting is often relatively inaccurate. Nevertheless, we cannot avoid the tasks of planning appropriate stocks for even the low-volume parts. In Chapter 16, we discuss specific methods of managing these low-volume parts.

*Service parts and other low-volume
demands are very difficult to forecast.*

Manufacturers of Consumer Goods

Manufacturers of consumer goods must provide distribution channels that are responsive to the expectations of their markets. Most often we think of a consumer product as a good or service that is provided through retailers to the public. However, direct marketing via catalog sales and television sales has been increasing. Direct marketing of consumer goods will grow more rapidly as home communication centers make it easier to place orders. Today, and even more so in the future, manufacturers' and retailers' roles are merging.

For the moment, we will assume that the manufacturer's customers are wholesalers, distributors, and large chain retailers. Shipments direct from the manufacturer's plants to major customers are frequently made in truckloads of single or mixed products. The economics of mixing products made in two different plants onto one truck may suggest that some plant warehouses act as "full-service" warehouses by stocking products transferred from other plants, as illustrated in Figure 15–2. Shipments to regional distribution centers are also used to position the finished goods nearer to the distributors or smaller regional chain retailers.

FIGURE 15–2
Consumer-Goods Manufacturer

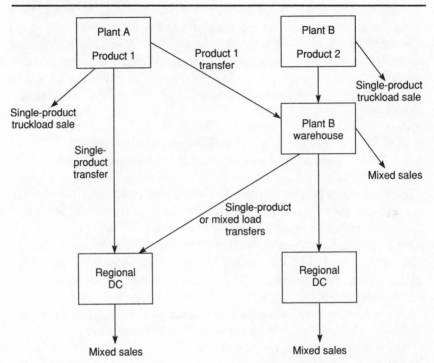

As with the service parts manufacturer who distributes products, the need for demand forecasts should be evident at each distribution center (DC), warehouse, or plant that sells or ships. If we have sales forecasts for each location and product, then the stocking plans and the timing of transfers from sources can be calculated. In turn, the production requirements can be fed to a production plan or master schedule.

The accuracy of consumer-goods forecasts is usually higher than service parts forecasts simply because of their larger volumes. But the difficulty of forecasting the demand for consumer goods centers on two related factors: (1) the effects of promotions or deals on the volumes, and (2) the choice or assignment of shipping location (plant, warehouse, or DC) to any given type of order for any particular product and for a particular customer. We discussed some of these issues in greater detail in Chapter 5.

As noted in Figure 15–2, the shipping location depends in part on the size of the customer order, which in many instances will be affected by the promotions offered on the item. One solution is to provide forecasts by product, location, and order size (e.g., less than truck load versus truck load). This also makes it easier to assign promoted product forecasts to the preferred economic shipping location for each order size, because they are likely to include a greater percentage of truckload orders for the promoted product.

Shipping-point forecasts for consumer goods
may depend on order size and promotions.

As business plans change, we expect the arrangements of DCs, warehouses, and plants to change as well. Demand forecasts in these changing circumstances should be quickly adaptable to the new structure of the distribution network. If the demand history has been retained in a useful form at a great enough level of detail, it is possible to recast the history to match the new structure of the distribution network with appropriate customer-product-order–size assignments to the shipping locations. By using this revised historical demand, more-accurate forecasts of the future demand can be made.

Revising the database by reassigning customers when modifying
the distribution network provides more-accurate forecasts.

Distributors

Distributors act as resellers in the supply chain, typically purchasing stock, which they hold in several DCs, for shipment to customers in various geographic areas. Demand forecasts by product and DC are needed to plan the stock and service levels at each DC.

Distributors do not operate manufacturing facilities as such, but, in some cases, perform packaging operations to label goods for private-label customers, or to combine items into kits for resale. These packaging operations do not necessarily require forecasts for each private label or kit, especially if those operations can be performed quickly in response to customer orders. Instead, the base items may be forecasted for their total demand. However, enough packaging capacity must be available to respond quickly, which suggests that these packaging operations may have to be performed by contractors to assure quick response.

Figure 15–3 shows the relationship of the packaging operations when some packaging is done for stock and when other packaging is done in response to customer orders. If the packaging for stock is done for all of an item's demand in *only one package*

FIGURE 15–3
Distributor with Packaging Operations

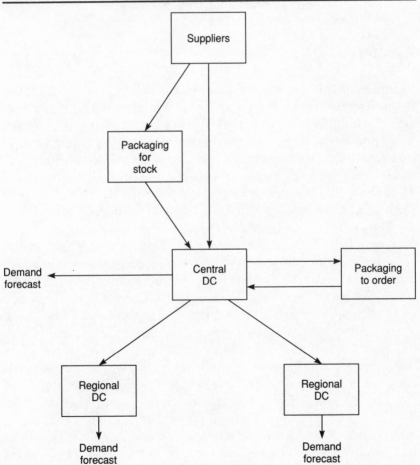

type, this causes no additional complexity in terms of forecasts. However, if packaging is done in order to *stock several versions* (labels, box types, and so on), then the forecasting system should assist with the decision to package specific quantities of the item by package type.

Distributors may be similar to a manufacturer of either consumer goods or service parts in terms of the forecasting tasks. The demand types and volumes will be quite similar because customers don't usually concern themselves with the distributor's source of products (be it a vendor to the distributor rather than a manufacturing plant owned by the distributor).

*Distributors who package products have
forecasting tasks similar to those of manufacturers.*

Retailers

Retailers of the size of a national chain will typically distribute to their stores from regional DCs that are supplied by many vendors. One distinguishing mark of retail forecasting is the very large number of items and stockkeeping units that must be forecast routinely. A general merchandise store may have 50,000 or more items, and the number of stores may be 2,000 or more. If all of these SKUs must be forecasted periodically, the number of records will require significant computer resources.

Forecasts can be provided through regional data centers, or even on a local computer at each store, thus avoiding the burden on a central host computer. Whether all forecasts must be available on one computer is an important management and user decision, but we still have the familiar task of using forecasts of store sales volumes to plan the stock quantities by item and store. Those stocking decisions may be made by the store management who has need for only that store's forecasts. Alternatively, the stocking decisions may be made by regional management who controls the inventory for many stores. There is a trade-off between these two approaches: Local store management should have a better feel for that particular store's market, but a regional manager may be better trained to interpret trends and make regional allocation decisions. The regional manager will need the support of a good data processing system to discern local trends and individual store differences. Unless a store's unique demand patterns are identified and used to make stocking decisions, that store's performance will be inferior in terms of stock availability and/or profitability.

Even in the same store chain and market (e.g., city) retail demand patterns are different, hence the need for store-specific forecasts.

Subjective managerial forecast modifications made by store management should be accommodated in most retail forecasting systems.

Retail sales forecasting is a good candidate for regionally distributed data processing support.

Regional or centralized allocation of inventory should not preclude store management input and modifications of forecasts.

Regulated Industries

Regulated industries deliver services and commodities to some confined groups of customers. These industries include water suppliers, gas and electric utilities, and telecommunications companies and could easily be interpreted to include city, state, and municipal governments (or government agencies) that have similar operating environments.

The demand forecasting tasks for these industries fall into three classes: (1) load forecasting based on changing demographics (which is beyond the scope of this book), (2) materials-related demand forecasts for purposes of providing maintenance, repair, and operating supplies (MRO), and (3) forecasting for purposes of purchasing and staging construction materials. Construction materials for particular projects (e.g., a new housing subdivision feeder line) will usually include many of the same items that are required for the ongoing maintenance of the existing operations.

MRO items are needed to support the unscheduled repairs that occur without warning. Demand forecasts are needed for pinpointing the inventory needs at a location (often called a *storeroom*) so that repair crews can quickly get what they need in their service territory. A few to several dozen geographic storerooms are used, depending on the size of the company.

Linking Electronic Stores Electronically

The Tandy Corporation sells electronics through approximately 6,000 retail stores and 3,000 dealer franchise outlets. To manage inventory better, Tandy developed a new inventory-management system in the early 1980s. The new system uses a microcomputer at each retail counter. The system provides management with the basic inventory information of what, how many, and when to place an order for an item. This assists in maintaining good inventory levels. When an order is necessary, the store transmits the order directly to the corporate data center. In the late 1980s, the system processed 50 million lines and 500,000 shipments each year. On a typical day, for example, a Fort Worth warehouse distributes 800 shipments that require 120,000 line-items to be taken from stock and shipped in 6,000 cartons to stores around the country.

Construction projects often have some repetitive characteristics and, thus, some similar material requirements. For example, two miles of gas feeder line will require approximately twice the materials of a similar one-mile project; yet engineering differences may exist for terrain features, bridges, tunnels, and so on. Construction-project materials estimates can be itemized from engineered bills of materials, and the construction schedules should disclose the timing of those material requirements. It would seem then that forecasting of construction material requirements is inappropriate. However, in the world of changing plans, the construction projects are juggled in response to funding and general building activity levels. As a result, the procurement department is often called on to be prepared for uncertain construction schedules. If this is the case, having historical construction material usage data organized in a way that (1) identifies frequently used materials and (2) identifies trends and material changes of the recent past is a definite advantage. This kind of data can help the procurement department enter into contracts for longer-leadtime, frequently used items, thus gaining advantages in terms of price and delivery leadtime.

INTERNAL DATA SOURCES–TRANSACTION SYSTEMS

To make various kinds of forecasts possible, the user must look first to the existing data systems for input of historical demands. The most frequently used sources of detailed historical data are the transaction systems of departments that need forecasts. These transaction systems include order, accounting, work order, and material-requisitioning systems. Typically, they are under direct control of the appropriate departments, so some important questions about the availability, quality, and completeness of the data should be answered first. Subsequently, if these data sources are deficient, some changes in the transaction systems may be made to improve the data.

Transaction systems are known by various names in different industries, even though their function is essentially the same. An *order processing system,* for example, will often be called a *customer order processing system* by a manufacturer or a *dealer order system* by a distributor. A customer order processing system (1) handles the requests for goods (a demand), (2) records the agreed conditions of the purchase, (3) tracks the status and changes to the order, (4) records picking and shipping activity, (5) triggers invoicing, and (6) provides historical data for sales analysis purposes. These same functions in retailing operations may be handled by the point-of-sale system.

Understanding that company-specific titles may vary, we can list the most frequently used transaction systems that are sources of historical data for forecasting:

Order Processing (of demand)
   Customer order processing
   Point of sale
   Dealer order processing
Accounting
   Inventory accounting
   Stock status
   Invoicing or billing
Work order system
   Production order
   Manufacturing order

Shop order
Job order
Material Requisitioning
  Issue ticket
  Move order
  Transfer order

Let us comment on the usefulness of these system in terms of data availability and quality. We will be concerned with the integrity, timing, accuracy, and units of measure of the data.

Order Processing Systems

Customer Order Processing Systems

Order processing systems have the distinct advantage in that they record recognized demand earlier than any other transaction system. In some companies, the order processing system captures tentative or unconfirmed orders and the demand for products that are not available but were requested for immediate delivery.

*The ability to capture demand whether fulfilled or not is
an important attribute for a good order processing system.*

However, most order processing systems do not provide these capabilities. The typical system provides data for the products or services that are scheduled for delivery only. However, they do not (1) capture actual demand when out of stock, including discussions of feasibility of delivery, (2) capture the requested delivery date, which may or may not be different from the actual delivery date, and (3) record substitutions of products if a stockout was discovered. In these instances, the typical order processing system will not capture accurate historical demand.

With order processing systems based on interaction with real-time inventory status systems, stock availability and delivery scheduling can be examined and resolved in a short time as part of the *order entry* process. The customer and order entry person may agree on the order, with any modifications that were required.

It is important that the recorded order shows the originally requested product and date, as well as the agreed-upon product and date. If both kinds of data are available, the demand data can be provided to the forecasting system for the *requested* products and for the *requested* dates to avoid the distortions caused by any unavailability of products. This provides a much better history of demand.

Thus, the precision of demand data from order entry is important in terms of the products and scheduled delivery dates. For accepting orders for future delivery, the *timing* of this *demand data* is also much better than that of *shipments data*, because this order entry data is available earlier than shipments data (sometimes as much as several weeks). By having the demand data earlier, the forecasting system can respond to new levels of demand sooner than if shipments data were used for forecasting.

If alternate units of measure are needed for the demand in the forecasting system, for example, dollars, cases, and pallets, the order processing system will usually have access to standard reference data about each product during the course of entering the order. Unit-of-measure conversions and summary data can be provided routinely to the forecasting system through use of the reference data.

It is difficult to imagine a situation in which the order processing system would not be *the* preferred source of demand data in an operation that uses order processing. The essential condition is that all recognized demand is processed and recorded, that no shipment or inventory usage is permitted without an appropriate order, and that the accuracy of products and quantities is assured during the order entry process.

The order processing system is the best source of demand data.

Some types of operations, however, do not use order processing systems. Table 15–3 organizes the data sources most often used in several forecast situations, including several that do not use order processing systems.

Point-of-Sale Systems
Point-of-sale (POS) systems for retailers are now commonplace, usually using bar coding with countertop or hand-held laser scanners. These systems offer great potential to the retailer not only for accounting and stock-replenishment purposes, but also for better responsiveness from their suppliers.

TABLE 15–3
Systems that Can Provide Historical Demand

Type of Business	Purpose of Forecasting	Possible Historical Demand Data Sources
Manufacturer	Finished goods planning at distribution centers or master scheduling	Customer order processing Invoicing Inventory accounting
Manufacturer	Maintenance, repair, and operating supplies planning	Material requisitioning Inventory accounting
Distributor	Stock planning and replenishment	Customer order processing Invoicing Inventory accounting
Retailer	Stock replenishment	Point of sale Purchasing
Public utility	Maintenance material replenishment	Material requisitioning Work orders Inventory accounting
Public utility	Construction-project–materials contracting	Project bills of materials Material requisitioning Work orders
Public schools	Food-service–materials procurement	School enrollments Food service sales Menus and recipes
Airline or cruise line	On-board food and beverage planning	Passenger reservations Passenger boardings Catering sales and transfers Menus and recipes
Banking or insurance	Form and supplies replenishment	Material requisitioning Purchasing

The potential of quick-response relationships between a customer (a retailer in this case) and suppliers (distributors or manufacturers of consumer goods) is being acted on by 70 percent or more of the major consumer-goods manufacturers in the United States. They are beginning to take advantage of the POS demand data to revise production, purchasing, and delivery plans for those major customers who are sharing the data with them.

UPC Bar Code Means Better Forecasting, Inventory Control, and Customer Service

The machine-readable patterns of alternating parallel bars and spaces that represent numbers and letters have revolutionized the collection of data for operations. UPC have been used in the grocery industry since they were pioneered there in the early 1970s. However, there are several industries that have been very slow in integrating this technology into their operations, even though companies in other industries could not compete without them. One retailer, the Toys "R" Us chain, is considered an industry leader in using bar coding and other technology to enhance operations. Some say that much of its rapid growth would not have been possible without point-of-sale scanning and computer cash registers. These registers let each Toys "R" Us store know what inventory is at the end of each day, thus allowing them to know sooner what merchandise the customer wants. Prior to bar coding systems, some customers would abandon full shopping carts in frustration while waiting in line and many would never come back again. Tests have shown that the checkout time is 30 percent faster with scanning than with the old manual cash registers. With bar coding, price checks are seldom needed, fewer and lower-skill checkers are needed, and customers get products they desire in less time. These advantages of improved forecasting and inventory control result from more timely and complete capture of POS information.

In turn, the retailers can get deliveries of replenishment inventories with dependably shorter leadtimes. The quick-response capabilities are achieved by the use of more-timely demand data and by revisions in the methods used to schedule and produce the best mix of products. In turn, manufacturers can expect a better evaluation of trends from their suppliers who also have access to the same POS data.

Accounting Systems

Inventory Accounting or Stock Status Systems
A transaction-based *inventory accounting* system will respond to and provide for all inventory receipts, transfers, adjustments, usage, and shipments. In more-comprehensive systems, the scope

of inventories for a manufacturer may include new materials, work in process, supply items, spare parts, and finished goods in one integrated system. A *stock status* system, however, is usually limited to finished goods and perhaps the work-in-process inventories.

When these accounting systems are the source of demand data, care is needed in the selection or specification of the types of transactions that will be recognized as demand for forecasting purposes. A comprehensive accounting system will provide precise transaction choices for each accounting purpose. Transfers of stock, for example, can and should be separated from shipments to customers. Likewise, the usage of materials for internal purposes (such as testing or samples) should not be included in the historical data that is to be used to forecast customer demand.

Carefully choose any accounting transactions
that will be used to provide demand history.

Both the order processing and inventory accounting systems should validate the items and locations associated with each transaction. Also, since these are usually real-time systems, the timing of data is good for forecasting purposes. Quantities may or may not be accurately recorded at the time of the transactions, but contemporary design and easy-to-use screens with color coding make it possible to achieve high levels of data accuracy.

With regard to the timing of demand data, accounting systems can provide shipments and returns data, but these are essentially historical and may occur several days or weeks after the customer order has been received. Returned quantities are usually netted from new demand so as to provide net demand for the period being entered into the forecasting system. This is usually precise enough except when quality problems or technological changes cause customer dissatisfaction with the product. In those instances, the forecast will need to be reevaluated by management.

An accounting system may be the only organized machine-readable source of demand data in some situations, especially noncommercial situations where no customer order is used.

Accounting system data may be the best source of demand
data in organizations where customer orders are not used.

Invoicing or Billing Systems

The preparation of an invoice for a shipment may occur in chronological order at the time of shipment or very soon after. But these data usually lag the other possible sources. There are, however, two reasons for using invoicing data.

The first reason is convenience or expediency when the inventory accounting or order processing procedures are slow or poorly automated. In this case, the invoicing system could have been given more attention in its automation to achieve better cash flow, a view we would expect if the MIS director reported to a financial department head.

The second reason has to do with the kind of data that may be needed for the forecasting system. Suppose that the stock status system can provide data for quantities shipped by item and location but has no dollar value data available. If the need arises for the forecasting system to project data in dollar values, the invoicing system may be the preferred source. This is especially true if the user desires information in terms of average net price per unit.

Work Order Systems

This kind of system by itself is primarily a source of demand data for labor, but is not as good a source for materials demand data. For example, work orders in a public utility for repair of home water service leaks could be used to capture the demand for repair crews. But the work order won't show whether a new fitting or meter was used. The work order must be coupled with the material-issue and return transactions to determine the materials used (see the section on material requisitioning, which follows).

Work orders then are a source of demand for emergency labor, which must be forecasted for purposes of planning the number of emergency crews and related support equipment—trucks, tools, and so on. However, the scheduled maintenance activities should not be confused with emergency labor because scheduled maintenance is normally planned without a forecast. Forecasting can benefit management of labor crews by recording trends and seasonal effects, thus providing better information for the hiring, training, and budgeting of service work.

Material-Requisitioning Systems for MRO Supplies

A material-requisitioning system is useful for getting demand data associated with the internal consumption of materials. The repair of production equipment or the scheduled and preventive maintenance activities will typically generate material-issue transactions that should be tied to the work orders that authorize labor and material expenditures (with some materials of high value being more carefully controlled). However, some issued quantities may be too high and others too low. There have been situations where crew supervisors held small inventories of critical parts because there had been a shortage in the recent past. They simply kept a leftover part or requisitioned more than needed at some earlier time. Behavior of this sort causes the demand to be more erratic over time and distorts its timing.

Crew supervisors also have been known to requisition the maximum required number of any one part with the intention of returning those unused to the store room after the repair work has been completed. Whether they are returned at all, and in a timely manner, depends on the discipline and training of those responsible. A good material-usage audit for the completed job is one way to reinforce good training.

These comments should make us aware that procedures and discipline may not be as good as necessary. We want to assure that the data are as accurate as can be afforded. How much is the increased accuracy worth? The answer lies in the reduced cost of the inventory of MRO items. If a forecast of a critical item's demand is in error by 30 percent and the error could be reduced to 20 percent by eliminating distortion from poor procedures and lack of discipline, then the safety stock should be reduced by a proportional amount. This can amount to a significant saving in terms of inventory carrying costs.

Disciplined requisitioning and return procedures of MROs are important for accurate demand data in repair operations.

Similar comments can be made about a customer order processing system and the discipline required to achieve complete and accurate data entry. But because customers act as an "external data source," firms are likely to have customer order data that are more accurate than material-requisitioning data. With an internal procedure, there may be less interest and control. Fundamentally, someone must see the value to the company and take responsibility for good procedures and discipline.

Move orders or transfer orders in a requisitioning system are usually not a good source of demand data for forecasting purposes. Since our intent is to estimate the demand at the point of use or consumption, a transfer of goods to another stocking location is not representative of the timing or the rate of consumption at the receiving location. It is far more precise to use the transactions associated with the date of issue to a repair job or to a construction project.

On the other hand, transfer orders may be the only data available for some materials issued to major projects for which there are no subsequent detailed accounting transactions. The materials are perhaps expensed at the end of the project in total or when they were issued to the project.

SUMMARY

Demand forecasts are needed for operational purposes in many different kinds of businesses. These forecasts are needed for several reasons: capacity planning, materials contracting, sales planning, replenishment planning, financial planning, and master scheduling, to name some of the most important.

These different purposes will be served by providing forecasts in varying degrees of detail and aggregation. By bringing several purposes and several related groups of users of those forecasts together, the firm may take advantage of the coordination of demand forecasts and better joint planning. Since forecasts are fundamental to planning in all departments, better forecast coordination is a key to success.

Historical demand to support these forecasting tasks is usually obtained from an order processing system or a related billing or inventory status system. While each of these systems is less than perfect as a source of complete demand data, the order processing system is the best source of demand in most applications. Less often, a material-requisitioning system or a work order system may be the best or only source of certain kinds of historical demand data.

REFERENCE

1. Joseph Orlicky, *Material Requirements Planning* (New York: McGraw-Hill, 1975), p. 240.

CHAPTER 16

FORECASTING AND INVENTORY MANAGEMENT

A danger foreseen is half avoided.

Independent demand inventory systems consist of decision rules that are used to answer three questions: what to order, when to order, and how much to order. For each question, there are several possible replies, and there are therefore many possible inventory-management systems. But no matter how we answer the question of inventory management, the effectiveness of the resulting system is determined in large part by the forecasting system. Combining the forecasting system with inventory methods forms an inventory-replenishment system.

Forecasts drive inventory-management decisions.

In this chapter, we develop the relationships between inventory systems and forecasting by discussing effective uses of forecasts in a reorder-point inventory-management system that uses statistically determined safety stock. An understanding of this type of system prepares you to understand the use of forecasts in almost any inventory-management system. A type of inventory-management system using distribution requirements planning (DRP) was presented in Chapter 5. The statistical inventory control methods presented here are equally applicable to DRP. This chapter will illustrate the statement below.

Accurate forecasts can yield lower inventory investment, higher customer service, and lower costs.

Unfortunately, the opposite is also true: inaccurate forecasts can yield higher investment, lower customer service, and higher costs.

We have been surprised over the years at the misunderstandings of some managers about the use and importance of forecasts in inventory management. Some managers have only a vague idea of how to effectively manage forecasts and inventory. To help clarify the important relationships between forecasting and inventory management, this chapter discusses measures of customer service, inventory systems, and methods of achieving the goals of inventory management through proper determination of safety stocks.

INVENTORY MANAGEMENT–
CUSTOMER SERVICE MEASURES

EFFECTIVE INVENTORY MANAGEMENT

The following are goals of effective inventory-management systems:

Purchase, produce, and distribute products profitably.

Provide high levels of product availability to customers.

Minimize costs and inventory investment.

Minimize investment in plant and equipment.

Maximize return on investment.

All inventory-management goals are affected by the forecasting system.

Simultaneous achievement of these goals requires considerable attention to the design of the forecasting and inventory replenishment system.

Good inventory management requires several types of forecasts to be effective. Short-term, Type 1 forecasts are needed to estimate demand during leadtimes and receipts of orders. Longer-term, Type 2 forecasts are needed to prepare production, marketing, finance, and inventory plans. In this chapter, we focus on the use of Type 1 forecasts for inventory management; Chapters 2 through 6 have already discussed Type 1 and Type 2 forecasts for general applications.

Safety Stock

Inventory provides an important buffer function under conditions of uncertainty. Firms keep extra finished goods inventory because of uncertainties in product demands (e.g., because of forecast error). However, there is some confusion over the use of inventory to protect against uncertainty. Some people mistakenly believe that more inventory should be ordered when demand is more uncertain as measured by the standard deviation of forecast errors. However, it is safety stock that should be increased to protect against forecast errors, not order quantities.

When demand is uncertain, increase safety stock, not order quantities.

To better understand the use of safety stock, consider its use in a reorder-point system.

REORDER–POINT SYSTEM AND SAFETY STOCK

One of the oldest and most-popular inventory-management systems is the order-point system, sometimes called a *reorder-point system*. Figure 16–1 illustrates the operation of this simple system; shown there is the level of inventory over time including several important points. Product M345 is ordered in quantities (Q) of 500 each time an order is placed. This Q was determined using some economic consideration such as the economic order quantity (EOQ) or minimum production or purchase lot size. While we discuss the economic order quantity later, a comprehensive discussion of the economic order quantity is not important for our purposes. There are many fine references on this topic.[1]

Instead, the focus in this chapter is on deciding how much safety stock is necessary to preclude stockouts. In an order-point system, orders are placed whenever the current items on hand (OH) and on order (OO) are equal to or less than the order point (R).

FIGURE 16–1
Reorder-Point System for Product M345 When Safety Stock Is Zero

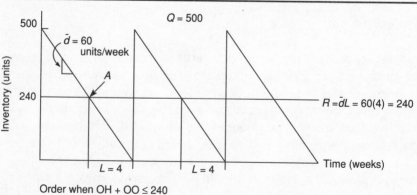

Place and order when OH plus OO is less than or equal to R.

The *order point* (R) is the quantity that equals the average demand or usage during leadtime. In this case, the leadtime for M345 is four weeks with a forecasted demand during leadtime of 60 units per week. As shown in Figure 16–1, inventory is depleted gradually from 500 units until the reorder point of 240 units is reached at Point A. At this time, an order is placed for an additional 500 units. The 240 units is calculated as follows.

$$R = L\overline{d} = 4*60 = 240 \qquad (16\text{--}1)$$

where

R = Order point (240 units) when safety stock is zero
L = Leadtime for an order (4 weeks)
$\overline{d}$ = Forecasted weekly usage during leadtime (60 units per week)

To preclude stockouts, an order is placed so that it will arrive exactly when inventories equal zero. Note the use and the importance of the forecast in determining the reorder point R. The point at which an order is placed depends on the forecast of demand during leadtime $(L\overline{d})$.

What and when to order is determined from forecasts of demand.

When Do Stockouts Occur?

As shown in Figure 16–1, if an item goes out of stock, it is during leadtime, that is, during the time between recognizing the need to place an order and the receipt of the order. Thus, by definition, a stockout occurs only during leadtime. In other words, when a firm runs out of stock, the out-of-stock condition triggers an order if one has not already been placed. To preclude a stockout, additional inventory called *safety stock* is added to the reorder point.

Stockouts occur during leadtime.

Safety Stock

The actual demand during leadtime is not known with certainty because the forecast is not perfect. If we place an order based on mean demand, then during 50 percent of the leadtimes there is insufficient stock, while during the other 50 percent there is too much stock. This is a characteristic of the mean. Because of the existence of forecast errors, the reorder point must include safety stock to avoid stockouts when the forecast is too low. The reorder point (R) is increased by the level of safety stock – in this case, 50 units.

$$R = L\bar{d} + \text{Safety stock} = 4*60 + 50 = 290 \qquad (16\text{–}2)$$

Therefore, when OH and OO get to 290 units, an order is placed for the order quantity. The additional 50 units protect (i.e., buffer) M345 from running out of stock when demand during lead-time exceeds 240 and is less than 291.

Safety stock is designed to preclude stockouts during leadtime.

In an order-point system, order earlier to preclude stockouts; don't increase the order quantity.

If the safety stock is large, the system will have fewer stock-outs, but this requires more investment in inventory.

Determining the optimal safety stock is a trade-off problem between customer service and inventory investment, a trade-off between marketing, finance, and operations.

As we will show, the objective of holding safety stock has to be established by management. After these objectives are defined, the best safety stock is calculated using the standard deviation of the forecast errors. Before illustrating the calculation of safety stock, it is important that the desired level of customer service be agreed upon by management. That is, it is important that the firm has clearly expressed customer service objectives before calculating safety stock. The next section defines several important measures of customer service.

Safety-stock objectives are defined by management; resulting safety-stock calculations are driven by the forecast error.

CUSTOMER SERVICE MEASURES

There are several measures of customer service, including those that measure in-stock, out-of-stock, and backorder occurrences. In this section, we first define seven specific measures of customer service in make-to-stock firms and then make-to-order firms.

Make-To-Stock Customer Service

Seven specific make-to-stock measures of customer service are discussed here:

Leadtime service level (LSL)–percentage of leadtimes without stockouts.

Annual service level (ASL)–the number of stockouts per year.

Item percent fill rate (IPF)–percent of an item's quantity demanded in stock when requested.

Line-item percent fill rate (LPF)–percent of line items in stock across all orders.

Order percent fill rate (OPF)–percentage of multi-item orders filled directly from stock.

Backorder percent rate (BOP)–percentage of items, lines, or orders that were backordered.

Backorder recovery time (BRT)–average time needed to fill a backorder.

The first two concepts above, LSL and ASL, relate to the number or percentage of times stockouts occur, but not the number of units out of stock. The next three measures, IPF, LPF, and OPF, relate to the percentage of an item's units, line items, and orders, respectively, that are filled directly from stock. Finally, the last two, BOP and BRT, relate to the percentage of items backordered and the length of time items are on backorder, respectively. After defining the above measures, safety-stock calculations are discussed as methods of achieving desired customer service.

Leadtime Service Level

Leadtime service level (LSL) is the percentage of leadtimes in which no stockouts occur. For example, a 99 percent leadtime service level means that during 99 percent of the product's leadtimes there will be no stockouts. The number of leadtimes that occur during a year is equal to the annual demand (D) divided by the order quantity (Q). For example, if an item has an annual demand of 10,000 and 500 units are ordered each time, then there will be 20 orders and 20 leadtimes per year (i.e., 10,000/500). Remember: by definition, an item only runs out of stock during a leadtime.

Another valid definition of LSL is the probability of a stockout during a leadtime. Consider the following situation. A company monitors the number of times an item goes out of stock in a year. Item M109 is ordered 25 times per year. During this time, M109 was out of stock only once. Thus, M109 had a 96 percent leadtime service level $(1 - 1/25)$. That is, during 96 percent of the leadtimes, M109 *did not* run out of stock.

The number of leadtimes in a year for different items varies considerably. If an item is ordered 30 times a year, then it is exposed to stockouts 30 times. In contrast, if an item is ordered 12 times a year, then it is exposed only 12 times. Because leadtimes expose an item to stockouts, they are sometimes called *exposures*. Differences in the number of exposures of different products make LSL a dubious customer service measure.

Leadtimes expose items to stockouts.

Annual Service Level

Annual service level (ASL) measures and controls the number of stockouts in a year. Assume management finds one stockout per year acceptable. Based on this policy, set the desired LSL to achieve this level of service. Consider item M678, which is ordered 50 times per year. Given that management desires to have only one stockout per year, the question is: what should the probability of a stockout per leadtime be? In other words: What should the LSL be set to? To achieve only one stockout per year, management must set the LSL to 49/50, or 98 percent. The expected number of in-stock leadtimes needed to achieve an ASL of one stockout per year is 49.

ASL = n stockouts per year = 1 stockout per year

$$\text{LSL to achieve ASL} = \frac{\text{In-stock leadtimes}}{\text{Total leadtimes}} = \frac{49}{50} = .98 \quad (16\text{--}3)$$

On average, there will be 49 periods of no stockouts per 50-order year. Consider another example. Assume the firm desires to have only one stockout per year on average for M167. M167 has 30 order cycles per year. The required LSL is 29/30 or 97 percent.

ASL may appear to be a good method of measuring and controlling customer service; however, this is not usually the case.

The concept of an average number of stockouts may be misleading. In the M167 example above, on average, there will be 29 instock leadtimes out of 30 leadtimes per year. However, based on the laws of probability, the actual number of stockout periods will be 0, 1, 2, 3, or 4 per year with a frequency of 40 percent, 37 percent, 17 percent, 5 percent, and 1 percent, respectively. (These probability figures were generated using a binomial distribution.) Thus, approximately one out of four years will have two or more stockout periods (i.e., $17+5+1 = 23\%$ of the years). This may or may not be acceptable.

Also, you should note that the LSL and ASL measure the probability or number of stockouts, respectively. They do not measure the number of units that will be out of stock during leadtimes or per year. The negative consequences of stockouts are normally related to the number of units that are out of stock, not the number of leadtimes an item is out of stock. Additionally, depending on the number of order cycles there are per year, the ASL can vary dramatically from item to item even though the LSL is identical. Because of this, LSL and ASL are normally less effective measures of customer service level than the percent fill rates discussed below.

LSL and ASL are often dubious customer service measures.

The few cases in which LSL or ASL are good measures include those in which the number of leadtimes per year are the same for all items and the cost of a stockout is independent of the number of units out of stock. This situation does arise in some unusual applications.

Item Percent Fill Rate

Item percent fill rate (IPF) is the percentage of an item's quantity demanded that is supplied directly from stock when ordered or promised. For example, a 99 percent item fill rate means that 99 percent of an item's demand are in stock when requested. With a 99 percent fill rate, only 1 percent of the units demanded result in a stockout. Consider item M110. During the last year, the demand for item M110 was 10,000 units. Of the 10,000 units, 9,800 units were shipped directly from stock as requested. Consequently, 200 units were not in stock when requested; these resulted in stockouts. Thus, the IPF for M110 is 98 percent (9,800/10,000 = 98%).

The IPF concept is less abstract than the LSL and ASL. In this case, it is possible to measure and plan an item's percentage quantity that will be in stock when requested. As discussed previously, the IPF is superior to LSL and ASL.

Line-Item Percent Fill Rate

Line-item percent fill rate (LPF) is the percentage of line items on all orders that are shipped on time or when promised. The typical company sells many different items that are ordered from customers on the same order form. Thus, an order may be for 60 M345s, 30 M108s, 35 M678s, and 25 M123s. Each of the items is referred to as a *line item* on the order. When one of the line items on an order is incompletely filled or out of stock, this is a line item stockout. Consider the following situation. During the month of November, a company receives 1,000 orders from customers. Each order has an average of 10 different items on it; therefore, 10,000 (i.e., 10∗1,000) different line items were ordered. Of the 10,000, there were 200 line items out of stock or incompletely filled. Thus, this company had a 98 percent line-item fill rate during the month (i.e., 1 − 200/10,000).

The LPF is a very important measure for the typical firm, whether it is a manufacturer, distributor, or retailer. Customers expect all items to be available, particularly when ordered together. For the customer, an incomplete fulfillment of 1 out of 10 ordered items can be more costly than a single, independent item stockout. The customer expects to receive all of the ordered items in full. If an important project involving the use of 10 items is delayed, the out-of-stock line items may cause great problems for the customer. As we will discuss, management can control the line-item percent fill rate using item percent fill rates.

Order Percent Fill Rate

Order percent fill rate (OPF) is the percentage of customer orders for multiple items that are filled without any stockouts. Assume that part M345 is one of eight items on an order from customer A. If all eight items are shipped to customer A in the right quantity, then customer A's order has been filled. If any of the items were out of stock or not shipped in sufficient quantity, then customer A's order was not completely filled; thus, an order stockout occurred.

Suppose that a supplier ships 1,000 customer orders in the month of November. Of the 1,000 customer orders, 100 were only partially filled; thus, stockouts occurred on each of these 100 orders. Consequently, this supplier had a 90 percent order fill rate (900/1,000) during the month of November. An order is only filled if all items and quantities are shipped to the customer when demanded. If one item is short one unit, then the order is incomplete and an order stockout occurs. The OPF is a stringent measure of customer service. But, it may be appropriate where the items ordered are for a unique project, such as major equipment overhauls and repair kits. As in the case for LPF, OPF is managed through the control of IPF. The OPF will become used more widely in extremely competitive markets.

Measure customer service using item, line-item, and order percent fill rates.

Each of these five customer service measures has a slightly different purpose. It is recommended that a firm collect statistics on each of the percent fill rates of IPF, LPF, and OPF. Below, we develop ways of setting safety stock to achieve desired item percent fill rates (IPFs). In addition, we briefly discuss methods of setting line-item and order percent fill rates. Before describing the process of setting IPF rates, let's briefly describe several other measures of customer service. The most frequently used measures include determining the percentage of backorders that occur and the duration of these backorders.

Backorder Percentage

The *backorder percentage* (BOP) is a concept that can be applied to any of the above measures of customer service. The percentage of items, line items, and orders that are placed on backorder can be calculated directly from IPF, LPF, and OPF, respectively. Thus, these are normally simple complements of in-stock statistics.

Backorder Recovery Time

Another important backorder statistic is the average *backorder recovery time* (BRT). This is the average time between customer-requested ship date and actual ship date. For example, assume the following records exist for items M345 and M678. M345 was on backorder three times for six different orders. On average, it took 15 working days for each of the six orders to be filled. M678 was on backorder twice for five different orders that took an average of 20 working days to be filled. What is the average BRT by item and across items for the 11 backorders (6 + 5)?

The by-item BRTs are stated above as 15 and 20 working days each. The order BRT across all line items is a weighted average as shown below.

$$BRT = \frac{6*15 + 5*20}{11} = \frac{190}{11} = 17.3 \text{ days}$$

The BRT is an important statistic because the length of time a customer must wait is important. If the BRT is low, then the loss of customer goodwill may be minimum. In other words, loss of customer goodwill is frequently proportionate to the length of the BRT.

Make-To-Order Customer Service

The important determinant of customer service in engineer-to-order, make-to-order, and assemble-to-order operations is delivering products when promised. Modification of the make-to-stock measures discussed above can be used in these environments. Instead of focusing on being in stock when demanded, the measure of concern is whether the firm delivered the product on the promised delivery date and in the correct quantity. Consider the make-to-order measures below:

Leadtime service level (LSL)—probability of delivering an order when promised.

Annual service level (ASL)—percentage of promised deliveries on time in a year.

Item percent fill rate (IPF)—percentage of an item delivered on time when the order is for multiple units of the same item.

Line-item percent fill rate (LPF)—Percentge of line items that are delivered complete and on time.

Order percent fill rate (OPF)—Percentage of complete orders delivered on time.

Backorder percent rate (BOP)—percentage of items, line items, or orders that were backordered.

Backorder recovery time (BRT)—average time needed to fill an item, line item, or orders on backorder.

All of these make-to-order measures relate to achieving promised delivery dates. All of them highlight the importance of properly and realistically committing to delivery dates. Customer service may suffer only because of our inability to promise orders properly. In addition, this requires the proper recording of original and revised promised dates. Customer and supplier revisions of promised dates need to be recorded separately so as to assure an accurate customer service measure.

Customer service in make-to-order firms
includes accurate promised delivery dates.

Having defined these important measures of customer service, the section below discusses how to integrate forecasting and inventory management so as to achieve desired customer service goals.

STATISTICAL INVENTORY CONTROL

This section develops the use of forecasts in the statistical determination of safety stocks in inventory-management systems. This procedure and its variations are popular in make-to-stock environments. While presented only in the context of a reorder-point system, the concepts and calculations of this section are easily applied to other inventory systems, including, but not limited to, periodic review, distribution requirements planning (DRP), and time-phased order-point systems.[2]

STATISTICAL INVENTORY CONTROL— NORMAL DISTRIBUTION

As you will recall, the reorder point of Equation 16–1 assumes that the demand during leadtime $(L\overline{d})$ is known with certainty; however, this is rarely true. To preclude stockouts, Equation 16–1 was modified by adding safety stock to the reorder point as shown in Equation 16–2, which is repeated below.

$$R = L\bar{d} + \text{Safety stock} \qquad (16\text{–}2)$$

When safety stock is used, an order for inventory will be placed sooner. It is therefore less likely that there will be a stockout. Below we discuss how to calculate safety stock for use in Equation 16–2.

The forecast of demand $(\bar{d})$ is normally made in regular time periods such as weeks, months, or days. From the historical data, we can find the statistical distribution and standard deviation of the forecast errors. Usually, it is assumed that the forecast error is normally distributed. Even if the error in forecasting one period ahead is not normally distributed, the error during a multiple-period leadtime will most often be normally distributed (ND). (This is a result of the central limit theorem of statistical analysis.) While this is not always true, it is almost always assumed that the error during leadtime is ND, unless the demand for items is very low. Low item demands are discussed in the last section of this chapter.

Given a forecast of demand $\bar{d}$ and a standard deviation of forecast errors S_d, the following relationship describes the standard deviation of errors during leadtime and its use in the formula for safety stock.

$$S_L = \sqrt{\frac{L}{F} S_d^2} \qquad (16\text{–}4)$$

$$\text{Safety stock} = ZS_L \qquad (16\text{–}5)$$

where

Z = Safety factor chosen from the normal distribution
S_d = Standard deviation of errors in one forecast period
S_L = Standard deviation of forecast errors during leadtime
L = Leadtime in weeks, months, or quarters
F = Number of time periods in the forecast period

F and L are expressed in the same units, such as days, weeks, or months.

Equation 16–4 is called the variance law and describes the standard deviation of errors during leadtime assuming that the errors of each period (e.g., week) of leadtime are statistically independent. Again, this is an assumption that is sometimes violated, but almost always assumed to be true. The statistical reorder point R is expressed as:

$$R = L\bar{d} + ZS_L \qquad (16\text{-}6)$$

Because of the normal-distribution assumption, Equation 16–6 can be used to describe the probability of stockouts with any reorder point. For example, if Z is set to 2, then during approximately 97.5 percent of the leadtimes there will be sufficient stock. This means that there will be a stockout during approximately 2.5 percent of the leadtimes. The use of a safety factor of 2 ($Z = 2$) yields a 97.5 percent leadtime service level. The Z value is a characteristic of ND. These characteristics are defined in Table 16–1. Consider this use of this table in the applications below.

Safety Stocks Using LSL and ASL

By selecting the appropriate Z value in Equation 16–6, safety stocks can be set using the ND illustrated in Table 16–1. Columns 3 and 6 show $1 - \text{LSL}$ for the Z factor from the ND. For example, if management wanted to set safety stock so as to achieve a 95 percent LSL (i.e., $1 - \text{LSL} = 5\%$), then a Z of 1.65 should be used in Equation 16–6 (5% is midway between 1.60 and 1.70, thus the 1.65). Consider the following situation for item M164.

Forecasted demand $\bar{d} = 500$ units per week

Leadtime $L = 2$ weeks

Time periods in forecast $F = 1$ week

Standard deviation of forecast errors $S_d = 100$ units/week

Determine R to achieve a 95 percent LSL.

$$S_L = \sqrt{\frac{L}{F} S_d^2} = \sqrt{\frac{2}{1} (100)^2} = \sqrt{20{,}000} = 141$$

Therefore,

$$R = L\bar{d} + ZS_L = 500(2) + 1.65(141) = 1{,}233$$

By ordering when on hand plus on order equals 1,233 (OH + OO = 1,233), management will theoretically achieve a 95 percent LSL. Only during 5 out of 100 leadtimes will there be a stockout.

TABLE 16–1
Probability and Units of Stockouts

E(Z)	Z	1 – LSL Probability Demand > R = L̄d + ZS$_L$ P(X > Z)	E(Z)	Z	1 – LSL Probability Demand > R = L̄d + ZS$_L$ P(X > Z)
4.500	−4.50	100.00	0.399	0.00	50.00
4.400	−4.40	100.00	0.351	0.10	46.02
4.300	−4.30	100.00	0.307	0.20	42.07
4.200	−4.20	100.00	0.267	0.30	38.21
4.100	−4.10	100.00	0.230	0.40	34.46
4.000	−4.00	100.00	0.198	0.50	30.85
3.900	−3.90	100.00	0.169	0.60	27.43
3.800	−3.80	99.99	0.143	0.70	24.20
3.700	−3.70	99.99	0.120	0.80	21.19
3.600	−3.60	99.98	0.100	0.90	18.41
3.500	−3.50	99.98	0.083	1.00	15.87
3.400	−3.40	99.97	0.069	1.10	13.57
3.300	−3.30	99.95	0.056	1.20	11.51
3.200	−3.20	99.93	0.046	1.30	9.68
3.100	−3.10	99.90	0.037	1.40	8.08
3.000	−3.00	99.87	0.029	1.50	6.68
2.901	−2.90	99.81	0.023	1.60	5.48
2.801	−2.80	99.74	0.018	1.70	4.46
2.701	−2.70	99.63	0.014	1.80	3.59
2.601	−2.60	99.53	0.011	1.90	2.87
2.502	−2.50	99.38	0.008	2.00	2.28
2.403	−2.40	99.18	0.006	2.10	1.77
2.303	−2.30	98.93	0.005	2.20	1.39
2.205	−2.20	98.61	0.004	2.30	1.07
2.106	−2.10	98.21	0.003	2.40	0.82
2.008	−2.00	97.73	0.002	2.50	0.62
1.911	−1.90	97.13	0.001	2.60	0.47
1.814	−1.80	96.41	0.001	2.70	0.35
1.718	−1.70	95.54	0.001	2.80	0.26
1.623	−1.60	94.52	0.001	2.90	0.19
1.529	−1.50	93.32	0.000	3.00	0.13
1.437	−1.40	91.92	0.000	3.10	0.10
1.346	−1.30	90.32	0.000	3.20	0.07
1.256	−1.20	88.49	0.000	3.30	0.05
1.169	−1.10	86.43	0.000	3.40	0.03
1.083	−1.00	84.13	0.000	3.50	0.023
1.000	−0.90	81.59	0.000	3.60	0.016
0.920	−0.80	78.81	0.000	3.70	0.010
0.843	−0.70	75.80	0.000	3.80	0.007
0.769	−0.60	72.57	0.000	3.90	0.004
0.698	−0.50	69.15	0.000	4.00	0.003
0.630	−0.40	65.54	0.000	4.10	0.002
0.567	−0.30	61.79	0.000	4.20	0.001
0.507	−0.20	57.93	0.000	4.30	0.0009
0.451	−0.10	53.98	0.000	4.40	0.0005
0.399	−0.00	50.00	0.000	4.50	0.0003

Note: This table is standardized to a mean of zero and a standard deviation of 1.

Z = Number of standard deviations of safety stock

$E(Z)$ = Expected number of units short

$P(X > Z)$ = Probability that standardized demand will be greater than Z. Also, $P(X > Z) = 1 - LSL$.

Source: Revised from Robert G. Brown, *Advanced Service Parts Inventory Control*, 2nd ed. (Thetford, Vt.: Materials Management Systems, 1982).

For item M153, consider an ASL objective of having only one stockout per year. Item M153 is ordered 30 times a year. The LSL to achieve an average number of stockouts of one per year is calculated below using Equation 16–3.

$$\text{LSL} = 29/30 = .97 \text{ or } 97 \text{ percent}$$

Referring to Table 16–1 for the appropriate Z value of 1.90, R is:

$$R = L\bar{d} + ZS_L = 500(2) + 1.9(141) = 1{,}268$$

where Z is found in the last column of Table 16–1, choosing a value that has only approximately a 3 percent probability of demand exceeding it.

An ASL of one stockout per year yields a higher safety stock than the LSL of .95 because a LSL of .95 uses a Z value of only 1.65. Thus, the reorder point R is higher for the ASL.

Consider item M186, which is ordered 12 times a year. Management policy is to achieve an ASL of one stockout per year. At what should the LSL be set to achieve this objective?

$$\text{LSL} = 11/12 = .92$$

From Table 16–1, we see that a Z value of 1.40 achieves the ASL of one stockout per year. It has approximately an 8 percent probability that demand will exceed this value.

Table 16–2 illustrates the statistics of three different products, M186, M153, and M678. As the table shows, there is a considerable difference in the Z values necessary to achieve the same ASL for different products.

Because M678 is exposed to stockouts more frequently than M186 and M123, its safety stock is higher, everything else being equal. In general, the use of ASL to set LSL is more logical and effective than the use of a common Z value for items. Nonetheless, ASL is inferior to the use of the item percent fill rate (IPF), which is discussed below.

Safety Stocks Using Item Percent Fill Rate

Columns 1 and 4 of Table 16–1 illustrate a concept called the *expected Z value, E(Z)*. $E(Z)$ is equal to the average number of units out of stock during leadtimes when the standard deviation of error during leadtime S_L is 1. In other words, the $E(Z)$ is the aver-

TABLE 16–2
The Effect of the Number of Leadtimes or Orders per Year on Safety Stock

	M186	M153	M678
ASL (stockouts per year)	1	1	1
Number of leadtimes/year	12	30	50
Resulting LSL	11/12 = 92%	29/30 = 97%	49/50 = 98%
Resulting Z value	1.40	1.90	2.10

age or expected number of units out of stock if R were set using the Z value associated with that $E(Z)$ when the standard deviation of error during leadtime is 1. (The derivation of $E(Z)$ is beyond our purposes; however, this does not detract from our ability to apply the concept.) Consider the following relationships that result from these facts.

$E(Z)$ = Mean number of units short *per leadtime* if $S_L = 1$
$E(Z)S_L$ = Mean number of units short *per leadtime* for any S_L
D/Q = Number of leadtimes or orders *per year*

$$E(Z)S_L\left(\frac{D}{Q}\right) = \text{Mean number of units short } per\ year \qquad (16\text{–}7)$$

where

$$D = \text{Annual demand}$$
$$Q = \text{Quantity ordered each time}$$

Frequently, policy makers set the minimum IPF for items to maintain or achieve strategic customer service objectives. For example, assume top management sets the minimum IPF at .99. For brevity, P is used in formulas to designate IPF. Knowing P yields the following relationship.

$$(1 - P)D = \text{Mean number of units short per year} \qquad (16\text{–}8)$$

Setting Equation 16–7 equal to Equation 16–8 yields:

$$E(Z)S_L\left(\frac{D}{Q}\right) = (1 - P)D \qquad (16\text{–}9)$$

Rearranging Equation 16–9, $E(Z)$ can now be calculated directly:

$$E(Z) = \frac{(1 - P)Q}{S_L} \qquad (16\text{–}10)$$

Equation 16–10 is a very powerful one relating $E(Z)$, P, Q, and S_L directly to each other and indirectly to R, L, Z, and S_d. Knowing any three of the four values of Equation 16–10 makes possible the calculation of the fourth value. Consider several applications of this relationship.

Setting R to Achieve an IPF

Assume that management desires to achieve a 99 percent IPF for M123. What should the reorder point be to achieve this rate? Given:

$$\overline{d} = 500 \text{ units per week, mean demand}$$
$$S_d = 200 \text{ units per week}$$
$$F = 1 \text{ week in the forecast}$$
$$D = 26,000 \text{ units per year (52 times 500)}$$
$$L = 3\text{-week leadtime}$$
$$S_L = \sqrt{\frac{L}{F} S_d{}^2} = \sqrt{\frac{3}{1} (200)^2} = 346.4$$
$$R = L\overline{d} + ZS_L$$
$$Q = 850$$

Find the value of Z that will achieve a 99 percent IPF.

$$E(Z) = \frac{(1 - P)Q}{S_L} = \frac{(1 - .99)850}{346.4} = \frac{8.5}{346.4} = .02454$$

From Table 16–1, the appropriate Z value is 1.60. (Note: rather than interpolate, we choose to take the higher Z value.) Thus, the reorder point is:

$$R = 500(2) + 1.6(346.4) = 1,000 + 554 = 1,554$$

Whenever on hand plus on order reaches 1,554, place an order for 850 units. By doing so, 99 percent of the *units* are in stock when demanded. Let's review the statistics of M123 with different service objectives.

As shown in Table 16–3, there are differences in the resulting safety stocks and reorder points for each method. We do not suggest that you choose to use LSL, ASL, or IPF based on Table 16–3, but instead on the basis of the purposes of each of these methods.

It may appear from this table that there is little difference in the Z values of different methods; however, this is not true.

TABLE 16–3
Safety-Stock Calculations for Item M123

Method	Objective	Z	S_L	Safety Stock	Reorder Point
LSL	95% of leadtimes without stockouts	1.65	346.4	572	1,572
ASL	1 stockout per year	2.10	346.4	727.4	1,727.4
IPF	99% of units in stock	1.60	346.4	554	1,554

The difference between an ASL of 1 and an IPF of 99 percent is significant. The ASL requires approximately 31 percent more safety stock than IPF. More importantly, the use of LSL and ASL results in considerably different IPFs for different inventory items. Having different IPFs for items probably means we have too much of some and not enough of others.

If one chooses to use a single LSL for setting R for a number of items, the ASL and IPF will differ greatly between items with different numbers of orders per year and forecast errors. Alternatively, when one chooses to set Z and R using an ASL of one stockout per year, then each item has an equal expected number of stockout occurrences per year. This is more effective than setting a constant LSL and Z across all items. However, both methods suffer because the resulting IPF is unknown. Hence, LSL and ASL are not recommended.

If safety stock is managed using LSL or ASL, then there may be too much of some items and too little of others.

The use of IPF in setting stock policies is much more effective. A management policy of setting a corporate goal of 99 percent of units in stock is much more meaningful and defensible. The IPF for all items or classifications of items need not be the same. However, now management has a rationale for setting desired customer service by item, class of item, or even class of customer. Management has a strategic tool with which to achieve marketing, financial, and operational objectives. This tool makes trade-offs possible between customer service, inventory investment, cost, and return on investment.

In practice, the actual IPF can be lower or higher than the theoretical values of P in Equation 16–10, depending on the accuracy of the forecast over time. This can occur because the forecast model improves or worsens or because forecast errors are not normally and independently distributed. Consequently, if management wants to maintain at least 98 percent IPF, then the theoretical value should be increased to some larger value such as 99 percent.

The actual IPF may be higher or lower than the theoretical IPF; hedge by setting the theoretical IPF higher.

SAFETY STOCK AND ORDER QUANTITY INTERACTION

Equation 16–10 illustrates an important relationship between Q and safety stock. As a firm orders items more frequently and all other things remain constant, the resulting IPF will decrease. If S_L and $E(Z)$ remain constant and Q is decreased in Equation 16–10, then, mathematically, P must decrease. In other words, if a firm orders more frequently and does not recalculate $E(Z)$ and safety stocks, then the actual IPF will decrease. This is logical because, on average, we have less inventory on hand to preclude stockouts. To maintain IPF with smaller Qs requires more safety stock, because, as the $E(Z)$ decreases, Z increases.

If everything else remains constant, then ordering items more frequently requires more safety stock.

There are several other scenarios that we might build using Equation 16–10. Consider the numbers below, which illustrate the interactions between the required safety stock and order quantity. The example uses item M123. The question we address here is what value of Q will minimize the total cost of providing an IPF of 99 percent?

Table 16–4 illustrates the search for the best order quantity. Let's consider an order quantity of 850 while discussing this table. Column 1 illustrates the selected order quantities, columns 2 and 3 the resulting $E(Z)$ and Z values, respectively. The resulting

TABLE 16–4
Order Quantity, Safety Stock, and Cost Interactions for M123

(1) Order Quantity (Q)	(2) E(Z)	(3) Z†	(4) Safety Stock (Z*S_L)	(5) Average Inventory (Q/2 + ZS_L)	(6) Holding Cost (TAHC)	(7) Order Cost (TAOC)	(8) Total Cost
400	.01155	1.89	654.70	854.70	1,231	1,300	2,531
600	.01732	1.73	599.27	899.27	1,295	867	2,162
800	.02309	1.61	557.70	957.70	1,379	650	2,029
850	.02454	1.58	547.31	972.31	1,400	612	2,012
900	.02598	1.56	540.38	990.38	1,426	578	2,004
1,100*	.03176	1.47	509.21	1,059.21	1,525	473	1,998
1,300	.03753	1.39	481.50	1,131.50	1,629	400	2,029

*Lowest-cost order quantity.
†Interpolated values from Table 16–1.
$d = 500$ $D = 26,000$ $S_d = 200$ $S_L = 346.4$
$L = 3$ $C_P = 20$ $C_H = 1.44$ $P = .99$

safety stock and average inventory level are shown in columns 4 and 5, respectively. The average inventory when safety stock is held equals one half of the order quantity plus safety stock. This is shown for $Q = 850$ in Equation 16–11.

$$\text{Average inventory} = Q/2 + ZS_L$$
$$= 850/2 + 1.58(346.4) = 972.31 \qquad (16\text{–}11)$$

The safety stock in Equation 16–11 is assumed to be in stock all year because it is only used during 50 percent of the leadtimes, and then only during a very short period of time until the order arrives.

Suppose that the cost to hold one unit of M123 for a year is $1.44, where C_H is used to designate this cost. The cost of holding M123 is equal to C_H times average inventory. Thus, the total annual holding cost (TAHC), shown in column 6 of Table 16–4, equals C_H times average inventory. For $Q = 850$, TAHC is as follows:

$$\text{TAHC} = C_H[(Q/2) + ZS_L]$$
$$= 1.44(850/2 + 547.31) = \$1,400.13 \qquad (16\text{–}12)$$

(Note: The Z values of Table 16–4 were interpolated from Table 16–1. Your interpolated values may differ slightly.)

The cost of manufacturing or ordering M123 is assumed equal to $20 per order; as is common, we use C_P to denote cost per order.

Thus, there are D/Q orders per year. If a large quantity is ordered or manufactured each time, then there are fewer orders per year. The total annual order cost (TAOC) is shown in column 7 of Table 16–4. It is calculated for $Q = 850$ as shown below.

$$\text{TAOC} = C_P(D/Q)$$
$$= 20(26{,}000/850) = \$611.76 \tag{16–13}$$

As shown in Table 16–4, there is a considerable difference in the total cost of an order of 400 units versus the lowest-cost order quantity of 1,100 units. However, order quantities between 800 and 1,300 have about the same total cost.

Next, let's consider the impact of improving the accuracy of the forecast.

IMPROVING FORECAST ACCURACY

Suppose that, through an improved forecasting system, the standard deviation of the forecast error decreases from 200 to 100 units per week. What will the impact on the required safety stock and the total annual cost be given the desired IPF of 99 percent. Table 16–5 illustrates the relationship between total cost for this situation.

TABLE 16–5
Order Quantity, Safety Stock, and Cost Interactions for M123

(1) Order Quantity (Q)	(2) E(Z)	(3) Z	(4) Safety Stock (Z*S_L)	(5) Average Inventory (Q/2 + Z*S_L)	(6) Holding Cost (TAHC)	(7) Order Cost (TAOC)	(8) Total Cost
400	.02309	1.60	277.12	477.12	687	1,300	1,987
600	.03464	1.43	247.68	547.68	789	867	1,656
800	.04619	1.30	229.16	629.16	906	650	1,556
850	.04908	1.27	219.96	644.96	929	612	1,541
900*	.05196	1.24	214.77	664.77	957	578	1,535
1,100	.06351	1.14	197.45	747.45	1,076	473	1,549
1,300	.07506	1.06	183.59	833.59	1,200	400	1,600

*Lowest-cost order quantity.
$d = 500$ $D = 26{,}000$ $S_d = 100$ $S_L = 173.2$
$L = 3$ $C_P = 20$ $C_H = 1.44$ $P = .99$

The total costs of Table 16–5 behave similarly to those of Table 16–4, but they are lower in all cases. The optimal order quantity is now approximately 900 units as compared to 1,100 units in Table 16–4. To better understand the impact of the improved forecasts on inventory performance, consider the comparisons of Table 16–6.

As shown in Table 16-6, there is considerable difference in the cost (column 6) and inventory investment (column 8) of the old versus the new forecasting system. The old system required more inventory and had higher costs. The results of this simple example can only be generalized to the point of noting that improved forecasts can significantly reduce inventory costs and investment while maintaining a desired customer service level.

JIT, LEADTIMES, FORECAST ERROR, AND SAFETY STOCK

The widespread use of JIT methods and EDI has produced dramatic reductions in order leadtimes. What effects do reduced leadtimes have on forecast accuracy, safety stock, and costs? Equation 16–4 relates the standard deviation of the demand during leadtime (S_L) to the standard deviation of the forecast errors (S_d) and

TABLE 16–6
Total Cost Comparison of Old and New Forecasting System for M123

	$S_d = 200$		$S_d = 100$					
(1)	(2)	(3)	(4)	(5)	(6)	(7)	(8)	(9)
						Percent		Percent
Order					Cost	Cost	Inventory	Inventory
Quantity	Total	Average	Total	Average	Difference	Difference	Difference	Difference
(Q)	Cost	Inventory	Cost	Inventory	(2 – 4)	(2 – 4)/2	(3 – 5)	(3 – 5)/3
400	2,531	854.70	1,987	477.12	544	19	376	44
600	2,162	899.27	1,656	547.68	507	23	352	39
800	2,029	957.70	1,556	629.16	466	23	324	34
850	2,012	972.31	1,541	644.96	471	23	472	49
900*	2,004	990.38	1,535	664.77	469	23	326	33
1,100	1,998	1,059.21	1,549	747.45	449	22	312	29
1,300	2,029	1,131.50	1,600	833.60	429	21	298	26

*Lowest-cost order quantity.

leadtime (L). As shown by the formula, a decrease in leadtime decreases the standard deviation of demand during leadtime, which then reduces safety stock. However, there are two effects on safety stock from a reduction in leadtimes. These result from having a lower S_L in Equations 16–4 and 16–10. Let's see what the combined effect will be when reducing the leadtime for product M123 from three weeks to two weeks. All other factors will be held constant.

Table 16–7 compares the results of maintaining an IPF of .99 for item M123 with two- and three-week leadtimes. As the table shows, the two-week leadtime yields a 22 percent reduction in safety stock (column 5), a 13 percent reduction in average inventory and total annual holding costs, and an overall cost reduction of 8.8 percent. These reductions result from a 33 percent decrease in leadtime. Combining the cost reduction with an inventory investment reduction yields a multiplier effect on the return on investment. The return on investment that results from this system improvement is considerable—the firm invests less in inventory and has lower costs by reducing leadtimes. The average inventory investment is given below assuming each M123 costs $7.20 per unit. For a three-week leadtime:

$$C_H(\text{Average inventory}) = C_H(Q/2 + ZS_L) = 7.20(972.3) = \$7,000.56$$

For a two-week leadtime:

$$C_H(\text{Average inventory}) = C_H(Q/2 + ZS_L) = 7.20(849.2) = \$6,114.24$$

TABLE 16–7
Comparison of Two- and Three-Week Leadtime for Item M123

(1)	(2)	(3)	(4) Safety Factor	(5) Safety Stock	(6) Average Inventory	(7) Holding Cost	(8) Order Cost	(9)
L	S_L	$E(Z)$	(Z)	$(Z \cdot S_L)$	$(Q/2 + ZS_L)$	$(TAHC)$	$(TAOC)$	Total Cost
3	346.4	0.2454	1.58	547.3	972.3	1,400	611.76	2,011.9
2	282.8	.03000	1.50	424.2	849.2	1,223	611.76	1,834.6
Difference				−123.1	−123.1	−177		−177.3
Percent Difference*				−22%	−13%	−13%		−8.8%

*Percentage of reduction to three-week statistic.
$d = 500$ $D = 26,000$ $S_4 = 200$
$Q = 850$ $C_P = 20$ $C_H = 1.44$ $P = .99$

Thus, the reduced leadtime has resulted in an \$886.32 decrease in the average inventory investment in M123. This is not a trivial decrease in investment.

We have not measured the cost associated with the leadtime reduction. In many cases, leadtime reductions are not costly or difficult to obtain. However, in situations where leadtimes are at a minimum, it might be costly to reduce leadtimes. We caution you not to generalize these results further than the principles mentioned below.

Shorter leadtimes reduce forecast errors, safety stock, inventory carrying costs, and inventory investment.

There are significant cost and return on investment benefits from reducing order leadtimes.

Forecast accuracy, order frequency, leadtimes, and item percent fill rates can be managed to improve inventory-management performance.

STATISTICAL INVENTORY CONTROL– LOW–VOLUME DEMANDS

Low-Volume Demands

This section discusses forecasting and setting safety stock for items with very low demands. Items characterized by low-volume demands include maintenance and service items and some manufactured, remanufactured, and retail items. Frequently, the Poisson distribution describes demand for some spare parts, repair parts, slow-moving retail items, and other low-volume items. For example, the demand for replacement and repair parts at utilities commonly follows a Poisson distribution. The demand for many items at retail stores often follow a Poisson distribution instead of a normal distribution (ND). In the hardware and building materials industry, as in other retail industries, it is not uncommon for 40 percent of the stock to have a very low demand that can be accurately described by a Poisson or other non-normal distribution.

When a significant percentage of a firm's inventory or some expensive or important items have very low demands, benefits

---

Inventory Levels Crucial to Profits

Everex Computers Wins with Stock Controls;
Others Struggle with Excesses and Shortages

"If there are two words that send jitters through the computer hardware industry, they're *excess inventory.* Disk-drive makers, chip makers, and PC makers in the last six months have all seen profits fall in the face of mounting inventories." Reacting to last year's shortages of critical components, some companies overbought critical components. "Basically, the company forecast sales orders too aggressively and procured components in excess of what it needed."

Everex also faces the challenge of increasing sales, but it seems to have the inventory issue under control. Everex President Steve Hui is emphasizing a "zero-response-time" strategy in which PC resellers phone in customized orders. The goal is to ship orders within 48 hours after they arrive. "We have a lot of people focused on managing inventory, . . ." said Bruce Dunlevie. "That attention has begun to pay off."

Source: Richard March, *PC Week,* March 6, 1989, p. 65.

can accrue from using more accurate representations of forecast errors over leadtimes. As forecasting and inventory-management systems improve their capabilities to model demands and reduce errors, control of these slow-moving items may be improved. Some rules of thumb and research suggest that the normal distribution be used in all situations where the forecast of demand during leadtime is at least 10 units or greater even though the forecast errors might not be a normal distribution. In situations where the expected demand is less than 10 units during leadtime, other distributions are more likely to be appropriate for modeling forecast errors. As mentioned, one of the most frequently used statistical distributions for modeling low-volume forecast errors is the Poisson distribution.

Poisson Distribution

Using the Poisson is appropriate when the observed standard deviation of errors is nearly equal to the square root of the forecast. As we will see, this is characteristic of the Poisson distribution.

If the standard deviation of the errors is within 10 percent of the square root of the forecast value, then it is recommended that the Poisson distribution be used. If this condition does not exist, then other distributions—including the exponential, hypergeometric, negative binomial, or compound Poisson (sometimes called the stuttering Poisson)—might be used.

The Poisson describes the error in forecasting the number of orders per week or month when the probability of a single order is very low and independent of previous orders. The Poisson distribution is described by only one statistic—the mean (M). Let's assume the demand for a half-inch drill at the XYZ Hardware Store is very low. Over the last 48 months, the demand was distributed as shown in Figure 16–2. Assume also that this demand is patternless and is forecasted using the mean of 3 units per month. As shown in Figure 16–2, the Poisson distribution is skewed to the right; it is not symmetrical. The formula for the Poisson is given below.

$$P(X) = \frac{e^{-M}M^X}{X!} \text{ for } X = 0,1,2,3,4 \qquad (16\text{–}14)$$

where
$P(X)$ = Probability of demand equaling X
e = Natural number e = 2.7183
M = Mean number of orders per period
$X!$ = Factorial operation (e.g., $4! = 4*3*2*1 = 24$)

Consider the Poisson in setting safety stock for the half-inch variable-speed drills that have a mean demand of 3 units per month. Drills have a one-month leadtime and are ordered approximately once each month, using an order-point system. From this information, we describe the demand during leadtime and set safety stock so as to have a 99 percent leadtime service level (LSL). (We do not illustrate the derivation of IPF or other customer service levels because the calculations are beyond the purpose of this book. Many other fine inventory references exist for this purpose.[3])

Figure 16–2 illustrates the demand during leadtime for this product. While we do not show the actual calculations of the reorder point necessary to achieve management's objective of a 99 percent LSL, the reorder point equals eight units. However, if we had assumed that demand was ND, then the reorder point would

FIGURE 16-2
Poisson Distribution with Mean of 3 Units per Period

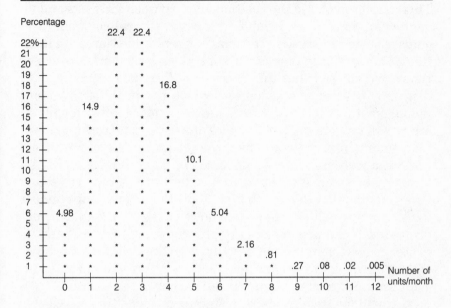

have been set too low, at seven units. The Poisson distribution calculations yielded a safety stock of five units (i.e., 8 − 3), while the ND yielded a safety stock of only four units (i.e., 7 − 3). While this one-unit difference does not appear significant, in general, it can be. The additional unit provides protection against stockouts; remove the extra unit, and we will have poorer customer service. The difference between the safety stocks of the ND and Poisson distributions becomes even greater with lower mean demands. Some important spare parts and service items have fractional mean demands during leadtimes.

When items are very important, then a stockout of a service or repair item can be very costly. The improved in-stock conditions achieved through better representation of forecast errors can mean the difference between effective or ineffective inventory management. Capturing forecast errors and investigating the nature of their distributions are necessary parts of good inventory management, particularly if demands and forecast errors are very non-normally distributed.

SUMMARY

This chapter explored the relationships between forecasts and inventory management. First, it discussed several common measures of customer service. The most important measures are item, line-item, and order percent fill rates and backorder recovery times. We showed that the accuracy of forecasts influences the cost and investment needed to achieve the goals of inventory management. A forecast with a lower standard deviation of the errors will provide customer service at a lower total cost and lower investment in inventory. Thus, the return on investment from improved forecasting is significant. We have illustrated the interaction between order quantities, safety stocks, total costs, and investments. Also, the search for the optimal order quantity under uncertainty was illustrated. We showed that, as order leadtimes decline and customer service remains constant, total cost and inventory investment decline. Finally, we discussed the importance of the Poisson distribution when the demand for items is very low. The assumptions of the normal distribution of the forecast errors do not hold for such items, and significant benefits are possible through the application of the Poisson distribution.

The next chapter discusses the design and selection of systems that will provide accurate and low-cost forecasts.

REFERENCES

1. D. W. Fogarty, J. H. Blackstone, Jr., and T. R. Hoffman, *Production and Inventory Management,* 2nd ed. (Cincinnati: South-Western Publishing, 1991); and T. E. Vollmann, W. L. Berry, and D. C. Whybark, *Manufacturing Planning and Control Systems,* 2nd ed. (Homewood, Ill.: Richard D. Irwin, 1984).
2. Vollmann et al., *Manufacturing Planning and Control Systems;* and R. G. Brown, *Advanced Service Parts Inventory Control,* 2nd ed. (Thetford Center, Vt.: Materials Management Systems, 1982).
3. Vollmann et al., *Manufacturing Planning and Control Systems;* and E. A. Silver and Rein Peterson, *Decision Systems for Inventory Management,* 2nd ed. (New York: John Wiley & Sons, 1985).

CHAPTER 17

FORECASTING SYSTEM DESIGN AND SELECTION

FORECASTING SYSTEM DEVELOPMENT
PAST FAILURES
ORGANIZATIONAL VERSUS TECHNICAL
  VALIDITY
SYSTEM–DEVELOPMENT PROCESS
  Project Organization
  System-Development Steps
  Implementation Strategy
  Implementation Project Activities
  Procedural Revision and Organizational
    Compatibility
  System-Development Time
SUMMARY
REFERENCE

> There is nothing more difficult to plan, more doubtful of suc-
> cess, nor more dangerous to manage than the creation of
> a new system. For the initiator has the enmity of all who
> would profit by the preservation of the old system and
> merely lukewarm defenders in those who would gain by the
> new one.
>
> Niccolo Machiavelli, *The Prince,* 1513

This chapter presents a summary of the important characteristics of good forecasting systems, a system-ranking checklist for
comparing different systems, and, finally, some comments about
implementing forecasting systems. Our purpose is to provide you
with information to assess, select, or design forecasting systems.
We caution you to not underestimate the many details necessary
to successfully implement forecasting systems. Almost all medium
to large firms should have operational forecasting systems with
the features presented here.

We have been surprised at the inability of firms to recognize
the multidimensional characteristics of integrated forecasting systems. Some firms have organizational structures or climates that
foster interdepartmental competition. Such competition interferes
with system integration; consequently, these corporations fail to
understand the integrative requirements of effective forecasting
systems. Too often, they search for a "black-box" solution to their
forecasting problems. They believe it is not necessary to under-

stand the forecasting system, merely to "put some data in and get some forecasts out." Such an attitude should be avoided.

Key personnel should be competent in forecasting system details.

The system-ranking checklist in this chapter enables you to develop a personalized ranking of required and desired functions in your system. Comparisons of prospective systems—whether purchased or developed in house—can be facilitated with this checklist. However, the decision to acquire versus to build a forecasting system is not just a matter of using the checklist, because time and risk also should be considered in the build-versus-buy decision. Well-designed forecasting systems from several vendors typically offer lower cost and risk in less time. The advantages of purchasing a system are even greater when a large number of users want or need the system immediately.

Included in the checklist are considerations of how easily the system can be adapted to unique requirements, either immediately or as the system evolves. The cost of modifications and their ongoing support should be part of any system evaluation. Whether these modifications can be made by the user company or the vendor is also an important characteristic. System documentation, database design, programming standards, programming language, vendor stability, vendor capabilities, and other factors often become important when unique features are to be added to a vendor's system.

Some firms decide to develop their own systems in house. They need to be very cautious when doing so. We have seen some firms attempt to build their own systems, yet have a history of failing miserably when it comes to designing complex systems. The attention to detail necessary to achieve an effective system is very great.

FORECASTING SYSTEM OVERVIEW

Figure 17–1 illustrates the major parts of a forecasting system. It is useful to view a system as having five logical modules and a database. Table 17–1 briefly outlines each of these modules. Our discussion of forecasting system capabilities is structured using the five modules presented in Table 17–1 and Figure 17–1.

FIGURE 17-1
The Modules of a Forecasting System

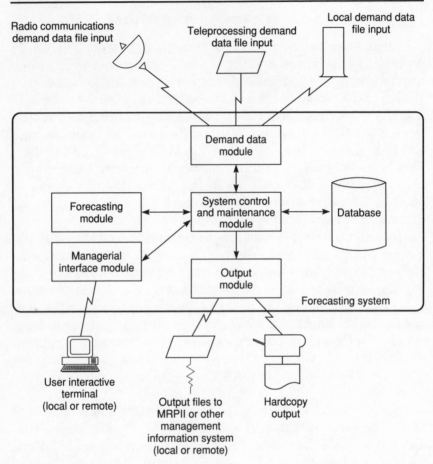

GENERAL CHARACTERISTICS
========================

The requirements of a good operational forecasting system are considerably greater than those of a good statistical forecasting package. These more general requirements include, but are not limited to, the ability to:

Provide ease of use to various types of users.

Process millions of records accurately and quickly.

TABLE 17–1
The Modules and Database of a Forecasting System

I. Demand Data Module
   Input of local and remote demand data
   Demand capturing
   Logical filtering (demand versus supply or shipments)
   Special-event filtering (promotions, price changes, product introductions)
   Initial outlier detection, adjustment, classification

II. Forecasting Module
   System forecast selection
   Outlier detection, adjustment, classification
   Reasonableness test
   Final forecast
   Error measures
   Tracking-signal control

III. Managerial Interface and Interaction Module
   Graphical user interface
   Screen displays
   Management forecasts
   User help
   Management feedback
   User notepad
   Expert advisory menu

IV. Output Module
   File generation
   Routine reports
   Ad hoc reports
   Exception reports

V. System Control and Maintenance Module
   Module and navigation control
   Simulation control
   Database updating and maintenance
   Detection of system malfunctions and bugs

VI. Database
   Actual demand history
   Adjusted demand history
   Promotional profiles
   Seasonal profiles
   Item and group relationships structure
   Performance measures
   Item relationships
   Item descriptions
   Demand forecasts

Provide accurate forecasts of item demands.

Group items with low demand to achieve good group forecasts.

Generate multilevel group forecasts.

Collect data from geographically diverse locations.

Generate hierarchical reports for several levels of management.

Provide management wiht diagnostic, graphical, and interactive interfaces with the system.

Be a means of integrating the market demand information needs of operations, marketing, and financial management.

In this chapter, we distinguish between system forecasts and management forecasts. The *system* forecast is the automatic forecast produced by the statistical model using historical demand or activity data. The *management* forecast is used to replace the system forecast when the user believes it is better during some periods. Consequently, management forecasts dominate the system forecasts for any periods in which management forecasts are entered.

FORECASTING SYSTEM RANKING CHECKLIST

A checklist of system characteristics is presented in Table 17–2. These characteristics are based on the principles developed throughout this book and the general requirements stated above. In many instances, we refer to other chapters that discuss the particular characteristic in detail. If Chapter 17 is listed as the source of a characteristic, then you will find a discussion of that characteristic following the checklist. Also, some characteristics are self-evident and are not referenced. With each characteristic, we provide a place to record its importance (I). Your use of this ranking checklist will be unique and subjective, which is an advantage of this method. Also, it is designed to be used as a point of discussion for design or selection purposes.

When assessing the characteristics of two or more designs and/or forecasting systems, they should be scored by using the

TABLE 17-2
Forecasting System Checklist and Ranking Criteria

General Characteristics

	I	*C*	*I*∗*C*	Chapter Reference
1. Produces forecasts at least once per month	___	___	___	
2. Produces different forecasting frequencies (e.g., per week, per month, per quarter)	___	___	___	
3. Provides item and item/location forecasts	___	___	___	2, 3
4. Provides group and family forecasts	___	___	___	2, 3
5. Provides top-down and bottom-up forecasts	___	___	___	2, 3
6. Provides forecasts at level of detail needed by each user	___	___	___	2
7. Processes new items automatically	___	___	___	
8. Allows management forecasting by exception	___	___	___	
9. Measures forecast accuracy by item/location	___	___	___	7
10. Permits mass maintenance of database	___	___	___	
11. Selects and updates models automatically	___	___	___	
12. Supports novice-to-expert range of users	___	___	___	
13. Processes large files quickly	___	___	___	
14. Selectively processes in a simulation mode	___	___	___	17
15. Adaptable to evolving business conditions	___	___	___	
16. Fully documented users and systems manuals	___	___	___	
17. Readily modified and supported if modified	___	___	___	17
18. Operates in an acceptable hardware and software environment	___	___	___	
19. Provides means to integrate forecasts with other systems or applications	___	___	___	3
Sum of *I*∗*C*s for general characteristics			___	
Section weight		×	___	
Section overall value			___	

Demand Data Module and Database

	I	*C*	*I*∗*C*	Chapter Reference
1. Interfaces with current database	___	___	___	3
2. Records and manages at least three years of history	___	___	___	
3. Maintains and adapts to the use of demand, orders received, or shipments data	___	___	___	3
4. Permits adjustments to the historical demand database (retroadjustments)	___	___	___	8
5. Filters and manages outliers and special events	___	___	___	8
6. Maintains actual, forecasted, and adjusted data	___	___	___	14
7. Provides full database management functions	___	___	___	
8. Maintains item and group promotional and seasonal profiles	___	___	___	5
Sum of *I*∗*C*s for demand data and database			___	
Section weight		×	___	
Section overall value			___	

TABLE 17–2   (continued)

Forecasting Module

	I	C	I∗C	Chapter Reference
1. Forecasts at least 12 months into future	——	——	——	
2. Offers choice of number of periods per year (4, 12, 13, 52 periods, etc.)	——	——	——	3
3. Permits user control of selected models	——	——	——	
4. Good automatic tracking signals and demand filters	——	——	——	14
5. Provides reasonableness test with warnings	——	——	——	14
6. Measures forecast error of each forecast	——	——	——	7, 14
7. Automatic, optimal selection of model parameters	——	——	——	10–14, 17
8. Provides combination of system and management forecasts	——	——	——	17
9. Provides a range of statistical models for random, trend, and seasonal data	——	——	——	14
10. Handles low-, medium-, and high-volume items	——	——	——	16
11. Permits user control of seasonal indexes	——	——	——	17
12. Provides seasonal indexes from group data	——	——	——	2, 3
13. Provides direct input of seasonal indexes	——	——	——	10–14
14. Detects and adjusts outliers in raw data	——	——	——	8
15. Reconciles group forecasts to item forecasts	——	——	——	3
16. Enables users to change defined groupings	——	——	——	17
17. Supports a hierarchy of forecast groups	——	——	——	3
18. Provides for allocation of management forecasts to items in a group	——	——	——	3
19. Flexible in methods available to relate group forecasts to item forecasts	——	——	——	17
20. Supports promotion and event management with appropriate models if necessary	——	——	——	5
21. System provides forecast performance measures for items and groups	——	——	——	
22. Adjusts demand for working days or weeks per month and so on	——	——	——	9
Sum of I∗Cs for forecasting module			——	
Section weight		×	——	
Section overall value			——	

Managerial Interface and Interaction Module

	I	C	I∗C	Chapter Reference
1. Enables easy, direct input of management forecasts at any level in the forecast hierarchy	——	——	——	17
2. Enables management forecasts to be entered for one or more periods in the future	——	——	——	
3. Provides conversion of units of measure for different user purposes, for example, currency, weight, volume, capacity	——	——	——	

TABLE 17-2   (continued)

	I	C	I*C	Chapter Reference
4. Provides graphical display of the results of overrides, historical data, and forecasts	___	___	___	17
5. Compares the historical accuracy of system and management forecasts	___	___	___	
6. Graphically presents forecast errors	___	___	___	7
7. Provides access to the database by various display screens or queries	___	___	___	17
8. Has navigation paths to support the most-frequent user actions and decisions	___	___	___	17
9. Supports new users with help keys	___	___	___	17
10. Provides expert advisory comments to improve model fitting simulation	___	___	___	
11. Provides notepad for users' comments tied to one or more forecasts	___	___	___	17
12. Supports promotion and event analysis with appropriate displays when necessary	___	___	___	5
13. Allows simulations with items and groups to proceed without changing the database	___	___	___	17
14. Allows simulation conditions to be applied to the database	___	___	___	17
15. For international operations, supports currency, date format, and language choice	___	___	___	
16. Provides graphical user interface	___	___	___	
Sum of I*Cs for managerial interface module			___	
Section weight		×	___	
Section overall value			___	

Output Module

	I	C	I*C	Chapter
1. Prints reports on request	___	___	___	
2. Creates files of selected items, groups, and so on, on request	___	___	___	
3. Provides routine interface data for use by other systems or applications (e.g., MRPII/JIT)	___	___	___	
4. Reports items whose forecast accuracy is below acceptable accuracy	___	___	___	
5. Provides variable exception criteria by item, group, class, or other meaningful category	___	___	___	
6. Provides useful summaries of forecasts for various management purposes	___	___	___	3
7. Supports summaries in common units of measure	___	___	___	
8. Provides quarterly, seasonal, and yearly data when necessary	___	___	___	
9. Reports historical data or future forecasts or both	___	___	___	

TABLE 17–2   (continued)

	I	*C*	*I*C*	*Chapter Reference*
10. Reports historical changes in demand, forecast accuracy, and other aspects of model performance	___	___	___	
Sum of I*Cs for output module			___	
Section weight		×	___	
Section overall value			___	

System Control and Maintenance Module

	I	*C*	*I*C*	*Chapter Reference*
1. Provides mass maintenance (many records with one transaction) based on user-specified conditions	___	___	___	
2. Provides audit trail of all maintenance	___	___	___	
3. Handles simulations apart from the permanent database when necessary	___	___	___	
4. Controls and informs the user of permissible and required steps in system use	___	___	___	
5. Controls user movement from functions of one module to any other module	___	___	___	
6. Retains common system-status data and item references across modules	___	___	___	
7. Provides user profiles and system security	___	___	___	
8. Provides diagnostic messages when system malfunctions	___	___	___	
9. Controls processing of batch tasks and reports results of processing	___	___	___	
Sum of I*Cs for system control and maintenance module			___	
Section weight		×	___	
Section overall value			___	

Software Vendor Criteria

	I	*C*	*I*C*	*Chapter Reference*
1. Available on company computer platforms	___	___	___	
2. Overall user flexibility for modification	___	___	___	
3. Time required to implement	___	___	___	
4. Overall cost	___	___	___	
5. Cost of additional hardware	___	___	___	
6. Current personnel capable of using	___	___	___	
7. Current DP personnel capable of maintaining and modifying system	___	___	___	
8. System uses well-structured design	___	___	___	
9. Good documentation	___	___	___	
10. Works on other computer platform(s)	___	___	___	

TABLE 17-2   (concluded)

	I	C	I∗C	Chapter Reference
11. System works with existing database management system	——	——	——	
12. Programmed in an industry-standard language	——	——	——	
13. Vendor offers a full line of integrated complementary software	——	——	——	
14. Vendor is financially sound	——	——	——	
15. Vendor in business minimum of 10 years	——	——	——	
16. Vendor has acceptable maintenance plan	——	——	——	
17. Vendor provides source code	——	——	——	
18. Vendor provides proper education support	——	——	——	
19. There is an independent users' group	——	——	——	
20. Vendor has good reputation in industry	——	——	——	
21. Program has good on-line documentation	——	——	——	
22. System has interactive and batch processes	——	——	——	
Sum of I∗Cs for software vendor criteria			——	
Section weight		×	——	
Section overall value			——	

Overall System Summary

General characteristic section value	——
Demand data module and database value	——
Forecasting module value	——
Managerial interface and interaction value	——
Output module value	——
System control and maintenance value	——
Software vendor criteria value	——
Total system value	══

capability (C) scale. The C scale indicates how well a system provides a characteristic. The following I and C scales are suggested as typical for your assessment. However, we encourage you to modify the scale in any way you deem appropriate.

I Scale: Importance

 0 = Not important in foreseeable future
 2 = Not needed until some future date
 4 = Good to have now, but not essential at this time
 6 = Important
 8 = Very important
16 = Essential to, or a must for, the system

C Scale: Capability and Flexibility for Modification

0 = Not cost effective to implement this feature
1 = Customer-implemented cost greater than $50,000
2 = Vendor-implemented cost greater than $50,000
3 = Customer-implemented cost less than $10,000
4 = Vendor-implemented cost less than $10,000
5 = Customer-implemented cost less than $5,000
6 = Vendor-implemented cost less than $5,000
7 = Customer-implemented cost less than $1,000
8 = Vendor-implemented cost less than $1,000
9 = Standard feature, limited modification flexibility
10 = Standard feature, great modification flexibility

By assigning numerical values to system features and sections, you can generate an overall effectiveness index for desired and actual systems. The values of characteristics can be calculated by multiplying each I value times its C value; then, by adding all the weighted factors, you can measure each section value.

In addition to weighting the importance of each characteristic in Table 17–2, it is important to weight the sum of the weights for each major section. Thus, each major section is followed by a subtotal weighting (sum of I*Cs for all characteristics in that section). These subtotal weights should then be multipled by another weight that reflects the importance of that group or section of characteristics. These second sets of weights are called *section weights*. The product of the section weight and section sums are called *section overall values*. It is suggested that the sum of all seven section weights should be 100 percent; however, any arbitrary total is valid so long as it remains constant during evaluations and there is meaning to the individual section weights and overall total value. Thus, each section can be weighted to provide the best combination of features for a specific application. The sum of the section weights should be calculated as shown at the end of Table 17–2.

The total system characteristics value can be used very effectively in designing and ranking alternative forecasting systems. While the system value is an important goal in itself, the actual process of identifying important characteristics yields the greatest benefits. Also, it is important to add characteristics unique to your application.

When comparing different systems, you should use the same importance (I) weight in each evaluation. This provides internal consistency in the evaluation process. Also, we caution you to be careful in assigning the importance weights of 8 and 16. A non-linear scale has been chosen for I so that features that are truly essential receive twice the weight of those features that are only very important. There may be some characteristics that your system must have. These can be given an extremely high I weight. If a system does not have this characteristic, then it is badly flawed. Also, while we suggest that you use an I weight of 0 cautiously, it is there to identify system features that are not important to your application.

We have noticed that many vendors provide excellent forecasting *methods*. However, their forecasting *systems* do not have many of the supporting features discussed in this book. To the extent that the customer does not need these features, no harm is done. However, the most effective system is one that has all the important features needed by the customer. Thus, the most cost-effective system either has all the features the customer needs or has the flexibility to allow easy modification and customization. The flexibility of the system for easy modification is one of the most important aspects of a system; that is why it receives a 10 on the C scale.

Finally, we caution you to view the final numeric results of your analyses as guides. You should not select one system over another based solely on its numeric superiority, but based on the importance of the differences highlighted by the numeric scales.

The following sections discuss the characteristics listed above that were referenced to Chapter 17. In addition, several of the previously presented principles are repeated for emphasis.

DEMAND DATA MODULE

The demand data module is used to record, track, and manage the demand data for product groups and items. It should utilize orders-received data as measures of demand. Shipment data represents a measure of how many units were shipped, but not necessarily what the demand was. Orders-received data, such as orders booked or orders-by-shipment data, are appropriate for most situations.

At any point in time, the user should be able to adjust the historical database to reflect unusual planned or unplanned events. Such retroadjustments are important in maintaining as accurate a demand database as possible.

Forecast accuracy can be improved if large unexplained variations in new demand data are validated and edited for reasonableness before being utilized by the system—a process called *demand filtering* and discussed in Chapter 14. The system should assist in editing the input demand or shipment data when it is substantially different from the history of data. All data entry should be edited automatically by the system for reasonableness, and unreasonably large or small data should be highlighted and altered. The system should maintain both actual and the adjusted data for comparison purposes.

FORECASTING MODULE

The system should be able to forecast every item at least 12 months into the future or longer depending on user needs. The ability to forecast groups further into the future is normally an important capability. The system should be capable of modeling demands using different demand periods per year, including 4, 12, 13, or 52.

When forecasting established and new items, the forecasting method should be capable of modeling at least three components of demand—average, seasonal, and trend. Table 17–3 summarizes these and other essential characteristics of forecasting systems.

Group Forecasting Capability

Group forecasting is important in achieving forecast accuracy. Chapter 3 presented group forecasting principles and the hierarchy (i.e., pyramid) that relates group and item forecasts. A good forecasting system will perform bottom-up and top-down forecasting as described there. In addition, the system should make

TABLE 17–3
Significant Characteristics of Item Forecasting Systems

Demand Data Characteristics	Capabilities
Demand	Actual demand, orders, or shipments
Number of historical periods	User specified (3 to 4 seasons)
Number of future forecasts	User specified (typically 12 months)
Number of periods per year	User specified (4, 12, 13, or 52)
Demand adjustments	By user and/or system

Statistical Forecast Generation	Capabilities
Type	Existing items and new items
Derivation	Data derived or management specified
Forecast generation	Uses system forecast, management forecast, or combination
Management interaction	Subjective adjustments and/or management overrides
Statistical model	Trend, seasonal, or single smoothed
Forecast bias	Tracking signals and automatic correction
Smoothing constants or model parameters	Automatic and optimal selection

Seasonality Factors	Capabilities
Derivation	Group, item, or management specified
Updating	Each periodic cycle or when management specified

Input/Output Reports	Capabilities
Maintenance	Auditing of item-level maintenance and group-change maintenance
Management	Managerial and analytical reports
Summarization	User specified

management overrides of group forecasts possible. The item forecasts and demands should be aggregated by groupings as specified by the user. The system should "force" the group forecast (either the system's forecast or management's override forecast) to the item level based on each item's forecast (which itself can be a system or management forecast).

Key characteristics of the combined group and item forecasts are that the detailed item demand should retain some of its essential characteristics while conforming to certain characteristics (e.g., seasonal indexes) specified by the group forecast. This characteristic produces stability at the item level that could not occur if the item had been forecasted independently. Also, an option should exist that causes the total of the item forecasts within a group to equal the group aggregate forecast, or some percentage of it.

Management Attention to Item and Group Forecasts

Using a two-level forecasting structure, management attention can be concentrated on the group level, which is the more significant forecasting activity. Management forecasts are one of the keys for good item forecasts. The system should allocate group forecasts to the item level.

Item forecasts may be produced using group and item data by using different methods. Four possible methods are discussed briefly. Method 1 relates the item forecasts within a group to the group's forecast in order to obtain a more accurate forecast. Each item's forecast is used to develop a percentage of the total of all item forecasts. Then this percentage is used to allocate the group forecast quantities to the item. This procedure was described in Chapter 3.

Method 2 is similar to Method 1, except that a user-input percentage relates the item's forecast to the group's forecast. This method is of particular value for new items that do not have relevant historical data on which to base percentages.

Method 3 utilizes a management forecast strictly as its forecast. This method is of particular relevance to items included primarily for completeness of the group. Also, it may be used for items for which the statistical methods cannot produce a forecast of acceptable accuracy.

Method 4 forecasts items independently without being related to a major group. This is most effective when item forecasts are accurate, for example, when demand patterns are stable and enough history exists to fit the pattern. Typically, it is high-demand items that have these characteristics.

Low-Demand Item Forecasts

When low-demand items are forecast, then the system should be able to stabilize these item forecasts by reference to product-group forecasts and group seasonal indexes. For example, a specific item such as a garment may have a very low demand rate, which makes it difficult to forecast. The system should maintain that item's specific stockkeeping unit while generating forecasts by allocating a share of the higher-level product group forecasts to that item.

Dynamic Model and Parameter Selection

The typical forecasting model will have coefficients or smoothing constants for each of the important patterns in demand— average, trend, and seasonal. The values for these smoothing constants will vary from item to item. A good forecasting system will, when necessary, recalculate the best smoothing constant for use in each item's forecast. These constants should be computed in such a way that the sum of the errors squared is minimized.

Weighted Sums of Squares and Parameter Estimates

The purpose of parameter optimization is to choose a model that is most accurate with recent demands. Therefore, when calculating sums of squares, the more recent errors should be weighted more heavily than distant-past errors. Parameters that minimize the sum of weighted squared errors are better than those that are based only on the sum of squares.

Automatic Computation of Group Seasonal Indexes

To develop more-accurate seasonal forecasts, the system should be able to compute group seasonal indexes and to automatically use them for forecasting some items. When items are assigned to seasonal groups, their data are combined and a group seasonal index is calculated by one of the methods discussed in Chapters 11, 12, and 13. These group seasonal indexes can be used for group forecasting and item forecasting.

Management Overrides

Management overrides of item-level and group-level forecasts should be possible at any level in the hierarchy. It is this capability that enables management to better control the forecasting process. Management may specify a forecast for one or more of the items in the group in addition to specifying the group forecast. Then the system will force the other item forecasts to be consistent with the management group and item forecasts.

Promotional Profiles

Frequently, demands are influenced by promotions. As discussed in Chapter 5, forecasts need to be adjusted to reflect the effect of the planned promotions. Additional data should be captured in the forecasting system to measure the effect of promotions. In addition, an optional file containing promotional profiles should be available.

Trend Dampening

In calculating the 12-month forecast, the trend component is reduced. Trend dampening has been shown to be effective, as discussed in Chapter 12.

MANAGERIAL INTERFACE AND INTERACTION MODULE

Simulations

Computer spreadsheet systems have made what-if analysis a part of many managers' and analysts' problem-solving approaches. A good forecasting system will make experimentation possible using various models as changes are made in the historical data,

> It is a truism that one learns how to read by reading and how to write by writing; this extends to forecasting. A forecasting system will be successful if it supports user interaction and involvement in the forecasting process.

forecast parameters, seasonality, smoothing constants, and so on. If the simulated results are preferred over the existing forecast, then the output of the simulation can be used as input to the next regular forecasting cycle.

The system should enable the user to select one or more forecasted items (or groups) with which to investigate possible changes to item history, model, management forecasts, and so on. These changes are tentative and should not change the database, but should be considered in a "working area" of extracted data. This provides a low-risk simulation environment. Any results of simulations that are found to be favorable to the user can then be directed to update the database.

Management Overrides to Forecasts

An important feature of a forecasting system should be its capability to utilize subjective forecasting techniques. It has been repeatedly proven that a blend of human and machine capabilities can produce results superior to those of a machine alone. However, in some firms, there are so many items that management interaction has to be focused only on the most critical problems. Nonetheless, override capability is essential to a good system.

Usually, subjective adjustments are made to higher-level group forecasts. Utilizing the product-group management forecast, the forecasting system proceeds "downward" to produce the best possible forecasts at the item level.

Management Forecast Accountability

In the early stages of using a forecasting system, management forecasts may be derived independently without reference to the system forecast. This independence changes as personnel gain experience with the system. The system should produce a percent error for both the management forecast and the system forecast. These comparative percent errors encourage management to utilize the system forecast, rather than to compete with it. Eventually, the management forecast should be better than the system forecast because it augments the system-forecast pattern projections with facts unknown to the statistical modeling process. For example, because of marketing management's knowledge of current customer activity, management should be able to better anticipate future demand by recognizing that certain products are going to be priced or promoted more or less competitively. The mathematical portion of the system has no way of detecting this. Consequently, the combined management and system forecast should be better than the system forecast for 75 to 80 percent of the products.

Graphical User Interfaces

Several aspects of user convenience and assistance should be considered. The navigation or movement from one screen to another (for example, from graphical to numeric tabular format) or from one function to another (graphical to model recomputation) should be easy for newer users. These navigation aids might even be facilitated by mouse-driven selections. Standard user interface design formats are being used across many systems today in an attempt to help users become proficient more quickly. Help keys often are provided to give users comments about the choices they have, the meaning of labels, and brief educational paragraphs.

Remarks capabilities should be included in a user interface for notepad purposes of the user. The user interface should allow notes about any information the user feels should be appended to the item. The remarks may apply to one or more forecasted records.

OUTPUT MODULE

We have restricted the meaning of *output* in this module to include only data files and printed reports. The output module takes instructions from the system control module, which, in turn, has been told what to do by other modules such as the managerial interface module. We have excluded screen displays from the meaning of *output*. Screen displays are essential to the managerial interface module discussed above.

Outputs may be routine, recurring files or reports, or may be created only on request. The range of choices may be very broad for reports that provide record selections, format controls, unit-of-measure choices, summary capabilities, and time-period consolidation. The user should be able to narrow the outputs to very clearly defined items by family and/or by exception conditions. An example could be to print a quarterly report (from a monthly system) of all products, by product group, totaled in cases and in dollars, and showing historical demand for the past three years and the forecasts for the next year.

SYSTEM CONTROL AND MAINTENANCE MODULE

Control of the total system by this module assures that data have been correctly and completely processed and that any exceptions have been provided to the user. This module provides tracking of all changes and keeps the user from performing sequences that are incomplete or illogical.

The maintenance of records in the database should be controllable one at a time, and by mass change steps. This offers flexibility to make either very few changes (for example, to change the description of only one item) or to change hundreds or more (i.e., mass) records with one transaction. Mass maintenance will allow the user to specify a logical condition (for example, all items in a single product line at a particular distribution center) and a related change to be made to all matching records (for example, to increase the forecast in selected periods by 25 percent).

Summary

The characteristics and features we discussed above may or may not exist in the system you are developing or purchasing. A specific characteristic may not be important now, but might be later. Often, users are unsure of which characteristics are of greatest importance and which are not. When in doubt, it is useful to re-search this with vendors or companies using similar software. This is why vendor user groups and referrals to other companies us-ing forecasting systems are so important. Answers to these in-quiries can be extremely beneficial to your application and decision.

Having discussed the many characteristics of good forecast-ing systems, we turn our attention to methods for developing these systems.

FORECASTING SYSTEM DEVELOPMENT AND IMPLEMENTATION

> All programmers are optimists. Perhaps this modern sorcery especially attracts those who believe in happy endings and fairy godmothers.
>
> Frederick P. Brooks, Jr., *The Mythical Man-Month*

FORECASTING SYSTEM DEVELOPMENT

The design or selection of a forecasting system should be done in the context of the longer-term goal—to use the system in rou-tine, ongoing control of the business. This goal must remain up-permost to avoid undesirable consequences or failure. The system that offers the highest expected return on investment should be chosen. It has been our experience that the return on investment in these systems is truly extraordinary, with payback times of a fraction of a year after full implementation. A good way to de-termine this is through use of the Du Pont model discussed in Chapter 1. The chosen system should have justifiable cost, lower risk, a proven record, a reasonable project time frame, and charac-teristics comparable to other evaluated systems.

The payback time of many forecasting systems is less than a year.

Highest long-term return on investment, not cost minimization, is the operable decision criterion for choosing a forecasting system.

The Du Pont financial planning model is a good tool for evaluating the financial impact of different forecasting systems.

PAST FAILURES

In the past, many information systems (IS) failed because of the lack of meaningful participation of managers who were functional or applications experts. Managers mistakenly thought that implementation required little of their expertise. Too often, control of the project was given to the IS specialist. Coincident to this was the lack of responsiveness of the IS specialist to the real needs of the system-development process. Both parties should have known better.

Functional (applications) management, not information system specialists, should head the system-development process.

The IS specialist is not normally a functional expert in the system he or she will help develop. Because neither the manager nor the system specialist can develop and implement effective systems alone, a number of integrated system-development approaches have become popular. These approaches are designed to reduce implementation problems associated with:

1. Lack of meaningful functional management involvement with system development.
2. Lack of compatibility between the system and the using organization.
3. Lack of managerial control.
4. Technically invalid (i.e., poorly designed) systems.
5. Ill-managed system-design processes.
6. Overly sophisticated and costly systems.

ORGANIZATIONAL VERSUS TECHNICAL VALIDITY

Those systems that have the highest success rates are those that are technically and organizationally valid. A technically valid system accomplishes its purpose (e.g., forecasting thousands of items accurately). Organizationally valid systems are those that have been designed, implemented, and introduced to an organizational setting that desires, understands, and is capable of using the system. Thus, the system is compatible with the user organization and the problems it must solve. It is consistent with organizational objectives, capabilities, and needs.

System developments fail most often because they are not organizationally valid, even though they may be a technical success.

SYSTEM–DEVELOPMENT PROCESS

Our presentation of the process of system implementation will be brief because there is already a wealth of literature available to developers.[1] The purchaser or designer of forecasting systems should be very familiar with this literature. However, we do have several comments about the process of successful implementation of forecasting systems.

Forecasting system implementers should be familiar with systematic system development processes.

Project Organization

The successful implementation of any information system requires an effective organizational structure. The typical hierarchical relationships in the system development process are:

Top management
Steering committee
Project manager
Project team
Team leaders
Team members

While it is obvious that top management is at the head of any organizational hierarchy, it is not obvious that we have the commitment and involvement of top management. This is essential for the success of the project. A "champion of the cause" in top-management ranks is important to assure success. Next, success requires an effective steering committee and project team. The steering committee is a decision-making committee of upper-level management from several functional areas, including information systems. Its responsibility is to oversee the project team, assure that adequate resources are available, and resolve any conflicting trade-offs facing the project team. Ultimate project ownership should reside in the steering committee.

A top manager should champion the implementation.

A good project organizational structure is important to implementation success.

The project team should be directed by a project manager who has a broad knowledge of the company's product and operating environment. If the system is to achieve its goals, a team of technical and managerial experts must be assembled. Usually, the project team is formed in a matrix organizational structure.

The project manager should have depth and breadth of knowledge regarding the needs for forecasts and system support.

The project team should consist of the project manager (application specialist), managers of each user department, systems analysts, a software engineer, and an organizational specialist. The relationships between the project manager and the project team members must be clearly defined. Team members need to be assigned to specific development efforts.

The following project team organization is typical for implementing forecasting systems.

1. Project Manager. The position of project manager is full time for the duration of the development and implementation process. Typically, this person is a representative of the user community. He or she should be an expert in the applications supported by the forecasting system. This will typically be someone from materials, marketing, operations, or inventory management. This project manager should have continuing overall responsibility for the planning, execution, and control of the system development and implementation process. He or she should also continually monitor key performance measures and milestones of the project, including the cost-benefit relationship.

2. Team Leaders. When the project is very large, team leaders can be assigned to lead the implementation of each of the major software application areas. This is often necessary when a system is being developed in house.

3. Team Members. Team members should include representatives from each department that will utilize the new software, as well as IS members who perform specific project tasks. Typically, user department representatives must devote 25 to 75 percent of their time to this activity, depending upon the impact that the new software will have on their department. The level of effort of data processing personnel will be a function of the specific tasks defined during the project planning activities.

System-Development Steps

There are a number of different approaches to the structured system-development process. These approaches proceed through a series of work steps or stages. Common system steps include:

Step	Explanation
1. Project feasibility study	Determine importance and feasibility of system
2. System definition and work plan	Define what the system will do and how to do it
3. System design	Define subsystem parts and their interfaces
4. System development	Develop subsystems
5. System integration	Put the subsystems together
6. System evaluation	Verify that the system works
7. Installation	Make the system operational
8. Operation and maintenance	Routinely use and maintain

Cooperative Organizations

If the members of an organization do not behave cooperatively, then their lives will probably be, in the words of 17th-century philosopher Thomas Hobbes, "solitary, poor, nasty, brutish and short."

Each of these system-development stages are well documented in other references. To complete these steps, users and systems analysts work together to:

Define system requirements.

Prepare functional specifications.

Prepare system specifications.

Prepare system flowcharts.

Design screens, forms, and reports.

Define database organization.

Define system calculations.

Define graphical user interface.

Design system documentation, on- and off-line.

After system analysis, programmers translate flowcharts into programs, test and debug programs, prepare test examples, maintain programs, and prepare operating instructions.

In summary, we see that a number of important conditions should exist to increase the probability of successful implementation. We, and others, have found that the attributes listed in Table 17–4 are important determinants of successful system implementation. While these are not strictly in the order of impor-

TABLE 17–4
Important Determinants of Successful System Implementation

Top-management education and indoctrination
Top-management support
Prudent use of outside consultants
Middle-management commitment
Non–information system project manager
Significant involvement of users
Data processing accountability to project management
Education and training for all users
Realistic time schedules
Good project management
Good project team
Adequate release time for team members

> As has been said about many functions, system development is too important to be left to the information system specialist.

tance, they are approximately so. However, all of these should exist for the project to be a success.

System developers should understand the relationships between the many important determinants of successful system implementation.

Implementation Strategy

A firm can choose one of two approaches in developing a forecasting system—make or buy. We strongly recommend the purchase of forecasting systems for the typical company because of the ineffective in-house systems we have encountered over the years. Only the large and well-managed firms have the capability to develop in-house systems. And even in those settings, it is often most cost effective to purchase and modify a vendor's system.

Developing a system in house is to be done very cautiously.

Implementation Project Activities

This section provides a brief outline of implementation activities in the development of systems either in house or purchased from vendors. It is important to emphasize the benefits derived from thorough planning prior to the implementation of a new system. Extra effort in early stages of the project yield the most significant benefits. Without the positive direction provided by an effective plan, the implementation of even the best applications software will flounder. It is important, therefore, to emphasize effective planning during the initial implementation phase.

In the early stages of system development, an ounce of prevention is worth a pound of cure.

1. Work Plan. After the organization of the project is complete, the first step is the definition of the work plan. The work

plan focuses on project scope, important milestones, tasks, timing, resource requirements, policies, procedures, and hardware and software issues. The objective is to confirm the project scope, develop an initial work plan, assess internal and external resource requirements, and identify other issues specific to your company's environment.

2. Team Training. Once the work plan and project team are in place, it is essential that individuals be thoroughly trained in the application and use of forecasting systems. Many times, companies will engage outside consultants to assist in this task. Also, it is very important to assure that adequate time is available for team members to do a thorough job.

Education of team members is essential to system success.

Providing adequate time to team members leads to system success.

3. Hardware Evaluation. It may be necessary to evaluate the hardware requirements of the new system. If new hardware is being acquired, it is important to include its acquisition time in the evaluation of requirements. Also, it may be helpful to engage outside assistance in the evaluation. With the rapid development of computer technology, it is difficult to stay current with the latest technology.

Figures 17–2 and 17–3 display two typical implementation plans. Figure 17–2 illustrates the plan of a system that is purchased from an outside vendor. Figure 17–3 shows the plan of a system that is developed in house. While these are brief, they do provide a macroview of the major tasks of forecasting system development. Obviously, these should be modified to agree with your company's situation. The time line at the bottom of each should agree with the time frame and milestones you establish.

Procedural Revision and Organizational Compatibility

The terms in Figure 17–3 are self-explanatory except for *procedural revision*. This term identifies the tasks of defining, designing, and implementing new user procedures in the new system.

FIGURE 17-2
Implementation Plan for Purchased Forecasting System

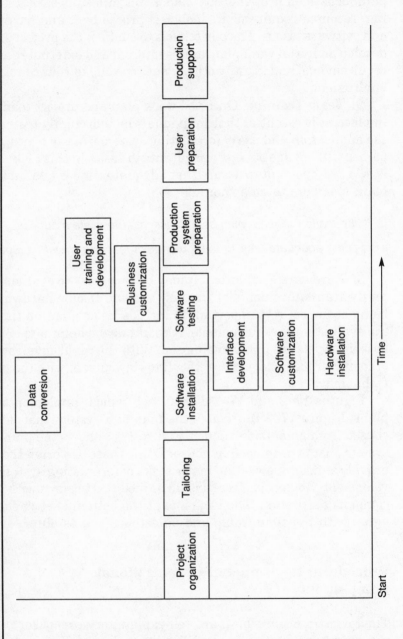

FIGURE 17–3
In-House Forecasting System Implementation Plan

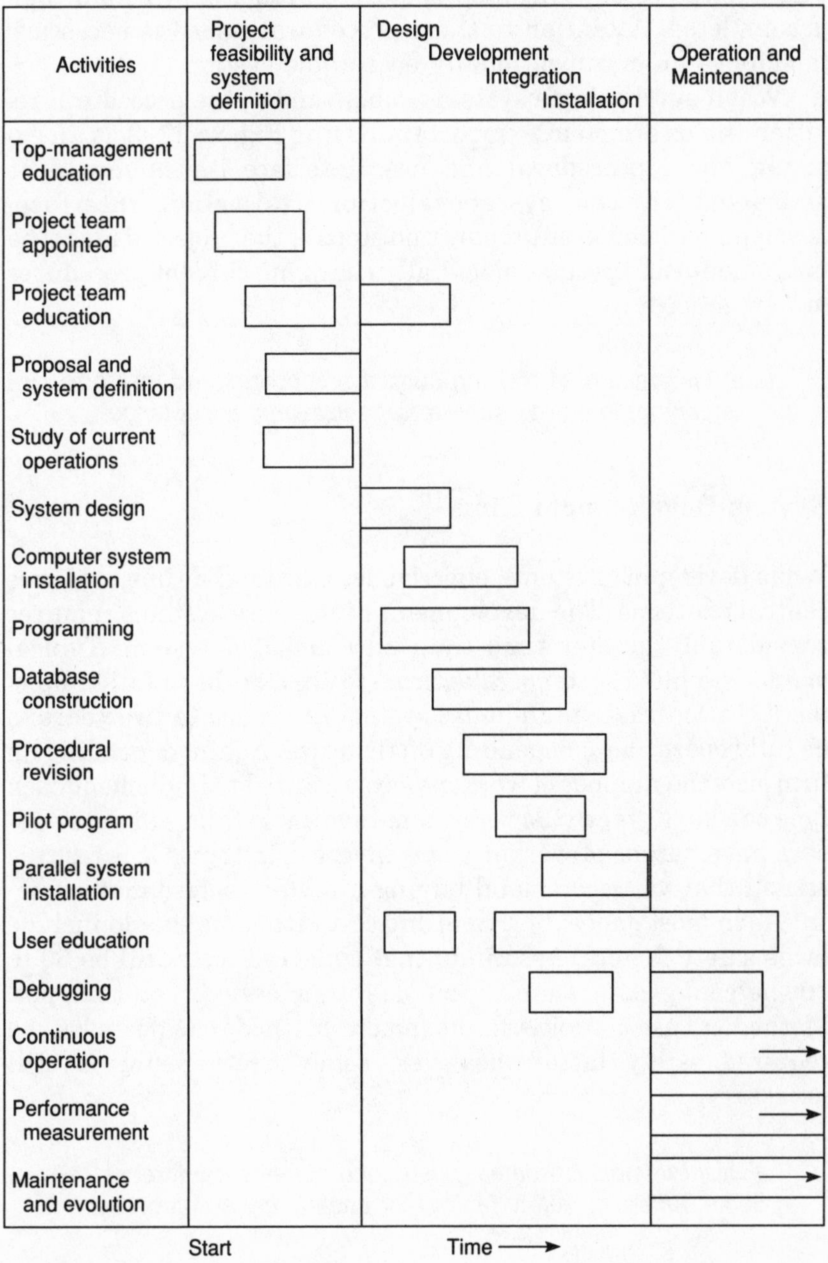

Activities	Project feasibility and system definition	Design Development Integration Installation	Operation and Maintenance
Top-management education	▭		
Project team appointed	▭		
Project team education	▭	▭	
Proposal and system definition	▭		
Study of current operations	▭		
System design		▭	
Computer system installation		▭	
Programming		▭	
Database construction		▭	
Procedural revision		▭	
Pilot program		▭	
Parallel system installation		▭	
User education	▭	▭	
Debugging		▭	▭
Continuous operation			⟶
Performance measurement			⟶
Maintenance and evolution			⟶

Start   Time ⟶

These can include user interface decisions such as actual procedures for order entry, order promising, master scheduling, forecasting, and so on. This step is started after the system design is completed. Attention to these procedural issues is necessary to achieve an organizationally acceptable system.

When purchasing a system from a vendor, the procedural revision issues are no less important. Using Figure 17–2 as an example, these procedural and user interface issues should be addressed in the system-selection, tailoring, interface-development, and user-preparation steps of the project. This is the implementation process of actually changing current procedures to new procedures.

User involvement in revising current procedures and methods
is very important to achieve organizational acceptance.

System-Development Time

When developing systems, effectiveness, costs, and time are three central concerns. The development of in-house systems requires considerably greater time than purchasing a system. Typical vendor-supplied systems take three to six months to fully implement. In contrast, an in-house system takes one to two years to be fully operational depending on firm size. Again, depending on firm size, the number of worker-years required to implement each type can vary greatly. Most systems available from software vendors have dozens of worker-years invested in them. It is for this reason that we recommend buying a system before making it.

As in most endeavors, time and cost estimates should include large safety factors. Assuming that time and costs will be 50 to 100 percent greater than expected is often more correct than not. Methodical use of project management methods can decrease the required safety factor; however, some safety factor is still necessary.

Project completion dates, costs, and benefits are forecasts.
Some buffers or safety factors for uncertainty are necessary.

Why Forecasting Systems Fail

1. Unrealistic expectations that:
   a. It's easy to achieve consensus about "good" forecasts. Good or accurate forecasts are sometimes thought to be without error.
   b. You can achieve a working, implemented system without a good implementation plan.
   c. Either a user or an MIS person can implement a system alone, without a team effort.
   d. Forecasting systems can operate apart from other systems or in an organizational vacuum.
2. The project team changes—new faces, new ideas—or team dissension. These lead to delays at best, and failure at worst.
3. Change in project leadership or sponsor.
4. Lack of training or loss of trained people.
5. a. Inadequate documentation of the system.
   b. Inadequate user-training materials to assist during a turnover period.
   c. Disinterest by management, especially new management of the using department, during a period of turnover.
6. Substitution of systems because of new management. New management styles may lead to simpler approaches, such as spreadsheets, with no objective basis for the choice of methods. Often the question of quality or accuracy of the forecasts is not put to an unbiased test because there is little understanding of how to do this; so, the simpler methods are chosen, even though they may be less accurate.
7. The system design may be inflexible to changing business needs. As the firm acquires new product lines or expands its scope, the system must be able to adapt.

SUMMARY

This chapter provided guidelines for project leaders and forecast users who must evaluate and select forecasting systems. The checklist format is organized by system module to identify desired and actual system characteristics. When there is a difference between actual and desired, then the importance and capability scales can be used to decide which system should be selected. In addition, this checklist is useful in organizing the discussions between users, systems personnel, and vendors. Checklists such as those presented in this chapter are important evaluation tools for selecting the correct system characteristics and the means to achieve those characteristics.

The second section of the chapter briefly discusses system development and implementation relevant to in-house or vendor-developed forecasting systems. Significant support is necessary from internal and external vendors during the system development and implementation process. Our experiences have shown a dangerous tendency on the part of companies to develop their own systems based only on perceived cost savings. It is not uncommon for companies to fail miserably in developing operational forecasting systems. It is so common that we most often recommend vendor-developed systems.

When in-house development takes place, it is important to assure that the correct expertise exists. When it does not exist, it must be acquired through training, new employees, or consultants. To ensure success, project team members should receive significant release time from other duties for the duration of the project.

Finally, it is important to emphasize the potential benefits of successful forecasting systems. The ability of all functional areas to perform their responsibilities more effectively is greatly enhanced through improved forecasting systems. Marketing has more-relevant data with which to plan, execute, and control all phases of providing the right product, at the right location, at the right time. Finance has the information it needs to plan, execute, and control financial plans and budgets. General management has the information with which to make important trade-offs among the many internal and external opportunities it faces. Finally, production and operations have the information with which to better plan, execute, and control production, inventory, quality, and cost. There is a synergism that occurs when the forecasting system provides integrated and coordinated information for all functions of the business. This synergism makes a forecasting system one of the most profitable investments facing an organization.

The next three chapters discuss recent developments that have influenced—and will continue to greatly influence—future forecasting systems.

REFERENCE

1. Rob Thomsett, *People Project Management* (New York: Yourdon Press, 1980); David King, *Current Practices in Software Development* (New York: Yourdon Press, 1984); Steve Eckols, *How to Design and Develop Business Systems* (Fresno, Calif.: Mike Murach & Associates, 1983); Tom DeMarco, *Controlling Software Projects* (New York: Yourdon Press, 1982); William Roetzheim, *Structured Computer Project Management* (Englewood Cliffs, N.J.: Prentice-Hall, 1988); and James Martin and Carma McClure, *Structured Techniques, The Basis for Case,* rev. ed. (Englewood Cliffs, N.J.: Prentice-Hall, 1988).

THE FUTURE OF
FORECASTING
SYSTEMS

Part 6 completes this book. Several important trends that will influence the future of forecasting systems are presented in this section.

Chapter 18 introduces expert systems (ES) and artificial intelligence (AI) in forecasting. The use of ES and AI will result in significant changes to the design and effectiveness of forecasting systems. Discussed in this chapter are several exciting ES/AI developments that are likely to cause significant changes and improvements in operational forecasting systems.

Chapter 19 discusses the current and future impacts of electronic data interchange (EDI) on forecasting systems. As we show, EDI has already altered the way in which data can be collected for planning and control purposes. However, current applications of EDI have only just started to influence and improve demand data collection and planning. This chapter discusses several important changes that will take place through the use of EDI. It answers the question of whether EDI will make short-term forecasting obsolete. It presents important principles and recommendations for using EDI data in forecasting.

Chapter 20 has two related sections. First, it speculates on the future of forecasting systems, defining the consequences of current and future developments in forecasting. The second section discusses sources of articles, research, and case studies about forecasting systems. These sources will provide information about the future developments that will affect your future forecasting system. Only by having access to state-of-the-art forecasting literature will you have a state-of-the-art forecasting system.

CHAPTER 18

FORECASTING EXPERT SYSTEMS AND ARTIFICIAL INTELLIGENCE

> Artificial intelligence is the study of how to make computers
> do things at which, at the moment, people are better.
>
> Elaine Rich, *Artificial Intelligence*

The forecasting systems discussed in this book are one of the most successful applications of conventional artificial intelligence (AI) programming procedures. Recent AI and expert system developments provide an extraordinary opportunity to improve the effectiveness of all modules of forecasting systems. The purpose of this chapter is to define artificial intelligence and expert systems (ESs), operational forecasting system (OFS) applications of AI/ES, and the tremendous potential of AI/ES in OFSs. Practical implications of expert systems for OFS design and development are stressed.

The most significant potential for improved forecasting system performance has been and will continue to be through increasing forecasting system intelligence, not through increasing forecasting model complexity or sophistication. Research into and development of improved forecasting methods continue, and some significant improvements in accuracy and effectiveness will occur as a result of these efforts; however, the greatest immediate need and potential benefits will be achieved through use of OFSs that use better artificial intelligence and expert systems.

> *The greatest potential for improving forecasting system performance is through more system intelligence.*

FORECAST ACCURACY AND MODEL COMPLEXITY

Chapter 14 discussed forecasting accuracy for most methods used in operational forecasting systems. These results were based on a study completed by Makridakis, et al.,[1] and showed that there was very little difference between the performance of the seasonally adjusted methods. Makridakis et al. reach these final conclusions.

> If the forecasting user can discriminate in his choice of methods depending upon the type of data (yearly, quarterly, monthly), the type of series (macro, micro, etc.) and the time horizon of forecasting, then he or she could do considerably better than using a single method across all situations—assuming, of course, that the results of the present study can be generalized. . . . Furthermore, combining the forecasts of a few methods improves overall fore-

casting accuracy over and above that of the individual forecasting method used in the combining. . . . Even though further research will be necessary to provide us with more specific reasons as to why this is happening, *a hypothesis may be advanced at this point stating that statistically sophisticated methods do not do better than simple methods (such as deseasonalized exponential smoothing) when there is considerable randomness in the data. . . . Finally, it seems that seasonal patterns can be predicted equally well by both simple and statistically sophisticated methods.*[2]

There are several important implications of these conclusions, and we believe two of the more important are the potential benefits and the necessity for improved expert-system support. That is, OFSs with simple AI and ES will be much more efficient and effective than systems that use more-complex and more-sophisticated forecasting models without expert assistance. Simple AI/ES–based forecasting systems will outperform more-sophisticated forecasting methods in many dimensions, including forecast accuracy, computational speed, user understanding, and cost effectiveness. This assertion is based upon our experiences and the results of the M-competition. The concepts, applications, and advantages of AI/ES in OFSs are developed below.

ARTIFICIAL INTELLIGENCE/EXPERT SYSTEMS

The field of artificial intelligence is exciting and is of particular importance to forecasting systems. *Artificial intelligence* is the capability of a computer to perform functions usually completed with human intelligence, such as reasoning, learning, and self-improvement. The general area of AI is broad, including the study of pattern recognition, robotics, process control methods, machine learning, expert systems, and cognitive learning.[3] To better understand AI in the context of forecasting systems, it is important to distinguish between two general areas and objectives of AI computer programs—the conventional program systems (CPS) approach and the expert-systems approach.

Conventional Program Systems versus Expert Systems

In the conventional program systems (CPS) approach, "the researcher wants to create a system that is able to deal with difficult intellectual tasks, regardless of whether the methods and techniques used are similar or identical to those used by humans. There is a job to accomplish inexpensively, efficiently, and reliably—that is all that matters."[4] The CPS is exemplified by the many conventional forecasting systems available from software houses such as D&B (formerly MSA), IBM, American Software, STSC, and Materials Management Systems.

In contrast, the ES approach "has the basic objective of trying to gain an understanding of the inside mechanisms of a real life system and to explain and predict its behavior. We can put in this category, for example, those projects that simulate human problem solving, decision making, or learning behavior by building models of neural networks."[5] The ES approach is the cutting edge of forecasting system development, and there have been a number of personal-computer-based forecasting packages that are being marketed as forecasting expert systems. However, in most cases, these systems are not expert systems, but instead are conventional program systems that have some expert system features. In fact, most ES programs fall some place between the two extremes of CPS and ES.

The difference between ES and CPS lies in ES's emphasis on symbol manipulation, whereas non-ES programming relies primarily on number crunching and, to a lesser extent, on logical relationships. ES programs solve problems by searching for patterns or logical relationships, not through simple algorithmic computations. ESs attempt to allow computers to act and react more like humans.

The major characteristics of an expert system are:

1. The ability to perform cognitive tasks at a level of an expert.
2. The representation of expert knowledge or recommendations in a domain-specific area.
3. The inclusion of explanations of why a decision or action is recommended.

4. Ways of handling uncertainty.
5. Systems directed to solving problems involving logical and symbolic representations as opposed to number crunching.[6]

Purpose of an Expert System

Another important distinction between an ES and a CPS is in the purpose of the systems. An ES is designed to:

1. Provide expert advice to nonexperts as they solve problems.
2. Assist experts as they solve problems.
3. Act as a teaching tool for the nonexpert.

Each of these purposes is relevant to operational forecasting systems.

Expert systems are best for problems that require linking large amounts of symbolic, unreliable, and uncertain inputs with detailed knowledge of the subject in the domain. Unlike ES, conventional programs do not normally process qualitative data. Also, expert systems are particularly effective when the expert's knowledge is largely heuristic, that is, based on rules of thumb developed over time under conditions of uncertainty. Therefore, an expert system must have corrections for uncertainty, and explanations must be built into the system so that the person using the system can understand how the conclusion has been derived.

Expert systems offer great benefits in
forecasting by processing qualitative information.

Parts of an Expert System

As shown in Figure 18–1, the components of an expert system consist of:

1. A user interface that supports conversation with the system; this is commonly called a *dialog structure*.
2. An inference engine that controls the decision process using logical search and "thought" processes.

FIGURE 18–1
Expert-System Modules

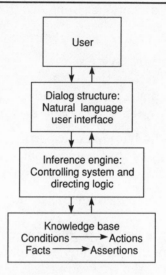

3. A knowledge base that contains the knowledge of the expert.

An ES combines the body of information that is agreed upon by experts in a field (i.e., the knowledge base) with heuristic solving techniques (i.e., the inference engine). The ES functions like a human expert—consulting others, asking questions, explaining reasoning when asked, and justifying conclusions. It should be able to function with incomplete data and without answers to questions, just as human consultants operate. To date, expert systems have only a limited, well-defined set of tasks through which they can reason. The expert system cannot as yet generate its own axioms or general theories; it cannot learn independently. But, human users can learn and adapt the ES program, adding new axioms and theories as that knowledge becomes available. Expert systems are designed to modify their queries as more information becomes known, allow users to move on to new goals, keep traces of solution paths for review, record responses given by users, and allow the user to record explanations and justifications for future reference.

Advantages of Expert Systems

An expert system has advantages over the human expert in terms of instant availability, consistency, and comprehensiveness of knowledge. Unlike the human expert, the ES never forgets to check every possibility and never forgets an axiom. Additionally, there are four other significant advantages provided by expert systems:

1. They are able to process qualitative information.
2. They process incomplete and/or uncertain information.
3. They provide permanent, documented, and duplicatable knowledge.
4. They are easy to maintain and modify.

In addition, expert systems may be applied to problems that occur infrequently and require a high level of expertise to solve or to frequently occurring problems at numerous sites dispersed throughout an organization.[7]

Disadvantages of Expert Systems

There are several disadvantages to ES, including:

1. The current scarcity of skilled people to create ES. This includes those who are, or would be, knowledge engineers, as well as those who provide the system support from a data processing perspective.

2. The lack of standardization of development tools and operating-system software, which makes it difficult to move ESs from one system or computer platform to another.

3. The risk associated with any body of knowledge. Will the prospective users accept the authority of the knowledge base?

4. The unrealistic expectations of those who expect the knowledge base of the ES to be more comprehensive than it is.

5. The possibility of contradictions or inconsistencies in the knowledge base if it has been provided by more than one "expert"; that is, finding the expert is a task with some risk in itself.

POTENTIAL EXPERT–SYSTEM APPLICATIONS IN FORECASTING

What ESs offer to users and their managers is the additional advice and problem-solving assistance of the people who have built the expert system. In turn, by proper use of the expert advice, the forecast calculations and related techniques are used to their greatest advantage to produce better forecasts and perhaps to achieve those forecasting results more efficiently. The ES can be thought of as a "cap" on the fundamental computational techniques. This is rather like having an assistant to the forecast analyst or primary user who is most familiar with the appropriate "knobs and levers" to use for particular forecast situations. When we look at the types of problems or questions that arise during implementation of a forecasting system, some of them will lend themselves to an ES analysis.

An ES should provide user-friendly interfaces to the forecast system.

Table 18–1 illustrates the parts of an OFS for purposes of discussion here. All parts of the system denote potential areas in which ESs offer solutions to ill-defined problems. We discuss three of the six modules here as if they are separate expert systems while in fact they are not. However, they can be developed independently if necessary. The three modules discussed here are the demand data, forecasting, and system control and maintenance modules. Each of these is discussed in detail below. Also, the other modules of Table 18–1 are potentially rich areas for expert systems applications.

A good ES should support all the functions of a good forecasting system.

Most commercially marketed forecasting expert systems are expert at selecting forecasting models, not expert in forecasting system support.

Demand Data Expert System

Forecasting systems can produce forecasts of future quantities using several different methods. Some methods are more appropriate to particular business situations or to the type of item that

TABLE 18-1
The Modules and Database of a Forecasting System

I. Demand Data Module
    Input of local and remote demand data
    Demand capturing
    Logical filtering (demand versus supply or shipments)
    Special-event filtering (promotions, price changes, product introductions)
    Initial outlier detection, adjustment, classification

II. Forecasting Module
    System forecast selection
    Outlier detection, adjustment, classification
    Reasonableness test
    Final forecast
    Error measures
    Tracking-signal control

III. Managerial Interface and Interaction Module
    Graphical user interface
    Screen displays
    Management forecasts
    User help
    Management feedback
    User notepad
    Expert advisory menu

IV. Output Module
    File generation
    Routine reports
    Ad hoc reports
    Exception reports

V. System Control and Maintenance Module
    Module and navigation control
    Simulation control
    Database updating and maintenance
    Detection of system malfunctions and bugs

VI. Database
    Actual demand history
    Adjusted demand history
    Promotional profiles
    Seasonal profiles
    Item and group relationships structure
    Performance measures
    Item relationships
    Item descriptions
    Demand forecasts

is being forecasted. Because the user of the forecasting system is (or should be) aware of the firm's business situation, the user should be able to guide the forecasting process in the selection of methods and data.

Logical filtering of data used in the forecasting system can improve the quality of the forecast and the resulting decisions. For example, shipments data may be distorted by supply restrictions. The ES can inquire and advise the user to modify the data to more closely reflect true demand.

As another example, the data may be distorted by an unusual mix of order processing transactions—perhaps an unusually high percentage of order cancellations or returns. A well-designed ES, behaving like a well-informed manager, will discover these conditions and suggest courses of action to modify the historical data.

An ES should provide initial outlier and special-event detection to the user.

Planned-event filtering manages the historical data adjustments associated with price changes, promotions, product introductions, product changes, and so on. These events are well identified ahead of time and may be organized in a database for analysis and recall, and thus can be treated more thoroughly than the unusual events of logical filtering. ESs offer convenient methods for programming the logical relationships that develop through experience in working with planned or special events. Experienced product managers may pass on to others, or simply organize for their own complete recall, the likely effects of each kind of promotion, or their distilled opinion regarding price increases. What percent demand increase occurred, for example, when a 3 percent price increase was announced one month ahead of the effective date? How did the effect vary among the product lines? Was there a difference in this market response when the inflation rate was twice as high?

An ES should assist in promotional and
deal analysis, particularly the deal profile.

The validation of data is an integral part of data entry. Validation should identify special events, unusual transactions, and poor data quality prior to model selection and forecasting.

While we are seeing an increase in the use of video training materials in support of users, the more specific questions of users are better handled by interactive use of the computer as the user performs system tasks. As a forecasting task progresses, the ES can conduct a dialog in which the user provides facts about the business situation and leads the user to draw conclusions and to take actions that are likely to improve the forecast accuracy.

An ES should assist the user in drawing conclusions during data validation.

A question-answer dialog that illustrates data validation could proceed as follows:

Q. Which of the following topics is selected? Move the arrow and hit the enter key:
  System diagnostics
  → Demand data characteristics
  Forecast model selection
  Forecast accuracy
  Graphics
  Input preparation

Q. Is the item believed to be seasonal?
  → Yes   No

Q. How much demand history is being used?
  Less than one year
  → One to two years
  Two to three years
  More than three years

Q. Is the seasonality caused by
  → Natural market demand conditions
  Managed events, promotions, and so on.

Q. Is the market changing?
  Yes   →No

Q. What is the annual volume of this item?
  Less than 100
  → 100 to 1,000
  Over 1,000

Q. Are other items sold with the same seasonality?
  → Yes   No

Q. Do any of these other items have greater volume?
  → Yes   No

Q. Would there be at least two years of history?
  → Yes   No

Q. Is that history distorted by either managed events or market changes?
→ Yes No

Q. Are these distortions identified well enough to be replaced by better history?
→ Yes No

Conclusion: Demand history should be adjusted on the selected larger-volume items to form a basis for seasonality estimates. This should be done before using the group seasonality method to assign the seasonality to the initial item.

Q. Do you want help with the procedure to adjust demand history?
→ Yes No

At this point in the dialog, the expert system has been asked to link to the input preparation portion of its knowledge base, a section that deals with screen inputs available to the user. The expert system will then link to the procedure for adjusting demand history. Subsequently, the appropriate items will be selected to make the adjustment to history to compute the group seasonality factors and then assign those group seasonality factors to the initial item.

In this example, the 12 questions took the user through many branches in a tree structure that could have had hundreds of different outcomes depending on the choices made during the dialog. In reality, some of the branches could lead to the same conclusions, but this is not a problem to the expert system or to the user. What has been done is to take advantage of a very efficient way to organize knowledge and to present it in a friendly and useful way to people who want to solve problems.

Model Selection and Forecasting Expert System

Because OFSs typically involve the processing of thousands of forecasts, routine forecasting will be done as in the past using background conventional program systems. However, when exceptions occur, the expert system can bring problems to the foreground so that they can very effectively and efficiently be resolved by a forecaster. Common problems requiring expert advice include initial selection of a forecasting model, resolution of outlier problems during the fitting/model-selection process, and checks for the reasonableness of a final forecast. One of the most important advantages of the ES is that novice and pro alike can be guided toward resolution of the problem.

*Under exceptional situations, an ES should guide
a human through the model-selection process.*

The initial selection of a forecasting model was illustrated earlier where the ES guided the analyst to select the use of group seasonality factors. There are many other possible considerations in the model-selection process that the ES can use to guide analysts. These considerations include several qualitative inputs such as cost (e.g., high, medium, or low), importance of or desire for accuracy (e.g., high, medium, or low), trends (e.g., likely or not likely), seasonality, relationship to other products, and the manner in which promotions might be included in the model. Makridakis et al.[8] and Kwong and Cheng[9] contain further discussions of model-selection criteria and their use in ESs. This is a very effective, routine use of a forecasting ES when the cost trade-offs justify analyst-ES interactions.

When outliers or exceptions are detected, an ES should be used to guide the analyst in identifying the causes of outliers and the means of correcting them. The ES can suggest possible explanations, ask questions, provide alternative solutions, and offer justifications. Outlier adjustments include ways to partition the outlier into classifications such as promotional, pricing, and unexplainable occurrences. Not only are the classifications important, but the numerical division of the outlier between normal demand and outlier effects is critical for forecast accuracy.

When unusually large or small forecasts are detected, the ES can guide the analyst in resolving the problem. For example, it is very common for CPS to include a reasonableness-of-the-forecast test in the software. For example, if the projected demand using a model for a product yielded an effective annual rate of growth of 200 percent, this might trip an exception report and an ES session. Such trip points can be set based on objective and subjective input.

System Control and Maintenance Expert System

As the actual demand for a product is realized, important measures of forecast validity and accuracy will be calculated and updated; these include several error statistics and tracking signals. At this time, the system may detect out-of-control situations and opportunities to improve forecasting performance. Tasks such as explaining, adjusting, and classifying outliers are part of both this ES and the system described in Table 18–1 above. In this case, the ES addresses an outlier as a real-time occurrence, not as a historical phenomenon. By having the ES generate a timely exception report, the analyst can devote the appropriate time and effort to resolving the problem through the guidance of the ES. Error statistics can be calculated in real time, and exceptions can trigger the ES to start an inquiry. Heuristic rules can be incorporated into the system and might even be tailored to the specific product or group of products.

An expert system should generate timely
exception reports for timely problem resolution.

There are several types of out-of-control situations that are detectable through the use of tracking signals. Again, these measures can be assessed each time an actual demand is realized either in interactive or batch-processing data input. The ES can decide which should be brought to the attention of management and which should not.

At times, there may be questions as to whether the software is processing the data according to its design specifications. These are the questions related to diagnosis of bugs or suspected bugs in the software. Diagnostic expert systems are one of the more popular chosen by first-time developers, perhaps because diagnostic services (problem solving) are a more traditional area in which special help is expected by customers.

Diagnostic expertise is usually supplied most effectively by the designer of the forecasting system. For larger, well-established forecasting packages, there may be a base of experienced users who share information regarding software problems. Some of those problems will be diagnosed by using the documentation, that is, deciding that the system does not do what the documentation says it is supposed to do. Some questions may revolve around uncertainties in the intended functionality when the documentation is unclear. Generally speaking, the diagnostic aids of an expert system will allow a user to check out the integrity of the data manipulation, calculations, and logic of the forecasting system.

An ES should assist in program malfunction
detection and problem resolution.

The evaluation of hardware and information systems is easier to perform with an expert system providing guidance in fault diagnosis. The expert system prompts the user for information concerning the symptoms of a particular malfunction. Using this information and the expert knowledge base, the expert system goes through the inference process to quickly provide the user with a diagnosis upon which corrective action can be taken. This enables the user to concentrate more effort on correcting the problem instead of spending hours, and maybe even days, trying to figure out what the problem is.

The diagnostic conclusions can fall into categories such as:

1. The system is performing as designed.
2. The system needs a fix in one or more particular modules.
3. No conclusion was reached; the inputs should be repeated for another item or forecast entity.

These three conclusions leave open the possibility of "design deficiency," which is what could be of concern to some users. When a user sees an unexpected output from the system, that in itself can be a problem. However, good documentation, good training aids, and a diagnostic expert system can guide the user to a better understanding of the design and intended capabilities of the system. The user needs to be confident that the system is doing what it is supposed to do with the data it is given.

EXPERT–SYSTEM DEVELOPMENT TOOLS

Much of the development of ES is similar to other software applications. The development process includes:

1. Problem identification and initial system specifications.
2. System design.
3. System development.
4. Implementation and maintenance.

We discuss only that which most distinguishes ES from other applications by computers—the system-development process. The choice of computer platform and language may not be as simple as in other software applications. In regards to the choice of language, there are at least three different types of system-development tools that can be used in the AI/ES system-development process. These are languages such as LISP and PROLOG, ES shells, and, finally, software tool kits.

AI languages such as LISP and PROLOG give greatest flexibility in the design of ESs. However, they are the most demanding languages in terms of the need for experienced programmers and software development.

ES development tools such as shells and tool kits are programs that are designed to make ES development more rapid and effective. They assist by making prototyping, knowledge engineering, and the structuring of the inference engine logic easier. The first step in AI/ES development, prototyping, is normally the hardest. It provides the knowledge engineer and the domain engineer a framework for further system development. Some products are designed to run only on a mainframe, minicomputer, microcomputer, or LISP machine. A LISP machine is typically a large, single-user machine with high-speed processors (typically faster than 33 Megahertz), large random access memory (approximately 30 megabytes), and large disk-drive storage (approximately 300 megabytes). Until recently, these machines were very costly, but prices continue to decline and these machines can now be purchased for several thousand dollars.

A useful compromise in regards to the cost-time and flexibility trade-off when using AI languages such as LISP or PROLOG is expert-system shells. These are very easily learned and have capabilities that reduce the required time to prototype a system. They typically have much less design flexibility and can make it difficult to use conventional software interfaces or subroutines. While constructing an ES using development tools is much simpler than use of LISP or PROLOG, the process is still complex enough to require both an applications expert (called a domain expert) and a software development expert (also called a knowledge expert).

A third approach to ES development involves the use of a number of development tool kits listed below. These tool kits require more-knowledgeable personnel and in some cases more-sophisticated computer hardware, including LISP machines. Shells and tool kits are priced from several hundred dollars to $50,000. The following list is very representative of those available, but it is not exhaustive. Harmon et al.[10] provides an excellent review of the available software development tools.

ART™ (Automated Reasoning Tool™) is a product of Inferences Corporation of Los Angeles. It is a full-scale commercial package for development of ESs in manufacturing planning, scheduling, and financial planning. It is available for LISP machines.

Expert Ease™ is available from Human Edge Software (HES) of Palo Alto, California. It is an ES development tool designed for use in decision support running on IBM-compatible computers. It is designed to be used by nonprogrammers.

EXSYS™ is a very low cost expert-system shell that works very well on IBM PCs. It is available from EXSYS of Albuquerque, New Mexico. It is very easy to use and may be the best starter system.

KEE™ (Knowledge Engineering Environment™) is available from Intellicorp, Menlo, California. It is a very sophisticated expert-system tool that is designed for LISP machines.

M.1™ is designed to run on personal computers such as the IBM compatibles. It is available from Teknowledge of Palo Alto, California.

Personal Consultant™ is a powerful ES developed by Texas Instruments and is designed to run on IBM-compatible PCs.

S.1™ is a product like M.1 but runs on LISP machines. It is also available from Teknowledge of Palo Alto, California.

The development of sophisticated ES forecasting systems is in its infancy. There are few actual systems that embody the attributes of forecasting systems developed in this book and highlighted in Chapter 17. Instead, there are several integrated systems under development. This will be an exciting area to watch and help develop. We discuss the future of AI/ES further in Chapter 20.

SUMMARY

Conventional programming solutions to forecasting system problems have existed for several decades and will continue to be very important in providing routine operational forecasts. The results of several forecasting studies have confirmed that increased forecast-model sophistication may not result in improved accuracy with the typical item data. Consequently, a more fruitful avenue for system improvement is the development of better AI and ES programs. However, the benefits from the use of AI/expert systems are just now being realized in some applications. This chapter has presented ES and CPS applications that can benefit from increased artificial intelligence in their implementations. These ES applications are currently under development at several firms and institutions. The probability of realizing very significant improvements in forecasting systems through ES is very high; these are the methods with greatest immediate and long-term potential benefit.

REFERENCES

1. S. Makridakis, A. Andersen, R. Carbone, R. Fildes, M. Hibon, R. Lewandowski, J. Newton, E. Parzen, and R. Winkler, "The Accuracy of Extrapolation (Time Series) Methods: Results of a Forecasting Competition," *Journal of Forecasting* 1, 1982, pp. 111–53.
2. Ibid.
3. R. I. Levine, D. E. Drang, and B. Edelson, *A Comprehensive Guide to AI and Expert Systems* (New York: McGraw-Hill, 1986); and A. Ralston and E. D. Reilly, Jr., eds. *Encyclopedia of Computer Science and Engineering*, 2nd ed. (New York: Van Nostrand Reinhold, 1983).
4. Ralston and Reilly, *Encyclopedia of Computer Science and Engineering*.
5. Ibid.
6. J. Liebowitz, *Introduction to Expert Systems* (Santa Cruz: Mitchell Publishing, 1988); and Kern K. Kwong and Donald Cheng, "A Prototype Microcomputer Forecasting Expert System," *The Journal of Business Forecasting*, Spring 1988, pp. 21–26.
7. Ralston and Reilly, *Encyclopedia of Computer Science and Engineering*.

8. Makridakis et al., "The Accuracy of Extrapolation (Time Series) Methods."

9. Kwong and Cheng, "Prototype Microcomputer Forecasting Expert System."

10. P. Harmon, R. Maus, and W. Morrissey, *Expert Systems: Tools and Applications* (New York: John Wiley & Sons, 1988).

CHAPTER 19

FORECASTING AND ELECTRONIC DATA INTERCHANGE

Where is the knowledge we have lost in information?
T. S. Elliot, 1888–1965

Data transmission between businesses has taken several forms in the past, evolving in terms of speed, format, medium, and usability. This evolution has spawned the growing field of electronic data interchange (EDI). EDI is often defined as the exchange of data from computer to computer. It is that, but even more. EDI is the exchange of data between computer applications in standard transaction formats that application programs in different computers and companies can process without reentry. What makes EDI important to business partners today is that data are immediately available for processing, having been standardized by national and international organizations. Some of the organizations that are important in the setting of standards are included in the discussion of the history of EDI in Appendix 19–B.

EDI provides valuable information immediately.

The growing use of EDI has raised some questions for specialists in the field of demand forecasting. Is it possible that by sharing demand data from point-of-sale devices with suppliers, retailers can eliminate the need to forecast their demand? Is it possible that the suppliers to those retailers can do away with their demand forecasting systems? And what about the next echelon in the supply chain—suppliers to suppliers—can they benefit in the same way by getting POS data from the retailers? We provide answers to these several questions in this chapter.

EDI USES

Because EDI provides data in standardized formats, new business partnerships can be established to share data more quickly without the need for manual intervention. Several data networks offer the service of EDI data transmission between network subscribers. These third-party networks hold data, if necessary, for various subscribers who sign on and retrieve it when needed. Some partners, however, work in direct communication without using an EDI third-party network, depending on the economics of their situation and the need for expandability (that is, to include additional partnerships).

EDI makes new business partnerships possible.

Numerous standard formats of EDI transactions have been defined by standards bodies; these standards are called *transaction sets*. They differ, of course, by type of data and the arrangement into sets of transactions that serve particular needs of the members. Table 19A–1 in Appendix 19–A presents several examples of the transaction sets and their similarities and differences. For purposes of this chapter, it is enough to know that data can be formatted into "transactions" that give business partners information about demand, forecasts of demand, inventories, orders, and so on.

The business needs and uses of EDI are evolving, and the transaction sets, accordingly, also are evolving. As major application requirements are identified and accepted by the standardization committees, the published standard transaction sets will be expanded. While the uses of EDI are being improved and expanded, the most frequent uses are as follows:

1. Placement of purchase orders.
2. Acknowledgement of customer orders.
3. Invoicing.
4. Bills of lading.
5. Freight bills.
6. Shipping notices.
7. Banking system fund transfers.
8. Inventory and demand data transfers.

For purposes of forecasting, we focus on the eighth use, the growing use of EDI to pass demand and inventory data between suppliers and customers in a supply chain.

EDI BENEFITS

Because EDI information shortens the response time in order processing, the reduced order cycle time enables alert buyers/customers to reduce inventory and carrying costs and to increase customer service. Both the retailer and supplier can benefit in terms of reduced document preparation and processing costs. The retailer benefits through shorter leadtimes and fewer order processing errors. As a result:

Shelf stock matches demand more closely.

Customers find what they want more often.

Sales are boosted.

Fewer markdowns are needed.

Stock turns increase.

From the supplier's perspective, EDI benefits may be:

Reduced order processing and invoicing costs.

An assured business relationship with major customers.

Better information about market trends.

Increased sales volume.

A major benefit of EDI is quick response to customer needs.

However, whether these benefits occur for the supplier may depend on the supplier's readiness and commitment to the new technology.

> Common wisdom suggests that implementing a "new" technology such as EDI can provide a competitive advantage. However, because many companies are coerced to implement EDI by their customers, they may be reluctant to make the significant financial or technical commitment to the technology necessary to give them a competitive edge. As a result, they derive little benefit from it, and may even lose money on their EDI project.[1]

A full commitment to EDI is necessary to gain a competitive edge.

Also, it is possible, as we explore partnership arrangements, that a retailer's time spent placing orders can be reduced significantly by enabling the supplier to have more-current and more-accurate market demand data via EDI from POS devices. Under a full-service arrangement, the supplier can provide routine stock replenishments without requiring time from store management.

Some of these EDI situations have been put into practice in recent years between apparel retailers, their apparel-manufacturing suppliers, and the next echelon as well—the textile manufacturers. The results are encouraging because of the reductions in the leadtimes required to replenish retail inventories. The unique phrase *quick response* was coined to refer to this tight linkage of data from the apparel retailers to their suppliers, although technologies other than EDI are also involved, for example, bar coding.

EDI is essential to quick response retail replenishments.

Quick Response Examples

The automatic direct replenishment of store inventories by manufacturers and other vendors is a growing and increasingly important function of business. Hanes Hosiery, for example, as a partner with Mercantile Stores Company, Inc., takes weekly POS sales data from the stores to determine the mix and quantity of hosiery to send to each store. The merchandise is shipped ready for the sales racks. The results have been a 35 percent increase in hosiery sales for Mercantile and a corresponding volume increase for Hanes.

The Dillard Department Stores have taken a different, but equally effective, approach to quick response relationships with their vendors of standard items like socks and T-shirts. The weekly POS data are used by Dillard to create a purchase order that is transmitted via EDI to the vendors over a value-added network. The vendors are expected to have the stock available, packed, and marked by store in three days. The goods are then sent to the appropriate Dillard regional distribution center for transfer to the stores. The order cycle time is about two weeks, but Ray Heflin, director of quick response for Dillard, would hope to see this reduced to about one week in the future.

The results at Dillard are very impressive: A 50 percent increase in sales, a 40 percent decrease in inventory, and corresponding improvements in turns, ROI, and gross margin.

Source: IBM *Newswire,* published by the Retail Distribution and Store Systems, Research Triangle Park, North Carolina, December 1989.

RETAIL USES OF EDI IN FORECASTING

Retailers in many industries are using direct communications to their consumer goods manufacturers. POS data are being provided to the manufacturer, who, in turn, sends the necessary resupply of goods to the retail stores from the plants or from regional warehouses operated by the manufacturer. These improved shipping procedures use POS data, EDI, and JIT to achieve rapid direct store delivery (DSD). Figure 19–1 illustrates EDI and DSD for a supplier of three retail stores. In this situation, the retailer need not carry any inventory other than the store inventories. The manufacturer-supplier is providing a value-added service to the retailer, and in so doing assures himself of a greater volume of sales and builds a strong relationship with the retailer.

Customers and suppliers benefit from sharing demand data via EDI.

   In some cases, the EDI demand data provided to the manufacturer are not from a POS system but from the transfer of inventory from the retailer's distribution center to several retail stores in the region. This situation is shown in Figure 19–2. The retailer has its own regional distribution operations. The retailer's stores frequently request resupply from the DCs; these resupply orders become demand on the retailer's warehouse.

FIGURE 19–1
EDI from Manufacturer to Retail Store with Direct Store Delivery (DSD)

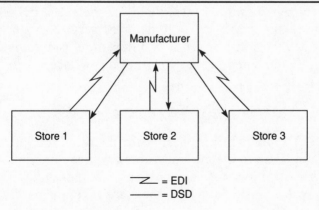

FIGURE 19–2
EDI from Manufacturer to Retail Warehouse

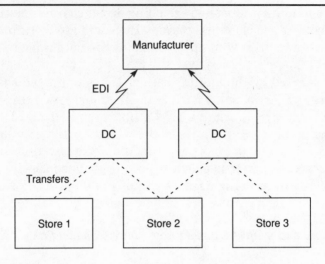

The manufacturer-supplier, in turn, is responsible for keeping the retailer's DCs replenished in a timely manner. The network being managed by the EDI linkage in this case is between the manufacturer and the retailer's warehouse.

Value-Added Resupply

Regardless of the delivery point—direct store delivery or the retailer's warehouse—the value-added service of the manufacturer is not a new idea to experienced distributors. For many years, major distributors have not only offered DSD, but have also marked the merchandise and stocked the shelves of the retailers. This sounds like a bakery route delivery service to stock retail stores. It is very similar. What is different, of course, is the frequency of delivery and the means whereby data are communicated.

Direct store delivery is not a new idea.

With EDI in place, it is possible for the retailer to provide not only demand data to the manufacturer but inventory data as well. Having the inventory data can be an advantage to manufacturers when they determine how long the store inventories will last so

---

Quick Response Example

"Sears has been actively pursuing quick response for many years. Since the mid 1970s, we have been sharing sales and inventory data to improve production planning and reduce order leadtime. Currently, we are transmitting sales and inventory information to 94 vendors across 138 softline and hardline product lines."

"Some examples. . . . We send weekly unit sales at the item level to Amory Garment so they can react to sales and adjust production accordingly. For Levi Strauss, we're transmitting weekly and monthly sales information and generating orders on a weekly basis."

"For Diehard batteries, mufflers, and shocks, we transmit actual point-of-sale data directly to the manufacturers. These vendors maintain a model stock by SKU and store to automatically replenish the merchandise based on the sales activity."

Source: *Quick Response 90 Proceedings,* AIM USA, March 20, 1990, Dallas.

as to anticipate the timing of future store replenishments. However, most EDI business partnerships have started more simply from the order entry, purchasing, invoicing, and payment application rather than with demand forecasting or quick response relationships. This is because many of the benefits of EDI are sought by the customer even if the suppliers aren't ready to take full advantage of the data-sharing potential.

EDI should provide demand and inventory information.

Continuous Replenishment

If a perfect retail world were devised, it would include some simple, low-cost means whereby the store shelf stock would be instantly replenished as sales are made. With only data of sales each day (or more often), the supplier would dispatch the correct replacement units from a nearby plant or distribution center. This flow of replacement stock would occur without formal orders because the supplier and retailer are committed to a close business partnership. As sales increase or decrease, the supplier increases or decreases the number of units sent to the retailer. The response to changes in the sales pattern is quick and without error because the supplier has the necessary stock.

A perfect retail replenishment is a continuous one.

This kind of replenishment can be described as *nearly continuous replenishment.* Goods from the supplier are provided in small, frequent lots, similar to what suppliers provide in a JIT manufacturing setting. From the customer's (retailer's) perspective, this is an effective process.

Figure 19–3 extends this flow process to the next level in the supply chain, where vendors provide materials just in time to the manufacturer. Thus, we can have JIT vendors supplying JIT manufacturers, who are supplying JIT retailers. JIT concepts are applicable here because the manufacturer's shipments determine the material requirements from their vendors.

Regardless of whether the supplier is a distributor or a manufacturer-distributor, one result of JIT and EDI is shorter response times at each level in the supply chain. Such reductions significantly improve supply-system performance.

JIT and EDI yield shorter response times throughout the supply chain.

FIGURE 19–3
EDI Supply-Chain Flow

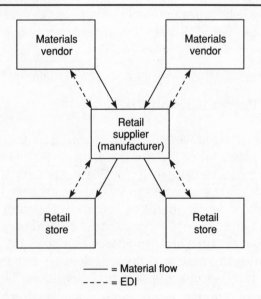

―――― = Material flow
- - - - = EDI

MANUFACTURER USES OF EDI IN FORECASTING

Now let us look at this process from the manufacturer's perspective. To "manage" a supply flow, a manufacturer needs information about the demand "downstream"—ultimately, at the retail level in a consumer-goods industry. With POS data more routinely available, it seems reasonable to examine the options open to manufacturers whose customers are all on EDI with them.

Assume that manufacturers can get daily POS data and store inventories. What other information should they try to get periodically? How should they use the data to help the retailer? How should they use the data to help themselves? As shown below, a retail supplier will be better off to have more-current and more-complete information if it is used properly.

Real-Time Retail Demand Data

Suppose all of the retail stores that are a manufacturer's customers have some means to provide POS data any time it is wanted. Would it be worthwhile for the manufacturer to accumulate that real-time demand for all customers? Would it be used? Watching real-time demand accumulate is similar to watching a population size sign in a major city, or watching the Detroit auto production sign. Usually, these real-time figures satisfy curiosity but lead to no immediate business decisions.

A more effective method is to process the POS data on a periodic basis—perhaps daily—to see what items have been selling and to plan the next round of replenishments. On a periodic basis, the simplest logic is to send to each store the quantities that sold since the last periodic review. This seems okay until we realize that current sales data don't fully reflect several aspects of retail life:

Returned goods.

Shrinkage.

Promotions.

Merchandising-plan changes.

Daily or weekly seasonality.

Processing only customer's demands in EDI may not be sufficient.

Each of these aspects can be handled to some degree in a data system, but not by using POS sales data alone. If we have no information about these aspects of the retail stores, we must replace what was sold in each store on the assumption that each stores' plan for items is unchanged. This is not a good assumption. What a manufacturer will be led to request from the retail business partner is a periodic inventory position of each item to see whether the returns, shrinkage, transaction errors, or changes in plans require an adjustment in the replenishment quantities. The manufacturer may be told, for example, that the inventory is less than it should be because the planned stock level has been increased by 20 units. The manufacturer must send an additional 20 units above the sales that were made for the day.

This adjustment can be thought of as a midcourse correction in a nearly continuous process. The manufacturer keeps all systems on "go," but checks to see whether the flow rate is keeping pace with the real situation. What may be needed is a one-time additional quantity or a one-time reduction in the replenishment.

The role of the manufacturer as a retail supplier is to be in a position to provide what the stores need. But when the stores' plans change and promotions dominate the demand, it isn't adequate to send what was sold yesterday. We need more than the POS demand data if we are going to be most effective as a supplier.

A manufacturer needs more than POS data
for effective customer service using EDI.

Manufacturer Responsibilities

We have assumed that if we are a manufacturer, we are attempting to provide what the stores need without the stores actually placing an order with us. To do this, we must anticipate (i.e., forecast) store needs at least through our internal lead-time so that production provides what the stores will be selling. This is essentially performing a replenishment function for the store with a very short-horizon demand forecast. This replenishment process at the store may be daily.

What has EDI done for us in this process? It has shortened the time delays in capturing demand and making decisions to replenish inventory at the stores. It has put us in a position to prepare a forecast and to plan our production with more-precise and more-current demand data because we don't have to wait for a retailer's order to give us a basis for anticipating over-the-counter sales. Instead, we are able to see the over-the-counter sales data as often as the retailer provides them to us.

We may use the POS data to prepare a forecast for production-planning purposes, but how often should we revise the forecast? If the POS data are analyzed each day instead of weekly, as a supplier, we may be as many as six or seven days ahead in sensing demand at our location. However, daily-demand data may have considerably greater random variation. It may vary more day to day than it does week to week. While we can analyze cumulative daily demand as the week progresses, these cumulative figures may also have too much variation. Thus, depending on the volume and randomness of sales, it may or may not be more effective to forecast using daily data.

Forecasting and planning using daily data may be too volatile.

Our responsibility to have goods in stock requires that we order materials now for production and shipments to the stores several weeks ahead of the retail sales. Figure 19–4 illustrates the timing of decisions and responses in the supply chain of Figure 19–3. As a retail supplier-manufacturer, we have an internal leadtime of 4 days to convert materials from our vendor to finished goods, and our vendors of materials have a 10-day leadtime to us as suppliers. Our commitments to materials now will affect our ability to ship to the retailers two weeks hence, and the coverage of retail sales three weeks hence. Figure 19–4 illustrates these effects of leadtimes in the supply chain.

FIGURE 19-4
Supply-Chain Calendar Days

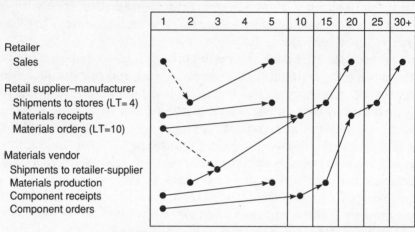

Retailer-supplier internal leadtime: 4 days (LT=4) ‑‑‑‑► Information flow
Retailer-supplier material leadtime:10 days (LT=10) ‑‑‑‑► Material flow

Our order to the vendor should be based on our next two weeks of planned production. In relationship to retail sales, the planned production should be based on the demand foreseen through the next 20 days at retail. This is a short horizon for purposes of forecasting, but, nevertheless, it is a forecast.

When manufacturers accept responsibility to replenish their customers' inventories without orders, it is important for the manufacturers to determine what to order from *their* suppliers. To do this, the manufacturers need to have short-range forecasts by item out to a horizon equal to the sum of their internal leadtime plus their suppliers' leadtime, even if they have ready access to their customers' demand data. While they may, with good systems and management skills, achieve better response with shorter leadtimes, the reality of leadtimes must be accepted and used in their decision process. Even with EDI, replenishment plans still have leadtimes, and forecasts are necessary.

EDI does not preclude the need to forecast.

Suppliers receiving EDI data from customers should have a forecast horizon equal to external plus internal leadtimes.

Retailer Responsibilities

In most instances of retailer-manufacturer partnerships, the retailer participates in the decision to replenish store inventories by placing specific item-quantity-date orders with the suppliers. This is a more practical and workable relationship, especially where retail merchandising of seasonal and fashion goods is involved. EDI can provide quick and accurate communication of the order and the acknowledgement to help shorten the order cycle.

The retailer's systems will determine what the current store inventory is by stockkeeping unit, compare that quantity to the model stock quantity, and issue the purchase order to the supplier by EDI. The supplier may acknowledge the order by EDI. Subsequently, the order is prepared for shipping and the supplier may send an EDI shipment notice to the retailer, which is used by the retailer to anticipate the receipt of merchandise. If direct store delivery is made frequently, the shipment notice may not be required.

Shipment notices or even order acknowledgements may not be needed if the retailer is able to see the supplier's available stock before placing an order. This inquiry-and-advice procedure is facilitated by specific EDI transactions. See Appendix 19–A, entry ID# 846. The retailer may send an inquiry directly to the supplier's computer, which will respond the next time it processes transactions from the retailer. The response interval may be very short if the EDI is supported by real-time direct communications, but this degree of commitment requires a significant investment in hardware and software. The investment in direct retailer-supplier communication is an indication that these business partners have recognized each other as strategically important, and they believe that their business volume will grow together.

Manufacturer Opportunities

Because the retailers are placing their own replenishment orders, the manufacturers may not foresee the benefit or opportunity in getting POS demand data from the retailers. However, the retailers' over-the-counter data may give the manufacturers a much earlier and more precise indication of market demand than do the retailers' orders. The orders are placed several days after the demand has occurred, and they reflect lot sizing and timing decisions of the retail buyer. These decisions often obscure the independent demand at the retail level. Thus, the manufacturers may receive discontinuous, lumpy demand even though the retailers face continuous uniform demand. The retailers' independent demand can provide valuable information to the manufacturers.

> *POS demand data provides valuable information*
> *that supplements periodic orders via EDI.*

If enough retailers of a product provide accurate POS data to that product's manufacturer, the manufacturer is in a position to compute market demand forecasts at whatever level of detail is appropriate. For example, forecasts from one region to another may be quite different in their rate of demand or their seasonality; this can affect the manufacturer's plans for distribution if he or she is stocking the product regionally. The total market demand forecast will provide an excellent basis for the planning that the manufacturer must do. Regression methods developed in Chapter 11 can forecast total market demand using POS demand data as an independent variable.

> *POS demand data from retailers can provide suppliers*
> *with ways to estimate total market forecasts.*

The required planning by the manufacturer is not greatly different, regardless of whether the retailer is placing his or her own replenishment orders. The manufacturer must plan production, at least at the level of detail required to determine the materials requirements, and he or she must place the orders for those materials. The importance of good communications with the retailers should not be overlooked, even when the market demand history and forecasts are routinely available.

EXTENSION TO THE MATERIALS VENDOR

We can imagine the materials vendor using the retail POS data for their own purposes. As indicated in Figure 19–4, the decisions being made by the materials vendor to order components (or other raw materials) will help to determine the availability of store merchandise many days into the future. In our example, if the materials vendor uses market demand to forecast retail demand for the next 30 days, he or she may have more responsive forecasts than if he or she waited to use orders from the manufacturer to forecast the manufacturer's demand. Whether those POS-based forecasts are more accurate is a matter of conjecture. However, with the forecast of retail demand, the materials vendor can anticipate the needs in the supply chain with the greatest possible leadtime. He or she can then set out a production rate or schedule that will satisfy the required "flow rate" in the supply chain, and can help to keep everybody from getting "whipsawed" with changes in the apparent demand that occurs when orders don't track the real demand.

Upstream suppliers should anticipate retail
trends so they can smooth supply-chain flow.

But is it reasonable that upstream suppliers should assume responsibility for forecasting retail demand? And if they did, how well would those forecasts help them be more responsive to the retail market?

WHO DOES THE DEMAND FORECASTING?

In principle, retail demand data can be provided routinely using EDI so that suppliers can process hundreds or even thousands of stores. Large-volume processing costs continue to decline. If the manufacturer performs retail demand forecasting, does the retailer also do this same forecasting work? Why should we have this redundancy? Perhaps we would say that the manufacturer's interests are not in store details, but rather in a national forecast. This is quite often true. But the manufacturer needs to plan production by finished good item, so considerable detail by item is needed. Thus the manufacturer does have interest in store details.

There are examples of suppliers of staple merchandise who have essentially taken the responsibility for retail forecasting. The relationships apply to a few key accounts, such as Wal-Mart and Sears Roebuck (see earlier box), who have insisted on vendor control of the store inventory replenishments to keep the stock at agreed levels in selected merchandise departments. Examples of these relationships will grow.

However, the most frequent solution to good customer-supplier planning is to expect the retailer to prepare his or her business plans, and to modify them as desired, based on his or her own demand forecasts and merchandising judgment. Those same forecasts then may be passed to the supplier and summed across customers. Furthermore, the retail plans may be changed by reason of promotions or the model stock altered to reflect new store conditions, so the retailer is in a better position than the supplier to establish the estimated demand that will be "pulled" through the supply chain. Therefore, as retail plans change, the actual orders placed on the upstream suppliers will differ from the POS demand data. The direction of the difference could be either plus or minus.

> *Retail plan changes are so important that retailers*
> *should provide their forecasts to suppliers.*

How prevalent is the sharing between customer and supplier of these business plans? Recent surveys of EDI usage in U.S. companies indicate that 50 to 60 percent of the surveyed companies are routinely processing orders and invoices. Only 10 to 15 percent reported using EDI for purposes of inventory control. Far fewer are using EDI in the way we have suggested here. The companies in the previous quick response examples boxes are leading-edge companies, but do not as yet represent mainstream U.S. suppliers.

At the same time, we should remember that the manufacturer's interests and benefits derive from better forecasts.

Manufacturers may have good reason to seek retail demand data for purposes of improving the national forecast. The retail data taken from several retailers may indicate changes in the mix of products that are not evident to any one retailer. We know too that many retailers still regard their demand forecasts and merchandise plans as too private to be shared, so, in some cases, it may be possible to obtain POS data more easily than the forecasts.

We believe that leading-edge manufacturers will seek ways to supplement the requirements data that they get from their immediate customers. This can be especially important in changing retail markets where second- and third-echelon members of the supply chain are making longer-term decisions to commit materials and capacity based on the ultimate sales they expect at retail. Selected retail segments may be sampled as indicators of market conditions. Processing costs and data collection costs are lower than in previous years and are continuing to decline. The feasibility of more-comprehensive forecasting systems will continue to increase.

Communicate, Don't Assume

We have been looking at the use of retail demand forecasts to drive decisions in the supply-chain flow using unstated assumptions regarding continuous flow of materials and information. One of the important assumptions is that business inventories are not changing significantly at either the retailer or manufacturer level in the chain. If, for example, the stock levels are increasing, the orders placed on the materials vendor will be greater than were anticipated by the retail demand forecasts. In this case, the production plan by the materials vendor will be too low.

Why would the retail or wholesale inventories be increasing? Several reasons are possible:

1. Seasonal demand increases are being anticipated by the retailers.
2. Promotions are being carried out by one or more large retailers.
3. The retailers may have bought more stock than they sold because their forecasts were too high.

4. The manufacturer may have produced in anticipation of retail demand that did not materialize.
5. The manufacturer may have bought materials in order to hedge for a price increase.
6. The manufacturer may be intentionally producing faster than demand in preparation for a scheduled vacation or plant maintenance period.
7. The product is becoming more of a commodity, with stock levels and service requirements rising across several markets.
8. The manufacturer may be hedging for an uncertain or increasing leadtime from the materials vendor. This behavior is still typical of supply-chain management when their suppliers are unresponsive and alternate sources are expensive or nonexistent.

What should the materials vendor do in the face of these inventory uncertainties? One reasonable and now-feasible choice is to request periodic inventory data from the downstream business via EDI. This is a necessary part of any thorough assessment of the supply-chain conditions. Today's EDI technology makes it possible to assess any changes that may be occurring in aggregate inventories in the chain. But the assessment procedures should also capture the reasons behind the changes; otherwise, the data could be easily misinterpreted.

An effective EDI system should detect changes and, if possible, the causes of those changes in demand.

The assessment procedures may well justify an investment in a model of the supply chain that will use both the demand forecasts and the inventory data to compute the expected required production by the materials supplier. An excellent model of a supply chain can be developed by using distribution resource planning (DRP) tools. Andre Martin has published important work regarding DRP. In his second edition, he has developed examples of DRP applied to supply-chain management, with new examples relating to retail and nonmanufacturing members of the supply chain.[2] The thrust of his book is the integration of connected customer-suppliers who pass time-phased requirements, and, if possible, also the inventory and demand forecasts, to the sources of supply. This integrating with DRP systems makes it possible for suppliers to anticipate the needs of their customers by seeing their customers' requirements for several weeks into the future. DRP is illustrated and discussed in Chapter 5 of this book.

In addition to using the supply-chain model to evaluate the inventories and demand data and the anticipated requirements, one may ask customers about the dynamics that are taking place in the market and in the supply chain. This evaluation is more important for the suppliers who are farther upstream in the supply chain from the retail markets. Supplier communications with their customers should be of two types then:

1. Obtain organized requirements, inventory, and demand data for not just this week and next, but for enough periods to cover their leadtimes. These are the data needed in the DRP model.
2. Obtain measures of changes occurring in downstream partners' business and see whether those changes are reflected in seasonal, temporary, or permanent changes in the requirements.

The first kind of communication can be entirely automated using EDI and the existing standard transaction sets. The second kind of communication requires more-inventive management behavior. Through this communication, however, downstream data can be used to verify supply and demand assumptions that are part of customer-supplier data sharing.

Partial Market EDI

When suppliers have all of their customers participating in EDI programs, they can quickly look at their total demand by summing all customers' requirements. However, most suppliers have some markets to which they are not as yet connected via EDI, though this number is decreasing. It should be clear that the use of EDI for acquiring market demand for some customers is worthwhile, even though the non-EDI demands must be forecasted by

FIGURE 19–5
Some Customers Not on EDI

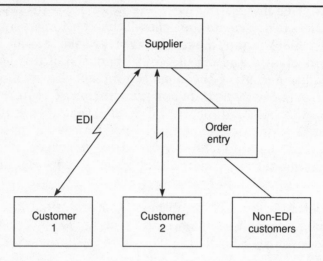

using orders received from the non-EDI customers. Or, with partial-market EDI, we have the ability to forecast non-EDI customer demands using the regression methods of Chapter 11.

If the supplier is fortunate to have major customers move into EDI, then they will benefit greatly from investment in hardware, software, and training.

Figure 19–5 illustrates the use of conventional demand forecasting for those market segments that are not connected via EDI. These forecasts use demand data based on orders received from non-EDI customers. At the same time, the EDI customers may provide more-precise planning data and receive commensurate benefits from the supplier.

SUMMARY

In this chapter, we have explored some alternate means whereby business partners may take advantage of EDI technology. An EDI implementation should yield significant benefits to suppliers in terms of cost reduction, more-accurate planning data, and customer service. To date, however, the benefits of EDI partnerships have more often been documented in terms of the customer benefits.

We discussed the operations of networked systems such as DRP. These systems use customers' requirements as demand on suppliers. To the extent that a supplier's customers will provide time-phased requirements that reach far enough into the future, the forecasting task is accomplished by the customers and need not be repeated by the supplier. The DRP net requirements provide dependent demands, which preclude forecasts; thus demand is passed by EDI to the suppliers.

Even with responsive data systems that enable second- and third-level suppliers to benefit from end-of-the-chain demand forecasting, there is a continuing need for demand forecasting by suppliers when:

1. Not all customers are sharing time-phased requirements with them.
2. The customer forecast horizon (and time-phased requirements) does not cover the supplier's total leadtime for materials and production.
3. Supplier decisions are being made for longer-range purposes such as capacity planning, materials contracts for price protection, or fiscal budgeting.
4. Selected independent demand data from customers down the supply chain (e.g., at retail level using POS data) may serve to give a few days or weeks of advanced warning to the supplier regarding market shifts on key products.

We conclude that EDI supports a valuable form of demand forecasting in the best of partnerships and that forecasting in its traditional form will continue to be needed for suppliers to do the best possible job.

REFERENCES

1. TDCC/EDIA, *EDI in North America: Status of Usage and Technology* (Alexandria, Va., December 1989), p. 49.
2. Andre J. Martin, *Distribution Resource Planning*, 2nd ed. (Essex Junction, Vt.: Oliver Wight Limited Publications, 1990).

APPENDIX 19-A

TABLE 19A-1
Examples of EDI Transaction Sets Illustrating Similarity of Some Sets between Standards

ID#	REF#	ANSI X12 TITLE	ID#	UCS/WINS TITLE
850	X12.1	Purchase order	875	Purchase order
n.a.			874	Purchase order multipoint
860	X12.15	Purchase order change	876	Purchase-order change
856	X12.10	Shipment notice/manifest	884	Shipment advice
810	X12.2	Invoice	880	Invoice
861	X12.12	Receiving advice	944	Stock transfer receipt advice
846	X12.28	Inventory inquiry/advice	941	Warehouse invoice status
852	X12.52	Product activity data	942	Warehouse activity report
867	X12.33	Product transfer and resale	n.a.	
n.a.			889	Promotion announcement
n.a.			879	Price change
n.a.			896	Product dimension maintenance

n.a. = Not available.

APPENDIX 19-B: History of EDI

The TDCC/EDIA report of 1989 indicates that 10,000 companies in more than 50 industries are using EDI in the form of standardized transaction sets. This growth has been rapid in recent years, but EDI began slowly in the late 1960s with mutual interests of railroads, airlines, motor carriers, and shipping companies to reduce delays in product deliveries and payments. The Transportation Data Coordinating Committee (TDCC) has been involved from the beginning, with special focus on the transportation industries. TDCC standards have also been used in other industries. TDCC is now the Electronic Data Interchange Association (EDIA).

Beginning in 1979 with the formation of the Accredited Standards Committee X12 (ASCX12) by the American National Standards Institute (ANSI), numerous standards have been reviewed and developed by the members of the ASCX12 working groups. Periodically, some of these standard transaction sets and their specific formats are approved officially by ANSI, but many more are in use across the 30 or so industries that have since endorsed the ASCX12 working-group results.

Apart from ANSI, specific industry-oriented transaction sets are in wide use, such as the Warehouse Information Network Standards (WINS), the Universal Common Standard (UCS) for the food industry, ORDERNET for the healthcare industry, and AIAG, used in the auto industry. Industry transaction sets are the first of three levels.

The ANSI ASCX12 standards represent the "national-level" standards, intended for cross-industry use. The subcommittees that develop these standards are comprised of representatives from many industries. The earliest official ANSI transaction sets were approved in 1986. As of January 1990, the various ASCX12 transaction sets and other standards were in several stages of evolution and use:

17 standards in development by subcommittees.

8 standards being reviewed in draft.

15 standards released in draft for trial use.

16 standards adopted by ANSI.

In addition, the ASCX12 subcommittees are working on many projects that include the consideration of international standards sponsored by the United Nations since 1988 through EDIFACT. EDIFACT represents the third "level" of standards. The acronym stands for the Electronic Data Interchange for Administration, Commerce, and Transport.

Recently, the ANSI X12 committee organized to consider the UCS/WINS and TDCC standards as part of their scope. This move has given ANSI X12 oversight of all North American standards for EDI.

Sources: TDCC/EDIA, *EDI in North America: Status of Usage and Technology* (Alexandria, Va.: December 1989); Council of Logistics Management, *Partnerships in Providing Customer Service* (Oak Brook, Ill.: 1989); and Data Interchange Standards Association (DISA), *ASCX12 Status Report* (Alexandria, Va.: January 1990).

CHAPTER 20

THE FUTURE OF FORECASTING SYSTEMS

Nothing is ever said that has not been said before.
Terence, 150 B.C.

Forecasting systems are not destinations but a continuing
  journey.

This book has been written to assist you in the use, design, development, selection, and purchase of forecasting systems. This chapter completes that purpose by discussing the future of forecasting systems and ways of staying current in the art of forecasting systems. We first speculate on the future of forecasting systems including important opportunities for improving system effectiveness. This is accomplished by presenting a number of trends and how these have and will continue to influence forecasting systems. The second part of this chapter discusses how managers and analysts can stay abreast of important forecasting developments. It provides a list of resources available to assist you in staying near the cutting edge of applications. This list includes journals, abstract services, on-line retrieval services, and publications specializing in the evaluation of commercial forecasting systems.

Both topics of this chapter are important in understanding and following the evolution of forecasting systems. By staying abreast of new developments in forecasting systems, your knowledge and systems can remain state of the art.

TRENDS IN FORECASTING SYSTEMS

Many best-selling management books speculate on the important technological changes in society that will impact us 10 to 20 years from now. Our purpose here is to speculate on what will occur in the next 5 to 10 years. We believe that this is more beneficial than making longer-term technological forecasts. Nonetheless, some of what follows is speculation. We hope to predict important opportunities for improving forecasting systems.

Figure 20–1 and Table 20–1 illustrate the important modules of a comprehensive forecasting system. In this section, we review recent developments that have and will continue to affect the design and use of these modules. These developments are summarized in Table 20–2. While we hope that this list is comprehensive, an important topic may have been unintentionally omitted. Current trends that will influence forecasting systems have been classified in Table 20–2 using the following:

FIGURE 20–1
The Modules of a Forecasting System

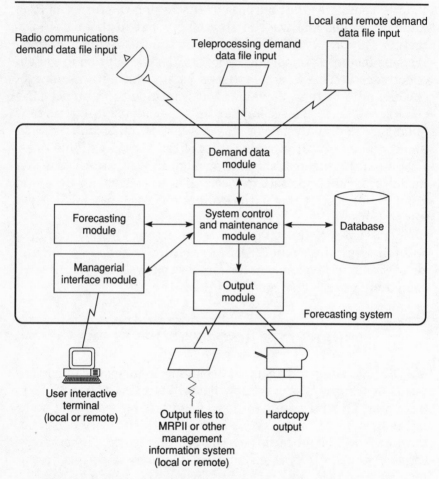

Technological and computer innovations.

Telecommunications.

Information systems and software.

Research.

Organizational and societal changes.

It is always difficult to classify interrelated concepts into meaningful, mutually exclusive groups. Consequently, there are

TABLE 20-1
The Modules and Database of a Forecasting System

I. Demand Data Module
   Input of local and remote demand data
   Demand capturing
   Logical filtering (demand versus supply or shipments)
   Special-event filtering (promotions, price changes, product introductions)
   Initial outlier detection, adjustment, classification

II. Forecasting Module
   System forecast selection
   Outlier detection, adjustment, classification
   Reasonableness test
   Final forecast
   Error measures
   Tracking-signal control

III. Managerial Interface and Interaction Module
   Graphical user interface
   Screen displays
   Management forecasts
   User help
   Management feedback
   User notepad
   Expert advisory menu

IV. Output Module
   File generation
   Routine reports
   Ad hoc reports
   Exception reports

V. System Control and Maintenance Module
   Module and navigation control
   Simulation control
   Database updating and maintenance
   Detection of system malfunctions and bugs

VI. Database
   Actual demand history
   Adjusted demand history
   Promotional profiles
   Seasonal profiles
   Item and group relationships structure
   Performance measures
   Item relationships
   Item descriptions
   Demand forecasts

many other possible classification schemes that might have been used; however, Table 20–2 seems an appropriate eclectic presentation. Our discussion of each is necessarily brief.

TECHNOLOGICAL AND COMPUTER INNOVATIONS

Computer Improvements

New, inexpensive technology will continue to increase the demand, supply, quality, and performance of forecasting systems. The number of forecasting system users will increase dramatically because of these improvements. The impact of the microelectronics and digital revolutions on all computer-based systems have been extraordinary.

The popularly priced microcomputers of tomorrow will have current mainframe capabilities, not only in processing capability, but also in mass storage devices such as read-and-write digital-optical storage devices. Thus, powerful microcomputers will be combined with mass storage and automated data entry devices. The continued integration of computer-based information systems will change the way all firms operate. Smaller firms will reap even more benefits as their larger numbers motivate the development of many new, user-friendly forecasting, inventory control, and planning systems. Also, larger firms will benefit greatly by having significant distributed data processing capabilities at each location.

Mass Storage Devices

Magnetic and digital-optical storage devices will result in improved demand data modules and bigger and more-relevant databases.

Point-of-Sale Equipment, Bar Coding, and Scanners

These will provide lower-cost and more-timely data for real-time, on-line forecasting systems. The data collected and the number of sources of data input to the demand database will increase greatly. These data will support the use of sophisticated group

A supercomputer performs calculations over 1 billion times faster than a human. That a half-dozen supercomputers have a computational processing speed in excess of all humankind is truly extraordinary. Technological advancements will increase this ability ten-fold in the near future.

and pyramid forecasting methods, along with the greater need for better management interfaces.

TELECOMMUNICATIONS

Satellite and Radio Communications and Networking

Telecommunications and information systems are mutually dependent. The combination of local radio teleprocessing and global satellite communications greatly decreases the cost of global data transmission and collection. Never before has there been more data collected on-line and in real time. While this will affect large firms more in the short term (most large firms are or have already implemented new telecommunications systems), in the long run, inexpensive communications will affect even the smallest manufacturer or retailer. Consider the effects that low-cost cellular telephones have had on mobile communications. Also, for example, it is now possible to communicate with palm-size, battery-operated radios from and to anywhere in the world. These developments will result in more demand data sources, larger databases, and significantly greater processing by the system control and maintenance module.

Electronic Data Interchange
EDI was discussed in detail in Chapter 19. It has resulted in greater integration, support for shorter leadtimes, quick response, more on-line and real-time systems, and greater interdependency of decisions in different organizations. Consequently, EDI will

TABLE 20–2
Developments Affecting the Future of Forecasting Systems

Development	Modules Primarily Affected by Development					
	Demand Data Module (DD)	Management Interface Module (MI)	Forecasting Module (FM)	System Control Module (SC)	Output Module (OM)	Database (DB)
I. Technological and Computer Innovations						
Computer improvements	DD	MI	FM	SC	OM	DB
Mass storage devices (CD ROMS, etc.)	DD					DB
Point-of-sale equipment, bar coding, and scanners	DD	MI	FM			DB
II. Telecommunications						
Satellite and radio communications and networking	DD			SC		DB
Electronic data interchange	DD			SC		DB
III. Information Systems and Software						
On-line, real-time systems	DD	MI	FM	SC		DB
Automated office	DD	MI			OM	DB

	DD	MI	FM	SC	OM	DB
Artificial intelligence/expert systems	DD	MI	FM	SC	OM	DB
Spreadsheets	DD	MI	FM	SC	OM	
Powerful statistical software		MI				
CAD/CAM/management information systems	DD	MI		SC	OM	DB
Better graphical user interfaces		MI		SC		DB
IV. Research						
New time series forecasting methods		MI	FM			DB
New theories on combining methods		MI	FM			DB
New tracking and control devices		MI	FM	SC		DB
New methods of combining judgmental and time series methods	DD	MI	FM			DB
More use of extrinsic (causal) methods	DD	MI	FM	SC		DB
V. Organizational and Societal Changes						
Education	DD	MI	FM	SC	OM	DB
Longer-term customer-vendor relationships	DD	MI	FM	SC	OM	DB
Integration through information systems	DD	MI	FM	SC		DB
Global competition	DD	MI				DB
Total mentions	16	18	13	13	7	18

place great demands on the interactive and on-line data-capturing capabilities of forecasting systems. Systems will have to interface more with remote data sources and users of data.

INFORMATION SYSTEMS AND SOFTWARE

Because of technological breakthroughs in equipment, new approaches to solving forecasting problems are possible. New automated information processing systems have familiarized many people with information systems and their capabilities. Clerks, managers, and analysts have learned to use and expect more-relevant information in decision making.

On-Line, Real-Time Systems
The ability to provide information with short leadtimes has always been an important attribute of computer-based systems. With the refinement of MRP II and JIT systems, there has been an even greater desire to reduce order and data processing leadtimes. Such reductions will result in even greater demands on the capabilities of future demand data, management interface, and database modules of the forecasting system.

Automated Office
As routine tasks in an office environment become more highly automated, users expect greater support from the forecasting system. Thus, there will be greater demands placed on all modules of future forecasting systems.

Artificial Intelligence/Expert Systems
Chapter 18 developed the use of AI/ES in forecasting systems. These developments will alter the functions of all modules of future forecasting systems. AI/ES offer an exciting potential for improving forecasting systems.

Spreadsheets and Graphical User Interfaces
Spreadsheets have provided natural and intuitive user interfaces for those doing both routine data entry and sophisticated analytical work. This tool has spawned more users expecting good graphi-

cal interfaces. These spreadsheets have improved the analytic abilities of many users while providing them with some independence from centralized MIS support staff. These users expect and need more support from the management interface and demand data modules of future forecasting systems. Also, forecasting systems will continue to interface with popular spreadsheets.

Powerful Statistical Software

The number of statistical software packages has increased dramatically in the last decade. These have been developed for many different computer platforms. This provides corporations with the option of using many alternative statistical forecasting methods. The forecasting methods that will be used in operational forecasting systems will be influenced by the acceptance and success of these statistically sophisticated software packages. Also, these new systems will eventually increase the number of competing comprehensive forecasting systems.

RESEARCH

More research is being directed to improving operational forecasting systems. The formation of three forecasting societies since 1982 has increased interest in all modules of forecasting systems. Their research literature and publications will provide important new findings for operational forecasting systems. The research thrusts discussed below will primarily influence the forecasting module of operational forecasting systems; however, several do have considerable effects on the management interface and demand data modules and the database.

New Time Series Forecasting Methods

Several recent research studies have suggested that some new methods of forecasting and model selection are better than existing methods. These were discussed in Chapters 13 and 14. For example, the methods of Lewandowski and Parzen may offer greater single-model effectiveness. Also, multimodel simulation methods might offer an exciting new forecasting approach.

New Theories on Combining Methods
Methods of combining forecasts have been researched for some time. Combining several forecasts using simple averaging methods has been found effective. However, as discussed in Chapter 14, other methods may be better than simple averages.

More-Complex Tracking and Control Devices
The uses of AI/ES and new statistical techniques offer opportunities to improve the performance of simple tracking signals. These improvements are possible because of the increased computational power of new computers.

New Methods of Combining Judgmental and Time Series Methods
Humans are better than statistical methods in identifying and using nonrepetitive or special-event influences in forecasting. The ability to know of events that will influence demands emphasizes the importance of management forecasts. Research continues on how to best combine management and system forecasts. We anticipate new ways of combining the distinct advantages of humans and computer programs.

More Use of Extrinsic (Causal) Methods
With the advent of more readily available external data and greater computational power, there will be more use of simple causal models of group and major-item demands. Expert systems can be used to replace human analysts in the fitting of these causal models. However, many of the disadvantages of causal models discussed in Chapters 8 and 9 will remain.

ORGANIZATIONAL AND SOCIETAL CHANGES

Education
Greater use of personal computers in education has spawned a new generation of literate computer users. These people will demand more capabilities from all modules of a forecasting system.

Longer-Term Customer-Vendor Relationships

We have learned that cooperative relationships between customers and suppliers decrease costs and increase the flexibility of the firm to respond to customer demands. Consequently, customers are more cooperative in sharing their demand data with suppliers. These trends will affect several modules of the forecasting system, particularly the demand data and system control modules and the database.

Integration through Information Systems

More and more types of firms are finding that the integration of operations, marketing, and finance is best accomplished through integrated planning, common forecasts, and shared databases. This will place great demand on the demand data module and the database of the forecasting system. Also, to better support marketing and the financial use of the forecasting system, the managerial interface and system control modules will be modified for their applications.

Global Competition

Globally competitive markets necessitate accurate and timely demand and forecast data. Global acquisition, sharing, and use of demand and forecast data will place greater demands on the demand data and management interface modules and the database of a forecasting system.

SUMMARY EFFECTS

The bottom of Table 20–2 totals the number of times a forecasting system data module has been mentioned as being affected by current or future developments. We use this as a crude measure of the impact of these developments on future forecasting systems. From this table and our experiences, we infer the following:

- In the future, there will be many:
    more-comprehensive forecasting systems on the market.

more user firms with forecasting systems.

small firms using forecasting systems.

new, competing, comprehensive forecasting systems.

new industry-specific forecasting systems.

more forecasters in a variety of industries.

forecasting systems using new methods such as multimodel simulation methods.

people rediscovering the importance of forecasting systems.

- The management interface of future forecasting systems will:

    be more user friendly.

    provide a good graphical user interface.

    be more versatile in their abilities to serve different users from operations, marketing, and finance.

    support more expert-system interactions.

    support more-complicated interactions of humans with more-sophisticated forecasting methods.

    provide more support for group forecasting and analysis.

    provide a much more powerful management-system forecast interface.

- The demand data module of future forecasting systems will:

    collect more-remote demand data.

    collect data using satellite and radio communications.

    collect more-timely data.

    collect more-detailed item data.

    receive and send data to and from significantly larger databases.

    interconnect with more-remote internal and external users, including international users.

- Future forecasting systems will have a database that will be:

    larger because of low-cost storage.

    more complex to support integrated forecasts.

    updated on-line and in real time.

    larger to capture actual demands, adjusted demands, seasonal profiles, promotional profiles, and more-

    complex hierarchical data structures.
    larger to support users throughout the world.
    larger to support users from finance, marketing, and operations.
    larger because of extrinsic data.
    larger and more complex to support expert systems.
    larger to store more-complex tracking signals and forecasts of multiple models.
- The forecasting module used in future systems will:
    use more-powerful hardware.
    forecast more items using more-detailed item-level data.
    use more-sophisticated forecasting methods.
    use more combinations of methods.
    use more-extrinsic forecasting methods.
    use more-complex methods of selecting best models.
    use more expert systems and intelligence in model selection.
    interface with management forecasts more.
- The system control and maintenance module of future forecasting systems will:
    be more complex to support the many new activities of the other modules.
    rely less on routine hardcopy batch processing from the output module.

INFORMATION SOURCES ON FUTURE FORECASTING SYSTEMS

> To live only for some future goal is shallow. It's the sides of the mountain that sustain life, not the top.
>
> Robert M. Pirsig

We feel that it is important to provide information about sources of continuing research and case studies in forecasting systems. The published research, case studies, and the experiences of others are valuable in making difficult trade-offs and decisions. Some managers may at first feel that the topic of this section is too academic or esoteric. However, to keep up with the state of the art in forecasting requires review of the evolving forecasting system literature.

Other than published books and monographs, there are four general sources of information on future developments in forecasting systems. These are journals, published index and abstract services, on-line literature-retrieval services, and published reviews about commercial software. Each of these is briefly reviewed below.

JOURNALS AND SOCIETIES

Since 1982, three new forecasting journals have been published by three new forecasting societies. Prior to these, there were no journals that were solely devoted to forecasting and forecasting systems. These journals vary in their level of quantitative and managerial emphasis. In addition to these, there are at least 18 other journals that include articles about forecasting. We briefly comment on the three new journals and list the other important journals.

The Journal of Business Forecasting Methods & Systems

The *Journal of Business Forecasting Methods & Systems,* first published in 1982, is associated with the International Association of Business Forecasting. This is a quarterly journal written for business managers who are responsible for evaluating forecasts prepared by technicians. This periodical provides very interesting reading for those desiring a managerial approach to forecasting.

International Journal of Forecasting

The *International Journal of Forecasting* is the official quarterly publication of the International Institute of Forecasters (IIF) and shares the society's aims. It started publication in 1985. The purpose of the journal is to bridge the gap between theory and practice. This journal places strong emphasis on empirical studies, forecast-method evaluation, implementation research, and ways of improving the practice of forecasting. Included in the 16 published areas of the journal are the following applications of forecasting systems:

Evaluation of forecasting methods and approaches.
Seasonal adjustments.
Organizational aspects of forecasting.
New-product forecasting.
Production forecasting.

This journal is more technical than the *Journal of Business Forecasting;* nonetheless, analysts and managers responsible for forecasting should have access to it.

The Journal of Forecasting
First published in 1982, the *Journal of Forecasting* is primarily academic and multidisciplinary in its approach. Like the *International Journal of Forecasting,* this journal publishes high-quality articles on operational forecasting.

Other Journals
Many other journals include research and case studies concerning operational forecasting systems. Most of these journals are more than three decades old and have a history of featuring articles on forecasting.

AIIE Transactions
Computers and Industrial Engineering
Computers and Operations Research
Decision Sciences
Econometrica
Harvard Business Review
Industrial Engineering
Interfaces
International Journal of Operations and Production Management
International Journal of Production Research
Journal of Business

Journal of Business and Economic Statistics
Journal of Operations Management
Journal of the American Statistical Association
Journal of the Operational Research Society
Journal of the Royal Statistical Society
Management Science
Operations Management Review
Operations Research
Production and Inventory Management
Sloan Management Review

In addition to these journals, many other academic, professional, and industry journals occasionally publish articles about forecasting systems.

INDEX AND ABSTRACT SERVICES

Most libraries subscribe to abstract services that review forecasting articles in business, engineering, and other fields. Several abstract services of value to one needing assistance in identifying past research in operational forecasting are given below in alphabetical order.

Applied Science and Technology, H. W. Wilson, New York. This is an index of several hundred periodicals that publish industrial engineering, production engineering, scheduling, quality control, and computer technology articles. While not management oriented, it does abstract periodicals such as *IBM Systems Journal, IBM Journal of Research and Development, Industrial Engineering, ACM Publications,* and *Bell Systems Technical Journal.*

Business Periodicals Index, H. W. Wilson, New York. This is a cumulative subject index of several hundred periodicals published in the United States and abroad. This index is valuable for finding articles about state-of-the-art topics written in a style that will appeal to managers and generalists.

Dissertation Abstracts, University Microfilm, Ann Arbor, Michigan. These are abstracts of Ph.D. dissertations published in the United States. This can be a very valuable resource of information concerning the research conducted by Ph.D.-granting universities in the United States, particularly those granting degrees in statistics, operations research, business, marketing, and production management.

Engineering Index, Engineering Information, Inc., New York. This is a subject-heading guide to engineering publications. Of the hundreds of society publications that are cited in the index are those of the following societies: ACM, AFIPS, IIE, SAE, SAM, and ORSA. Subject headings include production planning and control, industrial engineering, and computers.

Government-Reports Announcements and Government Reports Index, National Technical Information Service, Springfield, Virginia. This is an important source of government-sponsored research and development reports and other government analyses prepared by federal agencies, their contractors, or grantees. Sections are arranged in 22 subject fields with all entries abstracted.

International Abstracts in Operations Research, Operations Research Society of America, Baltimore. This source abstracts about 100 international journals. The abstracts are divided into small subject sectors, allowing rapid access to specific fields of interest.

Operations Research/Management Science Abstracts (ORMS), Executive Sciences Institute, Inc., Whippany, New Jersey. This service abstracts over 100 international journals, including the transactions and meetings of many learned societies in the United States and abroad.

Predicast Publications, Predicasts Inc., Cleveland. This company offers a wide variety of services, including abstract services, indexes, time series data, and forecasts. There are currently 1 million records on-line in their *Predicast Forecasts* and *Worldcasts* database services. Most of their services are available on-line using the Data-Star or DIALOG information services mentioned below.

Quality Control/Applied Statistics Abstracts (QC/AS), Executive Sciences Institutes, Inc., Whippany, New Jersey. This publication abstracts over 400 foreign and domestic periodicals and proceedings, including articles on forecasting, statistical process control, sampling, and quality control.

Readers' Guide to Periodical Literature, H. W. Wilson, New York. This is an author-subject index to about 400 selected general-interest periodicals. Included in the index are journals such as *Time, Life, OMNI, Science, Forbes, Fortune*, and *Futurists*.

Science Citation Index, Institute for Scientific Information, Philadelphia. This is an author-subject index of scientific publications in medicine, agriculture, technology, economics, management, demography, statistics, and the behavioral sciences. It is a useful resource for scientific applications and research in production and inventory management and forecasting. Articles from 1,400 journals are indexed and cited. The publications of IEEE, IIE, and IBM are included.

ON-LINE LITERATURE-RETRIEVAL SERVICES

The most effective way to research the forecasting systems literature is to use on-line literature-retrieval services. There are several on-line database services available to those seeking forecasting information. Almost all of the above indexes and abstract services are available on-line. On-line literature searches can be done at your local library or through computer services such as BRS, DIALOG, Data-Star, Compuserve, or Prodigy. Other electronic services include ABI/Inform, ERIC, Management Contents, COMPENDEX, INFOTRAC, PAIS International, Predicasts, and SciSearch, to name a few. Many of these services access multiple commercial databases. Unless you have studied several electronic services, it is highly recommended that you use a professional librarian to do on-line literature searches.

FORECASTING SOFTWARE LISTINGS
AND DESCRIPTIONS

The process of purchasing a forecasting system presupposes that we have identified potential systems from which to select a good system. Frequently, we can identify several software vendors from recommendations of others in our industry. These can be highly reliable sources. In addition to the journals and publications listed above, there are several commercial services that describe and list forecasting systems. Five of the most widely available are listed below.

Data Sources, Ziff-Davis Publications Co., New York.

Datapro, McGraw-Hill, Inc., Datapro Research, Delran, New Jersey.

ICP Software Directory, International Computer Programs, Inc., Indianapolis.

Reports on Applications Software, Faulkner Technical Reports, Inc., Pennsauken, New Jersey.

Survey of Logistics Software, Council of Logistics Management, Oak Brook, Illinois.

These five services differ in the degree of detail used to describe the software that is included. Because some of these services can be costly, we suggest investigating whether your corporate, community, or university libraries receive these publications. Our purpose in listing these publications is not to suggest that these are sufficient in deciding which forecasting system to select, but, instead, to help you identify a complete listing of potential software vendors from which a best system might be selected.

SUMMARY

In this chapter, we have reviewed the many current trends that will continue to influence forecasting systems. These are exciting times to be developing or purchasing operational forecasting systems. This field is evolving very rapidly, and to assist you in staying current in the forecasting system field, we have provided several important sources of continuing information.

After many years of stable growth, we believe that forecasting system developments and installations are poised for explosive growth. This growth will involve many more knowledgeable users, using more comprehensive forecasting systems to support other sophisticated computer-based systems.

We sincerely hope that this book has assisted and will continue to assist you in your effort to perfect current and future forecasting systems.

> The important thing is not to stop questioning. Curiosity has its own reason for existing.
>
> Albert Einstein

APPENDIX A: SIX DATA SERIES EXAMPLES

Series A: Boxes of computer paper
Series B: Price of a common stock
Series C: A brand of advanced microcomputers
Series D: A brand of diet soft drinks
Series E: 3.5" brand X floppy diskettes
Series F: AM/FM personal radios

Obs. No.	Series A	Series B	Series C	Series D	Series E	Series F
1	779.	476.	493.	518.	509.	546.
2	920.	574.	536.	572.	546.	578.
3	848.	589.	530.	599.	479.	660.
4	839.	649.	588.	652.	527.	707.
5	879.	712.	556.	692.	581.	738.
6	726.	691.	617.	759.	694.	781.
7	788.	659.	656.	705.	687.	848.
8	813.	600.	584.	643.	606.	818.
9	745.	587.	634.	600.	658.	729.
10	732.	658.	709.	546.	593.	691.
11	809.	719.	648.	518.	563.	658.
12	786.	747.	700.	426.	582.	604.
13	849.	818.	672.	554.	557.	629.
14	926.	782.	773.	585.	525.	711.
15	867.	766.	684.	633.	556.	729.
16	828.	679.	730.	688.	619.	798.
17	778.	634.	779.	731.	660.	861.
18	862.	583.	733.	794.	637.	903.
19	830.	561.	803.	805.	578.	968.
20	924.	495.	729.	726.	545.	894.
21	682.	426.	874.	717.	608.	860.
22	754.	442.	776.	651.	636.	792.
23	828.	475.	858.	605.	703.	739.
24	818.	558.	815.	550.	749.	699.
25	922.	597.	843.	463.	706.	773.
26	929.	654.	899.	497.	644.	818.
27	903.	695.	864.	564.	718.	871.
28	820.	746.	917.	582.	733.	882.
29	871.	814.	830.	633.	824.	959.
30	926.	826.	916.	686.	695.	979.
31	811.	867.	947.	676.	721.	955.
32	901.	844.	879.	657.	661.	925.
33	867.	806.	944.	602.	690.	843.
34	948.	727.	950.	534.	784.	790.
35	820.	751.	997.	499.	724.	746.
36	893.	805.	956.	472.	812.	822.
37	859.	864.	1,006.	459.	898.	857.
38	909.	888.	937.	519.	869.	876.
39	860.	970.	1,016.	552.	801.	959.
40	993.	991.	1,066.	589.	875.	981.
41	858.	1,041.	999.	653.	803.	1,051.
42	887.	1,105.	1,026.	684.	772.	1,124.
43	823.	1,159.	1,020.	766.	788.	1,073.
44	909.	1,077.	1,038.	678.	751.	1,020.
45	837.	1,053.	1,119.	649.	823.	933.
46	821.	984.	1,030.	582.	725.	787.
47	916.	965.	1,084.	537.	685.	830.
48	911.	903.	1,166.	475.	805.	922.

APPENDIX B: SIX SERIES PLOTS

FIGURE B–1

Demand for Computer Paper, Series with Random Behavior (Series A, Boxes of Computer Paper)

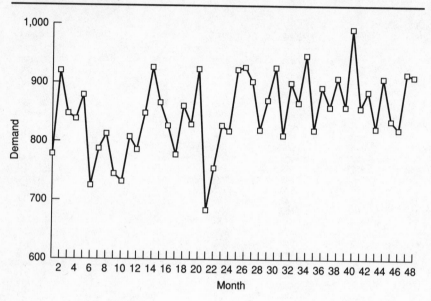

FIGURE B–2
Price of Common Stock with Highly Autocorrelated, Random-Walk Pattern
(Series B, Price of Common Stock)

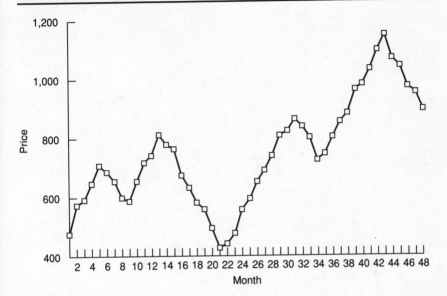

FIGURE B-3
Demand for a Product with Strong Trend (Series C, Demand for a Brand of Advanced Microcomputers)

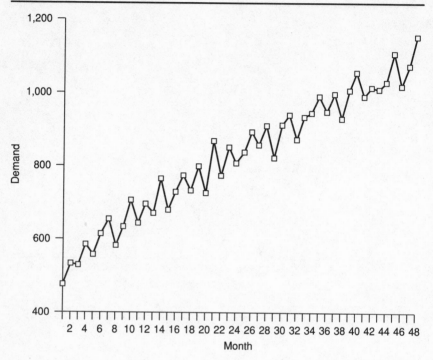

FIGURE B–4
Demand for a Product with Strong Seasonality (Series D, Demand for Brand D Diet Soft Drink)

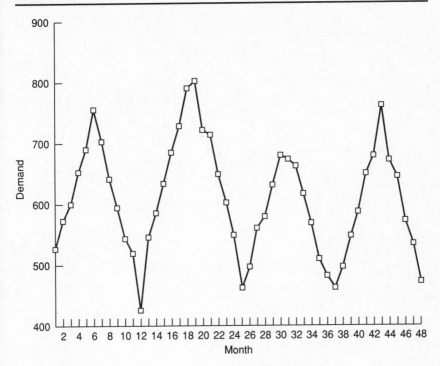

FIGURE B–5
Demand for a Product with Low Autocorrelation (Series E, 3.5-inch Brand X Floppy Diskettes)

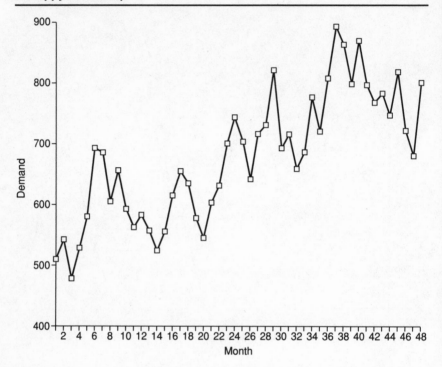

FIGURE B–6
Demand for a Product with Strong Trend and Seasonality (Series F, AM/FM Personal Radio)

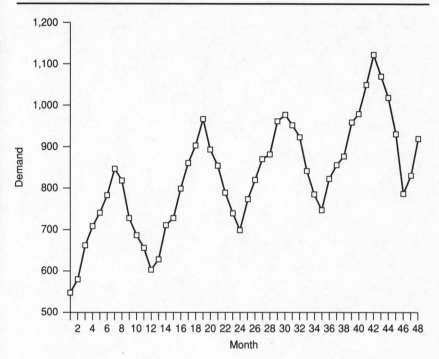

APPENDIX C: AREAS OF THE STANDARD NORMAL DISTRIBUTION

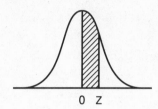

Z	.00	.01	.02	.03	.04	.05	.06	.07	.08	.09
0.0	.0000	.0040	.0080	.0120	.0160	.0199	.0239	.0279	.0319	.0359
0.1	.0398	.0438	.0478	.0517	.0557	.0596	.0636	.0675	.0714	.0753
0.2	.0793	.0832	.0871	.0910	.0948	.0987	.1026	.1064	.1103	.1141
0.3	.1179	.1217	.1255	.1293	.1331	.1368	.1406	.1443	.1480	.1517
0.4	.1554	.1591	.1628	.1664	.1700	.1736	.1772	.1808	.1844	.1879
0.5	.1915	.1950	.1985	.2019	.2054	.2088	.2123	.2157	.2190	.2224
0.6	.2257	.2291	.2324	.2357	.2389	.2422	.2454	.2486	.2517	.2549
0.7	.2580	.2611	.2642	.2673	.2703	.2734	.2764	.2794	.2823	.2852
0.8	.2881	.2910	.2939	.2967	.2995	.3023	.3051	.3078	.3106	.3133
0.9	.3159	.3186	.3212	.3238	.3264	.3289	.3315	.3340	.3365	.3389
1.0	.3413	.3438	.3461	.3485	.3508	.3531	.3554	.3577	.3599	.3621
1.1	.3643	.3665	.3686	.3708	.3729	.3749	.3770	.3790	.3810	.3830
1.2	.3849	.3869	.3888	.3907	.3925	.3944	.3962	.3980	.3997	.4015
1.3	.4032	.4049	.4066	.4082	.4099	.4115	.4131	.4147	.4162	.4177
1.4	.4192	.4207	.4222	.4236	.4251	.4265	.4279	.4292	.4306	.4319
1.5	.4332	.4345	.4357	.4370	.4382	.4394	.4406	.4418	.4429	.4441
1.6	.4452	.4463	.4474	.4484	.4495	.4505	.4515	.4525	.4535	.4545
1.7	.4554	.4564	.4573	.4582	.4591	.4599	.4608	.4616	.4625	.4633
1.8	.4641	.4649	.4656	.4664	.4671	.4678	.4686	.4693	.4699	.4706
1.9	.4713	.4719	.4726	.4732	.4738	.4744	.4750	.4756	.4761	.4767
2.0	.4772	.4778	.4783	.4788	.4793	.4798	.4803	.4808	.4812	.4817
2.1	.4821	.4826	.4830	.4834	.4838	.4842	.4846	.4850	.4854	.4857
2.2	.4861	.4864	.4868	.4871	.4875	.4878	.4881	.4884	.4887	.4890
2.3	.4893	.4896	.4898	.4901	.4904	.4906	.4909	.4911	.4913	.4916
2.4	.4918	.4920	.4922	.4925	.4927	.4929	.4931	.4932	.4934	.4936
2.5	.4938	.4940	.4941	.4943	.4945	.4946	.4948	.4949	.4951	.4952
2.6	.4953	.4955	.4956	.4957	.4959	.4960	.4961	.4962	.4963	.4964
2.7	.4965	.4966	.4967	.4968	.4969	.4970	.4971	.4972	.4973	.4974
2.8	.4974	.4975	.4976	.4977	.4977	.4978	.4979	.4979	.4980	.4981
2.9	.4981	.4982	.4982	.4983	.4984	.4984	.4985	.4985	.4986	.4986
3.0	.4987	.4987	.4987	.4988	.4988	.4989	.4989	.4989	.4990	.4990

An entry in the table is the proportion under the entire curve that is between Z = 0 and a positive value of Z. Areas for negative values of Z are obtained by symmetry.

Source: Paul G. Hoel, *Elementary Statistics* (New York: John Wiley & Sons, 1960), p. 240).

GLOSSARY

A

accuracy The degree of freedom from error or the degree of conformity to some standard. Accuracy is different from precision. For example, four-decimal-place numbers are less precise than six-decimal-place numbers. However, a properly computed four-decimal-place number might be more accurate than an improperly computed six-decimal-place number.

actual demand Customer orders (and often allocations of items/ingredients/raw materials to production or distribution). It nets against or "consumes" forecast, depending on rules chosen over a time horizon. For example, actual demand will totally replace forecast inside the "sold out" customer-order–backlog horizon, but will only replace forecast by planning period outside this horizon if it is greater than the period's forecast.

adaptive smoothing A term applied to a form of exponential smoothing in which the smoothing constant is automatically adjusted as a function of forecast error measurement.

aggregate forecast An estimate of sales, often time phased, for some grouping of products, perhaps for all products or within a family of products, produced by some manufacturing facility. Stated in terms of units or dollars or both, the aggregate forecast is used for sales and operations-planning purposes and to control the total company forecast.

algorithm A prescribed set of well-defined rules or processes for the solution of a problem in a finite number of steps; for example, the full statement of the arithmetic procedure for calculating the reorder point.

alpha The smoothing constant applied to the most recent forecast error in exponential smoothing forecasting.

amplitude In spectral analysis, the amplitude of a series is the magnitude of the wave, normally reflecting the magnitude of seasonality.

ARIMA Autoregressive integrated moving average (ARIMA) method of modeling a time series; also known as Box-Jenkins methods.

arithmetic mean See *mean*.

ARRES See *adaptive smoothing*.

assemble-to-order product A make-to-order product where all components (bulk, semifinished, intermediate, subassembly, fabricated, purchased, packaging, etc.) used in the assembly, packaging, or finishing process are planned and stocked in anticipation of a customer order. See *make-to-order product*.

autocorrelated errors When the errors in forecasting are autocorrelated, it indicates that the forecasting method has not removed all of the pattern or information from the data. See *autocorrelation*.

autocorrelation This term is used to describe the degree of association or mutual dependence between values of the same time series at different time lags. For example, it measures correlation between demand versus the same demand of three periods ago. The pattern of autocorrelations helps identify whether or not seasonality is present in a series and the length of seasonality. Also, importantly, it helps identify whether a series has a constant mean and the proper model for a series with trend, seasonality, or random walk.

autoregression (AR) Autoregression is regression of a dependent variable on its past values. For example, sales in period t are a function of sales in period t-1. An autoregressive model expresses the forecast as a function of past values of a time series.

available-to-promise The uncommitted portion of a company's inventory or planned production. This figure is normally calculated from the master production schedule and is maintained as a tool for customer-order promising.

average forecast error The arithmetic mean of the forecast errors, or the exponentially smoothed forecast error. See *forecast error, mean absolute deviation*.

B

backlog All of the customer orders received but not yet shipped. Sometimes referred to as open orders or the order board.

backorder An unfilled customer order or commitment. It is an immediate (or past-due) demand against an item whose inventory is insufficient to satisfy the demand. See *stockout*.

bar code A series of alternating bars and spaces printed or stamped on parts, containers, labels, or other media representing encoded information that can be read by electronic readers. Used to facilitate timely and accurate input of data to a computer system.

base index See *base series*.

base series A standard series of demand-over-time data used in forecasting seasonal items. This series of factors is usually based upon the relative level of demand during the corresponding period of previous years. The average value of the base series over a 12-month period will be 1.0. A figure higher than 1.0 indicates that the period is more than average; a figure less than 1.0 indicates less than average. For forecasting purposes, the base series is superimposed upon the average demand and trend in demand for the item in question. See *seasonality*. Synonym: *base index*.

bias The departure from the average of a set of values. See *skew*.

biased estimate When the estimate of a statistic (e.g., mean) is not on average equal to the true population value (e.g., the mean of the population), then the estimate will be called a *biased estimator*. In forecasting, we seek unbiased estimates of the future.

bill of material (BOM) A listing of all the subassemblies, intermediates, parts, and raw materials that go into a parent assembly showing the quantity of each required to make an assembly. There are a variety of display formats of bill of material, including single-level bill of material, indented bill of material, modular (planning) bill of material, transient bill of material, matrix bill of material, and costed bill of material. May also be called *formula, recipe,* and *ingredients list* in certain industries.

bottleneck A facility, function, department, or other that impedes production. For example, a machine or work center where jobs arrive at a faster rate than they can be completed.

Box-Jenkins models A forecasting approach based on regression and moving average models, where the model is based not on regression of independent variables, but on past observations of the item to be forecast, at varying time lags, and on previous error values from forecasting. See *ARIMA*.

business cycle Recurrent expansions of prosperity generally followed by contractions (i.e., recession) are called business cycles. Such cycles vary in length and amplitude. Cyclic influences are difficult to forecast because of their unknown period and complexity, but modeling past expansions and contraction is important in cyclical contingency planning. Cyclical influences are sometimes decomposed in a time series.

business plan A statement of long-range strategy and income, cost, and profit objectives usually accompanied by budgets, projected balance sheet, and a cash flow (source and application of funds) statement. It is usually stated in terms of dollars and grouped by product family. The business plan and the sales and operations plan, although frequently stated in different terms, should be in agreement with each other. See *manufacturing resource planning*.

C

capacity management   The function of establishing, measuring, monitoring, and adjusting limits or levels of capacity in order to execute all manufacturing schedules, that is, production plan, master production schedule, material requirements plan, and dispatch list. See *capacity requirements planning, rough-cut capacity planning*.

capacity requirements planning (CRP)   The function of establishing, measuring, and adjusting limits or levels of capacity. The term *capacity requirements planning* in this context is the process of determining how much labor and machine resources are required to accomplish the tasks of production. Open shop orders and planned orders in the MRP system are input to CRP, which "translates" these orders into hours of work by work center by time period. See *closed-loop MRP, rough-cut capacity planning*.

carrying cost   Cost of carrying inventory, usually defined as a percent of the dollar value of inventory per unit of time (generally one year). Depends mainly on cost of capital invested as well as the costs of maintaining the inventory such as taxes and insurance, obsolescence, spoilage, and space occupied. Such costs vary from 10–35 percent annually, depending on type of industry. Ultimately, carrying cost is a policy variable reflecting the opportunity cost of alternative uses for funds tied up in inventory.

causal or extrinsic model   A forecasting model that assumes that the demand being forecast is caused by one or more other external factors. Regression and econometric models are the most common forecasting types. See *extrinsic forecast*.

Census II   The Census II method of forecasting is a refinement of the classical decomposition method. It attempts to decompose a time series into seasonal, trend, cycle, and random components that can be analyzed separately, then recombined for predictive purposes. This method has been developed by using the empirical results obtained from its application at the United States Bureau of the Census and elsewhere.

centralized inventory control   Inventory decision making exercised for an entire company (all SKUs) from one office or department.

classical decomposition method This approach to forecasting a time series decomposes the patterns into cyclical, seasonal, trend, and random components. These components of demand are then extended into the future by recombining the individual values through multiplication or addition to obtain forecasts of the original series.

closed-loop MRP A system built around material requirements planning and also including the additional planning functions of sales and operations (production planning, master production scheduling, and capacity requirements planning). Further, once this planning phase is complete and the plans have been accepted as realistic and attainable, the execution functions come into play. These include the manufacturing control functions of input-output measurement, detailed scheduling and dispatching, as well as anticipated-delay reports from both the plant and vendors and vendor scheduling. The term *closed loop* implies that not only is each of these elements included in the overall system but also that there is feedback from the execution functions so that the planning can be kept valid at all times. See *manufacturing resource planning.*

coefficient of determination See R-*squared adjusted.*

coefficient of variation The ratio of the standard deviation to the mean, expressed as a percent. It is a measure of the relative scatter or variation in a series. A higher coefficient means greater variation in the values.

common parts bill (of material) A type of planning bill that groups common components for a product or family of products into one bill of material, structured to a "pseudo" parent item number. See *planning bill, modular bill.*

component A term used to identify a raw material, ingredient, part, or subassembly that goes into a higher-level assembly, compound, or other item. May also include packaging materials for finished items.

confidence limits A confidence interval is a probability statement about some value or range of values. Confidence limits can be placed on future forecast values. However, this must be done very cautiously because the past may not be repeated in the future.

constraint A limitation placed on the maximization or minimization of an objective function. These usually result from scarcity of the resources necessary for attaining some objective.

correlation The relationship between two sets of data such that when one changes the other is likely to make a corresponding change. If the changes are in the same direction, there is positive correlation. When changes tend to go in opposite directions, there is negative correlation. See *correlation coefficient* and *scatter chart.*

correlation coefficient A standardized measure of correlation between two variables, for example, X and Y. Designated as r, it ranges from -1 to $+1$, which denote a strong negative relationship and a strong positive association, respectively.

cross-correlation The correlation or association between one time series and the lead-lag values of another time series. This statistic is measured on a scale of -1 to $+1$ and is important in identifying leading indicators in regression or econometric methods.

cumulative forecasting Forecasting values for groups of equal time periods instead of forecasting the demand for individual time periods. For example, when sales are highly seasonal, it is typically more accurate to forecast monthly seasonal data than weekly seasonal data.

cumulative leadtime The longest planned length of time involved in accomplishing the activity in question. For any item planned through MRP, it is found by reviewing the leadtime for each bill of material path below the item. Whichever path adds up to the greatest number defines cumulative leadtime.

cumulative manufacturing leadtime The cumulative planned leadtime when all purchased items are assumed to be in stock.

cumulative sum The accumulated total of all forecast errors, both positive and negative. This will approach zero if the forecast is unbiased. See *tracking signal.* Synonym: *sum of deviations.*

curve fitting An approach to forecasting based upon a straight line, polynomial, or other curve that describes some historical time-series data.

customer-order servicing system System for order entry, where orders are keyed into a local terminal and a bill of material translator converts the catalog ordering numbers into required manufacturing part numbers and due dates for the MRP system. Advanced systems contain customer information, sales history, forecasting information, and product option compatibility checks to facilitate order processing, "cleaning up" orders prior to placing a demand on the manufacturing system. Synonyms: *sales order configurator, configuration system.*

customer service Delivery of product to the customer at the time that the customer or corporate policy specifies. See *percent of fill.*

customer service ratio A measure of delivery performance usually in the form of a percentage. In a make-to-stock company, this percentage usually represents the number of items or dollars (on one or more customer orders) that were shipped on schedule for a specific time period, compared to the total that were supposed to be shipped in that time period. In a make-to-order company, it is usually some comparison of the number of jobs shipped in a given time period (like a week) compared with the number of jobs that were supposed to be shipped in that time period. See *percent of fill, stockout percentage.*

cyclical index A cyclical index is a number, usually standardized around 100, that indicates the cyclical pattern of a given set of time-series data.

D

database A data processing file-management approach designed to establish the independence of computer programs from data files. Redundancy is minimized and data elements can be added to, or deleted from, the file designs without necessitating changes to existing computer programs.

decentralized inventory control Inventory decision making exercised at each stocking location for SKUs at that location.

degrees of freedom (df) The number of effective sample points is called the degrees of freedom. The higher the degrees of freedom, the better. For example, the degrees of freedom are defined as the number of observations included in a formula minus the number of parameters estimated using the data. For example, the mean statistic for 100 observations has 100 df because no other statistics must be estimated when calculating the mean. In contrast, the standard deviation has only 99 df because the mean has to be estimated before the standard deviation can be calculated. The degrees of freedom are important in trading off model complexity (the number of parameters in the model) versus the number of observations. Complex models require more observations to achieve the same level of degrees of freedom.

delivery policy The company's goal for the time to ship the product after the receipt of a customer's order. The policy is sometimes stated as "our quoted delivery time."

Delphi method A qualitative forecasting technique where the opinions of experts are combined in a series of iterations. The results of each iteration are used to develop the next, so that convergence of the expert opinion is obtained.

demand   A need for a particular product or component. The demand could come from any number of sources, for example, customer order, forecast, interplant, branch warehouse, service part, or for manufacturing another product. At the finished-goods level, "demand data" are usually different from "sales data" because demand does not necessarily result in sales, that is, if there is no stock, there will be no sale. See *dependent demand, independent demand.*

demand filter   A standard that is set to monitor individual sales data in forecasting models. Usually, it is set to be tripped when the demand for a period differs from the forecast by more than some number of mean absolute deviations or standard deviations.

demand management   The function of recognizing and managing all of the demands for products to ensure that the master scheduler is aware of them. It encompasses the activities of forecasting, order entry, order promising, branch warehouse requirements, interplant orders, and service parts requirements. See *master production schedule.*

demand uncertainty   The uncertainty or variability in errors as measured by the standard deviation, mean absolute deviation (MAD), or variance of forecast errors.

dependent demand   Demand is considered dependent when it is directly related to or derived from the schedule for other items or end products. Such demands are therefore calculated and need not and should not be forecast. A given inventory item may have both dependent and independent demand at any given time. See *independent demand.*

dependent variable   A variable that is a function of some other variables is called a dependent variable. In regression and econometric analysis, the variable being predicted is the dependent variable.

deseasonalized data   Removing the seasonal fluctuations in a series yields deseasonalized data. By removing seasonality, we can more easily identify trend, cyclical, promotional, and outlier influences in the data. Much of the economic data in the media is deseasonalized to add more continuity and comparability to reported statistics. Deseasonalization is an essential step in decomposition.

deviation   The difference between a number and the mean of a set of numbers, or between a forecast value and the actual datum.

diagnostic checking A step in forecast model building where the errors of a model are examined for normality, zero mean, constant standard deviation, and autocorrelation.

differencing When a time series is nonstationary, that is, has no constant mean, the series can be made to have a constant mean by taking first differences of the series ($Y_t - Y_{t-1}$). If first differences do not achieve a constant mean, then first differences of first differences, called *second differences,* or seasonal differences can be tried. Seasonal differences are defined as $Y_t - Y_{t-s}$ where s is the length of the seasonal cycle.

discontinuous demand A demand pattern that is characterized by large demands interrupted by periods with no demand, as opposed to a continuous or "steady" (e.g., daily) demand. See *lumpy demand.*

distributed processing A data processing organizational concept under which computer resources of a company are installed at more than one location with appropriate communication links. Processing is performed at the user's location generally on a smaller computer, and under the user's control and scheduling, as opposed to processing for all users being done on a large, centralized computer system.

distributed systems Refers to computer systems in multiple locations throughout an organization working in a cooperative fashion.

distribution center A warehouse with finished goods and/or service items. A company, for example, might have a manufacturing facility in Philadelphia and distribution centers in Atlanta, Dallas, Los Angeles, San Francisco, and Chicago. The term *distribution center* is synonymous with the term *branch warehouse,* although the former has become more commonly used recently. When there is a warehouse that serves a group of satellite warehouses, it is usually called a *regional distribution center.*

distribution of forecast errors Tabulation of the forecast errors according to the frequency of occurrence of each error value. The errors in forecasting are, in many cases, normally distributed even when the observed data do not come from a normal distribution. See *normal distribution.*

distribution requirements planning The function of determining the needs to replenish inventory at branch warehouses. A time-phased order-point approach is used where the planned orders at the branch warehouse level are "exploded" via MRP logic to become gross requirements on the supplying source. In the case of multilevel distribution networks, this explosion process can continue down through the various levels of master warehouse, factory warehouse, and so on and become input to the master production schedule. Demand on the supplying source(s) is recognized as dependent, and standard MRP logic applies. See *time-phased order point, physical distribution*.

distribution resource planning (DRP)   The extension of distribution requirements planning into the planning of the key resources contained in a distribution system: warehouse space, manpower, money, trucks, freight cars, and so on. See *distribution requirements planning*.

double moving average   A moving average of a moving average is taken so that changes in the average can be measured. This additional smoothing makes it possible to measure trends and other influences not evident in the single moving average.

double smoothing   See *second-order smoothing*.

DRP   Abbreviation for *distribution resource planning*.

dummy variable   Also referred to as a dichotomous or binary variable whose value is either 0 or 1. It is used to identify qualitative events such as promotions, seasonal periods, outliers, or supply interruptions. Multiple dummy variables can be used to model multiple qualities; for example, each quarter of the year can be modeled using three dummy variables. When all dummies are zero, it is quarter one; when the first equals one and all others zero, then that is quarter two. Thus the additive seasonal influence can be measured using dummy variables. Dummies are most commonly used in the application of multiple-regression analysis.

E

econometric forecasting   An econometric model is a set of equations intended to be used simultaneously to capture the way in which dependent and independent variables are interrelated. Using such a set of equations to forecast future values of key economic variables is known as econometric forecasting. The value of econometric forecasting is intimately connected to the value of the assumptions underlying the model equations.

economic indicator   An economic indicator is a time series that describes or predicts the movements of some other economic variable of interest such as industry or company demand. Indicators can be leading, lagging, or coincident. Leading indicators are particularly effective in forecasting and predicting the turning points in another variable.

error See *residual.*

expected value The average value that would be observed in taking an action an infinite number of times. The expected value of an action is calculated by multiplying the outcome of the action by the probability of achieving the outcome.

exponential distribution A continuous probability distribution where the probability of occurrence either steadily increases or decreases. The steady-increase case (positive exponential distribution) is used to model phenomena such as customer service level versus cost. The steady-decrease case (negative exponential distribution) is used to model things such as the weight given to any one time period of demand in exponential smoothing.

exponential smoothing A type of weighted moving average forecasting technique in which past observations are geometrically discounted according to their age. The heaviest weight is assigned to the most recent data. The smoothing is termed *exponential* because data points are weighted in accordance with an exponential function of their age. The technique makes use of a smoothing constant to apply to the difference between the most recent forecast and the actual demand data, which avoids the necessity of carrying historical sales data. The approach can be used for data that exhibit no trend or seasonal patterns or for data with either trend or seasonality or both. See *first-order smoothing, second-order smoothing.*

exponential smoothing, linear (Brown's) Linear exponential smoothing can model series that possess trend. The method is also known as double smoothing because two smoothed values are used and the difference between these smoothed values measures the trend in the original series.

exponential smoothing, linear (Holt's two-parameter model) This two-parameter method involves smoothing both the series and its trend. It has some greater appeal than Brown's in that different smoothing constants can be used to model the smoothed and trend values.

exponential smoothing, quadratic (Brown's one-parameter method) This approach involves smoothing three values using a single smoothing parameter. Nonlinear trends that can be described by a quadratic function (e.g., a *u*-shape) can be modeled using this method. This method is sometimes called *triple smoothing.* It is applicable to series that require second-order differences to achieve a constant mean.

exponential smoothing, seasonal (Winters' three-parameter method) Winters' method extends Holt's two-parameter smoothing by including a third equation to calculate seasonal indexes. Thus Winters' model includes random, trend, and seasonal components.

exponential smoothing, single This is the simplest of exponential smoothing methods. It models past demand as an exponentially weighted moving average of all past actual demands. It uses a single parameter, which can be optimized. It is popular in some automated forecasting systems, but is not versatile enough to model series with trend and seasonality. It is not recommended as a general approach to forecasting. Instead, methods such as Winters', Fourier, and classical decomposition are recommended.

extrapolation Estimating the future value of some data series based on past observations. Statistical forecasting represents a common example.

extrinsic forecast A forecast based on a correlated leading indicator, for example, estimating furniture sales based on housing starts. Extrinsic forecasts tend to be more useful for large aggregations, such as total company sales, than for individual product sales. Antonym: *intrinsic forecast*.

F

filter There are several meanings to filters in forecasting. 1. A forecasting model can be viewed as a filter through which past demand patterns are converted to forecasts and white noise errors. Theoretically, all forecast models are filters. 2. Demand filters are those that check the reasonableness of a past actual demand value. If this past demand value is too high or too low, then it is highlighted and investigated to determine whether it is an outlier. Demand filters are important in maintaining a valid demand database.

final assembly 1. The highest-level assembled product, as it is shipped to customers. 2. The name for the manufacturing department where the product is assembled.

final assembly schedule (FAS) Also referred to as *finishing schedule* since it may include operations other than simply the final ones. It may also not involve assembly but only final mixing, cutting, packaging, and so on. It is a schedule of end items to finish the product for specific customers' orders in a make-to-order or assemble-to-order environment. It is prepared after receipt of a customer order as constrained by the availability of material and capacity, and it schedules the operations required to complete the product from the level where it is stocked (or master scheduled) to the end-item level. Synonyms: *blending schedule, pack-out schedule.*

finished-products inventories Those items on which all manufacturing operations, including final test, have been completed. These products are now available for shipment to the customer either as end items or repair parts.

first-order smoothing This phrase refers to single exponential smoothing. First-order smoothing is best applied to forecasting problems where the data do not exhibit significant trend or seasonal patterns. Synonym: *single smoothing.* See *exponential smoothing.*

fixed-interval reorder system A periodic reordering system where the time interval between orders is fixed, such as weekly, monthly, or quarterly, but the size of the order is not fixed and orders vary according to usage since the last review. This type of inventory control system is employed where it is convenient to examine inventory stocks on a fixed time cycle in systems where orders are placed mechanically, such as in warehouse control systems, or for handling inventories involving a very large variety of items under some form of clerical control. Also called *fixed–reorder-cycle system.* See *fixed–order-quantity system.*

fixed–order-quantity system An inventory control method where the size of the order is fixed, but the time interval between orders depends on actual demand. The practice of ordering a fixed quantity when needed assumes that individual inventories are under constant watch. This system consists of placing an order of a fixed quantity (the reorder quantity) wherever the amount on hand plus the amount on order falls to or below a specified level (the order point or reorder point). See *fixed-interval reorder system.*

fluctuation inventory Inventories that are carried as a cushion to protect against forecast error. See *safety stock.*

focus forecasting™ A system that allows the user to simulate the effectiveness of numerous forecasting techniques, thereby being able to select the most effective one.

forecast An estimate of future demand. A forecast can be determined by mathematical means using historical data; it can be created subjectively by using estimates from informal sources; or it can represent a combination of both techniques. See *extrinsic forecast, intrinsic forecast.*

forecast consumption The process of replacing the forecast with customer orders, or other types of actual demands, as they are received.

forecast error The difference between actual demand and forecast demand.

forecast horizon The length of time into the future for which plans and forecasts are made. Horizons are short, intermediate, and long range and vary from less than one month to more than two years.

forecast period The time period for which forecasts are prepared, such as weekly, monthly, or quarterly time units.

Fourier series analysis A form of analysis useful for forecasting. The model uses sine and cosine waves to model the repeating patterns of seasonal demand. Pairs of sine and cosine waves can be added to model more-complex seasonal patterns.

frequency In spectral analysis, frequency is the number of peaks or troughs (i.e., the number of seasonal cycles) that exist in n observations. A frequency of 3 when there are 36 observations means that there are 3 peaks that are 12 periods apart. Similarly, a frequency of 4 for 48 observations denotes that there are 12 periods between peaks, that is, 12 periods in each season. See also *sine wave* and *line spectrum.*

frequency distribution A table that indicates the frequency with which data fall into each of any number of subdivisions of the variable. The subdivisions are usually called *classes.* See *histogram.*

function A function is a statement of relationship between variables in a model. For example, a variable Y is a function of X in the relationship $Y = 3 + 4X$. Almost all forecasting models are functional relationships between several variables such as current demand as a function of its past demand and other variables.

H

harmonic smoothing An approach to forecasting based upon fitting some set of sine and cosine functions to the historical pattern of a time series. See *Fourier series analysis.*

harmonic smoothing (Harrison's method) See *spectral analysis.*

heuristic A form of problem solving where the results or rules have been determined by experience or intuition instead of by optimization.

histogram A graph of contiguous vertical bars representing a frequency distribution in which the groups or classes of demands are marked on the X-axis, and the frequency in each class is indicated by a vertical bar segment drawn above the X-axis at a height equal to the number of observations in that class.

I

identification This is the process of identifying the best forecasting model to use in modeling a time series. Formal methods of ARIMA model building are used in the identification process. These methods focus on statistics that describe the autocorrelation of the time series. While formal model-building procedures are associated with ARIMA approaches, they are useful in any forecasting situation.

independent demand Demand for an item is considered independent when such demand is unrelated to the demand for other items. Demand for finished goods, parts required for destructive testing, and service parts requirements are some examples of independent demand. See *dependent demand.*

independent-demand inventory system The policies, methods, and procedures used to manage inventory items that have independent demand.

independent variable An independent variable is one used to predict the values of a dependent variable.

index numbers An index number is used to summarize several influences or indicators of economic activity. Many indexes are compiled by the Federal Reserve, Department of Commerce, and other government and trade organizations.

interactive forecasting Interactive forecasting is the use of on-line, real-time interaction with software and databases in identifying, estimating, and diagnosing alternative forecasts and forecasting models.

intercept The intercept is the constant term in regression analysis. It is the value of Y when all of the X variables are equal to 0. Frequently, the intercept is uninterpretable as a meaningful number. For example, it may be illogical or impossible for all X values to be equal to zero.

interdependence If two or more variables are dependent, then their values move together as measured by the correlation coefficient. Changes or values in one are associated with changes or values in the other. When independent variables in regression are highly dependent, there may be some problems in interpreting the regression coefficients.

intrinsic forecast A forecast based on internal factors, such as an average of past sales. See *extrinsic forecast.*

item number A number that serves to uniquely identify an item. Synonyms: *part number, product number, stock code.*

item record The "master" record for an item. Typically it contains identifying and descriptive data, status requirements, planned orders, and costs. Item records are linked together by bill of material records (for product-structure records), thus defining the bill of material.

J

JIT See *just-in-time.*

just-in-time (JIT) In the broad sense, an approach to achieving excellence in a manufacturing company based on the continuing elimination of waste (waste being considered as those things that do not add value to the product). In the narrow sense, just-in-time refers to the movement of material at the necessary place at the necessary time. The implication is that each operation is closely synchronized with the ones that make that possible.

L

leading indicator A specific business activity index that indicates future trends. For example, housing starts is a leading indicator for the industry that supplies builders' hardware. See *extrinsic forecast.* Turning points in such an indicator "lead" subsequent turning points in the general economy or some other economic series, thus signaling the likelihood of such a subsequent turning point.

leadtime A span of time required to perform an activity. In a logistics context, the time between recognition of the need for an order and the receipt of goods. Individual components of leadtime can include order preparation time, queue time, move or transportation time, receiving and inspection time.

least-squares method A method of curve fitting that selects a line of best fit through a plot of data to minimize the sum of squares of the deviations of the given points from the line. See *regression analysis.*

linear exponential smoothing See *exponential smoothing, linear.*

line item One item on an order, regardless of quantity.

line spectrum When a time series is modeled using Fourier analysis, it is possible to determine frequency (e.g., the length of the seasonal cycle) using a graph of the line spectrum. This graph illustrates frequencies and wavelength, which are important in modeling past sinusoidal patterns. See *spectral analysis, Fourier series analysis.*

logistics In an industrial context, this term refers to the art and science of obtaining and distributing material and product.

logistics curve This curve has the typical *s*-shape often associated with the product life cycle. It is frequently used in connection with long-term curve fitting as a technological forecasting method.

lumpy demand A demand pattern with large fluctuations from one time period to another. Synonym: *discontinuous demand.*

M

macroeconomic data This includes data such as GNP, interest rates, unemployment, inflation, and industrial production, which describes the behavior of the macroeconomy (the total national or international economy).

MAD See *mean absolute deviation.*

maintenance repair and operating supplies (MRO) Items used in support of general operations and maintenance such as spare parts and consumables used in the manufacturing process.

make-to-order product A product that is finished after receipt of a customer order. Frequently, long-leadtime components are bought prior to the order arriving so as to reduce the delivery time to the customer. Where options or other subassemblies are stocked prior to customer orders arriving, the term *assemble-to-order* is frequently used.

make-to-stock product A product that is shipped from finished goods, "off the shelf," and, therefore, is finished prior to a customer order arriving.

management information systems (MIS) A manual or computerized system that anticipates the wide use of data for management planning and control purposes. Accordingly, the data are organized in a database and are readily available for a variety of management functions.

manufacturing resource planning (MRP II)   A method for the effective planning of all resources of a manufacturing company. Ideally, it addresses operational planning in units and financial planning in dollars and has a simulation capability to answer what-if questions. It is made up of a variety of functions, each linked together: business planning, sales and operations (productions planning), master production scheduling, material requirements planning, capacity requirements planning, and the execution support systems for capacity and material. Output from these systems would be integrated with financial reports such as the business plan, purchase commitment report, shipping budget, and inventory projections in dollars. Manufacturing resource planning is a direct outgrowth and extension of closed-loop MRP. See *closed-loop MRP material requirements planning.*

market share   The actual portion of total market demand that a company and/or product achieves.

master production schedule (MPS)   The anticipated build schedule for those items assigned to the master scheduler. The master scheduler maintains this schedule, and, in turn, it becomes a set of planning numbers that "drive" material requirements planning. It represents what the company plans to produce as expressed in specific configurations, quantities, and dates. The master production schedule is not a sales forecast that represents a statement of demand. The master production schedule must take into account the forecast, the production plan, and other important considerations such as backlog, availability of material, availability of capacity, and management policy and goals. Synonym: *master schedule.* See *closed-loop MRP.*

master schedule item   A part number selected to be planned by the master scheduler. The item would be deemed critical in terms of its impact on lower-level components and/or resources such as skilled labor, key machines, and dollars. Therefore, the master scheduler, not the computer, would maintain the plan for these items. A master schedule item may be an end item, a component, a pseudo number, or a planning bill of material.

master scheduler   The job title of the person who manages the master production schedule. This person should be the best scheduler available, as the consequences of the planning done here have a great impact on material and capacity planning. Ideally, the person would have substantial product and plant knowledge.

material requirements planning (MRP) A set of techniques that uses bills of material, inventory data, and the master production schedule to calculate requirements for materials. It makes recommendations to release replenishment orders for material. Further, since it is time phased, it makes recommendations to reschedule open orders when due dates and need dates are not in phase. Originally seen as merely a better way to order inventory, today it is thought of as primarily a scheduling technique, that is, a method for establishing and maintaining valid due dates (priorities) on orders. See *closed-loop MRP, manufacturing resource planning.*

mean The arithmetic average of a group of values. It is used to measure the center of data. Also known as the *expected value.* See *median, mode.*

mean absolute deviation (MAD) The average of the absolute values of the deviations of some observed value from some expected value. MAD can be calculated based on observations and the arithmetic mean of those observations. An alternative is to calculate absolute deviations of actual sales data minus forecast data. These data can be averaged in the usual arithmetic way or with exponential smoothing.

mean absolute percentage error (MAPE) The mean absolute percentage error is the mean of the percentage errors without regard to sign. The absolute values are summed and the mean calculated. It is commonly used to judge forecast accuracy.

mean percentage error (MPE) The mean of all of the percentage errors in forecasting. Positive and negative percentage errors cancel one another. Its expected value is zero. Consequently, it can be used to detect bias in forecasts.

mean squared error (MSE) The mean squared error is the mean value of the squared error terms. The lower the MSE, the more accurate the resulting forecasts.

median The middle value in a set of measured values when the items are arranged in order of magnitude. If there is no middle value, the median is the average of the two middle values. See *mode, mean.*

mode The most common or frequent value in a group of values. See *mean, median.*

model A representation of a process or system that attempts to relate the most important variables in the system in such a way that analysis of the model leads to insights into the system. Frequently, the model is used to anticipate the result of some particular strategy in the real system.

modular bill (of material) A type of planning bill that is arranged in product modules or options. Often used in companies where the product has many optional features, e.g., automobiles. See *planning bill, common parts bill, super bill.*

moving average An arithmetic average of the *n* most-recent observations. As each new observation is added, the oldest one is dropped. The value of *n* (the number of periods to use for the average) reflects responsiveness versus stability in the same way that the choice of smoothing constant does in exponential smoothing. See *weighted average.*

multicollinearity The nonindependence in the independent variables of a regression relationship. When two variables are perfectly or highly correlated with each other, then inaccuracies exist in the estimated coefficients in a regression relationship. With perfect correlation, regression may be impossible because each variable provides the same information about the dependent variable. One variable has to be eliminated.

multiple-regression models A form of regression analysis where the model involves more than one independent variable such as sales being forecasted based upon housing starts, gross national product, and disposable income.

N

naive forecast Forecasts obtained with a minimal amount of effort and data manipulation and based solely on the most recent information available are frequently referred to as naive forecasts. One such naive method would be to use the most recent datum available as the future forecast. A slightly more sophisticated naive method would be to adjust that most recent datum for seasonality.

noise The unpredictable or random difference between the observed data and the forecasted data. See *residual.*

nonstationary If a time series has a nonconstant mean or variance, then it is nonstationary. This nonstationarity needs to be detected and modeled so that accurate forecasts result. Visual inspection can detect both forms of nonstationarity.

normal distribution A particular statistical distribution where most of the observations fall fairly close to one mean and a deviation from the mean is as likely to be plus as it is likely to be minus. When graphed, the normal distribution takes the form of a bell-shaped curve. See *frequency distribution.*

O

observation An observation is the actual value in a data set or database.

optimal parameter or coefficient The optimal value of a parameter or coefficient is that value that yields the desired forecasting property such as minimum sum of squared errors.

order entry The process of accepting and translating what a customer wants into terms used by the manufacturer or distributor. This can be as simple as creating shipping documents for a finished-goods product line, to a more complicated series of activities including engineering effort for make-to-order products.

order promising The process of making a delivery commitment, that is, answering the question "When can you ship?" For make-to-order products, this usually involves a check of uncommitted material and availability of capacity. Synonyms: *order dating, customer order promising.* See *available-to-promise.*

outlier A data point that differs significantly from other data for a similar phenomenon. For example, if the average sales for some product were 10 units per month and one month had sales of 500 units, this would be considered on outlier.

P

parameter estimation Use of numerical methods to estimate the best parameters or coefficients in exponential smoothing or regression analysis. Parameter values are chosen so as to minimize the sum of the squared errors and, consequently, minimize the resulting confidence intervals on projections. Exponential smoothing requires an iterative procedure to estimate minimum sum of squares parameters.

Pareto's law A concept developed by Vilfredo Pareto, an Italian economist, that states that a small percentage of a group accounts for the largest fraction of the impact, value, and so on. For example, 20 percent of the inventory items may comprise 80 percent of the inventory value. Synonym: *20/80 rule.*

parsimony The concept of parsimony denotes that models that are nearly as accurate as more-complex models are the better models.

Models with as few parameters as possible should be chosen over more-complex models. This principle almost always results in better forecasts even though the model might not fit the past as well as a more-complex model.

pattern The systematic movement in a time series that is modeled using a forecasting model. If this pattern repeats in the future, then models of the patterns yield good forecasts.

percent fill A measure of the effectiveness with which the inventory-management system responds to actual demand. The percent of customer orders filled off the shelf can be measured in either units or dollars. Antonym: *stockout percentage.*

periodic inventory A physical inventory taken at some recurring interval, for example, month, quarter, or year.

periodic replenishment A method of aggregating requirements to place deliveries of varying quantities at evenly spaced time intervals, rather than variably spaced deliveries of equal quantities.

periodic review system See *fixed-interval reorder system.*

perpetual inventory An inventory record-keeping system where each transaction in and out is recorded and a new balance is computed.

perpetual inventory record A computer record or manual document on which each inventory transaction is posted so that a current record of the inventory is maintained.

phase The phase of a sine wave is the horizontal shift of the whole wave. For example, given $Y = A*\sin(B + C)$, C is referred to as the *phase shift*. The wave will look identical for different values of C. However, it will shift right or left depending on the value of C.

physical distribution The activities associated with the movement of material, usually finished products or service parts, from the manufacturer to the customer. These activities encompass the functions of transportation, warehousing, inventory control, material handling, order administration, site/location analysis, industrial packaging, data processing, and the communications network necessary for effective management. In many cases, this movement is made through one or more levels of field warehouses. See *distribution requirements planning.*

pipeline stock Inventory to fill the transportation network and the distribution system including the flow through intermediate stocking points. The flow time through the pipeline has a major effect on the amount of inventory required in the pipeline. Time factors involve order transmission, order processing, shipping, transportation, receiving, stocking, and review time.

planning bill (of material) An artificial grouping of items and/or events in bill-of-material format, used to facilitate master scheduling and/or material planning. See *common parts bill, modular bill, super bill.*

point of sale (POS) The relief of inventory and computation of sales data at the time and place of sale, generally through the use of bar coding or magnetic media and equipment.

polynomial A polynomial expresses a dependent variable as a nonlinear function of one or more variables. For example, $Y = a + bX$ is a linear polynomial, $Y = a + bX + cX^2$ is a nonlinear, quadratic polynomial.

polynomial fitting Identifying the parameters in a polynomial regression relationship.

population The entire set of items from which a sample is drawn.

POS See *point of sale.*

post or out-of-sample validation Evaluating a forecasting model using data that were held out or unavailable at the time of estimating model form and parameters. This is important in model validation. The use of tracking signals is a form of model validation.

prediction An intuitive estimate of demand, taking into account changes and new factors influencing the market, as opposed to a forecast, which is an objective projection of the past into the future. See *forecast.*

probability Mathematically, a number between 0 and 1 that estimates the fraction of experiments (if the same experiment were being repeated many times) in which a particular result would occur. This number can either be subjective or can be based upon the empirical results of experimentation. It can also be derived theoretically to give the probable outcome of experimentation. See *expected value.*

probability distribution A table of numbers or a mathematical expression that indicates the frequency with which each of all possible results of an experiment should occur.

product family A group of products with similar characteristics, often used in sales and operations (production) planning.

product-group forecast A forecast for a number of similar products.

product life cycle The life cycle of many products evolves from slow growth in early stages of introduction to rapid and sustained growth before maturity during which sales decline. This cycle results in an *s*-shaped growth curve. Determining where the demand for product is on the life cycle curve is important in achieving good forecasts.

Currently, the lengths of the product life cycles of most products are much less than in the past.

product line A group of products whose similarity in manufacturing procedures, marketing characteristics, or specifications allows them to be aggregated for planning, marketing, or, occasionally, costing.

product load profile A listing of the required capacity and key resources required to manufacture one unit of a selected item or family. Often used to predict the impact of the item scheduled on the overall schedule and load of the key resources. Rough-cut capacity planning uses these profiles to calculate the approximate capacity requirements of the master production schedule and/or the production plan. Synonyms: *bill of labor, bill of resources, resource profile.*

product mix The proportion of individual products that make up the total production and/or sales volume. Changes in the product mix can mean drastic changes in the manufacturing requirements for certain types of labor and material.

production and inventory management General term referring to the body of knowledge and activities concerned with planning and controlling rates of purchasing, production, distribution, and related capacity resources to achieve target levels of customer service, backlogs, operating costs, inventory investment, manufacturing efficiency, and return on investment.

production forecast A predicted level of customer demand for an option, feature, and so on of an assemble-to-order product (or finish-to-order product). It is calculated by netting customer backlog against an overall family or product-line master production schedule and then factoring this product (available-to-promise) by the option percentage in a planning bill of material.

production plan The agreed-upon plan that comes from the sales and operations (production) planning function, specifically the overall level of manufacturing output planned to be produced. Usually stated as a monthly rate for each product family (group of products, items, options, features, etc). Various units of measure can be used to express the plan: units, tonnage, standard hours, number of workers, and so on. The production plan is management's authorization for the master scheduler to convert it into a more detailed plan, that is, the master production schedule. See *production planning, sales and operations planning.*

production planning An older name for sales and operations planning.

production rates   The rate of production usually expressed in units, hours or some other broad measure, expressed by a period of time, that is, per hour, shift, day, week. Synonym: *production levels.*

production schedule   A plan that authorizes the factory to manufacture a certain quantity of a specific item. Usually initiated by the production planning department.

Q

quadratic exponential smoothing   See *exponential smoothing, quadratic.*

qualitative or technological forecasting   Qualitative or technological methods of forecasting are used when objective data about the past are not available or are irrelevant as a predictor of the future (i.e., the past patterns are not expected to repeat).

quantitative forecasting   Quantitative forecasting methods are those statistical methods that model past patterns and assume those past patterns will repeat in the future.

R

random   Having no predictable pattern. For example, sales data may vary randomly about some mean value with no specific pattern. Thus, there is no method to obtain a more accurate sales estimate than the mean value.

random sample   A selection of observations taken from all of the observations of a phenomenon in such a way that each chosen observation had the same probability of selection. See *sampling.*

random variation   A fluctuation in data that is due to uncertain or random occurrences.

range   The statistical term referring to the spread in a series of observations. For example, the anticipated demand for a particular product might vary from a low of 10 to a high of 500 per week. The range would therefore be 500−10 or 490.

regression analysis   Models for determining the mathematical expression that best describes the functional relationship between two or more variables. Regression models are often used in forecasting. Regression analysis determines the functional relationship between a single dependent variable Y and several independent variables (Xs) and the error in using that relationship.

regression coefficients When Y is regressed against a set of independent measures, for example, X_1 through X_k, the regression coefficients measure the change in Y that is the result of a unit change in X_1, while controlling or adjusting for the influence of all other variables in the relationship. Because the regression relationship tries to measure the influence of a variable with other variables in the relationship, it is best to interpret the regression coefficient as the influence of X_1 on Y while the other variables are also influencing Y. The true influence of X_1 can be measured if all independent variables are statistically independent. If they are not, then interpretation of a regression coefficient may be confounded.

reorder quantity 1. In a fixed order-quantity system of inventory control, the fixed quantity that should be ordered each time the available stock (on hand plus on order) falls below the order point. 2. In a variable reorder-quantity system, the amount ordered from time period to time period will vary. Synonym: *replenishment order quantity.*

residual This is commonly used as a synonym for *forecast* or *model error.*

return on investment A financial measure of the relative return from an investment, usually expressed as a ratio of earnings produced by an asset to the amount invested in the asset.

review period The time between successive evaluations of inventory status to determine whether or not to reorder. See *leadtime.*

rough-cut capacity planning The process of converting the production plan and/or the master production schedule into capacity needs for key resources: manpower, machinery, warehouse space, vendors' capabilities, and, in some cases, money. Product load profiles are often used to accomplish this. Synonym: *resource requirements planning.* See *capacity requirements planning.*

R-squared adjusted or R-bar squared In modeling the relative accuracy of different forecasting methods, R-squared, also called the *coefficient of determination,* measures the percentage of the original variance in a series that has been eliminated or reduced through the model. For example, if the demand for a product has a mean of 900 and variance of 100 and this series is modeled with exponential smoothing, which yields a mean forecast error of 0 and an error variance of 4, then 96 percent (i.e., $100 - 4/100$) of the variance has been eliminated through the model; the R-square equals .96. The *unad-*

justed R-square is *R*-square unadjusted for the degrees of freedom or model complexity. For large samples or simple models, the values of adjusted and unadjusted *R*-square are nearly the same.

S

safety stock   1. In general, a quantity of stock planned to be in inventory to protect against fluctuations in demand and/or supply. 2. In the context of master production scheduling, safety stock can refer to additional inventory and/or capacity planned as protection against forecast errors and/or short-term changes in the backlog. Sometimes referred to as "overplanning" or a "market hedge." Synonym: *buffer stock*.

sales and operations planning (formerly called *production planning*)   The function of setting the overall level of manufacturing output (production plan) and other activities to best satisfy the current planned levels of sales (sales plan and/or forecasts), while meeting general business objectives of profitability, productivity, competitive customer leadtimes, and so on, as expressed in the overall business plan. One of its primary purposes is to establish production rates that will achieve management's objective of maintaining, raising, or lowering inventories or backlogs, while usually attempting to keep the work force relatively stable. It must extend through a planning horizon sufficient to plan the labor, equipment, facilities, material, and finances required to accomplish the production plan. As this plan affects many company functions, it is normally prepared with information from marketing, manufacturing, engineering, finance, materials, and so on.

sales mix   The proportion of individual product-type sales volumes that make up the total sales volume. See *product mix*.

sales plan   The overall level of sales expected to be achieved. Usually stated as a monthly rate of sales for a product family (group of products, items, options, features, etc.). It needs to be expressed in units identical to the production plan (as well as dollars) for planning purposes. It represents sales and marketing managements' commitment to take all reasonable steps necessary to make the sales forecast (a prediction) accurately represent actual customer orders received.

sample   A portion of a universe of data chosen to estimate some characteristic(s) about the whole universe. The universe of data could consist of sizes of customer orders, number of units of inventory, number of lines on a purchase order, and so on. See *sampling distribution*.

sampling A statistical process whereby generalizations regarding an entire body of phenomena are drawn from a relatively small number of observations.

sampling distribution The distribution of values of a statistic calculated from samples of a given size.

sampling error Sampling error occurs when a sample is taken. The standard error measures the expected level of sampling error.

scatter chart A graph showing the actual observed relationships between two variables by the use of plotted points.

s-curve A growth curve used to represent product or demand growth particularly as it relates to the product life cycle. Synonym: *logistics curve*.

seasonal differences A seasonal difference is the difference between Y_t and Y_{t-s} where s is the length of the seasonal cycle. These series are autocorrelated at seasonal lags. These high autocorrelations yield a simple strategy for modeling the series, Y_t equals Y_{t-s}. Other components can be added to the seasonal model to include trends and randomness. See *differencing*.

seasonal index A seasonal index (I) measures the amount by which a period is influenced by seasonal effects. The index typically measures the percentage difference between a typical period and the actual period. For example, if August has an I of 1.25, this indicates that August is 25 percent higher than the typical monthly demand.

seasonal influence or variation Variation in a series that is the result of recurrent and periodic influences. These influences are the result of things such as weather and societal conventions like holidays.

seasonal inventory Inventory built up in anticipation of a peak seasonal demand in order to smooth production.

seasonality A repetitive pattern from year to year with some periods considerably higher than others.

second-order smoothing A method of exponential smoothing for trend situations that employs two previously computed averages, the singly and doubly smoothed values, to extrapolate into the future. Synonym: *double smoothing*.

secular trend The general direction of the long-run change in the value of a particular time series.

serial correlation See *autocorrelation*.

service parts Items used for the repair and/or maintenance of an assembled product. Typically, they are ordered and shipped at a date later than the shipment of the product itself.

service parts demand The need for a component to be sold by itself, as opposed to being used in production to make a higher-level product. Synonyms: *repair parts demand, spare parts.*

setup cost The costs associated with a setup. Synonym: *changeover cost.*

sigma A Greek letter commonly used to designate the standard deviation, which is a measure of the dispersion of data or the spread of the distribution. See *standard deviation.*

simple regression Simple regression relates a single dependent variable with a single independent variable. The coefficients of the functional relationship are chosen using the method of least-squared deviations. It is a special case of multiple regression.

sine wave A trigonometric equation of the general form $Y = A \sin (W + P)$ that represents a wave with amplitude A, frequency and wavelength related to angle W, and a shift in its phase or horizontal position of P. See *amplitude, wavelength, frequency, phase,* and *line spectrum.*

single smoothing See *first-order smoothing.*

skew The degree of nonsymmetry shown by a frequency distribution.

SKU Abbreviation of *stockkeeping unit.*

slope The change in the Y value or dependent variable that results from a unit change in the independent variable is called the *slope*. In regression analysis, where demand is the dependent variable and time is the independent variable, the slope equals the trend or period-to-period increase.

smoothing Averaging data by a mathematical process or by curve fitting, such as the method of least squares or exponential smoothing. Extreme values are smoothed by averaging high and low values.

smoothing constant In exponential smoothing, the weighting factor that is multiplied against the most recent error. Synonym: *alpha factor.*

spectral analysis The decomposition of a time series into a set of sine waves and cosine waves with differing amplitudes, frequencies, and phase angles is known as *spectral analysis, harmonic analysis,* and *Fourier analysis.*

standard deviation A measure of dispersion of data or of a variable. The standard deviation is computed by finding the difference between the actual observations and the mean, squaring each difference, summing the squared differences, finding the average squared difference (called the variance), and taking the square root of the variance. See *sigma*.

standardizing   Standardizing is the process of transforming values to a normalized scale with a mean of zero and a standard deviation of one. This is accomplished by subtracting the mean from each value and dividing the difference by the standard deviation. For example, if the mean is 800 and the standard deviation is 100, the standardized value for 1,000 is 2, while the standardized value for 600 is −2. There are numerical advantages to using standardized values in statistical and graphical routines. It is a simple matter to convert the standardized values back to original values.

stationary   A time series is stationary if it has a constant mean and a constant variance. If a series has a trend or walks randomly up and down (i.e., is a random walk), then it is a nonstationary series. If we are to have a good forecast, then this nonstationarity must be modeled. Models that include trend estimates that follow the wanderings of the time series are valid ways of modeling nonstationary series.

statistic   A statistic is a value that is estimated from a sample of the population. A forecast is a mean value based on a sample of the past. All statistics have error or uncertainty when estimating the true population value. The degree of uncertainty or error in the statistic is measured by the standard error or deviation of the statistic.

statistical inventory control   The use of statistical methods to model the demands and leadtimes experienced by an inventory item or group of items. Demand during leadtimes and between reviews can be modeled, and reorder points, safety stocks, and maximum inventory levels can be defined to attempt to achieve desired customer service levels, inventory investments, manufacturing/distribution efficiency, and targeted returns on investments.

stock status   A periodic report showing the inventory on hand and usually showing the inventory on order and some sales and/or usage history for the products that are covered in the stock status report.

stockkeeping unit (SKU)   An item at a particular geographic location. For example, one product stocked at six different distribution centers would represent six SKUs, plus perhaps another for the plant at which it was manufactured.

stockout   The lack of materials or components that are needed. See *backorder*.

stockout costs   The lost sale and/or backorder cost incurred as a result of a stockout.

stockout percentage   A measure of the effectiveness with which a company responds to actual demand. The stockout percentage can be a measurement of total stockouts to total orders, or of line items incurring stockouts during a period to total line items ordered. See *customer service ratio*.

suboptimization   A problem solution that is best from a narrow point of view but not from a higher or overall company point of view. For example, a department manager who would not work his department overtime in order to minimize his department's costs may be doing so at the expense of overall company profitability.

super bill (of material)   A type of planning bill, located at the top level in the structure, that ties together various modular bills (and possibly a common parts bill) to define an entire product or product family. The "quantity per" relationships in the super bill represent the forecasted percentage of demand of each module. The master scheduled quantities of the super bill explode to create requirements for the modules that also are master scheduled. See *planning bill, modular bill, common parts bill*.

T

technological forecasting   See *qualitative forecasting*.

time fence   A policy or guideline established to note where various restrictions or changes in operating procedures take place. For example, changes to the master production schedule can be accomplished easily beyond the cumulative leadtime, whereas changes inside the cumulative leadtime become increasingly more difficult to a point where changes should be resisted. Time fences can be used to define these points.

time-phased order point (TPOP)   MRP (or DRP) for independent demand items, where gross requirements come from a forecast, not via explosion. This technique can be used to plan distribution center inventories as well as planning for service (repair) parts, since MRP logic can readily handle items with dependent demand, independent demand, or a combination of both. See *distribution requirements planning*.

time series A set of data that is distributed over time, such as demand data in monthly time-period occurrences.

time series model A time series model relates the values of a time series to previous values of that time series or its errors. See *intrinsic forecast* and *ARIMA*.

tracking signal Used to signal when the validity of the forecasting model might be in doubt. For example, the ratio of the cumulative algebraic sum of the deviations between the forecasts and the actual values to the mean absolute deviation.

trading-day adjustment A trading day is a day of business activity. The number of trading days in a month (e.g., January) may vary from year to year. Also, the number of trading days in different months can vary greatly. Methods exist to adjust for trading days. These normally involve adjusting the data so that it appears that each month of a year has the same number of trading days. Then, when forecasts are made, this adjustment is reversed to yield actual monthly forecasts, not average monthly forecasts. For example, if each month is divided by its number of trading days, then seasonality and trends in demand per day can be forecasted more accurately.

transformation Used to change the scale of measurement in variables. For example, a nonlinear relationship may be made linear by using a logarithmic or power transformation. Also, when a series variance or standard deviation is proportionate to the level of the series, a logarithmic transformation can be used to achieve a constant variance.

trend analysis Trend analysis includes a number of methods for estimating the consistent period-to-period increases in a series. Simple regression analysis, differences, or linear smoothing can be used to estimate trends.

trend forecasting models Methods for forecasting sales data when a definite upward or downward pattern exists. Models include double exponential smoothing, regression, and additive trend.

t-test The t-test is a general statistical test used to perform a simple hypothesis test. For example, in regression analysis, it tests the hypothesis that a regression coefficient is significantly different from 0. When modeling a series with trend using differences, it can be used to prove whether there is or is not a significant trend in the series. We use a t-test when degrees of freedom are less than 30 and a Z-test when degrees of freedom are greater than or equal to 30.

The tests are identical; only the table that is used to perform the test differs.

turning point A turning point is a change in the direction of a series. For example, when a cyclical influence changes from increasing demand to decreasing demand, then there has been a turning point. Turning points for seasonal patterns are frequently easy to predict because seasons have a known period, for example, every 12 months. In contrast, cyclical turning points are very difficult to predict unless we have identified a leading economic indicator. Cyclical influences have no known period.

U

unbiased A model or statistic is considered unbiased if on average its mean value equals the expected value of the population it is representing. In forecasting, a model is unbiased if the mean forecast error is zero.

universe The population, or large set of data, from which samples are drawn. Usually assumed to be infinitely large or at least very large relative to the sample. See *sampling*.

updating forecast Revising forecasts based on new data that has become available after the original forecasts.

V

validation The process of testing the stability and usefulness of a forecasting model. There are many different validation methods. These include holding out some data from a series being forecasted and seeing how well the model forecasts this holdout data. Other methods include dividing the series in two and fitting a model to the first half and seeing how well the model forecasts the second half. There are many other methods of validation.

variance The square of the standard deviation. It is the average of the mean squared error. It is a useful measure because the variances of independent events are additive. See *variance law*.

variance law If event X (e.g., demand during a three-week leadtime) is the sum of several independent events (i.e., demand per week for each of three weeks), then the variance of X equals the sum of the variance of each independent event (i.e., sum of the variances of each week). For example, the forecasted demand per week is 100 with a variance of the forecast errors equal to 16. If the leadtime is three weeks, then mean demand during leadtime is 300 with a variance of $16 + 16 + 16 = 48$. The standard deviation of demand during leadtime is the square root of 48, approximately 7.

W

warehouse demand The need for an item in order to replenish a branch warehouse. Synonym: *branch warehouse demand.*

wavelength In the context of Fourier analysis, the wavelength equals the number of periods between peaks or troughs. Thus, it is equal to the length of the modeled cycles. For example, with monthly seasonal demand, the expected wavelength will be 12 or integer fractions of 12 called harmonics.

weight The weights in a model measure the influence that an independent variable has on the dependent variable. For simple moving averages, each of the past demands are given equal weight in influencing future demand. In regression analysis, the weights are called *regression coefficients;* in exponential smoothing, the weights are called *smoothing constants.*

weighted average An averaging technique where the data to be averaged are not uniformly weighted and are given values according to their importance. The weights must always sum to 1.00 or 100 percent.

white noise A white noise series is one with no patterns in it. It is completely randomly distributed. A good forecasting model will yield errors that are distributed as white noise. We say that all information about past demand patterns have been identified if the errors from a model are white noise. White noise is normally and independently distributed.

Winters' exponential smoothing See *exponential smoothing, seasonal.*

Z

Z-test A test used to determine if a sample result (e.g., a forecast error) is significantly different than expected, that is, more than two or three standard deviations away from its expected or hypothetical mean. For example, forecast errors are not expected to be more than two or three standard deviations of the error away from zero. If they are, then something is unusual about the error. See *t-test.*

INDEX